THE WEST

Key Eras in the Transformation of the West

Western civilization has undergone many transformations throughout its history. Map 1 shows the Roman Empire at its greatest extent, an era when the basic intellectual, religious, political, and geographic outlines of what we call the West today were drawn. During the Carolingian Empire, seen in Map 2, Europe experienced greater political cohesion, as the Carolingian armies successfully reunified most of the western European territories of the ancient Roman Empire. A distinctive Latin Christian (or Roman Catholic) culture began to emerge in this region, distinguishing it further from Orthodox Christian culture of the Byzantine Empire in the east. Map 3 shows Europe after the Congress of

■ **MAP 1**
Roman Empire at Its Greatest Extent, ca. 117 C.E.

■ **MAP 2**
Carolingian Empire

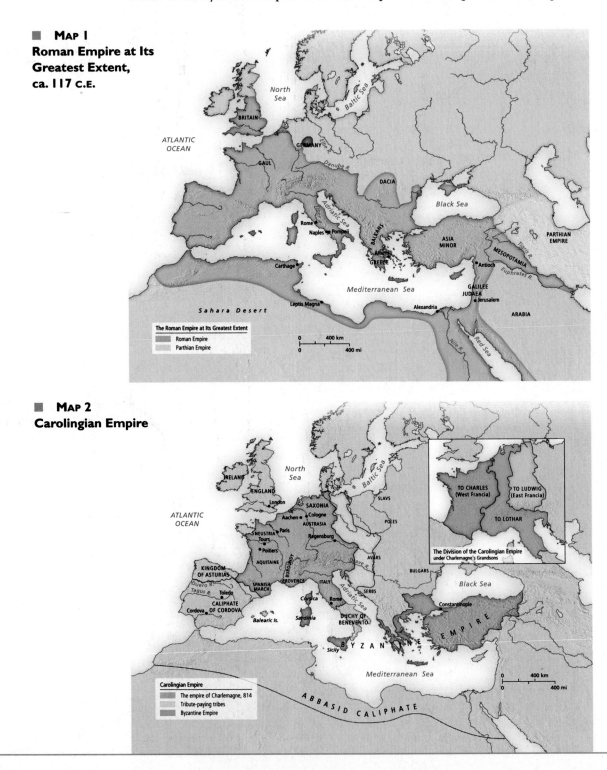

Vienna in 1815, when the major European powers re-drew the map of Europe after the defeat of Napoleon and the dismantlement of the massive empire France had acquired under his leadership. The settlement agreed upon at Vienna was intended to maintain a balance of power in the West. Map 4 shows Europe after World War I, when the map of Europe changed dramatically with the collapse of the old authoritarian empires and the creation of independent nation-states in eastern Europe. What neither Map 3 nor Map 4 can show, however, is the expansion of "the West" beyond European borders to embrace cultures on other continents, including Australia, Africa, and North America.

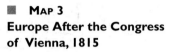

MAP 3
Europe After the Congress of Vienna, 1815

MAP 4
Europe After World War I

THE WEST

ENCOUNTERS & TRANSFORMATIONS

VOLUME C: SINCE 1789

BRIAN LEVACK
University of Texas at Austin

EDWARD MUIR
Northwestern University

MICHAEL MAAS
Rice University

MEREDITH VELDMAN
Louisiana State University

PEARSON
Longman

New York   San Francisco   Boston
London   Toronto   Sydney   Tokyo   Singapore   Madrid
Mexico City   Munich   Paris   Cape Town   Hong Kong   Montreal

Vice President and Publisher: Priscilla McGeehon
Acquisitions Editor: Erika Gutierrez
Development Manager: Lisa Pinto
Senior Development Editor: Dawn Groundwater
Executive Marketing Manager: Sue Westmoreland
Supplements Editor: Kristi Olson
Media Editor: Patrick McCarthy
Production Manager: Donna DeBenedictis
Project Coordination and Electronic Page Makeup: Elm Street Publishing Services, Inc.
Interior Design: Pearson Education Development
Cover and Frontispiece Art: Pierre Auguste Renoir (1841–1919), *Luncheon of the Boating Party*, 1880–81. Oil on canvas,
 51 $\frac{1}{4}$ × 68 $\frac{1}{8}$ in. Acquired 1923. The Phillips Collection, Washington, D.C.
Cover Designer/Manager: John Callahan
Cartography: Maps.com
Photo Researcher: Photosearch, Inc.
Manufacturing Buyer: Roy L. Pickering, Jr.
Printer and Binder: Quebecor World Versailles
Cover Printer: Coral Graphic Services, Inc.

For permission to use copyrighted material, grateful acknowledgment is made to the copyright holders on pp. C-1–C-2, which are hereby made part of this copyright page.

Library of Congress Cataloging-in-Publication Data

Levack, Brian P.
 The West : encounters & transformations / Brian Levack . . . [et al.].
 p. cm.
 Includes bibliographical references and index.
 ISBN 0-321-19833-6
 1. Civilization, Western—History. I. Title.

CB245.L485 2004
909'.09821—dc22

2003062213

Please visit our website at http://www.ablongman.com/levack

ISBN 0-321-19833-6 (single volume edition)
ISBN 0-673-98250-5 (volume I)
ISBN 0-673-98251-3 (volume II)
ISBN 0-321-18315-0 (volume A)
ISBN 0-321-18317-7 (volume B)
ISBN 0-321-18314-2 (volume C)

1 2 3 4 5 6 7 8 9 10—QWV—06 05 04 03

Brief Contents

Detailed Contents

What Is the West?   *3*

CHAPTER 20

The Industrial Revolution, 1760–1850   *655*

CHAPTER 21

Ideological Conflict and National Unification, 1815–1871   *685*

JUSTICE IN HISTORY

THE HUMAN BODY IN HISTORY

CHAPTER 22

The Coming of Mass Politics: Industrialization, Emancipation, and Instability, 1870–1914 *721*

CHAPTER 25

Reconstruction, Reaction, and Continuing Revolution: The 1920s and 1930s   *827*

Documents

Maps

Features

Chronologies

Preface

We wrote this textbook to answer questions about the identity of the civilization in which we live. Journalists, politicians, and scholars often refer to our civilization, its political ideologies, its economic systems, and its cultures as "Western" without fully considering what that label means and why it might be appropriate. The classification of our civilization as Western has become particularly problematic in the age of globalization. The creation of international markets, the rapid dissemination of ideas on a global scale, and the transmission of popular culture from one country to another often make it difficult to distinguish what is Western from what is not. *The West: Encounters & Transformations* offers students a history of Western civilization in which these issues of Western identity are given prominence. Our goal is neither to idealize nor to indict that civilization but to describe its main characteristics in different historical periods.

The West: Encounters & Transformations gives careful consideration to two basic questions. The first is how did the definition of the West change over time? In what ways did its boundaries shift and how did the distinguishing characteristics of its cultures change? The second question is by what means did the West—and the idea of the West—develop? We argue that the West is the product of a series of cultural encounters that occurred both outside and within its geographical boundaries. We explore these encounters and the transformations they produced by detailing the political, social, religious, and cultural history of the regions that have been, at one time or another, a part of the West.

Defining the West

What is the West? How did it come into being? How has it developed throughout history? Many textbooks take for granted which regions or peoples of the globe constitute the West. They treat the history of the West as a somewhat expanded version of European history. While not disputing the centrality of Europe to any definition of the West, we contend that the West is not only a geographical realm with ever-shifting boundaries but also a cultural realm, an area of cultural influence extending beyond the geographical and political boundaries of Europe. We so strongly believe in this notion that we have written the essay "What Is the West?" to encourage students to think about their understanding of Western civilization and to guide their understanding of each chapter. Many of the features of what we call Western civilization originated in regions that are not geographically part of Europe (such as northern Africa and the Middle East), while ever since the fifteenth century various social, ethnic, and political groups from non-European regions (such as North and South America, eastern Russia, Australia, New Zealand, and South Africa) have identified themselves, in one way or another, with the West. Throughout the text, we devote considerable attention to the boundaries of the West and show how borderlines between cultures have been created, especially in eastern and southeastern Europe.

Considered as a geographical and cultural realm, "the West" is a term of recent origin, and the civilization to which it refers did not become clearly defined until the eleventh century, especially during the Crusades, when western European Christians developed a distinct cultural identity. Before that time we can only talk about the powerful forces that created the West, especially the dynamic interaction of the civilizations of western Europe, the Byzantine Empire, and the Muslim world.

Over the centuries Western civilization has acquired many salient characteristics. These include two of the world's great legal systems (civil law and common law), three of the world's monotheistic religions (Judaism, Christianity, and Islam), certain political and social philosophies, forms of political organization (such as the modern bureaucratic state and democracy), methods of scientific inquiry, systems of economic organization (such as industrial capitalism), and distinctive styles of art, architecture, and music. At times one or more of these characteristics has served as a primary source of Western identity: Christianity in the Middle Ages, science and rationalism during the Enlightenment, industrialization in the nineteenth and twentieth centuries, and a defense of individual liberty and democracy in the late twentieth century. These sources of Western identity, however, have always been challenged and contested, both when they were coming into prominence and when they appeared to be most triumphant. Western culture has never been monolithic, and even today references to the West imply a wide range of meanings.

Cultural Encounters

The definition of the West is closely related to the central theme of our book, which is the process of cultural encounters. Throughout *The West: Encounters & Transformations,* we examine the West as a product of a series of cultural encounters both outside the West and within it. We show that the West originated and developed through a continuous process of inclusion and exclusion resulting from a series of encounters among and within different groups. These encounters can be described in a general sense as external, internal, or ideological.

EXTERNAL ENCOUNTERS

External encounters took place between peoples of different civilizations. Before the emergence of the West as a clearly defined entity, external encounters occurred between such diverse peoples as Greeks and Phoenicians, Macedonians and Egyptians, and Romans and Celts. After the eleventh century, external encounters between Western and non-Western peoples occurred mainly during periods of European exploration, expansion, and imperialism. In the sixteenth and seventeenth centuries, for example, a series of external encounters took place between Europeans on the one hand and Africans, Asians, and the indigenous people of the Americas on the other. Two chapters of *The West: Encounters & Transformations* (Chapters 12 and 19) and a large section of a third (Chapter 23) explore these external encounters in depth and discuss how they affected Western and non-Western civilizations alike.

INTERNAL ENCOUNTERS

Our discussion of encounters also includes similar interactions between different social groups *within* Western countries. These internal encounters often took place between dominant and subordinate groups, such as between lords and peasants, rulers and subjects, men and women, factory owners and workers, masters and slaves. Encounters between those who were educated and those who were illiterate, which recur frequently throughout Western history, also fall into this category. Encounters just as often took place between different religious and political groups, such as between Christians and Jews, Catholics and Protestants, royal absolutists and republicans.

IDEOLOGICAL ENCOUNTERS

Ideological encounters involve the interaction between comprehensive systems of thought, most notably religious doctrines, political philosophies, and scientific theories about the nature of the world. These ideological conflicts usually arose out of internal encounters, when various groups within Western societies subscribed to different theories of government or rival religious faiths. The encounters between Christianity and polytheism in the early Middle Ages, between liberalism and conservatism in the nineteenth century, and between fascism and communism in the twentieth century were ideological encounters. Some ideological encounters had an external dimension, such as when the forces of Islam and Christianity came into conflict during the Crusades and when the Cold War developed between Soviet communism and Western democracy in the second half of the twentieth century.

*   *   *

The West: Encounters & Transformations illuminates the variety of these encounters and clarifies their effects. By their very nature encounters are interactive, but they have taken different forms: they have been violent or peaceful, coercive or cooperative. Some have resulted in the imposition of Western ideas on areas lying outside the geographical boundaries of the West or the perpetuation of the dominant culture within Western societies. More often than not, however, encounters have resulted in a more reciprocal process of exchange in which both Western and non-Western cultures or the values of both dominant and subordinate groups have undergone significant transformation. Our book not only identifies these encounters but also discusses their significance by returning periodically to the issue of Western identity.

Coverage

The *West: Encounters & Transformations* offers both balanced coverage of political, social, and culture history and a broader coverage of the West and the world.

BALANCED COVERAGE

Our goal throughout the text has been to provide balanced coverage of political, social, and cultural history and to include significant coverage of religious and military history as well. Political history defines the basic structure of the book, and some chapters, such as those on building the classical world, the age of confessional divisions, absolutism and state building, the French Revolution, and the coming of mass politics, include sustained political narratives. Because we understand the West to be a cultural as well as a geographical realm, we give a prominent position to cultural history. Thus we include rich sections on Hellenistic philosophy and literature, the cultural environment of the Italian Renaissance, the creation of a new political culture at the time of the French Revolution, and the atmosphere of cultural despair and desire that prevailed in Europe after World War I. We also devote special attention to religious history, including the history of Islam as well as that of Christianity and Judaism. Unlike many other textbooks, our coverage of religion continues into the modern period.

The West: Encounters & Transformations also provides extensive coverage of the history of women and gender. Wherever possible the history of women is integrated into the broader social, cultural, and political history of the period. But there are also separate sections on women in our chapters on classical Greece, the Renaissance, the Reformation, the Enlightenment, the Industrial Revolution, World War I, World War II, and the postwar era.

THE WEST AND THE WORLD

Our book provides broad geographical coverage. Because the West is the product of a series of encounters, the external areas with which the West interacted are of major importance. Three chapters deal specifically with the West and the World.

- Chapter 12, "The West and the World: The Significance of Global Encounters, 1450–1650"
- Chapter 19, "The West and the World: Empire, Trade, and War, 1650–1850"
- Chapter 23, "The West and the World: Cultural Crisis and the New Imperialism, 1870–1914"

These chapters present substantial material on sub-Saharan Africa, Latin America, the Middle East, India, and East Asia. Our text is also distinctive in its coverage of eastern Europe and the Muslim world, areas which have often been considered outside the boundaries of the West. These regions were arenas within which significant cultural encounters took place. Finally we include material on the United States and Australia, both of which have become part of the West. We recognize that most American college and university students have the opportunity to study American history as a separate subject, but treatment of the United States as a Western nation provides a different perspective from that usually given in courses on American history. For example, this book treats the American Revolution as one of four Atlantic Revolutions, its national unification in the nineteenth century as part of a broader western European development, its pattern of industrialization as related to that of Britain, and its central role in the Cold War as part of an ideological encounter that was global in scope.

Organization

························■························

The chronological and thematic organization of our book conforms in its broad outline to the way in which Western civilization courses are generally taught. We have limited the number of chapters to twenty-nine, an effort to make the book more compatible with the traditional American semester calendar and to solve the frequent complaint that there is not enough time to cover all the material in the course. We have also made some significant changes in organization:

- Chapter 2, which covers the period from ca. 1600 to 550 B.C.E., is the first in a Western civilization textbook to examine the International Bronze Age and its aftermath as a period important in its own right because it saw the creation of expansionist, multiethnic empires, linked by trade and diplomacy.
- In Chapter 4 the Roman Republic, in keeping with contemporary scholarship, has been incorporated into a discussion of the Hellenistic world, dethroned slightly to emphasize how it was one of many competing Mediterranean civilizations.
- Chapter 12 covers the first period of European expansion, from 1450 to 1650. It examines the new European encounters with the civilizations of sub-Saharan Africa, the Americas, and East Asia. By paying careful attention to the characteristics of

these civilizations before the arrival of the Europeans, we show how this encounter affected indigenous peoples as well as Europeans.

- Chapter 16 is devoted entirely to the scientific revolution of the seventeenth century in order to emphasize the central importance of this development in the creation of Western identity.
- Chapter 19, which covers the second period of European expansion, from 1650 to 1850, studies the growth of European empires, the beginning of global warfare, and encounters between Europeans and the peoples of Asia and Africa.
- Chapter 27, "The Holocaust, the Bomb, and the Legacy of Mass Killing," explores the moral fissure in the history of the West created by World War II. This unique chapter looks in detail at the age of mass destruction inaugurated, in very different ways, by the Holocaust and by the aerial bombings of civilian centers that culminated in the use of the atomic bomb in August 1945.

Features and Pedagogical Aids

In writing this textbook we have endeavored to keep both the student reader and the classroom instructor in mind at all times. The text includes the following features and pedagogical aids, all of which are intended to support the themes of the book.

WHAT IS THE WEST?

The West: Encounters & Transformations begins with an essay to engage students in the task of defining the West and to introduce them to the notion of cultural encounters. "What Is the West?" guides students through the text by providing a framework for understanding how the West was shaped. Structured around the six questions of What? When? Where? Who? How? and Why?, this framework encourages students to think about their understanding of Western civilization. The essay serves as a blueprint for using this textbook.

JUSTICE IN HISTORY

Found in every chapter, the goal of this feature is to present a historically significant trial or episode in which different notions of justice (or injustice) were debated and resolved. The *Justice in History* features illustrate cultural encounters within communities as they try to determine the fate of individuals from all walks of life. Many famous trials dealt with conflicts over basic religious, philosophical, or political values, such as those of Socrates, Jesus, Joan of Arc, Charles I, Galileo, and Adolf Eichmann. Other *Justice in History* features show how judicial institutions, such as the ordeal, the inquisition, and revolutionary tribunals, handled adversarial situations in different societies. These essays, therefore, illustrate the way in which the basic values of the West have evolved through attempts to resolve disputes, contention, and conflict.

Each *Justice in History* feature includes two pedagogical aids. "Questions of Justice" helps students explore the historical significance of the episode just examined. These questions can also be used in classroom discussion or as student essay topics. "Taking It Further" provides the student with a few references that can be consulted in connection with a research project.

What Is the West?

MANY OF THE PEOPLE WHO INFLUENCE PUBLIC OPINION—POLITICIANS, teachers, clergy, journalists, and television commentators—frequently refer to "Western values," "the West," and "Western civilization." They often use these terms as if they do not require explanation. But what *do* these terms mean? The West has always been an arena within which different cultures, religions, values, and philosophies have interacted, and any definition of the West will inevitably arouse controversy.

The most basic definition of the West is of a place. Western civilization is now typically thought to comprise the regions of Europe, the Americas, Australia, and New Zealand. As we shall see, however, over time these boundaries have shifted considerably. In addition to being a place, Western civilization also encompasses a history—a tradition stretching back thousands of years to the ancient world. Over this long period the civilization we now identify as Western gradually took shape. The many characteristics that identify any civilization emerged over this time: forms of governments, economic systems, and methods of scientific inquiry, as well as religions, languages, literature, and art.

Throughout the development of Western civilization, the ways in which people identified themselves changed as well. People in the ancient world had no such idea of the common identity of the West, only of being subjects of an em-

JUSTICE IN HISTORY

The Trial of Joan of Arc

After only fifteen months as the inspiration of the French army, Joan of Arc fell into the hands of the English, who brought her to trial for witchcraft. The English needed to stage a kind of show trial to demonstrate to their own demoralized forces that Joan's remarkable victories had been the result not of military superiority but rather of witchcraft. In the English trial, conducted at Rouen in 1431, Joan testified that her mission to save France was in response to voices she heard that commanded her to wear men's clothing. On the basis of this evidence of a confused or double gender identity, the ecclesiastical tribunal de-

voices had the authority of divine commands. The problem the English judges faced was to demonstrate that the voices came not from God but from the Devil. If they could prove that, then they had evidence of witchcraft and sorcery. Following standard inquisitorial guidelines, the judges knew that authentic messages from God would always conform to church dogma. Any deviation from official doctrines would constitute evidence of demonic influence. Thus, during Joan's trial the judges demanded that she make theological distinctions that were alien to her. When they wanted to know if the voices were those of

THE HUMAN BODY IN HISTORY

**Shell Shock:
From Woman's Malady
to Soldier's Affliction**

Broken in mind as well as body, the casualties of World War I forced medical practitioners to think anew about the connections among emotional anguish, physical disabilities, and gender roles. Doctors discovered to their horror and surprise that in the trenches of total war, men's bodies began to act like women's. Pouring into hospital units came thousands of men with the symptoms of a malady that before the war was considered a woman's disease—hysteria.

The word *hysteria* comes from the Greek word *hystera*, for "womb" or "uterus," and for much of Western history doctors believed that women were doomed to suffer from hysteria because of their physical makeup—because they were afflicted with wombs. Physicians long considered the uterus to be an inherently weak and unstable organ, prone even to detach itself from its proper place and wander about the body causing havoc. By the end of the nineteenth century, however, the diagnosis had changed. Doctors continued

to regard hysteria as primaril were more inclined to view it emotional disorder. The sym included bouts of shrieking, pression or breakdown, and clear physical cause—rangin somnia to the inability to wal

With war came thousands of hysteria—men who could healthy limbs who could not were nibbling at their bodies. symptoms as signs of coward ness to avoid doing their duty accounting for 40 percent of zones alone, doctors realized demic of male hysteria.

The war illustrated that h uterus or the weak female ne environment of immobility length of time a soldier had horror of his combat experie ducing breakdowns. Instead, his level of immobility. Men found themselves in positior ment. Deprived of the ability mine their future, to act, ma

Yet the reincarnation of wl woman's malady as a soldier's

THE HUMAN BODY IN HISTORY

Found in most chapters, these features show that the human body, which many people tend to understand solely as a product of biology, also has a history. These essays reveal that the ways in which various religious and political groups have represented the body in art and literature, clothed it, treated it medically, and abused it tell a great deal about the history of Western culture. These features include essays on the classical nude male body, the signs of disease during the Black Death, bathing the body in the East and the West, and the contraceptive pill. Concluding each essay is a single question for discussion that directs students back to the broader issues with which the chapter deals.

PLACES OF ENCOUNTER

Found in four chapters of the book, these features show that cultural exchanges between groups of people often occurred in specific places. The four features discuss the Roman Colosseum, Protestant and Catholic churches at the time of the Reformation, the French salon during the Enlightenment, and the twentieth-century soccer stadium. Accompanied by innovative visuals and graphics, these features reinforce the theme of encounters and also show that culture, which students often think of in abstract terms, has a material dimension. Each essay concludes with a question for discussion.

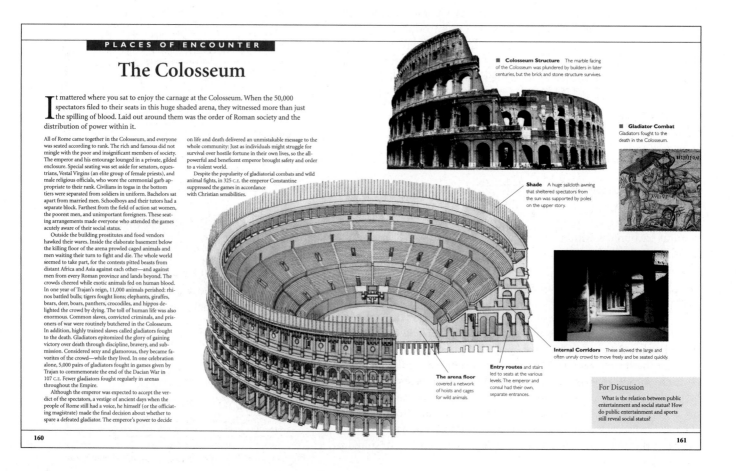

PLACES OF ENCOUNTER

The Colosseum

It mattered where you sat to enjoy the carnage at the Colosseum. When the 50,000 spectators filed to their seats in this huge shaded arena, they witnessed more than just the spilling of blood. Laid out around them was the order of Roman society and the distribution of power within it.

All of Rome came together in the Colosseum, and everyone was seated according to rank. The rich and famous did not mingle with the poor and insignificant members of society. The emperor and his entourage lounged in a private, gilded enclosure. Special seating was set aside for senators, equestrians, Vestal Virgins (an elite group of female priests), and male religious officials, who wore the ceremonial garb appropriate to their rank. Civilians in togas in the bottom tiers were separated from soldiers in uniform. Bachelors sat apart from married men. Schoolboys and their tutors had a separate block. Farthest from the field of action sat women, the poorest men, and unimportant foreigners. These seating arrangements made everyone who attended the games acutely aware of their social status.

Outside the building prostitutes and food vendors hawked their wares. Inside the elaborate basement below the killing floor of the arena prowled caged animals and men waiting their turn to fight and die. The whole world seemed to take part, for the contests pitted beasts from distant Africa and Asia against each other—and against men from every Roman province and lands beyond. The crowds cheered while exotic animals fed on human blood. In one year of Trajan's reign, 11,000 animals perished: rhinos battled bulls; tigers fought lions; elephants, giraffes, bears, deer, boars, panthers, crocodiles, and hippos delighted the crowd by dying. The toll of human life was also enormous. Common slaves, convicted criminals, and prisoners of war were routinely butchered in the Colosseum. In addition, highly trained slaves called gladiators fought to the death. Gladiators epitomized the glory of gaining victory over death through discipline, bravery, and submission. Considered sexy and glamorous, they became favorites of the crowd—while they lived. In one celebration alone, 5,000 pairs of gladiators fought in games given by Trajan to commemorate the end of the Dacian War in 107 C.E. Fewer gladiators fought regularly in arenas throughout the Empire.

Although the emperor was expected to accept the verdict of the spectators, a vestige of ancient days when the people of Rome still had a voice, he himself (or the officiating magistrate) made the final decision about whether to spare a defeated gladiator. The emperor's power to decide

on life and death delivered an unmistakable message to the whole community: Just as individuals might struggle for survival over hostile fortune in their own lives, so the all-powerful and beneficent emperor brought safety and order to a violent world.

Despite the popularity of gladiatorial combats and wild animal fights, in 325 C.E. the emperor Constantine suppressed the games in accordance with Christian sensibilities.

Colosseum Structure The marble facing of the Colosseum was plundered by builders in later centuries, but the brick and stone structure survives.

Gladiator Combat Gladiators fought to the death in the Colosseum.

Shade A huge saildoth awning that sheltered spectators from the sun was supported by poles on the upper story.

Internal Corridors These allowed the large and often unruly crowd to move freely and be seated quickly.

The arena floor covered a network of hoists and cages for wild animals.

Entry routes and stairs led to seats at the various levels. The emperor and consul had their own, separate entrances.

For Discussion

What is the relation between public entertainment and social status? How do public entertainment and sports still reveal social status?

PRIMARY SOURCE DOCUMENTS

In each chapter we have presented a number of excerpts from primary source documents—from "Tales of the Flood" to "A Ghetto Diary"—in order to reinforce or expand upon the points made in the text and to introduce students to the basic materials of historical research.

MAPS AND ILLUSTRATIONS

Artwork is a key component of our book. We recognize that many students often lack a strong familiarity with geography, and so we have taken great care to develop maps that help sharpen their geographic skills. Complementing the book's standard map program, we include maps focusing on areas outside the borders of Western civilization. These maps include a small thumbnail globe that highlights the geographic area under discussion in the context of the larger world. Fine art and photos also tell the story of Western civilization and we have included over 350 images to help students visualize the past: the way people lived, the events that shaped their lives, and how they viewed the world around them.

CHRONOLOGIES AND SUGGESTED READINGS

Each chapter includes chronological charts and suggested readings. Chronologies outline significant events, such as "The Road to the Atom Bomb," and serve as convenient references for students. Each chapter concludes with an annotated list of suggested readings. These are not scholarly bibliographies aimed at the professor, but suggestions for students who wish to explore a topic in greater depth or to write a research paper. A comprehensive list of suggested readings is available on our book-specific website, www.ablongman.com/levack.

GLOSSARY

We have sought to create a work that is accessible to students with little prior knowledge of the basic facts of Western history or geography. Throughout the book we have explained difficult concepts at length. For example, we present in-depth explanations of the concepts of Zoroastrianism, Neoplatonism, Renaissance humanism, the various Protestant denominations of the sixteenth century, capitalism, seventeenth-century absolutism, nineteenth-century liberalism and nationalism, fascism, and modernism. Key concepts such as these are identified in the chapters with a degree symbol (°) and defined as well in the end-of-text Glossary.

A NOTE ABOUT DATES AND TRANSLITERATIONS

In keeping with current academic practice, *The West: Encounters & Transformations* uses B.C.E. (before the common era) and C.E. (common era) to designate dates. We also follow the most current and widely accepted English transliterations of Arabic. Qur'an, for example, is used for Koran; Muslim is used for Moslem. Chinese words appearing in the text for the first time are written in *pinyin*, followed by the older Wade-Giles system in parentheses.

Supplements

FOR QUALIFIED COLLEGE ADOPTERS

Instructor's Resource Manual
0-673-97563-0
Written by Sharon Arnoult, Midwestern State University, each chapter contains a chapter outline, significant themes, learning objectives, lesson enrichment ideas, discussion suggestions, and questions for discussing the primary source documents in the text.

Test Bank
0-673-97564-9
Written by Susan Carrafiello, Wright State University, this supplement contains more than 1,200 multiple-choice, true/false, and essay questions. Multiple-choice and true/false questions are referenced by topic and text page number.

TestGen-EQ Computerized Testing System
0-673-97565-3
This flexible, easy-to-master computerized test bank on a dual-platform CD includes all of the items in the printed test bank and allows instructors to select specific questions, edit existing questions, and add their own items to create exams. Tests can be printed in several different fonts and formats and can include figures, such as graphs and tables.

Companion Website
www.ablongman.com/levack
Instructors can take advantage of the Companion Website that supports this text. The instructor section includes teaching links, downloadable maps, tables, and graphs from the text for use in PowerPoint™, PowerPoint™ lecture outlines, and a link to Supplements Central.

Supplements Central™
http://suppscentral.ablongman.com
A helpful website where instructors can download supplements including: Instructor's Manuals, Test Banks, TestGens, and PowerPoint™ presentations, as well as CourseCompass®, WebCT, and Blackboard materials. Instructors will need to request a password from their sales representative to gain access.

PowerPoint™ Presentations
These presentations contain an average of 15 PowerPoint™ slides for each chapter and may include key points and terms for a lecture on the chapter, as well as full-color slides of important maps, graphs, and charts. The presentations are available for download from www.ablongman.com/levack.

Text-Specific Transparency Set
0-673-97568-1
A set of full-color transparency map acetates taken from the text.

History Video Program

A list of over 100 videos from which qualified adopters can choose. Restrictions apply.

History Digital Media Archive CD-ROM
0-321-14976-9

This CD-ROM contains electronic images and interactive and static maps, along with media elements such as video. It is fully customizable and ready for classroom presentation. All images and maps are available in PowerPoint™ as well.

CourseCompass

http://www.ablongman.com/techsolutions

Focus on teaching the course, not the technology! CourseCompass combines the strength of Longman content with state-of-the-art technology that simplifies online course management for you. This easy-to-use and customizable program enables you to tailor the content and functionality to meet your individual needs. You can create an online presence—for ANY course you teach—in under an hour. This course contains several dozen primary sources, Western civilization maps from Longman textbooks, and the map exercises from both *Mapping Western Civilization* and *Western Civilization Map Workbook,* all of which you can customize for your own class and text.

BlackBoard

http://www.ablongman.com/techsolutions

Longman's rich Western civilization content is available in BlackBoard's course management system. The BlackBoard format enables you to quickly and easily customize any course to meet your specific needs. This course contains several dozen primary sources, Western civilization maps from Longman textbooks, and the map *Workbook,* all of which you can customize for your own class and text.

WebCT

http://www.ablongman.com/techsolutions

WebCT offers a host of online course management tools. Qualified college adopters can customize their own WebCT course with Longman content in a number of ways. Available content includes several dozen primary sources, Western civilization maps from Longman textbooks, and the map exercises from both *Mapping Western Civilization* and *Western Civilization Map Workbook,* all of which you can customize for your own class and text. Contact your sales representative for more information.

Discovering Western Civilization Through Maps and Views
0-673-97499-5

Created by Gerald Danzer, University of Illinois at Chicago, and David Buisseret, this unique set of 140 full-color acetates contains an introduction to teaching history through maps and a detailed commentary on each transparency. The collection includes cartographic and pictorial maps, views and photos, urban plans, building diagrams, and works of art. Available to qualified college adopters.

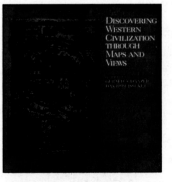

FOR STUDENTS

Study Guide
Volume I 0-673-98252-1
Volume II 0-673-98253-X

Containing activities and study aids for every chapter in the text, each chapter of the *Study Guide* written by Paul Brasil, Western Oregon University, includes a thorough chapter outline; timeline; map exercise; identification, multiple-choice, and thought questions; and critical-thinking questions based on primary source documents from the text.

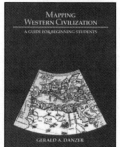

Companion Website

www.ablongman.com/levack

Providing a wealth of resources for students using *The West: Encounters & Transformations,* this Companion Website contains chapter summaries, interactive practice test questions, and Web links for every chapter in the text.

Research Navigator and Research Navigator Guide

0-205-40838-9

Research Navigator is a comprehensive website comprising three exclusive databases of credible and reliable source material for research and for student assignments: EBSCO's ContentSelect Academic Journal Database, the New York Times Search by Subject Archive, and "Best of the Web" Link Library. The site also includes an extensive help section. The Research Navigator Guide provides your students with access to the Research Navigator website and includes reference material and hints about conducting online research. **Free to qualified college adopters when packaged with the text.**

Multimedia Edition CD-ROM for
The West: Encounters & Transformations

0-321-18788-1

This unique CD-ROM takes students beyond the printed page, offering them a complete multimedia learning experience. It contains the full annotatable textbook on CD-ROM, with contextually placed media—audio, video, interactive maps, photos, and figures—that link students to additional content directly related to key concepts in the text. The CD also contains the *Study Guide,* Map Workbooks, a primary source reader, and more than a dozen supplementary books, most often assigned in Western civilization courses, including Plato, *The Republic,* and Machiavelli, *The Prince.* **Free to qualified college adopters when packaged with the text.**

Mapping Western Civilization:
Student Activities

0-673-53774-9

Created by Gerald Danzer, University of Illinois at Chicago, this FREE map workbook for students is designed as an accompaniment to *Discovering Western Civilization Through Maps and Views.* It features exercises designed to teach students to interpret and analyze cartographic materials such as historical documents. **Free to qualified college adopters when packaged with the text.**

Western Civilization Map Workbook

Volume I 0-321-01878-8
Volume II 0-321-01877-X

The map exercises in these volumes by Glee Wilson test and reinforce basic geography literacy while building critical-thinking skills. **Free to qualified college adopters when packaged with the text.**

Full-Color Longman Western Civilization Timeline

0-321-13004-9

Noting key events and trends in political and diplomatic, social and economic, and cultural and technological history, this fold-out illustrated timeline provides a thorough and accessible chronological reference guide for Western civilization. **Free to qualified college adopters when packaged with the text.**

Longman Atlas of Western Civilization

0-321-21626-1

This 52-page atlas features carefully selected historical maps that provide comprehensive coverage for the major historical periods. Each map has been designed to be colorful, easy-to-read, and informative, without sacrificing detailed accuracy. This atlas makes history—and geography—more comprehensible.

A Short Guide to Writing About History, Fourth Edition
0-321-09300-3
Written by Richard Marius, late of Harvard University, and Melvin E. Page, Eastern Tennessee State University, this engaging and practical text helps students get beyond merely compiling dates and facts; it teaches them how to incorporate their own ideas into their papers and to tell a story about history that interests them and their peers. Covering both brief essays and the documented resource paper, the text explores the writing and researching processes, identifies different modes of historical writing, including argument, and concludes with guidelines for improving style.

Longman World History—Primary Sources and Case Studies
Longmanworldhistory.com
The core of this website is its large database of thought-provoking primary sources, case studies, maps, and images—all carefully chosen and edited by scholars and teachers of world history. The content and organization of the site encourage students to analyze the themes, issues, and complexities of world history in a meaningful, exciting, and informative way. Offered at a significant discount to *The West: Encounters & Transformations* users, professors can visit the site for a free three-day trial.

PENGUIN-LONGMAN PARTNERSHIP

The partnership between Penguin Books and Longman Publishers offers your students a discount on the titles below when instructors bundle them with any Longman survey. Visit www.ablongman.com/penguin for more information.

Available Titles

Peter Abelard, *The Letters of Abelard and Heloise*
Dante Alighieri, *Divine Comedy: Inferno*
Dante Alighieri, *The Portable Dante*
Anonymous, *The Song of Roland*
Anonymous, *The Epic of Gilgamesh*
Anonymous, *Vinland Sagas*
Aristophanes, *The Knights, Peace, The Birds, Assemblywomen, Wealth*
Louis Auchincloss, *Woodrow Wilson* (Penguin Lives Series)
Jane Austen, *Emma*
Jane Austen, *Pride and Prejudice*
Jane Austen, *Persuasion*
Jane Austen, *Sense and Sensibility*
Edward Bellamy, *Looking Backward*
Richard Bowring, *Diary of Lady Murasaki*
Charlotte Brontë, *Jane Eyre*
Charlotte Brontë, *Villette*
Emily Brontë, *Wuthering Heights*
Benvenuto Cellini, *The Autobiography of Benvenuto Cellini*
Geoffrey Chaucer, *The Canterbury Tales*

Marcus Tullius Cicero, *Cicero: Selected Political Speeches*
Miguel de Cervantes, *The Adventures of Don Quixote*
Bartolome de las Casas, *A Short Account of the Destruction of the West Indies*
René Descartes, *Discourse on Method and The Meditations*
Charles Dickens, *Hard Times*
Charles Dickens, *Great Expectations*
John Dos Passos, *Three Soldiers*
Einhard, *Two Lives of Charlemagne*
Olaudah Equiano, *The Interesting Narrative and Other Writings*
Jeffrey Gantz (tr.), *Early Irish Myths and Sagas*
Peter Gay, *Mozart* (Penguin Lives Series)
William Golding, *Lord of the Flies*
Kenneth Grahame, *The Wind in the Willows*
Grimm & Grimm, *Grimms' Fairy Tales*
Thomas Hardy, *Jude the Obscure*
Herodotus, *The Histories*

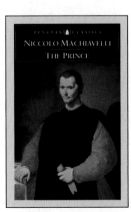

Thomas Hobbes, *Leviathan*
Homer, *The Iliad*
Homer, *Odyssey: Revised Prose Translation*
Homer, *Odyssey Deluxe*
The Koran
Lemisch, *B. Franklin*
Primo Levi, *If Not Now, When?*
Machiavelli, *The Prince*
Karl Marx, *The Communist Manifesto*
John Stuart Mill, *On Liberty*
Jean-Baptiste Molière, *Tartuffe and Other Plays*
Charles-Louis Montesquieu, *Persian Letters*
Sir Thomas More, *Utopia and Other Essential Writings*
Sherwin Nuland, *Leonardo DaVinci*
George Orwell, *1984*
George Orwell, *Animal Farm*
Plato, *Great Dialogues of Plato*
Plato, *The Republic*
Plato, *The Last Days of Socrates*
Marco Polo, *The Travels*
Procopius, *The Secret History*
Jean-Jacques Rousseau, *The Social Contract*
Sallust, *The Jugurthine Wars, The Conspiracy of Cataline*
William Shakespeare, *Hamlet*
William Shakespeare, *Macbeth*
William Shakespeare, *The Merchant of Venice* (Pelican Series)
William Shakespeare, *The Merchant of Venice* (Signet Classics)
William Shakespeare, *Othello*
William Shakespeare, *The Taming of the Shrew*

William Shakespeare, *Twelfth Night*
William Shakespeare, *King Lear*
William Shakespeare, *Four Great Comedies: The Taming of the Shrew, A Midsummer's Night Dream, Twelfth Night, The Tempest*
William Shakespeare, *Four Great Tragedies: Hamlet, Macbeth, King Lear, Othello*
William Shakespeare, *Four Histories: Richard II, Henry IV: Part I, Henry IV: Part II, Henry V*
William Shakespeare, *The Tempest*
Mary Shelley, *Frankenstein*
Aleksandr Solzhenitsyn, *One Day in the Life of Ivan Denisovich*
Sophocles, *The Three Theban Plays*
St. Augustine, *The Confessions of St. Augustine*
Robert Louis Stevenson, *The Strange Case of Dr. Jekyll and Mr. Hyde*
Suetonius, *The Twelve Caesars*
Jonathan Swift, *Gulliver's Travels*
Tacitus, *The Histories*
Voltaire, *Candide, Zadig and Selected Stories*
Goethe, *Faust, Part 1*
Goethe, *Faust, Part 2*
Edith Wharton, *Ethan Frome*
M. Willet, *The Signet World Atlas*
Gary Wills, *Saint Augustine* (Penguin Lives Series)
Virginia Woolf, *Jacob's Room*

Acknowledgments

In writing this book we have benefited from the guidance of many members of the superb editorial staff at Longman. Our first acquisitions editor, Bruce Borland, encouraged us to write a book emphasizing the theme of cultural encounters, while Jay O'Callaghan and Erika Gutierrez helped us refine that theme as the book progressed. Dawn Groundwater, our senior development editor, gave us valuable line-by-line criticisms of all our chapters and helped us keep our audience in mind as we revised them. Lisa Pinto, the director of development, read our chapters at different stages of composition and made sure that our arguments were logical and consistent. Priscilla McGeehon, publisher for the social sciences, facilitated the progress of the project at a number of crucial junctures. Susan Gallier superintended the copyediting and proofreading with skill and efficiency, while Jullie Chung helped us locate the most appropriate illustrations. Sue Westmoreland, the executive marketing manager for history, offered many creative ideas for promoting the book.

The authors wish to thank the following friends and colleagues for their assistance: Joseph Alehermes, Kenneth Alder, Karl Appuhn, Sharon Arnoult, Nicholas Baker, Paul-Alain Beaulieu, Paula Baskovits, Kamilia Bergen, Timothy Breen, Peter Brown, Peter Carroll, Patricia Crone, Tracey Cullen, Arthur Eckstein, Susanna Elm, Benjamin Frommer, Cynthia Gladstone, Dena Goodman, Matthias Henze, Stanley Hilton, Kenneth Holum, Mark Jurdjevic, Werner Kelber, Cathleen Keller, Anne Kilmer, Jacob Lassner, Robert Lerner, Nancy Levack, Richard Lim, David Lindenfeld, Sarah Maza, Laura McGough, Roderick McIntosh, Susan K. McIntosh, Glenn Markoe, William Monter, Randy Nichols, Scott Noegel, Monique O'Connell, Carl Petry, Michael Rogers, Karl Roider, Sarah Ross, Michele Salzman, Paula Sanders, Regina Schwartz, Ethan Shagan, Julia M. H. Smith, and James Sidbury.

We would also like to thank the many historians who gave generously of their time to review our manuscript at various stages of development. Their comments and suggestions have helped to improve the book. Thank you:

Henry Abramson, *Florida Atlantic University*

Patricia Ali, *Morris College*

Joseph Appiah, *J. Sergeant Reynolds Community College*

Sharon L. Arnoult, *Midwestern State University*

Arthur H. Auten, *University of Hartford*

Clifford Backman, *Boston University*

Suzanne Balch-Lindsay, *Eastern New Mexico University*

Wayne C. Bartee, *Southwest Miami State University*

Brandon Beck, *Shenandoah University*

James R. Belpedio, *Becker College*

Richard Berthold, *University of New Mexico*

Cynthia S. Bisson, *Belmont University*

Richard Bodek, *College of Charleston*

Melissa Bokovoy, *University of New Mexico*

William H. Brennan, *University of the Pacific*

Morgan R. Broadhead, *Jefferson Community College*

Theodore Bromund, *Yale University*

April A. Brooks, *South Dakota State University*

Nathan M. Brooks, *New Mexico State University*

Michael Burger, *Mississippi University for Women*

Susan Carrafiello, *Wright State University*

Kathleen S. Carter, *High Point University*

William L. Combs, *Western Illinois University*

Joseph Coohill, *Pennsylvania State University—New Kensington*

Richard A. Cosgrove, *University of Arizona*

Leonard Curtis, *Mississippi College*

Miriam Davis, *Delta State University*

Alexander DeGrand, *North Carolina State University*

Marion Deshmukh, *George Mason University*

Janusz Duzinkiewicz, *Purdue University, North Central*

Mary Beth Emmerichs, *University of Wisconsin, Sheboygan*

Steven Fanning, *University of Illinois at Chicago*

Bryan Ganaway, *University of Illinois at Urbana-Champaign*

Frank Garosi, *California State University—Sacramento*

Christina Gold, *Loyola Marymount University*

Ignacio Götz, *Hofstra University*

Louis Haas, *Duquesne University*

Linda Jones Hall, *Saint Mary's College of Maryland*

Paul Halsall, *University of North Florida*

Donald J. Harreld, *Brigham Young University*

Carmen V. Harris, *University of South Carolina at Spartanburg*

James C. Harrison, *Siena College*

Mark C. Herman, *Edison Community College*

Curry A. Herring, *University of Southern Alabama*

Patrick Holt, *Fordham University*

W. Robert Houston, *University of South Alabama*

Lester Hutton, *Westfield State College*

Jeffrey Hyson, *Saint Joseph's University*

Paul Jankowski, *Brandeis University*

Padraic Kennedy, *McNeese State University*

Joanne Klein, *Boise State University*

Theodore Kluz, *Troy State University*

Skip Knox, *Boise State University*

Cynthia Kosso, *Northern Arizona University*

Ann Kuzdale, *Chicago State University*

Lawrence Langer, *University of Connecticut*

Oscar E. Lansen, *University of North Carolina at Charlotte*

Michael V. Leggiere, *Louisiana State University at Shreveport*

Rhett Leverett, *Marymount University*

Alison Williams Lewin, *Saint Joseph's University*

Wendy Liu, *Miami University, Middletown*

Elizabeth Makowski, *Southwest Texas State University*

Daniel Meissner, *Marquette University*

Isabel Moreira, *University of Utah*

Kenneth Moure, *University of California—Santa Barbara*

Melva E. Newsom, *Clark State Community College*

John A. Nichols, *Slippery Rock University*

Susannah R. Ottaway, *Carleton College*

James H. Overfield, *University of Vermont*

Brian L. Peterson, *Florida International University*

Hugh Phillips, *Western Kentucky University*

Jeff Plaks, *University of Central Oklahoma*

Thomas L. Powers, *University of South Carolina, Sumter*

Carole Putko, *San Diego State University*

Barbara Ranieri, *University of Alabama at Birmingham*

Elsa M. E. Rapp, *Montgomery County Community College*

Marlette Rebhorn, *Austin Community College*

Roger Reese, *Texas A&M University*

Travis Ricketts, *Bryan College*

Thomas Robisheaux, *Duke University*

Bill Robison, *Southeastern Louisiana University*

Mark Ruff, *Concordia University*

Frank Russell, *Transylvania University*

Marylou Ruud, *The University of West Florida*

Michael Saler, *University of California—Davis*

Timothy D. Saxon, *Charleston Southern University*

Daniel A. Scalberg, *Multnomah Bible College*

Ronald Schechter, *College of William and Mary*

Philip Skaggs, *Grand Valley State University*

Helmut Walser Smith, *Vanderbilt University*

Eileen Solwedel, *Edmonds Community College*

Sister Maria Consuelo Sparks, *Immaculata University*

Ilicia J. Sprey, *Saint Joseph's College*

Charles R. Sullivan, *University of Dallas*

Frederick Suppe, *Ball State University*

Frank W. Thackery, *Indiana University Southeast*

Frances B. Titchener, *Utah State University*

Katherine Tosa, *Muskegon Community College*

Lawrence A. Tritle, *Loyola Marymount University*

Clifford F. Wargelin, *Georgetown College*

Theodore R. Weeks, *Southern Illinois University*

Elizabeth A. Williams, *Oklahoma State University*

Mary E. Zamon, *Marymount University*

BRIAN LEVACK
EDWARD MUIR
MICHAEL MAAS
MEREDITH VELDMAN

Meet the Authors

Brian Levack grew up in a family of teachers in the New York metropolitan area. From his father, a professor of French history, he acquired a love for studying the past, and he knew from an early age that he too would become a historian. He received his B.A. from Fordham University in 1965 and his Ph.D. from Yale in 1970. In graduate school he became fascinated by the history of the law and the interaction between law and politics, interests that he has maintained throughout his career. In 1969 he joined the History Department of the University of Texas at Austin, where he is now the John Green Regents Professor in History. The winner of several teaching awards, Levack teaches a wide variety of courses on British and European history, legal history, and the history of witchcraft. For eight years he served as the chair of his department, a rewarding but challenging assignment that made it difficult for him to devote as much time as he wished to his teaching and scholarship. His books include *The Civil Lawyers in England, 1603–1641: A Political Study* (1973), *The Formation of the British State: England, Scotland and the Union, 1603–1707* (1987), and *The Witch-Hunt in Early Modern Europe* (1987 and 1995), which has been translated into eight languages.

His study of the development of beliefs about witchcraft in Europe over the course of many centuries gave him the idea of writing a textbook on Western civilization that would illustrate a broader set of encounters between different cultures, societies, and ideologies. While writing the book, Levack and his two sons built a house on property that he and his wife, Nancy, own in the Texas hill country. He found that the two projects presented similar challenges: It was easy to draw up the design, but far more difficult to execute it. When not teaching, writing, or doing carpentry work, Levack runs along the jogging trails of Austin, and he has recently discovered the pleasures of scuba diving.

Edward Muir grew up in the foothills of the Wasatch Mountains in Utah, close to the Emigration Trail along which wagon trains of Mormon pioneers and California-bound settlers made their way westward. As a child he loved to explore the broken-down wagons and abandoned household goods left at the side of the trail and from that acquired a fascination with the past. Besides the material remains of the past, he grew up with stories of his Mormon pioneer ancestors and an appreciation for how the past continued to influence the present. During the turbulent 1960s, he became interested in Renaissance Italy as a period and a place that had been formative for Western civilization. His biggest challenge is finding the time to explore yet another new corner of Italy and its restaurants.

Muir received his Ph.D. from Rutgers University, where he specialized in the Italian Renaissance and did archival research in Venice and Florence, Italy. He is now the Clarence L. Ver Steeg Professor in the Arts and Sciences at Northwestern University and former chair of the History Department. At Northwestern he has won several teaching awards. His books include *Civic Ritual in Renaissance Venice* (Princeton, 1981); *Mad Blood Stirring: Vendetta in Renaissance Italy* (Johns Hopkins, 1993 and 1998); and *Ritual in Early Modern Europe* (Cambridge, 1997).

Some years ago Muir began to experiment with the use of historical trials in teaching and discovered that students loved them. From that experience he decided to write this textbook, which employs trials as a central feature. He lives beside Lake Michigan in Evanston, Illinois. His twin passions are skiing in the Rocky Mountains and rooting for the Chicago Cubs, who manage every summer to demonstrate that winning isn't everything.

Michael Maas was born in the Ohio River Valley, in a community that had been a frontier outpost during the late eighteenth century. He grew up reading the stories of the early settlers and their struggles with the native peoples, and seeing in the urban fabric how the city had subsequently developed into a prosperous coal and steel town with immigrants from all over the world. As a boy he developed a lifetime interest in the archaeology and history of the ancient Mediterranean world and began to study Latin. At Cornell University he combined his interests in cultural history and the Classical world by majoring in Classics and Anthropology. A semester in Rome clinched his commitment to these fields—and to Italian cooking. Maas went on to get his Ph.D. in the Graduate Program in Ancient History and Mediterranean Archaeology at University of California at Berkeley.

He has traveled widely in the Mediterranean and the Middle East and participated in several archaeological excavations, including an underwater dig in Greece. Since 1985 he has taught ancient history at Rice University in Houston, Texas, where he founded and directs the interdisciplinary B.A. Program in Ancient Mediterranean Civilizations. He has won several teaching awards.

Maas's special area of research is Late Antiquity, the period of transition from the Classical to the Medieval worlds, which saw the collapse of the Roman Empire in western Europe and the development of the Byzantine state in the east. During his last sabbatical, he was a member of the Institute for Advanced Study in Princeton, New Jersey, where he worked on his current book, *The Conqueror's Gift: Ethnography, Identity, and Imperial Power at the End of Antiquity* (forthcoming). His other books include *John Lydus and the Roman Past: Antiquarianism and Politics in the Age of Justinian* (1992); *Readings in Late Antiquity: A Sourcebook* (2000); and *Exegesis and Empire in the Early Byzantine Mediterranean* (2003).

Maas has always been interested in interdisciplinary teaching and the encounters among different cultures. He sees *The West: Encounters & Transformations* as an opportunity to explain how the modern civilization that we call "the West" had its origins in the diverse interactions among many peoples of antiquity.

Meredith Veldman grew up in the western suburbs of Chicago in a close-knit, closed-in Dutch Calvinist community. In this immigrant society, history mattered: the "Reformed tradition" structured not only religious beliefs but also social identity and political practice. This influence certainly played some role in shaping Veldman's early fascination with history. But probably just as important were the countless World War II re-enactment games she played with her five older brothers. Whatever the cause, Veldman majored in history at Calvin College in Grand Rapids, Michigan, and then earned a Ph.D. in modern European history, with a concentration in nineteenth- and twentieth-century Britain, from Northwestern University in 1988.

As Associate Professor of History at Louisiana State University, Veldman teaches courses in nineteenth- and twentieth-century British history and twentieth-century Europe, as well as the second half of "Western Civ." In her many semesters in the Western Civ. classroom, Veldman tried a number of different textbooks but found herself increasingly dissatisfied. She wanted a text that would convey to beginning students at least some of the complexities and ambiguities of historical interpretation, introduce them to the exciting work being done now in cultural history, and, most important, tell a good story. The search for this textbook led her to accept the offer made by Levack, Maas, and Muir to join them in writing *The West: Encounters & Transformations*.

The author of *Fantasy, the Bomb, and the Greening of Britain: Romantic Protest, 1945–1980* (1994), Veldman is also the wife of a Methodist minister and the mother of two young sons. They reside in Baton Rouge, Louisiana, where Veldman finds coping with the steamy climate a constant challenge. She and her family recently returned from Manchester, England, where they lived for three years and astonished the natives by their enthusiastic appreciation of English weather.

THE WEST

What Is the West?

MANY OF THE PEOPLE WHO INFLUENCE PUBLIC OPINION—POLITICIANS, teachers, clergy, journalists, and television commentators—frequently refer to "Western values," "the West," and "Western civilization." They often use these terms as if they do not require explanation. But what *do* these terms mean? The West has always been an arena within which different cultures, religions, values, and philosophies have interacted, and any definition of the West will inevitably arouse controversy.

The most basic definition of the West is of a place. Western civilization is now typically thought to comprise the regions of Europe, the Americas, Australia, and New Zealand. As we shall see, however, over time these boundaries have shifted considerably. In addition to being a place, Western civilization also encompasses a history—a tradition stretching back thousands of years to the ancient world. Over this long period the civilization we now identify as Western gradually took shape. The many characteristics that identify any civilization emerged over this time: forms of governments, economic systems, and methods of scientific inquiry, as well as religions, languages, literature, and art.

Throughout the development of Western civilization, the ways in which people identified themselves changed as well. People in the ancient world had no such idea of the common identity of the West, only of being subjects of an empire. But with the rise of Christianity and Islam between the third and seventh centuries C.E., the notion of a distinct civilization in these "Western" lands subtly changed. People came to identify themselves less as subjects of a particular empire and more as members of a community of faith—whether that community comprised followers of Christianity, Judaism, or Islam (see Chapter 7). These communities of faith drew lines of inclusion and exclusion that still exist today. Starting about 1,600 years ago, Christian monarchs obliterated polytheism (the worship of many gods) and marginalized Jews. Several centuries later they strove to expel Muslims from Christian kingdoms (see Chapter 9). Europeans developed definitions of the West that did not include Islamic communities. The Islamic countries themselves erected their own barriers, isolating themselves from the West. During the Renaissance in the fifteenth century an identity based on a continuous historical experience dating back to the ancient world was added to these religious definitions of the identity of the West.

The Temple of Hera at Paestum, Italy: Greek colonists in Italy built this temple in the sixth century B.C.E. Greek ideas and artistic styles spread throughout the ancient world both from Greek colonists, such as those at Paestum, and from other peoples who imitated the Greeks.

The definition of the West has also changed as a result of European colonialism, which began about 500 years ago. When European powers assembled large overseas empires, they introduced Western languages, religions, technology, and culture to many distant places in the world, making Western identity a transportable concept (see Chapters 12, 19, and 23). In some of these colonized areas—such as North America, Argentina, Australia, and New Zealand—the European newcomers so outnumbered the indigenous people that these regions became as much a part of the West as Britain, France, and Spain. In other European colonies, especially in European trading outposts on the Asian continent, Western culture failed to exercise a widespread influence.

As a result of colonialism Western culture sometimes merged with other cultures. Brazil, a South American country inhabited by large numbers of indigenous peoples, the descendants of African slaves, and European settlers, epitomizes the complexity of what defines the West. In Brazil, almost everyone speaks a Western language (Portuguese), practices a Western religion (Christianity), and enjoys the benefits of Western political and economic institutions (democracy and capitalism). Yet in Brazil all of these features of Western civilization have become part of a distinctive culture, in which indigenous, African, and European elements have been blended. During Carnival, for example, Brazilians dressed in indigenous costumes dance in African rhythms to the accompaniment of music played on European instruments.

For many people today, the most important definition of the West involves adherence to a certain set of values, the "Western" values. Values are the moral and philosophical principles that are held in esteem by a particular culture. The values typically identified as Western include universal human rights, toleration of religious diversity, equality before the law, democracy, and freedom of inquiry and expression. These values have a long history. Yet these values have not always been embraced by Western societies. For example, the rulers of ancient Rome extended the privileges of citizenship, the right to own property, and the ability to participate in trade to a select few inhabitants of their empire (see Chapter 5)—thus only the privileged enjoyed the benefits of equality before the law. The majority of medieval Europeans, who were Christian, expressed an intense intolerance for religious diversity expressed in the Crusades against Muslims and heretics and pogroms against Jews (see Chapter 9). As late as the nineteenth century, white men living in the United States enslaved blacks and into the twentieth excluded women from voting and equal access to jobs. And in Nazi Germany and the Soviet Union, totalitarian regimes terrorized their own population and millions of others beyond their borders (see Chapter 25). The history

■ **A Satellite View of Europe**
What is the West? Western civilization has undergone numerous transformations throughout history, but it has always included Europe.

of the West is riddled with examples of leaders who stifled free inquiry and who censored their followers. What are we to make of this contradiction in values? This text highlights and examines these contradictions, demonstrating how hard values were to formulate in the first place and how difficult they have been to preserve.

The Shifting Borders of the West

The geographical setting of the West has also shifted over time. This textbook begins about 10,000 years ago in southwestern Asia and Egypt. At that time the domestication of animals and crops began, and vast trading networks were being established. Cities, kingdoms, and empires gave birth to the first civilizations. By about 500 B.C.E., the civilizations that are the cultural ancestors of the modern West had spread from the Middle East to include the Mediterranean basin—areas influenced by Egyptian, Hebrew, Greek, and Roman thought, art, law, and religion. By the first century C.E. the Roman Empire drew the map of what historians consider the heartland of the West: most of western and southern Europe, the coastlands of the Mediterranean Sea, and the Middle East.

The West is now usually thought to include Europe and the Americas. However, the borders of the West have in recent decades come to be less about geography than identity. When Japan, an Asian country, accepted some Western values such as human rights and democracy after World War II, did it become part of the West? Or consider the Republic of South Africa, which until 1994 was ruled by the white minority, people descended from European immigrants. The oppressive regime violated human rights, rejected full legal equality for all citizens, and jailed or murdered those who questioned the government. Only when that government was replaced through democratic elections and a black man became president did South Africa grant full rights to non-Europeans. To what degree was South Africa part of the West before and after these developments?

Russia long saw itself as a Christian country with a tradition of culture, economic, and political ties with the rest of Europe. The Russians have intermittently identified with their western neighbors, but their neighbors were not always sure about the Russians. After the Mongol invasions of the thirteenth and fourteenth centuries much of Russia was isolated from the rest of the West (see Chapter 10) and during the Cold War from 1949 to 1989 (see Chapters 27–29) Russian communism and the Western democracies were polarized. When was Russia "Western" and when not?

Thus, when we talk about where the West is, we are almost always talking about the Mediterranean basin and much of Europe (and later, the Americas). But we will also show that countries that border "the West," and even countries far from it, might be considered Western in many aspects as well.

Asking the Right Questions

So how can we make sense of the West as a place and an identity, the shifting borders of the West, and Western civilization in general? In short, what has Western civilization been over the course of its long history—and what is it today?

Answering these questions is the friendly challenge this book poses. You may be alarmed to learn that there are no simple answers to any of these questions. On the other hand, you may be relieved to discover that there is a method for finding answers that have meaning for the different periods of history covered in this book. The method

■ **The Astrolabe**

The mariner's astrolabe was a navigational device intended for use primarily at sea. The astrolabe originated in the Islamic world and was adopted by Europeans in the twelfth century—a cultural encounter that enabled Europeans to embark on long ocean voyages around the world.

is straightforward. Always ask the *what*, the *when*, the *where*, the *who*, the *how*, and the *why* questions of the text. If you do so, you will surmount the challenge the book poses. To aid you, every chapter addresses the question of "What is the West," or "How was the West made" at its beginning following the story or event that opens the chapter. We revisit the question in the Conclusion at the end of every chapter. For example, in Chapter 11 we look at how the Italian Renaissance helped refashion the very concept of Western civilization. In the Conclusion, we see that the Renaissance interest in the history of the ancient world transformed the idea of the West from one defined primarily by religious identification with Christianity to one created by a common historical experience.

THE "WHAT" QUESTION

What is Western civilization? The answer to this question will vary according to time and place. In fact, for much of the early history covered in this book, Western civilization as we know it today did not exist as a single cultural entity. Rather, a number of distinctive civilizations were taking shape in the Middle East, northern Africa, and Europe, each of which contributed to what later became Western civilization (see Chapters 1–3). But throughout time the idea of Western civilization slowly began to form. Thus our understanding of Western civilization will change from chapter to chapter. For example, in Chapters 12, 19, and 23, we examine how the place of the West changed through the colonial expansion of the European nations. In Chapter 16 we learn how the West came to prize the values of scientific inquiry for solving human and philosophical problems, an approach that did not exist before the seventeenth century but became central to Western civilization.

THE "WHEN" QUESTION

When did the defining characteristics of Western civilization first emerge, and for how long did they prevail? To explore these questions you will want to refer to the dates that frame and organize each chapter, as well as the numerous short chronologies offered in each chapter. These resources will help you keep track of what happened when. Dates have no meaning by themselves, but the connections *between* them can be very revealing. For example, dates show that the agricultural revolution that permitted the birth of the first civilizations (see Chapter 1) unfolded over a long span of about 10,000 years—which is more time than was taken by all the other events and developments covered in this textbook. Wars of religion (see Chapter 14) plagued Europe for nearly 200 years before Enlightenment thinkers articulated the ideals of religious toleration (see Chapter 17). The American Civil War—the war to preserve the union as President Abraham Lincoln termed it—took place at exactly the same time as other wars were being fought to achieve national unity in Germany and Italy (see Chapter 21).

By learning when things happened, you can identify the major causes and consequences of events, and thus you can see the transformations of Western civilization. For instance, the ability to produce a surplus of food through agriculture and the domestication of animals was a prerequisite for the emergence of civilizations. The violent collapse of religious unity after the Protestant Reformation in the sixteenth century led some Europeans to propose the separation of church and state two centuries later. And during the nineteenth century many Western states—in response to the enormous diversity among their own peoples—became preoccupied with maintaining or establishing national unity.

THE "WHERE" QUESTION

Where has Western civilization been located? Geography, of course, does not change very rapidly, but the idea of where the West is does. The location of the West is not so much a matter of changing borders but of how people identify themselves. The key to understanding the shifting borders of the West is to study how the peoples within the West

■ **Map 1   Core Lands of the West**
The geographical borders of the West have changed substantially throughout history.

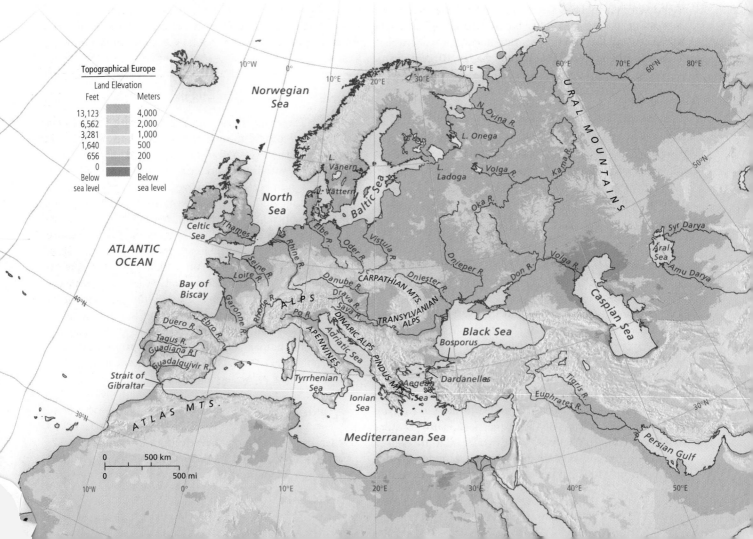

■ Cortés Meets Montezuma

As the Spanish fought, traded, and intermarried with the native peoples of the Americas during the fifteenth and sixteenth centuries, each culture changed.

thought of themselves. These groups include Muslims and the peoples of eastern Europe (such as the Soviet Union during the Cold War), which some people have wanted to exclude from the West. In addition, the chapters help you trace the relationships between the West (as it was constituted in different periods) and other, more distant civilizations with which it interacted. Those civilizations include not only those of East Asia and South Asia but also the indigenous peoples of sub-Saharan Africa, the Americas, and the Pacific islands (see Chapters 12, 19, and 23).

THE "WHO" QUESTION

Who were the people responsible for making Western civilization? Sometimes they were anonymous, such as the unknown geniuses who invented the mathematical systems of ancient Mesopotamia. At other times the makers of the West were famous—conquerors such as Julius Caesar, creative thinkers such as Galileo Galilei, or generals such as Napoleon. But history is not only made by great and famous people. Humble people, such as the many millions who migrated from Europe to North America or the unfortunate millions who suffered and died in the trenches of World War I, can also influence the course of events.

Perhaps most often in this book you will encounter people who were less the shapers of their own destinies than the subjects of forces that conditioned the kinds of choices they could make, often with unanticipated results. When during the eleventh century farmers throughout Europe began to employ a new kind of plow to till their fields, they were merely trying to do their work more efficiently. They certainly did not recognize that the increase in food they produced would stimulate the enormous population growth that made possible the medieval civilization of thriving cities and magnificent cathedrals. In answering the who question, you will always want to evaluate how much individuals and groups of people were in control of events and how much events controlled them.

THE "HOW" QUESTION

How did Western civilization develop? This is a question about processes—about how things change or stay the same over time. This book will help you identify these processes in several ways. First, we have woven the theme of encounters throughout the story. What do we mean by encounters? Here is an example from Chapter 12: When the Spanish *conquistadores* arrived in the Americas some 500 years ago, they came into contact with the cultures of the Caribs, the Aztecs, the Incas, and other peoples who had lived in the Americas for thousands of years. As the Spanish fought, traded with, and intermarried with the natives, each culture changed. The Spanish, for their part, borrowed from the Americas new plants for cultivation and responded to what they considered serious threats to their worldview. Many native Americans, in turn, adopted European religious practices and learned to speak European languages. At the same time, they were decimated by

European diseases to which they had never been exposed. They also witnessed the destruction of their own civilizations and governments at the hands of the colonial powers. Through many centuries of interaction and mutual influence, both sides became something other than what they had been.

The European encounter with the Americas is an obvious example of what was, in fact, a continuous process of encounters with other cultures. These encounters often occurred between peoples from different civilizations, such as the struggles between Greeks and Persians in the ancient world (see Chapter 3) or between Europeans and Chinese in the nineteenth century (see Chapter 23). Other encounters took place among people living in the same civilization. These include interactions between lords and peasants, men and women, Christians and Jews, Catholics and Protestants, factory owners and workers, and capitalists and communists. Western civilization developed and changed through a series of external and internal encounters.

Second, features in the chapters can also help you formulate answers to the question of how Western civilization developed. For example, each chapter contains an essay titled "Justice in History". These essays discuss a trial or some other episode involving questions of justice. Some "Justice in History" essays illustrate how Western civilization was forged in struggles over conflicting values, such as the discussion of the trial of Galileo in Chapter 16, which examines the conflict between religious and scientific concepts of truth. Others show how efforts to resolve internal cultural, political, and religious tensions helped shape Western ideas about justice, such as the essay on the *auto da fé* in Chapter 14, which illustrates how authorities attempted to enforce religious conformity. At the end of each "Justice in History" feature, you will find several questions tying that essay to the theme of the chapter. These questions will also ask you to explore the value-based conflicts or disputes embodied in the incident described in the essay.

Some chapters include two other features as well. Essays titled "The Human Body in History" demonstrate that even the body, which we typically understand as a product of genetics and biology, has a history. These essays show that the ways in which Western people understand their bodies, how they cure them, how they cover and uncover them, and how they adorn them tell us a great deal about the history of Western culture. We explore, for example, how the bodies of World War I soldiers afflicted with shell shock were treated differently from women experiencing similar symptoms of hysteria (see Chapter 24). Shell-shocked soldiers gave people a sense of the horrors of war and stimulated powerful movements in Europe to outlaw war as an instrument of government policy.

The "Places of Encounter" features show how encounters between different groups of people were not abstract historical processes but events that occurred in actual places, such as in the nineteenth-century soccer stadium (see Chapter 23). In the nineteenth century soccer was a sport reserved for gentlemen, but in the great industrial cities it became the favorite sport of the industrial workers. In the soccer stadiums they began to experience their common identity as a class.

THE "WHY" QUESTION

Why should you study Western civilization? Because everything around you depends on it—the education you receive, the books you read, the language you speak and those you study, the legal system that protects you, and the political one that guarantees you certain rights. The buildings you inhabit, the music and art you enjoy, and the science and technology that provides you with health, comfort, and prosperity are all artifacts of Western civilization. To appreciate all that, to contribute to it more fully yourself, and when necessary to question and critique it, requires that you understand the West was sometimes very different from the present—it was like a foreign country—and how it was sometimes very much like the present, the foundation upon which your world was made.

The Age of the French Revolution, 1789–1815

O N July 12, 1789, the French journalist Camille Desmoulins addressed an anxious crowd of Parisian citizens gathered outside the royal palace. Playing upon fears that had been mounting during the past two months, Desmoulins claimed that the royal government of Louis XVI was preparing a massacre of Parisians. "To arms, to arms," Desmoulins cried out, as he roused the citizens to their own defense. That night Parisians responded to his call by invading arsenals in the city in anticipation of the violence they thought was about to descend upon them. The next day they continued to seize weapons and declared themselves members of the National Guard, a volunteer militia of propertied citizens.

On the morning of July 14, crowds of Parisians moved into one of the suburbs of the city, where royal troops were stationed in an ancient fortress known as the Bastille. The Parisians feared that the troops in the Bastille would take violent action against them, and they also wanted to capture the ammunition stored inside the fortress, which served as both an arsenal and a prison. Negotiations with the governor of the Bastille were interrupted when some of the militia, moving into the courtyard of the fortress, demanded the surrender of the troops. Shots were fired from both sides, and the exchange led to a full-scale assault upon the Bastille by the National Guard.

After three hours of fighting and the death of eighty-three people, the governor surrendered. He was then led by his captors, bearing the arms they had seized, to face charges before the officers of the city government. The crowd, however, crying for vengeance against their oppressors, attacked the soldiers and crushed them one by one underfoot. The governor was stabbed hundreds of times, hacked to pieces, and decapitated. The chief magistrate of the city suffered

The Storming of the Bastille, July 14, 1789: The Bastille was attacked not because it was a symbol of the Old Regime, but because it contained weapons that the Parisian citizens needed to protect themselves from royalist troops.

the same fate for his reluctance to issue arms to its citizens. The crowd then placed the heads of the two men on spears and paraded through the city.

The storming of the Bastille was the first of many violent episodes that occurred during the sequence of events called the French Revolution. That revolution brought about some of the most fundamental changes in European political life since the end of Roman rule. It heralded the destruction of the Old Regime, the eighteenth-century political order that had been dominated by an absolute monarch and a privileged nobility and clergy. It led to the submission of the Catholic Church to state control. A more radical phase of the revolution, beginning in 1792, resulted in the destruction of the French monarchy and the declaration of a republic. It also led to a period of state-sponsored terrorism in 1793 and 1794, during which one group of revolutionaries engaged in a brutal campaign to eliminate their real and imagined enemies.

The excesses of the revolution led to a conservative reaction. Between 1795 and 1799 a moderate republican government, known as the Directory, modified the egalitarianism of the revolution by limiting the right to vote to men of property. Between 1799 and 1814 the reaction continued under the direction of Napoleon Bonaparte, a military officer who dominated the Consulate, a new political structure established in 1799, and then proclaimed himself emperor in 1804. Although Napoleon declared his loyalty to many of the principles of the revolution, his authoritarian rule undermined or reversed many of its achievements. In 1815 Napoleon fell from power and the monarchy was restored, marking the end of the revolutionary period. The ideas of the revolution, however, especially its commitment to democratic republicanism and its concept of the nation, continued to dominate politics in the West for the next hundred years. The French Revolution permanently changed the political culture of the West.

In this chapter we shall address five questions regarding the era of the French Revolution: (1) Why did the Old Regime in France collapse in 1789, and what revolutionary changes took place in French government and society during the next two years? (2) How did a second, more radical revolution, which began with the establishment of the Republic in 1792, lead to the creation of a regime that used the power of the state to institute the Reign of Terror? (3) In what ways did the political events of the revolution change French cultural institutions and create a new political culture? (4) How did the authoritarian rule of Napoleon Bonaparte from 1799 to 1814 confirm or betray the achievements of the French Revolution, and what impact did his military conquests have on Europe and the world? (5) What did the French Revolution ultimately achieve and in what ways did it change the course of European and Western history?

The First French Revolution, 1789–1791

One of the main characteristics of political revolutions is that they involve a fundamental change in the political *system*, not simply in the personnel of government. On the basis of this criterion the French Revolution consisted of two distinct revolutions. The first revolution, which began in 1789, resulted in a destruction of royal absolutism and the drafting of a constitution. The second and more radical revolution began in 1792 with the abolition of the monarchy and the formation of the French Republic.

Like all revolutions, the first French revolution had deep-seated causes. As we discussed in Chapter 17, a constant barrage of satirical literature directed at the royal family and the court lowered the prestige of the government and thus weakened its authority. The publication of thousands of pamphlets advocating reform, including many written by philosophes of the Enlightenment, fostered a critical attitude toward the French government and led to demands for political and economic change. Conflicts between the nobility and the crown over constitutional issues, a source of tension throughout the age of absolutism, led to charges that the government was acting despotically. Encounters between the landowning nobility and the peasantry, which increased in the last half of the eighteenth century, also contributed to the disaffection with the Old Regime and played a major role in stimulating demands for a restriction of the privileges enjoyed by the nobility. Ongoing food shortages in the cities created a militant citizenry ready to take action against authorities they considered responsible for the high price of bread.

The immediate cause of the revolution was a major economic crisis that bankrupted the monarchy and deprived it of its authority. This crisis led to a revolt of the nobles against the crown and brought down the entire system of royal absolutism. Only after this collapse of royal government did various groups that had had long-standing grievances against the regime take the initiative and establish a new political system. These groups never actually planned the revolution; they simply filled a void created by the absence of effective governmental power.

THE BEGINNING OF THE REVOLUTION

The financial crisis that brought about the collapse of the French government peaked in the late 1780s. The government of Louis XVI (r. 1774–1792) had inherited considerable debts from that of his grandfather, Louis XV (r. 1715–1774) as a result of protracted periods of warfare with Great Britain. The opening of a new phase of this warfare in 1778, when France intervened in the American War of Independence on the side of the United States, pushed the government further into debt and put a strain on the entire French economy. Attempts to solve the crisis by implementing financial reforms made the situation only worse. In 1787 the government had a revenue of 475 million livres and expenses of just under 600 million livres. More than half of the revenue went to pay interest on the accumulated debt. As the crisis deepened, protests from the ranks of the nobility against royal policy became more vocal.

In 1787 the king made efforts to win the support of the nobility by convening an Assembly of Notables, a handpicked group of 144 nominees, the great majority of whom were noblemen. The purpose of the meeting was to gain approval for a new system of taxation that would include a direct tax on all landowners. These proposals encountered formidable opposition from the members of the assembly, and the meeting was adjourned. Some of the nobles in the assembly had been willing to pay the taxes, but only if the king would convoke the Estates General, a national legislative body that had not met since 1614. Convening the Estates General, they argued, would provide them with guarantees against royal despotism. Louis resisted these pressures, since he did not want to give up the right to make law by his own authority.

The king then tried to gain approval of new taxes from the regional parlements, the provincial law courts whose powers included the registration of royal edicts. There too the crown met resistance. The Parlement of Paris, which was the most important of all the parlements, refused to comply with the king's request. The other parlements followed suit, claiming that only the Estates General had the power to approve new taxes. Constitutional tension was heightened when the king demanded the registration of edicts for new loans without the approval of the parlements, a step that even he acknowledged was illegal. He then suspended the parlements, thereby deepening the constitutional crisis.

The deterioration of the government's financial condition finally forced the king to yield to the demands of the nobles and the increasingly hostile popular press. When tax returns dried up as the result of an agricul-

tural crisis in the summer months of 1788, the government could no longer pay its creditors. In a desperate effort to save his regime, Louis announced that he would convene the Estates General. By this time there was little hope for Louis. His absolutist government had completely collapsed.

The meeting of the Estates General was set for May 1789, and during the months leading up to its opening, public debates arose over how the delegates should vote. The Estates General consisted of representatives of the three orders or social groups, known as estates, that made up French society: the clergy, the nobility, and the Third Estate.

CHRONOLOGY

The First French Revolution, 1789–1791

1787		
	February 22	Convening of the Assembly of Notables
1788		
	August 8	Announcement of the meeting of the Estates General
1789		
	May 5	The Estates General opens at Versailles
	June 17	The Third Estate adopts the title of the National Assembly
	June 20	Oath of the Tennis Court
	July 11	The king dismisses his finance minister, Jacques Necker
	July 14	The storming of the Bastille
	Late July	The Great Fear in rural areas
	August 4	Abolition of feudalism and privileges
	August 26	*Declaration of the Rights of Man and Citizen*
	October 5	March to Versailles; Louis XVI and National Assembly move to Paris
	November 2	Church property is nationalized
1790		
	July 12	Civil Constitution of the Clergy
	July 14	Feast of the Federation
	November 27	Decree requiring oath of loyalty from the clergy
1791		
	June 20	Royal family flees to Varennes, is apprehended by the National Guard
	October 1	Newly elected Legislative Assembly opens

The Third Estate technically contained all the commoners in the kingdom (about 96 percent of the population), ranging from the wealthiest merchant to the poorest peasant. The elected representatives of the Third Estate, whose numbers had doubled by a recent order of the king, were propertied nonnoble elements of lay society, including many lawyers and military officers.

Before the meeting a dispute arose among the representatives whether the three groups would vote by estate, in which case the first two estates would dominate the assembly, or by head, in which case the Third Estate would have numerical parity. Each side claimed that it was the best representative of the "nation," a term meaning the entire body of French people. The nobles maintained that the nation was represented by the nobility and clergy from all the provinces, especially the members of the provincial parlements, who had been critical of royal power during the past few decades. The members of the Third Estate advanced the claim that *they* represented the nation. The cleric Emmanuel-Joseph Sieyès (1748–1836), who joined the Third Estate during this dispute, claimed that it "has within itself all that is necessary to constitute a nation. . . . Nothing can go on without it, and everything would go on far better without the others . . . This privileged class (nobility and clergy) is assuredly foreign to the nation by its do-nothing uselessness."

The question of voting within the Estates General was not resolved when that body met at Versailles on May 5, 1789. After the king indicated that he would side with the clergy and nobility, the Third Estate took the dramatic step of declaring itself a National Assembly and asking members of the other estates to vote with them on the basis of "one man, one vote." Many members of the lower clergy and a few noblemen accepted this invitation. In a conciliatory response to this challenge, the king planned to summon all three estates to a special "royal session" to announce some concessions. In preparation for this meeting, however, he locked the Third Estate out of its meeting hall without explanation. The outraged members of the Third Estate went to a nearby indoor tennis court and took a solemn oath that they would not disband until the country had been given a constitution. One week later, after more clerics and noblemen had joined the ranks of the Third Estate, the king ordered the nobility and the clergy to join the National Assembly.

As this political crisis was reaching a climax, a major social crisis caused by the high price of bread was causing a breakdown of public order. For many years French agriculture had had difficulty meeting the demands of an expanding population. These problems, aggravated in the 1780s by a succession of poor harvests, climaxed in a widespread harvest failure in 1788. As the price of bread soared, demand for manufactured goods shrank, thus causing widespread unemployment among artisans. An increasing number of bread riots, peasant revolts, and urban strikes contributed to a sense of panic at the very time that the government's financial crisis deepened. In Paris the situation reached a critical point in June 1789.

At this point the king, a man with little political sense, made two ill-advised decisions. The first was to send 17,000 royal troops to Paris to restore order. The arrival of the troops gave the impression that the government was planning an attack on the people of the city. The second decision was the dismissal of the king's popular finance minister, Jacques Necker, who had favored the meeting of the Estates General and demonstrated real concern for the welfare of the populace. His dismissal sent a signal that the king was contemplating a move against the National Assembly. It was in this atmosphere of public paranoia that Parisians formed the National Guard and stormed the Bastille.

The fall of the Bastille unnerved the king. When he asked one of his aides, "Is it a revolt?" the aide replied, "No, sire, it is a revolution." The revolution had just begun. It moved into high gear two weeks later when the National Assembly responded to the outbreak of social unrest in the provinces. The scarcity of grain in the countryside gave rise to false rumors that the nobles were engaged in a plot to destroy crops and starve the people into submission. Peasants armed themselves and prepared to fight off the hired agents of the nobility. Some of these peasants burned the mansions of noblemen, together with the deeds that gave the nobles title to their lands and the right to collect dues from their tenants. A widespread panic, known as the "Great Fear," gripped the entire country. Townspeople and peasants amassed in large numbers to defend themselves and save the harvest. In response to this panic, which reached its peak in the last two weeks of July, the National Assembly began to pass legislation that destroyed the Old Regime and created a new political order.

THE CREATION OF A NEW POLITICAL SOCIETY

Between August 1789 and September 1790 the National Assembly took three revolutionary steps. The first was the elimination of noble and clerical privilege. In August the assembly abolished the feudal dues that peasants paid their lords, the private legal jurisdictions of noblemen, the collection of tithes by the clergy, and the exclusive rights of noblemen to hunt game on their lands. The privileges of provinces and local towns met the same fate, and ten months later the nobility lost their titles. Instead of a society divided into various corporate groups, each with its own privileges, France would now have only citizens, all of them equal at law. Social distinctions would be based on merit rather than birth. There were no longer any intermediary powers between the king and the individual subject.

The second step, taken on August 26, was the promulgation of the *Declaration of the Rights of Man and Citizen.*

DECLARATION OF THE RIGHTS OF MAN AND CITIZEN (1789)

....

The passage of the Declaration of the Rights of Man and Citizen *by the National Assembly on August 26, 1789, is one of the earliest and most enduring acts of the French Revolution. A document of great simplicity and power, it was hammered out during many weeks of debate. Its concern with the natural rights of all people and equality before the law reflected the ideas of the Enlightenment.*

1. Men are born free and remain free and equal in rights. Social distinctions may be founded only on the common good.

2. The aim of all political association is the preservation of the natural and imprescriptible rights of man. These rights are liberty, property, security and resistance to oppression.

3. The principle of all authority rests essentially in the nation. No body nor individual may exercise any authority which does not emanate expressly from the nation.

4. Liberty consists in the freedom to do whatever does not harm another; hence the exercise of the natural rights of each man has no limits except those which assure to the other members of society the enjoyment of the same rights. These limits can only be determined by law. . . .

6. Law is the expression of the general will. Every citizen has the right to participate personally or through his representative in its formation. It must be the same for all, whether it protects or punishes. All citizens, being equal in the eyes of the law, are equally eligible to all dignities and to all public positions and occupations, according to their abilities, and without distinction except that of their virtues and talents.

7. No man may be indicted, arrested, or imprisoned except in cases determined by the law and according to the forms prescribed by law. . . .

10. No one should be disturbed for his opinions, even in religion, provided that their manifestation does not trouble public order as established by law.

11. The free communication of thoughts and opinions is one of the most precious of the rights of man. Every citizen may therefore speak, write, and print freely, but shall be responsible for any abuse of this freedom in the cases set by the law. . . .

17. Property being an inviolable and sacred right, no one may be deprived of it except when public necessity, determined by law, obviously requires it, and then on the condition that the owner shall have been previously and equitably compensated.

Source: From P.-J.-B. Buchez and P.-C. Roux, *Histoire parlementaire de la Révolution française.* (Paris: Paulin, 1834).

This document reveals the main influence of the Enlightenment on the revolution. It declared that all men, not just Frenchmen, had a natural right to liberty, property, equality before the law, freedom from oppression, and religious toleration. The statement that the "law is the expression of the general will" reflects the influence of Rousseau's *The Social Contract* (1762), while the statement that every citizen has the right to participate in the formation of that law either personally or through a representative embodies the basic principle of democracy. The *Declaration* differed from the English Bill of Rights of 1689 by grounding the rights it proclaimed in the natural law rather than in the law of one country. The provisions of the French document therefore serve as statements of broad principle rather than as confirmations of specific rights that the government had allegedly been violating.

The third step in this revolutionary program was a complete reorganization of the Church. In order to solve the problem of the national debt, the National Assembly placed land owned by the Church (about 10 percent of all French territory) at the service of the nation. The Civil Constitution of the Clergy of July 1790 in effect made the Church a department of the state, with the government paying the clergy directly. In order to retain their positions, the clergy were required to take an oath of loyalty to the nation. At the same time the Church was reorganized into eighty-three dioceses, one for each of the *départments* or administrative units into which the country was also now divided. The bishops of these dioceses were to be elected by laymen. The parishes, which were the basic units of ecclesiastical administration, would become uniform in size, each administering to some 6,000 parishioners.

In 1791 a newly elected Legislative Assembly—replacing the National Assembly—confirmed and extended many of these changes. A constitution, put into effect in October, formalized the end of royal absolutism. The king became a constitutional monarch, retaining only the power to suspend legislation, direct foreign policy, and command the armed forces. The constitution did not, however, give all men the right to vote. Only "active citizens," who paid the equivalent of three days' wages in direct taxes, had the right to vote for electors, who in turn chose representatives to the legislature.

The new constitution formally abolished hereditary legal privileges, thus providing equality of all citizens before the law. Subsequent legislation granted Jews and Protestants full civil rights and toleration. A law eliminating primogeniture (inheritance of the entire estate by the eldest son) gave all heirs equal rights to inherited property. The establishment of marriage as a civil contract and the right to end a marriage in divorce supported the idea of the husband and wife as freely contracting individuals. The largely symbolic abolition of slavery in France was consistent with the proclamation of equality of all men, but the failure to extend that emancipation to French colonies suggests that there were limits to the concept of liberty proclaimed by the assembly.

This body of legislation amounted to nothing less than a revolution. The Old Regime had been destroyed and a new one had taken its place. Although the form of government remained a monarchy, the powers of that monarchy were drastically curtailed. Unlike the English Revolutions of the 1640s and 1688, this revolution did not disguise the extent of the changes that had transpired by using the language of conservatism, claiming that the revolution had recovered lost freedoms. It did not appeal to the French past at all. It promoted a new view of French society as a nation composed of equal citizens possessing natural rights, in place of the older concept of a society consisting of different corporate groups, each with its own privileges. Contemporaries recognized the significance of these changes. The Portuguese ambassador to France, who witnessed the events of 1789 firsthand, reported back to his government, "In all the world's annals there is no mention of a revolution like this."

RESPONSES TO THE FIRST FRENCH REVOLUTION

During the early years of the revolution, events in Paris and Versailles dominated the political scene. The revolution was not confined, however, to the metropolis. In the provinces groups of ordinary townspeople and peasants, frightened that the members of the nobility might be taking counteraction against them, took the law into their own hands and brought about a new revolutionary political and social order. In many places the local rulers who had exercised political power in towns and villages were overthrown and replaced by supporters of the new regime. At the same time there was considerable opposition to the revolutionary government. In many parts of the country the clergy's refusal to take the oath of loyalty to the nation led to violent clashes with the provincial authorities. In the south nobles began to organize resistance to the new regime, while militant Catholics attacked Protestants, who had been granted toleration and who generally supported the revolution.

The revolutionary events of 1789–1791 quickly gained the attention of countries outside France. In England the nonconformist Protestant minister Richard Price urged members of the British Parliament to follow the example of their French neighbors and abolish the laws that restricted hunting on aristocratic lands. Prussian reformers took heart that the events of the revolution would portend the destruction of absolutism in their country and in other European lands. A Prussian official who had studied with the philosopher Immanuel Kant called the revolution "the first practical triumph of philosophy . . . the hope and consolation for so many of those ancient ills under which mankind has suffered."

Not all foreign assessments of the revolution were positive. In November 1790 the British politician Edmund Burke published *Reflections on the Revolution in France,* in which he expressed horror at the way in which abstract philosophy had destroyed the traditional social order in France. Pope Pius VI condemned the *Declaration of the Rights of Man and Citizen* and then, outraged at the attack upon the Roman Catholic Church, issued a sweeping condemnation of the Civil Constitution of the Clergy. The absolute monarchs of western Europe, sensing rightly that their regimes were in danger of a contagious revolutionary ideology, not only planned an invasion of France to restore the old order but took action against dissent in their own territories. When Polish legislators wrote a new constitution in 1791, modeled on that of France, Catherine the Great of Russia, who controlled a portion of Poland at the time, claimed that it was the product of French radicalism. She shut down the presses, revived censorship, turned against the philosophes whom she had admired, and banned the works of Voltaire.

The French Republic, 1792–1799

Beginning in 1792 France experienced a second revolution that was much more radical than the first. During this revolution France was transformed from a constitutional monarchy into a republic. The state claimed far greater power than it possessed under the constitutional monarchy established in 1791, and it used that power to bring about a radical reform of French society.

THE ESTABLISHMENT OF THE REPUBLIC, 1792

During the first two years of the revolution it appeared that the building of a new French nation would take place within the framework of a constitutional monarchy. Absolutism had suffered an irreversible defeat, but there was little sentiment among the members of the Legislative Assembly, much less among the general population, in favor of abolishing the institution of monarchy. The only committed republicans—those supporting the establishment of a republic—in the Legislative Assembly belonged to a party known as the Jacobins°, who found support in political clubs in Paris and in other parts of the country. By

■ Sans-Culottes

Male and female dress of the *sans-culottes,* the armed Parisian radicals who supported the Republic. The men did not wear the breeches (*culottes*) that were in style among the members of the French nobility.

La Femme du Sans Culotte.

the late summer of 1792 this group of radicals, drawing upon the support of militant Parisian citizens known as *sans-culottes* (literally, those without breeches, the pants worn by noblemen), succeeded in bringing about the second, more radical revolution.

King Louis himself was in part responsible for this destruction of the monarchy. The success of constitutional monarchy depended on the king's willingness to play the new role assigned to him as a constitutional figurehead. In October 1789 Louis had agreed, under considerable pressure, to move his residence from Versailles to Paris, where the National Assembly had also relocated. The pressure came mainly from women, who formed the large majority of 10,000 demonstrators who marched from Paris to Versailles demanding a reduction in the price of bread. The king yielded to their demands and came to Paris. As he entered the city, accompanied by soldiers, monks, and women carrying guns and pikes, he reluctantly agreed to wear the liberty cap with the tricolor cockade (a badge) to symbolize his acceptance of the revolution. Louis, however, could not disguise his opposition to revolution, especially to the ecclesiastical settlement. This opposition led many people to suspect that he was encouraging the powers of Europe to invade France to restore the Old Regime.

Louis XVI had few personal resources upon which he might draw to win the confidence of his subjects. He was not as intelligent as his grandfather, Louis XV, nor did he have the skills necessary to dispel his subjects' growing distrust of him. Neither Louis nor his Austrian wife, Marie Antoinette, commanded much respect among the people. For many years the royal couple had been the object of relentless, sometimes pornographic satire. He had been lampooned for his rumored sexual inadequacies and she for a series of alleged infidelities with the king's brother and a succession of female partners. Whatever confidence Parisian citizens might have retained in the royal couple evaporated in June 1791, when the king and queen attempted to flee the country. The National Guard apprehended them at Varennes, close to the eastern French border, and forced them to return to Paris, where they were kept under guard at the palace of the Tuileries. Even that development, however, failed to destroy the monarchy, which had been preserved in the constitution implemented in October.

The development that actually precipitated the downfall of the monarchy and led to the establishment of a republic was the decision to go to war. Until the summer of 1791 European powers had been involved in various conflicts and had resisted pleas from French émigrés to support a counterrevolutionary offensive against the new French regime. After the flight to Varennes and the capture of the royal family, however, Frederick William II of Prussia (r. 1786–1797) and Emperor Leopold II of Austria (r. 1790–1792), the brother of Marie Antoinette, signed an alliance and called upon the other monarchs of Europe "to restore to the King of France complete liberty and to consolidate the bases of monarchical government." No action would be taken, however, unless all European sovereigns agreed to cooperate.

The actual declaration of war came not from the monarchs of Europe but from the French Legislative Assembly. A small group of republicans, headed by the eloquent orator Jacques-Pierre Brissot (1754–1793), convinced the assembly that an international conspiracy against the revolution would end in an invasion of their country. Brissot and his supporters also believed that if France could be lured into a foreign war, the king and queen would be revealed as traitors and the monarchy would be destroyed. Exploiting xenophobic as well as revolutionary sentiment, and claiming that the strength of a citizen army would win a quick and decisive victory, Brissot and his allies won the support of the entire assembly. They also appealed to the international goals of the revolution, claiming that the French army would inspire revolution against "the tyrants of Europe" everywhere they went.

The Legislative Assembly declared war on Austria in April 1792. Instead of a glorious victory, however, the war resulted in a series of disastrous defeats at the hands of Austrians and their Prussian allies in the Netherlands. This military failure contributed to a mood of paranoia in France, especially in Paris. Fears arose that invading armies, in alliance with nobles, would undermine the revolution. In May members of the assembly learned that the Austrian minister, in cooperation with a group of the king's advisers, was plotting the destruction of the assembly itself. In July the assembly officially proclaimed the nation to be in danger, calling for all citizens to rally against the enemies of liberty at home and abroad. Women petitioned for the right to bear arms. When the Austrians and Prussians threatened to torch the entire city of Paris and slaughter its population if anyone laid a hand on the royal family, citizens in Paris immediately demanded that the king be deposed.

On August 10 a radical republican committee overthrew the Paris commune, the city government that had

■ Tricolor Cockade
Louis XVI wearing the red liberty bonnet with the tricolor cockade in 1789. The king was forced to wear the liberty cap during his humiliating ride through Paris in October 1789.

been installed in 1789, and set up a new, revolutionary commune. A force of about 20,000 men, including volunteer troops from various parts of the kingdom, invaded the Tuileries, which was defended by about 900 Swiss guards. When the members of the royal bodyguard fled, they were pursued by members of the Paris crowds, who stripped them of their red uniforms and hacked 600 of them to death with knives, pikes, and hatchets. The attack on the Tuileries forced the king to take refuge in the nearby Legislative Assembly. The assembly promptly suspended the monarchy and turned the royal family over to the commune, which imprisoned them in the Temple, a medieval fortress in the suburbs of the city. The assembly then ordered its own dissolution and called for the election of a new legislative body that would draft a new constitution.

The fall of the monarchy did nothing to allay the siege mentality of the city, especially after further Prussian victories in early September escalated fears of a Prussian invasion. Individuals suspected of plotting against the regime were imprisoned, and when it was rumored that they would escape and support the Prussian enemy, angry crowds pulled 1,200 prisoners (most of whom were being held for nonpolitical crimes) from their cells and killed them. The feared foreign invasion that had inspired this "September Massacre" never did materialize. On September 20, 1792, a surprisingly well-disciplined and well-trained army of French citizens, inspired by dedication to France and the revolution, repulsed the armies of Austria and Prussia at Valmy. This victory saved the revolution. The German poet Johann Wolfgang von Goethe (1749–1832) claimed that the battle marked the beginning of "a new epoch in the history of the world." Delegates to a new National Convention, elected by universal male suffrage°, had already arrived in Paris to write a new constitution. On September 22 the convention declared that the monarchy was formally abolished and that France was a republic. France had now experienced a second revolution, more radical than the first, but dedicated to the same principles of liberty, equality, and fraternity.

■ The Attack on the Palace of the Tuileries

On the night of August 10, 1792, Parisian crowds and volunteer soldiers attacked the royal palace in Paris. The puffs of smoke in the building are coming from the Swiss guards, who were entrusted with the defense of the royal family and the palace. The royal family escaped and took refuge in the Legislative Assembly, but 600 of the Swiss guards were killed. Those that retreated were hunted down in the streets of Paris, stripped of their uniforms, and their heads placed on the end of spears.

THE JACOBINS AND THE REVOLUTION

Before the Republic was established, different political factions had begun to vie for power, both in the Legislative Assembly and in the country at large. The first major division to emerge was between the Feuillants, who supported a constitutional monarchy, and the Jacobins, many of whom favored the creation of a democratic republic. By the time the Republic had been declared, the Jacobins had become the major political party. Soon, however, factional divisions began to develop within Jacobin ranks. The main split occurred between the followers of Brissot, known as Girondins°, and the radicals known as Montagnards°, or "the Mountain." The latter acquired their name because they occupied the benches on the side of the convention hall, where the floor sloped upward. The Girondins occupied the lower side of the hall, while the uncommitted deputies, known as "the Plain," occupied the middle. Both the Mountain and the Girondins claimed to be advancing the goals of the revolution, but they differed widely on which tactics to pursue. The Mountain took the position that as long as the state was endangered by internal and external enemies, the government needed to centralize authority in the capital. The Mountain thought of themselves as the representatives of the common people, especially the *sans-culottes* in Paris. Many of their leaders, including Georges-Jacques Danton (1759–1794), Jean-Paul Marat (1743–1793), and Maximilien Robespierre (1758–1794), were in fact Parisians. Their mission was to make the revolution even more egalitarian and to establish a republic characterized by civic pride and patriotism, which they referred to as the Republic of Virtue.

The Girondins, known as such because many of their leaders came from the southwestern *département* of Gironde, took a more conservative position than the Mountain on these issues. Favoring the economic freedom and local control desired by merchants and manufacturers, they were reluctant to support further centralization of state power. They believed that the revolution had advanced far enough and should not become more radical. They were also afraid that the egalitarianism of the revolution, if unchecked, would lead to a leveling of French society and result in social anarchy.

The conflict between the Girondins and the Mountain became apparent in the debate over what to do with the deposed king. Louis had been suspected of conspiring with the enemies of the revolution, and the discovery of his correspondence with the Austrian government led to his trial for treason against the nation. The Girondins had originally expressed reluctance to bring him to trial, preferring to keep him in prison. Once the trial began, they joined the entire National Convention in voting to convict him, but they opposed his execution. This stance led the Mountain to accuse the Girondins of being secret collaborators with the monarchy. By a narrow vote the convention decided to put the king to death, and on January 21, 1793, Louis was executed at the Place de Revolution.

The instrument of death was the guillotine, an efficient and merciful but nonetheless terrifying decapitation machine first pressed into service in April 1792. It took its name from Dr. Joseph-Ignace Guillotin, who had the original idea for such a device, although he did not invent it. The guillotine was inspired by the conviction that all criminals, not just those of noble blood, should be executed in a swift, painless manner. The new device was to be put to extensive use during the next eighteen months, and many Girondins fell victim to it.

The split between the Mountain and the Girondins became more pronounced as the republican regime encountered increasing opposition from foreign and domestic enemies. Early in 1793 Great Britain and the Dutch Republic allied with Prussia and Austria to form the First Coalition against France, and within a month Spain and the kingdoms of Sardinia and Naples joined them. The armies of these allied powers defeated French forces in the Austrian Netherlands in March of that year, and once again an invasion seemed imminent. At the same time internal rebellions against the revolutionary regime took place in various outlying provinces, especially in the district of the Vendée in western France. These uprisings were led by nobleman and clerics, but they also had popular support, especially from tenant farmers who resented the increased taxation imposed by the new revolutionary government.

In the minds of Robespierre and his colleagues, the Girondins were linked to these provincial rebels, whom

CHRONOLOGY

The French Republic and the Terror, 1792–1794

1792

April 20	Declaration of war against Austria
August 10	Attack on the Tuileries; monarchy is suspended
September 2–6	September Massacre of prisoners in Paris
September 20	French victory at the Battle of Valmy
September 21	National Convention meets
September 22	Abolition of the monarchy and establishment of the Republic

1793

January 21	Execution of Louis XVI
February 1	Declaration of war against Great Britain and the Dutch Republic
March 11	Beginning of rebellion in the Vendée
June 2	Purge of Girondins from the Convention
June 24	Ratification of a republican constitution
July 27	Robespierre elected to the Committee of Public Safety
August 23	The Convention decrees the *levée en masse*
October 5	Adoption of the revolutionary calendar
October 16	Execution of Marie Antoinette

1794

July 28	10th of *Thermidor*; execution of Robespierre
November 12	Jacobin clubs are closed

they labeled as federalists° because they opposed the centralization of the French state and thus threatened the unity of the nation. In June twenty-nine Girondins were expelled from the convention for supporting local officials accused of hoarding grain. This purge made it apparent that any political opponent of the Mountain, even those with solid republican credentials, could now be identified as an enemy of the revolution.

In order to repel the coalition of foreign powers, the convention ordered a *levée en masse*, a conscription of troops from the entire population. This step, taken in August 1793, created an unprecedented military force, a massive citizen army drawn from all segments of the population and committed to the prosecution of the war. In the past the rank and file of European armies, whether mercenaries or regular troops, had been filled with men on the margins of society: the poor, the unemployed, and even criminal outcasts. The conscription of males from all ranks of society might have promoted a sense of national unity among the troops, but it also caused resentment and resistance against this use of state power. It led to increased federalist resistance to the radical Jacobin government.

THE REIGN OF TERROR, 1793–1794

In order to deal with its domestic enemies, the republican government claimed powers that far exceeded those exercised by the monarchy in the age of absolutism. The convention passed laws that set up special courts to prosecute enemies of the regime and authorized special procedures that deprived those accused of their legal rights. These laws laid the legal foundation for the Reign of Terror°, a campaign to rid the state of its internal enemies. A Committee of Public Safety, consisting of twelve members entrusted with the executive power of the state, superintended this process. Although technically subordinate to the convention, the Committee of Public Safety became in effect a revolutionary dictatorship.

The man who emerged as the main figure on the Committee of Public Safety was Maximilien Robespierre. A brilliant student as a youth, Robespierre was affronted when the king's carriage splashed him with mud as he was waiting to read an address to the king. A man with little sense of humor, he was passionate in his quest for justice. As a lawyer who defended indigent clients, Robespierre was elected to the Third Estate in 1789 and became a favorite of the *sans-culottes,* who called him "The Incorruptible." That he may have been, but he was also susceptible to the temptation to abuse power for partisan political purposes. Like Rousseau, whose work he admired, he was also willing to sacrifice individual liberty in the name of the collective General Will. His logic was that since the General Will was indivisible, it could not accommodate dissent. Robespierre was primarily responsible for pushing the revolution to new extremes and for establishing the program of state repression that began in the autumn of 1793.

The most intense prosecutions of the Terror took place between October 1793 and June 1794, but they continued until August 1794. By that time the revolutionary courts had executed 17,000 persons, while 500,000 had suffered imprisonment. Another 20,000 either died in prison or were killed without any form of trial. Among the victims of the Terror were substantial numbers of clergy and nobility, as we might expect, but the overwhelming majority were artisans and peasants. One Parisian stableboy was guillotined for having said "f . . . the Republic," while a baker from Alsace lost his head for predicting that "the Republic will go to hell with all its partisans." Many of the victims came from the outlying regions of the country, especially the northeast, where foreign armies were threatening the

Republic, and the west, where a brutal civil war between the French army and the advocates of federalism was raging. These provincial enemies of the regime were identified by special surveillance committees and then were tried by revolutionary tribunals. The guillotine was by no means the only method of execution. In November and December 1793, about 1,800 rebels captured during the uprising in the Vendée were tied to other prisoners, placed in sinking boats, and drowned in the chilly waters of the Loire River.

The most visible and alarming of the executions took place in the capital. The execution of Marie Antoinette and other royalists might have been justified on the basis of their active subversion of the regime, but trumped-up charges against Girondins exposed a process that would destroy republicans as well. As one victim of the Terror said in a speech before he went to the guillotine, the revolution, like the mythical Roman god Saturn, devoured its own children. Some of the most prominent figures of the Enlightenment fell victim to this paranoia. Among them was the Marquis de Condorcet, who believed passionately that all citizens, including women, had equal rights. Having campaigned against capital punishment, he committed suicide in a Parisian prison, just before he was to be executed. Another figure of the Enlightenment, the famous chemist Antoine Lavoisier (1743–1794), who had devoted himself to improving social and economic conditions in France, was executed at the same time. So too was the feminist Olympe de Gouges, who as we discussed in Chapter 17 had petitioned for the equal political rights of women. Many French revolutionaries, including Robespierre, used the political ideas of the Enlightenment to justify their actions, but the Terror struck down some of the most distinguished figures of that movement. In that sense the Terror marked the end of the Enlightenment in France.

The Committee of Public Safety then went after Danton and other so-called "Indulgents," who had decided that the Terror had gone too far. Danton's execution made everyone, especially moderate Jacobins, wonder who would be the next victim of a process that had spun completely out of control. In June 1794 the Terror reached a climax, as 1,300 people were sent to their deaths. In order to stop the process, a group of Jacobins in the convention, headed by Joseph Fouché (1759–1820) and Paul Barras (1755–1829), organized a plot against Robespierre. Calling him a tyrant, they arrested him and hundreds of his followers and guillotined them on July 28, 1794. An equally swift retaliation was exacted against the Jacobins in the provinces, when members of the White Terror, so named for the white Bourbon flag they displayed, executed leaders of the local revolutionary tribunals. With these reprisals, which used the very same methods that had been perfected by Robespierre and his followers, the most violent and radical phase of the French revolution came to an end.

The Reign of Terror had ended, but its memory would never be extinguished. Its horrors served as a constant

The Trial of Louis XVI

After the abolition of the monarchy and the proclamation of the French Republic in September 1792, the National Convention considered the fate of the deposed king. There was a broad consensus that Louis was guilty of treason against the nation and that he should answer for his crimes, but how he should do so was a matter of heated debate. The convention was divided between the Girondins and the Mountain. Of the two, the Girondins were more inclined to follow legal forms, whereas those of the Mountain considered themselves to be acting as a revolutionary tribunal that should adhere to standards of justice not specifically included in the law of the land. The convention thus became a forum where Louis's accusers expressed competing notions of revolutionary justice.

The most divisive and revealing issue was whether there should be a trial at all. The Mountain originally took the position that because the people had already judged the king on August 10, when the monarchy had fallen and the king taken prisoner, there was no need for a second judgment. They should proceed immediately to carrying out the death sentence. Robespierre argued that to have a trial would be counter-revolutionary, for it would allow the revolution itself to be brought before the court to be judged. A centrist majority, however, decided that the king had to be charged with specific offenses in a court of law and found guilty by due process before being sentenced.

A second issue, closely related to the first, was the technical legal question of whether the king could be subject to legal action. Even if the legislative branch of the government was considered the equal of the king in a constitutional monarchy, it did not possess authority over him. A further argument was that the king could not be tried for actions for which he had already suffered abdication. This claim was challenged on the most basic principle of the revolution—that the nation was higher than the king and his crimes were committed against that nation, which is the people. The king, moreover, was no longer king but was now a citizen and therefore subject to the law in the same way as anyone else.

The third issue was Louis's culpability for the specific charges in the indictment. These crimes included refusing to call the Estates General, sending an army to march against the citizens of Paris, and conducting secret negotiations with France's enemies. The journalist and deputy Jean-Paul Marat added that "he robbed the citizens of their gold as a subsidy for their foes" and "caused his hirelings to hoard, to create famine, to dry up the sources of abundance that the people might die from misery and hunger."

Nonetheless the king, who appeared personally to hear the indictment and then to respond to the charges on December 26, presented a plausible defense. He based it on the laws in force at the various times he was supposed to have committed his crimes. Thus he defended his sending of troops to Paris on the grounds that in June and July 1789 he could order troops wherever he wanted. In the same vein he argued that he had used force solely in response to illegal intimidation. These legalisms, however, only made the members of the convention more contemptuous of the king. His defense failed to persuade a single convention deputy. He was convicted of treason by a vote of 693–0.

This unanimous conviction of the king did not bring an end to the factional debates over the king's fate. Knowing that there was extensive support for the king in various parts of the country, the Girondins asked that the verdict be appealed to the people. Their argument was that the convention, dominated by the Mountain and supported by militants in Paris, had usurped the sovereignty of the people. Pierre-Victurnien Vergniaud, a lawyer from Bordeaux, pleaded that "To take this right from the people would be to take sovereignty from them, to transfer it . . . to the hands of the representatives chosen by the people, to transform their representatives into kings or tyrants." Vergniaud's motion to submit the verdict to the people for ratification lost by a vote of 424–283.

The last vote, the closest of all, determined the king's sentence. Originally it appeared that a majority might vote for noncapital punishment. The Marquis de Condorcet, for example, argued that although the king deserved death on the basis of the law of treason, he could not bring himself to vote for capital punishment on

MORT DE LOUIS CAPET 16ᵉ DU NOM, LE 21 JANVIER 1793.

■ **Execution of Louis XVI, January 21, 1793**
Although the king was convicted of treason by a unanimous vote, the vote to execute him carried by a slender majority of only twenty-seven votes.

principle. The radical response to this argument came from Robespierre, who appealed to the "principles of nature" in stating that the death penalty could be justified "only in those cases where it is vital to the safety of private citizens or of the public." Robespierre's impassioned oratory carried the day. By a vote of 361–334 the king was sentenced to "death within 24 hours" rather than the alternatives of imprisonment followed by banishment after the war or imprisonment in chains for life. The following day Louis was led to the guillotine.

All public trials, especially those for political crimes, are theatrical events, in that the various parties play specific roles and seek to convey certain mes-

sages to their audiences. The men who voted to put Louis XVI on trial wanted to create an educational spectacle in which the already deposed monarch would be stripped of any respect he might still have commanded among the people. Louis was to be tried like any other traitor, and he was to suffer the same fate, execution by the guillotine. The attempt to strip him of all privilege and status continued after his death. His corpse, with his head placed between his knees, was taken to a cemetery, placed in a wooden box, and buried in the common pit. The revolutionaries were determined to guarantee that even in death the king would have the same position as the humblest of his former subjects. ■

Questions of Justice

1. How would you describe the standard of justice that the members of the National Convention upheld in voting to execute the king? How did this standard of justice differ from the standard to which King Louis XVI appealed?

2. Evaluate the argument of Robespierre that the death penalty can be justified only in cases of public safety. Compare his argument to the Enlightenment critique of capital punishment presented by Cesare Beccaria. (See Chapter 17.)

Taking It Further

Jordan, David P. *The King's Trial: The French Revolution vs. Louis XVI.* 1979. The most thorough account of the trial.

Walzer, Michael (ed.). *Regicide and Revolution: Speeches at the Trial of Louis XVI.* 1974. A valuable collection of speeches with an extended commentary.

warning against the dangers inherent in revolutionary movements. The guillotine, the agent of a dysfunctional and indiscriminate state terrorism, became just as closely identified with the French Revolution as its famous slogan of "Liberty, Equality, Fraternity." The contrast between those two symbols, each of them emblematic of a different stage of the revolution, helps to explain how both conservatives and liberals in the nineteenth century would be able to appeal to the experience of the revolution to support their contradictory ideologies.

THE DIRECTORY, 1795–1799

A desire to end the violence of the Terror allowed moderates in the National Convention to regain control of the state apparatus that Robespierre and his allies had used to such devastating effect. The Paris Commune was dismantled and the Committee of Public Safety abolished. In November 1794 the Jacobin clubs throughout the country, which had provided support for the Terror, were closed. The moderates who now controlled the government still hoped to preserve the gains of the revolution, while returning the country to more familiar forms of authority. A new constitution of 1795 bestowed executive power on a five-man Directorate, while an assembly consisting of two houses, the Council of the Ancients and the Council of Five Hundred, proposed and voted on all legislation. The franchise was limited to property holders, allowing only 2,000,000 men out of an adult male population of 7,000,000 to vote. A system of indirect election, in which a person voted for electors who then selected representatives, guaranteed that only the wealthiest members of the country would sit in the legislative assembly.

The establishment of the Directory formed part of a more general reaction against the culture of the republic. The austere, egalitarian dress of the *sans-culottes* gave way once again to fancy and opulent clothes, at least among the bourgeoisie. Low necklines, officially out of favor during the Reign of Terror, once again came back into fashion among wealthier members of society. The high social life of the capital experienced a revival. Some dances took place on the sites of churches that Jacobins had desecrated. Jacobin theaters were shut down and Jacobin works of art destroyed. France was still a republic, but it was no longer Robespierre's Republic of Virtue.

Some of the more entrepreneurial citizens of Paris welcomed the new regime, but opposition soon arose, mainly from Jacobins and *sans-culottes*. When the government relaxed the strict price controls that had been in effect under the Jacobins, the soaring price of bread and other commodities caused widespread social discontent among the population. This situation was aggravated by the continuation of the interminable war against the foreign powers in the First Coalition. Wherever French troops went, their constant need of food and other goods resulted in serious shortages of these commodities.

By the end of 1798 conditions had grown even worse. Inflation was running out of control. The collection of taxes was intermittent at best. The paper money known as *assignats*, first issued by the government in 1791 and backed by the value of confiscated church lands, had become almost worthless. Late in 1797 the Directory had been forced to cancel more than half the national debt, a step that further alienated wealthy citizens who had lent money to the government. Military setbacks in 1798 and 1799 brought the situation to a critical point. An expedition to Egypt, which was intended to gain for France a

CHRONOLOGY		
The Directory, 1795–1799		
1795		
	August 22	The National Convention approves a new constitution
	October 5	Napoleon suppresses a royalist insurrection in Paris
	October 26	End of the Convention; beginning of the Directory
1796		
	February 19	The issuing of *assignats* is halted
	April 12	Beginning of a series of victories by Napoleon in Italy
1798		
	May 13	Napoleon's expedition departs for Egypt
	May	Second Coalition (Britain, Austria, Russia, Naples, and Turkey) is formed against Napoleon
	July 21	Napoleon wins the Battle of the Pyramids
	August 1	Nelson destroys the French fleet at the Battle of the Nile
1799		
	November 9–10	Napoleon's coup on the 18th of *Brumaire;* Consulate is established

■ **Jean Charles Tardieu, *The French Army Halts at Syene, Upper Egypt,***
on February 2, 1799
This painting depicts a cultural encounter between French soldiers and Egyptians in the city of Syene
(now Aswan) during the Egyptian campaign of 1798–1799. The soldiers are scribbling on the ruins of
ancient Egypt, indicating a lack of respect for Egyptian culture.

foothold in the Middle East, had resulted in a number of victories against the Turks, but the British destroyed the French fleet at the Battle of the Nile in 1798. The next year a series of revolts against French rule in Italy and in the Austrian Netherlands pushed the French armies back to France's earlier boundaries. The formation of a Second Coalition of European powers in 1799, which included Russia, Naples, and Turkey as well as Britain and Austria, represented a formidable challenge to French power and ensured that the war would not end soon. These military events produced a swing to the political left and raised the specter of another Jacobin coup.

In the face of this instability, Emmanuel-Joseph Sieyès, who had been elected as one of the directors two years earlier, decided to overthrow the government. Sieyès provided a link between the early years of the revolution, when he had defended the Third Estate, and the current government of the Directory. Unlike many other prominent political figures, he had managed to avoid prosecution as the revolution had become more radical. When asked what he had done during the Reign of Terror, Sieyès replied, "I survived." The goal of the planned coup was to provide the country with strong government, its greatest need in a period of political, economic, and social instability. The person Sieyès

selected as his partner in this enterprise, and the man who immediately assumed leadership of the coup, was Napoleon Bonaparte (1769–1821), a 30-year-old general who in 1795 had put down a royalist rebellion in Paris with a "whiff of grapeshot."

Napoleon had already established impressive credentials as a military leader. In 1796 and 1797 he had won major victories in Italy, leading to the Treaty of Campo Formio of 1797. Those victories and his short-lived success at the Battle of the Pyramids in Egypt had made him enormously popular in Paris, where he was received as a hero when he assumed command of the armed forces in 1799. His popularity, his demonstrated military leadership, and his control of a large armed force made this "man on horseback" appear to have the best chance to replace the enfeebled civilian regime of the Directory.

On November 9, 1799, Napoleon addressed the two legislative councils. He reported that another Jacobin conspiracy had been uncovered and that in order to deal with such insurrections a new constitution must be written to give the executive branch of the government more authority. Napoleon encountered resistance from some members of the Council of Five Hundred, who demanded that he be declared an outlaw. At this stage the president of the council,

Napoleon's brother Lucien, intervened and called in troops to evict the members who opposed him. The following day France had a new government, known as the Consulate.

Executive power in the new government was to be vested in three consuls—Napoleon, Sieyès, and Roger Ducos (1754–1816), a former member of the National Convention who had voted to execute Louis XVI. It soon became clear, however, that Napoleon would be the dominant member of this triumvirate, and in the new constitution of December 1799, which the electorate ratified by means of a plebiscite, Napoleon was named First Consul. This appointment made him the most powerful man in France and for all practical purposes a military dictator. Republican forms of government were preserved in the new constitution, but they were easily manipulated to produce what the consuls desired. A Senate appointed by the consuls chose men from a list of 6,000 "notables" to form a body known as the Tribunate, which would discuss legislation proposed by the consuls. Another assembly, the Legislative Body, would vote on those measures without debate.

With the establishment of the Consulate the French Republic was a thing of the past. It had been replaced by a military dictatorship in all but name. This transformation of the republic into a military dictatorship had been predicted by both the radical democrat Robespierre and the British conservative Edmund Burke many years before. The dictatorship became more apparent in 1802, when Napoleon was named Consul for Life, and in 1804, when he crowned himself emperor of the French.

Cultural Change in France During the Revolution

The French Revolution was primarily a political revolution. It brought about fundamental change in the system of government. It resulted in the destruction of the monarchy and the establishment of a republic. It inspired the drafting of new constitutions, led to the creation of new legislative assemblies, and endowed the state with unprecedented power. The French revolution also brought about profound changes in French culture. It transformed the cultural institutions of the Old Regime and created a new revolutionary culture.

THE TRANSFORMATION OF CULTURAL INSTITUTIONS

Between 1791 and 1794 most of the cultural institutions of the Old Regime were either destroyed or radically transformed, and new institutions under the control of the state took their place.

Schools

The confiscation of church property in 1790, followed by the abolition of the monastic religious orders, had a devastating effect on the traditional parish schools, colleges, and universities, most of which were run by the clergy. Without sufficient endowments, many of these schools were forced to close. During the Terror, schools suspected of having aristocratic associations and teaching counterrevolutionary doctrines came under further assault. Thousands of teachers lost their salaries and sought employment elsewhere. In September 1793 the universities were suppressed.

The government gradually realized that the entire educational process was collapsing. Recognizing the necessity of using education to encourage loyalty to the republican regime, the National Convention established a system of universal primary education. Instruction would be free, and the teachers would receive their salaries from the state. Unfortunately, the state did not have enough money to pay for the system, so the schools continued to languish.

The state was only slightly more successful in providing secondary education by converting abandoned colleges, monasteries, and libraries into "central schools," which were intended to provide a standardized form of state education. By 1799, the central schools had 10,000 students, 40,000 fewer than were in the colleges in 1789. The system was improved significantly during the Napoleonic period when the government established thirty-six secondary schools known as *lycées* while also allowing private and religious schools to continue to function.

Academies

The Parisian scientific and artistic academies established by Louis XIV (see Chapter 15) had a monopoly over the promotion and transmission of knowledge in the sciences and the visual arts. The academies were the epitome of privilege. They controlled their own membership, determined the recipients of their prizes, and had a monopoly of their particular branch of knowledge. They were also heavily aristocratic institutions; as many as three-quarters of their members were nobles or clergy.

During the revolution the academies were abolished as part of a general attack on corporate bodies. The work they did was taken over by various government committees. For example, the Commission on Weights and Measures, which had been part of the Academy of Science, became an independent commission. Its task had been to provide uniform weights and measures for the entire kingdom. In 1795 it established the meter, calculated as one ten-millionth of the distance from the North Pole to the equator, as the standard measure of distance. The metric system and the decimal system, which were introduced at the same time, have subsequently been adopted as universal standards in all European countries except Great Britain.

The Royal Academy of Arts, dissolved by a vote of the National Convention in 1793, was replaced by the Popular

■ **Destruction of the Statue of Louis XIV in the Place de Victoires, August 11, 1792**

The leaders of the Republic attempted to eliminate the memory of the institution of monarchy by destroying statues as well as the tombs of France's kings.

Le XI Aout 1792, les parisiens reprennent une mesure qu'ils avoient eu tort de ne pas mettre à exécution le 20 Juin 1791. Ils abbatirent les Statues de Louis XIV, Place des victoires, et place vendôme.

and Republican Society of the Arts. The inspiration for this new republican society, which was open to artists of all social ranks, was Jacques-Louis David (1748–1825), the greatest painter of his generation. Employed at the court of Louis XVI, David became a vocal main critic of the academy at the time of the revolution. He painted some of the most memorable scenes of the revolution, including the oath taken at the tennis court by the members of the National Assembly in 1789. During the Republic David depicted heroes of the revolution such as Jean-Paul Marat, and after the empire was established he was appointed First Painter to Napoleon. David presided over a revival of classicism in French painting, employing Greek and Roman motifs and exhibiting a rationalism and lack of sentiment in his work.

Libraries

Shortly after the revolution had begun, thousands of books and manuscripts from the libraries of monasteries, royal castles, residences of the nobility, and academies came into the possession of the state. Many of these were funneled into the Royal Library, which grew five times in size between 1789 and 1794 and was appropriately renamed the National Library. The government also intended to inventory and catalog all the books held in libraries throughout the country. This effort to create the General Bibliography of France was never completed, and while the books were being cataloged, the government decided to get rid of those that dealt with "theology, mysticism, feudalism, and royal-

ism" by sending them to foreign countries. This decision did not lead to the export of books to other parts of Europe, but it initiated a frenzy of book sales, mainly to private individuals. Altogether about five million books were lost or sold during these years.

Museums and Monuments

The day after the abolition of the monarchy the National Assembly created a Commission of the Museum, whose function was "to collect paintings, statues and other precious objects from the crown possessions" as well as from the churches and houses of the émigrés. The museum was to be located in the Louvre, a royal palace that also served as an art gallery. When it opened in August 1793 the Louvre included a majority of paintings with religious themes, most of them confiscated from royal and émigré residences. The incompatibility of these religious works of art with the republican rejection of Christianity can be explained only by the assumption that this museum was intended to be entirely historical and to have no relevance to contemporary politics. The Louvre and the Museum of French Monuments represented an attempt to quarantine the religious French past from its secular present, lest it contaminate the revolution itself.

The revolutionaries did not have the same respect for the bodies of their former kings. On August 10, 1793, the first anniversary of the deposition of Louis XVI, the National Convention ordered the destruction of all the tombs of past French kings. One by one the tombs were opened and the corpses, embalmed in lead, were removed. Metals and valuables were melted down for use in the war effort. The corpses were either left to disintegrate in the atmosphere or dragged unceremoniously to the cemetery, where they were thrown into the common pit. The corpse of Louis XIV landed on top of that of Henry IV. This disrespectful treatment of the remains of France's former kings was intended to erase the memory of monarchy.

THE CREATION OF A NEW POLITICAL CULTURE

As the state was taking over and adapting the cultural institutions of the Old Regime, revolutionaries engaged in a much bolder and original undertaking: the production of a new, revolutionary political culture. Its sole purpose was to legitimate and glorify the new regime. It symbolized the political values of that regime: liberty, equality, and fraternity in 1789 and republicanism after 1792. This culture was almost entirely political; all forms of cultural expression were subordinated to the realization of a pressing political agenda.

One of the main characteristics of this culture was that it was popular—it was shared by the entire populace, not simply by a small upper-class or literate elite. The fundamental political doctrine of the revolution was popular sovereignty°: the claim that the people were the highest political power in the state. The revolutionaries claimed that this power could never be alienated. The move of the National Assembly from Versailles to Paris actually enabled the people to be present in the gallery during political debate, and deputies were always conscious of their presence. "Learn," claimed one of them in 1789, "that we are deliberating here in front of our masters and we are answerable to them for our opinions." The political culture that emerged—the textual and literary symbols spoken, written, and drawn to reflect this sovereignty of the people—would become the property of the entire population, especially in Paris, where the revolutionary cause found its most passionate popular support. The very words used to identify revolutionary institutions, such as the National Assembly and the National Guard, formed the texture of this new political culture.

The common people who embraced this new culture most enthusiastically were the *sans-culottes*—the radical shopkeepers, artisans, and laborers of Paris. The dress of these people influenced a change in fashion among the wealthier segments of society. A simple jacket replaced the ruffled coat worn by members of the upper classes, their powdered wigs gave way to natural hair, and they too now wore long trousers. They also donned the red liberty cap, to which a tricolor cockade was affixed. The tricolor, which combined the red and blue colors of Paris with the white symbol of the Bourbon monarchy, identified the adherents of the revolution.

Symbols of revolution could be found everywhere. The commercialization of the revolution guaranteed that the tricolor flag, portraits of revolutionary figures, and images of the Bastille would appear on household objects as constant reminders of the public's support for the revolution. By an order of the government in 1792 all men were required to wear the tricolor cockade. Liberty trees, first planted by peasants as protests against local landlords, became a symbol of the revolution. By May 1792 more than 60,000 had been planted throughout the country.

The press, no longer tightly controlled by the government and the printers' guild, became a crucial agent of revolutionary propaganda and a producer of the new culture. Pamphlets, newspapers, brochures, and posters all promoted a distinctive revolutionary language, which became one of the permanent legacies of the revolution. Political leaders used the same rhetoric in their political speeches. *Sans-culottes* sang satirical songs and ballads, many of them to the same tunes well known in the Old Regime. The most popular of the songs of the revolutionary period was the *Marseillaise,* first sung by soldiers preparing for battle against the Austrians but soon adopted by the civilian population and sung at political gatherings. The theaters, which had been privileged corporations in the Old Regime but also carefully regulated, were now free to engage in political satire that strengthened the ties of the people to the revolution.

Much of this new political culture stemmed from the conviction that the doctrine of popular sovereignty should be practiced in everyday life. *Sans-culottes* did this by joining the political clubs organized by different factions within the National Assembly, by addressing others as citizens, and by using the more familiar form of the pronoun *you* (*tu* rather than *vous*) in all conversations. They also participated in the revolution by taking public oaths. On the first anniversary of the fall of the Bastille, as many as 350,000 people, many of them members of the "federations" of National Guards throughout the country, gathered on the royal parade ground outside Paris to take an oath "to the Nation, to the Law, to the King." Direct democracy was not possible in a society of 27 million people, but these cultural practices allowed people to believe that they were participating actively in the political process.

The new revolutionary culture was emphatically secular. In its most extreme form, it was blatantly anti-Christian. In September 1793 the radical Jacobin and former priest Joseph Fouché inaugurated a program of de-Christianization°. Under his leadership, radical Jacobins closed churches and removed religious symbols such as crosses from cemeteries and public venues. In an effort to establish a purely civic religion, they forbade the public practice of religion and renamed churches "temples of reason." In their public pronouncements the architects of de-Christianization avoided reference to the Christian period of French history, which covered the entire national past.

This de-Christianization campaign became the official policy of the Paris Commune, and the National Convention issued a few edicts to enforce it. The program, however, did not win widespread support, and even some Jacobins claimed that in rejecting Christianity it had undermined a belief in God and the afterlife. In 1794 Robespierre attempted to modify the excesses of de-Christianization by launching the Cult of the Supreme Being. He promoted a series of festivals acknowledging the existence of a deity and the immortality of the soul. This new cult paid lip service to traditional religious beliefs, but it still served secular purposes. In fact, the cult was designed to direct the spiritual yearnings of the French people into patriotic undertakings and promote republican virtue.

The new secular revolutionary culture incorporated many elements of the Christian culture that had prevailed before the revolution began. The new pageants and festivals designed to promote a civic religion were modeled on traditional Catholic processions. Revolutionaries co-opted some of the religious holy days for their own purposes. Churches were converted to temples honoring revolutionary heroes. An effigy of Jean-Paul Marat, who was murdered in 1793, appeared on the altar of a Parisian church, next to a female statue of liberty. Jacques-Louis David's portrait of the murdered Marat depicted the slain victim in the manner of the dead Christ in Michelangelo's *Pietà*. Meetings of revolutionaries often took on the atmosphere of religious revivals, as men and women wept in response to orations. Secular catechisms taught young children the virtues of republicanism in the same way that they had instructed them in Christian doctrine during the Old Regime.

■ **Oath Taking**
On July 14, 1790, the first anniversary of the fall of the Bastille, as many as 350,000 people gathered on a field outside Paris to take an oath of loyalty to the new French nation. The event was referred to as the Feast of the Federation, since most of the oath takers were members of the regional federations of National Guards. The oath taking, which had many characteristics of a religious gathering, was led by the king himself, and it marked the most optimistic period of the revolution.

■ **Jacques-Louis David, *The Death of Marat* (1793)**
The Jacobin journalist Jean-Paul Marat was stabbed to death in his bathtub by a noblewoman, Charlotte Corday, in July 1793. The painting depicts Marat as having suffered a martyr's death. Marat holds the letter from his murderer that gave her entrance to his residence.

In order to destroy all vestiges of the Old Regime, the government also instituted a new calendar in October 1793. The dates on the calendar began with September 22, 1792, the day the Republic was established. That became the first day of the year I, while the weeks now had ten days instead of seven. The new months were given names to evoke the different seasons, such as *Brumaire* for the first month of wintry weather, *Germinal* for the season of planting, and *Thermidor* for the warmest month of the summer. Hostile British contemporaries gave their own humorous renditions of these names, translating them as Freezy, Flowery, Heaty, and so on. The new calendar was intended to make the revolution a part of people's everyday consciousness. It remained in effect until the last day of 1805.

The new revolutionary culture was disseminated widely, but it was always contested. Royalists trampled on the tricolor cockade, refused to adopt the new style of dress, and pulled up the liberty trees. This resistance from counter-revolutionary forces guaranteed that when the revolution

was reversed, much of the new political culture would disappear. Napoleon did little to perpetuate it, and the restored monarchy was openly hostile to it. Like the political revolution, however, some elements of revolutionary culture, such as the tricolor and the rhetoric of the revolutionary press, could never be suppressed. Not only did these cultural innovations inspire revolutionaries for the next hundred years, but they also became part of the mainstream of Western civilization.

CULTURAL UNIFORMITY

One of the most striking features of the new revolutionary culture was its concern for standardization and simplicity. The division of France into *départments,* all roughly equal in size, population, and wealth, and the further subdivision of each *départment* into uniform districts and communes, serves as one manifestation of this compulsion. The establishment of a national school system, at least on paper, serves as another. When the *lycées* were founded by Napoleon, each of the schools was given the exact same curriculum, and the same 3,000 books, chosen by a central committee, were deposited in all *lycée* libraries. The adoption of the metric system and the decimal system and the plan to establish one body of French law for the entire country, eventually brought to fruition by Napoleon, reflected the same impulse. So too did the efforts begun during the Terror to make French the official language in regions of the country that spoke Breton, Occitan, Basque, or other regional dialects.

The main source of this drive toward cultural uniformity was the desire to build a new French nation composed of equal citizens. Linguistic, legal, educational, or administrative diversity only made the realization of that program more difficult. The quest for cultural and political standardization did not, however, originate during the revolution. Many of the projects of the 1790s, especially the desire to establish standard weights and measures, began during the Old Regime. They were often the product of the rationalism of the Enlightenment, which, as we have seen in Chapter 17, sought to make society conform to the operation of universal laws.

The Napoleonic Era, 1799–1815

The coup d'état on November 9, 1799, or the eighteenth of *Brumaire* on the revolutionary calendar, marked a turning point in the political history of France. The Consulate ushered in a period of authoritarian rule. Liberty was restricted in the interest of order; republicanism gave way to dictatorship. The French Revolution had apparently run its course. But the period between 1799 and 1815 was also a time of considerable innovation, especially in the realm of politics and diplomacy. Those innovations were primarily the work of one man, Napoleon Bonaparte, who controlled the French government for the next fifteen years.

NAPOLEON'S RISE TO POWER

Napoleon Bonaparte was born on the Mediterranean island of Corsica. His father, Charles-Marie de Buonaparte, was an attorney who had supported the Corsican patriot Pascale de Paoli in winning the independence of the island from the Italian state of Genoa. His mother, Letizia, had come from an old noble family from Lombardy in Italy. In 1770 the new French government, which had gained control of the island the previous year, accepted the Buonaparte family as nobility. In 1779 the young Napoleon, whose native language was Corsican, received an appointment to a French military school. He survived both the rigors of the course of study and the taunting of his classmates, who mocked him for his accent and his poverty. Displaying a natural gift for military science, he won a position in the artillery section of the national military academy in Paris.

Until the beginning of the French Revolution, Napoleon seemed destined to pursue a successful but unspectacular career as an officer in the royal army. The events of the revolution made possible his rapid ascent to military prominence and political power. When the revolution broke out,

Napoleon returned to Corsica, where he organized the National Guard and petitioned the government to grant full rights of citizenship to his people. As the revolution became more radical he became a Jacobin, and he was commissioned to attack federalist and royalist positions in the south of France. Unlike many of his fellow Jacobins, he managed to survive the Terror and then found favor with the Directory. In 1796 Napoleon was given command of the Army of Italy, at which time he abandoned the Italian spelling of his name for Bonaparte. His decisive victories against the Austrians and his popularity in Paris attracted the attention of Sieyès and others who wished to give the country strong, charismatic leadership.

Napoleon's personality was ideally suited to the acquisition and maintenance of political power. A man of unparalleled ambition, he was driven by an extraordinarily high assessment of his abilities. After one of his military victories he wrote, "I realized I was a superior being and conceived the ambition of performing great things." To the pursuit of his destiny he harnessed a determined and a stubborn will. Temporary setbacks never seemed to thwart his single-minded pursuit of glory. He brought enormous energy to his military and political pursuits. He wrote more than 80,000 letters during his life, many of them transmitting orders to his officers and ministers. Authoritarian by nature, he used intimidation as well as paternal concern to cultivate the loyalty of his subordinates. Like many

■ **Charles Meynier,**
Napoleon on the Island of Lobau after the Battle of Essling, 1807
This painting depicts the loyalty of Napoleon's troops to him and his concern for those who had been injured in battle.

THE FRENCH PEOPLE ACCEPT NAPOLEON AS EMPEROR, 1804

The Countess de Rémusat was the wife of one of Napoleon's chamberlains. In this letter she explains why the French people accepted Napoleon as their emperor. Her comments reflect the fear of disorder that permeated French society at the end of the eighteenth century.

I can understand how it was that men worn out by the turmoil of the Revolution, and afraid of that liberty which had long been associated with death, looked for repose under the dominion of an able ruler on whom fortune was seemingly resolved to smile. I can conceive that they regarded his elevation as a decree of destiny and fondly believed that in the irrevocable they should find peace. I may confidently assert that those persons believed quite sincerely that Bonaparte, whether as Consul or Emperor, would exert his authority to oppose the intrigues of faction and would save us from the perils of anarchy.

None dared to utter the word Republic, so deeply had the Terror stained that name, and Directorial Government had perished in the contempt with which its chiefs were regarded. The return of the Bourbons could only be brought about by the aid of a revolution; and the slightest disturbance terrified the French people, in whom enthusiasm of every kind seemed dead. Besides, the men in whom they had trusted had one after the other deceived them; and as, this time, they were yielding to force, they were at least certain that they were not deceiving themselves.

The belief, or rather the error, that only despotism could at that epoch maintain order in France, was very widespread. It became the mainstay of Bonaparte; and it is due to him to say that he also believed it. The factions played into his hands by imprudent attempts which he turned to his own advantage; he had some grounds for his belief that he was necessary; France believed it too; and he even succeeded in persuading foreign sovereigns that he constituted a barrier against Republican influences which, but for him, might spread widely. At the moment when Bonaparte placed the imperial crown upon his head, there was not a king in Europe who did not believe that he wore his own crown more securely because of that event. Had the new emperor granted a liberal constitution, the peace of nations and of kings might, in sober seriousness, have been for ever secured.

Source: *Memoirs of Madame de Rémusat,* translated by C. Hoey and John Lillie (D. Appleton and Co., 1880).

---

authoritarian leaders, he had difficulty delegating authority, a trait that was to weaken his regime. Finally, in an age dominated by high-minded causes, he exhibited an instinctive distrust of ideology and the doctrinaire pronouncements of philosophes like Rousseau. Napoleon's military training led him to take a pragmatic, disciplined approach to politics, in which he always sought the most effective means to the desired end.

Napoleon's acquisition of power was systematic and shrewd. Playing on the need for a strong leader, and using the army he controlled as his main political tool, he maneuvered himself into the position of first consul in 1799. In 1802 he became consul for life, and two years later he crowned himself emperor of the French and his wife Josephine empress. The title of emperor traditionally denoted the height of monarchical power. It identified a ruler who not only ruled more than one kingdom or state but also did not share power with any other political authority. That was certainly the case with Napoleon. During his rule the Legislative Body, the Senate, and the Tribunate, all of which had been instituted during the Consulate, were reduced to performing only ceremonial functions.

It is certainly ironic that Napoleon, while continuing to hunt down and execute royalists, accepted a title of royalty himself and made his position, just like the French kingship, hereditary. In 1804 a group of royalists, including the members of the Bourbon family, were convicted of and executed for trying to assassinate Napoleon. One of them declared ironically, "We have done more than we hoped. We meant to give France a king, and we have given her an emperor." That emperor moreover, appeared to the royalists and to many others to be a tyrant who would trample on the rights of the French people. Napoleon's coronation also made a negative impression outside France. The great German composer Ludwig van Beethoven, having dedicated his *Third Symphony* (1803) to Napoleon for overthrowing tyranny in France, scratched Napoleon's name from the dedication after Napoleon assumed his new position as emperor.

NAPOLEON AND THE REVOLUTION

What was the relationship between Napoleon's rule and the French Revolution? Did Napoleon consolidate the gains of the revolution or destroy them? Did he simply redirect the revolutionary commitment to liberty, equality, and fraternity into new and more disciplined channels of expression after 1799? Or did he reverse the political trends that had prevailed from 1789 to 1799, crushing liberty in all its forms and establishing a ruthless, authoritarian dictatorship? Napoleon always thought of himself as the heir of the revolution rather than its undertaker. Certainly he was able to use the radical vocabulary of the revolution to characterize his domestic programs and his military campaigns. He presented himself as the ally of the common man against entrenched aristocratic privilege. He proclaimed a love for the French people and gave his support to the doctrine of popular sovereignty. He often referred to the rulers of other European countries as tyrants and presented himself as the liberator of their subjects.

This view of Napoleon as a true revolutionary, however, ignores the fact that his commitment to liberty was almost entirely rhetorical. Behind the appeals to the slogans of the revolution lurked an authoritarian will that was far stronger than that of any eighteenth-century absolute monarch. He used the language of liberty and democracy to disguise a thoroughgoing authoritarianism, just as he used the rhetoric of republicanism to legitimize his own dictatorial regime. The practice of holding carefully orchestrated and controlled elections to ratify the changes he made in French government guaranteed that his rule would appear to have emanated from the will of the people. At the establishment of the Consulate, Napoleon paid lip service to representative forms of government, which he maintained but then proceeded to render totally ineffective. When the empire was established he told his troops that they had the freedom to vote for or against the new form of government but then told them that if they voted against it, they would be shot.

We can make a stronger case for Napoleon's egalitarianism. He spoke of equality of opportunity. He synthesized the egalitarianism of the revolution with the authoritarianism of the Old Regime. He supported the equality of all Frenchmen (but not Frenchwomen) before the law. This egalitarianism laid the foundation for the support he received from the peasants, soldiers, and workers. It might be said that he brought both equality and political stability to France in exchange for political liberty.

There are two other ways in which we might legitimately consider Napoleon the heir of the revolution. The first is that he continued the centralization and growth of state power and the rational organization of the administration that had begun in 1789. Each of the successive regimes between 1789 and 1815, even the Directory, had contributed to this pattern of state building, and Napoleon's contribution was monumental. The second was his continuation and extension of France's military mission to export the revolution to its European neighbors. The two achievements are related to each other, since it was the war effort that necessitated the further growth and centralization of state power.

NAPOLEON AND THE FRENCH STATE

Once Napoleon had gained effective control of the French state, he set about the task of strengthening it, making it more efficient, highly organized, and powerful. In addition to turning the government into a de facto dictatorship, he settled the long struggle between Church and state, laid down an entirely new law code that imposed legal uniformity on the entire country, and made the civil bureaucracy more centralized, uniform, and efficient. All of this was done with the intention of making the state an effective instrument of social and political control.

Concordat with the Papacy

Napoleon's first contribution to the development of the French state, achieved during the Consulate, was to bring about a resolution of the bitter struggle between Church and state. A committed secularist, Napoleon was determined to bring the Church under the direct control of the state. This had been the main purpose of the Civil Constitution of the Clergy of 1790. Napoleon also realized, however, that this policy had divided the clergy between those who had taken an oath to the nation and those who had refused. Clerical independence had also become a major rallying cry of royalists against the new regime, thereby threatening the stability of the country.

Napoleon's solution to this problem was to reach an agreement with the Church that would satisfy clerics and royalists yet not deprive the state of its authority over the Church. With the Church safely under state control, Napoleon could also use religion to maintain respect for authority and to encourage loyalty and service to the state. "In religion," he wrote, "I do not see the mystery of the Incarnation but the mystery of the social order." In a new catechism published after Napoleon became emperor, children were taught: "Christians owe to the princes who govern them, and we owe in particular to Napoleon I, our Emperor, love, respect, obedience, fidelity, military service, and the tributes laid for the preservation and defense of the Empire."

The death of Pope Pius VI (r. 1775–1799), the implacable foe of the revolution, gave Napoleon the opportunity to address this problem. The new pope, Pius VII (r. 1800–1823), who was more sympathetic to liberal causes, was eager to come to terms with a French government that had become more moderate under the Consulate. The Concordat, which Napoleon and Pope Pius agreed to in 1801 and which was published the following year, gave something to both sides, although Napoleon gained more than he conceded. The pope agreed that all the clergy who refused to swear their loyalty to the nation would resign their posts, thus ending the bitter divisions of the past twelve years. The pope would appoint new bishops, but only with the prior approval of Napoleon. The state would pay all clerical salaries, and the Church would abandon any claims it still had to the ecclesiastical lands seized by the state at the beginning of the revolution.

These provisions represented formidable concessions to state power, and many French bishops found the terms of the Concordat too unfavorable to the Church. But the pope did manage to secure a statement that Roman Catholicism was the religion of the majority of citizens, and Napoleon agreed to scrap the secular calendar introduced in 1793, thereby restoring Sundays and holy days. Church attendance began to increase after having reached historic lows during the period of the Republic. The Church regained its respect as well as its legitimacy and its freedom to function in French society. More young recruits joined the clergy. Napoleon did not make many concessions to the Church, but they were significant enough to alienate a group of liberal philosophers and writers known as the Ideologues°, who objected to what they saw as the return of "monkish superstition."

With the pope at least somewhat appeased, Napoleon took unilateral steps to regulate the administration of the French Church. In a set of regulations known as the Organic Articles, which were added to the Concordat in 1802, the French church became a department of state, controlled by a minister of religion, just like the treasury or any other bureaucratic ministry. Pronouncements from the pope required prior government approval, and the clergy were obliged to read government decrees from the pulpit. Protestant congregations, which were also given freedom of worship and state protection by the terms of the Concordat, were likewise brought under state control, and their ministers were paid by the state. Jews received the protection of the state, but the government did not pay the salaries of rabbis.

The Civil Code

Napoleon's most enduring achievement in the realm of state building was the promulgation of a new legal code, the Civil Code of 1804, later known as the Napoleonic Code°. A legal code is an authoritative and comprehensive statement of the law of a particular country. The model for modern legal codes in Europe was the *Corpus Juris Civilis* of the Roman Empire, which Justinian decreed at Constantinople between 529 and 534 C.E. That code had replaced the thousands of constitutions, customs, and judicial decisions that had been in effect during the Roman republic and empire. In compiling the new French code Napoleon, who had just proclaimed himself emperor of the French, was imitating Justinian's legal achievement.

The Napoleonic Code also met a long-standing set of demands to reform the confusing and irregular body of French law. Ever since the Middle Ages, France had been governed by a multiplicity of laws. In the southern provinces of the country, those closest to Italy, the law had been influenced by Roman law. The *Corpus Juris Civilis* had

CHRONOLOGY	
The Consulate and the Early Years of the Empire, 1799–1806	
1799	
December 15	Proclamation of the Constitution of the Consulate
1801	
July 15	Signing of the Concordat with the Papacy
1802	
March 27	Peace of Amiens
April 8	Organic Articles added to the Concordat
1803	
May	Renewal of the war with Britain
1804	
March 21	The Civil Code is promulgated
December 2	Napoleon is crowned emperor of the French
1805	
August	Third Coalition (Britain, Austria, and Russia) is formed against France
October 21	Defeat of the French navy in the Battle of Trafalgar
October 29	The French defeat the Austrian army at Ulm
December 2	The French defeat Russian and Austrian armies at Austerlitz
December 31	End of the revolutionary calendar
1806	
October 14	French victories at the battles of Jena and Auerstädt
November 21	Proclamation of the Continental Blockade of British goods
August 6	Formal dissolution of the Holy Roman Empire

been revived in the Middle Ages and had been incorporated into the written law of these southern French provinces and municipalities. In the north the law was based on local or provincial customs that had not originally existed in written form. France needed a common law for all its people. Efforts to produce an authoritative written code began during the revolution, but Napoleon completed the project and published the code.

The Civil Code, which consisted of more than 2,000 articles, reflected the values that were ascendant in Napoleonic French society. The ideals of the revolution were enshrined in the articles guaranteeing the rights of private property, the equality of all people before the law, and freedom of religion. The values it promoted, however, did not include the equality of the sexes. It granted men control of all family property. Women could not buy or sell property without the consent of their husbands. Only adult men could witness legal documents. All male heirs were entitled to inherit equal shares of a family estate, but daughters were excluded from the settlement.

The Civil Code, which dealt only with the rights and relationships of private individuals, was the first and most important of six law codes promulgated by Napoleon. Others dealt with civil procedure (1806), commerce (1807), and criminal law (1811). Renamed the Napoleonic Code in 1806, the Civil Code had an impact on the law of several countries outside France. It became the basis for the codification of the laws of Switzerland, northern Italy, and the Netherlands, and it served as a model for the numerous codes that were compiled in the German territories controlled by France during the Napoleonic period. The Napoleonic Code also influenced the law of French-speaking North America, including the civil law of the state of Louisiana, which bears signs of its influence even today.

Administrative Centralization

Napoleon laid the foundation of modern French civil administration, which acquired the characteristics of rational organization, uniformity, and centralization. All power emanated from Paris, where Napoleon presided over a Council of State. This body consisted of his main ministers, who handled all matters of finance, domestic affairs, and war and oversaw a vast bureaucracy of salaried, trained officials. The central government also exercised direct control over the provinces, which lost the local privileges they had possessed under the Old Regime. In each of the departments an official known as a *prefect,* appointed by the central government, implemented orders emanating from Paris. Paid the handsome annual salary of 20,000 francs, the prefects were responsible for the maintenance of public order. The power of the prefects was far greater than that of the *intendants* of the Old Regime. The prefects enforced conscription, collected taxes, and supervised local public works, such as the construction and improvement of roads.

The men who served in the government of the French Empire belonged to one of two elaborate, hierarchical institutions: the civil bureaucracy and the army officer corps. The two were closely related, since the main purpose of the administrative bureaucracy was to prepare for and sustain the war effort. Both institutions were organized hierarchically, and those who held positions in them were trained and salaried. Appointment and promotion were based primarily on talent rather than birth.

The idea of "a career open to all talents," as Napoleon described it, ran counter to the tradition of noble privilege. This was one of the achievements of the revolution that Napoleon perpetuated during the empire. All of the twenty-six marshals who served under him in the army were of nonnoble blood. Three of them had been sergeants in the army before 1789 and another three had been privates. The new system did not amount to a pure meritocracy, in which advancement is determined solely by ability and performance, since many appointments were made or influenced by Napoleon himself on the basis of friendship or kinship. Napoleon's brother, Lucien, for example, became minister of the interior. The system did, however, allow people from the ranks of the bourgeoisie to achieve rapid upward social mobility. In order to recognize their new status, Napoleon created a new order of nonhereditary noblemen, known as *notables.* As men ascended through the ranks of the bureaucracy and army they were given the titles of duke, count, baron, and chevalier. Instead of basing their status on their ancestry, these men acquired their titles by virtue of their service to the state. Napoleon created more than 3,500 notables during his rule. In this way he encouraged service to the state while also strengthening loyalty to it.

NAPOLEON, THE EMPIRE, AND EUROPE

Closely related to Napoleon's efforts to build the French state was his creation of a massive European empire. The empire was the product of a series of military victories against the armies of Austria, Prussia, Russia, and Spain between 1797 and 1809. By the latter date France controlled, either directly or indirectly, the Dutch Republic, the Austrian Netherlands, Italy, Spain, and large parts of Germany and Poland. The instrument of these victories was the massive citizen army that Napoleon was able to assemble. Building on the *levée en masse* of 1793, which he supplemented with soldiers from the countries he conquered, Napoleon had more than one million men under arms by 1812. More than three times the size of Louis XIV's army in 1700, it was the largest military force raised under the control of one man up to this time in European history.

These troops engaged in a military offensive that was more massive, wide-ranging, and sustained than Alexander the Great's invasion of Egypt, Persia, and northern India between 334 and 326 B.C.E. Napoleon's invasion began with the great victories against Austria and Prussia in 1797. Two years later, shortly after Napoleon had become first consul, he directed his army to further military successes that paved the way to French dominance of Europe. The defeat of Austria in 1800 confirmed earlier territorial gains in Italy as well as French control over the southern Netherlands, now called Belgium. With Austria defeated and Russia involved with the Ottoman Turks, France and Britain concluded peace at Amiens in 1802. This peace gave Napoleon free rein to reorganize the countries that bordered on France's eastern and southeastern boundaries. In Italy he named himself the president of the newly established Cisalpine Republic, and he transformed the cantons of Switzerland

■ **Emperor Napoleon Crowning His Wife, Josephine, Empress of the French in the Cathedral of Notre Dame, 1804**

This painting by Jacques-Louis David depicts secular and religious figures gathered around Napoleon not as members of privileged orders but as representatives of the nation. Pope Pius VII remains seated as Napoleon places the crown on Josephine's head. Napoleon had already crowned himself emperor of the French.

into the Helvetic Republic. These acquisitions gave substance to the title of emperor that he assumed in 1804, since now he controlled many different kingdoms. France had not had an emperor since the ninth century, when Charlemagne and his heirs had ruled as Roman emperors, and Napoleon's territories were more extensive than those under Charlemagne's jurisdiction.

These stunning military successes as well as those that were to follow have secured Napoleon's reputation as one of the most brilliant and successful military leaders in modern history. The reasons for that reputation are a matter of some controversy. Napoleon made terrible strategic blunders in many of his campaigns and tactical mistakes in many of his battles. Somehow he seemed to make up for these mistakes by his careful planning, unbounded energy, and decisive moves. He spent hours studying his opponents' position beforehand but made quick decisions once the battle had begun. "Everything," he once said, "is in the execution." The combination of infantry, artillery, and cavalry in the same units or *corps* allowed him to move these forces easily on the battlefield. He struck quickly, usually at the center of en-

emy lines, using superior numbers to overwhelm his opponent. Attacks on enemy lines of communication often prevented his opponents from calling up reinforcements. Once they began their retreat, he would pursue them rather than stop to celebrate. In his campaigns he benefited from the loyalty of his troops and the ideological zeal that continued to inspire them, even as his wars lost their ideological purpose of exporting the ideals of the revolution.

Napoleon was far less successful at sea than on land. With no real experience in naval warfare, he could not match the dominance of the British navy, which retained its mastery of the seas throughout the entire revolutionary period. Only in the West Indies, where Britain was never able to send sufficient naval forces, did the French navy manage to hold its own. This naval weakness also explains Napoleon's failure to build or regain an overseas empire. His expedition to Egypt in 1798, which was dominated by dreams of colonial conquest in the Middle East and South Asia, was checked by the British destruction of the French fleet at the Battle of the Nile. In the Western Hemisphere financial problems and a false hope of limiting British power induced Napoleon to sell the vast North American territory of Louisiana, which he had acquired from Spain in 1796, to the United States in 1803. The following year the French Caribbean colony of St. Domingue became independent as the result of the violent revolution staged by free blacks and slaves, which we shall discuss in the next chapter. Informed of that loss, Napoleon shouted "Damn sugar, damn coffee, damn colonies!"

The most significant French naval defeat came in 1805, shortly after Britain, Austria, and Russia had formed the Third Coalition against France. As Napoleon was preparing for an invasion of Britain from northern French ports, the British navy, under the command of the diminutive, one-eyed Admiral Horatio Nelson, won one of the most decisive battles in the history of naval warfare. Nelson broke the line of a Franco-Spanish fleet that was preparing to strike off the Cape of Trafalgar near Gibraltar. The British destroyed or captured half the enemy ships, thus breaking the back of French sea power. The battle is commemorated at Trafalgar Square in London, which is overlooked by a towering statue of Nelson, who died of wounds inflicted during the battle.

Nelson might have survived if he had not insisted on wearing glimmering medals on his uniform, thereby attracting the notice of French marksmen.

The monumental naval defeat at Trafalgar did not prevent Napoleon from continuing his wars of conquest in central Europe. In October 1805 he defeated an Austrian army at Ulm, and in December of that year he overwhelmed the combined forces of Austria and Russia at Austerlitz. These victories brought him new German and Italian territory, which he ceded to some of the larger German states; the smaller German states became satellites of France and fought with him until the collapse of his empire. A defeat of Prussian forces at Jena and Auerstedt in 1806 and the subsequent occupation of Berlin gave him the opportunity to carve the new German kingdom of Westphalia out of Prussian territory in the Rhineland and to install his brother Jerome as its ruler. In the East he created the duchy of Warsaw out of Polish lands controlled by Prussia. In 1806 he formally dissolved the ancient Holy Roman Empire and replaced it with a loose association of sixteen German states known as the Confederation of the Rhine. By 1807, in the

THE FRENCH ENCOUNTER THE EGYPTIANS

....

When the French army occupied Egypt in 1798, Napoleon brought with him 165 scholars who were organized into a Commission of Science and Arts. Their purpose was to give Napoleon information on the people and the resources of the country so that he could more easily control the country. A small group of these scholars set up an Institute of Egypt, whose mission was to propagate the Enlightenment and to undertake research on the history, people, and economy of the country. One of the members of the Institute, Vivant Denon, published Travels in Upper and Lower Egypt *in 1803. The following excerpt describes three of the ethnic groups in Egypt whom the French encountered: Arabs, Turks, and Greeks.*

After the Copts come the Arabs, the most numerous of the inhabitants of modern Egypt. Without possessing an influence proportioned to their numbers, they seem to be placed there to people the country, to cultivate the lands, to tend the flocks, or to be themselves in the degraded state of animals. They are, however, lively, and have a penetrating physiognomy. Their eyes, which are sunk in and overarched, are replete with vivacity and character; all their proportions are angular; their beard is short and hanging in filaments; their lips are thin and open, displaying fine teeth; their arms are fleshy and, in other respects, they are more active than handsome and more muscular than well shaped. . . .

The beauties of the Turks are more dignified and their shape more delicate. Their thick eyelids allow little expression in the eyes; the nose is thick; the mouth and lips handsome; the beard long and heavy; and this solemnity of gait, which, notwithstanding the nullity of their authority, inspires a certain degree of awe, they mistake for dignity. They possess a beauty which cannot be defined, or a reason given why it should be considered as such. This is not the case with the Greeks, who must be classed among the foreigners by whom societies distinct from those of the indigenous inhabitants are formed. The fine delineations of their form, their arch and penetrating eyes, and the delicacy and flexibility of their traits bring to the remembrance all that their monuments have transmitted to us to attest their elegance and taste. The degraded state to which they have been reduced, through a dread which the superiority of their intellectual faculties still inspires, has rendered many of them wily knaves. Were they, however, left to themselves, they would perhaps become, in a little time, who they formerly were, subtle and ambitious. Of all the nations on earth, this is the one which longs the most ardently for a revolution from whatever quarter it may come.

Source: From Vivant Denon, *Travels in Upper and Lower Egypt During the Campaigns of General Bonaparte in Their Country, Volume I* (Heard and Foreman, 1803).

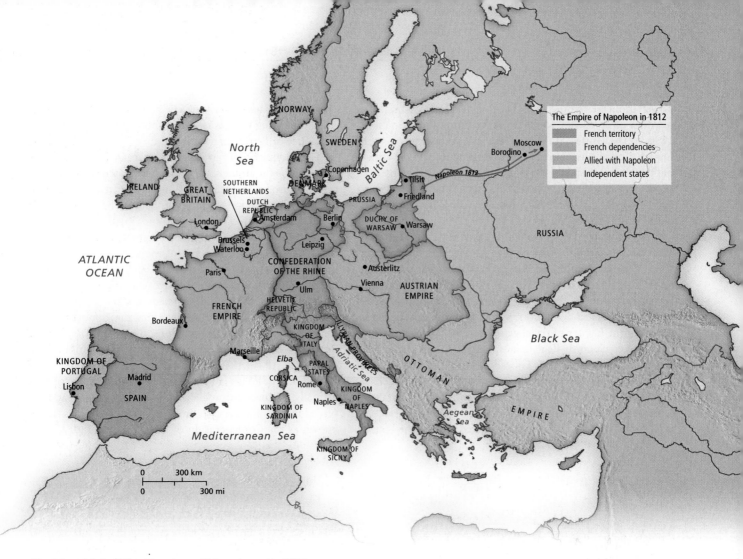

■ **Map 18.1 The Empire of Napoleon in 1812**

By establishing dependent states in Spain, Italy, Germany, and Poland, France controlled far more territory than the areas technically within the French Empire.

words of one historian, Napoleon had "only allies and victims" on the Continent (see Map 18.1).

Napoleon inserted the last piece in this imperial puzzle by invading and occupying the kingdom of Spain in 1807. This campaign began as an effort to crush Portugal, the ally of Britain, which he was never able to defeat. In May 1808, as French armies marched through Spain en route to Lisbon, the Portuguese capital, a popular insurrection against Spanish rule occurred in Madrid. This spontaneous revolt, which led to the abdication of King Charles IV and the succession of his son Ferdinand VII, was the first of many developments that caused the collapse of the Spanish Empire in America. In Europe it led to the absorption of Spain into the French Empire. Sensing that he could easily add one more territory to his list of conquests, Napoleon forced Ferdinand to abdicate and summoned his own brother, Joseph Bonaparte, who was then ruling the dependent kingdom of Naples, to become king of Spain.

Joseph instituted some reforms in Spain, but the abolition of the Spanish Inquisition and the closing of two-thirds of the Spanish convents triggered a visceral reaction from the Spanish clergy and the general populace. Fighting for Church and king, small bands of local guerillas subjected French forces to intermittent and effective sabotage. An invasion by British forces under the command of Arthur Wellesley, later the Duke of Wellington (1769–1852), in what has become known as the Peninsula War (1808–1813), strengthened Spanish and Portuguese resistance.

The reception of the French in Spain revealed that the export of revolution, which had begun with the French armies of 1792, was a double-edged sword. The overthrow of authoritarian regimes in other European states won the support of progressive, capitalist, and anticlerical forces in those countries, but it also triggered deep resentment against French rule. The ideology of nationalism in Germany and Italy arose more because of a reaction against French rule than because the armies of France had tried to stimulate it. In Italy during the 1790s young educated *patrioti*, imbued with enthusiasm for liberty, equality, and progress, supported the newly proclaimed republics and envisioned the establishment of a single Italian state, at least in the north of Italy. By the middle of the Napoleonic years that vision had changed. Many of the *patrioti* had become disillusioned and joined secret societies to press for further political and social change and to plot insurrections against the new republics.

In Germany many of those who supported the French cause during the early years of the Republic turned away from it during Napoleon's wars of expansion. In 1809 a German student who attempted to assassinate Napoleon shouted "Long live Germany" at his execution. In 1813 the German writer Johann Gottlieb Fichte (1762–1814) appealed to the German nation to resist Napoleon in order to regain their liberty. For all his political astuteness, Napoleon could not comprehend that his own policies were responsible for the growth of this reactive sentiment, which formed one of the foundations of nineteenth-century nationalism. We shall discuss this topic more fully in Chapter 21.

THE DOWNFALL OF NAPOLEON

The turning point in Napoleon's personal fortunes and those of his empire came in 1810. After securing an annulment of his marriage to Josephine in late 1809, he married Marie-Louise, the daughter of the Habsburg emperor. This marriage, which the following year produced a son and heir to the throne, should have made the French Empire more secure, but it had the opposite effect. For the first time during his rule, dissent from both the right and the left became widespread. Despite the most stringent efforts at censorship, royalist and Jacobin literature poured off the presses. The number of military deserters and those evading conscription increased. Relations with the papacy reached a breaking point when Napoleon annexed the Papal States, at which point Pope Pius VII, who had negotiated the Concordat of 1801, excommunicated him.

Dissent at home had the effect of driving the megalomaniacal emperor to seek more glory and further conquests. In this frame of mind Napoleon made the ill-advised decision to invade Russia. The motives for engaging in this overly ambitious military campaign were not completely irrational. Victory over Russia promised to give France control of the Black Sea, and that in turn would ultimately lead to the control of Constantinople and the entire Middle East. More immediately, defeating Russia would be necessary to enforce the French blockade of British goods, which Russia had refused to support.

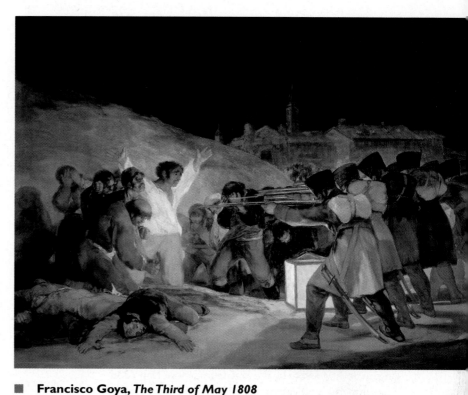

■ **Francisco Goya, *The Third of May 1808***
This painting of the suppression of the popular revolt in Madrid in 1808 captures the brutality of the French occupation of Spain. A French unit executes Spanish citizens, including a monk in the foreground. Goya was a figure of the Enlightenment and a Spanish patriot.

The problem with a Russian invasion was that it stretched Napoleon's lines of communication too far and his resources too thin, despite the support of the Austrians and Prussians whom he had defeated. Even before the invasion it was becoming increasingly difficult to feed, equip, and train the huge army he had assembled. The Grand Army that crossed from Poland into Russia in 1812 was not the efficient military force that Napoleon had commanded in the early years of the empire. Many of his best soldiers were fighting in the guerilla war in Spain. Casualties and desertions had forced Napoleon to call up new recruits who were not properly trained. Half the army, moreover, had been recruited from the population of conquered countries, making their loyalty to Napoleon uncertain.

The tactics of the Russians contributed to the failure of the invasion. Instead of engaging the Grand Army in combat, the Russian army kept retreating, pulling Napoleon further east toward Moscow. On September 7 the two armies clashed at Borodino, suffering a staggering 77,000 casualties in all. The Russian army then continued its retreat eastward. When Napoleon reached Moscow he found it deserted, and fires deliberately set by Muscovites had destroyed more than two-thirds of the city. Napoleon, facing the onset of a dreaded Russian winter and rapidly diminishing supplies, began the long retreat back to France. Skirmishes with the Russians along the way, which cost him 25,000 lives just crossing the Beresina River, conspired with the cold and hunger to destroy his army. During the entire Russian campaign his army lost a total of 380,000 men to death, imprisonment, or desertion. In the midst of this horror Napoleon, oblivious to the suffering of his troops, reported back to Paris, "The health of the emperor has never been better."

Not to be discouraged, Napoleon soon began preparing for further conquests. Once again his enemies formed a coalition against him, pledging to restore the independence of the countries that had become his satellites or dependents. Napoleon scored a few victories in the late summer of 1813, but in October allied forces inflicted a crushing defeat on him in the Battle of the Nations at Leipzig. Austrian troops administered another blow to the French in northern Italy, and the British finally drove them out of Spain. As a result of these defeats, Napoleon's army was pushed back into France. A massive allied force advanced into Paris and occupied the city. After extensive political maneuvering, including a vote by the Senate to depose Napoleon, the emperor abdicated on April 6, 1814. The allies promptly exiled him to the Mediterranean island of Elba. As he made the journey to the coast, crowds surrounding his coach shouted "Down with the tyrant!" while some villagers hanged him in effigy.

This course of events led to the restoration of the Bourbon monarchy. By the terms of the first Treaty of Paris of May 1814, the allies restored the brother of Louis XVI, the Count of Provence, to the French throne as Louis XVIII (r. 1814–1824). Louis was an implacable foe of the revolution, and much of what he did was intended to undermine its achievements. The white Bourbon flag replaced the revolutionary tricolor. Catholicism was once again recognized as the state religion. Exiled royalists returned to their high-ranking positions in the army. Nonetheless, Louis accepted a Constitutional Charter that incorporated many of the changes made between 1789 and 1791. Representative government, with a relatively limited franchise, replaced the absolutism of the Old Regime. Equality before the law, freedom of religion, and freedom of expression were all reaffirmed. Even more important, the powers of the state that the National Assembly and the Directory had extended and Napoleon had enhanced were maintained. The administrative division of France into departments continued, and the Napoleonic Code remained in force. France had experienced a counterrevolution in 1814, but it did not simply turn the political clock back to 1788. Some of the political achievements of the previous twenty-five years were indeed preserved.

Despite his disgrace and exile, Napoleon still commanded loyalty from his troops and from large segments of the population. While in power he had constructed a legend that drew on strong patriotic sentiment. Supporters throughout France continued to promote his cause in the same way that royalists had maintained that of the Bourbon monarchy since 1792. The Napoleonic legend held great appeal among the lower classes, who were persuaded that Napoleon, the patriot and the savior of the revolution, had made it possible for every Frenchman to achieve wealth and fame. The strength of the Napoleonic legend became apparent in March 1815, when Napoleon escaped from Elba and landed in southern France. Promising to rid the coun-

CHRONOLOGY

The Downfall of Napoleon, 1807–1815

1807	
November–December	French military intervention in Spain and Portugal begins
1808	
May	Beginning of the Spanish rebellion
July 20	Joseph Bonaparte appointed king of Spain
1809	
December 15	Annulment of marriage of Napoleon and Empress Josephine
1810	
April 2	Marriage of Napoleon to Marie-Louise
1812	
September 7	Battle of Borodino
September 14	Napoleon enters Moscow
October	Retreat from Moscow begins
1813	
October 16–19	Battle of the Nations at Leipzig
1814	
April 6	Abdication of Napoleon
May 30	First Treaty of Paris
September	Congress of Vienna assembles
1815	
March	Napoleon escapes from Elba
June 18	Battle of Waterloo
November 20	Second Treaty of Paris

try of the exiled royalists who had returned and to save the revolutionary cause that he claimed had been abandoned, he won over peasants, workers, and soldiers. Regiment after regiment joined him as he marched toward Paris. By the time he arrived, Louis XVIII had gone into exile once again, and Napoleon found himself back in power.

But not for long. The allied European powers quickly began to assemble yet another coalition. Fearing that the allies would launch a massive invasion of France, Napoleon decided to strike first. He marched an army of 200,000 men into the Austrian Netherlands, where the allies responded by amassing 700,000 troops. Near the small village of Waterloo, south of Brussels, he met the British forces of the

Duke of Wellington, who had turned the tide against him during the Peninsula War. Reinforced by Prussian troops, Wellington inflicted a devastating defeat on the French army, which lost 28,000 men and went into a full-scale retreat. Napoleon, captured in the battle, abdicated once again. He was exiled to the remote South Atlantic island of St. Helena, from which escape was impossible. He died there in 1821.

Even before the battle of Waterloo, the major powers of Europe had gathered in Vienna to redraw the boundaries of the European states that had been created, dismembered, or transformed during the preceding twenty-five years (see Map 18.2). Under the leadership of the Austrian foreign

■ **Map 18.2   Europe After the Congress of Vienna, 1815**

The four most important territorial changes that took place in 1815 were the scaling back of the boundaries of France to their status in 1790, the Austrian acquisition of territory in western and northeastern Italy, the establishment of the new kingdom of the Netherlands, and the formation of the new German Confederation.

minister, Prince Clemens von Metternich (1773–1859), this conference, known as the Congress of Vienna°, worked out a settlement that was intended to preserve the balance of power in Europe and at the same time uphold the principle of dynastic legitimacy. By the terms of a separate Treaty of Paris (the second in two years) the boundaries of France were scaled back to what they had been in 1790, before it had begun its wars of expansion. To create a buffer state on the northern boundary of France, the Congress annexed the Austrian Netherlands to the Dutch Republic, which now became the kingdom of the Netherlands with William I, a prince of the House of Orange, as its king. Territory along the Rhineland in the state of Westphalia was ceded to Prussia, while Austria gained territory in Italy, both along the French border in the west and in northern Italy to the east. In place of the defunct Holy Roman Empire, the Congress established a new German Confederation, a loose coalition of thirty-nine separate territories with a weak legislative assembly, whose members were appointed and instructed by their governments. The five major powers that had drawn this new map of Europe—Britain, Austria, Prussia, Russia, and France—agreed to meet annually to prevent any one country, especially France but also Russia, from achieving military dominance of the European Continent.

The Legacy of the French Revolution

With the conclusion of the Congress of Vienna a tumultuous period of European and Western history finally came to an end. Not only had France experienced a revolution, but every country in Europe and America had felt its effects. Governments were toppled in countries as far apart as Poland and Peru. Added to this turbulence was the experience of incessant warfare. France was at war for more than twenty years during the period of the Republic and the empire, and it had brought almost all European powers into the struggle. With armies constantly in need of provisions and supplies, high taxation, galloping inflation, and food shortages inflicted economic hardship on a large portion of the European population.

The cost of all this instability and warfare in terms of human life is staggering. Within the space of one generation almost two million European soldiers were killed in action, wasted by disease, or starved or frozen to death. In France alone just under 500,000 soldiers died during the revolutionary wars of 1792–1802 and another 916,000 during the wars of the empire. Internal political disturbances took the lives of hundreds of thousands of civilians from all

ranks of society, not only in France but throughout Europe. The violence was fed at all levels by unprecedented fears of internal and external subversion. Government officials, collaborators, counterrevolutionaries, and imagined enemies of the state were all executed. This spate of violence and death—much of it in the name of liberty—was inflicted almost entirely by the state or its enemies.

What was achieved at this extraordinary price? How did the France of 1815 differ from the France of 1788? What on balance had changed? For many years historians, especially those who believed that economic forces determined the course of history, claimed that as a result of the revolution the bourgeoisie, composed of merchants, manufacturers, and other commoners of substantial wealth, had replaced the nobility as the dominant social and political class in the country. The bourgeoisie, so they argued, had started the revolution in order to acquire political power that was commensurate with their economic power, and they had ultimately prevailed.

This assessment can no longer be sustained. The nobility certainly lost many of their privileges in 1789, and many of them went into exile during the revolutionary period; however, the position they had in French society in 1815 did not differ greatly from what it had been under the Old Regime. In both periods there was considerable blurring of the distinctions between nobility and bourgeoisie. Nor did the revolutionary period witness the emergence of a new class of industrial entrepreneurs. The only group who definitely profited from the revolution in the long run were men of property, regardless which social category or "class" they may have belonged to. Men of property emerged triumphant in the Directory, they found favor during the Napoleonic period, and they became the most important members of political society after the monarchy was restored.

It would be difficult to argue that *women* of any social rank benefited from the revolution. During the early years of the revolution, women participated actively in public life. They were involved in many demonstrations in Paris, including the storming of the Bastille and the march to Versailles to pressure the king to move to Paris. Women as well as men filled the ranks of the *sans-culottes,* and women donned their own female version of nonaristocratic dress. During the early years of the revolution, many women joined patriotic clubs, such as the Club of Knitters or the unisex Fraternal Society of Patriots of Both Sexes. In 1790 the Marquis de Condorcet had published *On the Admission of Women to the Rights of Citizenship,* and the following year Olympe de Gouges published *The Rights of Women,* in which she called for the granting of women's equal rights. Both of these advocates of women's rights had been influenced by Enlightenment thought, as we have discussed in Chapter 17.

The goal advanced by Condorcet and de Gouges was not to be realized. The radical Jacobins dealt it a terrible setback when they banned all women's clubs and societies on the grounds that their participation in public life would be harmful to the institution of the family. This action, coupled with the imprisonment and death of both de Gouges and Condorcet during the Terror, signaled an end to the extensive participation of women in political life, which had begun during the eighteenth century, especially in the salons. During the nineteenth century women were generally considered to occupy a separate sphere of activity from that of men. They were expected to exercise influence in the private sphere of the home, but not in the public sphere of politics. As we shall discuss in Chapter 20, the changes wrought by the Industrial Revolution reinforced this segregation of men and women by excluding many married women from the workforce.

It is even more difficult to identify permanent economic changes as a result of the revolution. The elimination of the remnants of feudalism may have made France marginally more capitalist than it had been before the revolution, but agricultural and mercantile capitalism had long been entrenched in French society. Nor did the Continental System, the blockade of British goods from all European ports initiated in 1806, allow French industry to catch up with that of Great Britain. Whatever economic gains were made under the protective shield of the state were offset by the adverse economic effects of twenty-two years of nearly continuous warfare. In the long run the revolutionary period delayed the process of industrialization that had entered its preliminary stages in France during the 1780s and retarded the growth of the French economy for the remainder of the nineteenth century.

The permanent legacy of the French Revolution lies in the realm of politics. First, the period from 1789 to 1815 triggered an enormous growth in the competence and power of the state. This was a trend that had begun before the revolution, but the desire of the revolutionaries to transform every aspect of human life in the service of the revolution, coupled with the necessity of utilizing all the country's resources in the war effort, gave the state more control over the everyday life of its citizens than ever before. Fifteen years of Napoleonic rule only accentuated this trend, and after 1815 many of those powers remained with the government.

An even more significant and permanent achievement of the French Revolution was the promotion of the doctrine of popular sovereignty. The belief that the people constituted the highest political authority in the state became so entrenched during the revolution that it could never be completely suppressed, either in France or in the other countries of Europe. Napoleon recognized its power when he asked the people to approve political changes he had already made by his own authority. He also arranged for such plebiscites to secure approval of the new states he had set up in Europe. After the restoration of the monarchy the doctrine of popular sovereignty was promoted mainly by the press, which continued to employ the new revolutionary rhetoric to keep alive the high ideals and aspirations of the revolution. The doctrine also contributed to the formation of two nineteenth-century ideologies, liberalism and nationalism, which will be discussed in Chapter 21.

The third permanent political change was the active participation of the citizens in the political life of the nation. This participation had been cultivated during the early years of the revolution, and it had been accompanied by the creation of a new political culture. Much of that culture was suppressed during the Napoleonic period, but the actual habit of participating in politics was not. The franchise was gradually expanded in Europe during the nineteenth century. The press spread political ideas to a large segment of the population. People from all walks of life participated in marches, processions, and demonstrations. All of this followed from the acceptance of the French revolutionary doctrine that the people are sovereign and have a right therefore to participate in the political life of the state.

CONCLUSION

The French Revolution and Western Civilization

The French Revolution was a central event in the history of the West. It began as an internal French affair, reflecting the social and political tensions of the Old Regime, but it soon became a turning point in European and Western history. Proclamations of the natural rights of humanity gave the ideals of the revolution widespread appeal, and a period of protracted warfare succeeded in disseminating those ideals outside the boundaries of France.

Underlying the export of French revolutionary ideology was the belief that France had become the standard-bearer of Western civilization. French people believed they were *la grande nation,* the country that had reached the highest level of political and social organization. They did not believe they had acquired this exalted status by inheritance. Unlike the English revolutionaries of the seventeenth century, they did not claim that they were the heirs of a medieval constitution. French republicans of the 1790s attributed none of their national preeminence to the monarchy, whose memory they took drastic steps to erase. They considered the secular political culture that emerged during the French Revolution to be an entirely novel development.

The export of French revolutionary political culture during the Republic and the empire brought about widespread changes in the established order. Regimes were toppled, French puppets acquired political power, boundaries of states were completely redrawn, and traditional authorities were challenged. Liberal reforms were enacted, new constitutions were written, and new law codes were promulgated. The Europe of 1815 could not be mistaken for the Europe of 1789.

The ideas of the French Revolution, like those of the Enlightenment that had helped to inspire them, did not go unchallenged. From the very early years of the revolution they encountered determined opposition, both in France and abroad. As the revolution lost its appeal in France, the forces of conservatism and reaction gathered strength. At the end of the Napoleonic period, the Congress of Vienna took steps to restore the legitimate rulers of European states and to prevent revolution from recurring. It appeared that the revolution would be completely reversed, but that was not the case. The ideas born of the revolution would continue to inspire demands for political reform in Europe during the nineteenth century, and those demands, just like those in the 1790s, would meet with fierce resistance.

Suggestions for Further Reading

For a comprehensive list of suggested readings, please go to www.ablongman.com/levack/chapter18

Blanning, T. C. W. *The French Revolutionary Wars 1787–1802.* 1996. An authoritative political and military narrative that assesses the impact of the wars on French politics.

Chartier, Roger. *The Cultural Origins of the French Revolution.* 1991. Explores the connections between the culture of the Enlightenment and the cultural transformations of the revolutionary period.

Cobban, Alfred. *The Social Interpretation of the French Revolution.* 1971. Challenges the Marxist interpretation of the causes and effects of the revolution.

Doyle, William. *The Oxford History of the French Revolution.* 1989. An excellent synthesis.

Ellis, Geoffrey. *Napoleon.* 1997. A study of the nature and mechanics of Napoleon's power and an analysis of his imperial policy.

Furet, François. *The French Revolution, 1770–1814.* 1992. A provocative narrative that sees Napoleon as the architect of a second, authoritarian revolution that reversed the gains of the first.

Hardman, John. *Louis XVI: The Silent King.* 2000. A reassessment of the king that mixes sympathy with criticism.

Higgonnet, Patrice. *Goodness beyond Virtue: Jacobins during the French Revolution.* 1998. Explores the contradictions of Jacobin ideology and its descent into the Terror.

Hunt, Lynn. *Politics, Culture and Class in the French Revolution.* 1984. Analyzes the formation of a revolutionary political culture.

Kennedy, Emmet. *The Culture of the French Revolution.* 1989. A comprehensive study of all cultural developments before and during the revolution.

Landes, Joan B. *Women and the Public Sphere in the Age of the French Revolution.* 1988. Explores how the new political culture of the revolution changed the position of women in society.

Lefebvre, Georges. *The Great Fear of 1789: Rural Panic in Revolutionary France.* 1973. Shows the importance of the rural unrest of July 1793 that provided the backdrop of the legislation of August 1789.

Schama, Simon. *Citizens: A Chronicle of the French Revolution.* 1989. Depicts the tragic unraveling of a vision of liberty and happiness into a scenario of hunger, anger, violence, and death.

The West and the World: Empire, Trade, and War, 1650–1850

I N 1789 OLAUDAH EQUIANO, A FREED SLAVE LIVING IN GREAT BRITAIN, PUBLISHED an autobiographical account of his experiences in captivity. In this narrative Equiano recounted his seizure in the Gambia region of Africa and his transportation on a slave ship to the British Caribbean colony of Barbados. He described the unmerciful floggings to which the Africans on his ship were subjected, the unrelieved hunger they experienced, and the insufferable heat and smells they endured in the hold of the ship. He witnessed the suicide of those who threw themselves into the sea in order to avoid further misery. He was terrified that his white captors would eat him, and he wished for a merciful death.

Once the ship had reached its destination Equiano related how the Africans were herded into pens where white plantation owners examined, purchased, and branded them. The most moving part of Equiano's narrative is his account of the cries he heard as family members were sold to different masters. "O you nominal Christians," wrote Equiano, "might not an African ask you, learned you this from your God? Is it not enough that we are torn from our country and friends to toil for your luxury and lust of gain? Must every tender feeling be sacrificed to your avarice? Surely this is a new refinement in cruelty, which, while it has no advantage to atone for it, thus aggravates distress and adds fresh horrors to the wretchedness of slavery."

The journey that Equiano was forced to take across the Atlantic Ocean and the emotions he described were experienced by millions of African men and women during the period from 1650 to 1850. The forced emigration of Africans from their homelands, their sale to white landlords, and their subjection to inhumane treatment number among the abiding horrors of Western civilization. To understand how these horrors could have occurred, especially at the hands of men who proclaimed a commitment to human freedom, we must study the growth of European empires during these centuries.

Chapter Outline

- European Empires in the Americas and Asia

- Warfare in Europe, North America, and Asia

- The Atlantic World

- Encounters Between Europeans and Asians

- The Crisis of Empire and the Atlantic Revolutions

Samuel Scott, *A Thames Wharf* (1750s): British merchants conducted a brisk trade with Asia and the Americas in the eighteenth century.

As European states grew in size, wealth, and military power in the sixteenth and seventeenth centuries, the most powerful of them acquired large overseas empires. By the end of the seventeenth century the British, French, and Dutch had joined the Portuguese and the Spanish as overseas imperial powers. As we discussed in Chapter 12, the first stage of empire building, which lasted from 1500 until about 1650, had many different motives. The search for gold and silver, the mission to Christianize the indigenous populations, the desire of some colonists to escape religious persecution, the urge to plunder, the efforts of monarchs to expand the size of their dominions, and the desire to profit from international trade all figured in the process. In 1625 the English government recognized many of these motives when it declared the purpose of the colony of Virginia to be "the propagation of the Christian religion, the increase of trade, and the enlarging of the royal empire."

During the second stage of empire building, which lasted from roughly 1650 to 1850, the economic motive for acquiring overseas possessions became dominant. More than anything else, imperial policy was shaped by the desire for profit within a world economy. As far as the governments of western Europe were concerned, all colonies were economic enterprises. Whether these colonies were primarily involved in commerce or agriculture or mining was only a minor distinction. The main consideration was that they provided economic benefits to the European countries. They supplied the parent country, often referred to as the metropolis°, with agricultural products, raw materials, and minerals. Overseas colonies also provided the metropolis with markets for its manufactured goods.

The growth of these empires resulted in the expansion of the geographical boundaries of the West. It also resulted in the spread of Western ideas, political institutions, and economic systems to Asia and the Americas. At the same time, encounters between Europeans and non-Western peoples, especially those of Asia, brought about significant changes in the cultures of the West.

To understand the relationship between empire, trade, and war during this period, and their impact on the changing definition of the West, this chapter will address five main questions: (1) How did the composition and the organization of European empires change during the seventeenth and eighteenth centuries? (2) In what ways did the wars waged by European powers during this period involve competition for overseas possessions and trading routes? (3) How did European empires create an Atlantic economy in which the traffic in slaves was a major feature? (4) What cultural encounters took place between European and Asian peoples during this period of empire building, and how did these encounters change Western attitudes toward outsiders? (5) Why did European powers begin to lose control of some of their colonies, especially those in the Americas, between 1775 and 1825?

European Empires in the Americas and Asia

The main political units in Europe during this long period of history are usually referred to as states°. A state is a consolidated territorial area that has its own political institutions and recognizes no higher authority. Thus we refer to France, England (which became Great Britain after its union with Scotland in 1707), Prussia, the Dutch Republic, and Portugal as states. As we have discussed in Chapter 15, most of these states acquired larger armies and administrative bureaucracies during the sixteenth and seventeenth centuries, mainly to meet the demands of war. Consequently they became more highly integrated and cohesive political structures.

Many European states formed the center or core of much larger political formations known as empires°. The main characteristic of an empire in the seventeenth and eighteenth centuries was that it comprised many different kingdoms or territorial possessions outside the geographical boundaries of the state itself. These imperial territories were controlled by the metropolis, but they were not fully integrated into its administrative structure. Some of the territories that formed a part of these empires were located in Europe. The Austrian Habsburg monarchy, for example, had jurisdiction over a host of separate kingdoms and principalities in central and eastern Europe, including Hungary and Bohemia. This arrangement made Austria an empire, a designation it formally acquired in 1806. In like manner the Spanish monarchy, which also was an empire, controlled many different kingdoms and provinces in the Iberian peninsula as well as territories in southern Italy and the Netherlands. On the eastern and southeastern periphery of Europe lay two other empires: the Russian and the Ottoman, which controlled vast expanses of land not only in eastern Europe but also in the adjacent areas of Asia. As in previous centuries, the Russian and Ottoman empires marked the ever-shifting and often blurred boundaries between East and West.

Beginning in the fifteenth century, as the result of transoceanic voyages of exploration and the establishment of overseas colonies, western European states acquired, settled, or controlled territories in the Americas, Africa, and Asia. Mastery of these lands came much more quickly in the New World than in Asia. The peoples of North and South America whom the Europeans encountered when they arrived were able fighters, but they were not organized politically, and diseases introduced by the Europeans drastically reduced their numbers. European settlers, who had the added advantage of superior military technology, were able to gain the upper hand in battle, seize or purchase their lands, and force those who survived to retreat into less inhabited areas.

When Europeans started to develop extensive trading routes in Asia, however, that continent was already highly developed politically and militarily. Three Muslim empires—the Ottoman, the Safavid (Persia), and the Mughal (India)—as well as the neighboring Chinese Empire in East Asia occupied the mass of land from the Balkans to the Pacific Ocean. It was only when these Asian empires began to fall apart, giving greater autonomy to the smaller, subordinate states within their boundaries, that Europeans were able to exploit the situation and secure favorable trading arrangements and ultimately control of Asian territory itself.

Until the late eighteenth century European governments usually allowed their colonies a considerable degree of political autonomy. Although monarchs claimed sovereignty over all their imperial possessions, the distance of these lands from the metropolis made direct rule difficult. The solution to this problem was to delegate the functions of government either to officials who represented royal authority in the colony or to some corporate body. In the British, Dutch, and French empires, trading companies that engaged in commerce with the East Indies assumed many of these functions. These companies could negotiate treaties, raise military forces, and govern the population of the colonies. In many ways the companies became small states themselves, operating under the authority of the Crown. In North America and the Caribbean, imperial governments usually granted charters to their colonies, authorizing them to establish their own legislative assemblies.

Colonists were granted considerable autonomy as long as they conducted trade exclusively with the metropolis. Metropolitan governments were determined to use the colonies to realize the objectives of gaining the largest possible share of world trade, acquiring a supply of gold and other precious metals, and collecting import and export duties on the colonial trade. To accomplish these ends they passed legislation forcing the colonists to trade exclusively with the metropolis. When colonists tried to break this monopoly by trading with other nations or colonies, they came into direct conflict with their own governments in Europe.

The earliest of the European overseas empires were established by the Spanish and the Portuguese. During the period we are considering here, three rising European powers—Great Britain, France, and the Dutch Republic—began to rival the older empires. By the end of the period the British had emerged as the dominant imperial power. During the third period of imperial expansion in the late nineteenth and early twentieth centuries, the imperial rivalries that had developed in earlier years continued in different forms, and new European powers, most notably Germany and Italy, joined in the competition.

THE RISE OF THE BRITISH EMPIRE

The fastest-growing of these new European overseas empires during this period was that of Great Britain. England had begun its overseas empire in the late twelfth century, when it conquered the neighboring island of Ireland, but only in the seventeenth century did it begin to acquire lands in the New World and Asia. Attempts to establish colonies on the Atlantic coast of North America in the late sixteenth century had failed, most notably at Roanoke (in present-day North Carolina) in 1584. After Spain agreed not to contest English claims of territory north of Florida, the English succeed in settling a series of colonies along the Atlantic seaboard, the first of which was at Jamestown, Virginia, in 1607.

By 1700 this English empire in the New World included a number of colonies on the North American mainland, a vast territory in the northern part of Canada, and a cluster of islands in the Caribbean, most notably Barbados, Jamaica, and the Bahamas. These West Indian colonies developed an economy that used slave labor, and therefore blacks brought there from Africa soon outnumbered Europeans by a significant margin. In the colonies on the mainland of North America, however, most of the colonists were white. This was true even in the southern colonies, where slave labor was also introduced. Only in South Carolina, which was settled by Caribbean planters, did the black population exceed 50 percent.

A number of English colonists, especially in the northern colonies, had emigrated so that they might practice their religion without legal restraint. During the 1630s communities of English Protestants known as Puritans settled in New England. They objected to the control of the English Church by bishops, especially during the period from 1633 to 1641, when William Laud served as Archbishop of Canterbury. Their main complaint was the church services authorized by Laud too closely resembled those of Roman Catholicism. At the same time small groups of English Catholics, who often faced prosecution in English courts for practicing their religion, had taken refuge in Maryland. In the late seventeenth century a dissenting Protestant sect known as Quakers (so called because their founder, George Fox, told them to quake at the word of the Lord), smarting under legislation that denied them religious freedom and political power, emigrated to Pennsylvania.

Many other British colonists had come to America as indentured servants, usually serving for a period of seven years in order to gain their freedom. By this time the size of the indigenous American population in the colonies had become negligible. The Indians of North America either had been pushed westward beyond the frontiers of these colonies, had died of diseases to which they were highly vulnerable, or had been killed in skirmishes with the English.

During the seventeenth century the English also established a number of trading posts, known as factories°, along the coast of India. The first of these factories was Surat, which was settled in 1612, and it was soon followed by Madras (1640), Bombay (1661), and Calcutta (1690). There were significant differences between these mercantile outposts and the colonies in the Caribbean and the North American mainland. The number of British settlers in India, most of whom were members of the East India Company, remained extremely small, and they did not establish large plantations like those in the Caribbean colonies and the southern mainland colonies. Consequently they did not introduce slave labor into these countries.

In contrast to the situation in North America and the Caribbean, the British in India had to deal with a large native population. At first they had contact with that population only when they were engaged in trade. In the second half of the eighteenth century, however, the British began to gain direct political control of Indian provinces, and by 1850 they controlled a large portion of the South Asian subcontinent. Not only did the British eventually subject the Indians to their rule, but they also drove out their French and Dutch commercial rivals, who had established their own factories along the coast.

In addition to their settlements in America and India, the British acquired influence and ultimately political control of the area from Southeast Asia stretching down into the South Pacific. In the late seventeenth century the British began to challenge the Dutch and the Portuguese for control of the trade with Indonesia, and in the second half of the eighteenth century British merchants established a thriving trade with the countries on the Malay peninsula. In the late eighteenth century the British also began to explore the South Pacific, which remained the last part of the inhabited world that Europeans had not yet visited and settled. In 1770 the British naval officer and explorer Captain James Cook (1728–1779) claimed the entire eastern coast of Australia for Great Britain, and in 1788 the British established a penal colony in the southeastern corner of the continent at Botany Bay. Cook also visited New Zealand and many of the islands in the South Pacific, including Fiji, but colonies were not established at those locations until the middle of the nineteenth century.

The British Empire of the late seventeenth and eighteenth centuries possessed little administrative coherence; it was a hodge-podge of colonies, factories, and territories that had different relationships to the royal government in Britain (see Map 19.1). In India the provinces brought under British control were run by a trading corporation that exercised many functions of government. Some colonies in America, such as Maryland and Pennsylvania, operated under charters granted to members of the aristocracy. Most of the colonies on the North American mainland and in the Caribbean had their own legislatures. None of these colonies, however, sent representatives to the British Parliament. The only bond of unity among all the colonists is that they, like British subjects living in England or Scotland, owed their allegiance to the monarch and were under the monarch's protection. All of these colonists were therefore British subjects.

THE SCATTERED FRENCH EMPIRE

French colonization of North America and India paralleled that of Great Britain, but it never achieved the same degree of success. As the British were establishing footholds in the West Indies and the mainland of North America, the French acquired their own islands in the Caribbean and laid claim to large sections of Canada and the Ohio and Mississippi River valleys in the present-day United States. In the West Indies the French began the process of colonization by introducing indentured servants for periods of three years, but in the eighteenth century they began to follow the British and Spanish pattern of importing slaves to provide the labor for the sugar plantations. In North America French settlers did not require a large labor supply, since their main economic undertakings were the fur trade and fishing. Consequently slaves were not introduced to those areas. The European population of French possessions in North America also stayed well below that of the British colonies.

The parallel between French and British overseas expansion extended to India, where in the early eighteenth century the French East India Company established factories at Pondicherry, Chandenagar, and other locations. Rivalry with the British also led the French to make alliances with native governors of Indian provinces, and with this support the French fought the British both on land and sea at different critical times between 1744 and 1815. The British ultimately prevailed in this struggle, and by the turn of the nineteenth century the French presence in India had been reduced to a few isolated factories.

The waning of French influence in India coincided with a series of territorial losses in the New World. Defeats suffered at the hands of the British during the Seven Years' War (1756–1763) resulted in the transfer of French Canada and the territory east of the Mississippi River to Great Britain. During that conflict France also ceded the vast region of Louisiana between the Mississippi River and the Rocky Mountains to Spain. France regained Louisiana in 1801 but then promptly sold the entire territory to the United States in 1803. The following year the French Caribbean colony of Saint Domingue became independent, although France retained possession of its other West Indian colonies.

The only overseas area where France continued to expand after 1800 was much closer to home, on the Mediterranean shores of North Africa. French influence in this area had begun in the seventeenth century, and it persisted until the twentieth century. France occupied Egypt briefly from 1798 until 1801, and it acquired Algeria in

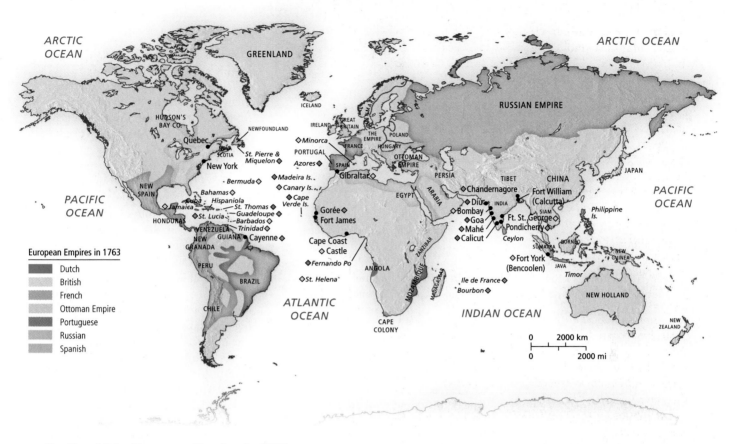

■ **Map 19.1 European Empires in 1763**
This map shows the overseas possessions of Britain, France, the Dutch Republic, Spain, and Portugal.
Russian overseas expansion into North America had not yet begun.

1830. It was not until the third stage of imperialism in the late nineteenth century that France took possession of large territories in the interior of Africa and in Asia (see Chapter 23).

THE COMMERCIAL DUTCH EMPIRE

The tiny Dutch Republic acquired almost all of its overseas possessions in the first half of the seventeenth century, at about the same time that the British and French were establishing their first colonies in Asia and the New World. The formation of the Dutch empire went hand in hand with the explosive growth of the Dutch economy in the seventeenth century. At that time the Dutch Republic became the very center of a global economy, and its overseas colonies in the New World, Asia, and Africa helped the republic maintain its commercial supremacy. Dutch overseas settlements, just like the port cities of the metropolis, were dedicated almost exclusively to serving the interests of trade.

The Dutch were more eager than other European powers to use military and naval power to acquire and fortify trading depots. They also used military force to seize factories that had been established earlier by other countries, es-

pecially Portugal. With more than 1,400 vessels that could be used as warships and 250,000 sailors, they had a distinct military advantage over the Portuguese, who could not muster half those numbers. They seized two trading posts from the Portuguese on the West African coast in 1637, and in 1641 they also acquired from Portugal the African islands of São Tomé and Principe. In 1624 the Dutch, operating through their West Indian Company, seized the northern coast of Brazil, and after its return to Portugal in 1654 they acquired two small West Indian islands and a number of small plantation colonies on the Guiana coast of South America, mainly in present-day Surinam. From these small settlements in Africa and the Caribbean the Dutch carried on trade with the Spanish, Portuguese, French, and British colonies. Through these ports the Dutch brought more than 500,000 slaves to Brazil, the Spanish colonies, and the French and British West Indies.

In addition to their African and Caribbean possessions, the Dutch established a presence in three other parts of the world. In the early seventeenth century they settled a colony in the Hudson River valley on the North American mainland. They named the colony New Netherland and its main port, at the mouth of the river, New Amsterdam. In

The Trial of the Mutineers on the *Bounty*

In December 1787 a British ship named the *Bounty,* under the captainship of William Bligh, left Portsmouth, England, on a momentous journey to Tahiti, an island in the South Pacific that Captain James Cook had first visited in 1769. The goal of the voyage of the *Bounty* was neither exploration nor colonial expansion but to bring home breadfruit trees that Cook had discovered on his second trip to the island in 1773. The trees, so it was hoped, would be introduced to the West Indies as a source of food for the slaves and hence the survival of the plantation economy. The voyage of the *Bounty* was therefore part of the operation of the new global economy that European expansion had made possible. The total size of the crew, all of whom had volunteered for service, was forty-six. The master's first mate, who became the main leader of a mutiny against Bligh, was Fletcher Christian.

The mutiny did not take place until after the ship had remained at Tahiti for a number of months, loaded its cargo of more than a thousand breadfruit plants, and begun its return voyage. The main reason for the mutiny was Captain Bligh's abusive and humiliating language. Unlike many other officers who faced the task of maintaining order on their ships and commanding the obedience of their crews, Bligh did not flog his men. In that regard Bligh's behavior was mild. Instead he went into tantrums and verbally abused them, belittling them and calling them scoundrels. Just before the mutiny Bligh called Fletcher Christian

a cowardly rascal and falsely accused him of stealing from him. On the morning of April 28, 1788 Christian arrested Bligh at bayonet point, tied his hands behind his back, and threatened him with instant death if he should speak a word. Claiming that "Captain Bligh had brought all this on himself," Christian and his associates put Bligh and eighteen other members of the crew into one of the ship's small launch boats and set them adrift, leaving them to reach a nearby island by their own power.

The mutineers sailed on to the island of Tubuai, where after a brief stay they split into two groups. Nine of them, headed by Christian and accompanied by six Tahitian men and twelve women, established a settlement on Pitcairn Island. The remaining sixteen mutineers returned to Tahiti. All but two of these men were apprehended in

1791 by Captain Edwards of the H.M.S. *Pandora,* which had been sent to Tahiti with the objective of arresting them and returning them to England for trial. At the beginning of its return voyage the *Pandora* was shipwrecked, and four of the prisoners drowned. The rest reached England aboard another ship in 1792. They were promptly charged before a navy court-martial with taking the *Bounty* away from its captain and with desertion, both of which were offenses under the Naval Discipline Act of 1766.

The trial took place aboard a British ship, H.M.S. *Duke,* in Portsmouth harbor in September 1792. The proceeding had all the markings of a state trial, one initiated by the government for offenses against the crown. Mutiny and desertion represented challenges to the state itself. During the second period of imperial expansion navies became major instruments of state power. Even when ships were used for purposes of exploration rather than naval combat, they served the interests of the state. The captain of the ship represented the power of the sovereign at sea. Because of the difficulty of maintaining order in such circumstances, he was given absolute authority. He could use whatever means necessary, including the infliction of corporal

■ **Sextant**
Eighteenth-century ships like the *Bounty* used this instrument to determine nautical position by means of the stars.

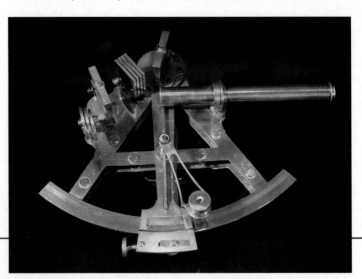

■ *The Mutineers Casting Bligh Adrift in the Launch,*
Engraving by Robert Dodd (1790)

This was the central act in the mutiny led by Fletcher Christian. Captain Bligh is standing in the launch in his nightclothes. Some of the breadfruit trees loaded on the ship at Tahiti can be seen on the top deck.

punishment, to preserve order. To disobey or challenge him was interpreted as an act of rebellion.

The trial was based on the assumption that the mutiny was illegal and seditious. The only question was the extent of individual involvement in the act itself. The degree of involvement was measured by evidence of one's cooperation with Christian or his loyalty to Bligh. The mere fact that some men had remained with Christian on the *Bounty* did not prove that they had supported the mutiny. Four of those men gave little evidence of having voluntarily cooperated with Christian, and those four men were eventually acquitted. The testimony of Captain Bligh, who testified that those four crew members had been reluctant to put him in the launch boat, was decisive in securing their nonguilty verdicts.

The remaining six men were convicted and sentenced to die by hanging. Three of those men were eventually spared their lives. Peter Heywood

and James Morrison were well connected to influential people in the navy and the government and received royal pardons. William Muspratt, one of only three mutineers to hire a lawyer, entered a protest against the procedures of the court. In a court-martial, unlike a criminal trial at the common law, a prisoner could not call witnesses in his own defense. At the time of his conviction Muspratt protested that he had been "debarred calling witnesses whose evidence I have reason to believe would have tended to prove my innocence." The difference between the two systems of criminal justice, he claimed, "is dreadful to the subject and fatal to me." On this ground Muspratt was reprieved.

The three men who were executed died as model prisoners, proclaiming the illegality of their rebellion. Although the government had executed only a small minority of the mutineers, by securing their conviction and dramatizing it with a widely publi-

cized hanging, it had upheld its authority and thus reinforced the power of the crown.   ■

Questions of Justice

1. How would you characterize the different ideals of justice used by the mutineers and the British admiralty court as the bases of their actions?

2. How would you explain the differences in the sentences handed down to the mutineers?

3. What does the journey of the *Bounty* tell us about the role of the British navy in the process of imperial expansion? What problems were inherent in using British ships for these purposes?

Taking It Further

Rutter, Owen, ed. *The Court-Martial of the "Bounty" Mutineers.* 1931. Contains a full transcript of the trial.

1664 the Dutch lost the colony to the English, who renamed the colony and the port New York. The second area was in Asia, where the Dutch East India Company established a fort at Batavia (now Jakarta in Indonesia) and factories in India, China, and Japan. These possessions allowed the Dutch to engage in trade throughout Asia. In the eighteenth century, however, the British began to take control of Dutch trading routes.

The third area was the southern tip of Africa, where in 1652 the Dutch settled a colony at the Cape of Good Hope, mainly to provide support for ships engaged in commerce with the East Indies. In this colony some 1,700 Dutch settlers, most of them farmers known as boers°, developed an agricultural economy on plantations that employed slave labor. The loss of this colony to the British at the end of the eighteenth century reflected a more general decline of Dutch military and imperial strength.

THE VAST SPANISH EMPIRE

Of all the European overseas empires, the lands under the control of the Spanish monarchy were the most extensive. At the height of its power in 1650, the Spanish Empire covered the western part of North America from California to Mexico and from Mexico down through Central America. It also included Florida and the Caribbean islands of Cuba, San Domingo, and Puerto Rico. It embraced almost all of South America except Brazil, which was under Portuguese control. In Asia the main Spanish possessions were the Philippine Islands, named for the future King Philip II in 1542 and conquered with little bloodshed after 1564. The Philippines served as the main base from which the Spanish engaged in trade with other Asian countries.

Spanish overseas possessions were never ruled as closely as the royal government in Madrid ruled the smaller kingdoms and principalities on the Iberian peninsula. Spanish overseas possessions were, however, integrated into a much more authoritative imperial system than were those of the British. Until the eighteenth century a hierarchy of councils, staffed by men appointed by the crown, exercised political control of the various large territories or viceroyalties into which the empire was divided. Like all mercantilist enterprises, the Spanish colonial empire was designed to serve the purposes of trade. Until the eighteenth century a council known as the House of Trade, situated in Seville, exercised a monopoly over all colonial commerce. It funneled trade with the colonies from the southwestern Spanish port of Cadiz and to selected ports on the eastern coasts of Spanish America, from which it was then redirected to other ports. The ships returned to Spain carrying the gold and silver that had been extracted from the mines of Mexico and Peru. The entire journey was made under the protection of Spanish warships.

The Bourbon kings of Spain, who were installed on the throne in 1700, introduced a number of political reforms

■ **The Dutch Factory of Batavia in Indonesia, ca. 1665**
The Dutch Republic dominated the Asian trade in the seventeenth century. Batavia (now Jakarta) was the most important of their settlements in Southeast Asia. The efforts of the Dutch to transplant their culture is evident in this building's Dutch style of architecture.

that were intended to increase the volume of the colonial trade and prevent the smuggling that had always threatened to undermine it. On the one hand, they opened up the colonial trade to more Spanish and American ports and also permitted more trade within the colonies. On the other hand, the Bourbons, especially Charles III (r. 1759–1788), brought the viceroyalties under more direct control of Spanish royal officials and increased the efficiency of the tax collection system. These Bourbon reforms made the empire more manageable and profitable, but they also created tension between the Spanish-born bureaucrats and the creoles°, the people of Spanish descent who had been born in the colonies. These tensions eventually led in the early nineteenth century to a series of wars of independence from Spain that we shall discuss in a later section.

THE DECLINING PORTUGUESE EMPIRE

The Portuguese had been the first European nation to engage in overseas exploration and colonization. During the late fifteenth and sixteenth centuries they had established colonies in Asia, South America, and Africa (see Chapter 12). By the beginning of the eighteenth century, however, the Portuguese Empire had declined in size and wealth in relation to its rivals. The Portuguese continued to hold a few ports in India, most notably the small island of Goa. They also retained a factory at Macao off the southeastern coast of China. In the New World the major Portuguese plantation colony was Brazil, which occupied almost half the land mass of South America and which supplied Europe with sugar, cacao (from which chocolate is made), and other agricultural commodities. Closely linked to Brazil were the Portuguese colonies along and off the West African coast. These possessions were all deeply involved in the transatlantic trade, especially in slaves. The Portuguese also had a series of trading stations and small settlements on the southeastern coast of Africa, including Mozambique.

The contraction of the Portuguese Empire in the seventeenth and eighteenth centuries resulted in the transfer of land to other European countries. A relatively weak European power, Portugal did not fare well in the fierce military conflicts that ensued in South America and Asia over control of the colonial trade. Portugal's main military

and economic competition came from the Dutch, who seized many of its Asian, African, and South American colonies, and who acquired many Portuguese trading routes. Most of those losses took place in Asia between 1600 and 1670. The Portuguese Empire suffered further losses when the crown relinquished Bombay and the northern African port of Tangier to the English as part of the dowry for the Portuguese princess Catherine of Braganza when she married King Charles II in 1661.

Brazil remained by far the most important of the Portuguese possessions during the late seventeenth and eighteenth centuries. The colony suffered from an unfavorable balance of trade with Portugal, but it expanded in population and wealth during this period, especially after the discovery of gold and diamonds led to large-scale mining in the interior. The slave trade increased in volume in order to provide additional labor in the mines and on the sugar plantations. In the first quarter of the nineteenth century, as the British slave trade declined and came to an end, Portuguese ships carried 871,600 slaves to Brazil. Between 1826 and 1850 the number increased to an astonishing 1,247,700. As a result of this massive influx of Africans,

■ **Rio de Janeiro, the Major Slave Port in Brazil, Receiving Slaves**
More slaves went to Brazil than to any other country in the Americas. The trade continued until 1851, and only in 1888 was the institution of slavery abolished.

slaves accounted for approximately 40 percent of the entire Brazilian population by the beginning of the nineteenth century.

Like most other European countries, Portugal tightened the control of its imperial possessions during the second half of the eighteenth century. During the ministry of the dictatorial Marquis of Pombal from 1755 to 1777, efforts were made to increase the control exercised by the crown over all aspects of colonial life. Pombal also took steps to encourage the growth of the colonial trade, and he legalized intermarriage between whites and indigenous peoples. Like the Bourbon reforms in Spanish America, this legislation created considerable resentment among the creoles against the Portuguese bureaucrats who controlled the government. As in Spanish America, these tensions led to demands for Brazil's autonomy in the nineteenth century.

THE RUSSIAN EMPIRE IN THE PACIFIC

The only eastern European state that established an overseas empire during the eighteenth century was Russia. Between the fifteenth and the early eighteenth centuries Russia had gradually acquired a massive overland empire stretching from St. Petersburg in the west across the frigid expanse of Siberia to the Pacific Ocean. The main impulse of Russian expansion had been the search for exotic furs that were in high demand in the colder climes of Russia and northern Europe. During the reign of the Empress Catherine the Great (r. 1762–1796), Russia entered a period of further territorial expansion. On its western frontier it took part in the successive partitions of Poland between 1772 and 1795, while to the south it held the Crimean region within the Ottoman Empire between 1783 and 1792.

During the late eighteenth and early nineteenth centuries Russia also extended its empire overseas. Russian traders and explorers undertook numerous expeditions to Hawaii and other islands in the Pacific Ocean, sailing as far south as Mexico. They did not, however establish colonies in these locations. Further expeditions brought Russia across the northern Pacific, where they encroached upon the hunting grounds of the native Aleuts in Alaska. The Russian-American Company, established in 1789, built a number of trading posts along the Pacific seaboard from Alaska down to Fort Ross in northern California. These claims led to a protracted territorial dispute with Spain, which had established a string of missions and settlements on the California coast as far north as San Francisco. In this way the two great European empires of Russia and Spain, advancing from opposite directions, confronted each other on the western coast of North America. Russian expansion into Alaska and California also led to territorial disputes with the United States, which was engaged in its own process of territorial expansion westward toward the Pacific during the nineteenth century.

Warfare in Europe, North America, and Asia

Until the middle of the seventeenth century, European states engaged each other in battle almost exclusively within their own continent. The farthest their armies ever traveled was to the Middle East to fight the Turks or to Ireland to conquer the native Celts. The acquisition of overseas empires and the conflicts that erupted between European powers over the control of global trade brought those European conflicts to new and distant military theaters. Wars that began over territory in Europe were readily extended to America in one direction and to Asia in the other. The military forces that fought in these imperial battles consisted not only of metropolitan government troops but also those of the colonists. These colonial forces were often supplemented by the troops drawn from the local population, such as when the French recruited Native Americans to fight with them against the British in North America. This pattern of recruiting soldiers from the indigenous population, which began in the eighteenth century, became the norm during the third and final phase of empire building in the nineteenth and early twentieth centuries.

Wars fought overseas placed a premium upon naval strength. Ground troops remained important, both in Europe and overseas, but naval power increasingly proved to be the crucial factor. All of the Western imperial powers either possessed or acquired large navies. Great Britain and the Dutch Republic rose to the status of world powers on the basis of sea power, while the French strengthened their navy considerably during the reign of Louis XIV. The Dutch used their naval power mainly against the Portuguese and the British, while the British directed theirs against the French and the Spanish as well as the Dutch. The overwhelming success that the British realized in these conflicts resulted in the establishment of British maritime supremacy.

MERCANTILE WARFARE

An increasingly important motive for engaging in warfare in the late seventeenth and eighteenth centuries was the protection and expansion of trade. The theory that underlay and inspired these imperial wars was mercantilism. As we discussed in Chapter 15, those who subscribed to this theory, such as Louis XIV's minister Jean-Baptiste Colbert, believed that the wealth of the state depended upon its ability to import fewer commodities than it exported and thus to acquire the largest possible share of the world's monetary supply. In order to achieve this goal, mercantilists encouraged domestic industry and placed heavy customs duties or tariffs on imported goods. Mercantilism was therefore a policy of protectionism°, the shielding of domestic industries from foreign competition. Mercantilists also sought to increase the size of the country's commercial fleet, establish colonies in order to promote trade, and import raw materials from the colonies to benefit domestic industry. The imperial wars of the seventeenth and eighteenth centuries, which were fought over the control of colonies and trading routes, thus formed part of a mercantilist policy.

Of course the older, more traditional motives for waging war, especially the desire of rulers for territorial expansion, did not disappear. The acquisitive impulses of France, Prussia, Austria, and Russia remained a recurrent source of international conflict throughout this period. But the mercantile motive, which began to emerge only in the 1650s, soon became a major feature of European warfare, and it explains why military conflict was extended from Europe to the colonies. As this motive for going to war became more important, wars fought primarily for religious or ideological reasons, which had been the norm during the period of the Reformation, virtually disappeared.

The first of the great mercantile wars that involved conflict overseas arose between England and the Dutch Republic in the middle and late seventeenth century (1652–1654, 1664–1667, 1672–1675). As these wars were fought between two Protestant powers, little about these conflicts could be attributed to religious zeal. Instead they were fought mainly for mercantile advantage between the two emerging commercial giants of Europe. The two countries were engaged in heated competition for control of the transatlantic trade, and the Dutch resented the passage of English laws, known as the Navigation Acts, that excluded them from trade with the English colonies. The Dutch claimed the right to trade with all ports in the world as well as to fish in the waters off British shores. Not surprisingly, many of the engagements in these wars took place at sea and in the colonies. The most significant outcome of these Anglo-Dutch wars was the loss of the port city of New Amsterdam to the English. That city, renamed New York, later became the leading port and financial center in the Western Hemisphere.

Shortly after the first Anglo-Dutch War, England also went to war against Spain (1655–1657). Although this conflict pitted a Protestant against a Catholic power, it too reflected the new emphasis on mercantile objectives. The main battles of this war were not fought in the English Channel, as they had been when the Spanish Armada had descended on England in 1588, but in the Caribbean. The war resulted in the British acquisition of one of its most important Caribbean colonies, Jamaica, in 1655. The Anglo-Spanish tensions that surfaced in this conflict continued into the eighteenth century, when Britain tried to smuggle more goods than it was allowed by the Treaty of Utrecht (1713) into the Spanish trading post of Portobelo on the isthmus of Panama. The Spanish retaliated by cutting off

the ear of Robert Jenkins, an English captain, and this incident led to the War of Jenkins' Ear in 1739. In 1762, during another war against Spain (as well as France), armed forces from Britain and the North American colonies seized the Cuban port of Havana as part of an effort to monopolize the Caribbean trade. The following year, however, Britain returned the city to Spain in exchange for Florida. This acquisition gave the British control of the entire North American eastern seaboard.

ANGLO-FRENCH MILITARY RIVALRY

Anglo-Spanish conflict paled in comparison with the bitter commercial rivalry between Great Britain and France during the eighteenth century. Anglo-French conflict was one of the few consistent patterns of eighteenth-century European warfare. It lasted so long and had so many different phases that it is known as the second Hundred Years' War, a recurrence of the bitter period of warfare between England and France from the middle of the fourteenth to the middle of the fifteenth century. The great difference between the two periods of warfare was that the first

---

CHRONOLOGY

A Century of Anglo-French Warfare

1701–1713	War of the Spanish Succession (Queen Anne's War in North America): Spain is allied with France
1740–1748	War of the Austrian Succession (Europe): France is allied with Spain, Prussia, and Russia; Britain is allied with Austria
1744–1748	King George's War (North America)
1754–1763	French and Indian War (North America): French and British are allied with different Indian tribes
1756–1763	Seven Years' War (Europe): France is allied with Austria; Britain is allied with Prussia
1775–1783	American War of Independence: France is allied with United States against Britain in 1778
1781–1783	Warfare in India
1792–1815	French Revolutionary and Napoleonic Wars: Britain is allied at various times with Austria, Prussia, Spain, and the Dutch Republic; warfare at various times in the West Indies as well as in India

Hundred Years' War involved military conflicts in France, while the second was marked by periodic naval and military engagements not only in Europe but in Asia and North America as well.

The Wars of the Spanish and Austrian Successions, 1701–1748

This eighteenth-century Anglo-French rivalry had its roots in the war of the Spanish Succession (1701–1713). The war began as an effort to prevent France from putting Louis XIV's grandson, Philip, on the Spanish throne (see Chapter 15). The implications of this dynastic conflict for the British and French colonial empires were monumental. By uniting French and Spanish territory the proposed succession would have created a massive French-Spanish empire not only in Europe but in the Western Hemisphere as well. This combination of French and Spanish territory and military power threatened to eclipse the British colonies along the North American coast and deprive British merchants of much of their valuable trade.

The ensuing struggle in North America, known by British colonists as Queen Anne's War, was settled in Britain's favor by the Treaty of Utrecht in 1713. Philip V, the first Spanish king from the Bourbon dynasty (r. 1700–1746), was allowed to remain on the throne, but French and Spanish territories in Europe and America were kept separate. Even more important, the French conceded their Canadian territories of Newfoundland and Nova Scotia to the British. The treaty, which also gave Britain the contract to ship slaves to the Spanish colonies for thirty years, marked the emergence of Britain as Europe's dominant colonial and maritime power.

The next phase of Anglo-French warfare, the War of the Austrian Succession (1740–1748), formed part of a European conflict that engaged the forces of Austria, Prussia, and Spain as well as those of Britain and France. In this conflict European dynastic struggles once again intersected with competition for colonial advantage overseas. The ostensible cause of this war was the impetuous decision by the new king of Prussia, the absolutist Frederick II (r. 1740–1786), to seize the large German-speaking province of Silesia from Austria upon the succession of Maria Theresa (r. 1740–1780) as the ruler of the hereditary Habsburg lands. Using the large army that his militaristic father Frederick William I had assembled, Frederick struck with devastating effectiveness, and by terms of the treaty that ended the war he acquired most of the province.

Frederick's aggression enticed other European powers to join the conflict. Eager to acquire some of the Habsburg territories in different parts of Europe, France and Russia both declared war on Austria. Britain then entered the war against France, mainly to keep France from acquiring Austria's possessions in the Netherlands. Britain's main concern in the European phase of this war, as it had been in the War of the Spanish Succession, was to maintain the balance of power among European states.

The colonial phase of this war, known in British North America as King George's War, opened in 1744, when the French supported the Spanish in a separate war that Spain had been waging against Britain since 1739 over the Caribbean trade. Clashes between French and British trading companies in India also began in the same year. The main military engagement of this war was the seizure of the French port and fortress of Louisbourg on Cape Breton Island in Canada by 4,000 New England colonial troops and a large British fleet. At the end of the war, however, the British returned Louisbourg to the French in exchange for the factory of Madras in India, which the French had taken during the war.

The Seven Years' War, 1756–1763

European and colonial rivalries became even more entangled in the next round of Anglo-French warfare, known as the Seven Years' War (1756–1763) in Europe and the French and Indian War (1754–1763) in North America. In Europe the conflict arose as a result of Maria Theresa's eventually unsuccessful attempt to regain Silesia. In this encounter, however, she joined forces with her former enemies, France and Russia, after Great Britain signed a defensive alliance with Prussia. This "diplomatic revolution" of 1756 shifted all the traditional alliances among European powers, but it did not affect Anglo-French rivalry in the colonies, which continued unabated.

The fighting in this North American theater of the war was particularly brutal and inflicted extensive casualties. In their struggle to gain control of eastern port cities and interior lands, the British and the French secured alliances with different Indian tribes. Among the many victims were some of France's Indian allies who contracted smallpox when British-American colonists sold them blankets deliberately contaminated with the disease—the first known use of germ warfare in the West. This colonial war also had an Asian theater, in which French and British forces, most of them drawn from the trading companies of their respective countries, vied for mercantile influence and the possession of factories along the coast of the Indian Ocean. This conflict led directly to the British acquisition of the Indian province of Bengal in 1765.

The Treaty of Paris, which ended this round of European and colonial warfare in 1763, had more profound implications in the colonies than in Europe. In Europe, Prussia managed to hold on to Silesia, although its army incurred heavy casualties and its economy suffered from the war. In North America, however, monumental changes occurred. As a result of British naval victories, all of French Canada east of the Mississippi, including the entire province of Quebec, with its predominantly French population and French system of civil law, passed into

British control (see Map 19.2). Even more important, the treaty secured British naval and mercantile superiority in the Atlantic, Caribbean, and Indian oceans. By virtue of its victories over France, Britain gained control of the lion's share of world commerce. This commercial superiority had profound implications for the economic development of Britain. Partially because of its ability to acquire raw materials from its colonies and to market its products throughout the world, Britain became the first country to experience the Industrial Revolution, as shall be discussed fully in Chapter 20.

The American and French Revolutionary Wars, 1775–1815

Despite the British victory over the French in 1763, the long conflict between the two countries continued into the early nineteenth century. During the American War of Independence (1775–1783), which we shall consider later, the North American colonists secured French military aid. During that war a British fleet attacked the French colony of Martinique, while the French dispatched an expedition against the British at Savannah that included hundreds of Africans and mulattos, or people of mixed race, drawn

■ **Map 19.2 British Possessions in North America and the Caribbean After the Treaty of Paris**
The British acquisition of French territory marked a decisive moment in the expansion of the British Empire.

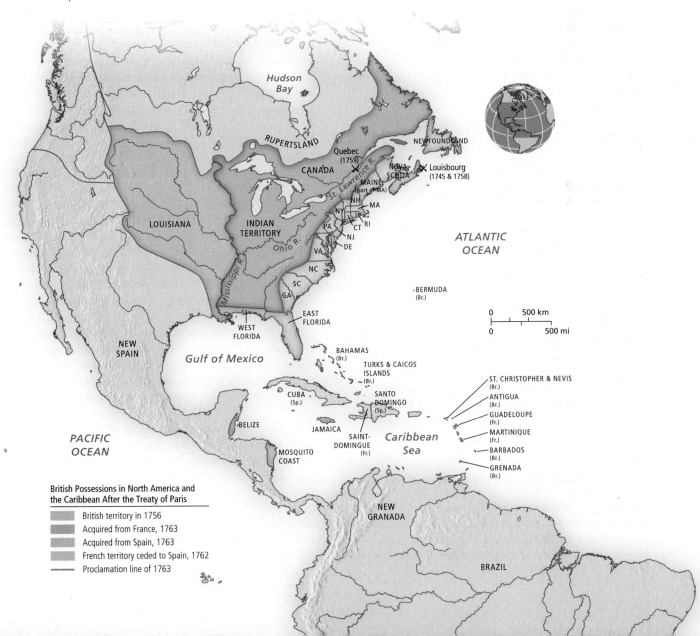

from the population of the West Indies. In India further conflicts between the French and British occurred, mainly between 1781 and 1783. These simultaneous military engagements in various parts of the world turned this phase of Anglo-French conflict into the first truly global war.

Anglo-French rivalry entered yet another phase between 1792 and 1815, during the era of the French Revolution (see Chapter 18). The British were able to maintain their military and naval superiority, although once again it required an alliance with many European powers and the creation of a new balance of power against France. Even during this later phase of this French-British rivalry the British pursued imperial objectives. They expanded their empire in India and consolidated their territory there under the governorship of Richard Wellesley (1760–1842). In 1795, in the midst of the war against France, the British also acquired the Dutch colony at the Cape of Good Hope, giving them a base for their claims to much larger African territories in the nineteenth century.

The Atlantic World

By the beginning of the eighteenth century, the territorial acquisitions of the five European maritime powers had moved the geographical center of the West from the European continent to the Atlantic Ocean itself. The Atlantic, rather than separating large geographical land masses, became a central, unifying geographical entity. The boundaries of this new Western world were the four continents that bordered the Atlantic: Europe, Africa, North America, and South America. The main thoroughfares that linked them were maritime routes across the Atlantic and up and down its coasts. The main points of commercial and cultural contact between the four continents, until the end of the eighteenth century, were the coastal areas and ports that bordered on the ocean. Within this Atlantic world arose new patterns of trade and economic activity, new interactions between ethnic and racial groups, and new political institutions. The Atlantic world also became the arena in which political and religious ideas were transmitted across the ocean and developed within a new environment.

THE ATLANTIC ECONOMY

The exchange of commercial goods and slaves between the western coasts of Europe, the African coasts, and the ports of North and South America created an economic enterprise that became one of the most active in the entire world

(see Map 19.3). The ships that had brought the slaves from Africa to the Americas used the profits gained from their transactions to acquire precious metals and agricultural products for the European market. They then returned to western European Atlantic ports, where the goods were sold.

This Atlantic economy was fueled ultimately by the demand of a growing European population for agricultural products that could not be obtained in Europe and were more costly to transport from Asia. Sugar was the most important of these commodities, but tobacco, cotton, rice, cacao, and coffee also became staples of the transatlantic trade. At the same time the North and South American colonists created a steady demand for manufactured goods, especially cutlery and metal tools, that were produced in Europe.

Two of the commodities that were imported from the colonies, tobacco and coffee, were criticized for the harmful effects they had on the human body. Both products had originally come from the Middle East or India, but lower transportation costs made the American source more desirable. Tobacco was the target of a number of attacks written in the seventeenth century. Even at that early date critics recognized the adverse physical effects of this product, which had been used widely among Native Americans. "Tobacco, that outlandish weed," read one popular rhyme, "It spends the brain and spoils the seed." Critics also believed that it had a hallucinatory effect on those who inhaled its smoke.

Coffee was another stimulant that originally came exclusively from the Middle East but later began to be shipped from Haiti and after 1809 from Brazil. Like tobacco, coffee was controversial because of the effects it had on the human body. In the late seventeenth and eighteenth centuries it was believed to be a source of political radicalism, probably because the coffeehouses where it was consumed served as gathering places for political dissidents. Contemporaries also identified coffee's capacity to produce irritability and depression.

The Atlantic economy had its own rhythms, but it was also part of a global economy that had taken shape during the seventeenth century. As Europeans had expanded the volume of their imports from Asia, those markets were fully integrated into this world system. The system was capitalist in the sense that the production and distribution of commodities were undertaken by private individuals, in a systematic way, for the purposes of profit. European governments had an interest in this capitalist economy because as mercantilists they wanted their countries to acquire the largest possible share of world trade, but they did not control the actual operations of the marketplace. Their role was mainly to authorize individuals or trading companies to conduct trade in a particular geographical area.

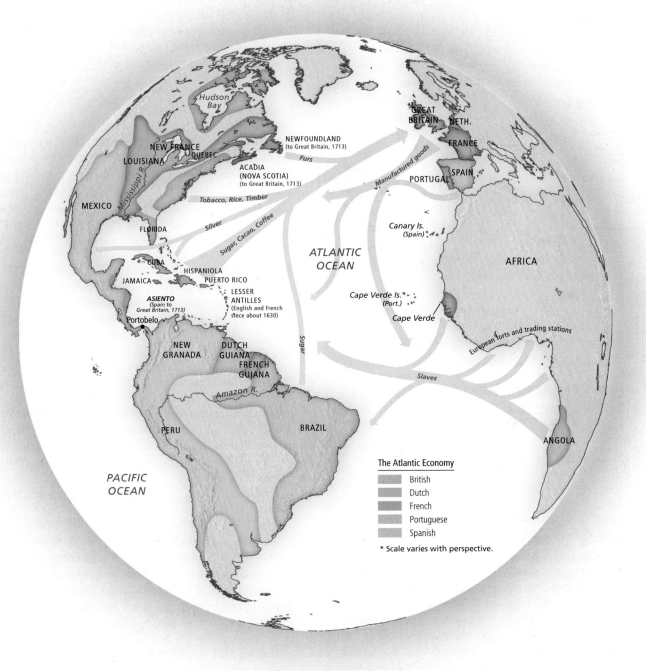

Hudson
Bay

NEW FRANCE
LOUISIANA
QUEBEC

NEWFOUNDLAND
(to Great Britain, 1713)

ACADIA
(NOVA SCOTIA)
(to Great Britain, 1713)

Furs

GREAT
BRITAIN   NETH.

FRANCE

PORTUGAL   SPAIN

Manufactured goods

MEXICO

Mississippi R.

Tobacco, Rice, Timber

FLORIDA

Silver

ATLANTIC
OCEAN

Canary Is.
(Spain)

AFRICA

CUBA

Sugar, Cacao, Coffee

JAMAICA

HISPANIOLA

PUERTO RICO

LESSER
ANTILLES
(English and French
since about 1630)

ASIENTO
(Spain to
Great Britain, 1713)

Portobelo

NEW
GRANADA

DUTCH
GUIANA

FRENCH
GUIANA

Amazon R.

PERU

BRAZIL

Sugar

Cape Verde Is.
(Port.)

Cape Verde

European forts and trading stations

Slaves

ANGOLA

PACIFIC
OCEAN

The Atlantic Economy
British
Dutch
French
Portuguese
Spanish
* Scale varies with perspective.

■ **Map 19.3   The Atlantic Economy in the Mid-Eighteenth Century**
Commodities and African slaves were exchanged between the four continents of North America,
South America, Europe, and Africa.

■ **A Satire Against Coffee and Tobacco**

A seventeenth-century satirical depiction of two European women smoking tobacco and drinking coffee. Turkey, represented by the figure to the right, was the main source of these products in the seventeenth century. An African servant, to the left, pours the coffee.

THE ATLANTIC SLAVE TRADE

The slave trade became the very linchpin of the Atlantic economy, and all five Western European imperial powers—Britain, France, the Dutch Republic, Spain, and Portugal—engaged in it. The trade arose to meet the demand of plantation owners in the New World for agricultural labor. In the seventeenth century, after the indigenous Indian population had been ravaged by disease and the indentured whites who emigrated from Europe in search of a more secure future had gained their freedom, this demand became urgent. Slave labor possessed a number of advantages over that of free labor. Slaves could be disciplined more easily, they could be forced to work longer hours, and they could be used to build a plantation economy in which the growing, harvesting, and processing of sugar and other agricultural commodities could be directed by one authority. The use of slave labor also allowed the economies of European countries, especially Great Britain, to develop. Those who had invested in the colonial trade received attractive returns on their investment, while agricultural profits acquired from crops produced by slaves encouraged the growth of domestic manufacturing.

The slave trade formed the crucial link in the triangular pattern of commercial routes that began when European vessels traveled to ports along the western coast of Africa. There they exchanged European goods, including guns, for slaves that African merchants had captured in the interior and had marched to the sea. At these ports the slaves were branded with initials indicating to which nation they belonged. They were then crowded into ships that transported them across the Atlantic to the coast of South America, to the Caribbean, or as far north as Maryland. This was the famous and often deadly Middle Passage, the second leg of the triangular journey, which was completed when the ships returned to their point of origin. Once they had arrived in the Americas, the slaves were sold to the owners of plantations in the tropical areas of the Caribbean and the south Atlantic and in the more moderate climates of the North American mainland.

Slavery has been present throughout world history. It was a major feature of classical civilization and it was also present in medieval Europe before 1200. In Greece and Rome it had often been the result of captivity in war, whereas in the Middle Ages it was reserved for individuals who had been denied certain liberties. As Islam expanded in the ninth century, Arabs began the enslavement of foreign peoples, including black slaves from east Africa, and they continued that traffic into the early modern period. In the sixteenth and seventeenth centuries Barbary pirates in the Mediterranean captured approximately 850,000 white Europeans during sea raids and forced them into slavery in Muslim North Africa.

Within this long history of world slavery, the African slave trade conducted by Europeans is unique in two respects. The first distinction is its size. As a demographic phenomenon this involuntary transportation of Africans to the New World is without parallel in world history. It is the largest transoceanic migration recorded in written documents. Between 1519 and 1867 more than 11 million slaves were shipped from Africa to the New World. Deaths at sea reduced the number of slaves who actually arrived in the Americas to about 9.5 million. The peak years of the trade were from 1751 to 1800, when nearly four million slaves left African shores. As the volume of the slave trade increased during the eighteenth century, the percentage of African slaves among all immigrants arriving in the New World rose to more than 75 percent. Nine out of every ten slaves were sent to Brazil or the Caribbean region, including the northern coast of South America. The great majority of these slaves were sold to the owners of sugar and coffee plantations. Only about 4 percent of all slaves were destined for the British colonies on the North American mainland (after 1776 the United States), and almost all of those slaves were sent to the southern colonies.

The second distinctive feature of the European slave trade was its highly commercial nature. Acting in concert with African chieftains, European slave traders seized people who had performed no acts of aggression in their homelands, transported them overseas and sold them to the highest bidders. In this way African slaves were turned into commercial commodities and treated in a manner that deprived them of all human dignity. Slaves have never been treated well in any society, but slavery in the Americas has acquired a reputation for being particularly exploitative and barbaric, and this has much to do with its commercial character.

One harrowing incident on the British slave ship *Zong* reveals the way in which financial calculations determined the fate of slaves. The *Zong* set sail in 1781 from the African island of São Tomé with 442 African slaves on board. When the slaves began to fall ill and die because of a shortage of water, the captain of the ship, Luke Collingwood, feared

Volume of the Transatlantic Slave Trade from Africa, 1519–1867

1519–1600	266,100
1601–1650	503,500
1651–1675	239,800
1676–1700	510,000
1701–1725	958,600
1725–1750	1,311,300
1751–1775	1,905,200
1776–1800	1,921,100
1801–1825	1,645,100
1826–1850	1,621,000
1851–1867	180,800
Total	11,062,000

Source: David Eltis, "The Volume and Structure of the Transatlantic Slave Trade: A Reassessment," *William and Mary Quarterly*, 3rd series, 58 (2001), Table II. 6

■ **Carlos Julião,** *Extraction of Diamonds*

In addition to their labor on plantations, slaves in Latin America were put to work mining precious metals and jewels. This watercolor depicts African slaves mining diamonds in eighteenth-century Brazil.

that the owners of the ship would suffer a financial loss. If, however, the slaves were to be thrown overboard on the pretext that the safety of the crew was in jeopardy, the loss would be absorbed by those who had insured the voyage. Accordingly Collingwood decided to tie 132 slaves together, two by two, and fling them into the sea. When the ship owners went to court to collect the insurance, they argued that slaves were no different from horses and that they had a perfect right to throw the slaves overboard in order to preserve the safety of the ship.

Differences in the treatment and survival of slaves in the various parts of the New World had more to do with economic conditions, climate, and population trends than with the nationality or the religion of the slave masters. The crucial factor was the nature of the labor to which the slaves were subjected. Slaves who worked in the plantations, especially the sugar plantations, usually died within a few years. They were—simply said—worked to death. In the French colony of Saint Domingue, more than 500,000 of the 800,000 slaves brought to the colony between 1680 and 1780 perished. As long as the slave trade was still open, it was more profitable simply to replace those who died with new slaves than to try to extend the life of those the plantation owners already had. It was for this reason that the slave population did not start to grow internally in most areas until the slave trade ended in the nineteenth century.

Another factor influencing the treatment and survival of slaves was the ratio of the black to the white populations. When that ratio was high, as in all the Caribbean colonies, the codes regulating slave life were particularly harsh and created a reign of terror within the slave community. Yet another factor was climate. The absence of tropical diseases

A FORMER SLAVE PROTESTS AFRICAN SLAVERY

••••••••••••••••

In 1787 Quobna Ottobah Cugoano (1757–1791), a former slave, published an abolitionist treatise, Thoughts and Sentiments on the Evil and Wicked Traffic of the Slavery and Commerce of the Human Species. *Like the narrative written by Olaudah Equiano quoted at the beginning of this chapter, Cugoano's account describes the horrors of the African slave trade that he himself had experienced. In this passage Cugoano deplores the effect that the slave trade had on his native Africa.*

That base traffic of kid-napping and stealing men was begun by the Portuguese on the coast of Africa, and as they found the benefit of it for their own wicked purposes, they soon went on to commit further depredations. The Spaniards followed their infamous example, and the African slave trade was thought most advantageous for them, to enable themselves to live in ease and affluence by the cruel subjection and slavery of others. The French and English, and some other nations in Europe, as they founded settlements or colonies in the West Indies or in America, went on in the same manner, and joined hand in hand with the Portuguese and Spaniards to rob and pillage Africa as well as to waste and desolate the inhabitants of the western continent. But the European depredators and pirates have not only robbed and pillaged the people of Africa themselves; but, by their instigation, they have infested the inhabitants with some of the vilest combinations of fraudulent and treacherous villains, even among their own people, and have set up their forts and factories as a reservoir of public and abandoned thieves and as a den of desperadoes, where they may ensnare, entrap and catch men. So that Africa has been robbed of its inhabitants, its freeborn sons and daughters have been stole, and kid-napped and violently taken away and carried into captivity and cruel bondage. And it may be said in respect to that diabolical traffic which is still carried on by the European depredators, that Africa has suffered as much and more than any other quarters of the globe.

Source: Quobna Ottobah Cugoano, *Thoughts and Sentiments on the Evil and Wicked Traffic of the Slavery and Commerce of the Human Species* (London, 1787).

in the more temperate zone of the North American colonies provides the best explanation why in these colonies the numbers of births equaled and eventually exceeded the number of deaths long before they did in the Caribbean and South American colonies.

The slave trade itself became the object of intense competition, as each country tried to establish a monopoly over certain routes. During the seventeenth century the British managed to make inroads into the French slave trade, and eventually they surpassed the Portuguese and the Dutch as well. By 1700 British ships were transporting more than 50 percent of all slaves to the Americas. The dominance that Britain established in the slave trade was closely related to its growing maritime and commercial strength. With an enormous merchant marine and a navy that could support it, the British came to dominate the slave trade in the same way they came to dominate the entire world economy. Both revealed how far mercantile capitalism had triumphed in Britain and its overseas possessions.

For the British merchants who engaged in this trade there was no conflict between their traditional beliefs in individual liberty and their subjugation of African slaves. Theories of racial and national superiority removed Africans as well as other non-Europeans from the category of human beings who lived in a free society and who enjoyed individual rights. As long as those rights were tied to a particular national or racial group, such as freeborn Englishmen, slavery presented no challenge to British political ideas.

Not until the late eighteenth century did the enslavement of black Africans become a source of widespread moral concern. The movement to end the slave trade and slavery itself arose almost simultaneously in all European countries. It was inspired mainly by religious zeal, especially from evangelical Protestants in Great Britain and the Jesuits in Spain and Portugal. Societies were formed to campaign for the legislative prohibition of the transportation and sale of slaves. These appeals found support in the calculations by European capitalists, especially in Britain, that slavery was no longer economically advantageous. Goods produced by free labor, especially by machine, made slavery appear less cost-effective than in the past, and the entire system of slavery began to be viewed as a costly encumbrance.

By the first decade of the nineteenth century opposition to slavery began to achieve limited success, and by 1851 it had brought about an end to the entire slave trade. The United States refused to allow any of its ports to accept slave ships after 1808, the same year in which the British parliament legislated an end to the trade within its empire. The Dutch ended their slave trade in 1814, the French in 1815, and the Spanish in 1838. The Portuguese continued to import slaves to Brazil until 1851 and ended the practice only because the British were subjecting Portuguese slave traders to constant harassment. Liberation of the slaves generally came later, except in Haiti (formerly Saint Domingue), where slavery was abolished in 1794. The British dismantled the system within their empire between 1834 and 1838. Slavery persisted until 1848 in the French Caribbean, 1863 in the southern United States, 1886 in Cuba, and 1888 in Brazil.

CULTURAL ENCOUNTERS IN THE ATLANTIC WORLD

European countries had always possessed some ethnic diversity, but the emigration of people from many different parts of Europe and Africa to America, followed by their intermarriage, created societies of much greater complexity. Even the composition of the white European communities in the colonies was more varied than in the metropolis. In the British colonies, for example, English, Scots, and Irish were joined by large numbers of Germans, French, and Swiss. In 1776 Thomas Paine argued that all of Europe, rather than just England, was the true parent country of North American colonists. Ethnic divisions were further complicated by those of religion, especially in North America, where Protestants of many different denominations, as well as Roman Catholics, lived in close proximity to each other.

The ethnicity of colonial populations was more varied in Latin American colonies than in North America. The higher proportion of Africans in those colonies, more extensive patterns of intermarriage, and the free status achieved by large numbers of blacks and mulattos created highly stratified societies by the end of the eighteenth century. In these colonies divisions arose not only between the recently arrived Europeans and the creoles, but between the various groups considered by Europeans to be below them. The social structure of Brazil was more complex than that of any other country in the New World. At the top of the social hierarchy were Portuguese bureaucrats and below them was a large and wealthy group of planter creoles. These two elite groups dominated a lower-class social hierarchy of mestizos (people of mixed white and Indian ancestry), indigenous people, mulattos, freed blacks, and slaves.

Encounters between Europeans and Africans in the New World fostered the growth of ideas of white racial superiority that were grounded in the unbalanced power relationship between the dominant white and subordinate black populations. The circumstances under which physical contact between the races took place made the imbalance of this relationship readily apparent. Blacks appeared at the slave trading stations after having already been beaten into submission by their captives and forced to march hundreds of miles. The demeaning medical exams to which the slaves were subjected and their reduction to the status of a commodity for sale could readily deprive them of any sense of pride or self-respect. Their lack of formal education and literacy put them in a position of cultural inferiority, further reducing them to the status of beasts in the eyes of their white masters. In such circumstances references to the reputed blackness of the biblical Cain (Adam and Eve's first son, who murdered his brother Abel) only confirmed or reinforced the sense of superiority that white people took for granted.

THE TRANSMISSION OF IDEAS

The Atlantic Ocean became a corridor for the transmission of political and religious ideas. Political ideologies that developed in Europe were spread from the Old World to the New World mainly by the large volume of printed works that were exported during the eighteenth century. The ancient idea that a republic was the best form of government, which had found widespread support in Renaissance Italy and in seventeenth-century England, appealed to many political leaders in colonial North America. Eighteenth-century French and Scottish ideas regarding the rights of man and the responsibility of the government to bring about the improvement of society found fertile ground in many parts of North and South America. At the time of the French Revolution, ideals of liberty and equality were spread not only throughout Europe but in the Americas as well. Legal ideas embodied in English common law, French civil law, and Spanish customary law were also transported to the New World and became the legal foundation of the new societies that were formed there.

The traffic in political ideas did not flow in only one direction. Political ideologies that were formed out of British and European ideas of liberty at the time of the American Revolution were sent back to European countries in a new form, where they inspired reform and revolution in Britain, France, and Ireland. These same ideas of liberty exerted a powerful influence in the Caribbean colonies and in South America. In Haiti, where French and American ideas of liberty inspired a revolution in the 1790s, radical ideas of racial equality developed within the new republic and then spread outward to other colonies and the United States.

Religious ideas experienced a similar transmission and transportation. The Calvinist belief in predestination, which had been formulated in Switzerland and modified by Puritans in England during the sixteenth century, was adopted and further modified by colonists in New England during the seventeenth century. Catholic theological ideas that were introduced into Spanish and Portuguese America, including those regarding the role of the Devil in human society, interacted with those of indigenous peoples and African slaves and produced new religious syntheses. In religion as well as politics, these exchanges of ideas enriched the intellectual worlds of Europeans and colonists alike.

Encounters Between Europeans and Asians

The period from 1650 to 1850 was decisive in the development of European empires in Asia. These overseas possessions, like the American colonies, formed important components of the empires of European states and were also essential to the operation of the global economy. European dominance of world trade was exercised not only in the Atlantic world but also in the Middle East and Asia. The history of the European presence in these areas, however, is very different from that which occurred in the New World. A first difference was that of simple numbers. Prior to the eighteenth century the European presence in Asia had been limited to the activities of missionaries and merchants in places such as Jakarta, Macao, and Manila. During the eighteenth century the number of European colonists in Asia, even in India, remained relatively small in comparison with the numbers who settled in America, especially in British North America.

A second major difference between European empires in the East and in the West during the period from 1650 to 1850 is that in Asia European powers initially did not try to acquire and govern large land masses and subjugate their populations. Europeans first came to Asia to trade, not to conquer. They did not engage in fixed battles with Asians, take steps to reduce the size of their populations, or force them to migrate, as they did in the New World. Only in a handful of Southeast Asian islands did a pattern of conquest, similar to that which had occurred in the New World, take place. When Europeans used military force in Asia, it was almost always against rival European powers, not the indigenous population. When European countries did eventually use force against Asians, they discovered that victory was much more difficult than it had been in the New World. Indeed, Asian peoples already possessed or were acquiring sufficient military strength to respond to European military might. In China and Japan the possession of this military power prevented Europeans from even contemplating conquest or exploitation until the nineteenth century. Establishment of European hegemony in Asia, therefore, took longer and was achieved more gradually than in the Americas.

POLITICAL CONTROL OF INDIA

Despite their original intentions, Europeans eventually began to acquire political control over large land masses in Asia and subject Asians to European rule. The first decisive steps in this process took place in India during the second half of the eighteenth century. Until that time the British in India, most of whom were members of the British East India Company, remained confined to the factories that were established along the Indian coast. The main purpose of these factories was to engage in trade not only with Europe but also with other parts of Asia. In conducting this trade the British had to deal with local Indian merchants and to compete with the French, the Portuguese and the Dutch, who had established factories of their own. They also found it advantageous to make alliances with the provincial governors, known as nawabs°, who controlled the interior of the country. It became customary for each European power to have its own candidate for nawab, with the expectation that he would provide favors for his European patrons once he took office.

■ **Warren Hastings**

Hastings (1732–1818), who was appointed the first governor-general of India in 1773, represented the ambiguities of early British rule in that country. An officer in the British East India Company, he was sympathetic to Indian culture. He was, however, accused of gross misconduct in the management of Indian affairs. His impeachment by the British Parliament in 1786 for corruption in his administration, and cruelty toward some of the native people in Bengal, lasted 145 days but resulted in an acquittal in 1787.

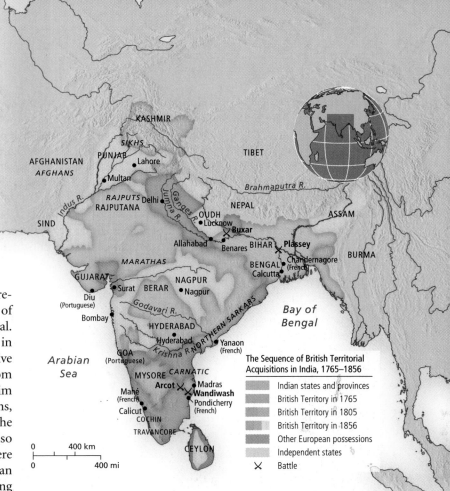

■ **Map 19.4 The Sequence of British Territorial Acquisitions in India, 1765–1856**
British political control of large territories on the South Asian subcontinent began more than a century after the establishment of the first factories along the coast.

The Sequence of British Territorial Acquisitions in India, 1765–1856

	Indian states and provinces
	British Territory in 1765
	British Territory in 1805
	British Territory in 1856
	Other European possessions
	Independent states
✕	Battle

Military Conflict and Territorial Acquisitions, 1756–1856

In 1756 this pattern of trading and negotiating resulted in armed military conflict in the city of Calcutta in the northeastern province of Bengal. The British had established a factory at Calcutta in 1690, and they continued to carry on an extensive trade there with Indian merchants, many of whom were Hindus. The nawab of Bengal, the Muslim Siraj-ud-Daulah, had contempt for all Europeans, especially the British, and he was determined that he would not be beholden to any of them. He was also deeply hostile to the Hindu merchants who were trading with the British. In June 1756 he sent an army of 50,000 Muslims against Calcutta, burning and plundering the city and beginning a siege of the East India Company's Fort William, which was manned by 515 troops in the service of the company. The entire British population of the city, together with more than 2,000 Hindus, had taken refuge in the fort. After a long struggle, which resulted in the death of hundreds of Indians, the fort fell to the nawab's forces, and some of the British officers and magistrates, including the governor of Calcutta, fled by sea.

During this siege the shooting death of a Bengali guard led to an incident that became permanently emblazoned on the emerging imperial consciousness of the British people. Officers in the nawab's army crammed the entire remaining British contingent, a total of 146 men and women, into the fort's lockup or prison, known as the Black Hole of Calcutta. Measuring 18′ × 14′ 10″, it was meant to hold only three or four prisoners overnight. The British prisoners were stifled by the insufferable heat and a lack of water and air. The stench was so bad that many prisoners vomited on the people squeezed next to them. Only twenty-two men and one woman survived until the next morning, when the nawab released them. The remainder had either been trampled to death or had asphyxiated.

The deaths of these British men and women in the Black Hole of Calcutta led the British to seek swift and brutal retribution against the nawab. In 1757, under the direction of the British military officer Robert Clive, a force of 800 British troops and 2,000 native Indian soldiers known as sepoys° retook Calcutta and routed Siraj-ud-Daulah's army

of 50,000 men at the battle of Plassey. Siraj-ud-Daulah was executed and replaced by a nawab more amenable to the British. A few years later the British East India Company secured the right to collect taxes and thus exercised political control over the entire province of Bengal. The enormous revenue from these taxes enabled the company to acquire a large army, composed mainly of sepoys. This force grew to 115,000 men by 1782. The British then used these military forces, which were equipped with Western military technology, to gain control of other provinces in India as well as to defeat their French rivals in subsequent engagements during the early nineteenth century.

These further acquisitions of Indian territory led to the eventual establishment of British rule throughout the south Asian subcontinent (see Map 19.4). New territories were brought under British control in the early years of the nineteenth century, and during the tenure of Lord Dalhousie as governor-general of India from 1848 to 1856 the British annexed eight Indian states, including the great Muslim state of Oudh in 1856. This policy of annexation went hand in hand with the introduction of Western technology and literature, the English language, and British criminal procedure.

The Sepoy Mutiny, 1857–1858

The British policy of annexation in India, coupled with the attitude of cultural superiority it encouraged, lay at the

641

root of the greatest act of rebellion by Indians against British rule in the nineteenth century. This rebellion, which began in 1857, is often known as the Sepoy Mutiny, since it originated in the ranks of the Indian troops serving in the armed forces of the British East India Company. The main source of resentment was the British annexation of Oudh, which many sepoys considered their homeland. The incident that actually provoked the rebellion was the issue of rifle cartridges coated with beef fat, which violated Hindu law, and pork fat, which violated Muslim law. Although this insensitivity to native Indian culture was not unprecedented, in this case it struck a particularly raw nerve and led to a mutiny by the Bengali army. The cities of Delhi and Lucknow came under siege, and dreadful atrocities, including the hacking to death of British women and children, occurred. British reprisals were equally savage and eventually succeeded in suppressing the rebellion.

In the wake of the mutiny the British government abolished the British East India Company and assumed direct rule of India. Queen Victoria (r. 1837–1901), the constitutional monarch of the United Kingdom, acquired much greater power over her Indian empire. Although the British government did take steps to confirm the lands and titles of Indian princes and to give them local power, their relationship with their British overlords remained one of strict subordination.

CHANGING EUROPEAN ATTITUDES TOWARD ASIAN CULTURES

This second phase of European imperialism in Asia, which lasted from 1650 to 1850, played a crucial role in the formation of Western identity. The steadily increasing numbers of Europeans who had contact with these lands—merchants, missionaries, writers and colonial administrators—and to a lesser extent the public who read about these foreign places, gained a clearer sense of who they were once they compared themselves to Indians, Chinese, and Polynesians. Until the seventeenth century Europeans thought of "the East" mainly as the Middle East, an area that was largely subsumed within the Ottoman Empire. Europeans expressed a generally negative view of the culture of this region (see Chapter 15), and over the years that perception had not changed. The political system of the Ottoman Empire was considered despotic and its religion, Islam, the antithesis of Christianity. The Far East, comprising South Asia (India), East Asia (China, Japan), and Southeast Asia (Burma, Siam, Indonesia), generally did not enter into these perceptions of "the Orient." There was little contact with this part of the world, and the little that was known about it was shrouded in mystery. During this period Europeans viewed the Far East mainly as an exotic land, rich in spices, silk, and other luxury commodities.

As Western missionaries and merchants made more frequent contacts with Asian society, Europeans developed more informed impressions of these distant lands and peoples. Some of those impressions were negative, especially when the power of Asian rulers was discussed, but many other characterizations of the East were positive. Interest in and admiration for both Indian and Chinese culture were most widespread during the middle years of the eighteenth century. The systematic study of Asian languages, especially Chinese and Sanskrit, began during this period. A preference for things Asian became characteristic of Enlightenment philosophes like Voltaire, who regarded

AN EIGHTEENTH-CENTURY CRITICISM OF NABOBS

The eighteenth-century English comedy The Nabob *reveals some popular prejudices against these merchants who had made fortunes in India and returned to England, where they flaunted their wealth. In this scene the mayor of the parliamentary borough of Bribe 'em has arrived at the house of the nabob, Sir Matthew Mite, to negotiate terms for the sale of the borough's seat. The mayor engages in this exchange with Mr. Touchit, who defends the nabob's wealth.*

Mayor: But how comes it about? And where do these here people get all their wealth?

Touchit: The way is plain enough; from our settlements and possessions abroad.

Mayor: Oh, may be so. I've been often minded to ask you what sort of things them there settlements are; because why as you know, I have been never beyond sea.

Touchit: Oh, Mr. Mayor, I will explain that in a moment; Why, here are a body of merchants that beg to be admitted as friends, and take possession of a small spot in a country, and carry on a beneficial commerce with the inoffensive and innocent people, to which kindly they give their consent.

Mayor: Don't you think that is very civil of them?

Touchit: Doubtless. Upon which, Mr. Mayor, we cunningly encroach upon and fortify by little and little, till at length, we growing too strong for the natives, we turn them out of their lands, and take possession of their money and jewels.

Mayor: And don't you think, Mr. Touchit, that is a little uncivil in us?

Touchit: Oh nothing at all, these people are but a little better than Tartars or Turks.

Mayor: No, no, Mr. Touchit, just the reverse; it is *they* have caught the Tartars in us.

Source: From *The Nabob: A Comedy, in Three Acts* by Samuel Foote (London: T. Sherlock, 1778), Act II.

■ Brighton Pavilion

This building, designed by John Nash, reflected the incorporation of Eastern styles into English architecture, and was inspired by the description of Kubla Khan's palace in Samuel Taylor Coleridge's poem "Kubla Khan" (1816).

Asian cultures as superior to those of a corrupt Europe. Voltaire also found the East unaffected by the superstition and the fanaticism that characterized Western Christianity, which he loathed. To him, the main philosophical tradition of China, Confucianism, which embodied a strict moral code, was a more attractive alternative. Eastern religion, especially Hinduism, was also admired for its ethical content and its underlying belief in one God.

This mid-eighteenth-century admiration of Asian culture even extended to Chinese and Indian political institutions. The despotic Chinese empire was transformed through Voltaire's perceptions into an enlightened monarchy. There was less to admire in the Mughal empire in India, but Guillaume Thomas Raynal's condemnation of European imperialism, which we discussed in Chapter 17, idealized the "purity and equity" of the ancient Indian political system. Comparison of contemporary Indian politics with the corruption of the old regime in Europe made native Asian political systems look good by comparison. In Britain there was more disrespect for the members of the East India Company known as nabobs°, who returned to England to flaunt the wealth they had recently acquired in India, than there was for native Indian officials. There was

also more interest in reforming the British East India Company than in reforming Indian politics.

This intellectual respect for Asian philosophy and politics coincided with a period of widespread Asian influences on Western art, architecture, and design. Eastern themes began to influence British buildings, such as in the Brighton Pavilion, designed by John Nash. Small cottages, known as bungalows, owed their inspiration to Indian models. French architects built pagodas (towers with the roof of each story turning upward) for their clients. Chinese gardens, which unlike classical European gardens were not arranged geometrically, became popular in England and France.

A new form of decorative art which combined Chinese and European motifs, known in French as chinoiserie°, became highly fashionable. Wealthy French people furnished their homes with Chinese wallpaper and hand-painted folding screens. The demand for Chinese porcelain, known in English simply as china, was insatiable. Vast quantities of this porcelain, which was technically and aesthetically superior to the stoneware produced in Germany and England, left China for the ports of western Europe. Even the dress of Europeans was influenced by Asian styles. Indian and Chinese silks were in high demand, and

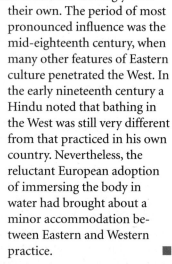

Bathing in the East and West

One of the most striking differences between Eastern and Western culture in the eighteenth century concerned the bathing of the human body. Among the Indians who practiced the Hindu religion, bathing had deep religious significance and was a daily ritual. The same was true for Muslims, for whom water possessed a sacred purifying role and prepared the bather for prayer or sacrifice. In the West bathing was not invested with similar religious significance. Christianity had emphasized purity of heart, not of the body. Without a religious inspiration, bathing the body rarely occurred in Western nations during the early modern period. Europeans might wash various parts of their body, especially the hands and face, but total immersion was almost unheard of. The few who did bathe usually did so no more than once a year, and tubs or basins were not widely available. Swimming in rivers and lakes was dangerous and often resulted in drowning. Even medical opinion conspired against bathing. According to one seventeenth-century French doctor, "bathing outside the practice of medicine was not only superfluous but very damaging to health."

By the beginning of the nineteenth century, many Europeans had begun to take regular baths. The sale of wash basins and commercially produced soap soared. This change occurred as a result of three distinct factors. The first was the insistence by many eighteenth-century Protestants that Christianity did indeed demand a clean body as well as a clean soul. The eighteenth-century founder of Methodism, the English preacher John Wesley, coined a new proverb when he declared that "cleanliness is indeed next to godliness."

A second reason was that cleanliness became associated with gentility and good manners. Bodily cleanliness became one of the ways in which members of society who considered themselves civilized made themselves attractive to the people with whom they associated. This explains why bathing the body all over first was adopted by the upper classes, who contrasted themselves with the dirty lower classes. It also became more common among women than men. The third reason was a change in medical opinion, which began to view bathing as a means to keep the pores of the skin open and thus promote perspiration. Bathing came to be viewed as a means of curing numerous diseases and as a key to long life.

The acceptance of bathing in the West owed something to Eastern influence. Eighteenth-century Western writers often commented on the daily bathing of Turks and Hindus, and Europeans who lived in the East had the opportunity to witness firsthand a custom that contrasted strikingly with their own. The period of most pronounced influence was the mid-eighteenth century, when many other features of Eastern culture penetrated the West. In the early nineteenth century a Hindu noted that bathing in the West was still very different from that practiced in his own country. Nevertheless, the reluctant European adoption of immersing the body in water had brought about a minor accommodation between Eastern and Western practice. ■

■ *Chaste Susanna at Her Bath* (1865), by Jean-Jacques Henner
By the nineteenth century, Europeans had adopted the practice of bathing the entire body.

For Discussion

What does the widespread practice of bathing in Asia and the reluctance of Europeans to adopt this practice tell us about the differences between Eastern and Western cultures in the eighteenth century?

Europeans expressed a preference for Indian cotton over that produced in the New World. A style of Indian nightwear, known as pajamas, became popular in England. Even a new sport, polo, which had originated to India, made its entry into upper-class European society at this time.

During the late eighteenth and early nineteenth centuries the European idealization of Asian culture came under direct attack. As the European presence in Asia became larger and more powerful, as the British began to exercise more control in India, and as merchants began to monopolize the Asian trade, Western images of the East became more unfavorable. Chinese philosophy, instead of being viewed as a repository of ancient ethical wisdom, was labeled as irrational when compared with that of the West. Confucianism fell out of favor, and Eastern religion in general was despised as being inferior to Christianity. Enlightenment thinkers such as Montesquieu and Diderot ranked Asian political systems below those of the more "advanced" countries of Europe. The English scholar George Anson claimed that the Chinese reputation for industry and ingenuity was undeserved and that their scientific thought was inferior to that of Europeans. The English writer Samuel Johnson (1709–1784) expressed this sense of Western intellectual superiority when he had an Arab poet in his novel *Rasselas* (1759) state that Europeans "are more powerful . . . than we, because they are wiser; knowledge will always predominate over ignorance."

Expressions of Western superiority over Asians were reinforced by emerging ideas of racial difference. Sixteenth- and seventeenth-century ideas of Europeans' superiority over black Africans and the indigenous peoples of the Americas on the basis of differences in skin color and facial features were now extended to the Chinese, dark-skinned South Asians, and Polynesians. Intellectual theories of race, which are a distinctly Western creation and were developed mainly during the late eighteenth century, provided an apparently empirical and scientific foundation for these assumptions. The color of one's skin in India, which had determined the position of a person in the Hindu caste system, was now used by Westerners to identify South Asians as "coloreds."

By the same token Chinese people, previously described as white by Westerners who admired China, were now referred to as being nonwhite or yellow. By the beginning of the nineteenth century, Westerners had acquired an ideology of superiority over Asians as well as Africans and indigenous American people that included racial difference as one of its main components. This ideology prepared Europeans intellectually and emotionally for the conquest of numerous countries in Asia and Africa in the second half of the nineteenth century. This third and final period of European imperial expansion, which began around 1870 and reached its peak around 1900, brought 84 percent of the Earth's surface under Western control.

The Crisis of Empire and the Atlantic Revolutions

During the period from 1780 to 1825, European empires experienced a crisis that marked the end of the second stage of European overseas expansion. As a result of this crisis British, French, and Spanish governments lost large segments of their empires, all in the Americas. New states and nations were carved out of the older sprawling empires. The crisis was to some extent administrative. Having acquired large expanses of territory overseas, European states were faced with the challenging problem of governing them from a distance. They not only had to rule large areas inhabited by non-European peoples (Indians and African slaves), but they also faced the difficulty of maintaining the loyalty of people of European descent who were born in the colonies.

These European colonials or creoles became the main protagonists in the struggles that led to the independence of the North American colonies from Britain in 1776 and the South American colonies from Spain a generation later. In the French colony of Saint Domingue, the location of the only successful revolution in the Caribbean region during this period, a very different set of pressures led to independence. In this colony, which became the republic of Haiti in 1804, the revolution was led not by white creoles but by people of color, including the slaves who worked on the plantations. In Britain's European colony of Ireland, where an unsuccessful revolution against British rule took place in 1798, the urge for independence came both from settlers of British descent and the native Irish population.

THE AMERICAN REVOLUTION, 1775–1783

The first Atlantic revolution was the revolt of the thirteen North American colonies and the establishment of their independence from British rule. During the second half of the eighteenth century, a number of tensions arose between the British government and its transatlantic colonies. All of these overseas colonies had developed traditions of self-government, and all of them had their own representative assemblies. At the same time the colonies were controlled by various governmental bodies responsible to the British Parliament, such as the Board of Trade. The colonies had their own militias, but they also received protection from British troops when conflicts developed with the French or other hostile powers.

The crisis that led to the American Revolution had its roots in the situation that emerged at the end of the French and Indian War. In order to maintain the peace agreed to in 1763, the government stationed British troops on the frontiers of the colonies. It argued that since the troops were protecting the colonists, they should contribute financially to their own defense. To this end the government began imposing a number of new taxes on the colonists. In 1765 the British Parliament passed the Stamp Act, which forced colonists to purchase stamps for almost anything that was printed. This piece of legislation raised the central constitutional issue of whether Parliament had the power to legislate for British subjects in lands that did not elect members of that Parliament. "Taxation without representation is tyranny" became the main rallying cry of the colonists. Opposition to the Stamp Act was so strong that Parliament repealed the act the following year, but at the same time it passed a statute declaring that it had the authority to tax the colonists as it pleased. When the government imposed new taxes on the tea imported from Britain in 1773, a number of colonists, dressed as Indians, threw the tea into the Boston Harbor.

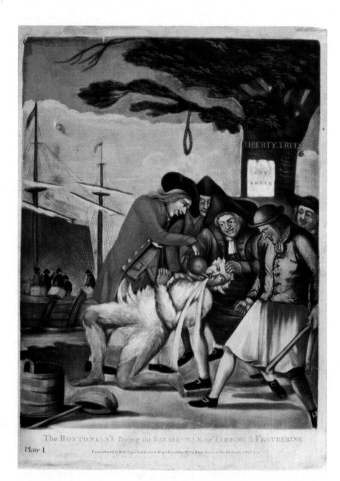

■ **The Bostonian's Paying the Excise Man or Tarring and Feathering (1774)**
This satirical engraving reflects the hatred of colonial Americans at the collection of taxes levied on them without their consent. The Boston Tea Party is depicted in the background. The colonists are forcing the tax collector to drink the tea on which he is trying to collect taxes.

The government responded to this "Boston Tea Party" by passing a series of statutes, known in the colonies as the Intolerable Acts, in 1774. One of these acts specified that the port of Boston be closed until the colonists had repaid the cost of the tea. The Intolerable Acts led to organized resistance to British rule, and in the following year military conflict broke out at Lexington and Concord in Massachusetts. On July 4, 1776, thirteen of the colonies on the North American mainland, stretching from New Hampshire to Georgia, approved a Declaration of Independence from Great Britain. A long revolutionary war, in which the colonists received assistance from France in 1778, ended with the defeat of British troops at Yorktown in 1781 and the recognition of the republic of the United States of America in the Treaty of Paris in 1783.

The case that the American colonists made for independence from Britain drew upon a body of ideas that were embodied in hundreds of printed pamphlets and in speeches made before colonial legislatures. The most prominent of these ideas were first expressed by John Locke and other radical Whigs in the late seventeenth century. Locke, who justified resistance against the Stuart monarchy at the time of the Glorious Revolution and who placed limits on legislative as well as executive power, became the main inspiration of the Declaration of Independence, which was drafted by Thomas Jefferson. These ideas found support in the customs and traditions embodied in the English common law, especially the principle that men could not be deprived of their rights without their own consent. Republican ideas, drawn both from ancient Greece and Rome and revived at the time of the Renaissance, gave colonists a model of a community of virtuous men joined in a commitment to the body politic, which they defined in colonial terms. Finally there was the influence of the ideas of the Enlightenment, which emphasized the natural right of all men to life, liberty, and the pursuit of happiness.

Although the American Revolution was inspired by many of the ideas that had originated in the two English revolutions of the seventeenth century, it differed from those earlier revolutions in that it was directed more against the British Parliament than the king. The Declaration of Independence severed the bonds between the colonists and King George III, to whom they formally owed allegiance, but the constitutional powers against which they protested, especially that of taxation, were those of Parliament. It was taxation by the British Parliament, rather than nonparliamentary taxes like those levied in the 1640s, that led to the American Revolution.

THE HAITIAN REVOLUTION, 1789–1804

The second successful revolution in the Atlantic world took place in the French Caribbean colony of Saint Domingue, known later as Haiti, which occupied the western portion of the island of Hispaniola. This revolution resulted in the establishment of the colony's independence, but the revolt was directed not so much against French rule as against the island's white planters. Just like their counterparts in Spanish and British Caribbean colonies, these planters, known in Haiti as colons°, had little desire for national independence. They wished to remain within the protective custody of the French state. Since they formed a distinct minority of the total population, they did not think of themselves as constituting a separate national community. Any resistance to imperial rule, moreover, would have required that they arm their slaves in order to make the movement succeed, and that would have threatened their control of the black population.

The real threat of revolution in all the Caribbean colonies came not from the elite or ruling class but from the subordinate members of the population. In Saint Domingue the revolution began in 1789 with a rebellion of people defined legally as free coloreds, most of whom were mulattos. The development that triggered this revolt, organized under the leadership of Vincent Ogé, was the refusal of the white planters, who were creoles, to give the free coloreds representation in the revolutionary French National Assembly as well as in local assemblies in Saint Domingue.

The free colored rebellion of 1789 led directly to a massive slave revolt in 1791. At that time slaves constituted about 90 percent of the population. Their uprising took place after the French National Assembly voted to abolish slavery in France but not in the French colonies. In this revolt 12,000 African slaves, armed with machetes and reacting to their brutal treatment by their masters, destroyed a thousand plantations and killed hundreds of whites. Their tactics, which included cutting white planters in half, raping their wives and daughters, and decapitating their children, were matched by those of the planters, who retaliated by torturing blacks and hanging them in the streets.

Spanish and British armies, frightened that this slave rebellion would spread to their colonies, occupied Saint Domingue and massacred thousands of slaves, many of them after they surrendered. In 1795, however, the Spanish withdrew from Saint Domingue and ceded their portion of the island of Hispaniola to France. The British were likewise forced to leave the colony in 1798, having lost as many as 40,000 soldiers, most of them from disease. The man who had assumed the leadership of the slave revolt, the freed slave Toussaint L'Ouverture, then proceeded to conquer the entire island in 1801, abolish slavery, and proclaim himself the governor-general of an autonomous province.

In 1801, after Napoleon had assumed control of the French government and the idealism of the French Revolution had evaporated, a French army of 20,000 men occupied Saint Domingue. The purpose was to make the colony the centerpiece of a restored French Empire, including Florida, Louisiana, French Guiana, and the French

THOMAS PAINE SUPPORTS THE AMERICAN CAUSE

....

Thomas Paine (1737–1809) was a radical Whig reformer who supported the cause for American independence. In Common Sense *(1776), a pamphlet written to support the American cause in the year of the Declaration of Independence, Paine refutes the arguments of the British that they served the interests of the American colonists. Paine protests not only the commercial exploitation of the colonies but also the way in which Great Britain has involved them in warfare with continental rivals.*

I have heard it asserted by some, that as America has flourished under her former connection with Great Britain, the same connection is necessary towards her future happiness, and will always have the same effect. Nothing can be more fallacious than this kind of argument. We may as well assert that because a child has thrived upon milk, that it is never to have meat, or that the first twenty years of our lives is to become a precedent for the next twenty. But even this is admitting more than is true; for I answer roundly that America would have flourished as much, probably much more, had no European power taken any notice of her. The commerce by which she hath enriched herself are the necessaries of life and will always have a market while eating is the custom of Europe.

But she has protected us, say some. That she hath engrossed us is true, and defended the Continent at our expense as well as her own, is admitted; and she would have defended Turkey from the same motive, *viz.* for the sake of trade and dominion.

Alas! We have been long led away by ancient prejudices and made large sacrifices to superstition. We have boasted the protection of Britain without considering that her motive was *interest*, not *attachment;* and that she did not protect us from *our enemies* on *our account* but from *her enemies* on *her own account,* from those who had no quarrel with us on any *other account*, and who will always be our enemies on the *same account*. Let Britain waive her pretensions to the Continent, or the Continent throw off the dependence, and we should be at peace with France and Spain, were they at war with Britain. The miseries of Hanover last war ought to warn us against connections.

Source: From Thomas Paine, *Common Sense* (Philadelphia: W.T. Bradford, 1776).

■ **The British Surrender at Yorktown in 1781**
This battle ended the American War of Independence, although the peace treaty was not signed for another two years.

West Indies. This assertion of French imperial control secured the surrender of L'Ouverture. When it was learned that the French were planning to reintroduce slavery, however, two black generals, Jean-Jacques Dessalines and Henri Christophe, whom the French had enlisted to suppress the revolt, united freed blacks and slaves against the French forces. In 1803 these united forces drove the French out of the colony, and in 1804 they established an independent state of Haiti.

This new state of Haiti was far different from that of the United States, in that it was governed entirely by people of color and it banned slavery. It proclaimed racial equality by defining all Haitians as black. The plantation system was destroyed and the land was redistributed among free blacks; foreigners were forbidden to hold property. Deciding upon the form of government took time, however, as the new rulers of the country were divided between those who wished to establish a monarchy and those who favored a republic. Those divisions led to a prolonged civil war from 1807 until 1822, when the warring northern and southern provinces were integrated into a single republic.

The Haitian revolution was the most radical and egalitarian of the Atlantic revolutions of the late eighteenth and early nineteenth centuries. Whereas the American Revolution was mainly a political movement that established a new republic, the Haitian revolution was a genuine social and economic revolution as well. Its unqualified declaration of human equality and its abolition of slavery served as an inspiration to abolitionist movements in other countries, including the United States, throughout the nineteenth century. The destruction of the plantation system, however, brought about a revolutionary transformation of the country's economy. As a French possession Saint Domingue was quite possibly the richest colony in the world, producing about two-fifths of the world's sugar and half of its coffee. After the revolution, with its economy severed from that of France, the country could no longer compete successfully in the Atlantic economy.

THE IRISH REBELLION, 1798–1799

Within the British Empire the country that was most directly inspired by the success of the American Revolution was the kingdom of Ireland. Unlike the residents of the thirteen colonies in North America, the Gaelic people of Ireland had long thought of themselves as a distinct nation.

The English, however, had begun a conquest of this Irish nation in the eleventh century, and during the next 500 years they had struggled to rule it effectively. One of their methods was to settle English landlords on Irish lands. They had done this in the Middle Ages by giving large estates to English feudal lords, but those old Anglo-Irish families had gradually begun to think of themselves as Irish, and after the Reformation they had remained Catholic, while most English people had become Protestant.

In the sixteenth century the English government had begun to settle colonies of English Protestants on plantations in various parts of Ireland. The purpose of this policy was to gain tighter control over the country and to promote the loyalty of Irish landowners to the English government. In the early seventeenth century James VI of Scotland (who had also become James I of England in 1603) had settled both Scottish Presbyterians, later known as the Scots Irish, as well as English Anglicans, in the northern Irish province of Ulster. These Protestants of Scottish and English descent had become the core of the ruling establishment throughout Ireland, especially after Catholic rebellions in 1641–1649 and again in 1689–1690 had failed.

In the eighteenth century Irish Protestants began to resent their subservient relationship to the British government. Just like the American colonists, they recognized the way in which the Irish economy was serving British rather than Irish interests, and they resented the control that Britain had over the Irish parliament. A reform association known as the Society of United Irishmen, led by the Protestant Ulsterman Wolfe Tone, succeeded in building common ground between Protestants and Catholics. The United Irishmen demanded the repeal of the laws that denied Catholics the right to hold office and sit in the Irish parliament.

The ideals of the United Irishmen drew on many different sources. A long tradition of Presbyterian republican radicalism found reinforcement in the ideals of the American Revolution. The Irish objected to paying tithes to the established Anglican church, and like the American colonists in the 1760s they resented the taxes they were asked to pay to aid in the British war against the French during the 1790s. French revolutionary ideas of liberty, equality, and fraternity had a pervasive influence in Ireland as well.

In 1798 the United Irishmen aligned themselves with lower-class Catholic peasants known as Defenders, and these Irish groups staged a rebellion against British rule with the intention of establishing an Irish republic. Like the American colonists, the Irish revolutionaries sought French aid, but it came too little and too late, and the rebellion failed. The revolt, which was marred by atrocities on both sides, resulted in the death of 30,000 people.

The British government recognized that its arrangement for ruling Ireland, in which the nationalist republican movement had originated, could no longer work. The British government decided therefore to bring about a complete union between Great Britain and Ireland. By the terms of this arrangement, which took effect in 1801, Ireland's parliament ceased to meet; instead the Irish were to elect a limited number of representatives to sit in the British parliament. Ireland thus became a part of the United Kingdom, just as Scotland had done in 1707. The proximity of Ireland to Britain, which made the prospect of Irish independence much more dangerous, was a major factor in making the British determined to hold on to this "internal colony." The forces of Irish nationalism could not be contained, however, and during the nineteenth century new movements for Irish independence arose.

NATIONAL REVOLUTIONS IN SPANISH AMERICA, 1810–1824

The final set of revolutions against European imperial powers occurred between 1810 and 1824 in a number of Spanish American colonies. These struggles, like the American Revolution, turned colonies into new states and led to the building of new nations. The first of these revolutions began in Mexico in 1810; others soon arose in Argentina, Colombia, Chile, and Peru. In these revolutions creoles played a leading role, just as they had in the American War of Independence. The main sources of creole discontent were the Bourbon reforms, which ironically had been intended to make the Spanish Empire more efficient and thus to preserve it. The reforms had achieved this goal, however, by favoring commercial interests at the expense of the traditional aristocracy, thereby reversing or threatening the position of many creole elites. The creoles also faced increasingly heavy taxation, as the Spanish government sought to make them support the expenses of colonial administration.

CHRONOLOGY

The Atlantic Revolutions, 1775–1824

1775–1783	United States of America
1789–1804	Haiti
1798–1799	Ireland
1810–1822	Mexico
1810–1819	Colombia
1810–1821	Venezuela
1810–1816	Argentina
1810–1818	Chile
1821–1824	Peru

Símon Bolívar Presenting the Flag of Liberation to Soldiers After the Battle of Carabobo, 1821

Bolívar was the man most directly responsible for liberating South American countries from Spanish rule. He liberated his native Venezuela in 1821 and defeated Spanish forces in Peru in 1824.

During the late eighteenth century Spanish creole discontent had crystallized into demands for greater political autonomy, similar to the objectives of British American colonists. South American creoles began to think of themselves as Spanish Americans and sometimes simply as Americans. Like British American colonists, they also read and were inspired by the works of Enlightenment political philosophers. They protested against the Bourbon reforms. Nevertheless, the Spanish creole struggle against imperial rule did not commence until some thirty years after the North American colonies had won their independence. One reason for this slow development of revolutionary action was that Spanish American creoles still looked to the Spanish government to provide them with military support against the threat of lower-class rebellion. When, for example, a rebellion of this sort against Spanish rule occurred in Peru in 1780, creole planters not only refused an invitation to join the revolt but also supported the Spanish forces that crushed it. Faced with this lower-class threat, which continued to plague them even after independence, creoles were cautious about abandoning the military and police support provided by the metropolis.

The event that eventually precipitated these wars for national independence was the collapse of the Spanish monarchy after Napoleon's French army invaded Spain in 1807 (see Chapter 18). This development left the Spanish Empire, which had always been more centralized than the British Empire, in a weakened position. In any effort to reconstitute the political order in their colonies, creoles sought to establish greater autonomy. Once the monarchy was restored, this demand for autonomy led quickly to armed resistance. This resistance began in Mexico, but it soon spread throughout Spanish America and quickly acquired popular support.

The man who took the lead in these early revolts against Spanish rule was the fiery Venezuelan aristocrat Símon Bolívar (1783–1830). Educated in the ideas of the Enlightenment, Bolívar led uprisings in his homeland in 1812 and 1814 and eventually defeated the Spanish there in 1819. Unlike most creoles, Bolívar was not afraid to recruit free coloreds and blacks into his armies. His hatred of European colonial governors knew few boundaries. At one point he reportedly commanded his soldiers to shoot and kill any European on sight. He vowed never to rest until all of Spanish America was free. Bolívar carried the struggle for liberation to Peru, which became independent in 1824, and created the state of Bolivia in 1825. Often compared to George Washington, he was more responsible than any one individual for the liberation of Spanish America from Spanish rule. Independent states were established in Argentina in 1816, Chile in 1818, Colombia in 1819, and Mexico in 1822. By then the Spanish, who in the sixteenth century had the largest empire in the world, retained control of only two colonies in the Western Hemisphere: Puerto Rico and Cuba.

CONCLUSION

The Rise and Reshaping of the West

During the second period of European empire building, from 1650 until 1850, the West not only expanded geographically but also acquired a large share of the world's resources. By dominating the world's carrying trade, and by exploiting the agricultural and mineral resources of the Americas, Western states gained control of the world economy. The slave trade, with all its horrors, formed an important part of this economy and served as one of the main sources of Western wealth.

Western economic power laid the foundations for Western political control. In Asia European states assumed political control over territories slowly and reluctantly, as Britain's gradual and piecemeal acquisition of territory in India revealed. In the Americas, European powers acquired territory with relative ease, and European possessions in the New World soon became part of the West. By 1700, as we have seen, the geographical center of the West had become the Atlantic Ocean.

The American territories that were brought under European political control also became, at least to some extent, culturally part of the West. The European colonists who settled in the Americas preserved the languages, the religions, and many of the cultural traditions of the European countries from which they came. When some of the British and Spanish colonies in the Americas rebelled against European regimes in the late eighteenth and early nineteenth centuries, the identity of the colonists who led the resistance remained essentially Western. Even the political ideas that inspired national resistance to European regimes had their origins in Europe.

The assertion of Western political and economic power in the world cultivated a sense of Western superiority. The belief that Europeans, regardless of their nationality, were superior to those from other parts of the world originated in the encounters that took place between Europeans and both African slaves and the indigenous peoples in the Americas. In the late eighteenth century a conviction also developed, although much more slowly, that the West was culturally superior to the civilizations of Asia. This belief in Western superiority became even more pronounced when the economies of Western nations began to experience more rapid growth than those of Asia. We now turn to the source of this new Western economic strength, the Industrial Revolution.

Suggestions for Further Reading

For a comprehensive list of suggested readings, please go to www.ablongman.com/levack/chapter19

Bailyn, Bernard. *Ideological Origins of the American Revolution.* 1967. A probing analysis of the different intellectual traditions upon which the American colonists based their arguments for independence.

Blackburn, Robin. *The Making of New World Slavery: From the Baroque to the Modern, 1492–1800.* 1997. Places European slavery in a broad world perspective.

Boxer, C. R. *The Dutch Seaborne Empire, 1600–1800.* 1965. A thorough account covering the entire period of Dutch expansion.

Davis, Ralph. *The Rise of the Atlantic Economies.* 1973. A readable study of economic development on both sides of the Atlantic.

Eltis, David, *The Rise of African Slavery in the Americas.* 2000. An analysis of the different dimensions of the slave trade based on a database of slave ships and passengers.

Goody, Jack. *The East in the West.* 1996. Challenges the idea that Western cultures are more rational than those of Asia.

Greene, Jack P. *Peripheries and Center: Constitutional Development in the Extended Polities of the British Empire and the United States 1607–1788.* 1986. A study of the composition of the British Empire and its disintegration in North America.

Kamen, Henry. *Empire: How Spain Became a World Power.* 2003. Explains how Spain established the most extensive empire the world had ever known.

Langley, Lester D. *The Americas in the Age of Revolution, 1750–1850.* 1996. A broad comparative study of revolutions in the United States, Haiti, and Latin America.

Liss, Peggy K. *The Atlantic Empires: The Network of Trade and Revolutions, 1713–1826.* 1983. Places the American Revolution in a broader comparative setting and includes material on early Latin American independence movements.

Mungello, D. E. *The Great Encounter of China and the West, 1500–1800.* 1999. Studies China's acceptance and rejection of Western culture as well as the parallel Western reception of China.

Pagden, Anthony. *Lords of All the World: Ideologies of Empire in Spain, Britain and France ca. 1500–ca. 1800.* 1996. Discusses the theoretical foundations of the Atlantic Empires.

Said, Edward. *Orientalism.* 1979. A study of the way in which Western views of the East have assumed its inferiority.

The Industrial Revolution, 1760–1850

N 1842 A 17-YEAR-OLD GIRL, PATIENCE KERSHAW, TESTIFIED BEFORE A BRITISH PAR-liamentary committee regarding the practice of employing children and women in the nation's mines. When the girl made her appearance, the members of the committee observed that she was "an ignorant, filthy, ragged, and deplorable-looking object, such as one of uncivilized natives of the prairies would be shocked to look upon." Patience, who had never been to school and could not read or write, told the committee that she was one of ten children, all of whom had at one time worked in the coal mines, although three of her sisters now worked in a textile mill. She went to the pit at five in the morning and came out at five at night. Her job in the mines was to hurry coal, that is, to pull carts of coal through the narrow tunnels of the mine. Each cart weighed 300 pounds, and every day she hauled eleven of them one mile. The carts were attached to her head and shoulders by a chain and belt, and the pressure of the cart had worn a bald spot on her head. Patience hurried coal for twelve hours straight, not taking any time for her midday meal, which she ate as she worked. While she was working, the men and boys who dug the coal and put it in the carts would often beat her and take sexual liberties with her. Patience told the committee, "I am the only girl in the pit; there are about 20 boys and 15 men. All the men are naked. I would rather work in a mill than a coal pit."

Patience Kershaw was one of the human casualties of an extraordinary development that historians usually refer to as the Industrial Revolution. This process, which brought about a fundamental transformation of human life, involved the extensive use of machinery in the production of goods. Much of that machinery was driven by steam engines, which required coal to produce the steam. Coal mining itself became a major industry, and the men who owned and operated the mines tried to hire workers, many of them children, at the lowest possible wage. It was this desire to maximize profits that led to the employment, physical hardship, and abuse of girls like Patience Kershaw.

Exhibit of Machinery at the Crystal Palace Exhibition in London in 1851: During the Industrial Revolution the manufacture of heavy machinery itself became an industry.

■ **Child Labor in the Mines**
A child hurrying coal through a tunnel in a mine.

The story of the Industrial Revolution cannot be told solely in terms of the exploitation of child or even adult workers. Many of its effects can be described in positive or at least morally neutral terms. The Industrial Revolution resulted in a staggering increase in the volume and range of products made available to consumers, from machine-produced clothing to household utensils. It made possible unprecedented and sustained economic growth. The Industrial Revolution facilitated the rapid transportation of passengers as well as goods across large expanses of territory, mainly on the railroads that were constructed in all industrialized countries. It brought about a new awareness of the position of workers in the economic system, and it unleashed powerful political forces intended to improve the lot of these workers.

The Industrial Revolution played a crucial role in redefining and reshaping the West. Until the late nineteenth century industrialization took place only in Western nations. During that century "the West" gradually became identified with those countries which had industrial economies. When some non-Western countries introduced mechanized industry in the twentieth century, largely in imitation of Western example, the geographical boundaries of the West underwent a significant alteration.

In this chapter we shall consider five basic questions: (1) To what economic and social developments does the term Industrial Revolution refer? (2) What social and economic changes made industrial development possible? (3) How did industrialization spread from Great Britain to the European continent and America? (4) What were the economic, social, and cultural effects of the Industrial

Revolution? (5) What was the relationship between the growth of industry and Britain's dominance in trade and imperial strength during the middle years of the nineteenth century?

The Nature of the Industrial Revolution

The Industrial Revolution was a series of economic and social changes that took place in Great Britain during the late eighteenth and early nineteenth centuries and on the European continent and in the United States after 1815. Some economic historians claim that the use of the term *revolution,* which suggests radical and abrupt change, is misleading in this context, since the economic and social changes to which the term refers occurred gradually over a long period of time. Even so, the term is still appropriate because it conveys the radical nature and profound significance of the changes it identifies. Like the Scientific Revolution of the seventeenth century, which also took place gradually, the Industrial Revolution reshaped Western civilization.

The Industrial Revolution consisted of four closely related developments: the introduction of new industrial technology, the utilization of mineral sources of energy, the concentration of labor in factories, and the development of new methods of transportation.

NEW INDUSTRIAL TECHNOLOGY

The Industrial Revolution ushered in the machine age, and to this day machines are the most striking feature of modern industrial economies. In countries that have become industrialized, virtually every human-made commodity can be mass-produced by some kind of machine. In the late eighteenth century such machines were novelties, but their numbers increased dramatically in the early nineteenth century. For example, the power loom, a machine used for weaving cloth, was invented in Britain in 1787 but not put into widespread use until the 1820s. By 1836 there were more than 60,000 power looms in just one English county.

Machines became so common in Britain that machine making itself became a major industry, supplying its products to other manufacturers rather than to individual consumers. Machines were introduced in the textile, iron, printing, papermaking, and engineering industries and were used in every stage of manufacture. Machines extracted minerals that were used as either raw materials or sources of energy, transported those materials to the factories, saved time and labor in the actual manufacturing of commodities, and carried the finished products to market. Eventually machines were used in agriculture itself, facilitating both the plowing of fields and the harvesting of crops.

The most significant of the new machines, which changed the entire industrial process, were those used for spinning and weaving in the textile industry and the steam engine, first used in mining and the iron industry. These pieces of machinery became almost synonymous with the Industrial Revolution, and their invention in the 1760s appropriately marks its beginning.

Textile Machinery

Until the late eighteenth century, the production of textiles throughout Europe, which involved both the spinning of yarn and the weaving of cloth, was done entirely by hand, on spinning wheels and hand looms respectively. This was the practice for wool, which was the main textile produced in Europe during the early modern period, as well as for a new material, cotton, which became immensely popular in the early eighteenth century, mainly because of its greater comfort. The demand for cotton yarn was greater than the quantities spinners could supply. To meet this demand a British inventor, James Hargreaves, in 1767 constructed a new machine, the spinning jenny, which greatly increased the amount of cotton yarn that could be spun and thus made available for weaving. The original jenny, a hand machine used in the homes of spinners, consisted of only eight spindles, but it later accommodated as many as 120.

The spinning of yarn on the jenny required a stronger warp, the yarn that ran lengthwise on a loom. A power-driven machine, the water frame, introduced by the barber and wigmaker Richard Arkwright in 1769, made the pro-

CHRONOLOGY

Technological Innovations of the Industrial Revolution

1763	James Watts's rotative steam engine
1767	James Hargreaves's spinning jenny
1769	Richard Arkwright's water frame
1779	Samuel Crompton's mule
1787	Edmund Cartwright's power loom
1815	George Stephenson's steam locomotive
1846	Elias Howe's sewing machine

duction of this stronger warp possible. In 1779 Samuel Crompton, using tools he had purchased with his earnings as a fiddle player at a local theater, combined the jenny and the frame in one machine, called the mule. Crompton worked on his machine only at night, in order to keep it secret, and the strange noises that came out of his workshop made his neighbors think his house was haunted. The mule, which could spin as much as 300 times the amount of yarn produced by one spinning wheel, became the main spinning machine of the early Industrial Revolution. Both the water frame and the mule required power, and that requirement led to the centralization of the textile industry in large rural mills located near rivers so that their water wheels could drive the machinery.

The tremendous success of the mule eventually produced more yarn than the weavers could handle on their hand looms. Edmund Cartwright, an Oxford-educated clergyman, supported by monies from his heiress wife, addressed that need with the invention of the power loom in 1787. In that same year he put his new invention to use in a weaving mill he built near the town of Doncaster. The power loom, like the spinning jenny, the water frame, and the mule, met a specific need within the industry. It also gave the producer a competitive advantage by saving time, reducing the cost of labor, and increasing production. Two power looms run by a 15-year-old boy, for example, could produce more than three times what a skilled hand loom weaver could turn out in the same time using only the old hand device, the flying shuttle. The net effect of all these machines was the production of more than 200 times as much cotton cloth in 1850 as in 1780. By 1800 cotton became Britain's largest industry, producing more than 20 percent of the world's cloth, and by 1850 that percentage had risen to more than 50 percent. Indeed, by midcentury, cotton accounted for 70 percent of the value of all British exports.

The Steam Engine

The steam engine was even more important than the new textile machinery since it was used in almost every stage of the productive process, including the operation of textile machinery itself. The steam engine was invented by a Scottish engineer, James Watt, in 1763. It represented an improvement over the engine invented by Thomas Newcomen in 1709, which had been intended mainly to drain water from deep mines. The problem with Newcomen's engine was that the steam, which was produced in a cylinder heated by coal, had to be cooled in order to make the piston return, and the process of heating and cooling had to be repeated for each stroke of the piston. The engine was therefore inefficient and expensive to operate. Watt created a separate chamber where the steam could be condensed without affecting the heat of the cylinder. The result was a more efficient and cost-effective machine that could provide more power than any other source. Watt's pride in his invention was matched only by his pride in his Scottish nationality. Upon receiving a patent for the new device, he boasted, "This was made by a Scot."

After designing the steam engine, Watt teamed up with a Birmingham metal manufacturer, Matthew Boulton, to produce it on a large scale. Boulton provided the capital necessary to begin this process and to hire the skilled laborers to assemble the machines. He also had ambitious plans for marketing the new invention throughout the world. "It would not be worth my while to make for three countries only," Boulton said, "but I find it well worth my while to make for the whole world."

The steam engine soon became the workhorse of the Industrial Revolution. Not only did it pump water from mines, but it helped raise minerals like iron ore that were extracted from those mines. It provided the intense blast of heat that was necessary to re-smelt pig iron into cast iron, which in turn was used to make industrial machinery, buildings, bridges, locomotives, and ships. Once the engine was equipped with a rotating device, it was used to drive the factory machinery in the textile mills, and it eventually powered the railroad locomotives that carried industrial goods to market.

The widespread adoption of steam power came fairly late in the Industrial Revolution. Only in the 1840s and 1850s, after its efficiency had been greatly improved, did it become the main source of energy in the textile industry. Until then rural water power was the preferred method of running the cotton mills. Only after the introduction of coal-driven steam power did the factories locate in the cities, especially those of northern England, such as Manchester. The 1840s and 1850s were also the decades when the railroads, using the steam locomotive invented by the English engineer George Stephenson in 1815, began to crisscross the European continent. By midcentury the steam engine had become the predominant symbol of the Industrial Revolution.

MINERAL SOURCES OF ENERGY

Until the late eighteenth century, most economic activity, including the transportation of goods, was powered by either humans or beasts. Either people tilled the soil themselves, using a spade, or they yoked oxen to pull a plow. Either they carried materials and goods on their backs or they used horses to transport them. In either case the energy for these tasks came ultimately from organic sources, the food that was needed to feed farmers or their animals. If workers needed heat, they had to burn an organic material, wood or charcoal, to produce it. The amount of energy that could be generated in a particular region was therefore limited by its capacity to produce sufficient wood, charcoal, or food. By the middle of the eighteenth century, for example, the forests in Britain were no longer capable of producing sufficient quantities of charcoal for use in the iron industry.

Organic sources of energy were of course renewable, in that new crops could be grown and forests replanted, but the long periods of time that these processes took, coupled with the limited volume of organic material that could be extracted from an acre of land, made it difficult to sustain economic growth. The only viable alternatives to these organic sources of energy before the eighteenth century were those that tapped the forces of nature: windmills, which were used mainly in the Netherlands for purposes of field drainage, and water wheels, which were driven by water pressure from river currents, waterfalls, or human-made channels that regulated the flow of water. The potential of those natural sources of energy was both limited and difficult to harness, and it could be tapped only in certain locations or at certain times. Moreover, those sources could not produce heat.

The decisive change in the harnessing of energy for industrial purposes was the successful use of minerals, originally coal but in the twentieth century oil and uranium as well, as the main sources of energy used in the production and transportation of goods. These minerals were not inexhaustible, as the decline of coal deposits in Europe during the twentieth century has shown, but the supplies could last for centuries, and they were much more efficient than any form of energy produced from organic materials, including charcoal and peat. Coal produced the high combustion temperatures necessary to smelt iron, and unlike charcoal it was not limited by the size of a region's forests. Coal therefore became the key to the expansion of the British iron industry in the nineteenth century. That industry's dependence on coal was reflected by the relocation of iron works from the mines that supplied the ore itself to the coal fields that supplied the energy. Coal also became the sole source of heat for the new steam engine.

As the Industrial Revolution progressed, it relied increasingly on coal as its main fuel. The change, however, occurred gradually. In 1830 a majority of factories still used

■ **Philippe Jacques de Loutherbourg, *Coalbrookdale by Night* (1801)**
This painting depicts the intense heat produced by the coal bellows used to smelt iron in
Coalbrookdale, an English town in the Severn Valley that was one of the key centers of industrial ac-
tivity at the beginning of the nineteenth century.

water power, and steam power did not realize its most spectacular increases until after 1870. Nevertheless, largely because of the demands of the mining, textile, and metal industries, coal mining became a major industry itself with
an enormous labor force. By 1850 British mines employed
about 5 percent of the entire national workforce. These
miners were just as instrumental as textile workers in making Britain an industrial nation.

THE GROWTH OF FACTORIES

One of the most enduring images of the Industrial
Revolution is that of the large factory, filled with workers,
laboring amid massive machinery driven by either water or
steam power. Mechanized factory production evolved out
of forms of industry that had emerged only during the early
modern period (1500–1750). In the Middle Ages virtually
all industry in Europe was undertaken by skilled craftsmen
who belonged to urban guilds. These artisans, working
either by themselves or with the assistance of apprentices or
journeymen, produced everything from candlesticks and
hats to oxcarts and beds. During the early modern period
the urban craftsman's shop gave way to two different types
of industrial workplaces, the rural cottage and the large
handicraft workshop. Both of these served as halfway
houses to the large factory.

Beginning in the sixteenth century, entrepreneurs began
employing families in the countryside to spin and weave
cloth and make nails and cutlery. By locating industry in
the countryside the entrepreneurs were able to escape the
regulations imposed by the guilds regarding employment
and the price of finished products. They also paid lower
wages, since the rural workers, who also received an income
from farming, were willing to work for less than the residents of towns. Another attraction of rural industry was
that all the members of the family, including children, participated in the process. In this "domestic system" a capitalist entrepreneur provided the workers with the raw materials and sometimes the tools they needed. He later paid them
a fixed rate for each finished product. The entrepreneur was
also responsible for having the finished cloth dyed and for
marketing the commodities in regional towns.

Rural household industry was widespread not only in
certain regions of Britain but also in most European countries. In the late eighteenth century it gradually gave way to
the factory system. The great attraction of factory production was mechanization, which became cost-efficient only
when it was introduced in a central industrial workplace. In
factories, moreover, the entrepreneur could reduce the cost
of labor and transportation, exercise tighter control over
the quality of goods, and increase productivity by concen-
trating workers in one location. Temporary labor shortages

■ **Mule Spinning**
A large mechanized spinning mill in northern England, about 1835. The workers did not require any great skill to run the machinery.

sometimes made the transition from rural industry to factory production imperative.

The second type of industrial workplace that emerged during the early modern period was the large handicraft workshop. Usually located in the towns and cities, rather than in the countryside, these workshops employed relatively small numbers of people with different skills who worked collectively on the manufacture of a variety of items, such as pottery and munitions. The owner of the workshop supplied the raw materials, paid the workers' wages, and gained a profit from selling the finished products.

The large handicraft workshop made possible a division of labor°—the assignment of one stage of production to each worker or group of workers. The effect of the division of labor on productivity was evident even in the manufacture of simple items such as buttons and pins. In *The Wealth of Nations* (1776), the economist Adam Smith (1723–1790) used a pin factory in London to illustrate how the division of labor could increase per capita productivity from no more than twenty pins a day to the astonishing total of 4,800.

Like the cottages engaged in rural industry, the large handicraft workshop eventually gave way to the mechanized factory. The main difference between the workshop and the factory was that the factory did not require a body of skilled workers. When production become mechanized,

the worker's job was simply to tend to the machinery. The only skill factory workers needed was manual dexterity to operate the machinery. Only those workers who made industrial machinery remained craftsmen or skilled workers in the traditional sense of the word.

With the advent of mechanization, factory owners gained much tighter control over the entire productive process. Indeed, they began to enforce an unprecedented discipline among their workers, who had to accommodate themselves to the boredom of repetitive work and a timetable set by the machines. Craftsmen who had been accustomed to working at their own pace now had to adjust to an entirely new and more demanding schedule. "While the engine runs," wrote one critical contemporary, "the people must work—men, women, and children yoked together with iron and steam. The animal machine—breakable in the best case, subject to a thousand sources of suffering—is chained fast to the iron machine which knows no suffering and no weariness."

Despite the growth and development of the factory system, the factory did not become the most common type of industrial workplace until the early twentieth century. In Britain, Germany, France, and the United States most manufacturing continued to take place in handicraft workshops in the cities or in rural households. Indeed, many of the industries that became mechanized spawned a variety of secondary crafts and trades, such as the dyeing and finishing of cloth and the sewing of clothes, which were conducted mainly in rural households.

NEW METHODS OF TRANSPORTATION

As industry became more extensive and increased its output, transport facilities, such as roads, bridges, canals, and eventually railroads, grew in number and quality. Increased industrial productivity has always depended on efficient movement of raw materials to places of production and transportation of finished products to the market. During the early phase of the Industrial Revolution in Britain, water transportation supplied most of these needs. A vast network of navigable rivers and human-made canals, eventually more than 4,000 miles in length, was used to transport goods in areas that did not have access to the coast. The canals that were built after 1760, with their systems of locks and their aqueducts spanning roads and rivers, were a product of the technology that the Scientific Revolution had made possible. For routes that could not be reached by water, the most common method of transportation was by horse-drawn carriages on newly built turnpikes or toll roads, many of them made of stone so that they were passable even in wet weather.

The most significant innovation in transport during the nineteenth century was the railroad. Introduced as the Industrial Revolution was gaining momentum, the railroad provided quick, cheap transportation of heavy materials like coal and iron over long distances. Its introduction in Britain during the 1820s and throughout Europe and America during the following decades serves as one of the best illustrations of the transition from an economy based on organic sources of energy to one based on mineral sources of energy. Driven by coal-burning, steam-powered locomotives, the railroads freed transport from a dependence on animal power, especially the horses that were used to pull coaches along turnpikes, barges along canals, and even carts along parallel tracks in mines. Railroads rapidly became the main economic thoroughfares of the industrial economy. They linked towns and regions that earlier had not been easily accessible to each other. They also changed the travel habits of Europeans by making it possible to cover distances in one-fifth the time it took by coach.

ADAM SMITH DESCRIBES THE DIVISION OF LABOR

·················

Adam Smith, a Scottish economist who is considered the founder of the classical school of economics, was the great theorist of modern laissez-faire *capitalism. In* An Inquiry into the Nature and Causes of the Wealth of Nations *(1776), he challenged the mercantilist assumption that there was only a fixed supply of wealth for which nations had to compete. He also argued that in an unregulated economy, the pursuit of self-interest would work in the interest of the public welfare. In this selection Smith discusses the division of labor. Smith wrote* The Wealth of Nations *during the very early stages of industrialization. The place of production that he uses in this example is not a large mechanized factory but a small urban workshop, often referred to as a manufactory.*

To take an example, therefore, from a very trifling manufacture; but one in which the division of labour has been very often taken notice of, the trade of the pin-maker; a workman not educated to this business (which the division of labour has rendered a distinct trade), nor acquainted with the use of the machinery employed in it (to the invention of which the same division of labour has probably given occasion), could scarce, perhaps, with his utmost industry, make one pin in a day, and certainly could not make twenty. But in the way in which this business is now carried on, not only the whole work is a peculiar trade, but it is divided into a number of branches, of which the greater part are likewise peculiar trades. One man draws out the wire, another straits it, a third cuts it, a fourth points it, a fifth grinds it at the top for receiving the head; to make the head requires two or three distinct operations; to put it on is a peculiar business, to whiten the pins is another; it is even a trade by itself to put them into the paper; and the important business of making a pin is in this manner, divided into about eighteen distinct operations, which in some manufactories, are all performed by distinct hands, though in others the same man will sometimes perform two or three of them. I have seen a small manufactory of this kind where ten men only were employed, and where some of them consequently performed two or three distinct operations. But though they were very poor and indifferently accommodated with the necessary machinery, they could, when they exerted themselves, make about twelve pounds of pins a day. There are in a pound upwards of four thousand pins of a middling size. Those ten persons, therefore, could make among them upwards of forty-eight thousand pins in a day. Each person, therefore making a tenth part of forty-eight thousand pins, might be considered as making four thousand eight hundred pins in a day.

Source: From Adam Smith, *An Inquiry into the Nature and Cause of the Wealth of Nations, 5th Edition,* 1789, Book I, Chapter 1.

■ The Stockton and Darlington Railway
A locomotive and two cars used on the first major railroad in Britain, which opened in 1825. The railroad carried materials and goods to and from towns producing iron in the northern counties of England.

The construction and operation of railroads became a major new industry, employing thousands of skilled and unskilled workers and providing opportunities for investment and profit. The industry created an unprecedented demand for iron and other materials used to build and equip locomotives, tracks, freight cars, passenger cars, and signals, thus giving a tremendous boost to the iron industry and the metalworking and engineering trades. By the 1840s the railroads had become the main stimulus to economic growth throughout western Europe and the United States. Transport in industrialized economies continues to experience frequent innovation. During the twentieth century, for example, new methods of transportation, including automobiles, airplanes, and high-speed rails, have sustained economic growth in all industrialized countries, and like the railroads they have become major industries themselves.

Transport facilities, unlike factories, can seldom be built entirely by their individual owners. The cost of building locomotives and laying railroad tracks is almost always too great to come from the profits accumulated in the normal conduct of one's business. The funds for these facilities must come from either private investment, governments, or international financial institutions. In Britain the capital for the railroads came entirely from individual investors. In the United States, which built the world's largest railroad system in the nineteenth century, most of the capital also came from private investment, but many state and city governments helped finance early railroads. In other industrialized countries, governments played a more important role. In Belgium, which was the second European country to experience an Industrial Revolution, and in Russia, which was one of the last, the governments of those countries assumed the responsibility for building a national railroad system.

Conditions Favoring Industrial Growth

The immediate causes of the Industrial Revolution were the competitive pressures that encouraged technological innovation, the transition to coal power, the growth of factories, and the building of the railroads. These developments, however, do not provide a full explanation for this unprecedented economic transformation. Certain social and economic conditions were present in Britain that allowed industrialization to progress—a large population, improved agricultural productivity, the accumulation of capital, a group of people with scientific knowledge and entrepreneurial skill, and sufficient demand for manufactured goods. In this section we will look at the historical experience of Great Britain, which was the first country to industrialize, to see how these conditions made industrial economic development possible.

POPULATION GROWTH

Industrialization requires a sufficiently large pool of labor to staff the factories and workshops of the new industries. One of the main reasons why the Industrial Revolution occurred first in Britain is that its population during the eighteenth century increased more rapidly than that of any country in continental Europe. Between 1680 and 1820 the population of England more than doubled, while that of France grew at less than one-third that rate, and that of the Dutch Republic hardly grew at all. One of the reasons this growth took place was that famines, which had occurred periodically throughout the early modern period, became less frequent during the eighteenth century. The last great

Increase in European Population, 1680–1820

Population Totals (millions)

	1680	1820
France	21.9	30.5
Italy	12.0	18.4
Germany	12.0	18.1
Spain	8.5	14.0
England	4.9	11.5
Netherlands	1.9	2.0
Western Europe	71.9	116.5

Percentage Growth Rates, 1680–1820

England	133%
Spain	64
Italy	53
Germany	51
France	39
Netherlands	8
Western Europe	73

Source: E. A. Wrigley, "The Growth of Population in Eighteenth-Century England: A Conundrum Resolved," *Past and Present* 98 (1983), 122.

famine in Britain took place in 1740, only a generation before industrialization began. There was also a decrease in mortality from epidemic diseases, especially typhus, influenza, and smallpox. Bubonic plague, which had decimated the European population periodically since the fourteenth century, struck England for the last time in the Great Plague of London of 1665. It made its last European appearance at Marseilles in 1720 but did not spread beyond the southern parts of France.

Even more important than this reduction in mortality was an increase in fertility. More people were marrying, and at a younger age, which increased the birth rate. The spread of rural industry seems to have encouraged this early-marriage pattern. Wage-earning textile workers tended to marry a little earlier than agricultural workers, probably because wage earners did not have to postpone marriage to inherit land or to become self-employed, as was the case with farm workers.

This increase in population facilitated industrialization in two ways. First, it increased demand for the goods that were being manufactured in large quantities in the factories. The desire for these products, especially the new cottons, played an important role in enlarging the domestic market for manufactured goods, as we shall see shortly. Second, it increased the supply of labor, freeing a substantial portion of the population for industry, especially for factory labor. At the same time, however, this increase was not so large as to have had a negative effect on industrializa-

tion, as it did in a number of underdeveloped countries in the twentieth century. If population growth is too rapid, it can lead to declining incomes, put pressure on agriculture to feed more people than is possible, and prevent the accumulation of wealth. Most important, it can discourage factory owners from introducing costly machinery, because if labor is plentiful and cheap, it might very well cost less for workers to produce the same volume of goods by hand. Industrialization therefore requires a significant but not too rapid increase in population—the exact scenario that occurred in Britain during the eighteenth century.

AGRICULTURAL PRODUCTIVITY

Between 1700 and 1800 British agriculture experienced a revolution, resulting in a substantial increase in productivity. A major reason for this increase was the consolidation of all the land farmed by one tenant into compact fields. During the Middle Ages and most of the early modern period, each tenant on a manorial estate leased and farmed strips of land that were scattered throughout the estate. The decisions regarding the planting and harvesting of crops in these open fields were made collectively in the manorial court. Beginning in the sixteenth century, some of the wealthier tenants on these estates agreed to exchange their strips of land with their neighbors in order to consolidate their holdings into large compact fields, whose boundaries were defined by hedges, bushes, or walls. The main benefit of this process of enclosure° was that it allowed individual farmers to exercise complete control over the use of their land. In the eighteenth and nineteenth centuries the number of these enclosures increased dramatically, as the British Parliament passed legislation that divided entire estates into a number of enclosed fields. This legislation benefited all landowners, including the members of the aristocracy who passed the legislation.

With control of their lands, farmers could make them more productive. The most profitable change was to introduce new crop rotations, often involving the alternation of grains like rye or barley with root crops like turnips or grasses like clover. These new crops and grasses restored nutrients to the soil and therefore made it unnecessary to let fields lie fallow once every three years. Farmers also introduced a variety of new fertilizers and soil additives that made harvests more bountiful. Farmers who raised sheep took advantage of discoveries regarding scientific breeding that improved the quality of their flocks.

More productive farming meant that fewer agricultural workers were required to feed the population. This made it possible for more people to leave the farms to work in the factories and mines. The expanded labor pool of industrial workers, moreover, was large enough that factory owners did not have to pay workers high wages; otherwise the prospect of industrializing would have lost much of its appeal. The hiring of children and women to work in the factories and mines also kept the labor pool large and the costs of labor low.

CAPITAL FORMATION AND ACCUMULATION

The term capital° refers to all the assets used in production. These include the factories and machines that are used to produce other goods (fixed capital) as well as the raw materials and finished products that are sent to market (circulating capital). Other forms of capital are the railroads and barges used for transporting raw materials to the place of production and finished products to market. Mechanized industry involves the extensive and intensive use of capital to do the work formerly assigned to human beings. An industrial economy therefore requires large amounts of capital, especially fixed capital.

Capital more generally refers to the money that is necessary to purchase these physical assets. This capital can come from a number of different sources: It can come from individuals, such as wealthy landlords, merchants, or industrialists who invest the profits they have accumulated in industrial machinery or equipment. In many cases the profits derived from industrial production are reinvested in the firm itself. Alternatively, capital can come from financial institutions in the form of loans. Very often a number of individuals make their wealth available to an industrial firm by buying shares of stock in that company's operations. This of course is the main way in which most capital is accumulated today. In countries that have only recently begun to industrialize in Latin America and Southeast Asia, capital often comes from public sources, such as governments, or from international institutions, such as the International Monetary Fund.

In Great Britain the capital that was needed to achieve industrial transformation came almost entirely from private sources. Some of it was raised by selling shares of stock to people from the middle and upper levels of society, but an even larger amount came from merchants who engaged in domestic and international trade, landowners who profited from the production of agricultural goods (including those who owned plantations in America), and the industrial entrepreneurs who owned mines, ironworks, and factories. In Britain, where all three groups were more successful than in other parts of Europe, the volume of capital made available from these sources was substantial. These people could invest directly in industrial machinery and mines or, more commonly, make their wealth available to others indirectly in the form of loans from banks where they kept their financial assets.

Banks supplied a considerable amount of the funds necessary for industrialization. In Britain the possibilities for such capital were maximized in the late eighteenth century when financial institutions offered loans at low interest rates, and when the development of a national banking system made these funds readily available throughout the country, especially in the new industrial cities such as Leeds, Sheffield, and Manchester. The number of English banks went from a mere dozen in 1750 to more than 300 in 1800. Many bankers had close ties with industrialists, thereby facilitating the flow of capital from the financial to the industrial sector of the economy. Banks played an even more central role in the industrialization of Germany, which was economically not as advanced as Britain and less capable, therefore, of generating capital through the accumulation of profits.

TECHNOLOGICAL KNOWLEDGE AND ENTREPRENEURSHIP

The process of industrialization involves the application of technological knowledge to the manufacturing process. It also involves entrepreneurship, the ability to make business ventures profitable. The mechanization of industry demanded scientifically trained people not only to introduce new forms of machinery but also to mass produce that machinery for other manufacturers. The development of new modes of transportation required the skill of an entire class of civil engineers who could design and construct locomotives, ships, canals, railroads, and bridges. At the same time, industrialization required a group of business experts who knew how to run the factories and market their products. These requirements help explain why countries that are industrializing today often import technological and financial personnel from other countries to assist them in the process of industrialization and take steps to train and educate people from their own countries to carry on this work.

As we have discussed in Chapter 16, the geographical center of the Scientific Revolution shifted from the Mediterranean to the North Atlantic, especially to England, in the late seventeenth century. At the same time, England took the lead in making science an integral part of the nation's culture. In no other European country was so much attention given to the dissemination of scientific knowledge in public lectures, the meetings of local scientific societies, and the publication of scientific textbooks. Much of this popular scientific education focused on Newtonian mechanics and dynamics. These were precisely the areas of science that lent themselves most readily to technological application. The only area that was developed more fully in France than in Britain was thermodynamics, the branch of physics dealing with heat and its conversion into other forms of energy, such as steam power. To some extent the technological innovations and engineering achievements that took place in Britain during the Industrial Revolution can be considered the product of this unparalleled diffusion of scientific knowledge. Those who made these innovations also required extensive mathematical skill. The education given to British schoolchildren in the eighteenth century included more instruction in mathematics than was given in any other European country.

Industrial entrepreneurs, the people who actually ran the factories and superintended the industrial process, also needed a certain level of technological and mathematical skill, but their talents lay much more in their ability to run a variety of capitalist enterprises for a profit. Britain had no shortage of this type of talent in the eighteenth century. Even before the advent of mechanization there had developed an entire class of merchant capitalists who had organized the domestic system of rural industry or run the large handicraft workshops in London and other towns.

The invention and production of the steam engine readily illustrate the way in which technological and entrepreneurial skills reinforced and complemented each other. The partnership between the Scotsman James Watt, who invented the steam engine, and the Englishman Matthew Boulton represented a dynamic British alliance of science and capitalism. Of the two men, Watt had more scientific and mathematical knowledge, having taught himself geometry and trigonometry as well as having read textbooks on mechanics. He was familiar with the work of Joseph Black, the chemist at the University of Glasgow who studied steam, and he had acquired a knowledge of scientific instruments from his father's business as an outfitter of ships. Even though he was not an academic, he thought he was as smart as the famous French chemist Antoine Lavoisier. He was also a shrewd businessman who figured out various ways to use his knowledge of engineering to turn a profit and acquire a competitive advantage over others. Boulton was the classic eighteenth-century English entrepreneur who manufactured a variety of small metal objects from toys and buttons to teakettles and watch chains. His contribution to the partnership was assembling workers with the requisite skills to mass-produce the engine. Boulton was also scientifically knowledgeable, and both he and Watt were members of the Lunar Society of Birmingham, a voluntary scientific society where they shared similar interests. Both men thought of themselves as scientists, just as both of them acted as entrepreneurs.

DEMAND FROM CONSUMERS AND PRODUCERS

The conditions for industrialization that we have discussed so far all deal with supply°, that is, the amounts of capital, labor, food, and skill that are necessary to support the industrial process. The other side of the economic equation is demand°, that is, the desire of consumers to purchase industrial goods and of producers to acquire raw materials and machinery. Much of the extraordinary productivity of the Industrial Revolution arose from the demand for industrial products. Many of the technological innovations that occurred at the beginning of the revolution also originated as responses to the demand for more goods. For example, the demand for more cotton goods spurred the introduction of the spinning jenny, the water frame, and the mule.

Likewise the demand for coal for industrial and domestic use led to the development of an efficient steam engine in order to drain mines so that those supplies of coal could be extracted.

During the early years of industrialization, only about 35 percent of all British manufactured goods were exported. This statistic indicates that as the Industrial Revolution was taking hold, the domestic market was still the main source of demand for industrial products. The demand was especially strong among the bourgeoisie. Within that group a "consumer revolution" had taken place during the eighteenth century. This revolution was based on an unprecedented desire to acquire goods of all sorts, especially clothing and housewares, such as pottery, cutlery, furniture, and curtains. The consumer revolution was fueled in large part by a desire to imitate the spending habits of the aristocracy. It was assisted by commercial manipulation of all sorts, including newspaper advertising, warehouse displays, product demonstrations, and the distribution of samples. An entirely new consumer culture arose, one in which women played a leading role. Advertisements promoting the latest female fashions, housewares, and children's toys became more common than those directed at adult male consumers. One ad in a local British paper in 1777, capitalizing on reports that mice were getting into ladies' hair at night, promoted "night caps made of silver wire so strong that no mouse or even a rat can gnaw through them." Advertisements therefore created a demand for new products as well as increasing the demand for those already on the market.

If this consumer revolution had been restricted to the middle class, it would have had only a limited effect on the Industrial Revolution. The bourgeoisie in the eighteenth century constituted at most only 20 percent of the entire population of Britain, and most of the goods they craved, with the exception of the pottery produced in Josiah Wedgwood's factories (which is still made today), were luxury items rather than the types of products that could be easily mass-produced. A strong demand for manufactured goods could develop only if workers were to buy consumer goods such as knitted stockings and caps, cotton shirts, earthenware, coffeepots, nails, candlesticks, watches, lace, and ribbon. The demand for these products came from small cottagers and laborers as well as the middle class. The demand for stockings for both men and women was particularly strong. In 1831 the author of a study of the impact of machinery on British society declared, "Two centuries ago not one person in a thousand wore stockings; one century ago not one person in five hundred wore them; now not one person in a thousand is without them."

Demand for manufactured products from the lower classes was obviously limited by the amount of money that wage earners had available for non-essential goods, and real wages did not increase very much, if at all, during the eighteenth century. Nevertheless the income of families in which the wife and children as well as the father worked for wages did increase significantly both during the heyday of rural industry and during the early years of industrialization. With these funds available, a substantial number of workers could actually afford to buy the products that they desired. As the population increased, so too did this lower-class demand, which helped to sustain an economy built around industrial production.

The Spread of Industrialization

The Industrial Revolution, like the Scientific Revolution of the sixteenth and seventeenth centuries, did not occur in all European countries at the same time. As we have seen, it began in Britain in the 1760s and for more than four decades was confined exclusively to that country (see Map 20.1). It eventually spread to other European and North American countries, where many industrial innovations were modeled on those that had taken place in Britain. Belgium, France, Germany, Switzerland, Austria, Sweden, and the United States all experienced their own Industrial Revolutions by the middle of the nineteenth century. Only in the late nineteenth century did countries outside the traditional boundaries of the West, mainly Russia and Japan, begin to industrialize. By the middle of the twentieth century, industrialization had become a truly global process, transforming the economies of a number of Asian and Latin American countries.

GREAT BRITAIN AND THE CONTINENT

Industrialization occurred on the European continent much later than it did in Great Britain. Only after 1815 did Belgium and France begin to industrialize on a large scale, and it was not until 1840 that Germany, Switzerland, and Austria showed significant signs of industrial growth. Other European countries, such as Italy and Spain, did not begin serious efforts in this direction until the late nineteenth century. It took continental European nations even longer to rival the economic strength of Britain. Germany, which emerged as Britain's main competitor in the late nineteenth century, did not match British industrial output until the twentieth century.

Why did it take so long for other countries to industrialize? Virtually all of them had developed extensive rural industry in the late eighteenth century. The governments of European countries, in keeping with mercantilist philosophy, had a long tradition of encouraging the development of domestic industry. Population growth on the Continent during the late eighteenth century, while less dramatic than in Great Britain, should have been sufficient to stimulate consumer demand and increase the supply of labor. Overall

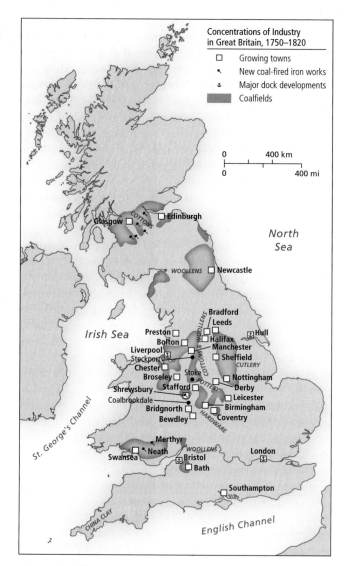

■ **Map 20.1   The Concentrations of Industry in Great Britain, 1750–1820**
The most heavily industrialized regions were in the north, where the population of cities such as Manchester, Liverpool, and Sheffield grew rapidly.

economic growth in France during that time almost matched that of Great Britain. Scientific education, while not as widespread as in Britain, was hardly lacking, especially in France. Nonetheless, industrialization on the Continent, especially in heavy industry, lagged far behind that of Great Britain, and the process was for the most part painfully slow.

One explanation for the slower development of industrialization on the Continent relates to the political situations in those countries. Well into the nineteenth century, most continental European countries had numerous internal political barriers that could impede the transportation of raw materials and goods from one part of the country to another. In Germany, for example, which was not politically united until 1871, scores of small sovereign territorial units charged tariffs whenever goods crossed their territorial boundaries. Only in 1834 was a customs union, the *Zollverein,* created to eliminate some of these barriers. In France, which had achieved a formal territorial unity during the reign of Louis XIV, local rights and privileges impeded internal trade until the early nineteenth century. This political situation was aggravated by the relatively poor state of continental roads and the inaccessibility of many seaports from production sites.

The contrast between the situation on the Continent and that which prevailed in Great Britain is striking. After 1707, when Scotland was united to England and freedom of internal trade was established between the two countries, the United Kingdom of Great Britain constituted the largest free trade zone in Europe. Thus raw materials and finished products could pass from one place within Great Britain to another, up to a distance of more than 800 miles, without payment of any internal customs or duties. The system of inland waterways was complete by 1780, and seaports were accessible from all parts of the country.

The industrial potential of many continental European countries was also weakened by the imposition of protective tariffs on goods imported from other countries. The purpose of this mercantilist policy was to develop national self-sufficiency and to maintain a favorable balance of trade, but it also had the negative effect of limiting economic growth. For example, in the Dutch Republic (the kingdom of the Netherlands after 1815) a long tradition of protecting established industries prevented that country from importing the raw materials and machines needed to develop new industries. Since protectionism invited retaliation from trading partners, it also tended to shrink the size of potential overseas markets. Britain adopted a policy of free trade during the 1840s, and it applied pressure on other European countries to adopt the same policy.

A further obstacle to European industrialization was aristocratic hostility, or at least indifference, to industrial development. In Britain the aristocracy, which consisted of noblemen and gentry, were themselves often involved in capitalist enterprise and did not have the same suspicion of industry and trade that their counterparts in France and Spain often harbored. Many members of the British aristocracy, such as the entrepreneur "Turnip Townshend" (see Chapter 17), were agricultural capitalists who improved the productivity of their estates. Others were involved in mining. The Duke of Devonshire encouraged the exploitation of the copper mines on his estate, while the Duke of Bridgewater employed the engineer James Brindley to build a canal from the duke's coal mines in Worsley to Manchester in 1759. He later had Brindley extend the canal from Manchester to the mouth of the Mersey River, connecting the textile region of Manchester with the large northern industrial city of Liverpool.

One reason for the British aristocracy's support for economic growth was that many of its members, especially the gentry, rose into its ranks from other social and economic groups. These individuals tended to be sympathetic to the values of a commercial and an industrial society. The same attitude toward commerce and industry simply did not exist among the nobility in France before the revolution, much less among German *Junkers.* These groups had little connection with industrial or commercial society, whose values they held in very low regard. Consequently they rarely invested in industry.

Even among the European middle classes, the same type of competitive entrepreneurial spirit that was exhibited by men like Matthew Boulton seems to have been in large part lacking. Capitalism was by no means absent in European countries, but the conduct of business was characterized by greater caution and less willingness to obtain new capital from loans or the sale of stock to investors. This went hand in hand with a reluctance to innovate as well as a distaste for competition and the maximizing of profits. Consequently continental European countries failed to produce many counterparts to the captains of industry who had contributed much of the capital, technology, and entrepreneurial spirit to the Industrial Revolution in Britain.

A final reason for the slow industrialization of continental European countries was that they lacked the abundant raw materials that were readily accessible in Britain. The natural resources that Britain had in greatest quantities were coal and iron ore, both of which were indispensable to industrialization. At the same time British farms provided ample supplies of raw materials for the wool and leather industries. The French and the Germans had some coal deposits, but they were more difficult to mine, and they were not located near ocean ports. Continental countries also lacked the access to other raw materials that Britain could import through its vast trading network, and in particular from its overseas colonies. With a large empire on four continents and the world's largest merchant marine, Britain had abundant supplies of raw materials such as cotton as well as the capacity to import them cheaply and in large quantities. The greater difficulty European countries had in obtaining these raw materials did not prevent them from industrializing; it simply made the process slower.

FEATURES OF CONTINENTAL INDUSTRIALIZATION

During the first half of the nineteenth century, especially after 1830, Belgium, France, Switzerland, Germany, and Austria began to introduce machinery into the industrial process, use steam power in production, concentrate labor in large factories, and build railroads. This continental European version of the Industrial Revolution is usually described as an imitative process, one in which entrepreneurs or government officials simply tried to duplicate the economic success that Britain had achieved by following British example. Continental European nations did indeed rely to some extent on British industrial machinery. Some of them also relied on British skilled labor when they began to build their first factories and ironworks. In a few instances, in violation of British law, foreign agents actually smuggled blueprints, models, or machine parts out of Britain. British engineers, entrepreneurs, and managers were also occasionally hired to run British-style factories in France and Germany. But each European nation, responding to its own unique combination of political, economic, and social conditions, followed its own course of industrialization.

■ **Medal Struck in 1835 to Commemorate the First German Railroad, from Nuremberg to Fürth**

Industry is depicted as a female figure with her arm resting on a winged wheel. The first railroad in Europe had opened in England in 1825. German engineers had modeled their first locomotive on that of George Stephenson.

One distinctive feature of continental European industrialization was that once countries like Belgium and Germany began to industrialize, their governments played a much more active role in encouraging and assisting in the process. In contrast to Britain, whose government allowed private industry to function with few economic controls, continental governments became active partners in the industrial process. They supplied capital for many economic ventures, especially the railroads and roads. In Prussia the government ran the mines. Many continental governments also imposed protective tariffs to prevent an influx of cheap British goods from underselling the products of their own fledgling industries. In a few cases continental European governments even provided financial support for investors in an effort to encourage capital formation. In some places, such as Austria, the state eliminated the regulations of urban guilds that had restricted industrial development in rural regions.

A second major feature of continental European industrialization is that banks, particularly in Germany and Belgium, played a central role in industrial development. This was necessitated by the low level of capital formation on the Continent and the reluctance of entrepreneurs to take risks by investing money themselves. Banks in Germany and Belgium played a particularly active role in stimulating industry. Drawing on the resources of both small and large investors, these corporate banks became in effect industrial banks, building railroads and factories themselves in addition to making capital available for a variety of industrial ventures.

A third distinct feature of continental European industrialization is that the railroads actually contributed to the beginning of industrial development. In Great Britain the railroads were introduced some sixty years after industrial-

ization had begun and thus helped sustain a process of economic development that had been long afoot. By contrast the railroads on the Continent provided the basic infrastructure of its new economy and became a major stimulus to the development of all other industries. Railroads also gave continental European governments the ability to transport military troops quickly in time of war, which helps to explain why governments supported railroad construction with such enthusiasm. In Belgium, which was the first continental European nation to industrialize, the new government built a national railroad system during the 1830s and 1840s, not only to stimulate industry but also to unify the newly independent nation.

Of all the European countries that industrialized, only Belgium appears to have followed the British model closely by developing coal, iron, and textiles as the three main sectors of the new economy. Other countries tended to concentrate their activity in one specific area. France emphasized textiles, especially those like worsted woolens that did not compete with British cottons. France's coal production and consumption never matched that of Great Britain or Belgium, and after 1850 it fell behind that of Germany as well. In 1860 France was importing 43 percent of its coal, and it was still relying on charcoal rather than coal to smelt pig iron. In Germany the main economic advances, which did not begin until 1850, occurred mainly in the area of heavy industry, that is, coal, iron, and engineering rather than textiles. Together with the United States, Germany began to offer the main economic competition to the British economy by the end of the nineteenth century.

INDUSTRIALIZATION IN THE UNITED STATES

Industrialization in the United States began during the 1820s, not long after Belgium and France had begun to experience their own industrial revolutions. It occurred first in the textile industry in New England, where factories using water power produced goods for largely rural markets. New England also began producing two domestic hardware products—clocks and guns—for the same market. Between 1850 and 1880 a second region between Pittsburgh and Cleveland became industrialized. This region specialized in heavy industry, especially steelmaking and the manufacture of large machinery, and it relied on coal for fuel.

American industrialization conformed to many of the patterns established in Britain and on the European continent. As in Britain and France, the development of cottage industry preceded industrialization. Most of the industrial machinery used in the United States during the nineteenth century was modeled on imports from Britain. The most significant American technological innovation before 1900 was the sewing machine, which was patented by Elias Howe in 1846 and then developed and improved upon by Isaac Singer in the 1850s. This new machine was then introduced in Europe, where it was used in the production of ready-to-wear garments.

After 1865, when American industrialization began to spread rapidly across the entire country, American entrepreneurs made a distinctive contribution to the industrial process in the area of business organization, especially the operation of international firms. Toward the beginning of the twentieth century, American manufacturers streamlined the production process by introducing the assembly line, a division of labor in which the product passes from one operation to the next until it is fully assembled. The assembly line required the production of interchangeable parts, another American innovation, first used in the manufacture of rifles for the U.S. government.

Like Great Britain, the United States possessed vast natural resources, including coal. It also resembled Britain in the absence of governmental involvement in the process of industrialization. The main difference between the industrialization of the two countries is that during the nineteenth century labor in America was in relatively short supply. This placed workers in a more advantageous situation in dealing with their employers and prevented some of the horrors of early British industrialization from recurring on the other side of the Atlantic. Only with the influx of European immigrants in the late nineteenth century did the condition of American workers deteriorate and begin to resemble the early nineteenth-century British pattern.

INDUSTRIAL REGIONALISM

Although we have discussed the industrialization of entire nations, the process usually took place within smaller geographical regions. There had always been regional specialization in agriculture, with some areas emphasizing crops and others livestock. During the Industrial Revolution, however, entire economies acquired a distinctly regional character. Regional economies began to take shape during the days of the domestic system, when merchants employed families in certain geographical areas, such as Lancashire in England, to produce textiles. In these regions there was a close relationship between agricultural and industrial production, in that members of the same household participated in both processes. Related industries, such as those for finishing or dyeing cloth, also sprang up close to where the cotton or wool yarn was spun and the cloth woven.

As industrialization spread outside Britain, this regional pattern became even more pronounced. In France the centers of the textile industry were situated near the northeastern border near Belgium and in the area surrounding Lyons in the east-central part of the country. Both of these areas had attracted rural household industry before the introduction of textile machinery. In Germany the iron industry was centered in the Ruhr region, where most of the country's coal was mined. In the city of Essen on the Ruhr River the industrialist Alfred Krupp (1812–1887) established an enormous steelmaking complex that produced industrial machinery, railroad equipment, and guns for the Prussian army. Within the Habsburg Empire most industry was located in parts of Bohemia (now the Czech Republic). The region in Ireland that experienced the most significant measure of industrialization was the northern province of Ulster, a linen-producing area that became Europe's leading producer of ready-to-wear women's undergarments and men's shirts in the 1850s.

The development of regional economies did not mean that markets were regional. The goods produced in one region almost always served the needs of people outside that particular area. Markets for most industrial goods were national and international, and even people in small agricultural villages created a demand for manufactured goods. The French iron industry, for example, was centered in the eastern part of the country, but it catered to the needs of the wealthier segments of its own and other European populations, as did the iron industry in the Ruhr region in Germany and the textile industry in the north of England.

The development of regional industrial economies helps to explain the striking contrast that persisted well into the twentieth century between the parts of countries that had become heavily industrialized and those that retained at least many of the appearances of a preindustrial life. In Britain and the rest of Europe industrial machinery and factories were not introduced into every village. Some areas remained exclusively agricultural, while others continued a tradition of rural industry. This pattern was particularly evident in France, where mechanized industry was concentrated in a limited number of centers in the northeastern half of the country. In 1870 more than two-thirds of the French population still lived in rural areas. As economic growth and industrial development continued, however, agricultural regions eventually began to lose their traditional character. Even if industry itself did not arrive, the

■ **A Colossal Steam-Driven Hammer, Nicknamed "Fritz," Installed by Alfred Krupp at His Steelworks in Essen in 1861**
Krupp's factory was located in the Ruhr region of Germany, the main center in that country for heavy industry.

larger industrial economy made its mark. Agriculture itself became mechanized, while railroads and other forms of mechanized transport integrated these areas in a national economy.

The Effects of Industrialization

The Industrial Revolution had a profound impact on virtually every aspect of human life. It encouraged the growth of the population and the economy, affected the conditions in which people lived, changed family life, created new divisions within society, and transformed the traditional rural landscape. The changes that it brought about were most evident in Britain, but in time they have occurred in every country that has industrialized, including the United States.

POPULATION AND ECONOMIC GROWTH

The most significant of these changes was the sustained expansion of both the population and the economy. As we have seen, the Industrial Revolution in Britain was facilitated by a significant population increase in the eighteenth century. That growth had created a plentiful supply of relatively cheap labor, which in turn had helped to bring about a marked increase in industrial output. As industry grew, population kept pace, and each provided a stimulus to the growth of the other.

Most contemporary observers in the late eighteenth century did not believe that this expansion of both the population and the economy could be sustained indefinitely. The most pessimistic of these commentators was Thomas Malthus (1766–1834), an English cleric who wrote *An Essay on the Principle of Population* in 1798. Malthus argued that population had a natural tendency to grow faster than the food supply. Thus, unless couples exercised restraint by marrying late and producing fewer children, the population would eventually outstrip the resources necessary to sustain it, resulting in poor nutrition, famine, and disease. These "positive checks" on population growth, which sometimes were initiated or aggravated by war, would drive population back to sustainable levels. These checks would also end periods of economic expansion, which generally accompany increases in population. For example, in the fourteenth century the Black Death, which killed about one-third of the European population, also ended a significant period of economic growth. A similar but less severe contraction of the European population and economy occurred in the second half of the seventeenth century, marking the end of the economic expansion that had begun in the sixteenth century. In both these instances the increase in population put pressure on the food supply, raised the price of food, reduced employment, and lowered wages. The scarcity of food and the reduced nutritional levels that followed had made the population vulnerable to disease. If these demographic and economic patterns were to recur, we might expect that the significant expansion of the population and the economy that took place in eighteenth-century England would likewise reach its limits, just around the time that Malthus was writing.

This predicted cyclical contraction of both the population and the economy did not take place. Europe for the first time in its history managed to escape the "Malthusian population trap." Instead of being sharply reduced after 1800, the population continued to expand at an ever faster rate, doubling in Great Britain between 1800 and 1850 and following a similar pattern of rapid growth in all other countries that had industrialized. At the same time the economy, instead of contracting or collapsing, continued to grow and diversify.

It is not absolutely clear how Europe avoided the Malthusian trap in the nineteenth century. Part of the answer lies in the greater productivity of agriculture, which resulted from either private initiative, as in Britain, or governmental agrarian reforms, as in Austria. The importation of grain from central and eastern Europe also helped to feed the larger, more urbanized population. Improvements in medicine and public health reduced mortality during the

THOMAS MALTHUS WRITES ABOUT THE LIMITATION OF POPULATION

·················

Thomas Malthus was an English cleric who studied at Cambridge University and then took a position as a curate in a country parish in Surrey. In 1798 he published anonymously An Essay on the Principle of Population, *in which he advanced the argument that population tends to grow faster than the food supply, resulting in periodic subsistence crises that keep population in check. In the greatly expanded second edition of this book, published in 1803, Malthus distinguished between preventive and positive checks on the growth of population.*

The checks to population, which are constantly operating with more or less force in every society, and keep down the number to the level of the means of subsistence, may be classed under two general heads: the preventive and the positive.

The preventive check is peculiar to man and arises from that distinctive superiority in his reasoning faculties, which enables him to calculate distant consequences. . . . But man cannot look around him and see the distress which frequently presses upon those who have large families . . . These considerations are calculated to prevent a great number of persons in all civilized nations from pursuing the dictate of nature in an early attachment to one woman.

The positive checks to population are extremely various and include every cause, whether arising from vice or misery, which in any degree contributes to shorten the natural duration of human life. Under this head therefore may be enumerated all unwholesome occupations, severe labour and exposure to the seasons, extreme poverty, bad nursing of children, great towns, excesses of all kinds, the whole train of common diseases and epidemics, wars, pestilence, plague and famine.

On examining the obstacles to the increase of population which I have classed under the heads of preventive and positive checks, it will appear they are all resolvable into moral restraint, vice and misery. Of the preventive checks, the restraint from marriage, which if not followed by irregular gratifications may properly be termed moral restraint. Promiscuous intercourse, unnatural passions, violations of the marriage bed, and improper arts to conceal the consequences of irregular connexions clearly come under the head of vice. Of the positive checks, those which appear to arise unavoidably from the law of nature may be called exclusively misery; and those which we bring upon ourselves, such as wars, excesses and many others it would be in our power to avoid, are of a mixed nature. They are brought upon us by vice, and their consequences are misery.

Source: From Thomas Malthus, *An Essay on the Principle of Population, 2nd Edition*, 1803.

nineteenth century, helping to maintain the size of the industrial population. But it was mainly developments in industry itself, especially the increased accumulation of capital, that kept Europe from succumbing to yet another cycle of depopulation and economic contraction. The accumulation of capital over a long period of time was so great that industry was able to employ large numbers of workers even during the 1790s and 1800s, when Europe was at war. Since they had income from wages, workers were willing to marry earlier and have larger families, and with lower food prices because of higher agricultural productivity they could afford to maintain a healthier diet and purchase more manufactured goods as well. Thus the Industrial Revolution itself, coupled with the changes in agriculture that accompanied it, proved Malthus wrong.

While the rapid growth of population in industrialized societies up until the late twentieth century is incontestable, the record of economic growth is not so clear. In order to claim that the Industrial Revolution has resulted in sustained economic growth, we have to take a broad view, looking at an overall pattern of growth and ignoring certain cyclical recessions and depressions. Nations that have industrialized, beginning with European countries in the nineteenth century, have all experienced a significant increase in both gross national product and per capita income over the long run. Although the contrast between the size of these industrial economies and those of preindustrial, agrarian countries is staggering, economic growth in industrialized countries was not always rapid or continuous. During the first six decades of industrialization in Britain, for example, economic growth was actually fairly slow, mainly because so much capital went into subsidizing the long war against France (1792–1802; 1804–1815). During this period Britain spent an average of 60 million English pounds, or 25 percent of its national income, on war. Nevertheless, there still was steady growth, and more important, the type of Malthusian economic contraction or collapse that had followed all previous periods of expansion did not occur. To that extent we can say that the Industrial Revolution has resulted in sustained economic growth in the West.

STANDARDS OF LIVING

Ever since the early years of the Industrial Revolution, a debate has raged over the effect of industrialization on the standard of living and the quality of life of the laboring population. The supporters of the two main schools of thought on this issue have been called the optimists and the pessimists. The optimists have always emphasized the positive effects of both the process of mechanization and the system of industrial capitalism that arose during the revolution. They have focused on the success that industrialized nations have achieved in escaping the Malthusian trap and in achieving sustained economic growth. The Industrial

Revolution, so they argue, has resulted in an unprecedented rise in individual income, which has made it possible for the mass of a country's population to avoid poverty for the first time in human history. In the second half of the twentieth century many optimists claimed that the industrialization of Western nations provided a blueprint for African, Asian, and Latin American countries that wished to escape from the poverty of a predominantly agrarian economy relying on organic sources of energy.

The main yardstick that the optimists have used to measure the improvement in living standards is per capita real income, that is, income measured in terms of its actual purchasing power. Real income in Great Britain rose about 50 percent between 1770 and 1850 and more than doubled during the entire nineteenth century. This increase in income allowed workers to improve their diets as well as to purchase more clothing and other basic commodities. These improvements, however, did not affect the lives of most workers for a long period of time—in Great Britain not until 1820, about sixty years after the beginning of industrialization. The increases that occurred after that date, moreover, were only averages, concealing disparities among workers with different levels of skill. Only in the late nineteenth and twentieth centuries did industrialization raise the real income of all workers to a level that made the benefits of industrialization apparent.

Even if the pessimists concede a long-term increase in real income, it has never been substantial enough to persuade them that industrialization was on balance a positive good, at least for the working class. The pessimists have always stressed the negative effects of industrial development on the life of the lower classes. In their way of thinking, industrialization was an unmitigated disaster. The cause of this disaster in their eyes was not the process of mechanization but the system of industrial capitalism°. This form of capitalism is characterized by the ownership of factories by private individuals and by the employment of wage labor. Like earlier forms of mercantile and agricultural capitalism, it involved a systematic effort to reduce costs and maximize profits. In the pursuit of this goal, employers tried to keep wages as low as possible and to increase production through labor-saving technology, thus preventing workers from improving their lot.

Pessimists regarding the Industrial Revolution over the past two centuries have usually claimed a moral basis for their position. In this respect they follow in a tradition begun by the poet William Blake (1757–1827), who referred to the new factories as "satanic mills," and the socialist Friedrich Engels, who in *The Condition of the Working Class in England in 1844* (1845) accused the factory owners in England of mass murder and robbery. Much pessimist writing has also been used to support a program of social or political reform. The German social philosopher Karl Marx (1818–1883), with whom Engels often collaborated and whose views we shall discuss more fully in Chapter 21, used his critique of industrial capitalism to call for a communist revolution in which the working class would seize political power and acquire ownership of the means of production.

Most of the evidence that social critics have used to support the pessimist position has come from the early period of industrialization in Britain, when incomes were either stagnant or declining and when conditions in factories and industrial and mining towns were most appalling. It is difficult to measure these living standards statistically, but the weight of qualitative evidence suggests that they deteriorated during the nineteenth century. Working-class housing was makeshift and crowded, and there were few sanitary facilities. A new word, *slum,* was coined to refer to these poverty-stricken working-class neighborhoods. Poor drainage and raw sewage gave rise to a host of new hygienic problems, especially outbreaks of typhus and cholera. Between 1831 and 1866 four epidemics of cholera killed at least 140,000 people in Britain, most of whom lived in poorer districts.

The impact of industrialization and urbanization on the environment was no less harrowing. The burning of coal and the use of industrial chemicals polluted the urban atmosphere. The famous London fogs, which were actually smogs caused by industrial pollutants, presented a serious public health problem throughout the nineteenth century and did not begin to disappear until the introduction of strict regulations on the burning of coal in the 1950s.

While life in the city was bleak and unhealthy, working conditions in the factory were monotonous and demeaning. Forced to submit to a regimen governed by the operation of the machine, workers lost their independence as well as any control whatsoever over the products of their labor. They were required to work long hours, often fourteen hours a day, six days a week, with few breaks. Factory masters locked the doors during working hours, and they assessed fines for infractions such as opening a window when the temperature was unbearable, whistling while working, and having dirty hands while spinning yarn. Work in the mines was a little less monotonous, but it was physically more demanding and far more dangerous.

WOMEN, CHILDREN, AND INDUSTRY

During the early Industrial Revolution in Great Britain, large numbers of children and women were recruited into the workforce, especially the textile and mining industries. In the woolen industry in the western part of England, for example, female and child labor together accounted for 75 percent of the workforce. Children under age 13 made up 13 percent of the cotton factory workforce, and those under age 18 made up 51 percent. This pattern of employment reflects the demands of industrialists, who valued the hand skills and dexterity that children possessed as well as the greater amenability of both children and women to the discipline of factory labor. Some of the machines that were introduced into the textile industry in the late eighteenth century were specifically designed for women and children.

Female and child labor was both plentiful and cheap. Children received only one-sixth to one-third the wages of a grown man, while women generally took home only one-third to one-half of that adult male income. There was no lack of incentive for women and children to take one of these low-paying jobs. In a family dependent on wages, everyone needed to work, even when a large labor pool kept wages depressed.

The participation of both women and children in the workforce was not new. In an agricultural economy all members of the family contributed to the work, with parents and children, young and old, all being assigned specific roles. Rural industry also involved the labor of all members of the family. When people began working in the factories, however, they were physically separated from the home, making it impossible for workers to combine domestic and occupational labor.

As the workplace became distinct from the household, family life underwent a fundamental change, although this change did not occur immediately. During the early years of the Industrial Revolution, members of many families found employment together in the factories and mines. Factory owners also tried to perpetuate many aspects of family life in the new industrial setting, defining the entire factory community as an extended family, in which the factory owner played the paternalistic role. Gradually, however, mothers found it impossible to care for their youngest children on the job, and most of them dropped out of the full-time workforce. The restriction of child labor by the British Factory Act of 1833 reinforced this trend and led to the establishment of a fairly common situation in which the male wage earner worked outside the home while his wife stayed home with the children. As one young girl who worked in the mines testified before a parliamentary commission investigation of child labor in 1842, "Mother takes care of the children."

As more and more mothers left the factories, the female workforce became increasingly dominated by those who were unmarried. The few female workers who were married with children either came from the very poorest segments of society or took jobs only because their husbands were ill or unemployed. Neither the pay these women received nor the jobs they performed gave them financial autonomy or social prestige. Becoming an independent wage earner meant little when women's wages were on average one-third to one-half those of men. The jobs assigned to women within industry, such as operating textile machinery, generally required the least skill. When men and women were employed in the same workplace, the women were invariably subordinated to the authority of male workers or foremen, thereby perpetuating the patriarchal patterns that prevailed in preindustrial society. The Industrial Revolution did nothing to improve the status of women, and even their

The Sadler Committee on Child Labor

The widespread use of child labor in Britain during the early decades of the Industrial Revolution led to efforts by social reformers and members of Parliament to regulate the conditions under which children worked. Parliament passed legislation restricting the number of hours that all children could work in textile mills in 1819 and 1829, but neither of these laws were enforced effectively, and they did not apply to all industries. Complaints of inhumane treatment, moral degradation, and exploitation of child workers continued to surface. In 1831 Michael Sadler (1780–1835), a Tory member of the British Parliament, introduced a bill in Parliament to limit the number of hours that all children could work to ten hours per day. Like many social reformers, Sadler was inspired by what he considered his Christian duty to protect dependent members of the community.

Sadler chaired the committee to which his bill was referred. In order to muster support for the bill, Sadler held hearings in which child workers themselves came before the committee to report on the conditions under which they lived and worked. The success of his bill was by no means guaranteed. Many members of Parliament were deeply committed to the policy of *laissez-faire,* according to which the government should not intervene in the operation of the economy, treating it instead as a self-regulating machine. Sadler had to convince his colleagues

that they should modify that policy in the case of children, on the grounds that the state was obliged to provide for the welfare of children when their parents were unable to do so. He also needed to make the members of Parliament and the broader public aware of the brutality of the conditions under which the children worked.

The hearings that took place were not a trial in the strict sense of the word, but they possessed many of the features of a judicial investigation, not unlike those conducted by grand juries in criminal cases. The committee's proceedings were intended to expose, condemn, and ultimately remedy misconduct by the factory owners. Procedurally the committee members had more latitude than did courts of law. Since these parliamentary committees were designed to extract information rather than to bring offenders to trial, they did not need to adhere to any established judicial guidelines. There was no cross-examination of witnesses, nor could factory owners present a defense. The witnesses in this investigation were chosen because Sadler knew they would reveal the evils of the factory system.

The testimony presented to the Sadler Committee produced abundant

Child Workers
These children are on their way to work in the Yorkshire textile mills.

evidence of the exploitation and physical abuse of child workers. Some of the most harrowing testimony came from the examination of a 17-year-old boy, Joseph Hebergam, on July 1, 1832. Hebergam revealed that he had begun the work of worsted spinning at age 7, that he worked at the factory from five A.M. until eight P.M., and that he had only thirty minutes for lunch at noon, leaving him to eat his other meals while standing on the job. In the factory there were three overlookers, one of whom was responsible for greasing the machinery and another for whipping the workers. The latter overlooker walked continually up and down the factory with whip in hand.

When asked where his brother John was working, Joseph replied that he had died three years before at age 16. Sadler then inquired into the cause of his brother's death. The boy responded, "It was attributed to this, that he died from working such long hours and that it had been brought on by the factory. They have to stop the flies [part of the textile machinery] with their knees, because they go so swift they cannot stop them with their hands; he got a bruise on the shin by a spindle-board, and it went on to that degree that it burst; the surgeon cured that, then he was better; then he went to work again; but when he had worked about two months more his spine became affected, and he died." The witness went on to explain that his own severe labor had damaged his knees and ankles so much so that he found it painful to walk. His brother and sister would help carry him to the factory, but when they arrived late, even by as little as five minutes, the overlooker beat all three of them "till we were black and blue." At the request of the committee, Joseph then stood up to show the condition of his limbs. He reported the death of another boy who had sustained massive injuries when he was caught in the shaft of the machinery he was running. Joseph concluded his testimony by recounting how the factory owners had threatened him and his younger brothers with losing their jobs if they testified before the committee.

The hearings of the Sadler Committee were widely publicized, but they fell short of realizing their original objective. The bill, which eventually was approved by Parliament as the Factory Regulations Act of 1833, prohibited the employment of children under age 9 in all factories. Boys and girls were allowed to work up to nine hours a day from age 9 until their thirteenth birthdays, and up to twelve hours a day from age 13 until their eighteenth birthdays. The long-term effect of this legislation was to establish in Western industrialized countries the principle that childhood was a period of life set aside for education rather than work. ■

■ **Child Labor in the Textile Industry**
Factory girls operate machinery in a textile mill under the tight supervision of the factory owner.

Questions of Justice

1. Sadler's opponents could have objected that his "investigation" was a setup, since Sadler had chosen and coached the witnesses. In what ways was this proceeding fair? In what ways was it unfair?

2. This investigation was concerned with the achievement of social justice rather than the determination of criminal culpability. What were the advantages of using legislative committees in such an undertaking?

3. Child labor was not a new phenomenon in the early eighteenth century. Why did the Industrial Revolution draw attention to this age-old practice?

Taking It Further

Horn, Pamela. *Children's Work and Welfare, 1780–1890.* 1996. An examination of the scale and nature of child employment in Britain and changing attitudes toward the practice.

exclusion from certain occupations, such as mining by an act of Parliament in 1842, only reinforced a new sexual division of labor that was even more rigid than that which had prevailed in preindustrial society.

CLASS AND CLASS CONSCIOUSNESS

As Europe became more industrialized and urbanized, and as the system of industrial capitalism became more entrenched, writers began to use a new terminology to describe the structure of society. Instead of claiming that society consisted of a finely graded hierarchy of ranks to which individuals belonged by virtue of their occupations or their legal status, they divided society into three classes that could be distinguished by the type of property people owned and the manner in which they acquired it. At the top of this new social hierarchy was the aristocracy, consisting of those who owned land and received their income in the form of rent. The middle class or bourgeoisie, which included the new factory owners, possessed capital and derived their income from profits, whereas the working class

owned nothing but their own labor and received their income from wages.

This new model of society served a number of different purposes. Marx and Engels used it to construct a comprehensive theory of historical development. According to this theory, the middle class had struggled for centuries to seize power from the aristocracy, while the working class would eventually take power from the middle class. For Marx and Engels, conflicts over control of the means of production created a state of continuous class conflict. David Ricardo (1772–1823), an English social philosopher whose political and social allegiances were very different from those of Marx, used a similar model of society to illustrate the crucial role that the middle class played in the economy. Ricardo compared society to a coach in which the middle class was the driver guiding the vehicle, the working class was the horse that provided the labor, and the aristocracy was the nonpaying passenger.

Historians and social scientists disagree over the extent to which men and women in the nineteenth century were actually conscious of their membership in these classes. Marxist historians have claimed that the growth of wage

---

THE EMPLOYMENT OF WOMEN

The German social philosopher Friedrich Engels (1820–1895) was one of the founders of modern socialism. He and Karl Marx collaborated in writing The Communist Manifesto (1848), *and he edited the final two volumes of Marx's* Capital *after Marx died. Having served as a manager in a factory in Manchester, Engels described these conditions throughout Britain in one of his earliest works,* The Condition of the Working Class in England in 1844 (1845). *He emphasized the exploitation and brutalization of the lower classes as they were turned into a wage-earning proletariat. In this passage Engels describes the negative effects of factory labor on women and the family.*

The employment of women at once breaks up the family; for when the wife spends twelve or thirteen hours every day in the mill, and the husband works the same length of time there or elsewhere, what becomes of the children? They grow up like weeds; they are put out to nurse for a shilling or eighteen pence a week, and how they are treated may be imagined. Hence the accidents to which little children fall victims in the factory districts multiply to a terrible extent . . . Women often return to the mill three or four days after confinement, leaving the baby of course; in the dinner hour they must hurry home to feed the children and eat something, and what kind of suckling that can be is also evident. Lord Ashley repeats the testimony of several work women: "M.H., twenty

years old, has two children, the youngest a baby, that is tended by the other, a little older. The mother goes to the mill shortly after five o'clock in the morning, and comes home at eight at night; all day the milk pours from her breasts so that her clothing drips with it". . . . The use of narcotics to keep the children still is fostered by this infamous system and has reached a great extent in the factory districts. Dr. Johns, Registrar in Chief for Manchester, is of opinion that this custom is the chief source of the many deaths from convulsions. The employment of the wife dissolves the family utterly and of necessity, and this dissolution in our present society, which is based upon the family, brings the most demoralising consequences for parents and children. A mother who has no time to trouble herself about her child, to perform the most ordinary loving services for it during its first year, who scarcely indeed sees it, can be no real mother to the child, must inevitably grow indifferent to it, treat it unlovingly like a stranger. The children who grow up under such conditions are utterly ruined for later family life, can never feel at home in the family which they themselves found, because they have always been accustomed to isolation, and they contribute therefore to the already general undermining of the family in the working-class.

Source: From Friedrich Engels, *The Condition of the Working Class in England in 1844,* translated by F. K. Wischnewtzky (London: S. Sonnenshein, 1892).

■ Capital and Labor

This cartoon, drawn by the illustrator Gustave Doré, depicts wealthy industrialists gambling with workers tied together as chips.

labor, the exploitation of the working class, and conflicts between capital and labor encouraged workers to think of themselves not so much as individuals who claimed a certain social status but as members of a large class of workers who shared the same relationship to the means of production. These historians have pointed to the growth of trade unions, political campaigns for universal male suffrage, and other forms of working-class organization and communication as evidence of this awakening of class consciousness.

Other historians have claimed that people were less conscious of their class position. True, at certain times in the early nineteenth century some workers thought of themselves as members of a class whose interests were in conflict with those of factory owners and financiers. It was much more common, however, for them to think of themselves primarily as practitioners of a particular craft, as members of a local community, or as part of a distinct ethnic minority, such as the Irish. When they demanded the right to vote, workers based their claim on their historic constitutional rights, not on the interests of all wage earners. When they demonstrated in favor of the ten-hour working day, they did so to improve the conditions in which they worked, not to advance the struggle of all workers against the middle class. The work experiences of laborers were too varied to sustain an awareness among most of them that they belonged to one homogeneous group.

The various capitalists, shopkeepers, and factory owners who belonged to the bourgeoisie also lacked a clear sense of their membership in a single middle class. These people were capable of achieving solidarity on certain occasions, such as when they feared that workers threatened their in-

terests. As we discussed in Chapter 17, the bourgeoisie often criticized the lifestyle and values of the landed aristocracy in print. But like the working class, the bourgeoisie was too diverse to allow for the development of a unifying class consciousness inspired by an identity of economic interest against those who occupied social positions either above or below them.

Working men and women showed a marked reluctance to engage in militant or violent action against their employers. Appeals for working-class solidarity to a large extent fell on deaf ears. It is true that on certain occasions workers took violent action against their employers. In 1812 groups of hand-loom weavers in the highly industrialized Midland region of England engaged in a determined campaign to destroy the new power looms that they blamed for rising unemployment and low wages. Often disguised and operating at night, these "Luddites," who took their name from their mythical leader Ned Ludd, smashed the new textile machinery that factory owners had introduced. (Even today people who object to the introduction of new technology are referred to as Luddites.) The government sent an army of 12,000 men to suppress the Luddites, a task made difficult by the protection given them by their communities.

The Luddites did not, however, represent the majority of the English working class. Factory workers in particular seemed reluctant to join working-class organizations. Most of the workers who participated in these associations and who campaigned for the rights of the workers were independent artisans who had little interest in the struggle that Marx and Engels had predicted would result in the victory of the working class.

The incident that contributed most directly to the formation of working-class consciousness in Britain in the early decades of the nineteenth century was the so-called Peterloo Massacre. In August 1819 some 60,000 people, most of them workers and their families, gathered at St. Peter's Field in the northern English city of Manchester. The purpose of the meeting was to demonstrate support for universal male suffrage, annual parliaments, and relief from low wages, high prices, and long hours. Shortly after the meeting began, a violent confrontation took place between the demonstrators and the volunteer cavalry (known as yeomen), who belonged to the city's bourgeoisie. Frightened by the size of the demonstration and determined to prevent concessions that would reduce their profits, the yeomen decided to disperse the meeting by force. In the confrontation that ensued, the yeomen trampled hundreds of demonstrators and slashed many others with their swords, killing 11 people and wounding more than 400. "Over the whole field," wrote one observer, "were strewed caps, bonnets, hats, shawls, and shoes, and other parts of male and female dress, trampled, torn and bloody."

The Peterloo Massacre has been referred to as class warfare. The events of that day may have occurred too spontaneously to justify the claim that they conformed to a pattern of deliberate middle-class violence against the working class. There is little doubt, however, that the demonstration and the brutal response to it contributed to the growth of class solidarity, especially among the workers. The massacre inspired a number of calls for working-class revolution. The young poet Percy Shelley (1792–1822), upon hearing of what had occurred in Manchester, called the working class to action:

> *Rise like lions after slumber*
> *In unvanquishable numbers*
> *Shake your chains to earth like dew*
> *Which in sleep had fallen on you.*
> *You are many—they are few.*

The British working class did not respond to Shelley's summons. The Peterloo Massacre did not lead to a working-class revolution in Britain. This violent encounter did, however, lead to the further organization of British labor, most notably in the Chartist movement, which staged a number of demonstrations in favor of parliamentary reform and the improvement of working conditions. (We shall discuss the activities of the Chartists more fully in Chapter 21.) The Peterloo Massacre also contributed to the growth of class consciousness in Britain. In the age of the Industrial Revolution, the division of society on the basis of class became increasingly apparent to workers

■ **The Industrial City of Sheffield in 1858**
Factories dominated the landscape of the city of Sheffield, which specialized in the production of steel, silver-plated items, and other metal goods.

**■ Pont Cysyllte
Aqueduct in Wales**
This cast-iron bridge, 1,000 feet in length, carried the water of the Caledonian Canal across the River Dee, 127 feet below. It was built in 1805.

and members of the middle and working classes, as well as to social commentators such as David Ricardo and Karl Marx.

THE INDUSTRIAL LANDSCAPE

As industry spread throughout Europe and reached into areas that previously had been untouched by mechanization, urban and rural areas underwent dramatic changes. The most striking of these changes took place in the new industrial towns and cities, some of which had been little more than country towns before the factories were built. Manchester, for example, grew from a modest population of 23,000 people in 1773 to a burgeoning metropolis of 105,000 by 1820. Large factories with their smokestacks and warehouses, ringed by long rows of houses built to accommodate the armies of new industrial workers, gave these cities an entirely new and for the most part a grim appearance.

Cities experienced the most noticeable changes in physical appearance, but the countryside also began to take on a new look, mainly as a result of the transport revolution. The tunnels, bridges, and viaducts that were constructed to accommodate the railroad lines and the canals that were built to improve inland water transportation made an indelible imprint on the traditional terrain. In many ways this alteration of the landscape served as a statement of the mastery over nature that human beings had achieved at the time of the Scientific Revolution. The Industrial Revolution

finally fulfilled the technological promise of that earlier revolution, and one of its effects was the actual transformation of the physical world.

The advent of modern industry also brought about a change in attitudes toward the landscape. The destruction of natural beauty in the interest of economic progress stimulated an appreciation of nature that had not been widespread during the medieval and early modern periods. Before the Industrial Revolution many features of the countryside, especially mountains, were viewed as obstacles to either travel or human habitation, not as sources of aesthetic appreciation. Urbanization and industrialization changed those perceptions, triggering a nostalgic reaction that became one of the sources of the romantic movement, which we shall consider in greater detail in the next chapter. Some of the idyllic landscapes of the English romantic painter John Constable (1776–1837), for example, represented an imaginative recreation of a countryside that had already been transformed by the advent of industry by the time he painted them.

Industry did not always form a blight on the landscape or offend artistic sensibilities. Some of the new industrial architecture, especially the viaducts and aqueducts that traversed valleys in the mountainous regions of the country, were masterpieces of modern engineering and architecture. Sir Walter Scott (1771–1832), the Scottish romantic novelist, claimed that the cast-iron Pont Cysyllte aqueduct in Wales, which carried the waters of the Caledonian Canal 127 feet above the River Dee, was the most beautiful work

**■ Joseph M. W. Turner,
*Rain, Steam and Speed:
The Great Western Railway*
(1844)**
This was one of the first oil
paintings that had the railroad
locomotive as its theme.

of art he had ever seen. The railroads also had the ability to inspire the artistic imagination, as they did in Joseph Turner's (1775–1851) romantic painting *Rain, Steam and Speed,* which captured the railroad's speed and beauty.

Industry, Trade, and Empire

As the middle of the nineteenth century approached, Britain towered above all other nations in the volume of its industrial output, the extent of its international trade, and the size of its empire. In industrial production it easily outpaced all its competitors, producing two-thirds of the world's coal, about half of its cotton cloth, half of its iron, and 40 percent of its hardware. Little wonder that Britain became known as "the workshop of the world." Britain controlled about one-third of the world's trade, and London had emerged as the undisputed financial center of the global economy. Britain's overseas empire, which included colonies in Canada, the Caribbean, South America, India, Southeast Asia, and Australia, eclipsed that of all other European powers and would continue to grow during the second half of the century.

These three great British strengths—industry, trade, and empire—were closely linked. Britain's colonies in both Asia and in the Americas served as trading depots, while the promotion of trade led directly to the acquisition of new imperial possessions. Even when Britain did not formally acquire

territory, it often established exclusive trading relationships with those countries, thereby creating an informal "empire of trade." Trade and empire in turn served the purposes of industry. Many of the raw materials used in industrial production, especially cotton, came from Britain's imperial possessions. At the same time, those possessions provided markets for Britain's mass-produced manufactured goods. Such imperial markets proved immensely valuable when France blockaded its ports during the Napoleonic wars and thereby cut into British trade with the entire European continent (see Chapter 18).

The great challenge for Britain during the nineteenth century was to find new markets for its industrial products. Domestic demand had been strong at the beginning of the Industrial Revolution, but by the 1840s British workers did not possess sufficient wealth to purchase the increasingly large volume of hardwares and textiles manufactured in the mills and factories. Britain had to look overseas to find markets to sell the bulk of its industrial products. One possibility was to market them in other European countries, such as France and Germany, where demand for manufactured goods was high. These countries, however, were in the midst of their own industrial revolutions, and their governments had often legislated high protective tariffs against British goods to encourage the growth of their own industries. Britain therefore chose instead to market its goods in the less economically developed parts of the world, including its own colonies. We can see this trading pattern in the relationships that Britain had with three different regions: East Asia, India, and Latin America. In all three areas, moreover, British military power and diplomatic influence were enlisted in the cause of industry, trade, and empire.

EAST ASIA: THE OPIUM WAR, 1839–1842

British conflict with China provides the best illustration of the way in which the British desire to promote trade led to the acquisition of new colonies. For three centuries the Chinese had tightly controlled their trade with European powers. By 1842, however, British merchants, supported by the British government, managed to break down these barriers and give Britain a foothold in China, allowing it to exploit the East Asian market.

The conflict arose over the importation of opium, a narcotic made from poppy seeds and produced in great quantities in India. This drug, which numbed pain but also had hallucinogenic effects and could cause profound lethargy, was in widespread use in Europe and had an even larger market in Asia. In China opium had become a national addiction by the middle of the eighteenth century, and the situation became much worse when British merchants increased the volume of illegal imports from India to China in the early nineteenth century. The Chinese government prohibited the use of opium, but since it had difficulty enforcing its own edicts, it decided to put an end to the opium trade.

Chinese efforts to stop British merchants from importing opium led to an increase in tensions between China and Britain. The situation reached a climax in 1839, when the Chinese seized 20,000 chests of opium in the holds of British ships and spilled them into the China Sea. It is unknown what effect the opium had on the fish, but the incident led to a British attack on Chinese ports. In this conflict, the first Opium War (1839–1842), the British had the advantage of superior naval technology, itself a product of the Industrial Revolution. The first iron-clad, steam-driven gunboat used in combat, the *Nemesis,* destroyed Chinese batteries along the coast, and an assault by seventy-five British ships on Chinkiang forced the Chinese to come to terms. In a treaty signed in 1842 China ceded the island of Hong Kong to the British, reimbursed British merchants for the opium it had destroyed, and opened five Chinese ports to international trade. As part of this settlement, each of these ports was to be governed by a British consul who was not subject to Chinese law. In this way Britain expanded its empire, increased its already large share of world trade, and found new markets for British manufactured goods in East Asia.

INDIA: ANNEXATION AND TRADE

The interrelationship of industry, trade, and empire became even clearer in India, which became known as the jewel in Britain's imperial crown. As we have seen in Chapter 19, Britain gained control of the Indian province of Bengal in the eighteenth century and subsequently acquired a number of other Indian states. After the Sepoy Mutiny of 1857 the British government brought all of India under its direct control.

Political control of India during the nineteenth century served the interests of British trade in two ways. First, it gave British merchants control of the trade between India and other Asian countries. Second, Britain developed a favorable balance of trade with India, exporting more goods to that country than it imported. Taxes paid to the British government by India for administering the country and interest payments on British loans to India increased the flow of capital from Calcutta to London. The influx of capital from India was in large part responsible for the favorable balance of payments that Britain enjoyed with the rest of the world until World War I. The capital that Britain received from these sources as well as from trade with China was funneled into the British economy or invested in British economic ventures throughout the world.

Control of India also served British interests by supplying British industries with raw materials while giving them access to the foreign markets they needed to make a profit. This promotion of British industry was done at the expense of the local Indian economy. The transportation of cotton grown in India to British textile mills, only to be returned to India in the form of finished cloth certainly retarded, if it did not destroy, the existing Indian textile industry. Resentment of this economic exploitation of India became one of the main sources of Indian nationalism in the late nineteenth century.

LATIN AMERICA: AN EMPIRE OF TRADE

British policy in Latin America developed differently from the way it had in China and India, but it had the same effect of opening up new markets for British goods. Great Britain was a consistent supporter of the movements for independence that erupted in South America between 1810 and 1824 (see Chapter 19). Britain supported these movements not simply because it wished to undermine Spanish and Portuguese imperialism, but because it needed to acquire new markets for its industrial products. Britain did not need to use military force to open these areas to British trade, as it did in China. Once the countries became independent, they attracted large volumes of British exports. In 1840 the British cotton industry shipped 35 percent of all its exports to Latin American countries, especially to Argentina, Brazil, Uruguay, Mexico, and Chile. Britain also exported large amounts of capital to these Latin American countries by investing vast sums of money in their economies. Britain thus established an informal "empire of trade" in Latin America. These countries were not controlled by Britain, but they had the same economic relationship with Britain as did Canada, Australia, and other parts of the British Empire.

British investment and trade brought the newly independent nations of Latin America into the industrial world economy. In so doing, however, Britain assigned these countries to a dependent position in that economy, not unlike the position that India occupied in Asia about the same time. One effect of this dependence was to transform the small, self-sufficient village economies that had developed alongside the large plantations in Central and South America. Instead of producing goods themselves and selling them within their own markets, these villages now became suppliers of raw materials for British industry. At the same time the Latin American population became more dependent upon British manufactured goods. This transformation not only retarded or destroyed native Latin American industry but also created huge trade deficits for Latin American countries by the middle of the nineteenth century.

CONCLUSION
Industrialization and the West

By 1850 the Industrial Revolution had begun to bring about some of the most dramatic changes in human life recorded in historical documents. Not since the Neolithic Age, when people began to live in settled villages, cultivate grains, and domesticate animals, did the organization of society, the patterns of work, and the landscape undergo such profound changes. In many ways the Industrial Revolution marked the watershed between the old way of life and the new. It gave human beings unprecedented technological control over nature, made employment in the home the exception rather than the rule, and submitted industrial workers to a regimentation unknown in the past. It changed family life, gave cities an entirely new appearance, and unleashed new and highly potent political forces, including the ideologies of liberalism and socialism, which shall be discussed in depth in the next chapter.

Industrialization changed the very definition of the West. In the Middle Ages the predominant cultural values of Western countries were those of Christianity, while in the eighteenth century those values were more often associated with the rational, scientific culture of the Enlightenment. Now, in the nineteenth century, the West was increasingly becoming identified with industrialization and the system of industrial capitalism it had spawned. In discussing the prospects of industrialization in the Ottoman Empire in 1856, a British diplomat wrote that "Europe is at hand, with its science, its labor, and its capital," but that the Qur'an and other elements of traditional Turkish culture "are so many obstacles to advancement in a Western sense." The Industrial Revolution was creating new divisions between the West and the non-Western world.

Until the late nineteenth century, industrialization took place only in nations that have traditionally formed a part of the West. Beginning in the 1890s, however, countries that lay outside the West or on its margins began to introduce industrial technology and methods. Between 1890 and 1910 Russia and Japan underwent a period of rapid industrialization, and in the second half of the twentieth century a number of countries in Asia and Latin America, as well as Turkey, followed suit. This process of industrialization and economic development is often described as one of Westernization, and it has usually led to conflicts within those countries between Western and non-Western values. The industrialization of these nations has not always been fully successful, and even when it has, doubt remains as to whether those nations should now be included within the West. Industrialization outside Europe and the United States reveals once again that the composition of the West changes from time to time and that its boundaries are often difficult to define.

Suggestions for Further Reading

For a comprehensive list of suggested readings, please go to www.ablongman.com/levack/chapter20

Ashton, T. A. *The Industrial Revolution,* reprint edition with preface by P. Hudson. 1992. The classic statement of the optimist position, identifying the benefits of the revolution.

Berg, Maxine. *The Age of Manufactures, 1700–1820: Industry, Innovation and Work in Britain.* 1994. A study of the process and character of specific industries, especially those employing women.

Brinley, Thomas. *The Industrial Revolution and the Atlantic Economy: Selected Essays.* 1993. Essays challenging the view that Britain's Industrial Revolution was a gradual process.

Deane, Phyllis. *The First Industrial Revolution.* 1967. The best study of technological innovation in Britain.

Gutmann, Myron. *Toward the Modern Economy: Early Industry in Europe, 1500–1800.* 1988. A study of cottage industry, especially in France.

Hobsbawm, E. J. *Industry and Empire.* 1968. A general economic history of Britain from 1750 to 1970 that analyzes the position of Britain in the world economy.

Jacob, Margaret. *Scientific Culture and the Making of the Industrial West.* 1997. An exploration of the spread of scientific knowledge and its connection with industrialization.

Morris. R. J. *Class and Class Consciousness in the Industrial Revolution, 1780–1850.* 1979. A balanced treatment of the link between industrialization and class formation.

Pollard, Sidney. *Peaceful Conquest: The Industrialization of Europe, 1760–1970.* 1981. A linking of coal supplies to economic development.

Rule, John. *The Vital Century, England's Developing Economy, 1714–1815.* 1992. A general economic history establishing the importance of early eighteenth-century developments.

Stearns, Peter. *The Industrial Revolution in World History,* 2nd ed. 1998. The best study of industrialization in a global context.

Teich, Mikulas, and Roy Porter, eds. *The Industrial Revolution in National Context: Europe and the USA.* 1981. Essays illustrating similarities as well as national differences in the process of industrialization.

Wrigley, E. A. *Continuity, Chance and Change: The Character of the Industrial Revolution in Britain.* 1988. Includes the best discussion of the transition from an advanced organic economy to one based on minerals.

Ideological Conflict and National Unification, 1815–1871

ON MARCH 18, 1871, THE PRESIDENT OF THE FRENCH GOVERNMENT, Adolphe Thiers, sent a small unit of troops to Paris to seize cannons that had been used against Prussian forces during their siege of the city a few months before. The artillery was in the possession of the National Guard, the citizen militia of Paris. The members of the National Guard felt that the government had abandoned them by recently concluding an armistice with the Prussians, who were still camped outside the city. They also believed that the government was determined to gain control of the city, which had refused to comply with the orders of the national government. When the troops reached the city, they encountered a hostile crowd of Parisians, many of whom were armed. The crowd surrounded the two generals who led the detachment, placed them up against a wall, and executed them.

This action by Parisian radicals led to a full-scale siege of Paris by government troops. In the city a committed group of radicals formed a new municipal government, the Paris Commune, which was a revival of the commune established during the French Revolution in 1792. The Commune took steps to defend the city against the government troops, and during its short life it implemented several social reforms. The Communards, as the members were known, set up a central employment bureau, established nurseries for working mothers, and recognized women's labor unions. For many decades the Commune served as a model of working-class government.

The Paris Commune lasted only a few weeks. On May 21 the troops of the provisional government poured through the gates of the city, and during the "bloody week" that followed they took the city street by street, demolishing the barricades and executing the Communards. The Communards retaliated by executing a number of hostages, including the archbishop of Paris. They also burned

The Proclamation of the German Empire in the Hall of Mirrors at Versailles, January 21, 1871: King William I of Prussia, standing on the dais, is being crowned Emperor of Germany. At the center of the picture, dressed in a white uniform jacket, is Otto von Bismarck, the person most responsible for the unification of all German territory in one empire.

down the Tuileries Palace, the hall of justice, and the city hall. During this one week at least 25,000 Communards were killed, and since many bodies were burned in the fires that consumed the city, the numbers were probably much higher.

The short life of the Paris Commune marks the climax of a tumultuous period of European history. Between 1815 and 1871 Europe witnessed numerous movements for reform, periodic uprisings, and several revolutions. The people who participated in these momentous developments were inspired in large part by ideologies°, theories of society and government that lay at the basis of political programs. The ideologies that developed during this period—liberalism, conservatism, socialism, and nationalism—were the product of historical developments that had arisen in the West, and they endowed the West with a distinctive political culture. These four ideologies also provide a framework for understanding the complex and often confusing political and social history of the West from 1815 until 1871.

In this chapter we shall address four questions: (1)What were the main features of the ideologies that inspired people to political action during those years? (2) How did the encounters among the people who espoused these ideologies shape the political history of Europe between 1815 and 1848? (3) How did liberal and conservative leaders use the ideology of nationalism as a tool to unite the people of various territories into nation-states between 1848 and 1871? (4) What role did ideology play in international warfare and diplomacy, especially in efforts to maintain the balance of power during this period?

New Ideologies in the Early Nineteenth Century

In the wake of the French Revolution, four new ideologies—liberalism, conservatism, socialism, and nationalism—led thousands of Europeans to call for profound changes in the established political order. These ideologies had their roots in the works of eighteenth-century writers, but they developed into integrated systems of thought and inspired political programs in the first half of the nineteenth century. All four were influenced by the two great transformations of the West that we have discussed in Chapters 18 and 20: the French Revolution and the Industrial Revolution.

LIBERALISM: THE PROTECTION OF INDIVIDUAL FREEDOM

Liberalism° is anchored in the beliefs that political, social, and economic freedoms are of supreme importance and that the main function of government is to protect those freedoms. The political agendas of nineteenth-century liberals varied from one country to another, but they all pursued three main objectives. The first objective was to establish and protect individual rights, such as the freedom of the press, freedom of religion, and freedom from arbitrary arrest and imprisonment. Liberals sought to guarantee these rights by having them enumerated in written constitutions. Opposed to aristocratic privilege, liberals supported the principle of equality before the law. They also tended to be anticlerical, a position that led to frequent tension between them and the Roman Catholic Church. As defenders of individual freedom they often campaigned to end slavery and serfdom.

The second objective of liberals was the extension of the franchise (the right to vote) to all property owners, especially those in the middle class. For the most part liberals were opposed to giving the vote to the lower classes, on the grounds that poor people, with little property of their own, could not be trusted to elect representatives who would protect property rights. Liberals also were opposed to giving the vote or any other form of political power to women. They justified the exclusion on the grounds that the proper arena for female activity was the home, where women occupied their natural domain. In this way liberals subscribed to the theory of separate spheres, which assigned men and women different gender roles. As we know from Chapter 17, this theory was based on the belief that women were different in nature from men and that they should be confined to an exclusively domestic role as chaste wives and mothers. Liberals believed that only male property holders should be allowed to participate in public affairs.

The third objective of liberals was to promote free trade with other nations and to resist government regulation of the domestic economy. This economic dimension of liberal ideology, which is grounded in the writings of the Scottish economist Adam Smith and other advocates of free-market capitalism, is usually referred to as laissez-faire°, a phrase that means "let (people) do (as they choose)." Advocates of *laissez-faire* held that the government should intervene in the economy only if it is necessary to maintain public order and protect property rights. As merchants and manufacturers, liberals favored a policy of *laissez-faire* because it offered them the freedom to pursue their own self-interest without governmental interference and thereby realize greater profits.

Some of the earliest expressions of liberal ideology appear in the works of John Locke and his fellow Whigs in England during the late seventeenth century (see Chapter 15). In arguing against the absolutist policies of Charles II and James II, the Whigs emphasized the inviolability of private property rights, freedom from state economic control, and the rights of those who held property to participate in government. In the eighteenth century these ideas were developed by Enlightenment thinkers who defended natural rights, and they found eloquent expression at the time of the American Revolution and the early years of the French

Revolution. Liberal ideas were also embodied in the constitutions implemented in France, Germany, and Spain at the end of the Napoleonic period. When those constitutions and their principles came under attack after 1815, liberals sought to restore the freedoms they had lost without destroying public order. At that time liberalism became a distinct ideology.

Some liberals sought to realize their goals through the establishment of a republic, but the ideal form of government for most early nineteenth-century liberals was a limited monarchy—one in which the ruler did not act arbitrarily and suppress representative assemblies. As we shall see, liberal reformers in Britain during the 1830s wished to preserve the monarchy, and in France Louis-Philippe, the bourgeois citizen king installed during the Revolution of 1830, sought to implement liberal programs. In Germany, Belgium, and Greece, liberal revolts ended in the establishment of a constitutional monarchy.

Liberalism found its greatest strength among the urban middle class: merchants, manufacturers, and members of the professions. These people formed the group that felt most aggrieved by their exclusion from political life during the eighteenth and early nineteenth centuries and most eager to have government protect their property. Their substantial wealth provided the basis for their claim to acquire a share of political power, and as manufacturers and merchants they had the most to gain from an economy unfettered by government regulations.

Liberal economic theory found its most articulate proponents in England, where industrial capitalism achieved its earliest and most significant successes. Two of the most prominent liberals in early nineteenth-century Britain were the utilitarians Jeremy Bentham and David Ricardo. Utilitarians° advocated economic and social policies which in their view would provide the greatest good to the greatest number of people. In pursuit of that goal, Bentham (1748–1832), a legal scholar and political philosopher, proposed that a government should give its people as much freedom as possible and impose only those laws that were socially useful. The economist Ricardo (1772–1823), the son of a Dutch Jewish banker, argued that the absence of government intervention would spur economic growth and thus contribute to the benefit of all people. This *laissez-faire* argument was far more persuasive to manufacturers than to workers. In *Principles of Political Economy and Taxation* (1819), Ricardo argued that if wages were left to the law of supply and demand, they would fall to near subsistence levels. This "iron law of wages" made it clear that *laissez-faire* liberalism would not benefit the working class.

CONSERVATISM: PRESERVING THE ESTABLISHED ORDER

Throughout human history people have demonstrated a desire to maintain the established order and to resist change. In the early nineteenth century, however, the ideals of the Enlightenment and the radical changes ushered in by the French Revolution led to the formulation of a new ideology of conservatism°, a set of ideas intended to prevent a recurrence of the revolutionary changes of the 1790s. The main goal of conservatives after 1815 was to preserve the monarchies and aristocracies of Europe against liberal and national movements.

The new conservatism justified the existing political order as the product of gradual change. This defense was most clearly expressed in the writings of the fiery, Irish-born parliamentary orator Edmund Burke (1729–1797). Burke was no reactionary; he advocated a number of changes in British public life, including electoral reform and a reorganization of the British Empire. But Burke, who is regarded as the founder of modern conservatism, had enormous respect for the existing social order, which he considered the handiwork of God. Society according to Burke was a partnership between the living, the dead, and those who had yet to be born. Only within this historical partnership could change take place, and all changes would have to be gradual.

On the basis of this view of the social order, Burke attacked the liberal and radical ideas that had inspired the French Revolution. In *Reflections on the Revolution in France* (1790), he asserted that equality was a dangerous myth; its effect would be to allow those at the bottom to plunder those at the top and thus destroy the social order. Unlike the French revolutionaries, Burke had no faith in the people, whom he referred to as the "swinish multitude." In Burke's view rights did not derive from human nature, as they did for the philosophes of the Enlightenment; rights were privileges that had been passed down through the ages and could be preserved only by a hereditary monarchy. By claiming abstract rights for all men, the French had rejected their inheritance.

Conservative ideology justified the institution of monarchy on the basis of religion. The French writer Louis de Bonald (1754–1840) argued that Christian monarchies were the final creation in the development of both religious and political society. Only monarchies of this sort could preserve public order and prevent society from degenerating into the savagery witnessed during the French Revolution. De Bonald and his fellow French writer, Joseph de Maistre (1754–1821), rejected the entire concept of natural rights and reiterated the traditional doctrine of divine right, by which all political power came from God. De Maistre also reinforced the alliance between the throne and the altar by considering the monarchy and the Church as the foundations of the social order. In the nineteenth century, conservatives throughout Europe thought of religion as the basis of society. This view was especially strong in Catholic countries such as France and Austria, but Burke had put forth the same argument in Protestant England.

A fine line separates conservatism, which allows for gradual change, and reaction, which is the effort to reject any changes that have taken place and return to the old order. Early nineteenth-century conservatism provided an ideological foundation for the reactionary movements that arose throughout Europe after 1815. These movements had both national and international dimensions. In all western European countries, groups of influential and powerful individuals, usually nobles and churchmen, were determined to return to the days when they had more power. Internationally, the rulers of Europe, under the leadership of the Austrian foreign minister Clemens von Metternich, established a mechanism known as the Concert of Europe° to preserve the map of Europe as it was drawn at the Congress of Vienna (see Chapter 18). To do so meant taking concerted action against liberals and nationalists who attempted to unseat dynastic rulers.

In keeping with the identification of conservatism with religion, three of the four original powers in the Concert of Europe—Prussia, Russia, and Austria—gave their alliance a religious mission. At the Congress of Vienna Tsar Alexander I drafted a document in which the cooperation among European monarchs, whom he referred to as "the delegates of Providence," would be based "upon the sublime truths which the holy religion of Our Savior teaches." The British refused to subscribe to this document, claiming that it was "sublime mysticism and nonsense." So too did the future Louis XVIII of France (which was only a probationary member of the Concert of Europe until 1818) and even the pope. But Alexander's commitment to defend Christian values in what he called the Holy Alliance provided a religious foundation for the reactionary and repressive policies that Russia, Prussia, and Austria took steps to implement.

SOCIALISM: THE DEMAND FOR EQUALITY

Socialism, the third new ideology of the early nineteenth century, arose in response to the development of industrial capitalism and the liberal ideas that justified it. Socialism calls for the ownership of the means of production (such as factories, machines, and railroads) by the community, with the purpose of reducing inequalities of income, wealth, opportunity, and economic power. In small communities, such as some early nineteenth-century socialist settlements, ownership could be genuinely collective. In a large country, however, the only practical way to introduce socialism would be to give the ownership of property to the state, which represents the people.

The main appeal of socialism was the prospect of remedying the deplorable social and economic effects of the Industrial Revolution. As we have seen in Chapter 20, the short-term effects of industrialization included wretched working conditions, low wages, a regimentation of the labor force, and a declining standard of living. Socialists did not object to the mechanization of industry as such. Like liberals, they wanted society to be as productive as possible.

They did, however, object to the system of industrial capitalism that accompanied industrialization and the liberal economic theory that justified it.

The earliest socialists were known as Utopian socialists, a name given to them because they envisioned the creation of ideal communities in which perfect social harmony and cooperation would prevail. One of these Utopian socialists, the British industrialist and philanthropist Robert Owen (1771–1858), actually turned his mill in New Lanark, Scotland, into a model socialist community in which the principles of cooperation prevailed and where the workers were housed and their children were educated. In 1825 he established a similar community in New Harmony, Indiana. Utopian socialism was not particularly concerned with the granting of political rights to workers, nor did it encourage class consciousness or class tensions.

A second generation of socialists became more concerned with using the power of the state to improve their lot. The most influential of these socialists was the French democrat Louis Blanc (1811–1882), who proposed that the state guarantee workers' wages as well as employment in times of economic depression. He also wanted the state to support the creation of workshops in which workers would sell the product of their labor directly without a intermediary. The principle underlying Blanc's concept of the social order was, "From each according to his abilities; to each according to his needs." Blanc's brand of socialism began a long tradition in which workers tried to improve their lot by influencing government. This initiative was closely related to the radical democratic goal of universal male suffrage, which became one of the main objectives of many socialists after 1840.

The most radical form of nineteenth-century socialism was formulated by the German social philosopher Karl Marx (1818–1883). Marx was much more preoccupied than other socialists with the collective identity and political activities of the working class. Reading about working conditions in France during the early 1840s, he became convinced that workers in industrial society were the ultimate example of human alienation and degradation. In 1844 he began a lifetime association with another German-born philosopher, Friedrich Engels (1820–1895), who as we have seen in the preceding chapter exposed the wretchedness of working class life in Manchester. Marx and Engels began to think of workers as part of a capitalist system, in which they owned nothing but their labor, which they sold to capitalist producers for wages.

Marx and Engels worked these ideas into a broad account of historical change in which society moved inevitably and progressively from one stage to another. They referred to the process by which history advanced as the dialectic°. Marx acquired the idea of the dialectic from the German philosopher Georg Wilhelm Friedrich Hegel (1770–1831), who believed that history advanced in stages as the result of the conflict between one idea and

■ **Karl Marx**

Karl Marx, the German social philosopher who developed the revolutionary socialist doctrine of communism.

another. Marx disagreed with Hegel on the source of historical change, arguing that material or economic factors rather than ideas determined the course of history. Hence Marx's socialist philosophy became known as dialectical materialism°.

According to Marx and Engels, the first stage of the dialectic had taken place when the bourgeoisie, who received their income from capital, seized political power from the aristocracy, who received their income from land, during the English and French revolutions. Marx and Engels predicted that the next stage of the dialectic would be a conflict between the bourgeoisie and the working class or proletariat°, which received its income from wages. This conflict, according to Marx and Engels, would result in the triumph of the working class. Led by a committed band of revolutionaries, the proletariat would take control of the state, establish a dictatorship so that they could implement their program without opposition, and usher in a classless society.

Marx and Engels issued this call to action in *The Communist Manifesto* (1848), which ended with the famous words, "Working men of all countries unite!" Marx's brand of socialism, communism°, takes its name from this book. Communism is a revolutionary ideology that advocates the overthrow of "bourgeois" or capitalist institutions and the transfer of political power to the proletariat. Communism differs from other forms of socialism in its call for revolution, its emphasis on class conflict, and its insistence on complete economic equality. Communism belongs to a tradition that originated among members of the extreme wing of the democratic movement at the height of the French Revolution. One of those radicals, François-Noël Babeuf (1760–1797), demanded economic as well as political equality, called for the common ownership of land, and spoke in terms of class warfare. Marx's achievement was to place Babeuf's radical ideas in a new philosophical and historical framework. That framework, dialectical materialism, was explained in great detail in Marx's monumental three-volume work, *Das Kapital,* or *Capital* (1867–1894).

Nationalism: The Unity of the People

Nationalism, the fourth new ideology of the early nineteenth century, also took shape during and after the French Revolution. A nation° in the nineteenth-century sense of the word refers to a large community of people who possess a sense of unity based on a belief that they have a common homeland and share a similar culture. The ideology of nationalism° is the belief that the people who form this nation should have their own political institutions and that the interests of the nation should be defended and promoted at all costs.

The geographical boundaries of nations do not often correspond to the geographical boundaries of states, which are administrative and legal units of political organization. For example, in the early nineteenth century Germans often referred to their nation as comprising all people who spoke German. At that time, however, there were several German states, such as Prussia, Bavaria, and Baden. A primary goal of nationalists is to create a nation-state°, a single political entity that governs all the members of a particular nation. The doctrine that justifies this goal is national self-determination°, the claim that any group that considers itself a nation has the right to be ruled only by members of its own nation and to have all the members of the nation included in this state.

The ideology of nationalism had roots in the French Revolution. Most of the revolutionary steps taken in France during the 1790s were undertaken in the name of a united French people. Article 3 of the *Declaration of the Rights of Man and Citizen* (1789) declared that "the principle of all authority rests essentially in the nation." The French Republic was constructed as the embodiment of the French nation. It gave an administrative unity to the French people and encouraged them to think of themselves as sharing a

KARL MARX AND FRIEDRICH ENGELS, *THE COMMUNIST MANIFESTO* (1848)

These excerpts from the final pages of The Communist Manifesto *provide a summary of the communist plan for establishing a socialist society by means of revolution. They reveal Marx's view of history as a succession of class conflicts and his prediction that the proletariat will become the ruling class. The appeal for working-class solidarity and revolution illustrates the power of socialist ideology to inspire people to action.*

The history of all past society has consisted in the development of class antagonisms, antagonisms that have assumed different forms at different epochs. But whatever form they may have taken, one fact is common to all past ages, viz., the exploitation of one part of society by the other . . .

We have seen above that the first step in the revolution by the working class is to raise the proletariat to the position of ruling class, to win the battle of democracy. The proletariat will use its political supremacy to wrest, by degrees, all capital from the bourgeoisie, to centralize all means of production in the hands of the state, i.e., of the proletariat organized as the ruling class, and to increase the total of productive forces as rapidly as possible.

If the proletariat during its contest with the bourgeoisie is compelled by the force of circumstances, to organize itself as a class, if by means of a revolution it makes itself the ruling class, and as such sweeps away by force the old conditions of production, then it will, along with these conditions, have swept away the conditions for the existence of class antagonisms and of classes generally, and will thereby have abolished its own supremacy as a class. . . .

Communists disdain to conceal their views and aims. They openly declare that their ends can be attained only by the violent overthrow of all existing social conditions. Let the ruling classes tremble at a Communist revolution. The proletarians have nothing to lose but their chains. They have a world to win. WORKING MEN OF ALL COUNTRIES UNITE!

Source: From Karl Marx and Friedrich Engels, *The Communist Manifesto*, 1848, translated in English by Friedrich Engels in 1888.

---

common cultural bond. Instead of a collection of regions, France had become *la patrie*, or the people's native land.

Nationalists emphasized the antiquity of nations, arguing that there had always been a distinct German, French, English, Swiss, or Italian people living in their respective homelands. This claim involved a certain amount of fiction, since in the past the people living in those lands possessed little cultural unity. There was little uniformity, for example, in the languages spoken by people who were identified as German, French, or Italian. Until the eighteenth century most educated Germans wrote in French, not German. Only a small percentage of Italians spoke Italian, and the main language of many Italian nationalists of the nineteenth century was French. Even after nation-states were formed, a large measure of linguistic, religious, and ethnic diversity has persisted within those states and has made true cultural unity impossible. The nation is therefore something of a myth—an imagined community to which nationalists believe they belong, but which in reality has never existed.

The ideal of the nation-state has proved almost impossible to realize. The boundaries of nations and states have never fully coincided. Patterns of human settlement are too fluid to prevent some members of a particular cultural group from living as a minority in a neighboring state. Germans, for example, have always lived in Poland, Spaniards in Portugal, and Italians in Switzerland. France at the time of the French Revolution probably came closest to realizing the ideal of a nation-state, claiming jurisdiction over most French people. Nevertheless, different regional identities and languages, such as that of the people of the southern province of Languedoc who spoke their own dialect, prevented the emergence of a powerful sense of national identity in all parts of France until the late nineteenth or early twentieth century.

In Britain the creation of a nation-state has been a complicated process. National consciousness, which is a people's belief that they belong to a nation, developed earlier in England than in any other country in Europe. In the sixteenth century almost all English people spoke the same language, and they were also subject to the same common law. In 1536, however, Wales was united to the kingdom of England, thereby including two nations, the English and the Welsh, in the same state. In 1707 England and Scotland were united in a new state, the United Kingdom of Great Britain, and in 1801 Ireland was brought into the United Kingdom as well. Thus the United Kingdom now included four nations: the English, the Welsh, the Scots, and the Irish. The task of building a British, as opposed to an English or a Scottish, nation in this multinational state has taken time, and to this day Britons are more accustomed to think of themselves as primarily English or Scottish than as British.

Other peoples have faced even more daunting obstacles than the British in constructing nation-states. Many nations have been subsumed within large empires, such as Hungarians and Croatians in the Habsburg Empire and Greeks and Serbs in the Ottoman Empire. In those empires, nationalist movements have often taken the form of separatist revolts or wars of independence, in which a nationalist group attempted to break off and form a nation-state of its own. A very different situation prevailed in Germany and Italy, where people who shared some linguistic and cultural traditions lived under the control of many different sovereign states of varying size. In these cases nationalist movements have sought to unite the smaller states into a larger nation-state.

One of the great paradoxes of nationalism is that the acquisition of colonies overseas often strengthened nationalist sentiment at home. The military conquest of these lands became a source of pride for the people in the metropolis, and also gave them a sense of cultural superiority. The main source of British national pride was the rapid spread of British control over one-quarter of the world's surface during the eighteenth and nineteenth centuries. Nationalism could also promote the supremacy of one's own nation over others. The French revolutionaries who conquered a large part of the European continent in the early nineteenth century justified their expansion on the grounds that they were superior to the rest of the human race. In 1848 a fervent German nationalist declared his support for "the preponderance of the German race over most Slav races." The Italian national leader Giuseppe Mazzini (1805–1872), whom we shall discuss in detail shortly, preferred to be called a patriot rather than a nationalist on the grounds that nationalists were imperialists who sought to encroach on the rights of other peoples.

Nationalism was often linked to liberalism during the early nineteenth century, when both movements supported revolutionary programs to realize the goal of national self-determination. Liberals believed that representative government and a limited expansion of the franchise would provide a firm foundation for the establishment of the nation-state, both in nations like Spain with a long tradition of self-rule as well as in countries like Greece that were seeking their independence from autocratic rulers. In Germany and Italy, where there was no central state, nationalists and liberals joined together to create one. There was, however, a difference of emphasis between the two ideologies, even in the early years of the nineteenth century. Liberalism stressed individual freedom, whereas nationalism was more concerned with political unity. At times those different ideals came into conflict with each other. The liberal doctrine of free trade, for example, ran into conflict with the doctrine of economic nationalism, which encouraged the protection of national industries. The nationalist German economist Friedrich List (1780–1846) claimed that free trade benefited only the wealthy and the powerful; he advocated instead protective tariffs to benefit German businesses.

Nationalism was just as capable of supporting conservatism as liberalism in the early nineteenth century. Since the nation was often viewed as having deep roots in the distant past, some nationalists glorified the monarchical and hierarchical political arrangements that prevailed in the Middle Ages. In 1848 conservative Prussian landlords rallied around the cause of "God, King, and Fatherland." Later in the nineteenth century, nationalism became identified almost exclusively with conservatism when the lower middle classes began to prefer the achievement of national glory, either in warfare or in imperialistic pursuits, to the establishment of individual freedom.

CULTURE AND IDEOLOGY

As the four great ideologies of the Western world were developing during the nineteenth century, they were influenced by two powerful cultural traditions: scientific rationalism and romanticism. These two traditions represented two sharply divergent sides of modern Western culture.

Scientific Rationalism

Scientific rationalism is a manner of thinking that traces its origins to the Scientific Revolution and reached its full flowering in the Enlightenment. This tradition has provided a major source of Western identity ever since the late eighteenth century. It has stressed the powers of human reason and considered science superior to all other forms of knowledge. Scientific rationalism is essentially a secular tradition, in that it does not rely on theology or Christian revelation for its legitimacy. The effort to construct a science of human nature, which was central to Enlightenment thought, belongs to this tradition, while the Industrial Revolution, which involved the application of scientific knowledge to production, was one of its products.

During the nineteenth century, scientific rationalism continued to have a powerful influence on Western thought and action. As scientific knowledge continued to grow, and as more people received a scientific education, the values of science and reason were proclaimed more boldly. Scientific knowledge and an emphasis on the importance of empirical data (that which can be tested) became essential components of much social thought. The clearest statement that science was the highest form of knowledge and would lead inevitably to human progress was the secular philosophy of positivism°.

The main elements of positivism were set forth by the French philosopher Auguste Comte (1798–1857). Like many thinkers in the Enlightenment tradition, Comte argued that human society passed through a succession of historical stages, each leading to a higher level. It had already passed through two stages, the theological and the metaphysical, and it was now in the third, the positive or scientific stage. The word *positive* in this context means that which has substance or concrete reality, as opposed to that which is abstract or speculative. Comte predicted that in the final positive stage of history the accumulation of factual or scientific knowledge would enable thinkers, whom we now call sociologists, to discover the laws of human behavior and thus make possible the improvement of society. This prediction of human progress, and Comte's celebration of the liberation of knowledge from its theological shackles, had particular appeal to liberals, especially those who harbored hostility to the Roman Catholic Church.

The values of science and the belief in its inevitable advance also influenced the social thought of Karl Marx. His ideology of communism has been referred to as scientific socialism, in that it too is based on a vision of history determined solely by positive, in this case material or economic, developments. Marxism rejects the metaphysical, idealistic world of Hegel and the theology of all Christian religion and thus fits into the same scientific tradition to which positivism and earlier Enlightenment thought belongs.

Romanticism

The cultural tradition that posed the greatest challenge to scientific rationalism was romanticism°. This tradition originated as an artistic and literary movement in the late eighteenth century, but it soon developed into a more general worldview. The artists and writers who identified themselves as romantics recognized the limits of human reason in comprehending reality. Unlike scientific rationalists, they used intuition and imagination to penetrate deeper levels of being and to comprehend the entire cosmos. Romantic art, music, and literature therefore appealed to the passions rather than the intellect.

Romantics did not think of reality as being simply material, as did the positivists. For them it was also spiritual and emotional, and their purpose as writers and artists was to communicate that non-empirical dimension of reality to their audiences. Romantics also had a different view of the relationship between human beings and nature. Instead of standing outside nature and viewing it objectively, in the manner of a scientist analyzing data derived from experiments, they considered themselves a part of nature and emphasized its beauty and power.

As an art form, romanticism was a protest against classicism and in particular the classicism that prevailed in the late eighteenth century. As we discussed in Chapter 17, classicism reflects a worldview in which the principles of orderliness and rationality prevail. Classicism is a disciplined style that demands adherence to formal rules that governed the structure as well as the content of literature, art, architecture, and music. By contrast romanticism allows the artist much greater freedom. In literature the romantic protest against classicism led to the introduction of a new

poetic style involving the use of imagery, symbols, and myth. One example of this new approach is "Rime of the Ancient Mariner" (1798) by the English romantic poet Samuel Taylor Coleridge (1772–1834), which uses the sun and moon as powerful symbols in describing a nightmarish sea voyage.

Many romantic works of literature, such as the novels of the Scottish author Sir Walter Scott (1771–1832), were set in the Middle Ages, a period often associated with superstition rather than science and enlightenment. Other romantic prose works explore the exotic, the weird, the mysterious, and even the satanic elements in human nature. Mary Shelley's introspective novel *Frankenstein* (1818), an early example of science fiction that embodies a critique of scientific rationalism, incorporates many of these themes.

Within the visual arts, romanticism also marked a rebellion against the classicism that had dominated eighteenth-century culture. Classicism emphasized formality and symmetry in art, and it celebrated the culture of an ideal Greek and Roman past. By contrast, romantic painters depicted landscapes that evoked a mood and an emotion rather than an objective pictorial account of the surroundings. Romantic paintings were intended to evoke feeling rather than to help the viewer achieve intellectual comprehension. John Martin's landscape *Sadak in Search of the Waters of Oblivion* (1812) conveys the power of nature and the eeriness of its animal life.

Romantic music, which also appealed to the emotions, marked a similar but more gradual departure from the formal classicism that was triumphant during the eighteenth century. The inspirational music of Ludwig van Beethoven (1770–1827), the son of a German court musician from Bonn, marked the transition from classical to romantic forms. Beethoven's early work conformed to the conventions of classical music, but his later compositions, which were completed as he became progressively deaf and which defied traditional classical harmonies, were intended to evoke an emotional response. His famous "Ode to Joy," in his ninth and final symphony, remains unequaled in its ability to rouse the passions. In the view of one critic, Beethoven's music "opens the floodgates of fear, of terror, of horror, of pain, and aroused that longing for the eternal which is the essence of romanticism."

Another early romantic composer, Franz Schubert (1797–1828), who was born in Vienna, blended classical forms with romantic themes by incorporating Hungarian and gypsy folk music into his compositions. The emotionally powerful operas of the German composer Richard Wagner (1813–1883), which were set in the mythical German past, marked the height of the romantic movement in music. That style attained its greatest popularity during the second half of the nineteenth century with the lyrical symphonies and concertos of Johannes Brahms (1833–1897) in Germany and the symphonies, ballets, and operas of Peter Tchaikovsky (1840–1893) in Russia.

■ **John Martin, *Sadak in Search of the Waters of Oblivion* (1812)**
This painting reflects the romantic concern with the fantastic or the bizarre as well as its intention to convey the power of nature.

Romanticism, like the rational and scientific culture it rejected, had powerful political implications, leaving its mark on the ideologies of the modern world. In the early nineteenth century, romanticism appealed to many liberals because it involved a protest against the established order and emphasized the freedom of the individual. Romantic writers were themselves often outsiders, and therefore their protests took many different forms. The French romantic author Victor Hugo (1802–1885), whose epic novels *The Hunchback of Notre Dame* (1831) and *Les Misérables* (1862) depicted human suffering with great compassion, identified romanticism as "liberalism in literature." For Hugo a relationship existed between liberty in art and liberty in society. In France wealthy liberal bourgeoisie generally patronized romantic music and literature, while nobles and clerics denounced them. Romanticism could, however, provide support for conservatism by idealizing the traditional social and political order of the Middle Ages and the central importance of religion in society. The hostility of romantics to the culture of the Enlightenment could also lead to political conservatism. Sir Walter Scott and Samuel Taylor Coleridge were both conservatives, while the German writer Johann Wolfgang von Goethe (1749–1832), whose poems reflected many of the themes of romantic literature, opposed all liberal and republican movements in Germany.

Romanticism has a closer association with nationalism than with any other ideology. In the most general sense romanticism invested the idea of "the nation" with mystical qualities, thus inspiring devotion to it. Romantics also had an obsessive interest in the cultural, literary, and historical roots of national identity. This connection between romanticism and nationalism can be seen in the work of the German philosopher and literary critic Johann Gottfried von Herder (1744–1803), who was one of the leaders of the *Sturm und Drang* (storm and stress) literary movement. This movement, which developed in the 1770s and 1780s and included works by Goethe and Friedrich von Schiller (1759–1805), encouraged subjectivity and the youthful revolt of genius against accepted classical standards. Herder promoted the study of German language, literature, and history with the explicit purpose of giving the German people a common sense of national unity. He claimed that "a people may lose its independence, but it will survive as long as its language survives." Like many romantics, Herder idealized the Middle Ages and cultivated many of the myths that surrounded that epoch in Germany's history.

In other parts of Europe, especially in Poland and the Balkans, romantic writers and artists gave nationalists the tools necessary to construct a common culture and history of their nations. The Polish romantic composer Frédéric

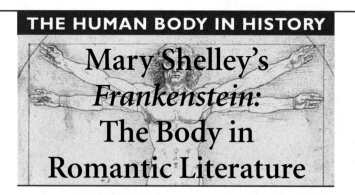

Mary Shelley's *Frankenstein:* The Body in Romantic Literature

I n 1818, Mary Shelley, the twenty-year-old daughter of the feminist Mary Wollstonecraft and the wife of the poet Percy Shelley, published a novel, *Frankenstein: or, The Modern Prometheus,* that became a literary sensation in contemporary England and has inspired books and films down to the present day. The depiction of the human body in the novel reflects the attitude of romantic writers toward nineteenth-century science.

The novel tells the story of an idealistic Swiss scientist, Victor Frankenstein, who discovers the secret of giving life to

■ Depiction of the Monster Created by Victor Frankenstein

The creation of the monster in Mary Shelley's novel embodied a critique of scientific rationalism.

inanimate matter. Using his knowledge of chemistry, anatomy, and physiology, Frankenstein pieces together bones and flesh from corpses to construct the frame of a human being, which he then infuses with life. The creature turns out to be a freak of nature: a gigantic, ugly, and deformed monster with watery eyes, yellow shriveled skin, and straight black lips. Frankenstein is horrified by what he has wrought, and his rejection leads the monster to turn on his creator, eventually killing his brother, his friend, and his wife on their wedding night. Frankenstein pursues the creature to the Arctic region, but the monster brings about Frankenstein's death. Filled with self-loathing for having murdered "the lovely and the helpless," the monster declares that Frankenstein will be his last victim and sets off to throw himself on his own funeral pyre.

The body of the monster created by Frankenstein is unnatural in the manner of creation, its size, its features, and its preternatural strength. The depiction of monstrous creatures in literature was common during the early modern period, as a way of indicating supernatural intervention in the world. Shelley's depiction of this monster, which reflects the preoccupation of romantic literature with the exotic and the mysterious, differs from that older tradition in that it identifies modern science, not supernatural forces, as the source of the monster's abnormality. In trying to unite the body and the soul, Frankenstein produced a creature he called a daemon, a body inhabited by an evil spirit who commits multiple murders. Science had produced a moral and a physical aberration.

One of the important theological questions in the history of Christianity has been whether an evil spirit or demon can inhabit or possess a human body. Shelley was preoccupied by this issue, as evidenced by Victor Frankenstein's deep interest in the figure of Satan in the novel. Frankenstein's monster was a demonic figure, but unlike the Satan of the Bible, he was the product of science and its attempt to control nature. The real monster becomes science itself, whose power nineteenth-century intellectuals desired but at the same time feared.

Mary Shelley, like many romantic writers, thought of nature as a life force with which human beings should be in harmony. The novel reinforces this theme by showing how a human being's attempt to control nature leads to nature's revenge. Frankenstein's loss of physical and mental health, the thwarting of his ability to have children with his wife, and his eventual death are all penalties for his violation of nature. ■

For Discussion

How does *Frankenstein* reflect the themes of romanticism and in particular its critique of scientific rationalism?

Chopin (1810–1849), who emigrated to Paris in 1831, inspired Polish nationalists by drawing on native Polish dances in his works for the piano. At the same time the romantic poet Adam Mickiewicz (1798–1855), another Polish exile in Paris, wrote *The Books of the Polish Nation* (1832), exalting his country as the embodiment of freedom and predicting that by its long suffering it would eventually liberate the human race.

Ideological Encounters in Europe, 1815–1848

The four new ideologies of the nineteenth century—liberalism, conservatism, socialism, and nationalism—interacted in a variety of ways, sometimes reinforcing each other and at other times leading to direct and violent political conflict. During the years between 1815 and 1831 the main ideological encounters occurred between liberalism, sometimes infused with nationalism, and conservatism. In 1815, at the time of the Congress of Vienna, it appeared that conservatism would carry the day. The determination of Metternich, the Austrian minister, to employ all the resources of the Holy Alliance to suppress any signs of revolutionary activity made the future of liberalism and nationalism appear bleak. The power of the new ideologies, however, could not be completely contained. Liberal and nationalist revolts took place in three distinct periods: the early 1820s, 1830, and 1848. During the latter two periods the demands of workers, sometimes expressed in socialist terms, added to the ideological mixture. In all these encounters conservatives had their say, and in most cases they emerged victorious.

LIBERAL AND NATIONALIST REVOLTS, 1820–1825

Between 1820 and 1825 a sequence of revolts in Europe revealed the explosive potential of liberalism and nationalism and the determination of conservatives to crush those ideologies. These revolts also reflected the strength of movements for national self-determination. The three most significant revolts took place in Spain, Greece, and Russia.

The Liberal Revolts of 1820 in Spain and Portugal

The earliest clash between liberalism and conservatism occurred in Spain, where liberals ran into determined opposition from their king, Ferdinand VII (r. 1808–1833). Ferdinand had been restored to power in 1814 after his forced abdication in 1808. In 1812, during the rule of

CHRONOLOGY

Liberal and Nationalist Revolts, 1820–1833

1820	Liberal Revolt in Spain; liberal army officers seize power in Portugal
1821	Beginning of Greek revolt against the Ottoman Empire
1825	Decembrist Revolt in Russia against Nicholas I
1829	Liberals gain majority in French Chamber of Deputies
1830	Revolution in Paris, Louis-Philippe I becomes king of France; Belgium becomes independent and adopts a liberal constitution; beginning of the Polish Rebellion against Nicholas I of Russia
1833	Greece becomes independent; Otto I becomes king

Joseph Bonaparte, the Spanish *cortes*—the representative assembly in that kingdom—had approved a liberal constitution. This constitution provided a foundation for a limited monarchy and the protection of Spanish civil liberties. In keeping with the ideas of the French Revolution, it also declared that the Spanish nation, not the king, possessed sovereignty. The tension began when King Ferdinand declared that he would not recognize this constitution. Even worse for the disheartened liberals was Ferdinand's decision to reestablish the Spanish Inquisition, invite exiled Jesuits to return, and refuse to summon the *cortes*. In 1820, when the Spanish Empire in the New World had already begun to collapse (see Chapter 19), liberals in Madrid, in alliance with some military officers, seized power.

This liberal revolt proved to be a test for the Concert of Europe. Metternich urged intervention, and although the British refused because they wanted to protect their trading interests with the Spanish colonies, the members of the Holy Alliance supported the invasion of Spain by a French army of 200,000 men. Ferdinand was restored once again to the throne, and once again he renounced the liberal constitution of 1812. The liberals not only lost this struggle, but they also suffered bitter reprisals from the government, which tortured and executed their leaders. The situation became only marginally better in 1833, when Ferdinand died and the liberal ministers of his young daughter, Queen Isabella II (r. 1833–1868), drew up another constitution. Her reign was marked by civil war, instability, and factional strife in which liberals made few substantial gains.

Shortly after the Spanish revolt of 1820, a similar rebellion based on liberal ideas took place in Portugal. The royal family had fled to Brazil during the Napoleonic wars, leaving Portugal to be governed by a regent. A group of army officers removed the regent and installed a liberal government, which proceeded to suppress the Portuguese Inquisition, confiscate church lands, and invite King John (r. 1816–1826) to return to his native land as a constitutional monarch. After the king returned in 1822, his enthusiasm for liberal government waned. His granddaughter, Maria II (r. 1826–1853), kept the liberal cause alive, relying on support from Portugal's traditional ally, Britain, but she struggled against the forces of conservatism and had only limited success.

The Nationalist Revolt of 1821 in Greece

A revolt in Greece in 1821, inspired more by nationalism than liberalism, achieved greater success than did the rebellions of 1820 in Spain and Portugal. It succeeded because other members of the Concert of Europe, not just Britain, lent their support to the revolt. Greece had long been a province in the sprawling Ottoman Empire, but a nationalist movement, organized by Prince Alexander Ypsilantis (1792–1828), created a distinct Greek national identity and inspired the demand for a separate Greek state. In 1821 a

series of revolts against Ottoman rule took place on the mainland of Greece and on some of the surrounding islands. These rebellions received widespread support in Europe from scholars who considered Greece the cradle of Western civilization and from religiously inspired individuals who saw this as a struggle of Christianity against Islam. Hundreds of European volunteers joined the Greek rebel forces. Thus the insurrection became not only a liberal and national revolt but a broad cultural encounter between East and West. The English romantic poets George Lord Byron (1788–1824) and Percy Shelley (1792–1822) became active and passionate advocates for Greek independence, while the romantic painter Eugène Delacroix (1798–1863) depicted the horror of the Turkish massacre of the entire population at the island of Chios in 1822. The link between nationalism and romanticism could not have been made more explicit.

The Greek revolt placed the powers allied in the Concert of Europe in a quandary. On the one hand they were committed to intervene on behalf of the established order to crush any nationalist or liberal revolts, and they condemned the insurrection on those grounds when it first erupted. On the other hand they were Western rulers who identified the Ottoman Turks with everything that was alien to Christian civilization. Moreover, Russia wanted to

■ **Eugène Delacroix,**
***The Massacre at Chios* (1824)**

In 1821 the Greeks on the Aegean Islands rebelled against their Turkish rulers, and in April 1822 Turkish reprisals reached their peak in the massacre of the inhabitants of Chios. Romantic paintings were intended to evoke feelings, in this case horror, at the genocide perpetrated by the Turks against the Greek rebels. The painting reveals the close association of romantic art with the causes of liberalism and nationalism.

use this opportunity to dismember its ancient enemy, the Ottoman Empire. The European powers eventually took the side of the Greek rebels. In 1827 Britain, France, and Russia threatened the Turks with military intervention if they did not agree to an armistice and grant the Greeks their independence. When the Turks refused, the combined naval forces of those three countries destroyed the fleet of the Turks' main ally, Egypt, at Navarino off the Greek coast. This naval action turned the tide in favor of the Greeks, who in 1833 finally won their independence and placed a Bavarian prince, Otto I (r. 1833–1862), on the throne. Thus the Greek war of independence effectively ended the Concert of Europe. Originally intended to crush nationalist and liberal revolts, the Concert had in this case helped one succeed.

The Decembrist Revolt of 1825 in Russia

The least successful of the early liberal revolts took place in Russia, where a number of army officers, influenced by liberal ideas while serving in western Europe during the Napoleonic wars, staged a rebellion against the government of Tsar Nicholas I (r. 1825–1855) on the first day of his reign. The officers, together with other members of the nobility, had been meeting for almost a decade in political clubs, such as the Society of True and Faithful Sons of the Fatherland in St. Petersburg. In these societies they articulated their goals of establishing a constitutional monarchy and emancipating the serfs.

The rebels, known as Decembrists° for the month in which their rebellion took place, could not agree on the precise form of government they wished to institute. That disagreement, coupled with a reluctance to take action at the critical moment, led to their failure. When Tsar Alexander I died suddenly in 1825, the Decembrists hoped to persuade his brother Constantine to assume the throne and establish a representative form of government. Their hopes were dashed when Constantine refused to tamper with the succession and accepted the reign of his brother Nicholas. The reactionary Nicholas had no difficulty suppressing the revolt, executing its leaders, and leaving Russian liberals to struggle against police repression for the remainder of the nineteenth century.

LIBERAL AND NATIONALIST REVOLTS, 1830

A second cluster of early nineteenth century liberal and national revolts in 1830 achieved a greater measure of success than the revolts of the early 1820s. These revolutions took place in France, the kingdom of the Netherlands, and the kingdom of Poland.

The French Revolution: The Success of Liberalism

The most striking triumph of liberalism in Europe during the early nineteenth century occurred in France, where a revolution took place fifteen years after the final defeat of Napoleon at Waterloo. This liberal success did not come easily. During the first few years of the restored monarchy conservatives had their way, as they did elsewhere in Europe. Louis XVIII had approved a Charter of Liberties in 1814, but he was hardly receptive to any further liberal reforms. Between 1815 and 1828 French politics was dominated by the ultraroyalists, who sponsored a "white terror" (so called because they displayed the white flag of the Bourbon monarchy) against liberals and Protestants. The terror was led by two men nicknamed Three Slices and Four Slices, indicating the number of pieces into which they butchered their Protestant enemies.

In 1824, when the conservative Charles X (r. 1824–1830) ascended the throne and took steps to strengthen the Church and the nobility, there appeared to be little hope for liberalism. Nevertheless liberal opposition to the monarchy gained support from merchants and manufacturers, as well as from soldiers who still kept the memory of Napoleon alive. When liberals became frightened that Charles would claim absolute power, and when a serious economic crisis afflicted the country in 1829, liberals at last gained a majority in the Chamber of Deputies, the French legislature.

Charles then embarked upon a perilous course. In what became known as the July Ordinances he effectively undermined the principles of the Charter of 1814. These ordinances dissolved the new Chamber of Deputies, ordered new elections under a highly restrictive franchise, and censored the press. The public reaction to this maneuver caught the king by surprise. Thousands of students and workers, liberals and republicans alike, poured onto the streets of Paris to demonstrate. Skirmishes with the king's troops only made the situation worse, and when the tricolor flag of the French Revolution appeared on top of Notre Dame Cathedral, protesters blocked the streets with barricades. Unable to restore order, the king abdicated in favor of his grandson, but the liberals offered the crown instead to the Duke of Orléans, who was crowned as Louis-Philippe I (r. 1830–1848).

Louis-Philippe accepted a revised version of the Charter of 1814 and doubled the franchise, giving the vote to middle-class merchants and industrialists. The king catered to this bourgeois constituency by encouraging economic growth and restricting noble privilege. His reign, which is often referred to as the "bourgeois monarchy," also achieved a measure of secularization when the Chamber of Deputies declared that Roman Catholicism was no longer the state religion. In keeping with mainstream liberal ideals, however, he did nothing to encourage republicanism or radical democracy, much less socialism. Efforts to depict him as the heir to the French Revolution did not persuade the bulk of the population. When the government brought the ashes of Napoleon from St. Helena to Paris, thousands of French men and women turned out to pay homage to the former emperor. Much to his disappointment, Louis-Philippe

■ **Scene from the French Revolution of 1830 in Paris**

Demonstrations by students and workers led to the abdication of King Charles X and the establishment of a liberal government. Tricolor flags of the French Revolution hang from the windows.

gained little political benefit from the move. France had acquired a liberal monarchy, but it stood on a precarious foundation.

The Belgian Revolution: The Success of Nationalism

The French Revolution of 1830 triggered the outbreak of a liberal and nationalist revolution in the neighboring country of Belgium. At the Congress of Vienna the Austrian Netherlands were united with the Dutch Republic in a new kingdom of the Netherlands. This union of the Low Countries did not work out, and soon after the formation of the new kingdom the Belgians began pressing for their independence as a nation. With a Dutchman, William I, as king and with the seat of government in Holland, the Dutch were the dominant partner in this union, a situation that cause considerable resentment in Belgium. Belgians spoke Flemish or French rather than Dutch, which had become the kingdom's official language. Moreover, most Belgians were Catholics, whereas the majority of Dutch people were Protestants. With their own language, religion, and culture, as well as their own history, Belgians thought of themselves as a separate nation. They also were more liberal than their

Dutch neighbors, advocating free trade and the promotion of industry, while resenting the high tariffs imposed by the Dutch government.

The two main political parties in Belgium, the Liberals and the Clericals, joined forces to achieve autonomy. When the news of the Revolution in Paris reached Brussels, fighting broke out between workers and government troops. A national congress gathered to write a new constitution, and when the Dutch tried to thwart the rebellion by bombarding the Belgian city of Antwerp, Britain assembled a conference of European powers to devise a settlement. The powers agreed to recognize Belgium's independence, and they arranged for a German prince, Leopold of Saxe-Coburg, uncle of the future British Queen Victoria, to become king. The Dutch, however, refused to recognize the new government, and they renewed their military attacks on Belgium. Only in 1839 did all sides accept the new political arrangement.

The Polish Rebellion: The Failure of Nationalism

The French Revolution of 1830 triggered a second uprising, this one unsuccessful, in the kingdom of Poland (see

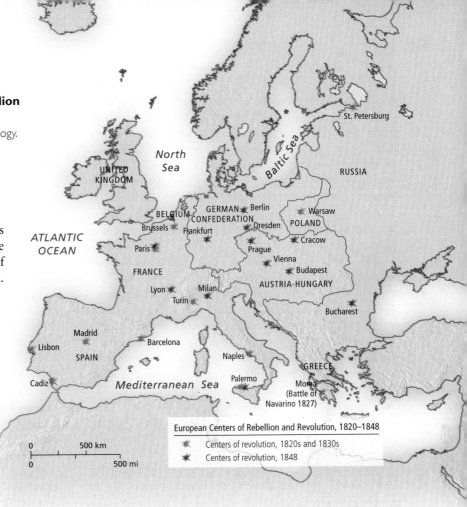

Map 21.1). Poland had suffered many partitions at the hands of European powers during the eighteenth century, and in 1815 the Congress of Vienna had redefined its borders once again. After incorporating much of the eastern portion of the country into the Russian Empire, the Congress established a separate Polish kingdom, with Warsaw as its capital and the Russian Tsar, Alexander I, as its king (r. 1815–1825).

With a Russian king the independence of Poland was a mere fiction, but Alexander had approved a liberal Polish constitution in 1815. He grew to regret this decision, and his rule as king of Poland gradually alienated Polish liberals within the national legislature, the *sejm*. The accession of Nicholas in 1825 only aggravated those tensions. An uncompromising conservative, Nicholas accused the Polish opposition of complicity with the Russian Decembrist rebels, and he brought them to the brink of rebellion when he made plans to send the Polish army, together with Russian troops, to suppress the French revolution of 1830 and to prevent the Belgians from receiving their independence.

The revolt began within the school of army cadets, who attacked the residence of the Grand Duke Constantine, but it quickly gained the support of the entire army and the urban populace. The revolt appealed to both liberals and nationalists, and it drew inspiration from a group of romantic poets who celebrated the achievements of the Polish past. A provisional government was established at Warsaw, but the liberal members of the elected national assembly were unwilling to enlist the peasantry in the conflict, fearful that they would rise against Polish landlords rather than the Russians. When the powers of western Europe refused to intervene on behalf of this liberal cause, Nicholas was able to crush the rebellion, abolish the *sejm*, and deprive the kingdom of Poland of its autonomous status. Nicholas visited a terrible revenge upon the leaders of the revolt, confiscated the lands of those who had emigrated, and shut down the University of Warsaw. His brutal repression set back the cause of liberalism and nationalism in Poland for another two generations.

LIBERAL REFORM IN BRITAIN, 1815–1848

The challenges that liberals faced in Britain were somewhat different from those they confronted in most other European countries. Having maintained the status quo during the era of the French Revolution, the forces of British conservatism, which bore the ideological stamp of Edmund Burke, remained formidable. At the same time, however, Britons already enjoyed many of the rights that liberals on the European continent demanded, such as freedom of the press and protection from arbitrary imprisonment. The power of the British monarchy was more limited than in almost any other European country. The ideology of liberalism, which originated in England and had deep roots in British political and social philosophy, defined the political creed of many Whigs, who formed the main opposition to the ruling Conservative or Tory party after 1815.

In this relatively favorable political climate, British liberals pursued three major goals, which amounted to a program for reform rather than revolution. The first was parliamentary reform and the expansion of the franchise. The British had a long tradition of representative government, which had been secured by the Glorious Revolution of 1688, but the titled nobility in the House of Lords effectively

699

controlled elections to the House of Commons, while the members of the gentry or lesser aristocracy held most of the seats in the House of Commons. In some boroughs real representation was a sham; the electorate consisted entirely of the borough councils, who elected the nominees of the noblemen who controlled them. Very few people lived in some of these "rotten boroughs"—one was nothing but a pasture—whereas large segments of the population in the recently industrialized north had no representation at all in Parliament.

The Great Reform Bill of 1832, which was pushed through Parliament by the Whig prime minister, Lord Grey, marked a victory for British liberalism. The bill expanded the franchise to include most of the urban middle class. It eliminated the rotten boroughs and created a number of new ones in heavily populated areas. It also established a uniform standard for the right to vote in all parliamentary boroughs. In keeping with the principles of liberalism, however, the bill restricted the vote, and hence active citizenship, to property owners. It rejected the demands of radicals for universal male suffrage, and by using the phrase "male person" to identify eligible voters, the bill denied all women the vote.

The second liberal cause was the repeal of legislation that denied political power to Catholics and also to Protestants who did not attend the service of the Anglican Church. In the seventeenth century a body of legislation had denied both of these religious minorities the right to hold national or local political office. Catholics suffered the additional liability of being denied the right to sit in Parliament. Liberals provided the basis of support for the political "emancipation" of Catholics and Protestant nonconformists. Liberals were opposed on principle to religious discrimination, and many of them belonged to Protestant nonconformist congregations. Conservatives opposed the repeal of this legislation, but they feared a civil war in Ireland if Catholics were not allowed to sit in the British Parliament. The Tory prime minister, the Duke of Wellington, who had defeated Napoleon at Waterloo, eventually agreed to liberal demands. The Protestant nonconformists were emancipated in 1828, while the Catholics had to wait until one year later. One of the first Catholics elected to Parliament in 1830 was Daniel O'Connell (1775–1847), an Irishman who worked tirelessly to improve the lot of his countrymen within the limits of the Irish union with Britain.

The third liberal cause was free trade. The target of this campaign was a series of protective tariffs on the import or export of hundreds of commodities, including raw materials used in production. The most hated protective tariff was on grain (known in Britain as corn), which kept the price of basic food commodities high in order to protect the interests of landlords and farmers. In this respect the desire of liberals for free trade collided against the desire of Parliament to defend the economic interests of its largely aristocratic membership. In 1837 a group of indus-

AN IRISH OFFICIAL CRITICIZES BRITISH POLICY DURING THE POTATO FAMINE
....

The potato famine of 1845–1848, which was caused by a blight on Ireland's staple crop, the potato, killed thousands of Irish people and drove more than one million others to emigrate. As the extent of the famine became apparent in November 1845, the Lord Mayor of Dublin sent the following resolution to the Lord Lieutenant of Ireland, the highest-ranking official of the British government in that country.

. . . . That we have ascertained beyond the shadow of doubt that considerably more than one-third of the entire of the potato crop in Ireland has been already destroyed by the potato disease; and that such disease has not, by any means, ceased its ravages . . . That we arraign in the strongest terms, consistent with personal respect to ourselves, the culpable conduct of the present administration, as well in refusing to take any efficacious measure for alleviating the present calamity with all its approaching hideous and necessary consequences; as also for the un-

equivocal crime of keeping the ports closed against the importation of foreign provisions, thus either abdicating their duty to the people or their sovereign, whose servants they are, or involving themselves in the enormous guilt of aggravating starvation and famine, by unnaturally keeping up the price of provisions, and doing this for the benefit of a selfish class who derive at the present awful crisis pecuniary advantage to themselves by the maintenance of the oppressive Corn laws . . . Yet, whilst the Irish harbours are closed against the importation of foreign food, they are left open for the exportation of Irish grain, which has already amounted in the present season to a quantity nearly adequate to feed the entire people of Ireland, and to avert the now certain famine; thus inflicting upon the Irish people the abject misery of having their own provisions carried away to feed others, while they themselves are left contemptuously to starve.

Source: From John O'Rourke. *The History of the Great Irish Famine of 1847.* Dublin: 1902.

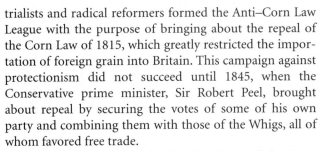

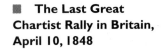

The Last Great Chartist Rally in Britain, April 10, 1848

Government precautions, including the appointment of special constables to handle the crowd, and rain kept the number of demonstrators in London lower than anticipated. The government ordered the leader of the movement, Feargus O'Connor, to stop the planned march to Parliament.

trialists and radical reformers formed the Anti–Corn Law League with the purpose of bringing about the repeal of the Corn Law of 1815, which greatly restricted the importation of foreign grain into Britain. This campaign against protectionism did not succeed until 1845, when the Conservative prime minister, Sir Robert Peel, brought about repeal by securing the votes of some of his own party and combining them with those of the Whigs, all of whom favored free trade.

Peel took this action only after the advent of the Great Famine in Ireland (1845–1848), which was caused by a blight on potatoes, the main crop on which the Irish population relied. The repeal of the corn laws allowed the importation of foreign grain into Ireland, but it did not solve the problem. More than one million Irish people died as a result of the famine, and another million were forced to emigrate, many of them to the United States and Canada.

Unlike the liberals, socialists and radical democrats achieved little success in Britain during the first half of the nineteenth century. In 1834 the Utopian socialist Robert Owen established the Grand National Consolidated Trades Union, the purpose of which was to unite all workers in a peaceful struggle to realize his idealist goals. Owen had hoped that his union would give "the productive classes a complete dominion over the fruits of their own industry."

The refusal of many unions to join this association, coupled with opposition from the government, led to its disintegration. In its wake workers and radicals decided that economic improvement could come only through political means. In 1837 the newly formed London Workingman's Association, in collaboration with a few radical Members of Parliament, drew up a People's Charter, calling for the implementation of a program of radical democracy. Their demands included universal male suffrage, annual parliaments, voting by secret ballot, equal electoral districts, the elimination of property qualifications for Members of Parliament, and the payment of salaries to those same members. The workers who supported this cause became known as Chartists.

The strength of the Chartist movement fluctuated between 1837 and 1848, gaining the greatest popular participation when economic conditions deteriorated. Most Chartists restricted their activities to meetings to support candidates for Parliament and petitioning Parliament. A few of the more militant, like the Irish immigrant Feargus O'Connor, called for "a holy and irresistible crusade" against the government. The British government and the upper classes became most frightened in 1848, when revolution broke out in France, Italy, and Germany, and when the Chartists decided to draft a new charter and threatened to form a revolutionary national assembly like that of France if Parliament were to reject the new document.

Within the next few years the Chartist movement died. British workers revealed, as they would throughout the remainder of the nineteenth century, that they had little inclination to take to the streets, especially after good economic times returned. The government's reduction of indirect taxes during the 1840s, coupled with the effective use of the police force and the strict enforcement of the criminal law, also helped prevent Britain from experiencing revolution in 1848. The price of this failure was that further liberal reforms, such as the extension of the franchise, did not take place in Britain for another two decades.

THE REVOLUTIONS OF 1848

Unlike Britain, almost every country in Europe experienced revolution in 1848. A wave of revolutionary activity spread rapidly throughout the Continent. The revolutions took place during a period of widespread economic discontent. European countries had suffered bad harvests in 1845 and 1846 and an economic recession in 1847, leading to a temporary decline in the standard of living among industrial as well as agricultural workers. Discontent took the form of mass protests and demonstrations, which increased the likelihood of violent confrontation. The revolutions of 1848 were more widespread than the revolts of the 1820s and 1830, and they involved greater popular participation. These revolutions also gave greater attention to both nationalist and socialists issues.

The French Revolutions of 1848

The first of the revolutions of 1848 took place in France, where the liberal government of Louis-Philippe faced mounting criticism. Declining economic conditions, which prevailed throughout Europe during the 1840s, provided an environment that brought the country to a crisis point. A series of demonstrations in Paris in favor of the right of workers to vote and to receive state assistance for their trades was the final precipitant. When troops from the Paris National Guard fired on the demonstrators and killed forty people, the barricades once again appeared in the streets and the rebels seized government buildings. France was experiencing its third revolution in sixty years. In an effort to

CHRONOLOGY		
The Revolutions of 1848		
1848		
February	Revolution in Paris	
March	Insurrection in Berlin, peasant unrest in the countryside, formation of liberal governments in Prussia and other German states; revolutions in Milan and Venice, Ferdinand II issues a new constitution in Naples	
April	Elections for a new National Assembly in France	
May	Meeting of the Frankfurt Parliament; meeting of the Prussian Assembly	
June	Suppression of working-class resistance in Paris; Pan-Slav Congress in Prague; suppression of the rebellion in Prague	
October	Suppression of revolution in Vienna	
December	Election of Louis-Napoleon as president of the Second French Republic; Frankfurt Parliament issues *Declaration of the Basic Rights of the German People*; Frederick William dissolves Prussian Assembly	
1849		
March	King Frederick William rejects the German crown offered by the Frankfurt Parliament	
April	Frankfurt Parliament promulgates a new constitution; Hungarian Diet proclaims Magyar independence	
May–June	Fall of the liberal ministries in German states	
August	Venetian Republic surrenders to Austrian forces; suppression of the Hungarian movement for independence	

save his regime, Louis-Philippe abdicated in favor of his grandson, but the revolutionaries abolished the monarchy and declared the Second French Republic.

A provisional government selected by the Chamber of Deputies was headed by nine republicans, but it included liberals and radical democrats. Most significantly it also included two socialists, Louis Blanc and a worker who preferred to be called by the single name of Albert. The French Revolution of 1848 offered the socialists the first opportunity to realize their goal of a democratic and socialist republic. Many of the 200 clubs formed in Paris at this time, some of which were exclusively female, were either republican or socialist in their orientation. The socialist agenda included not only universal male suffrage, which was granted immediately by the government, but also active support for the masses of unemployed workers. Louis Blanc secured the establishment of national workshops to give the unemployed jobs on public projects. Ordinances reduced the length of the workday to ten hours in the city and twelve hours in rural areas, and the government authorized a commission to study working conditions.

These bold socialist initiatives did not last long. By the summer the euphoria of the revolution had dissipated and the aspirations of workers had been crushed. The elections held in April 1848 to constitute a new National Assembly and write a new constitution seated an overwhelming majority of conservative monarchists and only a small minority of republicans and socialists. Resentment of the provisional government's assistance to urban workers and anger at the levying of a surtax to pay for government programs revealed the lack of broad popular support for radical political programs. Tension between the new conservative assembly and the forces of the left mounted when the government closed the workshops and Parisian workers were either drafted into the army or sent to the provinces.

These newly adopted policies led to further working-class violence in Paris in June 1848. When General Louis Cavaignac, known as "the butcher," was called in to suppress this insurgency with regular army troops, there was a devastating loss of life. No fewer than 1,500 insurgents were killed in the streets or in summary executions, while another 4,000 were sent into exile in French colonies. These confrontations appeared to Karl Marx to constitute class warfare, a prelude to the proletarian revolution he predicted for the future. Louis Blanc, who was implicated in these uprisings, fled to England, where Marx himself would soon arrive and spend the rest of his life.

The revolution ended with the election of Napoleon's nephew, Louis-Napoleon Bonaparte (1808–1873), as the president of the Second French Republic in December 1848. Until the February Revolution it seemed highly unlikely that Louis-Napoleon, an impetuous adventurer and conspirator, would ever come to power. After staging two unsuccessful coups against the government of Louis-Philippe in 1836 and 1840, he was sentenced to life imprisonment. He managed to escape to England, however, and the events of February 1848 gave him the opportunity to return to France. He became a member of the new National Assembly, and then easily defeated Cavaignac in the presidential election.

As president, Louis-Napoleon drew support from conservatives, liberals, and moderate republicans. He also benefited from the legend that his uncle had created and the nationalist sentiment it inspired. Because the first Napoleon had become emperor, even those who preferred an empire to a republic could vote for his nephew. The younger Napoleon followed in his uncle's footsteps, seizing power in December 1851 and proclaiming himself emperor of the French one year later. He called himself Napoleon III, in deference to the dynastic rights of the uncrowned Napoleon II, the son of Napoleon I who had died in 1823.

The Revolutions of 1848 in Germany, Austria, Hungary, and Bohemia

Until French revolutionaries built barricades in the streets of Paris in 1848, liberalism and nationalism had achieved little success in Germany. German university students, inspired by the slogan "Honor, Freedom, Fatherland," had staged a number of large rallies during the early years of the nineteenth century, but the forces of conservatism had kept them in check. The Carlsbad Decrees of 1819, intended to suppress university radicalism, inaugurated a period of severe repression throughout Germany. The only success achieved by German liberals and nationalists prior to 1848 was the establishment of the *Zollverein*, a customs union of the various German states, in 1834. Even that project, which promoted free trade within German lands, did not attract support from all liberals.

A major opportunity for the liberal cause in Germany came in 1848 in the immediate wake of the February Revolution in France. As in France, however, this opportunity was complicated by the more radical demands of democrats and socialists for universal suffrage, including equal rights for women. German radicals also demanded government assistance to artisans and workers who had suffered economic hardship as a result of industrialization. In Berlin, the capital of Prussia, these discontents led radicals to barricade the streets. The situation became more serious after troops fired into the crowd, killing some 250 people. The violence spread to the countryside, where peasants demanded that landlords renounce their privileges and grant them free use of their lands. In response to these pressures, King Frederick William IV summoned an assembly, elected by universal male suffrage, to write a new Prussian constitution. Other German states also yielded to liberal pressure, establishing liberal governments known as the "March ministries."

As these events were unfolding, the contagion of revolution spread to Austria, the other major German kingdom, which formed the nucleus of the sprawling Habsburg Empire. News of the revolution in Paris led to demonstrations by students and workers in Vienna. An assortment of Austrian liberal aristocrats, middle-class professionals, and discontented workers demanded an end to the long rule of the conservative minister, Clemens von Metternich. In response to the demands of these groups, Emperor Ferdinand I (r. 1835–1848) summoned a constitutional assembly and installed a moderate government. A conservative Prussian observer feared that these concessions had broken "the most secure dam against the revolutionary tide."

The main difference between the revolutions of 1848 in Austria and the other German lands was that events in

THE CARLSBAD DECREES, 1819

The main source of liberal and national ideas in Germany after 1815 were university students, who often belonged to secret societies or fraternities. Conservatives considered these students dangerous revolutionaries and tried to expel them from the universities. When a student assassinated a conservative writer in 1819, the princes of the German Confederation issued a set of decrees that called for the monitoring of the lectures given at the universities, the removal of liberal professors, the expulsion of students, and the censorship of the press.

2. The confederated governments mutually pledge themselves to remove from the universities or other public educational institutions all teachers who, by obvious deviation from their duty, or by exceeding the limits of their functions, or by the abuse of their legitimate influence over youthful minds, or by propagating harmful doctrines hostile to public order or subversive to existing governmental institutions, shall have unmistakably proven their unfitness for the important office entrusted to them. No teacher who shall have been removed in this manner shall be again appointed to a position in any public institution of learning in another state of the Confederation.

3. Those laws which have for a long period been directed against secret and unauthorized societies in the universities shall be strictly enforced. The governments mutually agree that such persons as shall hereafter be shown to have remained in secret or unauthorized associations, or shall have entered such associations, shall not be admitted to any public office.

4. No student who shall be expelled from a university by a decision of the university senate which was ratified or prompted by the agent of the government, or shall have left the institution in order to escape expulsion, shall be received in any other university.

So long as this decree shall remain in force no publication which appears in the form of daily issues, or as a serial not exceeding twenty sheets of printed matter, shall go to press in any state of the union without the previous knowledge and approval of the state officials.

Vienna awakened demands of Hungarians and Czechs for national autonomy within the Empire. In Hungary the nationalist leader Lajos Kossuth (1802–1894) pushed for a program of liberal reform and national autonomy. This initiative created further tensions between the Magyars and the various national minorities within the kingdom of Hungary. Similar problems arose in Bohemia, where a revolution in Prague led to demands from the Czechs for autonomy within the Habsburg Empire. In June 1848 the Czech rebels hosted a Pan-Slav Congress in Prague to advance a nationalist plan for achieving unity of all Slavic people within the empire. This idealistic proposal could not be realized, for there were many distinct Slavic nationalities, each of which had a desire to preserve its autonomy. In addition, there was a large German-speaking population within Bohemia that identified with other German territories in the Confederation.

The most idealistic and ambitious undertaking of the revolution in central Europe was the meeting of the Frankfurt Parliament in May 1848. Some 800 middle-class liberals, many of whom were lawyers, officials, and university professors, came from all the German states to draft a constitution for a united Germany. The Parliament produced powerful speeches in support of both liberal and nationalist ideals, and in December 1848 it promulgated a *Declaration of the Basic Rights of the German People*. This document recognized the equality of all German people before the law; freedom of speech, assembly, and religion; and the right to private property. Like so many liberal assemblies, however, the Frankfurt Parliament failed to address the needs of the workers and peasants. The delegates rejected universal male suffrage as a "dangerous experiment" and refused to provide protection for craftsmen who were being squeezed out of work by industrialization. For these reasons the Parliament failed to win broad popular support.

In April 1849 the Frankfurt Parliament drafted a new constitution for a united Germany, which would have a hereditary "emperor of the Germans" and two houses of parliament, one of which would be elected by universal male suffrage. Austria, however, voted against the new plan, and without Austrian support the new constitution had little hope of success. The final blow to German liberal hopes came when King Frederick William of Prussia refused the Frankfurt Parliament's offer of the crown, which he referred to as coming from the gutter and "reeking of the stench of revolution." At that point the Frankfurt Parliament disbanded and the efforts of German liberals to unite their country and give it a new constitution came to an inglorious end.

By the middle of 1849, conservative forces had triumphed in the various German territories and the

■ **The German National Assembly Gathered in St. Paul's Church in Frankfurt, 1848**
The Parliament ultimately failed in its goal to give a liberal constitution to a united Germany.

Habsburg Empire. In Prussia the efforts of the newly elected assembly to restrict noble privilege triggered a reaction from the conservative nobles known as *Junkers*. Frederick William dismissed his liberal appointees, sent troops to Berlin, and disbanded the assembly. A similar fate befell the other German states, such as Saxony, Baden, and Hanover, all of which had installed liberal governments in the early months of the revolution. In Austria Prince Alfred Windischgrätz, who had crushed the Czech rebels in June, dispersed the rebels in Vienna in October. When Hungary proclaimed its independence from the empire in April 1849, Austrian and Russian forces marched on the country and crushed the movement.

The Revolutions of 1848 in Italy

The revolutions of 1848 also spread to Austrian possessions in the northern Italian territories of Lombardy and Venetia. In Milan, the main city in Lombardy, revolutionary developments followed the same pattern as those in Paris, Berlin, and Vienna. When the barricades went up, some of the Milanese insurgents used medieval pikes stolen from the opera house to fight off Austrian troops. Their success triggered rebellions in other towns in Lombardy, in Venice, and in the southern kingdom of the

Two Sicilies. In that kingdom the Spanish Bourbon king, Ferdinand II (r. 1830–1859), after suppressing a republican revolt in January, was forced to grant a liberal constitution. The spread of these revolts inspired the hope of bringing about the unification of all Italian people in one state.

This Italian nationalist dream had originated among some liberals and republicans during the first half of the nineteenth century. Its most articulate proponent was Giuseppe Mazzini, a revolutionary from Genoa who envisioned the establishment of a united Italian republic through direct popular action. In his youth Mazzini had been a member of the *Carbonari*, a secret conspiratorial society pledged to drive foreigners out of the Italian states, to secure constitutional liberties, and to bring about some form of Italian unity. His arrest led to one of many periods of exile in London, where he continued to pursue the cause of republicanism and democracy. In 1831 Mazzini founded Italy's first organized political party, Young Italy, which was pledged to realize national unification, democracy, and greater social equality. Mazzini combined a passionate commitment to the ideals of liberalism, republicanism, and nationalism. For him the nation was the highest ideal to which one could pledge devotion, one possessing almost mystical qualities. "We have beheld in Italy," he wrote, "the purpose,

Prostitution, Corporal Punishment, and Liberalism in Germany

In March 1822 Gesche Rudolph, a poor, uneducated twenty-five-year old woman from the northern German city of Bremen, was arrested by municipal authorities for engaging in prostitution without registering with the police. Ever since the days when troops from five different European nations had occupied her neighborhood, Rudolph had been selling her sexual services as her only form of livelihood. After her arrest she was not given a formal trial but was summarily expelled from the city and banned from ever returning. Unable to earn a living through prostitution in a village outside the city, where she resided with a brother who physically abused her, Rudolph returned to the city, where she was arrested once again for prostitution. This time she was sentenced to fifty strokes of the cane and six weeks in jail, after which she was once again expelled from the city. Returning again to Bremen, she was arrested in a drunken stupor in a whorehouse and subjected to a harsher sentence of three months' imprisonment and 150 strokes before another expulsion. This pattern of arrest and punishment, expulsion and return occurred repeatedly during the next two decades, with the number of strokes rising to 275 and the period of imprisonment to six years. During a portion of her prison sentence she was given only bread and water for nourishment.

Rudolph's arrest in 1845 at the end of a six-year imprisonment and her subsequent expulsion and return to Bremen led to the appointment of a liberal lawyer, Georg Wilhelm Gröning, to represent her. After reviewing her case and calculating that she had been whipped a total of 893 times and imprisoned for a cumulative period of eighteen years, Gröning appealed her sentence to the senate of Bremen on the grounds that her treatment was not only futile but immoral. His appeal addressed an issue that went far beyond this particular case or even the prosecution of the crime of prostitution. Gröning's action raised the highly controversial issue of the legitimacy and value of corporal punishment, an issue that pitted liberals and conservatives, who had different notions of justice.

Until the eighteenth century the penal systems of Europe had prescribed corporal punishments, administered publicly, for most crimes. These punishments ranged from whippings and placement in the stocks for minor offenses to mutilation, hanging, and decapitation for felonies. They were justified mainly on the grounds that they provided retribution for the crime and deterred the criminal and those who witnessed the punishment from committing further crimes. These two main functions of retribution and deterrence are the same functions that capital punishment allegedly serves today. Corporal punishments were also intended to humiliate the criminal both by violating the integrity of the body and by subjecting the prisoner to the mockery and sometimes the maltreatment of the crowd. The torture of suspects to obtain evidence also served some of these functions, although judicial torture took place during the trial, not as part of the sentence.

The entire system of corporal punishment, as well as that of torture, came under attack during the eighteenth century. In Prussia torture was abolished in 1754, and the General Law Code of 1794 eliminated many forms of corporal punishment. The General Law Code reflected the concern of Enlightenment thinkers that all such assaults on the body were inhumane and a denial of the moral dignity of the individual. Because corporal punishments in Prussia and elsewhere were administered mainly against people from the lower classes, they also were a violation of the liberal principle of equality before the law.

Despite these efforts at reform, the illegal administration of corporal punishment by public and private authorities continued in Prussia and the other German states. Conservatives, who had a different notion of justice from that of the liberals, defended these sentences on the grounds that all punishment, including imprisonment, was intended to deny the criminal freedom and hence his or her dignity. For them any reference to natural rights and human dignity were "axioms derived from abstract philanthropic speculation." The president of the Prussian police, Julius Baron von Minutoli, expressing the conservative position on the issue, claimed that corporal punishment was more effective than imprisonment in preventing crime, since it alone could instill terror in the criminal.

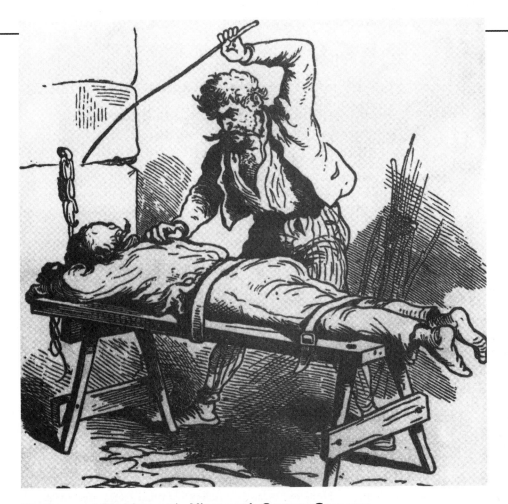

■ Corporal Punishment in Nineteenth-Century Germany

Whipping in prisons continued long after public corporal punishment was abolished in the middle of the nineteenth century.

It was apparent that in the case of Gesche Rudolph, 893 strokes had not instilled terror in her or brought about any transformation of her spirit. The Senate made the young woman Gröning's ward and suspended her sentence. Gröning arranged for Rudolph to live in the countryside under the strict supervision of a competent countryman. This compromise solution at least broke the cycle of expulsion, return, and punishment that had failed to reform her. We do not know whether she gave up her life of prostitution.

Soon after Gesche Rudolph became Gröning's ward, the liberal critics of corporal punishment in Germany celebrated a victory. King Frederick William IV of Prussia formally abolished the practice in his kingdom in May 1848. Shortly thereafter the Frankfurt Parliament included freedom from physical punishment by the state in its *Declaration of the Basic Rights of the German People.* Most German states and municipalities, including Bremen, wrote this right into law in 1849. The failure of the Frankfurt Parliament, however, and the more general failure of liberalism in Germany after 1849 led to a strong conservative campaign to reinstate corporal punishment in the 1850s. They succeeded only in maintaining corporal punishment within the family, on manorial estates, and in the prisons. Liberalism had not succeeded in completely establishing its standard of justice, but it did end exposure to public shame as a punishment for crime. ■

Questions of Justice

1. Many societies equate "justice" with the administration of punishments. In what ways were the authorities who whipped and imprisoned Gesche Rudolph upholding a standard of justice?

2. Why did liberals object to corporal punishment?

3. In addition to inflicting physical pain, corporal punishment produces social shame. What is the difference between social shame and legal guilt? In what ways does shame still play a role in punishments today?

Taking It Further

Evans, Richard. *Tales from the German Underworld: Crime and Punishment in the Nineteenth Century.* 1998. Provides a full account of the prosecution of Gesche Rudolph.

the soul, the consolidation of our thoughts, the country chosen of God and oppressed by men."

The ruler who assumed the nationalist mantle in 1848 was Charles Albert of Piedmont-Sardinia, the most economically advanced of the Italian states. This initiative began successfully, as Charles Albert's army, which included volunteers from various parts of Italy, marched into Lombardy and defeated Austrian forces. Instead of moving forward against Austria, however, Charles Albert decided to consolidate his gains, hoping to annex Lombardy to his own kingdom. This decision alienated republicans in Lombardy and in other parts of Italy as well as the rulers of the other Italian states, who feared that Charles Albert's main goal was to expand the limits of his own kingdom at their expense. By August 1848 the military tide had turned. Fresh Austrian troops defeated the Italian nationalists outside Milan. The people of that city turned against Charles Albert, forcing him to return to his own capital of Turin. The Italian revolutions of 1848 had suffered a complete defeat.

The Failure of the Revolutions of 1848

The revolutions of 1848 in France, Germany, the Habsburg Empire, and Italy resulted in victory for conservatives and defeat for liberals, nationalists, and socialists. All the liberal constitutions passed during the early phase of the revolutions were eventually repealed or withdrawn. The high hopes of national unity in Germany, Italy, and Hungary were dashed. Workers who built the barricades in the hope of achieving improvements in their working conditions gained little from their efforts.

Divisions among the different groups that began the revolutions were in large part responsible for their failure. The most serious division—in fact, one that was fatal—was the split between the liberals who formulated the original goals of the revolution and the lower-class participants who took to the streets. Liberals used the support of the masses to bring down the governments they opposed, but their ideological opposition to broad-based political movements and their fear of further disorder sapped their revolutionary fervor. Divisions also emerged between liberals and nationalists, whose goals of national self-determination required different strategies from those of the liberals who supported individual freedom.

The failure of nationalism in the revolutions of 1848 did not, however, portend the death of the ideologies of liberalism, nationalism, and socialism. They all continued to manifest strength during the following two decades, and they often influenced the policies of the conservative governments that returned to power after the revolutions. In Germany, for example, the goal of nationalists was realized under conservative auspices and even mustered a measure of liberal support, while in France liberalism made some inroads into the conservative and nationalist government of the Second French Empire after 1860.

National Unification in Europe and America, 1848–1871

Prior to 1848 the forces of nationalism, especially when combined with those of liberalism, had little to show for their efforts. Besides the Greek rebellion of 1821, which succeeded largely because of international opposition to the Turks, the only successful nationalist revolution in Europe took place in Belgium. Both of these nationalist movements were secessionist in that they involved the separation of smaller states from larger empires. Efforts in 1848 to form nations by combining smaller states and territories, as in Italy and Germany, or by uniting all Slavic people, as proposed at the Pan-Slav Congress, had failed. Between 1848 and 1871, however, movements for national unification succeeded in Italy, Germany, and the United States, each in a different way. In the vast Habsburg Empire a different type of unity was achieved, but it did little to promote the cause of nationalism.

ITALIAN UNIFICATION: BUILDING A FRAGILE NATION-STATE

The great project of Italian nationalists, the unification of Italy, faced formidable obstacles. Austrian military control over the northern territories, which in the end had thwarted the nationalist movement of 1848, meant that national unification would not be achieved peacefully. The dramatic economic disparities between the prosperous north and the much poorer south posed a challenge to any plan for economic integration. A long tradition of local autonomy within the kingdoms, states, and principalities made submission to a strong central government unappealing. The unique status of the papacy, which controlled its own territory and which influenced the decisions of many other states, served as another challenge. Despite these obstacles, the dream of a resurgence of Italian power, reviving the achievements of ancient Rome, had great emotive appeal. Hatred of foreigners who controlled Italian territory, which dates back to the fifteenth century, gave further impetus to the nationalist movement.

The main question for Italian nationalism after the failure of 1848 was who could provide effective leadership of the movement. It stood to reason that Piedmont-Sardinia, the strongest and most prosperous Italian kingdom, would be central to that undertaking. Unfortunately the king, Victor Emmanuel II (r. 1849–1861), was more known for his hunting, his carousing, and his affair with a teenage mistress than his statesmanship. Victor Emmanuel did, however, appoint as his prime minister a nobleman with liberal leanings, Count Camillio di Cavour (1810–1861). Cavour displayed many of the characteristics of nineteenth-

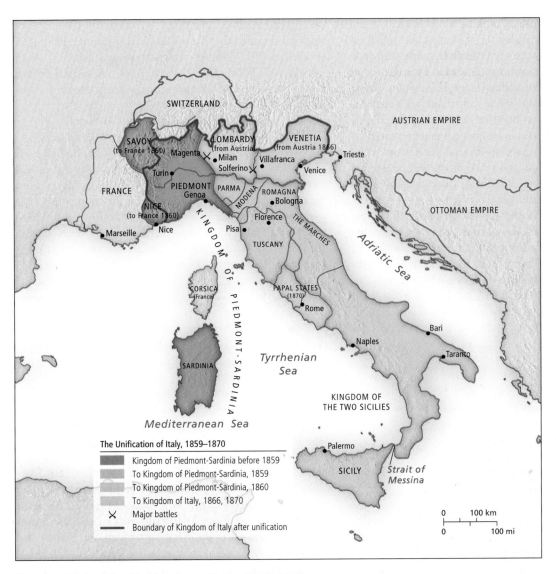

SWITZERLAND

AUSTRIAN EMPIRE

SAVOY
(to France 1860)

LOMBARDY
(from Austria)

VENETIA
(from Austria 1866)

Magenta ✕   Milan
Solferino ✕

Villafranca

Trieste

Turin

PIEDMONT

Genoa

PARMA

MODENA

ROMAGNA
• Bologna

Venice

FRANCE

NICE
(to France 1860)

Florence •

THE MARCHES

OTTOMAN EMPIRE

Marseille •   Nice •

Pisa •

TUSCANY

Adriatic Sea

CORSICA
(France)

PAPAL STATES
(1870)

Rome •

Bari •

Naples •

Taranto •

SARDINIA

Tyrrhenian
Sea

KINGDOM OF
THE TWO SICILIES

Mediterranean Sea

The Unification of Italy, 1859–1870

Kingdom of Piedmont-Sardinia before 1859
To Kingdom of Piedmont-Sardinia, 1859
To Kingdom of Piedmont-Sardinia, 1860
To Kingdom of Italy, 1866, 1870
✕   Major battles
—   Boundary of Kingdom of Italy after unification

Palermo •

SICILY

Strait of
Messina

0   100 km
0   100 mi

■ **Map 21.2   The Unification of Italy, 1859–1870**
The main steps to unification took place in 1860, when Piedmont-Sardinia acquired Tuscany, Parma, Modena, and the Romagna and when Garibaldi seized control of the Kingdom of the Two Sicilies in the name of King Victor Emmanuel of Piedmont-Sardinia.

century liberalism. He favored a constitutional monarchy, the restriction of clerical privilege and influence, and the development of a capitalist and industrial economy. He was deeply committed to the unification of the Italian peninsula, but only under Piedmontese leadership, and preferably as a federation of states. In many ways he was the antithesis of the republican Mazzini, the other central figure in Italian unification. Mazzini's idealism and romanticism led him to think of national unification as a moral force that would lead to the establishment of a democratic republic, which would then undertake an extensive program of social reform. Mazzini often wore black, claiming that he was in mourning for the unrealized cause of unification.

Mazzini's strategy for national unification involved a succession of uprisings and invasions. Cavour, however, adopted a diplomatic course of action intended to gain the military assistance of France against Austria. In 1859 French and Piedmontese forces defeated the Austrians at Magenta and Solferino and drove them out of Lombardy. One year later Napoleon III signed the Treaty of Turin with Cavour, allowing Piedmont-Sardinia to annex Tuscany, Parma, Modena, and the Romagna, while ceding to France the Italian territories of Savoy and Nice. This treaty resulted in the unification of all of northern and central Italy except Venetia in the northeast and the Papal States in the center of the peninsula (see Map 21.2).

The main focus of unification efforts now turned to the Kingdom of the Two Sicilies in the south. A rebellion against the Bourbon monarch Francis II, protesting new taxes and the high price of bread, had taken place there in 1860. At that point the militant republican adventurer Giuseppe Garibaldi (1807–1882) intervened with decisive force. Garibaldi, who was born in Nice and spoke French rather than Italian as his main language, was determined no less than Cavour and Mazzini to drive all foreigners out of Italy and achieve its unification. Originally a supporter of Mazzini's republican goals, Garibaldi gave his support in the 1860s for Italian unification within the framework of a monarchy. A charismatic military leader, Garibaldi put together an army of volunteers, known as the Red Shirts for their colorful makeshift uniforms. In 1860 he landed in Sicily with an army of 1,000 men, took the main Sicilian city of Palermo, and established a dictatorship on behalf of King Victor Emmanuel. He then landed on the mainland and took Naples. Shortly thereafter the people of Naples, Sicily, and most of the Papal States voted their support for union with Piedmont-Sardinia. In March 1861 the king of Sardinia assumed the title of King Victor Emmanuel of Italy (r. 1861–1878). Complete unification was achieved when Austria ceded Venetia to Italy in 1866 and when French troops, which had been protecting a portion of the Papal States, withdrew from Rome in 1870.

The unification of Italy owed more to the statecraft of Cavour than the passion of Mazzini and Garibaldi. Their achievement did not fully realize the lofty nationalist goals of creating a culturally unified people or a powerful central state. Economic differences between northern and southern Italy became even greater after unification than before. The overwhelming majority of the people continued to speak their local dialects or even French rather than Italian. Traditions of local political autonomy and resentment against the concentration of wealth in the north retarded the development of loyalty to the new Italian state and inspired a series of bloody rebellions in the former Kingdom of the Two Sicilies during the 1870s and 1880s.

This instability was aggravated by the widespread practice of banditry in the southern mainland. Bandits were peasants who, in the hope of maintaining a world that appeared to be vanishing, swept through towns, opened jails, stole from the wealthy, and sacked their houses. Closely related to banditry was the growth in Sicily of the Mafia°, organizations of armed men who took control of local politics and the economy. The Mafia originated during the struggle for unification in the 1860s and strengthened their position in Sicily once the country had been unified. Their power, the prevalence of banditry, and the enduring strength of Italian loyalty to the local community all made it difficult for the new Italian state to flourish. The movement for national unification had driven the French and the Austrians out of the peninsula, but it had failed to create a model nation-state.

GERMAN UNIFICATION: CONSERVATIVE NATION-BUILDING

Like Italy, Germany experienced a successful movement for national unification after the disappointments of 1848. The German movement, like the Italian, benefited from the actions of crafty statesmen and from the decisions made by other states. Unlike Italy, however, Germany achieved unification under the direction of highly conservative rather than liberal forces. One reason for this was that the severity of the reaction to the Revolution of 1848 had forced the emigration of many German liberals and nationalists to Great Britain and the Netherlands and as far west as the hill country of central Texas. Nevertheless a number of liberals, such as those who belonged to a Pan-German association known as the National Union, still kept alive the hopes of the Frankfurt Parliament for a German constitutional republic.

■ **Giuseppe Garibaldi**
The uniform he is wearing was derived from his days as a guerilla fighting in the civil war in Uruguay, 1842–1846. Garibaldi also spent two years in asylum in the United States.

The main dilemma regarding German unification was whether Prussia or Austria would form the nucleus of any new political structure. In the end, Prussia, with its almost entirely German-speaking population, its wealth, and its strong army, assumed leadership of the movement. The key figure in this process was Count Otto von Bismarck (1815–1898), a lawyer and bureaucrat from an old *Junker* family whom King William I of Prussia appointed as his prime minister in 1862. By birth, training, and instinct Bismarck was an inflexible conservative, determined to preserve and strengthen the Prussian nobility and monarchy and to make the Prussian state strong and powerful. In the words of the liberal British ambassador to Berlin, Robert Morier, "not one mustard seed of faith in liberal principles exists in Count Bismarck's nature." Bismarck did not hesitate, however, to make alliances with any political party, including the liberals, to achieve his goals. This subordination of political means to their ends, and Bismarck's willingness to use whatever tactics were necessary, regardless of any moral considerations, made him a proponent of *Realpolitik*, the adoption of political tactics solely on the basis of their realistic chances of success.

Bismarck pursued the goal of national unification through the exercise of raw military and political power. "The great questions of the time," he said in 1862, "are not determined by speeches and majority decisions—that was the error of 1848 and 1849—but by iron and blood." Bismarck did not share the romantic devotion of other German nationalists to the fatherland or their desire to have a state that embodied the spirit of the German people. His determination to achieve German national unification became synonymous with his goal of strengthening the Prussian state. This commitment to the supremacy of Prussia within a united Germany explains his steadfast exclusion of the other great German power, Austria, from his plans for national unification.

Bismarck's achievement of German unification was based mainly on Prussian success in two wars (see Map 21.3). The first, the Austro-Prussian War of 1866, resulted in the formation of a new union of twenty-two states, the North German Confederation. This new structure replaced the old German Confederation, the loose association of thirty-nine states, including Austria, that had been established in 1815 by the Congress of Vienna. The North German Confederation had a centralized political structure with its own legislature, the *Reichstag;* the king of Prussia became its president and Bismarck its chancellor. The foundation of the North German Confederation was, however, only one step toward the unification of all Germany. Bismarck laid the foundation for the realization of this larger goal by strengthening the *Zollverein*, which included the southern German states. By encouraging free trade among all the German states he also won support for unification from German liberals.

■ **Otto von Bismarck, Chancellor of Prussia**
Bismarck used state power to achieve the unification of Germany. He became known as the "iron chancellor," a reference to his exercise of raw political power.

The second war, which completed the unification of Germany, was the Franco-Prussian War of 1870–1871. This conflict began when Napoleon III, the French emperor, challenged Prussian efforts to place a member of the Prussian royal family on the vacant Spanish throne. Bismarck welcomed this opportunity to take on the French, who controlled German-speaking territories on their eastern frontier and who had cultivated alliances with the southern German states. Bismarck played his diplomatic cards brilliantly, guaranteeing that the Russians, Austrians, and British would not support France. He then used the army that he had modernized to invade France and seize the towns of Metz and Sedan. The capture of Napoleon III during this military offensive precipitated the end of France's Second Empire and the establishment of the Third French Republic in September 1870.

As a result of the war Prussia annexed the predominantly German-speaking territories of Alsace and Lorraine. Much more important, it led to the proclamation of the German Empire with William I of Prussia as emperor.

Officially the structure of the new empire, a term used to indicate that it embraced many separate states, was that of a federation, just like that of the North German Confederation that preceded it. In fact the government of the empire, like that of Prussia, was highly centralized as well as autocratic, and the liberal middle classes did not participate in it, as they did in the governments of Britain, France, and Italy. The German imperial government won the support of the middle class by adopting policies supporting free trade, but the ideologies that underpinned the new German Empire were those of conservatism and na-

tionalism, which encouraged devotion to "God, King, and Fatherland."

UNIFICATION IN THE UNITED STATES: CREATING A NATION OF NATIONS

At the same time that Italy and Germany were achieving national unification, the United States of America engaged in a bitter process that preserved and strengthened the federal union it had instituted in 1787. The thirteen colonies

■ **Map 21.3   The Unification of Germany, 1866–1871**
Prussia assumed leadership in uniting all German territories except Austria. Prussia was responsible for the formation of the North German Confederation in 1866 and the German Empire in 1871.

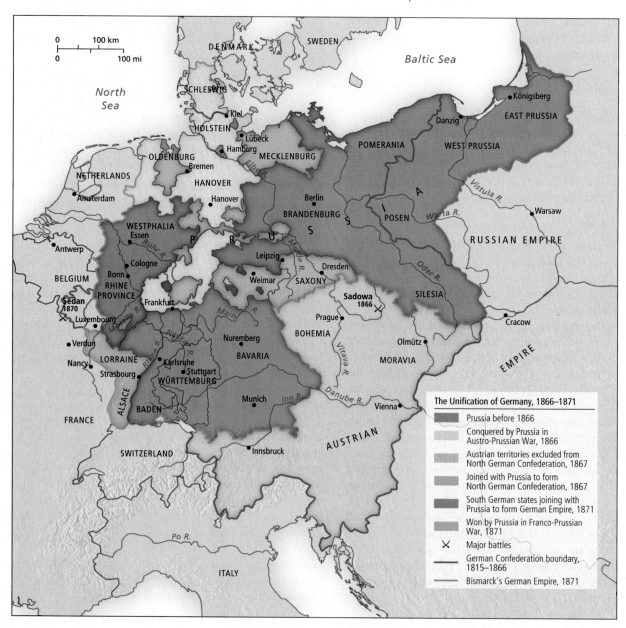

that proclaimed their independence from Great Britain in 1776 shared common constitutional grievances against the mother country or metropolis, but each colony had its own identity. The U.S. Constitution, drawn up in 1787, sought to preserve this balance between the states and the federal government by dividing sovereignty between them, leaving to the states control over all matters it had not specifically given to the federal government. This arrangement generated friction and debate between the Federalists, who wished to strengthen the central government, and the Anti-Federalists, who feared that a strong central government would lead to corrupt, arbitrary rule. The Federalists won some early victories, including the establishment of a national bank, but they were unable to create a truly united people. The great victory of the Anti-Federalists was the Bill of Rights, the first ten amendments to the U.S. constitution, which was ratified by the states in 1791. By enumerating the rights of the citizens in a formal constitution, including freedom of speech and freedom of assembly, the Bill of Rights embodied one of the main elements of liberal ideology.

Throughout the early years of the republic Americans continued to think of themselves as citizens of particular states more than as members of a single national community. In the early nineteenth century, President Thomas Jefferson (1801–1809) imagined a new American nation, a people "with one heart and one mind," but nationalist sentiment, such as had developed in European countries on the basis of a common language and culture, had difficulty materializing in the United States. The American republic was originally the product of English-speaking colonists who shared the same language and culture as the British against whom they had rebelled. After the revolution, efforts were made to build a new nation on the basis of a distinctly American culture. *The American Dictionary of the English Language,* compiled by Noah Webster (1758–1843) in 1812, made one contribution to this endeavor by listing thousands of American words that had never been included in English dictionaries. Patriotic sentiment, especially after the defeat of British forces at the battle of New Orleans in 1815, also helped to give Americans a sense of common purpose and destiny.

These efforts at building an American nation became more challenging as the young republic began to incorporate Western territories into the federal union. Lands acquired by purchase or conquest were formed into territories and then gradually admitted into the union as states. This process of unification, which proceeded in a piecemeal fashion, took much longer than the unifications of Italy and Germany in the 1860s. It was marked by sustained military action against the Native American population and a war against Mexico between 1846 and 1848. Florida was annexed in 1819, while Texas, an independent republic for nine years, was admitted in 1845 and California in 1850. This process of gradual unification did not end until 1912,

when New Mexico and Arizona, the last territories in the contiguous forty-eight states, were admitted to the union.

As the United States expanded westward into the Spanish-speaking Southwest, and as immigrants from various European nations swelled the population of the eastern as well as the western states, the country became more rather than less culturally diverse. Assimilation to a dominant Protestant English-speaking culture, even one that was gradually becoming distinct from that of Great Britain, could not provide the same commitment to the homeland that inspired Italians and Germans to support national unification. Americans might be patriotic, in that they proclaimed their allegiance to the federal republic, but they had more difficulty thinking that they shared a common culture with the people from different parts of the country. Building a nation-state in America was a task fraught with obstacles.

The great test of American national unity came during the 1860s, when eleven southern states, committed to the preservation of the economic system of slavery, and determined that it should be extended into new territories acquired by the federal government, seceded from the union and formed a confederation of their own. The issue of slavery had helped to polarize North and South, creating deep cultural and ideological divisions that made the goal of national unity appear even more distant. America had its own ideological and cultural encounters that paralleled those that prevailed in European countries.

The constitutional issue underlying the civil war was the preservation of the union. In a famous speech President Abraham Lincoln (1861–1865) declared that "a house divided against itself cannot stand . . . this government cannot endure permanently half slave and half free." When the war ended, and slavery was abolished, that union was not only preserved but strengthened. Amendments to the U.S. Constitution provided for equal protection of all citizens under the law. The South, which had its own regional economy, was integrated into the increasingly commercial and industrial North. The whole process of national unification, both economic and social, was greatly facilitated by the building of railways. In the United States, even more than in Europe, railroads linked otherwise isolated communities and facilitated the spread of products and ideas across vast distances. Gradually the people of the United States began to think of themselves as a united people, drawn from many different nations of the world. The United States became "a nation of nations."

NATIONALISM IN EASTERN EUROPE: PRESERVING MULTINATIONAL EMPIRES

The national unifications that took place in Germany, Italy, and the United States formed part of a *western* European pattern in which the main units of political organization

■ **Map 21.4 Nationalities Within the Habsburg Empire**
The large number of different nationalities within the Habsburg Empire made it impossible to accommodate the demands of all nationalities for their own state.

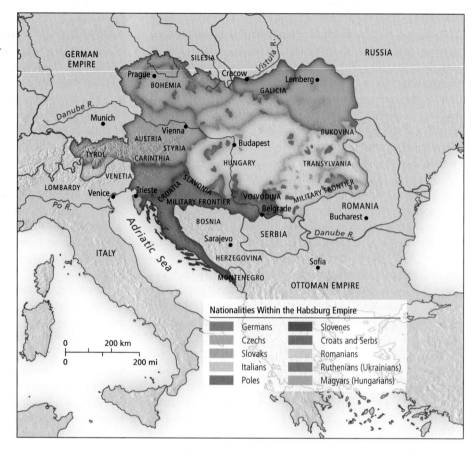

would be nation-states. Ethnic minorities would of course always live within the boundaries of these states, but the state itself would encourage the growth of a national identity among all its citizens. We can observe this process at work in France, Britain, and Spain, all of which had undergone a process of national unification before the nineteenth century. Minority populations within these large western European states have occasionally threatened to establish a separate political identity as nations, but with the one notable exception of Ireland, the southern portion of which became independent of Britain in the twentieth century, the large states of western Europe have maintained their unity and promoted nationalist sentiment to sustain it.

In *eastern* Europe a very different pattern prevailed, especially in the Habsburg and Russian Empires. Instead of becoming unified nation-states, these two empires remained large, multinational political formations, embracing many different nationalities. This pattern was most obvious in the large, sprawling Habsburg Empire, which encompassed no fewer than twenty different ethnic groups, each of which thought of itself as a nation (see Map 21.4). The largest of these nationalities were the Germans in Austria and Bohemia and the Magyars in Hungary, but the Czechs, Slovaks, Poles, Slovenes, Croats, Rumanians, Bulgarians, and Italians (before 1866) all formed sizable minority populations. Map 21.4 only begins to reveal the full complexity of this diversity. The various nationalities

within the empire had little in common except loyalty to the Habsburg emperor, who defended the Catholic faith and the privileges of the nobility. National unification of the empire would have presented a much more formidable task than the ones that confronted Cavour and Bismarck.

During the era of national unification the ideology of nationalism threatened to tear apart this precariously unified empire. It awakened demands of Hungarians, Czechs, and others for national autonomy and also spawned a movement for the national unity of all Slavs. The emperor, Francis Joseph, recognized the danger of nationalist ideology. He also feared that liberalism, which was often linked to nationalism, would at the same time undermine his authority, which he had reasserted with a vengeance after the failure of the revolutions of 1848. He therefore repressed these nationalist aspirations at every turn. This policy had disastrous consequences for the future history of Europe, since Slavic nationalism and separatism have remained a source of political instability of southeastern Europe until the present day.

The one concession that Francis Joseph did make during this volatile period was to establish the Dual Monarchy of Austria-Hungary in 1867. This significant increase of Hungarian power within the empire came in the wake of the disastrous defeats of Austrian forces by the French and Piedmontese in 1859 and the Prussians in 1866. Austrian liberals took this opportunity to call for the introduction of constitutional government, while the second-largest ethnic group within the empire, the Magyars, demanded more autonomy for Hungary. The *Ausgleich* (Settlement) of 1867, which was proposed by the wealthy Hungarian nobleman and lawyer Ferenc Deák (1803–1876), created a dual monarchy in which Francis Joseph would be both king of Hungary and emperor of Austria. Each monarchy would have its own parliament and bureaucracy, although matters of foreign policy and finance would be handled in Vienna. This arrangement represented a concession to Magyar nationalism but gave very little to all the other nationalities within both kingdoms. The *Ausgleich* officially recognized the equality of all nationalities within the empire, and allowed schooling to be conducted in the local language, but it permitted only Germans in Austria and Magyars in Hungary to acquire their own political identity. Instead of a unified nation-state the emperor now presided over two multinational monarchies.

Ideology, Empire, and the Balance of Power

The new ideologies of the early nineteenth century, and the movements for national unification to which they gave rise, had a disruptive impact on the conduct of international affairs. The original framework for international action after 1815 was the Concert of Europe, which was intended to prevent the recurrence of revolution and preserve the balance of power. It achieved much greater success in pursuing the second goal than it did the first. The five European powers in the Concert—Britain, Austria, Russia, Prussia, and France—could never contain the liberal and national forces that the French Revolution had unleashed, but as a group the five powers prevented any one of them from establishing a dominant position in Europe.

Challenges to the balance of power during this period came mainly from governments engaged in a process of imperial expansion. The first of these challenges arose in the Western Hemisphere during the 1820s, the second occurred in the 1850s in the Balkans, and the third took place after the Franco-Prussian War of 1870–1871.

BRITAIN, THE UNITED STATES, AND THE MONROE DOCTRINE OF 1823

In North America a clash of empires threatened to engulf European powers in a new round of imperial expansion and warfare during the early 1820s. As Spanish power in the Western Hemisphere began to collapse, the young republic of the United States feared that Austria or France might intervene in the new Latin American nations. The United

States was also alarmed about Russian expansion down the western coast of North America, as we have discussed in Chapter 19. In order to prevent imperial expansion by any of these European powers, the United Sates found an ally in Britain, which even after the loss of the thirteen North American colonies still ruled a large empire of its own in Canada, the Caribbean, and South America. Britain did not wish to compromise the dominant influence it exercised in this area.

British and U.S. resistance to continental European imperialism in the Western hemisphere had a foundation in liberal ideology. The United States, with its constitutional protection of individual liberty and its success in achieving national self-determination in the American Revolution, had become the very embodiment of European liberalism. No wonder it supported the independence of Latin American nations on ideological as well as diplomatic grounds. In Britain, as we have already seen, the liberal tradition was stronger than in other parts of Europe. Britain's liberal heritage also helps to explain its refusal to join the Holy Alliance of 1815. The British government viewed the Concert of Europe as a mechanism for preserving the balance of power, not for supporting autocratic regimes.

In 1823, President James Monroe (1817–1825) declared that the United States would consider any future attempts by European powers to colonize the Americas as hostile acts. The enforcement of this policy, which became known as the Monroe Doctrine, depended mainly on the support of the British navy, since the United States was not yet capable of taking on the powers of Europe by itself. During the next ten years Britain provided that naval support.

The main effect of the Monroe Doctrine, and Britain's enforcement of it, was to preserve the balance of power in the Western Hemisphere. The doctrine also created the concept of two hemispheres, one old and one new, each refraining from interference in each other's affairs. The broader ideological significance of the Monroe Doctrine was that it provided support for liberalism and nationalism both in Europe and in the Americas. Monroe's speech made explicit reference to the opposition of the United States to the repressive political systems of the allied powers, support for the liberal revolutions that had taken place in Spain and Portugal in 1820, and approval of the revolutions against Spanish rule in Latin America.

RUSSIA, THE OTTOMAN EMPIRE, AND THE CRIMEAN WAR, 1853–1856

The second major challenge to the balance of power occurred as a result of Russian imperial ambitions in the Balkans, resulting in the first major war among European powers since the defeat of Napoleon at Waterloo in 1815. The Crimean War (1853–1856), which claimed almost a million casualties on all sides, was the direct result of Russian imperial expansion. It began when Russia occupied the principalities of Moldavia and Wallachia (present-day Romania) in the Ottoman Empire in order to gain access to the Straits of Constantinople and thus to the Aegean and Mediterranean seas. The weakness of the Ottoman Empire had invited Russian expansion into this area, which Russians justified by claiming they were protecting the Orthodox Christianity of people in the Balkans from their Turkish Muslim oppressors. They also claimed that they were promoting the national unity of all Slavic people under Russian auspices. This Russian version of Pan-Slavism differed from that developed by Czech Slavs at the Pan-Slav Congress of 1848. In effect it was an extreme form of Russian imperialism that rivaled the nationalism of individual Slavic nationalities.

Britain resisted the Russian occupation of Moldavia and Wallachia, ostensibly to protect its trade with the Turks but more urgently to prevent Russia from becoming too powerful. In this respect it was adhering to the principles of the Concert of Europe by trying to preserve the balance of power in Europe. The underlying British fear was that Russia might invade India, Britain's most important colony. When the Turks declared war on the Russians, therefore, the British followed suit and were joined by the French. Both powers sent large armies to begin a siege of the port of Sebastopol on the Black Sea.

The poorly trained British forces, commanded by officers who had purchased their commissions and who had no sound knowledge of military tactics, suffered staggering losses, more of them from disease than from battle. The most senseless episode of the war occurred when a British cavalry unit, the Light Brigade, rode into a deep valley, only to be cut down by Russian artillery perched on the surrounding hills. The slaughter was memorialized in a poem by the British poet Alfred Lord Tennyson (1850–1892), "The Charge of the Light Brigade."

Nevertheless, the British, French, and Turks prevailed, handing Russia its most humiliating defeat of the nineteenth century. The defeat led to a curtailment of Russian expansion for the next twenty years and preserved the balance of power in Europe. Within Russia the defeat contributed to a crisis that led to a series of liberal reforms during the rule of Tsar Alexander II (1855–1881). Alexander, an indecisive man who had inherited the throne in the middle of the Crimean War, was hardly a liberal (he once referred to the French system of government as "vile"), but he did yield to mounting liberal pressure to emancipate the serfs in 1861, a step that occurred two years before the emancipation of slaves in the United States.

THE GERMAN EMPIRE AND THE PARIS COMMUNE, 1870–1871

A third, and in the long run the most serious, challenge to the balance of power in Europe came from Prussia. As we have seen, Prussian victories over Austria in 1866 and France in 1871 allowed Bismarck to complete the unification of Germany. The newly created German Empire, which now possessed the strongest army in Europe, replaced Austria as the predominant power in central Europe. The growth of German military power, coupled with its expansionist territorial ambitions, soon made it a formidable rival to other European countries and threatened to upset the delicate balance of power. In the twentieth century Germany's territorial ambitions led ultimately to two world wars.

German military success in the Franco-Prussian War of 1870–1871 played a crucial role in French politics, exposing the complex ideological contradictions of the Second French Empire and laying the groundwork for the Third French Republic. After Napoleon III had established the Second Empire in 1852, he tried to mask his usurpation of power by preserving the tradition of universal male suffrage and by submitting his rule to popular ratification, just as his uncle had done. During the 1860s his government became known as "the Liberal Empire," a strange mixture of conservatism, liberalism, and nationalism. Although "the little Napoleon" ruled as an emperor, he gradually allowed a semblance of real parliamentary government to return, relaxed the censorship of the press, and encouraged industrial development. To this mixture he added a strong dose of nationalist sentiment by evoking the memory of Napoleon I.

These efforts failed to save Napoleon III's regime. His moderate liberal policies angered conservatives on the one hand and failed to satisfy the demands of republicans and socialists on the other. These complex ideological encounters came to a head in 1870 during the Franco-Prussian War, which Napoleon himself was in large part responsible for starting. Napoleon took the field at the Battle of Sedan and was captured. The Prussians allowed him to go into exile in England, where he lived until his death in 1873. On September 4, 1870, a large crowd invaded the Legislative Assembly in Paris and forced the deputies who still remained to join them in declaring the end of the Second Empire and the beginning of the Third Republic. Shortly thereafter Prussian troops surrounded Paris and began a long siege of the city, forcing hungry city dwellers to eat cats and dogs roaming the streets and an elephant seized from the Paris zoo.

In January 1871 Adolphe Thiers (1797–1877), a veteran statesman who had served as prime minister during the liberal government of the 1830s, negotiated an armistice with Bismarck. Thiers hoped to establish a conservative republican regime or possibly a restoration of the monarchy at the conclusion of the war. This prospect gained strength when elections to the new National Assembly, which Bismarck permitted so that the French legislature could conclude a formal peace treaty, returned a majority of monarchists. The National Assembly then elected Thiers as president of the provisional government.

■ **Execution of Paris Communards, May 1871**
Troops of the provisional French government killed at least 25,000 Parisians during the uprising.

The National Assembly, which sat at Bordeaux, and the provisional government, which took up residence at Versailles, were determined to assert their authority over the entire French nation. In particular, they wanted to curb the independence of the city of Paris, which was determined to carry on the struggle against Prussia and to keep alive the French radical tradition that had flourished in the city in 1792 and again in 1848. The radicalism of the Paris Commune drew its strength from the large working-class population in the industrialized districts on the northern,

eastern, and southern edges of the city. The socialist and republican ideals of the Commune's leaders, coupled with their determination to preserve the independence of the city, culminated in the bloodshed described at the beginning of this chapter. The crushing of the Commune marked a bitter defeat for the forces of French socialism and radicalism. The Third French Republic that was established in September 1870 endured, but its ideological foundation was conservative nationalism, not liberalism or socialism.

CONCLUSION
The Ideological Transformation of the West

■

The ideological encounters that took place between 1815 and 1871 resulted in significant changes in the political culture of the West. As the early nineteenth-century ideologies of liberalism, conservatism, socialism, and nationalism played out in political movements and revolutions, the people who subscribed to these ideologies often redefined their political objectives. Many British and French socialists, for example, recognizing the necessity of assistance from liberals, abandoned their call for creating a classless society and sought instead to increase wages and improve working conditions of the lower classes. The demands of so-cialists for greater economic equality pressured liberals to accept the need for more state inter-vention in the economy. The realities of conservative politics led liberal nationalists in Germany and Italy to accept newly formed nation-states that were more authoritarian than they had originally hoped to establish. Recognizing the strength of the ideologies to which they were opposed, conservative rulers like Emperor Napoleon III and Tsar Alexander II agreed to adopt liberal reforms. Liberals, conservatives, socialists, and nationalists would con-tinue to modify and adjust their political and ideological positions during the period of mass politics, which began in 1870 and which will be the subject of the next chapter.

The Western ideologies that underwent this process of adaptation and modification had a broad influence on world history. In the twentieth century, three of the four ideologies dis-cussed in this chapter have inspired political change in parts of the world that lie outside the geographical and cultural boundaries of the West. Liberalism has provided the language for movements seeking to establish fundamental civil liberties in India, Japan, and several African countries. In its radical communist form, socialism inspired revolutions in Russia, a country which for many centuries had straddled the boundary between East and West, and in China. Nationalism has revealed its explosive potential in countries as diverse as Nepal, Thailand, and Zaire. Ever since the nineteenth century, Western ideologies have demonstrated a capacity both to shape and to adapt to a variety of political and social political circumstances.

Suggestions for Further Reading

For a comprehensive list of suggested readings, please go to www.ablongman.com/levack/chapter21

Anderson, Benedict. *Imagined Communities: Reflections on the Origin and Spread of Nationalism.* 1991. A discussion of the ways in which people conceptualize the nation.

Clark, Martin. *The Italian Risorgimento.* 1999. A comprehen-sive study of the social, economic, and religious context of Italian unification as well as its political and diplomatic dimensions.

Gellner, Ernest. *Nations and Nationalism.* 1983. An interpretive study that emphasizes the social roots of nationalism.

Hamerow, Theodore S. *Restoration, Revolution, Reaction: Economics and Politics in Germany, 1815–1871.* 1966. An investiga-tion of the social basis of ideological encounters in Germany.

Honour, Hugh. *Romanticism.* 1979. A comprehensive study of romantic painting.

Hunczak, Tara, ed. *Russian Imperialism from Ivan the Great to the Revolution.* 1974. A collection of essays that illuminate Russian nationalism as well as imperialism over a long period of time.

Lichtheim, George. *A Short History of Socialism.* 1970. A good general treatment of the subject.

Nipperdey, Thomas. *Germany from Napoleon to Bismarck, 1800–1866.* 1996. An exploration of the creation of German na-tionalism as well as the failure of liberalism.

Onuf, Peter S. *Jefferson's Empire: The Language of American Nationhood.* 2000. A study of Jefferson's expansionary nationalism.

Pflanze, Otto. *Bismarck and the Development of Germany: The Period of Unification, 1815–1871.* 1963. The classic study of both Bismarck and the unification movement.

Pinckney, David. *The French Revolution of 1830.* 1972. The best treatment of this revolution.

Seton-Watson, Hugh. *Nations and States.* 1977. A clearly writ-ten study of the nation-state.

Sperber, Jonathan. *The European Revolutions, 1848–1851.* 1994. The best study of the revolutions of 1848.

Tombs, Robert. *The War Against Paris, 1871.* 1981. A narrative history of the Paris Commune.

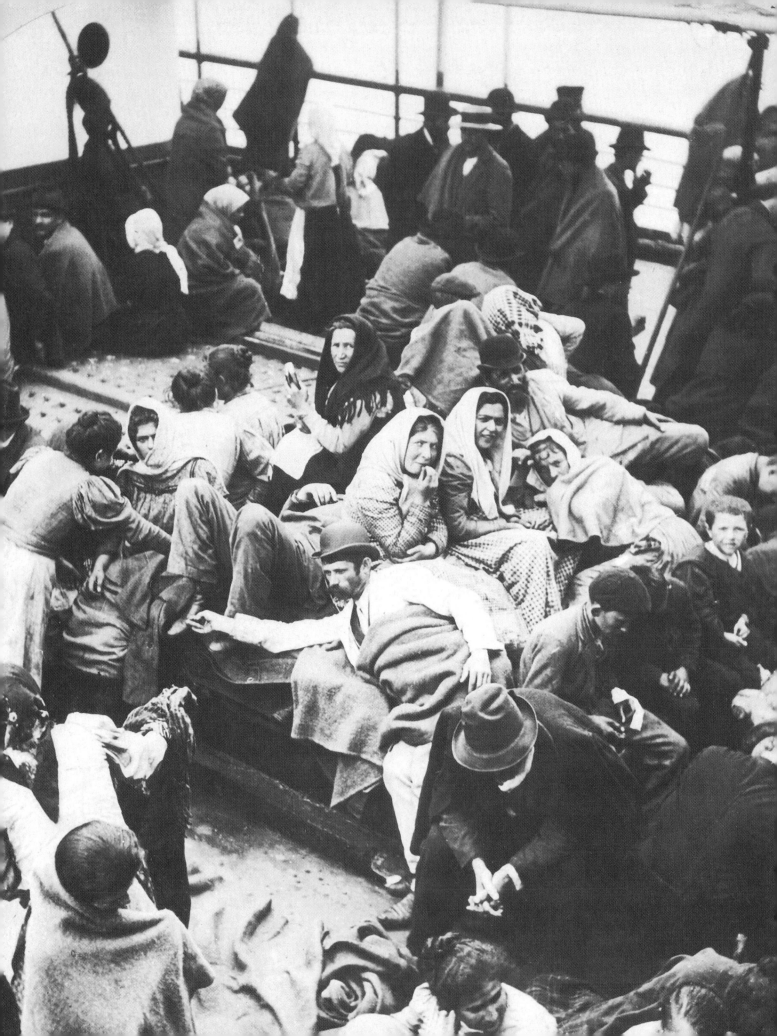

The Coming of Mass Politics: Industrialization, Emancipation, and Instability, 1870–1914

I N THE SPRING OF 1881, A HARROWING SCENE TOOK PLACE IN ST. PETERSBURG, CAPI-tal of the vast Russian Empire. A 28-year-old woman, Sofiia Perovskaia, was scheduled to be executed for her part in the assassination of Tsar Alexander II. Born into the ranks of wealth and privilege, Perovskaia had rejected her traditional role in order to join the revolutionary socialist movement. She became a leader of the People's Will, a small revolutionary group that sought to undermine the tsarist regime through a program of sabotage and assassination. These revolutionaries dared to set their sights on assassinating the tsar himself, and on March 1, 1881, they achieved this goal. Led by Perovskaia, six People's Will members (all under age 30) stationed themselves at prearranged points along the streets of St. Petersburg. At Perovskaia's signal, they released their bombs and assassinated one of the most powerful men in Europe.

Despite the death of the tsar and the audacity of the crime, however, the tsarist regime did not crumble. The six assassins were quickly arrested and sentenced to death by hanging. (One of the six was pregnant and therefore allowed to live.) On the day of Perovskaia's execution, she mounted the scaffold calmly, but when the noose was placed around her neck, she grabbed hold of the platform below with her feet. It took the strength of two men to pry her feet loose so that she could hang.

The image of Sofiia Perovskaia clinging to the platform with her bare feet while her two executioners strained to push her to her death captures the ferocity of political struggle not only in Russia but throughout Europe at the end of the nineteenth century. As Chapter 21 explained, the ideological competition among liberalism, conservatism, socialism, and nationalism shaped the political culture of the West in the nineteenth century. Economic developments after 1870 both intensified and widened this competition. Individuals and groups that had traditionally been excluded from power demanded a voice in political affairs. Even in

Chapter Outline

- Economic Transformation

- Defining the Political Nation

- Broadening the Political Nation

- Outside the Political Nation? The Experience of Women

Mass Society on the Move: European immigrants arriving in the United States, New York Harbor, 1906.

authoritarian Russia, the political nation could not long remain the preserve of the titled and wealthy. Neither economic modernization nor the coming of mass politics ensured the victory of democracy, however. Like Sofiia Perovskaia's executioners, the governing classes often struggled hard to pry newcomers off the platform of political power—and they often won.

Four questions will structure our exploration of this period: (1) How did the economic transformation of Europe after 1870 help shape the encounters between established political elites and newcomers to the political process? (2) How did the ruling classes of the Western powers respond to the new threats and opportunities provided by mass political participation? (3) What was the relationship between modern nationalism and the emergence of mass politics? (4) In what ways did the emergence of feminism in this period demonstrate the potential as well as the limits of political change?

Economic Transformation

Europe's political development between 1870 and 1914 is inextricably linked to its economic transformation. Four important economic developments helped shape European actions and attitudes during these years: the onset of economic depression in 1873, the expansion of the Industrial Revolution into new geographic regions and economic sectors, the emergence of new patterns in the production and consumption of industrial goods, and accelerated urbanization and immigration. Together, these developments not only altered the daily life of the ordinary European, they also exacerbated social tensions and accelerated political change. The resulting series of often violent encounters within societies helped transform the political structures and ideologies of the West.

ECONOMIC DEPRESSION

In 1873, Europe's economy tilted sharply downward—prices, interest rates, and profits all fell, and remained low in many regions until the mid-1890s. Contemporaries referred to this as the Great Depression in Trade and Agriculture°. In hindsight, "Great Depression" may seem an inaccurate label for a period that saw a continuing rise in world production and growing levels of foreign investment in new industrial economies, but to many Europeans living in these decades, this Great Depression seemed depressing indeed. Agriculture was hardest hit of all economic sectors. By the 1890s, the price of wheat had fallen to only one-third of what it had been in the 1860s. Farm owners and laborers across Europe found it difficult to remain on the land and make a living. Business, too, faced hard times after 1873.

Profit margins were squeezed as the prices of finished products fell, often by as much as 50 percent, while labor and production costs tended to remain much more static.

What caused this depression? Ironically, it was rooted in the very success of the Industrial Revolution. The development of the steamship and the expansion of railway lines across Europe and the United States sharply reduced the cost of transporting both agricultural and industrial goods. Cheaper transportation costs opened the breadbaskets of the American Midwest and Ukraine to European consumption. With wheat and other agricultural goods now flooding the market, farmers were forced to accept increasingly lower prices for their products. More generally, as regions and nations industrialized, they of course produced more goods. Yet many industrial workers, agricultural laborers, and landowning peasants still stood on the very edge of subsistence, with little money to spend on industrial products. In other words, by the 1870s, a mass consumer society had not yet emerged. Thus in many regions of Europe production exceeded consumption, and the result was a long-term agricultural and industrial depression.

INDUSTRIAL EXPANSION

The onset and impact of economic depression is, then, closely linked to the second important economic development of this period—the continued expansion of the Industrial Revolution. As Chapter 20 detailed, the period between 1760 and 1860 saw gradual, spotty, but still dramatic changes in economic production, first in Britain, then in portions of western Europe. But throughout much of the nineteenth century many of the inhabitants of central, eastern, and southern Europe continued to live and work in ways not far removed from those of their great-grandparents. They used simple horse- or oxen-drawn plows, they harvested with scythes fueled by their own arms and backs, they celebrated births and mourned deaths with rituals embedded in centuries-old peasant cultures. And they had little contact with unsettling ideas as high rates of illiteracy continued—almost 90 percent in some rural regions of the Austrian Empire, for example.

This cultural and economic isolation was breaking down by the time World War I erupted in 1914. Railways, which increasingly linked Europe's diverse regions into a single economic network, played a crucial role. Between 1870 and 1914 the world's rail network grew by 500 percent. In the 1880s, agriculture still employed the majority of Europe's population in all countries except Britain, Belgium, France, the Netherlands, and Switzerland, but even peasants still farming in traditional ways were caught up in the momentum of the industrial economy.

Imperial Russia serves as a good example of the breakdown of social and cultural isolation. By 1914 Russia had developed a significant industrial zone, one that tied it more closely than ever before to Western economic struc-

■ **Pre-Industrial Continuities**

This photograph of French peasant women taking time off for a meal highlights the patchy nature of industrialization even in western Europe. Not until the 1880s and 1890s did many rural regions come within the embrace of the modern industrial economy.

tures. In the 1890s, Russia underwent dramatic industrialization under the leadership of Sergei Witte (1849–1915), Alexander III's finance minister. Before serving the tsar in this capacity, Witte had a successful career in the railway industry. He used this experience to carry out a program of planned economic development. The state-owned railway network doubled in size. This impressive engineering achievement, which included the 5,000-mile Trans-Siberian railway (begun in 1891), accelerated the movement of both goods and laborers across the vast expanse of Russian territory. Witte also placed Russia on the gold standard, making the Russian ruble easily convertible into other currencies and so fostering international trade. High taxes and protective tariffs generated some of the capital to fuel industrial expansion, but foreign investment was also crucial. French, British, German, and Belgian capital poured into Russia, up from 98 million rubles in 1880 to 911 million by 1900. By the turn of the century, as a result of such policies, Russian steel production was ranked fourth worldwide, behind only Britain, Germany, and the United States And Russia supplied 50 percent of the oil used by the industrialized world. Coal mines and steel mills dotted Ukraine, and huge state-run factories dominated Moscow and St. Petersburg.

THE SECOND INDUSTRIAL REVOLUTION

The expansion of the Industrial Revolution coincided with a shift in the processes of industrialization itself. The decades after 1870 witnessed a new phase in the techniques and technologies of both production and consumption, a phase that some historians regard as so important that they call it the "Second Industrial Revolution°." Mechanical processes were altered with the development of more specialized lathes and the mechanization of tasks such as grinding that had previously been completed by hand. By the late 1870s, a series of technological innovations ensured that for the first time steel could be produced cheaply and in huge quantities. The availability of steel, more durable and more flexible than iron, expanded production in industries such as railroads, shipbuilding, and construction.

The construction industry itself was transformed. New technological advances in the production of not only steel but also iron, cement, and plate glass, combined with the inventions of the mechanical crane and stone cutter, allowed architects and builders to reach to the skies. Cityscapes changed dramatically as these spectacular new constructions thrust upward. In 1885, the engineering firm of Gustave Eiffel (1832–1923) proposed the construction of an iron and steel tower to celebrate the Paris World's Fair of 1889. Modeled on the structural supports of railway viaducts, the Eiffel Tower was ridiculed by critics as a "truly tragic street lamp" and a "half-built factory pipe," but it soon came to symbolize both Paris and the new age of modernity.

This same era saw the development of electric power. In 1866 the English scientist Michael Faraday (1791–1867) designed the first electromagnetic generator. Four years later the first commercially viable generator was produced. Once electricity could be cheaply generated and delivered to homes and shops, it then needed to be converted into usable forms. In 1879, the American Thomas Edison (1847–1931) invented the light bulb and illuminated the

14 Août 1888   14 Septembre 1888   26 Décembre 1888   20 Janvier 1889

■ **The Eiffel Tower Reaches to the Sky**
Engineer Gustave Eiffel designed the Eiffel Tower for an international exposition in Paris in 1889.

practical possibilities of electric power. These developments created a huge new energy-producing industry. They also accelerated the production and distribution of other industrial goods as factories and shops, as well as the train and tram lines that serviced them, were linked to the city power grid.

One important characteristic that distinguished this new phase of industrialization was the role of the state in encouraging economic modernization. Governments implemented policies of economic regulation and intervention, such as the construction of state-owned and -operated railway networks and the provision of financial assistance to private business ventures. The challenge posed by the Great Depression hastened the retreat from the free-trade principles of economic liberalism. Faced with declining profits and increased competition, businessmen demanded that their governments act to protect domestic industries from foreign competition. In this period, only Britain, Denmark, and the Netherlands retained the liberal commitment to free trade and refused to construct tariff walls designed to overprice the goods of outside competitors.

The emergence of much larger and more complicated organizational structures also characterized this new industrial phase. As a result of the economic pressures of the Great Depression, businesses grew much bigger. Faced with the necessity of trimming production costs in a time of declining profits, business owners developed new organizational forms, including both *vertical integration*—buying up the companies that supplied their raw materials and those that bought their finished products—and *horizontal inte-*

gration—linking up with companies in the same industry to fix prices, control competition, and ensure a steady profit. The Standard Oil Company exemplifies both trends. Formed in 1870 by the American industrialist John D. Rockefeller (1839–1937), Standard Oil monopolized 75 percent of the petroleum business in the United States by the 1890s, and in addition controlled iron mines, timberland, and various manufacturing and transportation businesses.

Within these new, huge, often multinational companies, organization grew more complex and impersonal. The small family firm run by the owner who knew the name of every employee grew increasingly rare as an ever-expanding layer of managers and clerical staff separated worker from owner. Moreover, identifying "the owner" grew increasingly difficult. The need for capital to fuel these huge enterprises drove businesses to incorporation—the sale of "shares" in the business to numerous stockholders, each of whom now shared ownership in the company.

The development of more complicated organizational patterns at the production end of the economic process interacted with changes in the way goods were marketed. During these decades, a revolution in retailing occurred, one that culminated in a new type of business aimed at middle-class customers—the department store. In a traditional shop, the retailer (who was often also the producer) offered a single product—gloves, for example—in limited quantity at a fairly high price. Often, this price was not set. The customer haggled with the tradesperson until they agreed on a price. "Browsing" was unheard of; an individual who entered a shop was expected to make a purchase. The department stores changed these practices. These new commercial establishments—Bon Marche in Paris, Macy's in New York, Marshall Field's in Chicago, Whiteley's in London—offered a vast array of products in huge quantities. They made their profits not from high prices, but from a quick turnover of a very large volume of low-priced goods. To stimulate sales, they sought to make shopping a pleasant experience. Thus, they provided huge, well-lighted expanses filled with appealing goods sold by courteous, well-trained clerks. In-store reading rooms and restaurants pampered the weary shopper. Another innovation, mail-order catalogs, offered the store's delights to potential customers stranded in distant rural regions and traditionally reliant for their goods on the itinerant peddler and the seasonal fair. Advertising became a crucial industry in its own right, as business sought to persuade potential customers of new needs and desires.

ON THE MOVE: EMIGRATION AND URBANIZATION

These three economic developments—the onset of the Great Depression, the expansion of industrialization, and the Second Industrial Revolution—accelerated already existing patterns of urbanization and immigration, and so helped widen the borders of local, regional, and national communities across Europe. The Great Depression hit agricultural regions particularly hard, at just the same time that continuing population growth exerted greater pressure on land and jobs. In addition, industrial expansion undercut rural manufacturing and handicraft production, crucial sources of income for rural populations. As a result, men and women from traditional villages sought new economic opportunities in the industrializing cities of Europe, or further abroad, in the United States, Canada, South America, and Australia.

European cities grew dramatically after 1870. In 1800, only 23 European cities had more than 100,000 inhabitants. By 1900, 135 cities of such a size had sprung up. The European population as a whole continued to expand in this period, but the cities increased at a much faster pace. For example, in 1800 the city of Odessa in Ukraine held 6,000 inhabitants. By 1914, Odessa contained 480,000 people. In the same period, Hungary's Budapest expanded from 50,000 to 900,000 inhabitants. Even within these expanding cities, Europeans were on the move. Take the example of Berlin. In 1890, 12 percent of the city's population had arrived just that year; 8.5 percent of the population was on its way out. Another 56 percent moved to a new location within the city itself.

The migration flow was not all one-way. Farm laborers moved to the cities when times were tough and then moved home again after they had earned some money. Most urban immigrants came to the cities from the surrounding countryside, and often stayed for less than a year. Duisberg, a steel and tool-making center located in Germany's Ruhr Valley, grew in population from 8,900 to 106,700 between 1848 and 1904. Almost one-third of its newcomers in the 1890s came from villages less than fifteen miles away. No fewer than two-thirds of these immigrants eventually returned to their rural villages.

By 1910, however, one-sixth of Duisberg's immigrants came from other countries, particularly Italy and the Netherlands. The combined impact of agricultural crisis and urban industrial expansion broke down national boundaries to create an international industrial workforce by 1914. Inhabitants of industrially underdeveloped regions were drawn to more economically advanced areas. Italians

■ The Bicycle Revolution

The bicycle revolutionized daily life for ordinary Europeans. The introduction of equal-sized wheels in 1886 and of pneumatic tires in 1890 allowed for a far more comfortable ride than had been the case with the bone-breaking cycles built earlier. Mass industrial production made the bicycle affordable, and for the first time, ordinary individuals, far too poor to afford a horse or motorcar, could dare to purchase their own private means of transportation, which would get them where they wanted to go in one-quarter of the time that walking required. No longer confined to their village for work opportunities or social contacts, bicycle owners discovered that their daily world had widened fourfold.

A LETTER HOME

·············

For immigrants to the United States, the "new world" offered the chance to break free from the cultural and religious restraints that had governed their lives in their villages at home. Many found the changes unsettling and distressing. Others were thrilled with their new freedom, as this letter reveals. The letter never made it to Goodstein's "auntie," but was instead confiscated by Russian tsarist authorities in an effort to discourage illegal emigration from its Polish territories.

San Bernadino [California], 28 November 1890

Dearest Auntie!

How happy I was a little while ago when finally I received a letter from You. Reading it and hearing about your good health gave me great pleasure and joy. . . .

This past 4 November, it was exactly one year since I left home. On 4 December I arrived in New York and on the 12th I reached San Bernadino. I can tell You for sure that I should have left home 15 years earlier. It would have been much better for me, a thousand times better because I am not able even to describe it to You, how I looked at first and how different I look now. I do not want to write about it because if I start I may never finish with it. I would like to ask the people at home just this one question: why is it forbidden for a young man to take a walk with a girl, to talk to her and to become acquainted with her. I do not consider it a sin. . . . Only You [the Jews in Poland] . . . are so backward. . . .

I do not mean to insult You, but it is especially true that in Your small towns within a half hour everything is known all over and becomes gossip. And so when a young man from there arrives here, what kind of an impression does he make? . . . when he gets together with people, he does not know how to behave and how to have a good time. . . . He also does not know how to hold a knife or a fork or a table napkin. And he does not know how to sing or raise a toast in company. At home we only used to say, "*Lehayim*." At home we only sang *zmires*.*
. . .

In our store, we also sell women's dresses and even underwear. And it may happen that a young man has to sell to some young girl some such things or whatever. We also sell, here, undershirts, shirts, collars, fine ties, pocket watches, top hats and overcoats. All this the young man was not acquainted with at home. . . .

Be well, Dear Auntie, and please write again to Your forever loving nephew.

Your nephew,
M. Goodstein

––––––––––
*"*Lehayim*" = "to life"; a toast. "*Zmires*" = sabbath songs.

Source: From Witold Kula et al., *Writing Home: Immigrants in Brazil and the United States 1890–1891*, edited and translated by Josephine Wtulich (New York: Columbia University Press, 1986). Reprinted by permission of East European Monographs.

---

headed to France and Switzerland, while the Irish poured across the Irish Sea into Liverpool and Glasgow. Earlier in the century large numbers of Germans had sought new lives in the United States, but after 1880 emigration from Germany dwindled. As its industrial economy boomed, Germany became a net importer of labor from Poland and other eastern and central European regions.

Some immigrants headed not for the nearest city, but for an entirely different continent. Between 1860 and 1914, over 52 million Europeans crossed the ocean in quest of a better life. Seventy-two percent of these transoceanic immigrants traveled to North America, 21 percent to South America, and the rest to Australia and New Zealand.[1] Irish and English immigration to the United States remained high throughout this period, but after the 1880s eastern Europeans accounted for an ever-larger share of those bound for America. One hundred thousand Poles moved to the United States over the course of the 1880s; in the first decades of the twentieth century, between 130,000 and 175,000 Poles were immigrating to the United States each year.

By the 1890s, a truly global labor market had developed. Both technological developments (primarily the shift from sailing to steam ships) and competition among shipping firms considerably reduced the cost of transoceanic travel. As a result, men from villages in southern Italy and Spain could cross the Atlantic in time for the fall harvest of wheat in Argentina, travel to Brazil to pick coffee beans, and then head back home in May. Clearly, in such societies, the borders between local villages and the rest of the world had become permeable.

GROWING SOCIAL UNREST

Rapid economic change, combined with accelerated urbanization and immigration, heightened social tensions and destabilized political structures. The freefall in prices that characterized the Great Depression eroded capitalist profit margins, shattered business confidence, and increased middle-class resistance to workers' demands. Class hostilities rose as workers responded angrily to businessmen's efforts to protect their profit margins by reducing the number of their employees and increasing labor productivity. In rural regions such as Spain and Ireland, the devastating collapse in agricultural prices fostered serious social and economic crises. Increasingly desperate, agricultural laborers and peasants turned to violence to enforce their calls for a fairer distribution of land. The spread of industrialization into southern and eastern Europe also led to social unrest as handicraft producers and independent artisans fought to maintain their traditional livelihoods in the face of the industrial onslaught.

In regions such as Britain and parts of Germany, traditional producers had lost their battle against industrialization in the preceding generation, but the onset of the Second Industrial Revolution brought new social strains. The expansion of office and sales jobs widened the ranks of the lower middle class (or *petty bourgeoisie*). This increasingly important social group exhibited extreme class consciousness and an often fierce hostility toward the working class. With an income no higher than that of a skilled worker, the clerk had to fight hard to maintain middle-class status. The erosion of objective differences such as income levels accentuated the importance of subjective differences—wearing the correct clothing, speaking with the proper accent, living on the right street, keeping the children in school.

The flow of immigrants into Europe's cities also sent social and ethnic tensions soaring. Cities were often unable to cope with the sudden and dramatic increases in population, despite the spread of public health provisions such as water and sewer systems. Housing shortages and poor living conditions exacerbated social tensions as newcomers battled with established residents for jobs and apartments. The mixture of different nationalities and ethnic groups often proved particularly explosive.

Defining the Political Nation

These encounters between rival social groups within European societies changed European politics. Faced with rising social tensions, political leaders sought ways to quell social discontent and to ensure the political loyalty of their populations. At the same time, they faced a new world of mass politics—a new political culture characterized by the participation of men outside the upper and middle classes. Across Europe in the decades after 1870, those in power had to figure out how to stay there. They had to devise ways to incorporate the newly politicized masses into the nation while at the same time suppressing actual and potential unrest.

MAKING NATIONS

After 1870, all but the most authoritarian of European political leaders recognized the importance of "making nations," of creating a sense of national identity powerful enough to overcome the conflicting regional, social, and political loyalties that divided their citizens and subjects. In this nation-making effort, both education and nationalistic ritual proved essential. (See Map 22.1).

State elementary schools served as important tools in the effort to build internally united and externally competitive nation-states. During the last third of the nineteenth century, most of the nations of western and central Europe established free public elementary education systems. In Austria-Hungary, for example, free and compulsory education was decreed in 1869. Of course, passing legislation is one thing, ensuring compliance another. Because children's wages contributed to the family income, many poor families deeply resented the laws that made school attendance mandatory. In poorer districts of Austria-Hungary such as Bukovina, only 36 percent of children attended school, despite the law. In Italy communities were required to provide free education to needy children as early as 1859, but as late as 1912 only 31 percent of the children in the southern region of Calabria were in school.

Despite these difficulties, the schools constituted an essential link in the chain of national identity. Schools broke the cultural barriers imposed by illiteracy. Individuals who could read had access to newspapers, magazines, and books that drew them far beyond the borders of their local village or neighborhood. Both political leaders and intellectuals recognized the power of education in creating a national community. In the 1880s, for example, French student teachers were instructed that "their first duty is to make [their pupils] love and understand the fatherland."[2]

Schools thus helped forge a national identity in very specific ways. First, they ensured the triumph of the national language. Required to abandon their regional dialect (and sometimes brutally punished if they did not), children learned to read and write in the national language. Second, history and geography lessons taught children particular versions of the past that buttressed their sense of belonging to a superior people, and often served a specific political agenda. For example, French classrooms after 1870 displayed wall maps of France—maps that clearly included the provinces of Alsace and Lorraine, even though these regions belonged to Germany, which had seized them as the spoils of victory after the Franco-Prussian War. Finally, the schools, with their essentially captive populations, participated fully in newly designed nationalistic rituals, such as singing aggressive patriotic songs like "Deutschland Über Alles" ("Germany Over All") or "Rule Britannia," and observing special days to commemorate military victories or national heroes.

Nationalistic ritual was not confined to the schoolroom and playground. Making nations often meant *inventing* traditions to captivate the imagination and capture the loyalty of the mass electorate. German policymakers, for example, developed "Sedan Day." This national holiday, which celebrated the battle that helped create the new German state, featured parades, flag raisings, and special services to foster a sense of German nationalism among its citizens. At the same time, the person of the emperor, or *kaiser,* became the center of nationalistic ceremony and loyalty, particularly after the accession of William II (r. 1888–1918), the first emperor to identify himself as truly German rather than Prussian. William used personal appearances, militaristic pageantry, and civic ritual to link together monarchy and subjects in a sturdy chain of nationalism.

The monarchy was even more central to British nationalism. Whereas Queen Victoria's coronation in 1837 had been a small, disorganized affair, by the final decades of the century the anniversaries of her accession to the throne (the Silver Jubilee of 1887 and the Diamond Jubilee of 1897) were dramatically different. Elaborately staged, beautifully costumed, and carefully orchestrated, these events were designed to make ordinary individuals feel part of a wider,

powerful, meaningful national community. The new technologies of mass printing and mass production helped support this new mass politics of nationality. At the Jubilees, participants could purchase colorfully illustrated commemorative pamphlets, ceramic plates etched with the Queen's silhouette, teapots in the shape of Victoria's head, or even an automated musical bustle that played "God Save the Queen" whenever the wearer sat down.

RUSSIA: REVOLUTION AND REACTION

Across Europe, politicians and policymakers used both education and nationalistic ritual to blend disparate groups into a cohesive national community. As the example of Russia illustrates, failure to construct such a national com-

■ **Map 22.1 Europe at the End of the Nineteenth Century**

A comparison of this map with Map 18.2 ("Europe After the Congress of Vienna in 1815," p. 615) shows the impact of modern nationalism on European political geography. The most striking change is the formation of the new states of Italy and Germany (the German Empire). In addition, nationalist movements succeeded in carving away large chunks of the Ottoman Empire's European territories. By the 1880s, Bosnia and Herzegovina were under Austrian administration, and Greece, Serbia, Montenegro, Rumania, and Bulgaria had all achieved independence.

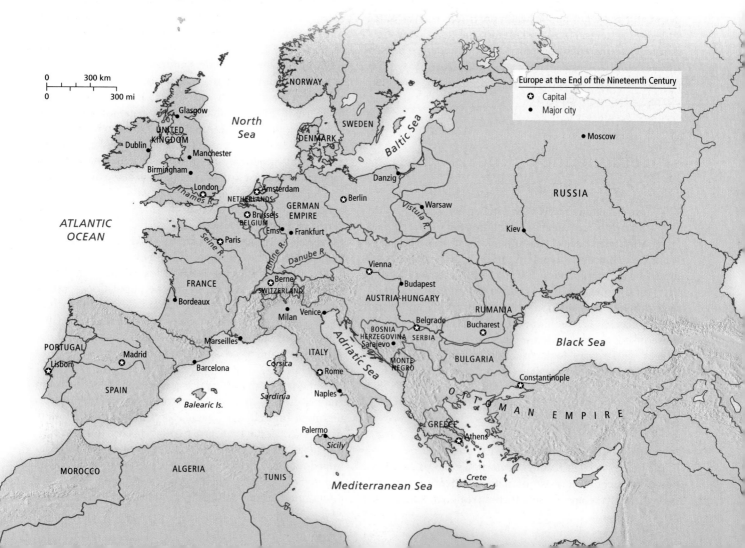

■ The Mass Marketing of National Identity

Advertising and mass production allowed ordinary Britons to participate in the glamour of royalty by purchasing inexpensive trinkets, like this 1902 coronation souvenir.

munity threatened political rulers with revolutionary consequences. Convinced that God had appointed them to rule, Russia's tsars clung to absolutism. To catch up with the West, the tsarist regime adopted Western industrialization but it had no intentions of accepting Western ideas of representative government. It could not, however, completely block the flow of these ideas into the Russian Empire. By the 1880s, many members of Russia's small but growing middle class espoused liberal political goals such as a written constitution and limited representational government. Other Russians went further and embraced socialism. Both liberalism and socialism constituted revolutionary ideological challenges to tsarist absolutism, and both met with fierce repression.

Socialists faced not only harsh political repression but also a major intellectual dilemma—the problem of adapting the political and economic ideas of Karl Marx to the

Russian situation. As we saw in Chapter 21, Marx stressed that revolution would come from the ranks of the urban working class, but in Russia, the number of urban workers remained relatively small (3 million in 1914, out of a population of 170 million) and the chances of a genuinely working-class revolution appeared slight. Many Russian revolutionaries, then, rejected Marx's brand of socialism as a Western ideology unsuited for export eastward. Arguing that Russia must follow its own, non-Western path, they looked not to the urban working class but to the peasantry as the source of a genuinely popular socialist revolution. Calling themselves *Populists* ("of the people") they fanned out across the countryside, living and working with peasants and endeavoring to build a new Russia from the bottom up. Some, such as Sofiia Perovskaia and the other members of the People's Will, turned to terrorism.

As we saw at the opening of this chapter, revolutionary populists succeeded in assassinating Tsar Alexander II, but not in toppling the tsarist regime. With the use of repressive legislation and an ever-expanding secret police force, both Alexander III (r. 1881–1894) and Nicholas II (r. 1894–1917) drove political dissenters—liberal, Marxist, and populist—underground or into exile. They could not, however, quell the social unrest produced by economic change. By the turn of the century, rapid, state-sponsored industrialization had built an industrial structure in Russia, but it stood on a very faulty foundation. Russia remained a largely agricultural nation, with peasants still accounting for over 75 percent of the population. Heavy taxation and rapid population growth, which increased competition for land, heightened social and economic anxiety among the peasant masses.

Within the industrial cities, social unrest also simmered. Factory workers labored more than twelve hours a day in wretched working conditions for very little pay. Any protest against these conditions was regarded as protest against the tsar and was quickly repressed. The workers

CHRONOLOGY

Instability Within the Russian Empire

1881	Assassination of Tsar Alexander II; accession of Alexander III
1882	May Laws reimpose restrictions on Russian Jews
1890s	Industrialization accelerates under Witte
1894	Accession of Nicholas II
1904	Outbreak of Russo-Japanese War
1905	Revolution
1906–1910	Nicholas II stifles political revolution

■ **The Revolution of 1905 in the Movies**

On Bloody Sunday, January 22, 1905, Russian troops opened fire on more than 100,000 citizens who had gathered in St. Petersburg to present a petition to the tsar. Rather than subduing the revolt, the massacre sparked a revolution. This photograph, supposedly of the moment when the tsar's troops began to shoot the demonstrators, is one of the most familiar images of the twentieth century—yet it is *not* in fact a documentary record. Instead, it is a still taken from *The Ninth of January*, a Soviet film made in 1925.

themselves remained peasants in their loyalties and mindset. Separated from their families who remained behind in the village, they lived in crowded state dormitories and traveled regularly back to their villages to plant and harvest. They had little sense of belonging to the Russian nation, or of participating in the political structures that governed their lives.

In 1905, popular discontent flared into revolution. That year Japan trounced Russia in a war sparked by competition for territory in Asia. The military debacle of the Russo-Japanese War revealed the incompetence of the tsarist regime and provided an opening for reformers to demand political change. On a day that became known as "Bloody Sunday" (January 22, 1905), a group of 100,000 workers and their families attempted to present to the tsar a petition calling for higher wages, better working conditions, and the right to participate in political decision making. Government troops opened fire on the unarmed crowd; at least 70 people were killed and more than 240 were wounded.

The massacre horrified and radicalized much of Russian society. Across the Russian Empire, cities came to a standstill as workers went on strike and demanded both economic and political rights. In June, portions of the navy mutinied. By the fall, the empire was in chaos, with transportation, communications, energy, and water supplies all facing disruption. Taking advantage of this upheaval, states on the fringes of the empire, such as the Baltic regions, rose up in revolt against imperial rule, and middle-class liberals demanded limited representative government. In October, Tsar Nicholas II gave in and acceded to demands for the election of a legislative assembly. The Revolution of 1905 appeared to be a success.

By 1910, however, the tsar had regained much of his autocratic power. Revolutionary fervor dissipated as rival groups jostled for political influence. The tsar, with his army still loyal, refused to carry out many of the promised reforms. Tsarist autocracy remained intact, but so too did the causes of the discontent that had led to the revolution. Russia lacked an authentic national community, as Nicholas would discover during the First World War. We shall see in Chapter 24 that total war finally snapped the very fragile links that connected the tsarist regime to the peasant masses, and a new revolution destroyed the Russian imperial state.

GERMANY: IDENTIFYING THE ENEMY

In the new states of Germany and Italy, political rulers made a concerted effort to shape a national community, in contrast to the tsarist regime in Russia. Military victories constructed the borders of the new united Germany. Constructing a sense of nationhood within these borders, however, turned out to be more difficult. We saw in Chapter 21 that the new German state remained politically authoritarian, despite its democratic appearance. All adult males had the right to elect representatives to the German Reichstag (the lower house of parliament) but the Reichstag was fairly powerless. Real power lay in the hands of William I (r. 1861–1888), the first emperor (or *kaiser*) of the unified Germany, and his chancellor, the conservative aristocrat Otto von Bismarck. Appointed—and fired—at the emperor's whim, Bismarck did not answer to the legislature or the electorate. He could not entirely ignore the Reichstag, however, because it possessed the power of the purse. It had to approve the budget and appropriate the funds necessary to run the government. Bismarck thus faced the task of ensuring a sympathetic majority in the Reichstag while at the same time maintaining the emperor's authority, protecting the social and political privileges of the aristocracy, and pacifying the masses.

One way to unite these disparate interests was by identifying a common enemy. In the 1870s, that enemy was the Catholic Church. Convinced that loyalty to the Roman papacy compromised German Catholics' loyalty to the new state, Bismarck initiated what he rather grandly called the *Kulturkampf* (the "struggle of civilization"), a series of measures designed to limit the power of the Catholic Church in Germany. But Bismarck lost this battle. Catholics organized into an opposition political party and resisted Bismarck's efforts to marginalize them or to paint them as in any way "non-German." In 1874 the Catholic Center party won 25 percent of the seats in the Reichstag, and by 1878 Bismarck was forced to recognize that his anti-Catholic policies were threatening rather than strengthening his hold on German politics.

At this point Bismarck shifted his aim to a new target: German socialists. As we will see in the next section, powerful socialist political parties emerged in Europe during this era. To Bismarck, socialist loyalty to an international workers' movement was like the Roman Catholics' loyalty to the pope—an outside allegiance that weakened national unity.

CHRONOLOGY

The Coming of Mass Politics in Germany

1870	Franco-Prussian War
1871	Unification of Germany; Jewish emancipation
1878	*Kulturkampf* ended; antisocialist law enacted
1883	First social welfare legislation enacted under Bismarck
1888	Accession of William II
1890	Bismarck dismissed by Emperor William II; SPD becomes the largest political party in Germany
1900	Promulgation of German Civil Code: single law code for German Empire
1901	Women admitted to full-time university study

Alarmed by socialist electoral victories, Bismarck outlawed the German Social Democratic Party (SPD) in 1878 and authorized the federal police to disband all socialist meetings and organizations.

This attack on the SPD appealed to antisocialist groups such as conservative landowners, Roman Catholics, and liberal businessmen, and thus gave Bismarck the Reichstag majority that he needed. The antisocialist strategy, however, risked alienating the growing urban working class. To attract the support of this vital social segment and weaken the

■ **German Emperor William II and His Entourage**

William preferred to wear military regalia when he appeared in public. In this way, William himself symbolized the link between the German state and Germany's military might.

appeal of the SPD at the same time, Bismarck introduced some of the most thoroughgoing social welfare measures yet seen in Europe. He initiated sickness benefits in 1883, coverage for industrial accidents in 1884, and old-age pensions and disability insurance in 1889. Even so, the outlawed SPD continued to attract growing numbers of working-class supporters.

In 1890, however, the new German emperor, William II (r. 1888–1918), fired Bismarck and let the antisocialist legislation lapse. William believed he could cement a sense of common German national identity among its various social groups—Catholics and socialists, aristocrats and workers, liberals and military officers, industrialists and landowners—through aggressive militarization and imperial expansion. These policies helped clear the way for World War I, a war that would at first unify but then destroy the German imperial state.

ITALY: THE ILLUSION OF TRANSFORMATION

The development of national unity in Italy ran up against two key obstacles: the papacy and poverty. As we saw in Chapter 21, Rome and the surrounding region remained outside the borders of the new Italian nation-state until 1870, when the French troops that had been protecting the pope withdrew to fight in the Franco-Prussian War. The Italian army marched in and claimed Rome as the capital of Italy. Pope Pius IX (r. 1846–1878) shut himself within the Vatican, refused to recognize the new state, and forbade Catholics (almost the entire Italian population) from voting or running for office. Many Catholics ignored the pope's prohibition, but the hostility between the papacy and the new government undermined the state's legitimacy.

An even more serious obstacle to national unity was raised by severe levels of poverty and economic underdevelopment, particularly in southern Italy. The south remained a region of huge, inefficiently run agricultural estates, unable to support its expanding population, particularly after cheap North American grain flooded the European markets and gutted agricultural prices. Small landowners were unable to make a profit, while the large aristocratic landholders responded to the economic crisis by "rationalizing" the management of their estates, a practice that usually included firing large numbers of agricultural laborers. As a result, much of the south seethed with social discontent. Immigration to France, Switzerland, South America, and the United States relieved some of the pressure, but both small landholders and the landless laborers who worked on the large estates found it increasingly difficult to make ends meet. Economically desperate and receptive to radical political ideas, the rural poor began to demand the breakup of large landholdings.

By the 1880s, the social unrest resulting from the agricultural crisis and the spread of revolutionary socialist ideologies so frightened the upper classes that they voted to widen the franchise in the hopes of depriving socialism of some of its appeal. In 1882 the assembly expanded the franchise from 8 percent of the adult male population (2 percent of the total population) to 25 percent of adult males. This action alone could not make a nation, however. Most peasants remained disenfranchised, without any sense of ownership in the new national political system. Poverty persisted as a key obstacle to national unity. The wealthy southern landholders who formed a solid bloc in the national assembly insisted on maintaining high tariffs on imported grain—a policy that protected their profits while increasing food prices. Taxes also rose rapidly as politicians favored balancing the budget over alleviating the plight of the poor.

The political system could not meet the challenge of creating a national community. No single party had a majority in the national assembly. Instead, Italian politicians developed a system of *trasformismo*, building and maintaining coalition governments by transforming opponents into allies through bribery and patronage. Because political leaders needed the votes of southern landowners to stay in power, the system stifled any chance to implement programs of economic development or land reform. Thus the politics of transformation actually ensured that no real social transformation occurred in Italy. By the 1890s, the government had to call out the army to put down labor strikes in the northern industrial cities, and imposed martial law over much of the south, which had erupted in revolt.

In a vain attempt to build national consensus through military glory, the Prime Minister Francesco Crispi (1819–1901), one of the heroes of Italian unification and a dominant figure in post-unification politics, authorized a disastrous invasion of Ethiopia. Italy's defeat in Ethiopia led to the fall of the Crispi government in 1896 and to a period of political confusion. Anarchist bombings, socialist-led

---

CHRONOLOGY

The Coming of Mass Politics in Italy

1870	Rome occupied by Italian army
1896	Italian invasion of Ethiopia defeated; fall of Crispi government
1900	Anarchists assassinate King Humbert
1903	First ministry of Giovanni Giolitti
1911	Universal manhood suffrage enacted
1912	Successful invasion of Libya
1914	Red Week

urban uprisings, violent labor strikes, and agricultural riots escalated.

In the first decade of the twentieth century, however, Italy appeared to take a new course under the premiership of Giovanni Giolitti (1842–1928), who sought ways for both rural and urban workers to feel a part of the nation. Alarmed by the growing appeal of Italy's revolutionary socialist parties, Giolitti embarked on a conscious policy of improving workers' lives and so convincing their political leaders that real change did not require revolution. Giolitti legalized trade unions, nationalized the railroads, established public health and life insurance programs, cracked down on child labor, established a six-day workweek, and in 1911 introduced universal manhood suffrage to Italy. Like Crispi, he turned to imperial expansion to foster a sense of "Italianness" among diverse groups. Unlike Crispi's humiliating failure in Ethiopia, however, Giolitti's colonial venture succeeded. In 1912 Italy annexed Libya.

Yet Giolitti's efforts to create a more inclusive political nation in Italy faltered. The Italian Socialist Party rejected his plan to incorporate it within the existing political system. During "Red Week" in June 1914, anarchist and socialist-inspired revolts spread across northern Italy. Perhaps most seriously, Giolitti, like his predecessors relied on the support of southern landowners in the assembly and therefore ignored the crying need for economic development in the south. On the eve of the First World War, Italy remained seriously divided between north and south, between peasant and landowner, between industrialist and worker. No single vision of "Italianness" fused these groups into a single nation.

FRANCE: A CRISIS OF LEGITIMACY

Unlike Germany and Italy, France had long existed as a nation-state, but a century of almost continuous political revolution ensured that in the final decades of the nineteenth century no consensus existed on who or what France actually was. After Napoleon III's capture by Prussian troops in 1871, his empire collapsed and the French returned to a republican form of government, based on universal manhood suffrage. Born in the humiliation of military defeat, the Third Republic faced a crisis of legitimacy. Key sectors of the population argued that the Republic had been foisted on the French by their Prussian conquerors, and that it was therefore not a legitimate state and not worthy of their loyalty or support. This crisis of legitimacy was worsened by the failure of French politicians to generate much enthusiasm. A dozen different parties jostled for control of the legislature. Because no single party controlled a majority, the only way to form a government was through forging coalitions, and thus compromise, political wheeling and dealing, financial corruption, and constant reshuffling of officeholders became the common tools of parliamentary politics.

The lackluster nature of French politics accentuated the appeal of those who wished to destroy the French Republic—monarchists who wanted a king back on the throne, Bonapartists longing for the glory days of Napoleonic empire, Roman Catholics disturbed by republican efforts to curb the political power of the Church, aristocrats opposed to democracy. To perceive the depth of opposition to the Republic, it is essential to understand that "republicanism" in France meant more than "no king, no emperor." Rooted in the radical Jacobin Republic of 1792, republicanism rested on a vision of an ideal France consisting of male equals—small shopkeepers and independent artisans, governed by reason rather than religion. Such a vision directly conflicted with the interests and ideals of monarchists, Bonapartists, and Roman Catholics, as well as of the growing number of working-class socialists. The encounter of these rival ideologies generated chaos in French politics throughout this era.

This fundamental lack of consensus about the nature or shape of France was strikingly revealed by the eruption of the Dreyfus Affair°. In 1894, on the basis of hearsay evidence and forged documentation, a French military court convicted Captain Alfred Dreyfus (1859–1935) of espionage. Prominent French intellectuals took up Dreyfus's case, and it became a full-fledged "affair," as supporters and opponents of Dreyfus battled in the streets and in the legislature. Support for Dreyfus, who was Jewish, became linked to support for the secular and egalitarian ideals of the Republic; the anti-Dreyfusards, in contrast, saw Dreyfus's Jewishness as a threat to France's Catholic identity and argued that to question the army hierarchy was to undermine France's military might. The Dreyfus Affair so dominated French politics that in 1899, when René Waldeck-Rousseau, a prominent politician, formed a governing coalition comprising members of a number of political parties, its unifying principle was support for Dreyfus.

The Dreyfus Affair: Defining National Identity in France

On September 27, 1894, the five officers that made up the counterespionage section of France's War Ministry examined a disturbing document—an unsigned, undated, torn piece of paper that had clearly served as a cover letter for a packet of documents containing information on French military equipment and training. The officers found no envelope, but they concluded that the letter was intended for Lieutenant Colonel Maximilian von Schwartzkoppen, the German military attaché in Paris. Thus, this torn piece of paper constituted evidence of treason. Someone in the French officer corps was selling military secrets to the Germans.

After a brief investigation and a cursory comparison of handwriting samples, the French investigators concluded that the traitor was Captain Alfred Dreyfus, a candidate officer on the General Staff. An unlikely traitor, Dreyfus had compiled a strong record during his military career and, by all accounts, was a staunch French patriot. Moreover, because of his marriage to a wealthy woman, he had no need to sell his country for money. He was, however, an aloof and arrogant man, disliked by most of his fellow officers and without a strong backer among his superiors. He was also a Jew.

Despite the lack of solid evidence, Dreyfus was convicted of treason. After a ceremony of military degradation, he was exiled in 1895 to a specially constructed prison hut on Devil's Island, a former leper colony twelve miles off

the coast of French Guyana. Many French men and women believed he had gotten off too lightly. Both public and press clamored for his execution.

With Dreyfus safely imprisoned on his island, his case seemed closed. But in July 1895, Major Marie-Georges Picquart was named chief of the Intelligence Bureau. An ambitious man determined to make a name for himself, Picquart soon discovered that the sale of military secrets to the Germans had continued even after Dreyfus's imprisonment. Ignoring his superiors' instructions to leave the Dreyfus case alone, Picquart set out to trap the man he first believed to be Dreyfus's accomplice. The evidence he uncovered, however, led him to conclude that Dreyfus was in fact innocent.

Picquart's investigations raised serious doubts about Dreyfus's conviction. These doubts were transformed into sensational charges on January 13, 1898, when one of France's most famous authors, Émile Zola, alleged in a Paris daily newspaper that the French military was engaged in a colossal cover-up. In an article headlined "J'accuse!" ("I accuse!"), Zola charged that the General Staff had knowingly convicted an innocent man. Zola's accusations aroused enormous public attention, and over the next six weeks, riots broke out in French cities.

Retried before a second military court in 1899, Dreyfus was again found guilty—although this time "with extenuating circumstances," a ridiculous verdict (there are no extenuating circum-

stances for the crime of treason) concocted to salvage the military's position despite Dreyfus's obvious innocence. In the subsequent riots that broke out in Paris, 100 people were wounded and 200 jailed. Ten days later, the French president pardoned Dreyfus in an effort to heal the divisions opened by the trial. Finally, in 1906, a French high court set aside the court-martial verdict and exonerated Dreyfus. Not until 1995, however, did the French military acknowledge the captain's innocence.

The Dreyfus Affair drew international attention, polarized French politics, and tore apart Parisian society. It sparked not only violent protests but also numerous duels and a series of related trials for assault, defamation, and libel. To uphold Dreyfus's conviction, high-ranking military officials falsified evidence, even to the point of forging entire documents. The question "Are you for or against Dreyfus?" divided families and destroyed friendships. During the height of the controversy, for example, the painter Edgar Degas spoke contemptuously of paintings by Camille Pisarro. When reminded that he had once admired these very same works, Degas said, "Yes, but that was before the Dreyfus Affair." Degas was a passionate anti-Dreyfusard; Pisarro believed Dreyfus was innocent.[3]

What about the Dreyfus Affair so aroused personal passion as to alter one painter's perception of another's work? What made this trial not simply a case, but an *affair,* a matter of public debate and personal upheaval, a cause of violent rioting and political turmoil?

To comprehend the Dreyfus Affair, we must understand that it was less about Captain Alfred Dreyfus than about the very existence of the French Third Republic. The intellectuals and politicians who rallied in support of Dreyfus were defenders of the Republic, men and women who sought to limit the army's involvement in France's political life, who linked both monarchy and empire to national disaster rather than national glory, and who believed in a secular definition of the nation that would treat Roman

The Dreyfus Affair

Captain Alfred Dreyfus before his judges, 1899.

Catholics no differently from Protestants, Jews, or atheists. Dreyfus's opponents, in contrast, regarded the establishment of the Third Republic as a betrayal of the true France—a hierarchical, Roman Catholic, imperial state, steeped in military traditions. Defending the military conviction of Dreyfus became a way to express support not only for the army, but also for the authoritarian traditions that the Republic had jettisoned. The Dreyfus Affair was thus an encounter between competing versions of French national identity.

The question "What is France?" however, could not be answered without considering a second question: "Who belongs in France?"—or more specifically, "What about Jews?" France's small Jewish community (less than 1 percent of the total population) had enjoyed the rights of full citizenship since 1791—much longer than in most of Europe. Yet the Dreyfus Affair clearly demonstrated that even in France, the position of Jews in the national community was far from assured. Although anti-Semitism proba-

bly played little role in the initial charges against Dreyfus, it quickly became a dominating feature of the affair. More than seventy anti-Semitic riots ravaged France during this period. Anti-Semitic politicians and publications placed themselves in the vanguard of the anti-Dreyfus forces. For many anti-Dreyfusards, Dreyfus's Jewishness explained everything. The highly acclaimed novelist and political theorist Maurice Barres insisted, "I have no need to be told why Dreyfus committed treason . . . That Dreyfus is capable of treason I conclude from his race."[4]

Anti-Semites like Barres regarded Jewishness as a kind of genetic disease that made Jews unfit for French citizenship. To the anti-Semitic nationalist, the Jew was a person without a country, unconnected by racial or religious ties to the French nation—the very opposite of a patriot. As a symbol of rootlessness, "the Jew" came to represent for many anti-Dreyfusards the forces of unsettling economic and political change that appeared to be weakening the French nation. Anti-Semites

pointed to the successes of assimilated Jews such as Dreyfus—not only in the army but also in the universities, the professions, and business life—as evidence of what they perceived as the threat of Jewish "domination" of French culture.

Declared innocent in 1906, Dreyfus resumed his military career and served his country with distinction in the First World War. Like Dreyfus, the Third Republic survived the Dreyfus Affair. It was probably even strengthened by it. Outrage over the army's cover-up led republican politicians to limit the powers of the military and so lessened the chances of an anti-republican military coup. Anti-Semitism, however, remained a pervasive force in French politics and cultural life well into the twentieth century. ◼

Questions of Justice

1. Dreyfus was tried both in military courts and in public opinion. What does the Dreyfus Affair reveal about the emergence of the mass media as an agent of judgment in popular culture? What sorts of evidence were used to convict him in the court of public opinion? How did this evidence differ from that used in the military trial?

2. What does the Dreyfus Affair reveal about definitions of national identity in late-nineteenth-century Europe?

Taking It Further

Cahm, Eric. *The Dreyfus Affair in French Society and Politics.* 1994. A wide-ranging history.

Kleeblatt, Norman, ed. *The Dreyfus Affair: Art, Truth, and Justice.* 1987. This richly illustrated collection of essays explores the cultural as well as political and legal impact of the case.

Lindemann, Albert S. *The Jew Accused: Three Anti-Semitic Affairs (Dreyfus, Beilis, Frank) 1894–1915.* 1991. An illuminating comparative study.

Snyder, Louis L. *The Dreyfus Case: A Documentary History.* 1973. An accessible collection of primary documents.

Dreyfus was finally declared not guilty in 1906, but the consequences of the affair were far-reaching. The Dreyfus Affair revealed the strength of anti-republicanism in France, and so drove the Republic's supporters to seize the offensive. The government pushed through measures placing the army under civilian control, prohibiting members of Catholic religious orders from teaching in public *or private* schools, and removing the Catholic Church from its privileged position in French political life. With these measures politicians aimed to separate citizenship from religious affiliation and social rank and to redefine France in republican terms.

In 1914, the success of this effort at redefinition remained unclear. National political life was dominated by the Radical Party, which represented the interests of small shopkeepers and independent artisans, not industrial workers, and drew its support from rural and small-town constituencies, not the growing cities. The Radicals' grip on power thwarted any significant efforts to address the grievances of the urban working class. Radicals opposed the high taxes necessary to establish social welfare programs and dragged their feet on social legislation such as the ten-hour workday (not passed until 1904) and old-age provisions (not established until 1910). As a result, workers increasingly turned to violent ideologies and actions, such as anarchism and sabotage. Although by 1914 the Third Republic was far stronger than it had been in the early 1870s, it clearly had not yet gained the approval of all segments of French society.

BRITAIN: NATION, CLASS, AND RELIGION

Unlike Germany and Italy, Britain was not a new nation; unlike France, it did not have to reconstruct its political structures after the humiliation of military defeat. Yet in Britain, too, the upper classes faced the task of responding to working-class demands for a political voice. They also confronted the problem of a regional divide even wider than the gap between north and south in Italy. Although the single political entity of the United Kingdom comprised England, Wales, Scotland, and Ireland, a chasm yawned between the first three overwhelmingly Protestant and industrialized nations, and the Roman Catholic, economically backward, peasant culture of Ireland. By the end of the century, the British political nation had broadened to include working-class men but proved incapable of embracing the Irish peasantry.

CHRONOLOGY

The Coming of Mass Politics in Britain

1867	Vote extended to urban male workers; formation of National Society for Women's Suffrage
1873	Onset of Great Depression in Trade and Agriculture
1874–1880	Conservative government of Benjamin Disraeli passes social reform legislation
1880	Elementary education made compulsory
1886	Regulation of prostitution ended
1893	Defeat of Second Irish Home Rule Bill in Britain; dockworkers' strike in Hull met with navy gunboats
1897	Queen Victoria's Diamond Jubilee
1898	Formation of Sinn Fein in Ireland
1903	Formation of suffragette movement
1906	Formation of Labour Party
1905–1912	Liberal government lays foundation of British social welfare state

---

While the English, Scottish, and Welsh economies flourished under the impact of industrialization, the Irish economy stagnated. Still devastated by the famine of the 1840s, the island remained a land of absentee English Protestant landowners and poor Irish Catholic tenants. Peasant desperation fueled revolutionary Irish nationalism, as the economic grievances of the Irish fused with their sense of political and religious repression, and convinced many Irish Catholics of the need for independence from Britain. In the 1860s, the Irish Republican Brotherhood, or Fenian movement, endeavored to overthrow British rule by force. The Fenian "Rising" of 1867 failed dismally, but it planted a seed that took deep root in Irish soil—the belief that the British constituted an occupying force that must be violently resisted.

Faced with growing Irish nationalism, the British resorted to military rule, accompanied by attempts to alleviate peasant grievances through land reform. Such measures were always too little, too late. In the 1880s, the British Liberal leader William Gladstone (1809–1898) embraced the cause of Irish "Home Rule"—limited political autonomy for Ireland—and for a short time it appeared as if parliamentary measures would solve the Irish problem. Home Rule, however, met fierce opposition not only from British Conservatives, but also from Irish Protestants. The descendants of English and Scottish settlers in Ireland, these

Protestants constituted a minority of the Irish population as a whole, but made up the majority of the population in the northernmost province of Ulster. Frightened by the idea of belonging to a Catholic state, the Ulster Protestants made it clear that they would fight to the death to remain a part of Britain.

The defeat of Home Rule bills introduced in 1886 and 1893 persuaded Irish Catholic nationalists of the futility of working with the British. In 1898 they organized themselves as Sinn Fein (pronounced "shin fane"—Gaelic for "Ourselves Alone"), a political movement devoted to complete independence for Ireland by any means necessary. Sinn Fein grew rapidly, and by 1914 could call to arms a paramilitary force of 180,000 fighters. As the success of Sinn Fein demonstrated, Irish Catholics had developed their own sense of nationhood, which refused to be subordinate to or absorbed by the British political nation.

Unable to contain Catholic Ireland, the borders of the British political nation proved flexible enough to incorporate most adult men in England, Scotland, and Wales. In the first half of the nineteenth century, the landed elite had accommodated middle-class demands for greater influence without relinquishing its own grasp on political power. Aristocrats and landed gentlemen played leading roles in both major political parties—the Liberals and the Conservatives (also called "Tories")—but both parties also pursued policies that encouraged industrial growth and benefited the middle classes. In the last third of the century, this system expanded to include working-class men. In 1867, many urban working men won the right to vote, and in 1884 this right was extended to rural male laborers.

Both the Conservative and the Liberal parties sought the support of these new working-class voters with programs designed to benefit ordinary people. In the 1870s, the Conservative government of Benjamin Disraeli (1804–1881) strengthened trade union rights, established the beginnings of a public housing program, expanded the state's program of inspecting factories, and assumed some responsibility for the population's safety by beginning to monitor the sale of food and drugs. The most substantial foundations of Britain's welfare state were, however, constructed in the early twentieth century by the Liberal government. Between 1906 and 1912, the Liberals enacted a series of welfare measures, including state-funded lunches for schoolchildren, pensions for the elderly, and sickness and unemployment benefits for some workers. As with Bismarck's pioneering social measures in Germany and Giolitti's reforms in Italy, this legislation was intended not only to attract workers' votes, but also to ensure working-class loyalty to the nation and its political leaders. In 1906, however, an independent working-class Labour Party emerged, thus signaling that not all working-class voters were willing to accept upper- and middle-class versions of national identity.

Broadening the Political Nation

The expansion of the suffrage in Britain was not unusual. Across Europe in the last third of the nineteenth and opening decades of the twentieth centuries, both aristocratic and middle-class politicians enacted measures extending the vote to lower-class men. Many middle- and upper-class Europeans regarded franchise reform as a preventive measure, a way to avoid socialist revolution by incorporating potential revolutionaries within the system. Even conservative politicians came to realize that mass suffrage did not always mean radical political change.

THE POLITICS OF THE WORKING CLASS

Yet not all new voters from the laboring classes remained loyal to their traditional superiors. The era of franchise expansion also witnessed the escalation of class hostilities, expressed in the rise of working-class socialist political parties and the emergence of new, more radical forms of trade unionism. Workers often rejected the political vision offered by their bosses and landlords, and instead fought hard to broaden the political nation on their own terms.

The Workers' City

In the decades after 1870, the combined impact of agricultural crisis and industrial expansion created large working-class communities in the rapidly growing industrial cities. These working-class communities tended to be increasingly isolated from the middle and upper class. Technological developments such as electrified tram lines, together with the expansion of the railway system, enabled Europe's middle classes to retreat from overcrowded, dirty, disease-ridden city centers to new and burgeoning suburbs. Workers knew members of the middle class only within the limited context of the "boss-employee" relationship—a relationship that was growing more hostile as economic depression drove middle-class employers to try to limit wages and raise productivity.

Within the sprawling industrial cities, industrial workers created a vibrant community life. They developed what sociologists call "urban villages," closely knit neighborhoods in which each family had a clear and publicly acknowledged place. Sharply defined gender roles played an important part in ordering this world. The home became the woman's domain (although many working-class women continued to work outside the home as well). In many regions, the wife controlled the family income and made most of the decisions about family life. Men built up their own cultural and leisure institutions, free from middle-class (and from female) participation and control—the corner pub, the music hall, the football club, the choral society, the brass

■ **Urban Villages**
Crowded into slums, European workers developed a separate
working-class culture.

band. These institutions provided an escape from the physical and emotional confines of work and home; they also
secured the bonds of male working-class identity, one that
rested on a sharp distinction between "Us"—the ordinary
men, the workers, the neighbors—and "Them"—the
bosses, the owners, the landlords, the people with privilege
and power.

Working-Class Socialism and the Revolutionary Problem

This heightened class identity and hostility were embodied
in the emergence of working-class socialist political parties.
In the decades after 1870, socialism established itself as a
powerful force in European parliamentary politics, the
means by which workers sought to claim a place in the political nation. By 1914, socialist parties had been formed in
twenty European countries.

Why socialism? As we saw in Chapter 21, by 1870 Karl
Marx had published a series of books outlining his economic and political theory of revolutionary socialism. Not
many workers had the time, education, or energy necessary
for the study of Marx's complex ideas. But Marx's basic
points, presented to workers by socialist party activists and

organizers, resonated with many workers. Quite simply,
most workers had already identified their boss as the enemy, and Marx assured them that they were right. His insistence that class conflict was inherent within the industrial
system accorded with their own experience of social segregation and economic exploitation. In addition, the onset of
economic depression in the 1870s appeared to confirm
Marx's prediction that capitalism would produce ever more
serious economic crises, until finally it collapsed under its
own weight.

The most dramatic socialist success story was in
Germany. Even after it was outlawed in 1878, the German
Social Democratic Party (the SPD) continued to attract
supporters. In 1890, the SPD emerged from the underground as the largest political party in Germany. By 1914, it
held 40 percent of the seats in the German Reichstag, and
served as the model for socialist parties founded in the
Netherlands, Belgium, Austria, and Switzerland. Even more
important, German socialists constructed a set of institutions that provided German workers with an alternative
community. If they chose, they could send their children to
socialist day care centers and bury their parents in socialist
cemeteries. They could spend their leisure time in socialist
bicycling clubs and gymnastic groups and choral societies
and chess teams. They could read socialist newspapers, sing
socialist songs, save their money in socialist savings banks,
and shop at socialist co-operatives.

By the 1890s, the rapid growth of socialist parties such as
the SPD persuaded many socialists that working-class revolution was just around the corner. In 1885 SPD leader
August Bebel (1840–1913) told Marx's colleague Friedrich
Engels, "Every night I go to sleep with the thought that the
last hour of bourgeois society strikes soon."[5] Six years later
in a speech before the SPD congress, Bebel told the gathered
crowd, "I am convinced that the fulfillment of our aims is
so close, that there are few in this hall who will not live to
see the day."[6]

By the time Bebel made this promise, however, unexpected economic and political developments were creating
serious problems for Marxist theory and practice. When
Bismarck's antisocialist legislation was not renewed in
1890, the SPD faced a time of new opportunity, but also
new challenges. To improve workers' wages and working
conditions, the SPD worked in close connection with the
rapidly growing German trade union movement—from
300,000 members in 1890 to 2.5 million in 1913. Such
activity raised the fundamental question: What was the
role of a socialist party within a nonsocialist state? To continue to attract voters, the SPD needed to push through
legislation that would appeal to workers; yet the passage of
such legislation, by improving workers' lives within a
nonsocialist system, made the possibility of socialist revolution ever more remote. Why should workers resort to violent revolution when participation in parliamentary politics was clearly paying off?

The SPD's dilemma was shared by socialist parties across western Europe. According to Marx, capitalism would generate its own destruction—the growing misery of workers would fuel a social and political revolution. But in western European industrial nations in the last decades of the nineteenth century, working-class living standards were generally rising rather than deteriorating. In addition, the expansion of the franchise seemed to indicate that workers could gain political power without violent revolution. As socialist political parties grew in strength, then, they faced crucial and often divisive questions: Should they work for gradual reforms that would make life better for the worker—and risk making capitalism more acceptable? Could socialists participate in coalition governments with nonsocialists—and so lend legitimacy to parliamentary systems they condemned as oppressive and unequal?

The quest for answers to these questions led some socialists to socialist revisionism°, a set of political ideas most closely associated with the German socialist theorist Eduard Bernstein (1850–1932). Bernstein rejected the Marxist faith in inevitable violent revolution and argued instead for the gradual and peaceful evolution of socialism through parliamentary politics. Questioning Marx's insistence on the centrality of class struggle in modern politics, Bernstein called for German socialists to abandon their commitment to revolution, to form alliances with liberals, and to carry out immediate social and economic reforms.

In 1899, the German socialist party congress condemned Bernstein's revisionism and reaffirmed its faith in the inevitability of capitalism's collapse and working-class revolution. Bernstein had lost the battle—but he won the war. For regardless of what the congress affirmed as socialist theory, in practice the SPD acted like any other parliamentary party. It focused on improving the lot of its constituency through immediate and incremental legislative change. In the words of one socialist intellectual, the SPD was "a party which, while revolutionary, does not make a revolution."[7] Its effect, although not its aim, was thus to make the existing political system more responsive to the needs of working-class constituents. Despite the almost hysterical fears of many middle- and upper-class Europeans, the successes of socialist political parties probably worked less to foment revolution than to strengthen parliamentary political systems.

Radical Trade Unions and the Anarchist Threat

To many at the end of the nineteenth century, however, revolution appeared a genuine possibility. The Great Depression, which shattered middle-class confidence and shrank capitalists' profit margins, led businesses to look for ways to cut costs. As management sought to reduce the number of laborers, to increase the rate of production, and to decrease wages, workers began to organize themselves in new and threatening ways.

THE SOCIALIST CULTURE

Songs played a vital role in the socialist culture developed in Germany at the end of the nineteenth century. Workers organized singing societies, which competed in local, regional, and national competitions. Rejecting the nationalist and religious songs of the middle-class choral society repertoire, workers often expressed their political ideals in their music. These overly didactic lyrics reveal not only the rage against economic injustice that fueled the socialist movement, but also its fundamental faith in human rationality and in parliamentary politics as an avenue of change.

"YOU MEN, ALL OF YOU" BY ERNST KLAAR

Already on all sides and throughout the world
The proletariat rises up together—
The fate of the poor is to be changed,
And to be changed through the state.
O, if we stand together firmly,
Who will be able to refuse us our right?
Upward, upward, you new generation,
Defiant let your banner wave!
　　Put in the eight-hour day!
　　Reduce the misery of toil!
　　To our victorious march
　　The drum now beats.
　　Eight hours are enough!

Source: From "You Men, All of You" by Ernst Klaar, translated by Vernon L. Lidtke in *The Alternative Culture*, 1985. Reprinted by permission.

The expansion and radicalization of trade unions highlighted growing working-class militancy. For example, in Britain between 1882 and 1913, union membership increased from 750,000 to 4,000,000. While size alone set apart the new unions from their midcentury predecessors, two additional differences marked them as much more subversive. First, the new unions were much more willing to resort to large-scale strikes and to violence. Second, the unions sought to better the lives of a wide range of workers, not just an elite of the highly skilled. In contrast to the unions of the 1850s and 1860s, which had tended to be small, craft-based groupings of skilled workers, the new unions aimed to organize all the male workers in an entire industry—for example, all male textile workers, rather than just the skilled weavers. (Unionists, fighting for higher pay, often resisted the unionization of female workers both because women earned much less than did men and because a central union aim was the "family wage"—a pay rate high enough for a man to support a family without his wife's second income.)

■ **The Unions' Challenge**
In 1911 the British government deployed troops in the city of Liverpool to put down working-class labor unrest. In one confrontation, two people were killed.

Political leaders reacted ferociously to the unionist challenge. In the coastal port of Hull in Britain, striking dockworkers in 1893 confronted Royal Navy gunboats. A little over a decade later, the British government responded to a transport workers' strike in Liverpool by quartering 14,000 soldiers in the city and stationing two warships off the coast. Increasingly, "class war" seemed an appropriate label for interactions between workers and their middle-class employers. Even the simple act of getting a shave could prove dangerous for a member of the bourgeoisie: Unionized workers in barbershops were encouraged to "inflict nonfatal cuts on the clients of their capitalist masters."[8]

In the first decade of the twentieth century, the European labor movement became further radicalized by its encounter with the new ideology of syndicalism°. Syndicalists worked to overturn the existing social and political order by marshaling the economic might of the laboring classes. They focused on the general strike as a means of change. In the syndicalist vision, if every worker in a nation went on strike, the resulting disruption of the capitalist economy would lead to working-class revolution. Thus they placed their revolutionary faith in economic

rather than political action—in unions rather than parties, in the strike rather than the vote, and in compulsion rather than compromise. According to the French syndicalist theorist Georges Sorel (1847–1922), workers had to embrace violence to destroy the capitalist state. Sorel did not actually believe that a general strike was possible, but he believed that the idea of the general strike was crucial. In Sorel's view, the general strike served as an essential myth, an inspirational idea that would give workers the motivation and self-confidence they needed to overthrow the state.

In their rejection of parliamentary politics and in their willingness to utilize violent means to achieve their revolutionary ends, syndicalists were heavily influenced by anarchism°. In contrast to socialists who formed political parties to claim for workers a place in the political nation, anarchists shunned parliamentary politics. Opting for direct and violent action such as street fighting and assassination, anarchists aimed to destroy rather than control the state. The Russian anarchist Mikhail Bakunin (1814–1876) insisted that the great obstacle to achieving a just and egalitarian society was the state itself, not capitalism or the industrial middle class.

The combined impact of both syndicalism and anarchism created a climate of social unrest and political turmoil in much of Europe before 1914. In France, where a strong non-Marxist revolutionary tradition already existed, both syndicalism and anarchism possessed significant appeal. Impatient with parliamentary politics, anarchists resorted in the 1890s to a terrorist campaign in Paris, which began with a series of bombings and culminated in the fatal stabbing of President Sadi Carnot in 1894. Other prominent victims of assassination included Empress Elisabeth of Austria-Hungary in 1898, King Humbert of Italy in 1900, and U.S. president William McKinley in 1901.

NATIONALIST MASS POLITICS

The rise of socialist political parties and the spread of revolutionary ideologies such as anarchism and syndicalism fostered middle- and upper-class fears of a worker revolution. But the emergence of mass politics was not limited to left-wing ideologies. In the age of the masses, the right-wing ideas offered by nationalist, racist, and anti-Semitic parties also answered the demands of many ordinary people for a political voice. These parties possessed a special appeal in areas that industrialized late and so still contained a large peasant class profoundly threatened by the economic changes wrought by the continuing Industrial Revolution. Socialist politics also possessed little appeal for members of the petty bourgeoisie, who regarded the vision of working-class rule as a frightening nightmare. Instead, they turned to the new mass politics of nationalism.

Unlike the men who had dominated politics in the past, most newly enfranchised voters possessed only a basic education; they had little time for reading or sustained intellectual work; they worked long hours and therefore needed to be entertained. They needed a new style of politics—one based more on visual imagery and symbolism than on the written word, one that relied on emotional appeals rather than on intellectual debate. Nationalist politics fit the bill perfectly. Unlike socialists, who placed great faith in education and in rational persuasion, nationalist politicians did not recruit supporters with reasoned arguments. Instead, by waving flags, parading in historical costumes or military uniforms, and singing folk songs, they tapped into powerful personal and community memories to persuade voters of their common identity, one based not on shared political ideas or economic interests but rather on ethnic, religious, or linguistic ties. This was as much a politics of exclusion as of inclusion—it defined the nation by identifying who was "not in" as well as who belonged.

Austria-Hungary: The Politics of Division

Nationalist mass politics proved very powerful in the multiethnic, industrially underdeveloped Habsburg Empire. We saw in Chapter 21 that in 1867, Hungarian nationalism forced the administrative division of the empire into Austria in the west and the kingdom of Hungary in the east, thus creating what is called the Dual Monarchy, or simply Austria-Hungary. Straining under the social and economic pressures of late industrialization, Austria-Hungary contained numerous ethnic and linguistic groups competing for power and privileges. (See Map 21.4, p. 714.)This competition intensified as the franchise was gradually widened in the 1880s and 1890s. (The Austrian half of the empire achieved universal manhood suffrage in 1907.)

Language became a key battleground. In a multilingual empire, which language would be taught in the schools? Which language would be required in official communications? Which language would guarantee career advancement? Not surprisingly, individuals tended to agitate for the primacy of their own native language, and to jostle for the political power needed to ensure that primacy. In Hungary, the ruling Magyar-speaking Hungarian landlords redrew constituency boundaries to give maximum influence to Magyar speakers and to undercut the power of other ethnic and linguistic groups. This policy of "Magyarization" in governmental offices and in the schools bred widespread resentment among non-Hungarians and fostered their own nationalist ambitions.

At the same time in the Austrian half of the empire, Czechs succeeded in gaining greater political power and official support for the Czech language. Germans within Austria resented Czech gains and called for closer ties with Germany and even a complete break of the link with Hungary.

By 1900 the struggle over language laws in the Czech portion of the Austrian empire had become so intense that no party could establish a majority in the Reichsrat (the legislative assembly), and Emperor Francis Joseph (r. 1848–1916) resorted to ruling by decree.

The Appeal of Anti-Semitism

Anti-Semitism played a central role in the new nationalist mass politics. In the final third of the nineteenth century, Jews bore the brunt of the blame for Europe's economic, social, and cultural crises. They were charged with causing the Great Depression and masterminding terrorist conspiracies. Urban overcrowding, rising drug and alcohol addictions, the collapse of small corner shops unable to compete with large department stores, the rise of socialism—Jews received the blame for these diverse developments as well. As anti-Semitism grew, so too did anti-Jewish violence. In Russia, this violence often took the form of pogroms, mass attacks on Jewish homes and businesses, sometimes organized by local government officials. Although pogroms did not occur in western Europe, Jews in France, Britain, and other industrialized nations also experienced increasing hostility.

To explain the heightened anti-Semitism of this period, we need to understand three developments: the increased emphasis on racial identity, the upsurge in the numbers of Jewish immigrants into Western cities, and Jewish industrial and professional success. First, the triumph of nationalism meant a new concern with group boundaries and a greater focus on racial identity. Nationalism raised the question of "who does *not* belong?" For many Europeans and Americans, race provided the answer. The new nationalism meant new perceptions of common "racial roots." Ideas about "the English race" or of the shared racial heritage of the French had no scientific basis, but these perceptions of racial links nonetheless proved extremely powerful. In this new nationalistic climate, then, "Jewishness" was

CHRONOLOGY

The Coming of Mass Politics in Austria-Hungary

1867	Administrative division of Habsburg Empire: formation of Austria-Hungary; emancipation of Jews within Austria-Hungary
1869	Elementary education made compulsory and free
1881	Assassination of Russian Tsar Alexander II; upsurge in Jewish immigration into Vienna
1897	Karl Lueger elected mayor in Vienna on anti-Semitic platform
1898	Assassination of Empress Elisabeth
1907	Universal manhood suffrage enacted in Austria

increasingly defined not only as a matter of religious belief but also as a racial identity. As a racial marker, Jewishness was not a matter of choice but of blood—something that could not be changed. A Jew who no longer ascribed to the Jewish faith or even a Jew who converted to Christianity remained a Jew. This shift to a more racial definition of Jewishness is one of the factors behind the upsurge in anti-Semitic actions and attitudes at the end of the nineteenth century. If national identity grew from supposedly racial roots, then in the eyes of many Europeans, Jews were a foreign plant. They were non-English, or non-French, or non-German—essentially outsiders whose very presence could be seen as a threat to national unity.

This perception of Jews as outsiders was also exacerbated by the growth in immigrant Jewish urban populations after 1881. After the assassination of his father in 1881, Tsar Alexander III blamed Russia's Jewish community for his father's death. He responded by reimposing restrictions on Jewish economic and social life with the May Laws of 1882. Fleeing this repression, Jews from the Russian Empire settled in Paris, London, Vienna, and other European cities. The encounter between these immigrant Jewish communities and their hosts was often hostile. Extremely poor, the immigrants spoke Yiddish rather than the language of their new home, dressed in distinctive clothing, and sometimes practiced an ardently emotional style of Judaism that resisted assimilation. As the numbers of Jews escalated in Europe's cities, these new, impoverished, clearly identifiable immigrants were easily blamed for unemployment, the spread of disease, soaring crime rates, and any other difficulty for which desperate people sought easy explanations.

Many anti-Semites, however, associated Jews not with poverty but with wealth and power. One of the most striking developments of nineteenth-century history was what one historian has labeled the "rise of the Jews."[9] At the start of the nineteenth century, not only were Jews barred from political participation in most of Europe, but in the south and east they were also frequently confined to certain territories or city districts. Jews in Russia, for example, could not live outside the area defined as the "Pale of Settlement." Swiss Jews were confined to the canton of Aargau, and Jews in Rome had to reside in a certain district, or *ghetto*. The second half of the century, however, witnessed the emancipation of European Jewry as Jews gained civil and political rights. By 1900 many had benefited greatly from political and economic change.

Moving into new regions and new economic and political roles, Jewish communities quickly assumed a significant presence in European economic and political life. In Budapest in 1900, for example, Jews formed 25 percent of the population, yet they accounted for 45 percent of the city's lawyers, more than 40 percent of its journalists, over 60 percent of its doctors, and 50 percent of its qualified vot-

ers. A few Jewish families, such as the internationally connected Rothschild banking dynasty, possessed spectacular fortunes. Most important, in many cities Jewish businessmen clustered in certain areas of the emerging modern economy. In Germany, for example, almost all the large department stores were owned by Jewish businessmen, and in the cities of Frankfurt, Berlin, and Hamburg all the large daily newspapers were in the hands of Jewish proprietors. As a result, the small craftspeople and artisans with a great deal to lose from economic modernization often linked big-business capitalism to Jewishness. Like Tsar Nicholas II, who blamed the Russian Revolution of 1905 on Jewish conspirators, ordinary men and women reacted to their own personal reversals of fortune by seeking a scapegoat. Jews became the embodiment of threatening change to many newly enfranchised European voters.

Politicians quickly realized the power of anti-Semitism in the new age of mass politics. Across Europe, explicitly anti-Semitic parties emerged, while established conservative parties adopted anti-Semitic rhetoric to attract voters. In Germany, the widespread belief that Jews had conspired to cause the Great Depression fueled anti-Semitic politics; by the 1890s anti-Semitic parties had won seats in the Reichstag. In France, nationalists linked Jewish prosperity to French national decline and grew increasingly anti-Semitic in their ideology and rhetoric, until finally the Dreyfus Affair made explicit the connections between hatred of Jews and right-wing French nationalism. Many of Dreyfus's opponents saw "Jewishness" and "Frenchness" as incompatible, and regarded Dreyfus himself as part of a vast Jewish conspiracy to undermine France's religious, military, and national strength.

Anti-Semitic politics also proved extremely powerful in Vienna, capital of the Austrian half of the ancient Habsburg Empire. Vienna stood at the center of cultural, professional, and political life for German-speaking Austrians. As the city attracted both Austrian Jews from the surrounding countryside and Jewish emigrants fleeing Russian pogroms, Vienna's Jewish population grew from 118,000 in 1890 to 147,000 in 1900. Jews maintained a high profile in the city. At the University of Vienna, for example, one-quarter of the law students and almost one-half of the medical students were Jewish, although Jews made up only one-tenth of the Austrian population.

This growing Jewish presence provided the opportunity for Karl Lueger (1844–1910), a lawyer, self-made man, and power-hungry politician. Lueger's Christian Social party demonstrates how hate-based politics could overcome social and economic divisions among members of a single ethnic or religious community. Lueger used both anti-Semitism and promises of social reform to unite artisans and workers with conservative aristocrats in a German nationalist party. His proposals to exclude Jews from political and economic life proved so popular that he was elected mayor of Vienna in 1897, despite the opposition of Emperor Francis Joseph. Lueger was still the mayor in 1908, when 18-year-old Adolf Hitler, hoping to attend art school, moved to Vienna. Hitler's application to study art was denied, but he remained in Vienna for several years, soaking in the anti-Semitic political culture.

Zionism: Jewish Mass Politics

The heightened anti-Semitism of the last quarter of the nineteenth century convinced some Jews that the Jewish communities of Europe would be safe only when they gained a political state of their own. The ideology of Jewish nationalism was called Zionism°, as Jewish nationalists called for a return to Zion, the Biblical land of Palestine. Most Jews in western nations such as France and Britain viewed Zionism with skepticism, but it had a potent appeal in eastern Europe, home to more than 70 percent of the world's Jewish community—and to the most vicious forms of anti-Semitism.

Zionism became a mass movement under the guidance of Theodor Herzl (1860–1904). An Austrian Jew born in Budapest, Herzl was living in Vienna when Karl Lueger was elected mayor. Confronted with the appeal of anti-Semitism to the mass electorate, Herzl began to doubt whether Jews could ever be fully accepted as Austrian citizens. His experience as a journalist reporting on the Dreyfus Affair from Paris confirmed these doubts. The vicious display of anti-Jewish hatred in a prosperous, industrialized, western European state convinced Herzl that Jews would always be outsiders within the existing European nations. In 1896, he published *The Jewish State,* a call for Jews to build a nation-state in Palestine. Herzl gained the financial support of wealthy Jewish businessmen such as Baron Edmund James de Rothschild, but he recognized that for Zionism to succeed, it must capture the imagination and loyalties of ordinary Jews. Through newspapers, popular publications, large rallies, and his own enthusiasm, Herzl made Zionism into an international mass movement.

As a mass movement, Zionism faced strong opposition. Many Jewish leaders argued that Zionism played into the hands of anti-Semites by insisting that Jews did not belong in Europe. In addition, by marking out Palestine as the Jewish "homeland," Zionists ran into a huge political obstacle. Palestine still belonged to the Ottoman Empire, which opposed European Jewish immigration into the region as a destabilizing force. Nevertheless, 90,000 Jews had settled in Palestine, where they hoped to fulfill the Zionist dream, by 1914.

The Limits of Black Emancipation in the United States

The example of Jewish emancipation shows that the widening of the political nation to embrace adult working men in Europe did not always advance democratic values.

The process of extending the suffrage often accentuated perceptions of racial difference and so heightened rather than subdued racist rhetoric and violence. In the United States, efforts to widen the political nation to include African-American men largely foundered on the rocks of racism.

We saw in Chapter 21 that the end of the Civil War in 1865 led to black emancipation. Amendments to the Constitution abolished slavery, granted citizenship to former black slaves, and gave black men the right to vote. The stationing of federal troops in the former slave states enforced the efforts of the Republican Party to reconstruct the American South. Failure to carry out any sort of land reform in the region, however, limited the impact of these reforms. Wealthy, white landowners had lost their slaves but retained their economic supremacy.

Reconstruction ended in 1877 when President Rutherford Hayes (1822–1893) withdrew federal troops from the South. Over the next two decades, the dominant landowning class succeeded in effectively depriving black citizens (and many poor whites) of the right to vote and in ensuring that blacks remained in an inferior economic and social position. "Black Codes" passed by Southern legislatures limited the type of property and occupation open to blacks, while literacy tests, poll taxes, and violent intimidation ensured that few blacks dared to vote. The threat of lynching was omnipresent. In the decade after 1889, an average of 187 blacks were lynched in the United States each year, 80 percent of these in the Southern states.

At the same time, the passage of Jim Crow° legislation (named after a black minstrel singer) mandated racial segregation in almost every aspect of Southern American society. Jim Crow laws meant that blacks could not travel in the same train cars with whites; that white nurses could refuse to work on wards with black patients; that blacks and whites could not be educated in the same schools, fed in the same restaurants, or buried in the same cemeteries.

Interracial marriage was illegal. In the important case of *Plessy vs. Ferguson* in 1896, the U.S. Supreme Court declared Jim Crow to be constitutional. The Court ruled that "separate but equal" facilities did not violate the rights of black citizens. Yet the separate facilities reserved for blacks were never equal. Jim Crow, like the literacy tests and poll taxes that deprived black men of the right to vote, made it clear that in the eyes of many powerful whites, blacks were not and should not be members of the political nation.

Outside the Political Nation? The Experience of Women

Extending the suffrage to men outside the middle and upper classes also called attention to gender differences, as middle-class women demanded that they, too, be made part of the political nation. The campaign for women's suffrage, however, was only part of a multifaceted international middle-class feminist movement° that, by the 1870s, demanded a reconsideration of women's roles. To the feminist movement, the vote was not an end in itself, but a means to an end, a way of achieving a radical alteration in cultural values and expectations. At the core of nineteenth-century feminism stood a rejection of the liberal ideology of separate spheres—the insistence that both God and biology destined middle-class men for the public sphere of paid economic employment and political participation, and women for the private sphere of the home. In seeking a place in the political nation, feminists sought not just to enter the public, masculine sphere, but in fact to obliterate many of the distinctions between the public and private spheres altogether and so to reconfigure political and social life.

During this period the feminist movement remained largely middle-class in its membership and its concerns. Working-class and peasant women were occupied by the struggle for survival; obtaining the vote seemed fairly irrelevant to a woman listening to her children cry from hunger. Politically active working-class women tended to agree with Karl Marx that class, not gender, constituted the real dividing line in society. For help in bettering their lives, they turned to labor unions and to working-class political parties rather than middle-class feminist organizations. The British working-class feminist Selina Cooper (1868–1946), for example, fought hard for women's rights, but within the context of the British Labour movement. Cooper, who was sent to work in a textile mill at age 10, viewed the widening of women's opportunities and the achievement of working-class political power as two sides of the same coin. Similarly, in Germany, the SDP activist Clara Zetkin (1857–1933) argued that the fight against class oppression was inextricably linked to the fight against women's oppression.

CHANGES IN THE POSITION OF MIDDLE-CLASS WOMEN

The middle-class women's movement operated within changing economic and social conditions that were pushing middle-class women into more-public positions in European society. Married women moved into a new public role as consumers during this period. It was the woman who was the principal target of the new advertising industry, the woman whom the new department stores sought to entice with their lavish window displays and courteous shop clerks, the woman who rode the new tram lines and subways to take advantage of sale days.

The largest change for married middle-class women was much more basic, however. In the last third of the nineteenth century, middle-class men and women began to limit the size of their families. In Britain in the 1890s, the average middle-class family had 2.8 children, a sharp reduction in family size from the middle of the century, when the typical middle-class family had 6 children. This enormous change, characteristic of all the advanced industrial nations, reflected both economic and social developments. As the Great Depression cut into business profits and made economic ventures ever more precarious, middle-class families looked for ways to cut expenses and yet maintain a middle-class lifestyle. At the same time, the growing tendency to keep both boys and girls in school longer meant added financial obligations for the middle-class family. Limiting births, through the use of already well-known methods such as abstinence, withdrawal, and abortion, provided the answer. Smaller families meant middle-class married women no longer spent much of their married adult life pregnant or nursing. This change not only meant better health, it also freed women for other activities and interests, including feminist activism.

In contrast, working-class families continued to remain large because a worker's children were economic assets rather than liabilities. Working-class children left school by age 11 or 12 and so began to contribute to the family income much earlier. Middle-class women, then, were freed from the constant round of childbearing, while their working-class counterparts remained far more constrained by domestic duties.

The expectations of unmarried middle-class women were also transformed during this period. In 1850, the unmarried middle-class woman who had to support herself had little choice but to become a governess or a paid companion to an elderly widow. By 1900 her options had widened. As we shall see, the women's movement played a crucial role in this expansion of opportunity, but so also did two more general economic and political developments: the expansion of the state and the Second Industrial Revolution.

The expansion of state responsibilities in this period significantly widened opportunities for women. By the final

Men in Black

Within a span of about fifty years, upper- and middle-class European and American men transformed the way they presented their bodies to the world. Before the late eighteenth century, social rank outweighed gender in determining clothing styles. Thus an aristocratic man dressed more like an aristocratic woman than like a male laborer. Aristocrats, both men and women, decorated themselves with expensive jewels, shaped their bodies with corsets and pads, powdered their faces and hair, sported huge hats decorated with ribbons, carried lacy fans, wore high heels, and dressed in brightly colored and elaborately ruffled silks and taffetas. By the middle of the nineteenth century, however, the man had lost his plumage, and decoration had become a distinctly female attribute. The aristocratic man of the 1850s looked like his middle-class counterpart. He dressed in darkly colored, loose-fitting trousers and jackets; wore sensible shoes; and put on a top hat when he went outside. Cosmetics, perfume, ruffles and lace, elaborate jewelry, hats, and fans all retreated to the woman's sphere.

Whether he was engaged actively in business or lived a life of leisure, the new man in black now presented a sharp contrast to his female companions. His clothing associated him with the world of practicality and production; her costume, however, was designed to reinforce the prevailing notions about women's incapacity for public or economic roles.

Middle- and upper-class women's clothing not only remained brightly colored, decorative, and luxurious, it also became increasingly constrictive. The full crinolines and hoop skirts of the 1850s and 1860s, for example, made the simple task of sitting down a tricky endeavor, while tight corseting placed strenuous physical activity beyond reach of fashionable women.

Changes in clothing reflect new ideas about the relationships between a man's and a woman's identities and their physical bodies. After 1850 men's clothing styles de-emphasized their bodies. Whereas eighteenth-century aristocrats wore attention-grabbing colors, silk stockings that outlined their legs, short jackets that emphasized their waist, and tight-fitting breeches that highlighted the sexual aspects of the male body, the long loose jackets and trousers of the later nineteenth-century man masked rather than highlighted their wearer's physical characteristics. In contrast, women's fashions increasingly accentuated female sexuality. By shrinking the waist, tightly laced corsets made the bust and hips appear fuller. In the 1880s, the addition of the bustle emphasized the woman's bottom. Such clothing styles fortified the view that a woman's body in many ways determined her destiny, that women were designed to be wives and mothers.

Economic developments led to important changes in women's fashions in the 1890s. As middle-class women began to enter the workforce in large numbers, fashions adapted to fit their new roles. Dresses became more streamlined: Skirts moved slightly above the ankles and shrank in width, and bustles disappeared. But it took the demands of the First World War, when women assumed previously all-male positions in industry, agriculture, and transportation, to effect radical alterations in the way women presented their bodies and themselves to the world. ■

For Discussion

Changes in women's employment patterns clearly had an impact on women's dress styles. What other economic developments during this period may help explain changes in fashion?

■ **Men in Black**

Painting by James Tissot, *Cercle de la Rue Royale,* detail (1868). Although most are barons, marquises, or counts, the men whose portraits Tissot captured in this high-society painting dress like bankers or stockbrokers.

decade of the nineteenth century, local governments took over many tasks traditionally assigned to church volunteers and especially women charity workers, such as training the poor in proper hygiene and nutrition. Middle-class women quickly claimed both paying and elected positions in the new local bureaucracies, on the argument that women possessed an expertise in managing households and raising children that could be directly translated into managing poorhouses and running schools. Women served on school and welfare boards, staffed government inspectorates, voted in local elections, and were elected to local office. For example, in Britain between 1870 and 1914, approximately 3,000 women were elected to county and municipal governing bodies. In Germany, 18,000 women worked as local welfare officials by 1910. But the largest employers of middle-class women before 1914 were the new state-funded elementary schools. The implementation of compulsory mass education created a voracious demand for teachers and thus a new career path for unmarried women from the middle class as well as from the upper ranks of the working class.

The emergence of new technologies and the retail revolution also created new jobs for women, positions that did not involve manual labor and so did not mean a descent into the working class. Middle-class women moved into the work world as typists, telephone and telegraph operators, sales clerks, and bank tellers. During the 1860s in England, the number of women working as commercial clerks and accountants increased tenfold.

Middle-class women thus found new ways to make a living; they did not, however, find the same opportunities as their male counterparts. A woman earned an average of between one-third and two-thirds less than a man working in the same job. The entry of large numbers of women into any job was certain to result in a recasting of that position as unskilled and low-paying. Unlike men, women lost their jobs when they married and found most supervisory positions closed to them.

By the 1880s, an international women's movement had emerged to challenge the legal, political, and economic disabilities facing European and American women. Consisting of a vast web of interconnected organizations, publications, and correspondence networks, the middle-class women's movement sought to challenge the ideology of separate spheres and to establish a new basis for both private and public relations. Its multifaceted campaigns focused on four fronts: the legal impediments facing married women, employment opportunities and higher education for girls and women, the double standard of sexual conduct enshrined in European laws, and national women's suffrage.

WOMEN AND THE LAW

European legal systems strongly reinforced the liberal ideology of separate spheres for men and women. Law codes often classified women with children, criminals, and the insane. Article 231 of the Napoleonic Code, the legal system of France and the basis of the legal codes of much of western and central Europe, declared that the wife was the dependent of the husband; hence, "the husband owes protection to his wife; the wife owes obedience to her husband." The Russian legal code agreed: "The woman must obey her husband, reside with him in love, respect, and unlimited obedience, and offer him every pleasantness and affection as the ruler of the household." In Russia a woman could not travel without her father's or husband's permission. The

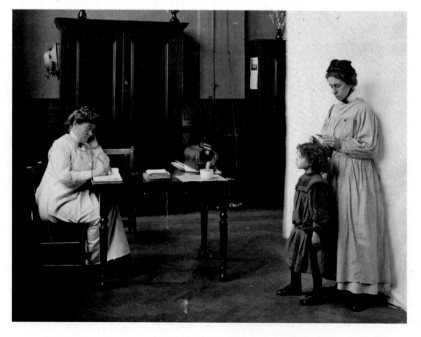

■ **Women at Work**

The expansion of local and central government interference in daily life created many opportunities for women's paid employment. Here government health inspectors check a schoolgirl for head lice.

husband was also the legal guardian of all children; he alone had the authority to pick their schools, determine their punishments, and approve their marriage partners. Similarly, in Prussia the law declared that only the husband could decide when his baby should stop breastfeeding. English common law, based on tradition and precedent rather than on a single, systematized code, proclaimed much the same idea. As Sir William Blackstone explained in his famous *Commentaries on the Laws of England* (1765–1769), "the husband and wife are one person in law," and that person was the husband. A married woman simply disappeared in the eyes of the British common law. Most property brought into a marriage, or given to her or earned by her while married, became the property of her husband.

From the middle of the nineteenth century on, women's groups fought to improve the legal rights of married women. By the end of the 1880s, English married women had won rights to own their own property, control their own income, and keep their children. Two decades later, French women could claim similar rights. In contrast, the German women's movement suffered a sharp defeat with the promulgation of the Civil Code in 1900. The Civil Code, which formulated a single uniform legal system for Germany, proclaimed that "the husband takes the decisions in all matters affecting married life." It granted all parental authority to the husband—over his stepchildren as well as his own children. By German law, "if the parents disagree, the father's opinion takes precedence." While it allowed married women to keep money they earned while married, it declared that all property owned by the wife before marriage or given to her after marriage became the husband's.

FINDING A PLACE: EMPLOYMENT AND EDUCATION

In addition to their legal campaigns, feminists also worked to widen women's educational and employment opportunities as part of their effort to enter the public sphere. At the core of this aspect of the women's movement was a simple demographic reality—women outnumbered men in almost every region in Europe. In England by 1900, the higher rates of male emigration and infant mortality meant that there were 1,064 females for every 1,000 males. Clearly, not all women could marry. Thus, providing respectable jobs for middle-class single women was a high priority for early European and American feminists.

The problem of women's jobs quickly proved to be inseparable from the issue of women's education. Even girls from privileged families rarely received rigorous educations before 1850. The minority of girls who did go to school spent their time learning ladylike occupations such as fancy embroidery, flower arranging, and piano playing. Proper posture was more important than any literary or scientific attainments. Widening the world of women's education, then, became a crucial feminist aim and proved to be an area in which they achieved considerable, but still limited, success.

Feminists' educational campaigns in the second half of the nineteenth century had two main emphases: first, improving the quality as well as expanding the number of girls' secondary schools, and second, opening universities to women. The fight to upgrade the quality of girls' secondary education was often difficult. Many parents opposed an academic curriculum for girls, a position reinforced by medical professionals who argued that girls' brains simply could not withstand the strain of an intellectual education. Dorothea Beale (1831–1906), a pioneer in girls' education in England, established one of the first academically oriented high schools for girls in London in the 1850s, but she faced an uphill battle in persuading reluctant parents to allow her to teach their daughters mathematics. In France, feminists achieved their goal of a state-funded and state-run system of secondary schools for girls in the 1880s. They lost the battle for a university-preparatory curriculum, however, which made it difficult for girls to pass the exams necessary to enter the French university system.

Not surprisingly, the number of women in French universities remained very small throughout this period. Opportunities for university education for women varied enormously. In the United States, women accounted for one-third of all students in higher education as early as 1880, while in Germany, women were not admitted to full-time university study until 1901. In Russia, the development of women's higher education was particularly sporadic. Full-time university study became available to women in Moscow in 1872, and by 1880, women in Russia had some of the best opportunities for higher education in all of Europe. But the involvement of Sofiia Perovskaia—an educated woman—in the assassination of Tsar Alexander II in 1881 convinced the authorities that revolutionary politics and advanced female education went hand in hand. Most educational avenues for Russian women were blocked for more than two decades after the assassination.

Despite such limitations and reverses, the range of jobs open to women did broaden during this period. In 1900, French women won the right to practice law, and in 1903 in the French city of Toulouse, a woman lawyer presented a case in a European court for the first time. In 1906, the physicist and Nobel Prize winner Marie Curie became the first woman to hold a university faculty position in France. By the opening decades of the twentieth century, women doctors, although still unusual, were not unheard of. In Russia, women accounted for 10 percent of all physicians by 1914.

NO MORE ANGELS

The campaigns for women's legal rights and an expansion of employment and educational opportunities helped women move out of the private and into the public sphere.

But the third goal of feminist activity—to eradicate the double standard of sexual conduct—posed a more radical challenge to nineteenth-century middle-class culture and its ideology of separate spheres. By arguing that the same moral standards should apply to both men and women, feminists questioned whether two separate spheres should exist at all.

The ideology of separate spheres glorified women's moral purity and held that the more aggressive, more animal-like natures of men naturally resulted in such male pastimes as heavy drinking and sexual adventurism. The laws as well as the wider culture reflected these assumptions. For example, in France, a woman with an illegitimate child could not institute a paternity suit against the father: Premarital sex was a crime for the woman, but not for the man. Similarly, the English divorce legislation of 1857 declared that a woman's adultery was all that was necessary for a husband to sue for divorce, but a man's adultery was not a sufficient reason to end a marriage. For a wife to divorce her husband, she had to prove that he had committed additional crimes such as bigamy, incest, or bestiality.

To feminists, applying different moral standards to men and women degraded men and blocked women's efforts to better their own lives and society as a whole. As the French feminist leader Maria Desraismes explained, "To say that woman is an angel is to impose on her, in a sentimental and admiring fashion, all duties, and to reserve for oneself all rights . . . I decline the honor of being an angel."[10]

In their effort to erase the moral distinctions between men and women, feminists fought on a variety of fronts. One key area of struggle was the regulation of prostitution. By the 1870s, many European countries, as well as the United States, had established procedures that made it safer for men to hire prostitutes, while still treating the women involved as criminals. In England, the Contagious Diseases Act, passed in 1870 to address the problem of venereal disease, declared that any woman suspected of being a prostitute could be stopped by the police and required to undergo a genital exam. Men, however, were subject to no such indignities. Feminists such as Josephine Butler (1857–1942) contended that such legislation made it easier for men to indulge their sexual appetites, while punishing the impoverished women who were forced to sell their bodies to feed themselves and their children. For almost twenty years Butler led a concerted campaign both to repeal the legislation that regulated prostitution and to focus public attention on the lack of employment opportunities for women.

Abuse of alcohol was another key battleground for the women's movement. Arguing that the socially accepted practice of heavy male drinking had devastating consequences for women, in the form of both family poverty and domestic violence, feminist activists backed the temperance or prohibitionist cause. The movement triumphed in the United States in 1919 when decades of agitation from groups such as the Women's Christian Temperance Union led to the passage of the Eighteenth Amendment prohibiting the manufacture and sale of alcoholic beverages. "Prohibition," however, did little to transform gender relations; instead, it simply created new ways for organized crime syndicates to make money. The American prohibition experiment ended in 1933 with the repeal of the Eighteenth Amendment.

In general, feminist moral reform campaigns achieved only limited success. The regulation of prostitution did end in England in 1886 and in the United States, France, and the Scandinavian countries by 1914, but remained in effect in Germany. By 1884 in France, a husband's adultery, like a wife's, could end a marriage, but in England, the grounds for divorce remained differentiated by gender until 1923. In all European countries and in the United States, the sexual double standard remained embedded in both middle- and working-class culture far into the twentieth century.

THE FIGHT FOR WOMEN'S SUFFRAGE

The slow pace and uneven progress on both the legal and moral fronts convinced many feminists that they would achieve their goals only if they possessed the political clout of the *national* suffrage. In 1867 the National Society for Women's Suffrage was founded in Britain; over the next three decades suffrage societies emerged on the Continent. The French suffragist Hubertine Auclert (1848–1914) described the vote as "the keystone that will give [women] all other rights." As the editor of *La Citoyenne* ("The Citizeness"), Auclert agitated for full citizenship rights for adult women. In an imaginative move, she refused to pay taxes, on the grounds of "no taxation without representation." Auclert was also the first woman to describe herself as a "feminist," a word that entered the English language from the French around 1890.

Auclert and other American and European suffragists had little success. Only in Finland (1906) and Norway (1913) did women gain the national franchise in this period. (By 1913, women also possessed the vote in twelve American states.) The social upheaval of World War I brought women the vote in Russia (1917), Britain (1918), Germany (1919), Austria (1919), the Netherlands (1919), and the United States (1920). Women in Italy had to wait until 1945; French women did not gain the vote until 1946, Greek women not until 1949. Women in Switzerland did not vote until 1971.

Feminists faced a number of significant obstacles in their battle for the national franchise. In Catholic countries such as France and Italy, the women's suffrage movement failed to become a political force not only because the Church remained fiercely opposed to the women's vote, but also because in Catholicism—in its veneration of the Virgin Mary and other female saints, in its exaltation of family life, in the opportunity for religious vocation as a nun—women found a great many avenues for emotional expression and

IN FAVOR OF THE VOTE FOR WOMEN

....

Many supporters of women's suffrage believed that education, reason, and persuasion would achieve the vote. If suffragists made their case in logical, reasonable terms, they would be able to convince a majority of male voters of the rightness of their cause. This excerpt from a French suffragist pamphlet, published in 1913, is very typical both in its effort to persuade its reader through a careful marshaling of factual evidence and in its belief that the women's vote would transform political life. French women did not win the vote for another thirty years.

We are going to try to prove that the vote for women is a just, possible and desirable reform.
. . .

A woman has responsibility in the family; she ought to be consulted about the laws establishing her rights and duties with respect to her husband, her children, her parents.

Women work—and in ever greater numbers; a statistic of 1896 established that . . . the number of women workers was 35 per cent of the total number of workers, both male and female.

If she is in business, she, like any businessman, has interests to protect. . . .

If a woman is a worker or a domestic, she ought to participate as a man does in voting on unionization laws, laws covering workers' retirement, social security, the limitation and regulation of work hours, weekly days off, labor contracts, etc.

. . .

Finally, her special characteristics of order, economy, patience and resourcefulness will be as useful to society as the characteristics of man and will favor the establishment of laws too often overlooked until now.

The woman's vote will assure the establishment of important social laws.

All women will want:

To fight against alcoholism, from which they suffer much more than men;

To establish laws of health and welfare;

To obtain the regulation of female and child labor;

To defend young women against prostitution;

Finally, to prevent wars and to submit conflicts among nations to courts of arbitration.

Source: From a report presented to Besancon Municipal Council by the Franc-Comtois Group of the Union Française pour le Suffrage des Femmes. Besancon, March 1913, pp. 6–9.

---

intellectual satisfaction. Feminism had a much harder time taking root in these countries.

In central and eastern Europe the obstacles were even greater. In much of this region, economic development was far behind that of the western areas of Europe, and thus middle-class culture—the social base of feminism—was also underdeveloped. In the Russian Empire, the middle class was small and any political organization independent of the tsar was seen as a form of treason. No women's suffrage movement existed there until the revolution of 1905 dramatically changed the political equation. After the Revolution won the vote for men but failed to extend it to women, an organized and vocal women's suffrage campaign emerged.

In contrast to Russia, in England the middle class was both large and politically powerful, and the political structure had shown itself capable of adaptation and evolution. Yet even in England, the site of the first and the strongest European female suffrage movement, women failed to win the vote in the nineteenth century. As a result, a small group of activists resorted to more radical tactics. Led by the imposing mother-and-daughters team of Emmeline (1858–1928), Christabel (1880–1958), and Sylvia Pankhurst (1882–1960), the suffragettes° formed a breakaway women's suffrage group in 1903. Convinced that the mainstream suf-

fragists' tactics such as signing petitions, publishing reasoned arguments, and lobbying politicians would never win the vote, the suffragettes threw respectability to the winds. They adopted as their motto the slogan "Deeds, Not Words," and declared that women would never earn the vote through rational persuasion. Instead, they had to grab it by force. The suffragettes broke up political meetings with the cry "Votes for Women!," they chained themselves to the steps of the Houses of Parliament, shattered shop windows, burned churches, destroyed mailboxes, and even, in a direct attack on a cherished citadel of male middle-class culture, vandalized golf courses.

In opting for violence, the suffragettes staged a full frontal assault on a central fortification of middle-class culture—the ideal of the passive, homebound woman. The fortress they were attacking proved well-defended, however. Their opponents reacted with fury. Police broke up suffragette rallies with sexually focused brutality: They dragged suffragettes by their hair, stomped on their crotches, punched their breasts, and tore off their blouses. Once in jail, hunger-striking suffragettes endured the horror of forced feedings. Several jailers pinned the woman to her bed while the doctor thrust a plastic tube down her throat, often lacerating her larynx in the process, and pumped in food until she gagged.

CONCLUSION

The West in an Age of Mass Politics

The clash between the suffragettes and their jailers was only one of a multitude of encounters, many of them violent, among those seeking access to political power and those seeking to limit that access, in the era from 1870 to the start of World War I in 1914. At the same time, changing patterns of industrialization and accelerated urbanization gave rise to other sorts of encounters–between the manager seeking to cut production costs and the employee aiming to protect his wages, for example, or among the newly arrived immigrants in the city, struggling to survive in an unfamiliar culture, and the long-established residents who spoke a different language.

Out of such encounters emerged key questions about the definition of "the West." Where, for example, did the West end? Did it include Russia? "Yes," replied the small revolutionary groups who embraced Karl Marx's socialist theories and argued that Russia would follow Western patterns of economic and political development. "No," replied the Russian populists who rejected Western models and sought a revolutionary path unique to Russia. The expansion of the franchise and the processes of making nations raised even more fundamental questions. Was the West defined by democracy? Should it be? Was it synonymous with white, western European men or could people with olive-colored or black skin—or women of any color—participate fully in Western culture and politics? Was "the West" defined by its rationality? In the eighteenth century, Enlightenment thinkers had praised the power of human rationality and looked to reason as the path to social improvement. The rise of a new style of politics, based on emotional appeal and often irrational racist hatred, challenged this faith in reason. But at the same time, developments in industrial organization and technologies, which helped expand European national incomes, seemed to point to the benefits of rational processes.

As we will see in the next chapter, the expansion of Western control over vast areas of Asia and Africa in this period led an increasing number of Europeans and Americans to highlight economic prosperity and technological superiority as the defining characteristics of the West. Confidence, however, was accompanied by anxiety as these years also witnessed a far-reaching cultural and intellectual crisis. Closely connected to the development of mass politics and changes in social and gender relations, this crisis slowly eroded many of the pillars of middle- and upper-class society and raised searching questions about Western assumptions and values.

Suggestions for Further Reading

For a comprehensive list of suggested readings, please go to www.ablongman.com/levack/chapter22

Evans, Richard. *The Feminists: Women's Emancipation Movements in Europe, America, and Australasia 1840–1920.* 1977. A helpful comparative overview.

Kern, Stephen. *The Culture of Time and Space 1880–1918.* 1983. An innovative work that explores the cultural impact of technological change.

Lidtke, Vernon. *The Alternative Culture: Socialist Labor in Imperial Germany.* 1985. Looks beyond the world of parliamentary politics to assess the meaning and impact of working-class socialism.

Lindemann, Albert. *Esau's Tears: Modern Anti-Semitism and the Rise of the Jews.* 1997. A comprehensive and detailed survey that challenges many assumptions about the roots and nature of modern anti-Semitism.

Mayer, Arno. *The Persistence of the Old Regime: Europe to the Great War.* 1981. Argues that landed elites maintained a considerable amount of economic and political power throughout the nineteenth century.

Milward, A. S., and S. B. Saul. *The Development of the Economies of Continental Europe, 1850–1914.* 1977. A helpful survey.

Moch, Leslie. *Moving Europeans: Migration in Western Europe Since 1650.* 1992. Filled with maps and packed with information, Moch's work explodes many easy assumptions about the movement of Europeans in the nineteenth century.

Nord, Philip. *The Republican Moment: Struggles for Democracy in Nineteenth-Century France.* 1996. Illuminates the struggle to define and redefine France.

Pilbeam, Pamela. *The Middle Classes in Europe, 1789–1914: France, Germany, Italy, and Russia.* 1990. A comparative approach that helps clarify the patterns of social change.

Richards, Thomas. *The Commodity Culture of Victorian England: Advertising and Spectacle 1851–1914.* 1990. Fascinating study of the manufacturing of desire.

Stearns, Peter N. *Lives of Labor: Work in a Maturing Industrial Society.* 1975. Explores changing economic and social patterns.

Steenson, Gary P. *After Marx, Before Lenin: Marxism and Socialist Working-Class Parties in Europe, 1884–1914.* 1991. Examines both ideology and political practice within Europe's socialist parties.

Weber, Eugen. *Peasants into Frenchmen: The Modernization of Rural France, 1870–1914.* 1976. A very important work that helped shape the way historians think about "nation making."

Notes

1. Leslie Moch, *Moving Europeans: Migration in Western Europe Since 1650* (1992), 147.
2. Quoted in Eugen Weber, *Peasants into Frenchmen: The Modernization of Rural France, 1870–1914* (1987), 332–333.
3. Norman Kleeblatt, *The Dreyfus Affair: Art, Truth, and Justice* (1987), 96.
4. Quoted in Eric Cahm, *The Dreyfus Affair in French Society and Politics* (1994), 167.
5. Quoted in Robert Gildea, *Barricades and Borders: Europe 1800–1914* (1987), 317.
6. Quoted in Leslie Derfler, *Socialism Since Marx: A Century of the European Left* (1973), 58.
7. Karl Kautsky, quoted in Eric Hobsbawm, *The Age of Empire 1875–1914* (1987), 133.
8. Eugen Weber, *France, Fin-de-Siecle* (1986), 126.
9. Albert Lindemann, *Esau's Tears: Modern Anti-Semitism and the Rise of the Jews* (1997).
10. Maria Desraismes, "La Femme et Le Droit," *Eve dans l'humanite* (1891), 16–17.

The West and the World: Cultural Crisis and the New Imperialism, 1870–1914

I N THE AUTUMN OF 1898, BRITISH TROOPS MOVED INTO THE SUDAN IN NORTHEAST Africa to claim the region for the British Empire. On September 2, the British Camel Corps faced an army of 40,000 fighters. The Sudanese soldiers, Islamic believers known as dervishes who possessed a reputation for military fierceness, were fighting on their home ground against an invading force. Nevertheless, after only five hours of fighting, 11,000 dervishes lay dead. Their opponents lost just forty men. While the dervishes, armed with swords and spears, surged forward in a full-scale frontal assault, the British troops sat safely behind fortified defenses, and, using repeating rifles and Maxim guns (a type of early machine gun), simply mowed down their attackers. According to one participant on the British side, the future prime minister Winston Churchill, the biggest danger to the British soldiers during the battle of Omdurman was boredom: "the mere physical act [of loading, firing, and reloading] became tedious." The dervishes had little chance of boredom. Churchill recalled, "And all the time out on the plain on the other side bullets were shearing through flesh, smashing and splintering bone; blood spouted from terrible wounds; valiant men were struggling through a hell of whistling metal, exploding shells, and spurting dust—suffering, despairing, dying."[1]

The slaughter of 11,000 Sudanese in just over five hours formed but one episode in what many historians call the age of new imperialism, a period that witnessed both the culmination of, and a new phase in, Europe's conquest of the globe. This often-violent encounter between Europe and the regions that Europeans emphatically defined as non-Western was closely connected to the political and economic upheavals examined in Chapter 22. An understanding of the new imperialism, however, demands a close look not only at political

Chapter Outline

- Scientific Transformations
- Cultural Crisis and the Birth of Modernism
- The New Imperialism

Paul Gauguin, *Matamoe* ("Peacocks in the Country"), 1892: The Fauvist painter Paul Gauguin fled Europe for Tahiti in an effort to restore to his art the strong colors and emotions that he believed characterized non-Western cultures. The sights, sensibilities, and symbolism of Tahitian society profoundly affected his painting—and helped shape modernist art.

rivalries and economic structures, but also at scientific, intellectual, and cultural developments in the last third of the nineteenth century. At the same time that European and American adventurers risked life and limb to chart Africa's rivers, exploit its resources, and subjugate its peoples, Western artists and scientists embarked on explorations into worlds of thought and perception far deeper than the surface reality accessible to the senses, and in so doing challenged the social order and even the meaning of reality itself.

The final decades of the nineteenth century and the opening years of the twentieth thus comprised an era of internal fragmentation and external expansion. The scientific, artistic, and physical explorations that are the subject of this chapter redefined the West and its relationship with the rest of the world. As Western dominance over Africa and Asia expanded, states such as Russia and Japan embarked on conscious efforts to westernize their societies and thereby compete successfully with the West's industrial and military might. Areas of white European settlement such as Australia, South Africa, and the United States moved more firmly inside Western boundaries. The tendency to color the West white, however, meant that members of the nonwhite populations of these regions were rarely accepted by whites as fully Western.

This chapter addresses three questions: (1) How did scientific developments during this period lead to not only greater intellectual and cultural optimism but also deepened anxiety? (2) What factors led many Europeans in this period to believe they were living in a time of cultural crisis? (3) What were the causes and consequences of the new imperialist ideology for both the West and non-Western societies?

Scientific Transformations

During the final third of the nineteenth century, Europeans encountered in new ways both the human body and the wider physical universe. Forced by urbanization to cram more bodies into limited space, men and women grew increasingly aware of the human body, and of the way it interacted with other bodies, both human and microscopic. At the same time, the work of geologists and biologists highlighted the way the body itself had evolved to meet the challenges of survival, while the experiments of chemists and physicists revealed the inadequacies of accepted models for understanding the physical world.

These developments affirmed a central assumption of the dominant middle-class worldview—that human reason

and endeavor can guarantee social, intellectual, and moral progress. Scientific advances in the final third of the nineteenth century helped improve the health and hygiene of the Western world. Yet these changes in scientific understandings of both the body and the cosmos also threatened to destabilize Western society and therefore deepened the cultural anxiety of Europeans and Americans in this period.

MEDICINE AND MICROBES

In the second half of the nineteenth century, and particularly after 1870, a series of developments transformed the practice of Western medicine. Before this time, Western physicians assumed that illness was caused by bad blood and so relied on practices such as leeching (attaching leeches to the skin) and bloodletting (slicing open a vein). These procedures drained large amounts of blood, further weakening already ill patients. Admission into a hospital was sometimes a death sentence. Ignorant of the existence of bacteria and viruses, doctors commonly attended one patient after another without bothering to wash their hands or surgical instruments. The only anesthetic available was alcohol; pain was regarded as inevitable, something to be endured rather than eased.

Urbanization posed a fundamental challenge to such traditional medical practice, and helped transform Western medicine. Expanding urban populations served as fertile seedbeds for contagious diseases. Cholera outbreaks, such as the epidemics that ravaged British cities in 1831 and 1848, forced doctors and public officials to pay attention to the relationship between overcrowding, polluted water, and epidemic disease. Hamburg was one of the first cities to undertake the construction of a modern water and sewer system in 1842; in 1848 the London cholera epidemic persuaded public officials to build a vast sewer system (most of which is still in use today).

It was not until the 1860s, however, that germ theory was developed. By exploring the transmission of disease among plants and animals in the French agricultural industry, the chemist Louis Pasteur (1822–1895) discovered that the source of contagion is not air, water, or odor, but microscopic living organisms—bacteria. Astonishingly productive, Pasteur developed vaccines against anthrax, hog fever, sheep pox, various poultry and cattle diseases, and rabies. (His process of purifying milk and fermented products is still known as pasteurization.) Following Pasteur, Robert Koch (1843–1910), professor of public health in Berlin, isolated the tuberculosis bacillus in 1882 and the bacteria that cause cholera in 1883.

The work of Pasteur, Koch, and other scientists in tracing the transmission of disease was crucial in improving Western medical practice. Between 1872 and 1900, the number of European deaths from infectious diseases dropped by 60 percent. Once physicians and surgeons

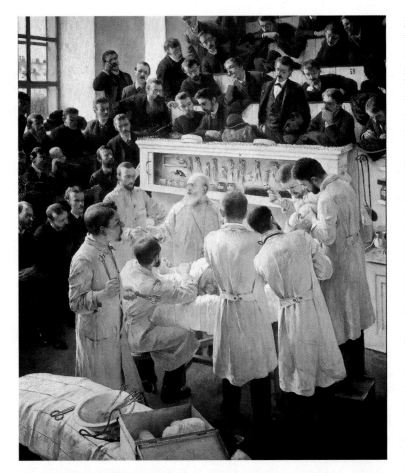

■ **Adelbert Seligmann, *German Surgeon Theodor Billroth at Work in Vienna* (1890)**
Modern surgery in the making: The patient has been anesthetized, but the modern operating room does not yet exist, nor are the doctors wearing gloves or masks. Billroth, the director of the Second Surgical Clinic in Vienna, pioneered surgical techniques for gastrointestinal illnesses and cancer.

genuine confidence that the conquest of nature through science would create a healthier environment. But the widespread awareness of germs also heightened anxiety. Isolation of the bacilli that caused an illness did not immediately translate into its cure, and viral infections remained often lethal. Measles, for example, continued to kill at least 7,000 people per year in Britain throughout the nineteenth century. After the 1870s, Europeans were aware that they lived in a world populated by potentially deadly but invisible organisms, carried on the bodies of their servants, their employees, their neighbors, and their family members. Those who could afford to isolate themselves from the danger often did so. As a result, this era witnessed striking growth in the number of seaside resorts, as middle- and upper-class Europeans fled from urban centers of contagion.

THE REVOLUTION IN PHYSICS

The transformation in medical practice was not the only dramatic scientific change that occurred in the late nineteenth century. Between 1880 and 1910 a revolution in physics occurred as well. Although the most dramatic consequences of this revolution—atomic weapons and nuclear energy—would not be realized for another half century, this transformation in scientific understanding contributed to both the exhilaration and the uncertainty that characterized the intellectual and cultural history of Europe in the decades before World War I.

At the core of this scientific revolution lay the question, "What is matter?" For most of the nineteenth century, the answer was simple: Matter was what close observation and measurement, as well as common sense, showed it to be. Material bodies, made up of the building blocks called atoms, rested and moved against a fixed backdrop of space and time. Matter was three-dimensional, defined by height, width, and depth. Accessible to reason, observation, and common sense, the material world could be understood and controlled.

As the new century opened, this picture of the universe began to crumble. A series of discoveries and experiments challenged this commonsense view of the universe and offered in its place a much more mysterious and unsettling vista. The discovery of the X ray in 1895 had already disrupted prevailing assumptions about the solidity and predictability of matter. They were shaken even further in 1898 when the Polish-French chemist Marie Curie (1867–1934) discovered a new element, radium, which did not behave the way matter was supposed to behave. Because

accepted that microscopic organisms caused disease, they began to develop techniques to control their spread. The development of antiseptic surgery in the later 1860s improved the patient's odds of surviving the operating table.

The increasing use of anesthetics in the second half of the nineteenth century also improved those odds. In 1847 a Scottish physician performed the first delivery of a baby using chloroform to dull the mother's pain. Although condemned by many Christian theologians (who regarded pain as both ennobling and a necessary part of sinful human existence), the use of anesthetics spread fairly quickly. Britain's Queen Victoria, who gave birth to nine children, probably articulated the feelings of many patients when she greeted the use of anesthetics in the delivery room with unfettered delight: "Oh blessed chloroform!"

Medical advances such as anesthetic techniques and an understanding of how diseases are spread gave Europeans it continually emitted subatomic particles, radium did not possess a constant atomic weight. Two years later, the German scientist Max Planck (1858–1947) theorized that a heated body radiates energy not in the continuous, steady, predictable stream most scientists envisaged, but rather in irregular clumps, which he called *quanta.* Although at first dismissed by most scientists as contrary to common sense, Planck's quantum theory accorded with the emerging picture of a changeable universe.

These scientific discoveries provide the context for the work of Albert Einstein (1879–1955), certainly the most famous and readily recognizable scientist of the twentieth century. Bored by his job as a patent clerk, Einstein passed the time speculating on the nature of the cosmos. In 1905, he rang the death knell for the Newtonian universe by publishing an article that introduced to the world the theory of relativity. Einstein rejected the nineteenth-century assumption of the absolute nature of time and space. Instead, he argued, time and space shift relative to the position of the observer. Similarly, matter itself shifts. Mass depends on motion, and thus time, space, and matter intermingle in a universe of relative flux. The result of Einstein's vision was a revolution in perspective. The universe is not three- but four-dimensional: To height, width, and depth, Einstein added *time.*

This new understanding was much harder to grasp than that offered by Newtonian science. With the revolution in physics, much of science became incomprehensible to ordinary men and women, even educated ones. The new science also challenged the basic assumptions that governed nineteenth-century thought by offering a vision of the universe in which what you see is *not* what you get, in which objective reality might well be the product of subjective perception.

SOCIAL THOUGHT: THE REVOLT AGAINST POSITIVISM

Just as the revolution in physics presented a new and more disturbing picture of the physical universe, so social thinkers in the last third of the nineteenth century began to formulate troubling theories about the nature of human society. As Chapter 21 explained, the mainstream of nineteenth-century thought was positivist: It placed great faith in human reason and therefore in the validity of applying methods drawn from the natural sciences to the study of human affairs. Positivism viewed the world as eminently knowable and progress as ultimately guaranteed, given the capacity of rational human beings to understand and therefore control both physical and human nature. This faith in human reason, however, came under attack in the last decades of the century. In this era, social thinkers (writers and scientists whose work would lay the foundations for new academic disciplines such as sociology, psy-

chology, and anthropology) began to emphasize the role of nonrational forces in determining human conduct.

Social thinkers confronted the power of the nonrational first in the new mass politics of this era. The rise of racist and nationalist political parties demonstrated that individuals were often swayed more by emotion than by rational argument. In an effort to understand and therefore to manipulate political demonstrations, the French theorist Gustave LeBon (1841–1931) developed the discipline of crowd or collective psychology. He showed how appeals to emotion, particularly in the form of symbols and myths, can influence crowd behavior. In LeBon's view, democracy relinquished political control to the easily swayed masses and so would lead only to disaster.

Unlike LeBon, the German social theorist Max Weber (1864–1920) believed in democracy, but he, too, recognized the role of the nonrational in influencing the mass electorate. Weber was both fascinated and frightened by the development of modern industrial society. His studies focused on the "bureaucratization" of modern life—the tendency of both political and economic institutions to become increasingly standardized and to grow ever larger and more impersonal. Weber judged the triumph of bureaucracy as the victory of reason and science over individual prejudice and interest-group politics, and so as a generally progressive force. But at the same time he recognized that because growing bureaucracies could crush both ideals and individuals, they posed a real threat to personal and political freedom. Troubled by the vision of individuals trapped within "the iron cage of modern life," Weber in 1898 suffered a nervous breakdown. After four years Weber was able to free himself from the grip of debilitating depression, but he remained profoundly pessimistic about the future, which he described as "a polar night of icy darkness and hardness."[2]

According to his wife, when Weber fell into depression, "an evil something out of the subterranean unconscious . . . grasped him by its claws."[3] This view of the individual as a captive of the unconscious was central to the revolt against positivism, and reached its fullest development in the highly influential work of the Viennese scientist and physician Sigmund Freud (1856–1939). Freud argued that the conscious mind plays only a very limited role in shaping the actions of each individual. His effort to treat patients suffering from nervous disorders led him to hypnosis and dream analysis, and to the conviction that behind the conscious exterior existed a deeper, far more significant reality—the unconscious. In *The Interpretation of Dreams* (1900), Freud argued that beneath the rational surface of each human being surge all kinds of hidden desires, including such irrational drives as the longing for death and destruction.

Freud thought of himself as a scientist. He believed that he could understand human behavior (and treat mental illness) by diving below the rational surface and exploring the submerged terrain of unconscious desire. Yet the emergence of Freudian psychology convinced many educated Western

individuals not that the irrational could be uncovered and controlled, but rather that the irrational was *in* control.

THE TRIUMPH OF EVOLUTIONARY THEORY

During the same period that social thought was
outlining new ways to understand human behavior and raising serious doubts about the essential
rationality of that behavior, developments in geology and biology also led to both confidence and
anxiety. Evolutionary theory provided a scientific
framework in which educated Europeans could
understand and justify their own superior social
and economic positions. It also, however, challenged basic religious assumptions and depicted
the natural world in new and unsettling ways.

Traditionally, Europeans had relied on the
opening chapters of the Bible to understand the
origins of both nature and humanity. By the
1830s, however, the work of geologists challenged the biblical account. Although a literal
reading of the Bible dated the Earth at only 6,000
years old, geologists such as Charles Lyell
(1797–1875) argued on the basis of the fossil
record and existing geological formations that
the Earth had formed over millions of years.
Lyell's most famous work was the *Principles of
Geology*, first published in 1830 and a nineteenth-century best-seller that went through
eleven editions. In three volumes of very readable prose, packed with illustrative examples,
Lyell gently but rigorously refuted the orthodox
Christian position that geological change and the
extinction of species could be explained by the
biblical account of the flood or other such supernatural interventions. Instead, he and others argued that
the material world must be seen as the product of natural
forces still at work, still observable today.

But how could one explain the tremendous variety of
plant and animal species in the world today on the basis of
natural processes? In 1859, the British scientist Charles
Darwin (1809–1882) answered this question in a way that
proved quite satisfying to large numbers of educated
Europeans—and quite horrifying to others. Darwin had
spent two decades thinking about the data he collected during a five-year expedition to the South Pacific in the 1830s.
Serving as an unpaid naturalist on the H.M.S. *Beagle* between 1831 and 1836, Darwin observed that certain species
of animal and plant life, isolated on islands, had developed
differently from related species on the coast. After returning
to Britain, Darwin read the population theory of Thomas
Malthus (1766–1834). Malthus argued that population

■ Darwin as a Monkey

Simplified and often ridiculous versions of Darwin's ideas almost immediately
entered popular culture. In this cartoon, he is being scolded by a woman for
his theory that women blush when men look at them because a man's gaze
directs a woman's attention to the visible parts of her body, which causes a
change in her "capillary circulation."

growth would outstrip food supply, and that in all species,
more offspring are produced than can actually survive.
Putting together Malthus's theory with his own observations, Darwin concluded that life is a struggle for survival,
and that even quite small biological variations might help
an individual member of a species win out in this struggle.
From this understanding came the Darwinian theory° of
the evolution of species.

Darwin's evolutionary theory rested on two basic ideas:
variation and *natural selection*. Variation refers to those
small but crucial biological advantages that assist in the
struggle for survival: A bird with a slightly longer beak, for
example, might gain easier access to scarce food supplies.
Over generations, the individuals more adapted for survival
displace those without the positive variation. Variation,
then, provides the means of natural selection, the process
by which new species evolve.

THE DESCENT OF MAN

First published in 1871, The Descent of Man *continued and completed Charles Darwin's theory of the evolution of species first introduced in his* Origin of Species *(1859). Darwin's work in many ways affirmed central prejudices and assumptions of his middle-class readers, as the following excerpts demonstrate.*

We have now seen that man is variable in body and mind; and that the variations are induced, either directly or indirectly, by the same general causes, and obey the same general laws, as with the lower animals. Man has spread widely over the face of the earth, and must have been exposed, during his incessant migration, to the most diversified conditions. . . . The early progenitors of man must also have tended, like all other animals, to have increased beyond their means of subsistence; they must, therefore, occasionally have been exposed to a struggle for existence, and consequently, to the rigid law of natural selection. Beneficial variations of all kinds will thus, either occasionally or habitually, have been preserved and injurious ones eliminated. . . .

Man in the rudest state in which he now exists is the most dominant animal that has ever appeared on this earth. He has spread more widely than any other highly organised form, and all others have yielded before him. He manifestly owes this immense superiority to his intellectual faculties, to his social habits, which lead him to aid and defend his fellows, and to his corporeal structure. . . .

The belief that there exists in man some close relation between the size of the brain and the development of the intellectual faculties is supported by the comparison of the skulls of savage and civilized races, of ancient and modern people, and by the analogy of the whole vertebrate series . . . the mean internal capacity of the skull in Europeans is 92.3 cubic inches; in Americans 87.5; in Asiatics 87.1; and in Australians only 81.9 inches . . . Nevertheless, it must be admitted that some skulls of very high antiquity, such as the famous one of the Neanderthal, are well developed and capacious.

Source: From *The Descent of Man,* 2nd edition, by Charles Darwin, 1874.

Darwin provided a persuasive explanation for evolutionary change, but the fact that the laws of genetic heredity were not yet understood resulted in two key weaknesses in his formulation—first, its extreme gradualness, in that the process of variation required many, many generations; and second, the lack of a precise explanation of how variations first emerge and how they are inherited. Answers to both problems lay embedded in the research of an Austrian monk, Gregor Mendel (1822–1884). Experimenting in his vegetable garden with what we now call selective breeding, Mendel developed the laws of genetic heredity. Mendel's work was ignored almost completely until the end of the century, when the Dutch botanist Hugo DeVries (1848–1935) used his data to hypothesize that evolution occurred through radical mutations in the reproductive cells of an organism. These mutations are passed on to offspring at the moment of reproduction and, if they offer an advantage in the struggle for existence, enable the offspring to survive and to produce more mutant offspring. Thus evolution can proceed by leaps, rather than gradually over a very long period of time.

Long before these genetic underpinnings of evolution were understood, however, Darwin's theories proved extraordinarily influential. Published in 1859, *The Origin of Species* aroused immediate interest and controversy. This controversy intensified when, in 1871, Darwin published *The Descent of Man,* in which he firmly placed humanity itself within the evolutionary process. Many Christians re-

acted with horror to a theory that they believed challenged the biblical narrative of Creation and denied a special place for humankind within the physical universe. But the most troubling aspect of Darwin's theory was its view of nature. According to orthodox Christian theology, nature, like the Bible, reveals God to the believer. In the Darwinian universe, however, nature was not a harmonious, well-ordered system that revealed the hand of God. Instead, it was the arena of brutal and bloody competition for survival— "nature red in tooth and claw," as the British poet Alfred Lord Tennyson put it. In such a universe, ideas of purpose and meaning seemed to disappear. Faced with this disturbing vision, many Christians opposed Darwinian evolutionary theory.

Many other Christians welcomed Darwin's theory, however. They argued that evolution did not banish divine purpose from the universe but instead showed God's hand at work in the gradual development of more perfect species. Enthusiastically applying the idea of evolution to the ethical universe, they contended that the history of humanity showed that the morally fittest proved victorious in the ethical sphere, just as the strongest triumphed in the natural world.

By 1870, three-quarters of British scientists surveyed accepted evolutionary theory. More important, many middle-class Europeans and Americans welcomed Darwin's ideas as providing a coherent explanation of change that accorded with their worldview. They saw Darwin's work as a scientific confirmation of their faith in the virtues of competition and in the inevitability of progress. As Darwin himself wrote in *The Origin of Species,* because "natural selection works solely by and for the good of each being, all corporeal [bodily] and mental development will tend to progress toward perfection."

SOCIAL DARWINISM AND RACIAL HIERARCHIES

Darwin's evolutionary theory contributed to a new understanding of biological relationships and of the connections between humanity and the natural world. In the last quarter of the nineteenth century, however, a growing number of writers and social theorists insisted that evolutionary theory could and should be applied more broadly. One of the most influential of this group was the British writer Herbert Spencer (1820–1902). Trained as a civil engineer, Spencer became convinced that evolution held the key to engineering a better human society. A self-confident, eminently practical thinker, Spencer coined the phrase "the survival of the fittest" to describe what he viewed as the most basic explanation of development in both nature and human society. He believed that human societies evolve like plant and animal species. Only the fittest, those able to adapt to changing conditions, survive. A great champion of *laissez-faire* economics (see Chapter 21), Spencer contended that government interference in economic and social affairs interfered with the natural evolutionary process and so hindered rather than assured progress.

Spencer's essentially biological vision of society proved influential in shaping the theories of Social Darwinism°. Arguing that racial hierarchy was the product of natural evolution, the Social Darwinists applied Spencer's ideas about the importance of individual competition and the survival of the fittest to entire races. In their view, the nonwhite races in Africa and Asia had lost the game. Their so-called backward way of life showed they had failed to compete successfully with white Europeans and thus displayed their biological inferiority. The very popular British novelist Rider Haggard, in his best-selling thriller *She* (1887), summed up the Social Darwinist worldview: "Those who are weak must perish; the earth is to the strong . . . We run to place and power over the dead bodies of those who fail and fall; ay, we win the food we eat from out the mouths of starving babes. It is the scheme of things."

In their effort to construct a scientifically based racial hierarchy, Social Darwinists made use not only of Darwin's idea of natural selection but also of the theory of "recapitulation," first proposed by the German zoologist Ernst Haeckel (1834–1919). According to Haeckel, as an individual matures, he or she moves through the same stages as did the human race during the course of its evolution. For example, the gill slits of a human embryo "recapitulate" the fish stage through which the human race had evolved. The idea of recapitulation enabled scientists to fill in the gaps left by the fossil record. By observing the development of children into adults, they argued, we can witness the evolutionary maturation of the human race.

Social Darwinists used the theory of recapitulation to argue that only white European males had reached the pinnacle of evolutionary development. They contended that nonwhite men, as well as all women, embodied the more primitive stages of evolution through which the white European male had already passed. In other words, the nonwhite races and white women were suffering from arrested development. Their bodies and brains bore witness to their low-ranking position on the evolutionary ladder. Such ideas permeated much of Western culture in the late nineteenth century. Sigmund Freud, for example, argued that "the female genitalia are more primitive than those of the male," while Gustave LeBon compared the average female brain to that of a gorilla. G. A. Henty, a best-selling British novelist, insisted that the "intelligence of the average negro is about equal to that of a European [male] child of ten years old."[4]

Firmly convinced that the inferiority of women and nonwhites was a biological fact, nineteenth-century scientists and large sections of the European public welcomed evolutionary theory as scientific proof of deeply embedded cultural assumptions, such as the benefits of competition, the rightness of white rule and male dominance, and the superiority of Western civilization. Yet evolutionary science also worked to undermine European confidence because with the idea of evolution came the possibility of regression: Was the traffic on the evolutionary ladder all one-way, or could species descend to a lower evolutionary level? Could humanity regress back to its animal origins?

The concept of the "inheritance of acquired characteristics," associated with the work of the French scientist Jean-Baptiste Lamarck (1744–1829), played a crucial role in fostering these fears of regression. More than fifty years before Darwin published his *Origin of Species,* Lamarck theorized that acquired characteristics—traits that an individual develops in response to experience or the environment, such as the stooped back of a miner, the poor vision of a lace maker, or the deep tan of an agricultural laborer—could be passed on to the individual's offspring. Because the process of genetic reproduction was not understood until the twentieth century, Lamarck's theories remained very influential throughout the nineteenth century, and possessed deeply disturbing implications. Middle-class Europeans began to speculate that the conditions of urban industrial life were producing undesirable characteristics among urban workers. In their view, characteristics such as physical weakness, sexual promiscuity, and violent criminality were being passed from one generation to the next, and were threatening to reverse the evolutionary ascent of Western civilization.

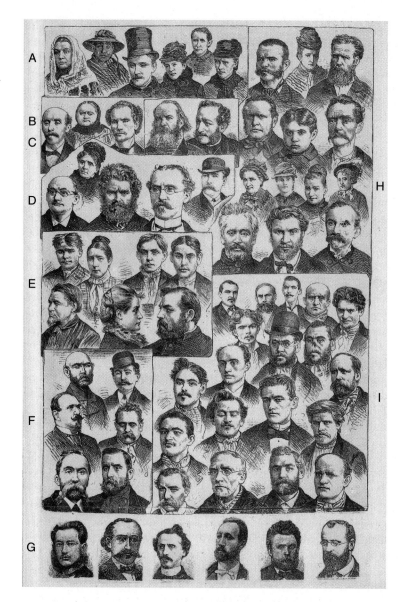

■ **A page from *Criminal Man* (1876), by Cesare Lombroso**

An Italian physician, Lombroso established the new social science of criminology. In *Criminal Man*, he argued that individuals with certain physical characteristics, such as a narrow forehead or linked eyebrows, are likely to be criminals. According to Lombroso, the criminal body is the result of evolutionary regression. In the face, skull, and physique of the criminal we can see evidence of a reversion to a more primitive evolutionary state. The images shown here are grouped alphabetically as follows: A: shoplifters; B, C, D, F: swindlers; E: murderers; G: fraudulent bankrupts; H: purse-snatchers; I: burglars.

Cultural Crisis: The Fin-de-Siècle and the Birth of Modernism

The fear of evolutionary regression contributed to a growing cultural crisis. The sense that Western civilization was declining, that degeneration and decay characterized the contemporary experience, was summed up in a single French phrase: *fin-de-siècle*°. Literally translated as "end of the century," fin-de-siècle served as a shorthand term for the mood of cultural uneasiness, and even despair, that characterized much of European society in the final decades of the nineteenth century and the opening years of the twentieth. Uncertainty colored many aspects of European thought and culture. Fast-moving economic and social change, coupled with the new scientific ideas, convinced many Europeans that old answers were no longer sufficient. The quest for new answers fostered the birth of what would become known as modernism, a broad label for a series of unsettling developments in thought, literature, and art. Many Europeans celebrated modernism as a release from the restraints imposed by middle-class cultural codes. Others, however, responded fearfully. Both exhilaration and anxiety, then, characterize this time of cultural crisis.

THE FIN-DE-SIÈCLE

A series of social problems common to increasingly urbanized nations reinforced Europeans' fear of degeneration. As cities spread, so too did the perception of a rising crime rate. This perception of a more criminal society went hand-in-hand with the reality of increasing drug and alcohol use. Diners in high society finished their sumptuous meals with a dessert course consisting of strawberries soaked in ether; respectable bourgeois men offered each other cocaine as a quick "pick-me-up" at the end of the working day; middle-class mothers fed restless babies opium-laced syrups; workers bought enough opium-derived laudanum on Saturday afternoon to render them unconscious until work on Monday morning. Using Lamarck's theory of the inheritance of acquired characteristics, scientists contended that addictions could be passed on from generation to generation, thus contributing to national decline and a culture of decadence.

Popular novels of the fin-de-siècle also contributed to the fear of degeneration by depicting Western culture as diseased or barbaric. In a twenty-volume work, the French novelist Émile Zola (1840–1902) traced the decline of a once-proud family to symbolize the decay of all of France. As alcoholism and sexual promiscuity pollute succeeding generations, the family disintegrates. In *Nana* (1880), Zola used the title character, a prostitute, to embody his country. Watching as French soldiers march off to defeat in the Franco-Prussian War, Nana is dying of smallpox, her face "a charnel-house, a heap of pus and blood, a shovelful of putrid flesh."[5] Novels such as *Dr. Jekyll and Mr. Hyde* (1886) and *Dracula* (1897) showed that beneath the cultured exterior of a civilized man lurked a primitive, bloodthirsty beast and so revealed a deep sense of anxiety.

The most influential advocate of the idea that Western culture had degenerated was the German philosopher and poet Friedrich Nietzsche (1844–1900). In Nietzsche's view, most people were little more than sheep, penned in by outdated customs and conventions. Bourgeois morality, rooted in Christianity, helped sap Western culture of its vitality. "Christianity has taken the side of everything weak," Nietzsche claimed. He traced the weakness of Western culture beyond Christianity, however, and back to ancient Greece, to Socrates's exaltation of rationality. In Nietzsche's view, an overemphasis on rational thought had deprived Western culture of the power of more primal urges, such as the irrational, emotional, and instinctive aspects of human nature.

Even more fundamentally, Nietzsche argued that the belief that human reason has direct access to scientific fact is an illusion. Trained as a classical philologist, Nietzsche's study of language convinced him that everything we know must be filtered through a symbolic system—through language or some other means of artistic or mathematic representation. We can know only the representation, not the thing itself. Not even science can uncover "reality." Even the style of Nietzsche's publications worked to expose the limits of reason. Rather than write carefully constructed essays that proceeded in a logical, linear fashion from fact to fact, Nietzsche adopted an elusive, poetic style characterized by

disconnected fragments, more accessible to intuitive understanding than to rational analysis.

Nietzsche's writings attracted little attention until the 1890s, when his ideas first exploded in Germany and Austria, and then spread throughout Europe. Nietzsche's call to "become what you are" attracted young enthusiasts, who embraced his conviction that the confining assumptions and aspirations of bourgeois society held back the individual from personal liberation. "God is dead," Nietzsche proclaimed, "and we have killed him." If God is dead, then "there is nobody who commands, nobody who obeys, nobody who trespasses."

TIGHTENING GENDER BOUNDARIES

The fear of degeneration evident throughout European culture and society in the last decades of the nineteenth century also expressed itself in a multifaceted effort to draw more tightly the boundaries around accepted definitions of "maleness" and femaleness." Both the feminist and the homosexual joined the alcoholic, the drug addict, the prostitute, and the criminal in the list of dangerous and degenerate beings.

As discussed in Chapter 22, the years after 1850 and particularly after 1880 witnessed the birth of modern feminism. The emergence of legal, educational, and political reform campaigns challenged nineteenth-century middle-class domestic ideology. Antifeminists viewed these campaigns with alarm. They insisted that a woman's physiology demanded that she remain in the home. In the view of antifeminists, a woman who chose political activism or paid employment not only risked her own physical and mental breakdown, she also tended to produce physically and morally degenerate children.

Like feminists, homosexuals were also singled out as threats to the social order. Before 1869, *homosexual* was not a word: Coined by a Hungarian scientist seeking a new label for a new concept, it entered the English language in 1890. Traditionally, Europeans and Americans had viewed same-sex sexual practice as a form of immoral behavior, indulged in by morally lax—but otherwise normal—men. (Few considered the possibility of female homosexual behavior.) In the last third of the nineteenth century, however, the emphasis shifted from *actions* to *identity*, from condemning a specific type of sexual behavior to denouncing a certain group of people now considered abnormal and dangerous. Scientists argued that "the homosexual" was diseased—and that he could communicate this disease to others.

These ideas gained in force as homosexual subcultures increased in number in European and American cities. The anonymity and mobility of urban life offered homosexuals the possibility of creating a space for themselves in which a new, more confident and assertive homosexual identity could be expressed. But these subcultures soon encountered fierce repression as the moral and medical condemnation

The Trial of Oscar Wilde

In March 1895 the Marquis of Queensberry left a message with the porter of a gentleman's club in London. The message, written on Queensberry's calling card, read "To Oscar Wilde, posing as a *somdomite*." What Queensberry meant to write was *sodomite,* a common term for a man who engaged in sexual relations with other men. By handing the card to the porter, Queensberry openly accused Wilde, a celebrated novelist and playwright, of homosexual—and therefore criminal—activity. Ten years earlier the British Parliament had declared illegal all homosexual activity, even consensual relations between adults in a private home. Queensberry's accusation, then, was extremely serious. Oscar Wilde responded by suing Queensberry for libel—and set in motion a legal process that led to Wilde's imprisonment, and indirectly, to his early death.

Wilde made a reckless mistake when he chose to sue for libel, for in fact Queensberry had not libeled him. Wilde was a homosexual, and he and Queensberry's son, Lord Alfred Douglas, were lovers. Why, then, did Wilde dare to challenge Queensberry? Perhaps the fact that he was married, with two children, seemed to provide a certain shield against the charge of homosexuality. Or perhaps Wilde's successes as a novelist and playwright gave him a misguided sense of invulnerability. With two of his plays currently appearing on the London stage to favorable reviews, Wilde stood at the pinnacle of his career in the spring of 1895.

Wilde had built that career on a deliberate flouting of middle-class codes of morality. He saw himself as an artist, and insisted that art should be freed from social convention and moral restraint. His "High Society" comedies about privileged elites living scandalous lives and exchanging witty epigrams were far from the morally uplifting drama expected by middle-class audiences. He also used his public persona to attack the conventional, the respectable, and the orthodox. Widely recognized for his outrageous clothing and conversation, Wilde had consciously adopted the mannerisms of what nineteenth-century Britons called a "dandy"—a well-dressed, irreverent, artistic, leisured, and most of all, effeminate man. Before the Oscar Wilde trial, such effeminacy did not serve as a sign of, or a code for, homosexual inclinations, but it did signal to many observers a lavish—and loose—lifestyle. Oscar Wilde, then, was a man many British men and women loved to hate.

Even so, when his trial opened Wilde appeared to be in a strong position, the prosecutor rather than the defendant. Because Wilde had Queensberry's card with the "sodomite" charge written right on it, Queensberry faced certain conviction unless he could show that Wilde had engaged in homosexual activity. Wilde knew, of course, that Queensberry would not risk bringing the legal spotlight to bear on his own son's homosexuality.

At first, Queensberry's attorney, Edward Carson, focused on Wilde's published works, trying to use Wilde's own words against him. It proved an ineffective strategy. On the witness stand, Wilde reveled in the attention, and ran circles around Carson.

On the second day of the libel trial, however, Wilde's witticisms proved insufficient as Carson began to question him about his frequent visits to a male brothel and his associations with a number of young, working-class men who worked as male prostitutes. Suddenly the issue was no longer the literary merit or moral worth of Wilde's published writings, but rather his sexual exploitation of working-class boys. At this point, Wilde withdrew his libel charge against Queensberry, and the court declared the Marquis not guilty.

If Queensberry was not guilty of libel in calling Wilde a sodomite, then by clear implication, Wilde was guilty of homosexual activity and therefore a criminal. Within days he was charged with "gross indecency" with another male. The jury in that case failed to reach a verdict, but the state was determined to obtain a conviction and brought the charges again. Wilde was refused bail, and on May 20 he was back in court.

On May 25, 1895—just three months after Queensberry had left his misspelled message with the club porter—Wilde's promising literary career ended. He was found guilty of seven counts of gross indecency with other men. The presiding judge, Sir Alfred Wills, characterized the trial as "the worst case I have ever tried," and declared, " I shall under the circumstances be expected to pass the severest sentence the law allows. In my judgment it is totally inadequate for such a case." He sentenced Wilde to two years at hard labor. The physical punishment took its toll. Wilde died in 1900 at age 46.

In sentencing Wilde, Wills described him as "the centre of a circle of extensive corruption of the most hideous kind." How do we account for the intensity of Wills's language, as well as the severity of Wilde's sentence? Homosexual activity had long been condemned on religious grounds, but this condemnation grew much more fierce in the closing decades of the nineteenth century. In a time of rapid and threatening change, the marking of gender boundaries became a way to create and enforce social order. Wilde crossed those boundaries, and so had to be punished. Moreover, by the end of the nineteenth century, the state had assumed new responsibilities. Desperate to enhance national strength in a period of heightened international competition, governments intervened in areas previously considered to be the domain of the private citizen. By the turn of the century, western European governments were compelling working-class parents to send their children to school, regulating the hours adults could work, supervising the sale of food and drugs, providing limited forms of old-age pensions and medical insurance—and policing sexual boundaries.

The policing of sexual boundaries became easier after the Wilde trial because it provided a homosexual personality profile, a "Wanted" poster to hang on the walls of Western culture. For many observers of his very well-publicized trial, Wilde became the embodiment of "the homosexual," a particular and peculiar type of person, and a menace to cultural stability. The Wilde trial linked "dandyism" to the new image of the homosexual. Outward stylistic choices such as effeminacy, artistic sensibilities, and flamboyant clothing and conversation became, for many observers, the telltale signs of substantial inner corruption. Thus the Wilde case marked an important turning point in the construction, as well as the condemnation, of a homosexual identity.

■ **Oscar Wilde and Lord Alfred Douglas**

Although the British government pursued its case against Wilde, it made no effort to put together a case against Douglas.

Questions of Justice

1. What does this trial reveal about changing definitions of "public" and "private" in the last decades of the nineteenth century?

2. How does this trial illustrate the role of medical, legal, and cultural assumptions in shaping sexual identity?

Taking It Further

An Ideal Husband. 1999. Film adaptation of Oscar Wilde's very funny play, which exemplifies his lighthearted but devastating critique of conventional manners and morals.

Ellman, Richard. *Oscar Wilde.* 1988. An important biography of Wilde.

Hyde, H. Montgomery. *The Trials of Oscar Wilde.* 1962. Includes extensive quotations from the trial transcripts as well as photographs of some of the documentary evidence.

McLaren, Angus. *The Trials of Masculinity: Policing Sexual Boundaries 1870–1930.* 1997. Places the Wilde trial within a wider cultural context.

of male homosexuality became enshrined in legislation. The Penal Code of the new Germany stipulated severe punishment for homosexuality, while the British government in 1885 made illegal all homosexual acts, even those between consenting adults in the privacy of their own home.

The new concern about homosexuality was nurtured by a wider anxiety about the man's role in society, an anxiety provoked not only by the challenge of feminism, but also by the economic changes associated with the rise of corporate capitalism (see Chapter 22). Required by liberal ideology to be aggressive, independent, self-reliant initiators, middle-class males increasingly found themselves bound to desks, demoted from being those who delivered orders to those who received them. No longer masters of their own fates, they were now bit players in the drama of corporate capitalism. Thus the fear of both feminism and homosexuality arose in part from the compelling need to shore up masculine identity.

The new science of sexuality also heightened this concern about the definition of the "normal" man and woman. During the final decades of the nineteenth century, scientists invaded the most intimate areas of human behavior and made important breakthroughs in the understanding of human reproduction and sexual physiology. In 1875, for example, a German physiologist discovered the basic process of fertilization—the union of male and female sex cells. Four years later, scientists for the first time witnessed, with the aid of the microscope, a sperm cell penetrating an egg. In the following decade, scientific research uncovered the link between hormonal secretions and sexual potency, affirmed the existence of erogenous zones, and began to explore the role of chromosomes in reproduction.

This greater understanding of sexual *physiology* went hand in hand with the effort to apply the scientific method to sexual *practice*. With data drawn from biology, anthropology, and human physiology, scientists in Europe and the United States sought to define "normal" sexual behavior. In seven weighty volumes, the British scientist Havelock Ellis (1859–1939) explored the range of child and adult sexuality. Ellis used his data to argue for sex education, legalization of contraception and nudism, and tolerance of homosexuality. Other sex researchers, however, turned to science to buttress middle-class moral codes. The German scientist Richard von Krafft-Ebing labeled homosexuality a pathology in 1886, while many publications condemned masturbation and frequent sexual intercourse. Other works offered support for antifeminism by arguing that female physiology incapacitated women for public life.

Heightened concern about gender boundaries also pervaded the visual art of late-nineteenth-century Europe. Women often appeared as elemental forces, creatures of nature rather than civilization, who threatened to trap, emasculate, engulf, suffocate, or destroy the unwary man. In *Medicine*, by the Austrian painter Gustav Klimt

---

SEX AND CHARACTER

Otto Weininger's Sex and Character, *first published in 1903, was an immediate best-seller. It quickly appeared in numerous translations, became the center of conversation among educated Europeans, and remained in print in Germany until the 1950s. In the enthusiastic response to the work, we can see that anxiety over changing gender roles permeated middle-class European society.*

. . . The female must be described as absolutely without the quality of genius. The male has everything within him . . . It is possible for him to attain to the loftiest heights, or to sink to the lowest depths; he can become like animals, or plants, or even like women, and so there exist women-like female men. The woman, on the other hand, can never become a man.

Woman's thought is a sliding and gliding through subjects, a superficial tasting of things that a man, who studies the depths, would scarcely notice; it is an extravagant and dainty method of skimming which has no grasp of accuracy. A woman's thought is superficial.

. . . no woman ever believes herself to be anything but beautiful and desirable . . . What is the source of this form of vanity, peculiar to the female? It comes from the absence of an intelligible ego, the only begetter of a constant and positive sense of value; it is, in fact, that she is devoid of a sense of personal value. As she sets no store by herself or on herself, she endeavours to attain to a value in the eyes of others by exciting their desire and admiration.

It has been exhaustively proved that the female is soulless and possesses neither ego nor individuality, personality nor freedom, character nor will.

Woman does not wish to be treated as an active agent; she wants to remain always and throughout—this is just her womanhood—purely passive, to feel herself under another's will. She demands only to be desired physically, to be taken possession of, like a new property . . . a woman is brought to a sense of her existence only by her husband or children.

Source: From *Sex and Character* by Otto Weininger. London: William Heinemann, 1906.

■ **Gustav Klimt, *Medicine* (1901)**
Klimt was commissioned by the University of Vienna to create a work that would celebrate medicine's great achievements. Not surprisingly, the painting he produced provoked great controversy. The woman in the forefront is Hygeia, the Greek goddess of health, but behind her swim images of female sexuality and death. Klimt's paintings often featured women as alluring but engulfing elemental forces.

(1862–1918), the liquid portraits of women flow between and into images of sex and death in a disturbing and powerful painting. Such images recur even more graphically in the work of Klimt's student, Egon Schiele (1890–1918). In his very short life Schiele created more than 3,000 works on paper and 300 paintings, many of these depictions of the dangerous female. In works such as *Black-Haired Girl with Raised Skirt* (1911), harsh colors and brazen postures present an unsettling vision of female sexuality. A series of Schiele's paintings with titles such as *Dead Mother* place children in the arms of dead or expressionless women—a direct challenge to the middle-class glorification of motherhood.

THE BIRTH OF MODERNISM

Schiele's disturbing paintings exemplify the new modernist movement. Although the term modernism° was not commonly used until the 1920s, the main developments it embraced were well underway by 1914. It is a difficult term to define, in part because it refers to a variety of artistic, literary, and intellectual styles. Despite this variety, however, modernist art and literature expressed a set of common attitudes and assumptions that centered on a rejection of established authority. In the final decades of the nineteenth century, many artists tossed aside accepted standards and rules and embarked on a series of bold experiments. Oscar Wilde (1854–1900), the British playwright whose dramas mocked Victorian conventions and outraged middle-class sensibilities, wrote, "It is enough that our fathers believed. They have exhausted the faith-faculty of the species. Their legacy to us is the skepticism of which they were afraid."[6] At the core of modernism was a questioning of all accepted standards and truths, particularly those that shaped the middle-class liberal worldview.

In that liberal worldview, the arts served a useful purpose and were a vital part of civilized society. Going to art galleries, for example, was a popular activity, rather like going to the movies today. Respectable workers and middle-class men and women crowded into exhibitions where they viewed paintings that told an entertaining story and had a clear moral message. Modernism shattered this community between artist and audience. It rejected the idea of art as an instrument of moral or emotional uplift. Modernists argued that art is autonomous—it stands alone, of value in and of itself rather than for any impact it may have on society. Modernist painters, for example, did not seek to tell a story or to preach a sermon, but rather to experiment with line, color, and composition.

In addition to rejecting the idea that art must be useful, modernists also challenged middle-class liberalism by insisting that history is irrelevant. Nineteenth-century culture was "historicist." Fascinated with the process of change over time—with the evolution not only of species but also of ideas and societies—the prevailing mindset viewed history as the orderly forward march of progress. In contrast, modernists argued that fast-moving industrial and technological change had shattered the lines connecting history and modernity. Painters such as the Futurists in Italy and the Vorticists in Britain (two of the many artistic movements that clustered under the modernist umbrella) reveled in the new machine age, a world cut off from anything that had gone before. In their paintings they depicted human beings as machines in motion, moving too fast to be tied down to history.

New musical styles emerging in both popular and high culture in these decades also demonstrated the modernist sense of discontinuity. Ragtime, for example, combined

The Soccer Stadium

On a typical Saturday in 1910, all across Britain, approximately 300,000 mostly working-class men paid their six pennies for a ticket, pushed past turnstiles, and headed up concrete steps. Their destination? The terraces—simple concrete expanses, without seats, without restrooms, and without roofs or any protection from the often cold and rainy British weather—on which hundreds of men packed together in order to cheer on and swear at a relatively new type of being: the professional soccer (in European terms, football) player.

The emergence of professional soccer was closely linked with the solidification of an urban working-class culture in Britain. Modern soccer originated in clubs formed by middle-class reformers who hoped to lure working-class boys away from the corruption of the streets and onto the healthy playing fields (and, then, they hoped, into church pews). But workers quickly made soccer their own. They not only took over the soccer clubs, they also rejected the middle-class value system that defined the true sportsman as the amateur who played strictly for love of the game. Love of the game could not pay the rent. By the mid-1880s, a significant number of clubs were recruiting skilled players from other cities, and paying for their services. These clubs found it made economic sense to enclose their fields and to charge for admission: Professional soccer was born. By 1910, six million people were attending professional soccer games in Britain each year. Every major city had at least one professional team, and large cities had two or more. In Glasgow, no fewer than six professional teams attracted thousands of supporters each Saturday of the season.

Soccer assumed a central role in urban working-class male culture. As cities grew, soccer became a way to create a sense of community, to overcome the anonymity of city life and forge bonds between men who were otherwise strangers. A shortened workweek (most factories released their employees at noon on Saturday by the 1880s), higher pay rates, and the construction of intracity rail networks all made possible regular outings to the soccer

■ **England vs. Scotland, 1905**
With the formation of national teams, professional soccer provided an important outlet for the expression of national identity.

■ **Wembley Stadium in England, ca. 1924** By the 1920s, professional sports had developed into a major industry with its own infrastructure. Sports stadia, such as Wembley pictured here, became an integral part of the urban landscape.

THE STADIUM, BRITISH E

stadium. At the stadium, working-class men constructed a world of their own, one that was separate from and opposed to both the woman-dominated space of the home and, even more important, the boss-controlled space of the factory. Both the players on the field and the supporters on the terraces expressed a set of values that sharply opposed the moral framework of the middle classes. To a team's supporters, winning was what mattered. Workers knew from their own brutal experience that the best man doesn't always win, and that life was not fair, so why value "fair play" on the field? Thus fans enthusiastically cheered illegal kicks and welcomed any referee error that benefited their side. At the Swindon vs. Barnsley Cup semifinal of 1912, the star player for Swindon was, unusually, a middle-class theological student. From the opening kickoff until he was carried off the field so badly injured that he could not play for a year, he was brutally kicked by the Barnsley players—to the delight of their cheering fans.

Even the game itself rejected middle-class values. The game first introduced by middle-class reformers to urban workers was intensely individualistic, with all the players scrambling to get the ball and then dribble it straight down the field for a goal. But workers changed the way soccer was played. By the 1890s, professional soccer had assumed its present form as a quintessential team sport with a clear division of labor: the defense holding off the opposing players, halfbacks linking up the defense and

■ **Bootham School Soccer Team, York, England, ca. 1885** Unlike the players on the professional teams, the boys on this school team would have been almost exclusively middle class.

offense, and forwards passing the ball into position. Victory on the field, like survival in the working-class world, depended not only on hard work and sheer ability, but also on possessing reliable mates and catching a good break now and then.

■ **Transportation for the Masses** By the turn of the century, the availability of cheap railway tickets not only made seaside excursions affordable for working people (as advertised here), but also enabled supporters to attend professional soccer matches.

For Discussion

What does the professionalization and division of labor in sport indicate about late-nineteenth century European society?

■ **Wyndham Lewis, *At the Seaside* (1913)**
Wyndham Lewis was one of the founders of Vorticism, a pre–World War I English modernist movement. The name *Vorticist* comes from the word "vortex"—a whirlwind, a constant flow of energy. The Vorticists passionately embraced the new machine age and argued that the art of the era needed to reflect its energy and ceaseless movement.

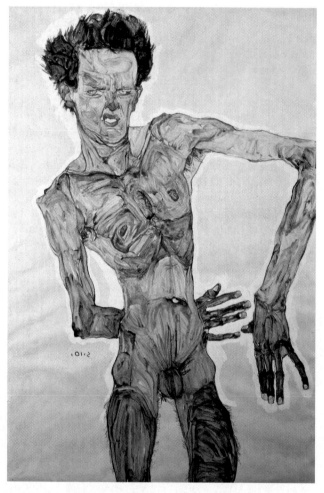

■ **Egon Schiele, *Nude Self-Portrait with Open Mouth* (1910)**
Schiele's paintings exemplify the Expressionist movement with their bold use of color and their no-holds-barred exploration of human emotion and sexuality.

syncopation with unexpected rhythms and sudden stops, while jazz, which developed around the turn of the century in black urban neighborhoods in the United States, created a musical universe of constant change. At the same time, symphonic musicians such as Russian composer Igor Stravinsky (1882–1971) and his Austrian counterpart Arnold Schoenberg (1874–1951) shocked their audiences by tossing aside the convention that a piece should state a central theme, which is then repeated in a sequence of variations. In Stravinsky's ballet *The Rite of Spring* (1913), the meter changes no fewer than twenty-eight times in the final thirty-four bars of the central dance. Similarly, Schoenberg eliminated repetition from his works and used rapid tempo changes.

Modernism also rejected the dominant nineteenth-century faith in the power of human reason and observation, and instead emphasized the role of individual emotion and experience in shaping human understanding. In Paris, for example, a group of artists centered on the Spaniard Pablo Picasso (1881–1973) dared to juxtapose different perspectives and points of view on a single can-

vas. They called themselves Cubists°. Just as Albert Einstein revolutionized physics by arguing that time and space shift as the position of the observer changes, so Cubism transformed Western visual culture by revealing the incompleteness and even incoherence of individual perception. In one cultural historian's apt description, "Cubists cracked the mirror of art."[7] Their fragmented, jagged, energetic works no longer reflected the world "out there," but instead revealed the artist's fluid and contradictory vision (see page 774).

This emphasis on art as a form of personal expression is also seen in the Expressionist° movement, centered not in France as was Cubism, but in central and eastern Europe. Expressionists such as Egon Schiele argued that art should express the artist's interior vision, not the exterior world. In nude self-portraits, Schiele depicted himself as ugly and emaciated, a graphic expression of his tormented internal universe. His fellow Expressionist, the Russian painter Wassily Kandinsky (1866–1944), went even further in shattering artistic boundaries and splashing his emotions all over the canvas. Kandinsky sought to remove all form from his painting, to create a universe of pure color that would express a fundamental spiritual reality. In the process, he produced the first purely abstract paintings in Western art.

Because they so radically challenged middle-class and liberal standards and assumptions, modernist works were greeted with incomprehension and outrage. At the first performance of Schoenberg's *Five Orchestral Pieces* (1909) in London in 1912, one listener reported that "the audience laughed audibly all through . . . and hissed vigorously at the end." The next year in Vienna, the performance of a different Schoenberg piece had to be abandoned after the audience rioted. Modernist painting was routinely condemned as sick, pornographic, anarchic, and simply insane. One London reviewer dismissed the painter Paul Cézanne

(1869–1954) as "an artist with diseased retinas." Most middle-class men and women remained firmly within a cultural milieu in which paintings revealed pretty scenes, novels told a moral tale, and music offered harmonious charm. At the same time that Picasso was shattering perspective, one of the most popular pieces of art in the English-speaking world was *The Light of the World* by William Holman Hunt (1827–1910) (see following page). This moralistic piece with its easy-to-understand and uplifting story, completely at odds with every modernist principle, triumphantly toured the British Empire from 1905 to 1907. In cities throughout Australia, South Africa, Canada, and Britain, enthusiastic crowds jostled for tickets and hailed the painting as both a religious and an artistic masterpiece.

POPULAR RELIGION AND SECULARIZATION

As the response to Holman Hunt's depiction of Jesus shows, religious belief remained a powerful force in the decades after 1870. In Britain, regular Sunday worship continued to be a central aspect of middle-class culture, and the still-strong Sunday School movement as well as religious instruction in state schools ensured that working-class children were taught the fundamentals of the Christian faith. On the Continent, many Europeans connected revolutionary anarchy with unbelief after revolutionaries executed the Archbishop of Paris in 1871 (see Chapter 21). The excesses of the Paris Commune thus contributed to a religious

■ **Wassily Kandinsky, *Composition VII* (1913)**
Kandinsky's experiments in color and form led him to pure abstraction.

■ **William Holman Hunt,**
***The Light of the World* (1903)**
This devotional painting is rich in Christian symbolism. Jesus, the light of the world, stands knocking at the closed door of a lost soul. The overgrown weeds and fallen fruit symbolize sin; the lantern stands for Christ's illuminating power, while the stars and crescents on it represent Christ's appeal to Jews and Muslims.

revival. Much of this popular Catholic religiosity focused on the cult of the Virgin Mary: By the 1870s, the shrine at Lourdes, site of Mary's miraculous appearance in 1858, was attracting hundreds of thousands of Catholic pilgrims.

Three additional factors contributed to the religiosity of late-nineteenth-century Europe. First, the high rate of immigration, which meant that large groups of people often found themselves searching for something familiar in foreign cities, fostered attachments to the religious cultures of the homeland. In English cities, for example, Irish immigrants looked to the local Roman Catholic Church for spir-

itual solace, material support, and social contacts. Second, in many regions nationalism also shored up religious belief and practice. Hence, for Polish nationalists dreaming of independence from Russian rule, Roman Catholicism was a key part of a separate national identity. Finally, as we shall see in the next section, imperialism became interwoven with Western Christianity. Missionary publications and societies not only lobbied intensely for continued Western expansion abroad, but also served to inspire and unite Western Christians at home. Foreign mission work gave Western Christians a sense of both purpose and power as imperial expansion appeared to provide clear evidence of the ongoing triumph of Christianity.

Yet this triumphalism met growing anxiety, as Christians faced a series of challenges, most obviously those posed by science. As we saw in our discussion of Darwin, developments in geology and biology undermined the orthodox Christian view of a harmonious, divinely directed, natural world. Medical advances also worked to narrow the appeal of traditional religion. Tragedies once accepted as "acts of God," such as epidemic disease, now appeared to be curable and controllable. Increasingly, scientists seemed able to answer questions once thought the province of the theologians.

At the same time, the emergence of the social sciences posed a direct challenge to Christian belief by simply dismissing the question of religious truth and asking instead, what is the function of religious belief in a society? Emile Durkheim (1858–1917), one of the founders of French sociology, dared to lump Christianity with "even the most barbarous and the most fantastic rites and the strangest myths." Durkheim insisted that no religion is more true than any other; each fills a social need.[8]

The Christian response to these challenges varied. Some Christians embraced the scientific method as a gift from God, and argued that the Christian faith must adapt to the ongoing expansion of human knowledge. To many theologians as well as ordinary believers, the study of the Bible as an historical and literary document—as a collection of divinely inspired texts produced by all-too-human writers—promised to free Christians *from* antiquated beliefs impossible to sustain in the new scientific age, and *for* a more worldly, reform-oriented religious life. Other Christians, however, resisted any accommodation to the scientific age. Protestant fundamentalists insisted on retaining a belief in the literal, historical, and scientific accuracy of the Christian scriptures, a stance that led them to oppose science as the enemy of religion.

Similarly, the Roman Catholic papacy adopted a defiant pose in the face of the scientific challenge. In 1864, Pope Pius IX (r. 1846–1878) issued a *Syllabus of Errors,* which condemned not only materialism but also the idea that the pope should "harmonize himself with progress, with liberalism, and with modern civilization." Five years later, a church council—the first called since the sixteenth-century Catholic Reformation—proclaimed the doctrine of papal infallibility. According to this doctrine, any decrees issued by the pope with regard to faith and morals were free from error and good for all time and all places. The proclamation of the doctrine of papal infallibility was a sharp rebuff to Catholic theologians who argued that Christianity must adapt to the modern world.

The Roman Catholic Church also faced a crucial political challenge from both liberal and socialist movements. In Roman Catholic countries, the Church's alliance with conservatism pushed anticlericalism° to a dominant position on the liberal agenda. In France, for example, Roman Catholics were in the forefront of the conservative forces seeking to overturn the Republic established in 1871 and to return to monarchical or authoritarian rule. As a result, Frenchmen who wanted the Republic to survive fought to reduce the Church's influence over French politics and culture. At the same time, the spread of socialism provided European workers with an alternative belief system and source of communal life. The result was to widen the secular sphere and limit the influence of traditional Christianity.

The most significant challenge faced by Christianity after 1870, however, emerged not from scientific laboratories, parliamentary assemblies, or socialist rallies but rather from the department stores and playing fields. In the growing industrial cities, both working- and middle-class individuals enjoyed new, secular sources of entertainment, inspiration, and desire. Energies once focused on Christian devotion were now increasingly displaced onto the activities of consumption and recreation. Whereas shared religious worship had once cemented community life, the increasingly elaborate rituals of spectator sports now forged new bonds of loyalty and identity. At the same time, the delectable array of colorful products displayed in shop windows promised fulfillment and satisfaction in the here and now, an earthly paradise rather than a heavenly reward.

The New Imperialism

M any of those items on display behind the new plate-glass shop windows were the products of imperial conquest. After 1870, Europe entered not only a new age of mass consumption but also a new era of imperialist expansion. Imperialism intertwined with many of the economic, scientific, and cultural developments already examined in this chapter. Telegraphs ensured rapid communication from far-flung empires while mass printing technologies guaranteed that illustrated tales of imperial achievement made their way into homes and schools; Social Darwinism supplied a supposedly scientific justification for the conquest of peoples deemed biologically inferior; swift and decisive victories over other lands and societies helped quell anxiety about European degeneration. For many Europeans, particularly the British who presided over the largest empire in the world, imperialist domination served as reassuring, even incontrovertible, evidence of the superiority of Western civilization.

UNDERSTANDING THE NEW IMPERIALISM

Imperialism was not, of course, new to Europe. In the fifteenth century, Europeans had embarked on the first phase of imperialism, with the extension of European control across coastal ports of Africa and India, and into the New World of the Americas. In the second phase, which began in the late seventeenth century, European colonial empires in both Asia and the Western Hemisphere expanded as governments sought to augment their profits from international trade. Trade motivated much of the imperial activity after 1870 as well, with the need to protect existing imperial possessions often impelling further imperialist conquests. The desire to protect India—the "Jewel in the Crown" of the British Empire—explains much of British imperial acquisition throughout the nineteenth century. Britain's annexation of Burma and Kashmir, its establishment of a sphere of influence in Persia, and its interests along the coast of Africa were all vitally linked to its concerns in India.

Neither defense of existing empires nor commercial considerations, however, fully explain the headlong rush into empire in the later nineteenth century. After 1870 and particularly after 1880, Europe's expansion into non-European territories became so much more aggressive that historians label this third phase the age of new imperialism°. A few figures illustrate the contrast: Between 1800 and 1880, European colonial empires grew by 6,500,000 square miles, but between 1880 and 1910, these empires increased by an astonishing 8,655,000. In just thirty years, European control of the globe's land surface swelled from 65 to 85 percent. In addition, new players joined the expansionist game. Recently formed nation-states such as Germany and Italy jostled for colonial territory in Africa, the United States began to extend its control over the western hemisphere, and Japan initiated its imperialist march into China and Korea. What factors lay behind this new imperialism?

Technology, Economics, and Politics

Part of the answer lies in the economic developments examined in Chapter 22. The new technologies characteristic of the Second Industrial Revolution meant that industrial Europe increasingly depended on raw materials available only in non-Western regions such as Asia, Africa, and South America. Rubber, for example, was essential not only for tires on the new automobiles, but also for insulating the electrical and telegraph wires now encircling the globe. Palm oil from Africa provided the lubricant needed for industrial machinery. Africa's once-plentiful elephant herds were slaughtered to provide the ivory for many of the new consumer goods now displayed prominently in department store windows and middle-class parlors—piano keys, billiard balls, knife handles. Increasingly dependent on these primary resources, European states were quick to respond to perceived threats to their economic interests. The Germans even coined a word to describe this fear of losing access to essential raw materials: *Torschlusspanik,* or "fear of the closing door."

Competition for markets also accelerated imperial acquisition. With the onset of economic depression in 1873 (discussed in Chapter 22), industrialists were faced with declining demand for their products in Europe. Imperial expansion seemed to provide a solution, with annexed territories seen as captive markets. As an editorial in the largest French mass circulation newspaper explained in 1891, "every gunshot opens another outlet for French industry."9

By the mid-1890s, however, the Great Depression had ended in most regions, and Europe embarked on the longest investment boom it had yet experienced. Western European capital spread across the globe, underwriting railway lines, digging mines, and erecting public utilities in the United States, Latin America, Russia, Asia, and Africa. This global investment boom also contributed to new imperialism. With each railroad or coal mine or dam, European interests in non-European regions expanded, and so did the pressure on European governments to assume formal political control should those interests be threatened, whether by the arrival of other European competitors or by local political instability.

Britain provides an important example of the link between empire and economics. By the end of the nineteenth century, the British Empire covered one-quarter of the globe and contained one-quarter of the world's population. This empire reflected Britain's position at the center of the world's economy, as the chief agent of global economic exchange. Despite the emergence of Germany and the United States as industrial powerhouses, Britain remained the world's largest trading nation. Even more important, British stockbrokers, currency traders, and banks managed the global exchange system that emerged in the last third of the nineteenth century. In this era British loans abroad were larger than the combined investments of its five largest competitors—France, Germany, the Netherlands, the United States, and Belgium.

Imperialism was motivated by more than economic concerns. Political pressures also contributed to imperialist acquisition. First, in the age of mass politics, political leaders needed to find issues that would both appeal to new voters and strengthen the status quo. Imperialism was one such issue. It assured ordinary men that they were part of a superior, conquering people. Tales of dangerous explorations and decisive military victories engaged the emotions and prodded the ordinary individual to identify more closely with the national group.

A second political factor motivating new imperialism was nationalist competition. As Chapter 21 outlined, the unification of Germany upset the balance of power in Europe. In this climate of tension, governments looked to enhance national strength. Newly formed nations such as Italy and Germany itself sought empires outside Europe as a way to gain both power and prestige within Europe. The nineteenth-century German historian Heinrich von Treitschke explained, "All great nations in the fullness of their strength have desired to set their mark on barbarian lands and those who fail to participate in this great rivalry will play a pitiable role in time to come." Similar concerns

The first step towards lightening

The White Man's Burden

is through teaching the virtues of cleanliness.

Pears' Soap

is a potent factor in brightening the dark corners of the earth as civilization advances, while amongst the cultured of all nations it holds the highest place—it is the ideal toilet soap.

■ **Pears' Soap Ad**

This advertisement brings together many of the assumptions of the imperial idea. Imperial rule is held to be a benevolent force, bringing both physical and moral hygiene to inferior peoples. At the same time, it brings profit to Western manufacturers.

about status and strategic advantages motivated nations such as Britain and France both to defend and expand their existing empires.

The Imperial Idea

New imperialism was not simply a policy embraced by elites for economic, political, and strategic advantage. One of its most distinctive features was the way it functioned as a belief system, as an idea that permeated middle-class and mass culture in the decades after 1870. Images of empire proliferated, appearing in boys' adventure stories, glossy ads for soap and chocolates, picture postcards, cookie tins, and cheap commemorative china plates and mugs. In the music halls and theaters, imperialist songs and dramas received popular applause. At exhibitions and world's fairs, both goods and peoples from conquered regions were put on display to educate the crowds of viewers in the "imperial idea."

At the center of this idea stood the assumption of the *rightness* of white European dominance over the world. Europeans would not have sought to remake the world in the European image had they not been convinced of the superiority of that image. What led white Europeans to believe they had both the right and the responsibility to take charge of other cultures and continents?

One key factor was the perceived link between Western Christianity and "civilization." Christian missionaries served as a vanguard of Western culture throughout the nineteenth century. The celebrated Scottish explorer David Livingstone (1813–1873), who mapped out much of central and southern Africa, was a Protestant missionary (although not a very successful one—his only convert eventually renounced the Christian faith). Moreover, missionary society publications introduced their readers to exotic territories, while the societies themselves served as powerful political interest groups that often lobbied for Western territorial expansion to promote the spread of Christian missionary activity.

Europeans also pointed to their advanced technologies as evidence of their material and moral superiority, and as a justification for their imperial rule. Before the nineteenth century, the technological gap between European and non-European societies had not loomed large; in some cases, such as China, non-European societies had held the technological advantage. Industrialization, however, gave Europe the technological edge. Thus Mary Kingsley (1862–1900), a British adventurer who was actually unusually admiring of African culture and customs, wrote, "when I come back from a spell in Africa, the thing that makes me proud of being one of the English is . . . a great railway engine . . . [I]t is the manifestation of the superiority of my race."[10]

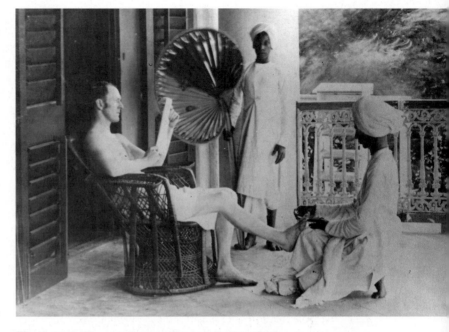

■ **British Men at Ease in Burma in the 1890s**
Ordinary middle-class men could live like aristocrats in the colonies, where labor was extremely cheap.

Although many European Christians regarded the West's technological advantages as a sign that God intended Europe to Christianize (that is, Westernize) the globe, a growing number of prominent thinkers, writers, and policymakers viewed the force that conferred this civilizing duty upon Europeans as natural rather than supernatural—biology rather than God. As we have already seen in this chapter, the age of new imperialism was also the age of pseudoscientific racism. Social Darwinism lent a seemingly scientific authority to the imperial idea by supposedly proving the mental and moral superiority of white Europeans over all peoples of color. Thus the British Lord Milner (1854–1925) explained in a speech in South Afric in 1903: "The white man must rule, because he is elev by many, many steps above the black man; steps v will take the latter centuries to climb, and whic possible that the vast bulk of the black po never be able to climb at all."

Often white Europeans presented t cally ordained imperial destiny ir saw imperial rule as a heavy re shouldered by the civilized. ' had a moral duty to bring to the rest of the worl' rialism was drama' (1865–1936), the pr alism. In 1899, Kipling complete their conquest words:

■ **Pablo Picasso, *Les Desmoiselles d'Avignon* (1907)**
Many art historians argue that Cubism was born with this painting. One of
Picasso's sources of inspiration was an exhibition of African masks held in Paris.
Like many modernists, Picasso saw in primitive art a passion and an elemental
clarity that he sought for in his own work.

> *Take up the White Man's burden—*
> *Send forth the best ye breed—*
> *Go bind your sons to exile,*
> *To serve your captives' need;*
> *To wait in heavy harness*
> *On fluttered folk and wild—*
> *Your new-caught sullen peoples,*
> *Half devil and half child.*

Not all Europeans embraced the idea of the "White
Man's burden," and many rejected the imperialist assumption of Western superiority. Some modernist artists, for example, looked to non-Western cultures for artistic inspira-
ion and argued that these societies had much to teach the
st. The Fauves ("wild beasts"), a Paris-based circle of
ts that included Henri Matisse (1869–1954) and Paul
uin (1848–1903), condemned most Western art as
ined and artificial, and sought in their own bril-
olored works to rediscover the vitality that they
non-Western cultures (see page 752).
f empire often focused on its domestic political
ic implications. The British economist J. A.
8–1940) charged that overseas empires bene-
thy capitalists while distracting public atten-

tion from the need for domestic political and
economic reform. Hobson argued that unregulated capitalism led almost inevitably to imperialist expansion. While impoverishing the
masses, the capitalist system generates huge
surpluses in capital for a very small elite, who
must then find somewhere to invest these surpluses. Hobson's ideas proved very influential
among European socialists, who condemned
imperialism along with capitalism.

Many liberals also condemned imperialism.
The British prime minister William Gladstone
(1809–1898) clung fast to the liberal belief that
free trade between independent nations fostered international peace. Gladstone and other
liberals were uneasy about the expense of empire and acutely aware of the contradictions
between liberal ideals and imperialist practice.
It was difficult, for example, to reconcile the
liberal commitment to individual freedom
with the widespread use of forced labor in
colonial Africa.

Yet between 1880 and 1885—while
Gladstone was prime minister—the British
Empire expanded at the rate of 87,000 square
miles per year, with Gladstone himself ordering the bombardment of Alexandria and the
military occupation of Egypt. When Gladstone
did hold firm to his anti-imperialist ideals and
ordered British troops to withdraw from the
Sudan in 1885, he outraged the British public.
Critics of empire were in the minority, not
only in Britain but throughout Europe. The
imperial idea permeated European and much of American
culture in the final decades of the nineteenth century.

THE SCRAMBLE FOR AFRICA

New imperialism reached its zenith in Africa. In 1875
European powers controlled only 11 percent of the African
continent. By 1905, 90 percent of Africa was under
European control. In just thirty years, between 1875 and
1905, Europeans established thirty new colonies and pro-
tectorates encompassing ten million square miles of territory and controlling 110 million Africans (see Map 23.1).
The conquest of the African continent was so rapid and
dramatic that as early as 1884 mystified Europeans began to
talk about the Scramble for Africa°.

Overcoming the Obstacles
When the nineteenth century began, Europeans knew little
more about the continent of Africa than the ancient Greeks
had known. A vast and profitable trading network between
European merchants and Africa's coastal regions had developed, centering on the exchange of European goods for
African gold and slaves. European efforts to establish settle-

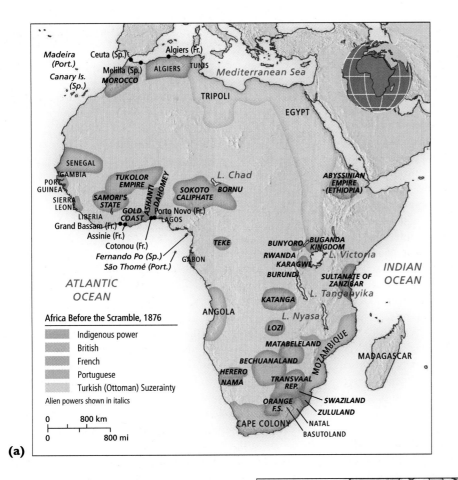

(a)

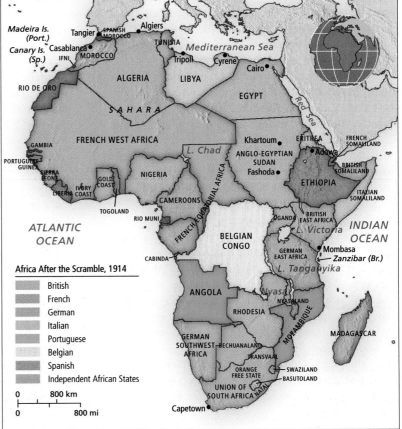

■ Map 23.1   (a) Africa Before the Scramble, 1876 and (b) Africa After the Scramble, 1914

A comparison of these two maps reveals the dramatic impact of the new imperialism on African societies. Indigenous empires such as the Sokoto Caliphate in West Africa came under Western rule, as did tribal societies such as the Herero. Even indigenous states ruled by whites of European descent came under European rule, as the examples of the Transvaal and the Orange Free State in South Africa illustrate. Only Ethiopia preserved its independence.

(b)

ments in the interior, however, faced three key obstacles—the climate, disease, and African resistance.

Africa was known as "the white man's grave," deservedly so. Seventy-seven percent of the white soldiers sent to West Africa in the early nineteenth century died there, and another 21 percent became invalids. Temperatures of over 100 degrees Fahrenheit in some regions and constant rainfall in others made travel extremely difficult. The mosquito and the tsetse fly made it deadly. Mosquito bites brought malaria, while the tsetse fly carried trypanosomiasis, or sleeping sickness, an infectious illness that began with a fever and ended in a deadly paralysis. Sleeping sickness also posed a grave danger to livestock and so aggravated the problem of transportation within the African interior. In regions with endemic trypanosomiasis, such as equatorial, southern, and eastern Africa, the use of horses and oxen was impossible. Despite the dangers posed by the climate and disease, Europeans did endeavor to establish inland settlements in Africa but then faced the obstacle of African resistance. In the seventeenth century, for example, the Portuguese set up forts and trading centers in modern Zimbabwe but were driven out by local African populations.

Beginning around 1830, a series of developments altered the relationship between Europe and Africa, and prepared the groundwork for European conquest. First, the efforts of European explorers changed the Western vision of Africa. Between 1830 and 1870, adventurers mapped out the chief geographical features of Africa's interior and so illuminated the "Dark Continent" for Europeans. They discovered that central Africa was not the vast, empty desert that Europeans had assumed, but rather a territory with abundant agricultural and mineral resources—and lots of people, all of them potential consumers of European goods.

The shift in the European vision of Africa—from empty desert to potential treasure house—coincided with important changes within Africa itself. In the first half of the nineteenth century, various forces destabilized African political structures and so weakened the African ability to withstand conquest in later decades. Although the precise nature of the destabilizing forces varied by region, one common denominator prevailed—the unsettling impact of early encounters with the West. In the 1830s, for example, Britain and other European powers, pressured by humanitarian and missionary lobby groups, embarked on an effort to stamp out the West African slave trade. They succeeded but only in West Africa. The slave trade shifted to the central and eastern regions of the continent and wreaked havoc with political arrangements there. African slaving nations relied on frequent military raids to obtain their human merchandise. These raids—carried out by Africans against Africans—disrupted agricultural production, shattered trade networks, and undermined the authority of existing political rulers. With political systems in disarray, many African regions were vulnerable to European encroachment.

Finally, three specific developments shifted the balance of power in the West's favor—the steamship, the "quinine prophylaxis," and the repeating, breech-loading rifle. The steam revolution was inaugurated in 1807 when the *Clermont,* a ship powered by a steam engine invented by the American Robert Fulton, chugged its way along the Hudson River between Albany and New York City. By the 1820s, steamships were widely in use on European lakes and rivers. Steam proved crucial in enabling Western imperialists to overcome the obstacles to traveling through Africa by allowing them to use the continent's extensive but shallow river system.

But until the 1850s and the development of the "quinine prophylaxis," such journeys almost guaranteed death sentences because of the risk of malaria. Steam enabled Westerners to penetrate the African interior; quinine helped them survive once they got there. Produced commercially from 1827 on, quinine was prescribed by doctors for malaria. Death and disability rates from the disease remained high, however, until a series of chance discoveries revealed the importance of taking quinine prophylactically—of saturating the system with quinine before any risk of infection. By the 1860s, Westerners were routinely ingesting quinine in preparation for postings in Africa—and their death rates dropped dramatically.

African death rates, however, soared because of the third crucial technology of imperialism—the repeating, breech-loading rifles carried by Europeans from the 1870s on. Before the invention of these rifles, Europeans used muskets or muzzle-loading rifles that had to be loaded one ball or cartridge at a time while standing up, and were prone to foul easily, particularly in damp weather. Such weapons did not provide Europeans with much of a military advantage, even over spears. With the repeating rifle, however, "any European infantryman could now fire lying down, undetected, in any weather, fifteen rounds of ammunition in as many seconds at targets up to half a mile away." As we saw at the beginning of this chapter, in regions such as the Sudan, where armor-clad cavalrymen fought with spears, swords, and arrows like medieval knights, the repeating breech-loader and its descendant the machine gun made the European conquest "more like hunting than war."[11]

Slicing the Cake: The Conquest of Africa

In the decades after 1870, convinced that the conquest of African territories would guarantee commercial prosperity and strengthen national power, European states moved quickly to beat out their rivals and grab a piece of the continent. As King Leopold II of Belgium (1865–1909) explained in a letter to his ambassador in London in 1876, "I do not want to miss a good chance of getting us a slice of this magnificent African cake."[12]

Leopold's slice proved to be enormous. Presenting himself as a humanitarian whose chief concern was the abolition of the slave trade, he called on the other European leaders to back his claim to the Congo, a huge region of central Africa comprising territory more than twice as large as central Europe. After a decade of controversy and quarreling, representatives of the European powers met in Berlin in 1884 and agreed to Leopold's demands. At the same time, they used the Berlin Conference to regulate the Scramble for Africa. According to the terms established in Berlin, any state claiming a territory in Africa had to establish "effective occupation" and to plan for the economic development of that region.

But as the history of the Congo Free State demonstrated, colonialism in Africa was far from a humanitarian endeavor. Leopold's personal mercenary army turned the Congo into a hellhole of slavery and death. By claiming all so-called vacant land, Leopold deprived villagers of the grazing, foraging, and hunting grounds they needed to survive. He levied impossibly high rubber quotas for each village, forcing villagers to harvest wild rubber for up to twenty-five days each month while their families starved. Brutal punishments ensured compliance: Soldiers chopped off the hands of villagers who failed to meet their rubber quota. In other cases, babies were chained in sweltering huts until their mothers delivered their quota. At the same time, the Belgians forced black Africans to serve as human mules. This practice spread sleeping sickness from the western coast into the interior. Between 1895 and 1908, an epidemic of sleeping sickness decimated the already weakened population. As an estimated three million people died from the combined effects of forced labor, brutal punishments, starvation, and disease, the enormous profits from the Congo enabled Leopold II to indulge his hobby of building elaborate tourist resorts on the Riviera.

King Leopold's personal brand of imperialism proved so scandalous that in 1908 the Belgian government replaced Leopold's personal rule with state control over the Congo. Yet the king's exploitation of the Congo differed

■ Congo Atrocities

Harsh punishments were used by Leopold's forces to subdue the Congoese people and increase his personal profits.

only in degree, not in kind, from the nature of European conquest elsewhere in Africa. Forced labor was common throughout European-controlled areas, as were brutal punishments for any Africans who dared resist. Faced with tribal revolt in Southwest Africa, the German colonial army commander in 1904 ordered that the entire Herero tribe be exterminated. Twenty thousand Africans, including children, were forcibly driven from their villages into the desert to die of thirst.

African Resistance

As the Herero rebellion demonstrates, Africans frequently resisted the imposition of these often-brutal imperial regimes, but to no avail. The only successful episode of African resistance to European conquest occurred in northern Africa, in the kingdom of Ethiopia (also called Abyssinia). After four centuries of isolation, Ethiopia modernized in the 1850s. By the time of the European Scramble for Africa, Ethiopia had developed not only a modern standing army but also an advanced infrastructure and communications system. These factors enabled the Ethiopian nation, in 1896, to defeat the Italian army at the battle of Adowa.

Adowa, however, was the exception. Most African resistance was doomed by the technological gap that yawned between the indigenous peoples and their European conquerors. A booming arms trade developed between European rifle manufacturers and African states desperate to obtain guns. Frequently, however, the arms shipped to Africa were inferior models—muskets or single-firing muzzle-loaders rather than the up-to-date and deadly efficient repeating rifles and early machine guns possessed by the European invaders.

African military leaders who did obtain advanced weaponry often did not make the strategic leap necessary to adapt their military tactics to new technologies. (As we will see in Chapter 24, European military leaders made similar mistakes in World War I.) In the 1890s, for example, the West African state of Dahomey imported repeating rifles to enable it to resist French annexation. A prosperous, highly centralized state, Dahomey possessed a 4,000-soldier standing army with a deservedly fierce reputation. Dahomey's military command, however, failed to change the attack drill devised for a musket-based regiment. The troops advanced forward at a run, fired from the hip, and withdrew—a strategy that worked well with muskets because they did not have to be aimed, but that proved disastrous with more advanced weapons. In 1892, French forces, outnumbered six to one, annihilated the Dahomian army. By 1900, Dahomey had become part of the French empire.

Yet even African resistance leaders who did adapt military strategy as well as adopt modern military weapons could not stand for long against the industrial might of Western powers. The most famous African resistance leader, Samori Ture (1830–1900), built a vast West African empire of 115,000 square miles and held off the forces of French imperialism for fifteen years, but he, too, was conquered in the end. Utilizing information obtained by spies sent to infiltrate the French military, Samori trained his massive infantry in modern military maneuvers and armed his elite cavalry troops with 6,000 repeating rifles, used with deadly effect against the French in a series of battles in the 1880s. Even more important, Samori was one of the first military commanders to conceive of the tactics of modern guerilla warfare—hit-and-run attacks, night battles, the crucial advantage of knowing the land. These measures enabled him to elude French capture for more than seven years after the French in 1891 sent a massive force to destroy the Samorian state. Yet 6,000 repeating ri-

CHRONOLOGY

Asia Encounters the West

1840–1842	The Opium War: "treaty port system" in China established
1853	Commodore Matthew Perry forces Japan to open its markets to the United States
1868	The Meiji Restoration in Japan: Japan begins rapid modernization
1885	Russia establishes control over Central Asia
1893	Union of French Indochina includes Laos, Cambodia, Tonkin, and Annam
1894–1895	The Sino-Japanese War
1898	Spanish-American War; United States annexes Puerto Rico, Philippines, Hawaii, and Guam; establishes protectorate over Cuba
1899	"Open door" policy in China proclaimed by United States
1900–1903	Boxer Rebellion in China
1901	Commonwealth of Australia formed
1904–1905	Russo-Japanese War
1911	Revolution in China: overthrow of Manchu Dynasty

fles and guerilla tactics could not hold off the vast weight of French imperialism. Ambushed in 1898, Samori died in exile two years later, with his empire in European control.

The Scramble for Africa provides the most dramatic illustration of new imperialism but certainly not the only one. The same era witnessed the extension of European empires throughout Asia. Moreover, it was in Asia that non-European powers—the United States and Japan—entered the imperial game, and that Russia made its bid for empire.

ASIAN ENCOUNTERS

Unlike most of Africa, many of the diverse states of Asia had already been woven into the web of the Western economy well before 1870. Pacific states such as Java and Malaysia formed a part of the eighteenth-century mercantilist empires established by Dutch, British, Portuguese, and French trading companies. Throughout the nineteenth century, European governments formalized their control over many of these island states, primarily to protect trade routes or to ensure access to profitable commodities such as rubber, tin, tobacco, and sugar. The Dutch, for example, gradually expanded their East Indies empire, moving from control of the island of Java in 1815 to domination over almost the entire archipelago several decades later. Similarly, Britain steadily expanded its control over India throughout the nineteenth century (see Map 23.2).

A number of factors accelerated the pace of imperialist acquisition in Asia beginning in the 1870s. In the age of steam, the Pacific islands took on strategic significance because European powers and the United States needed coaling stations for their commercial and naval fleets. At the same time, new industrial processes often heightened the economic value of many of these regions. The development of a process for producing dried coconut, for example, made Samoa so valuable that Germany, Britain, and the United States competed for control over the tiny islands. As in Africa, however, the most important factor in imperialist

expansion after 1870 was a phenomenon we can call the *scramble effect*: Imperialist gains by one power led to anxiety and a quicker pace of expansion by its rivals. The steady erosion of Chinese political stability—itself a result of encounters with the West—intensified this Asian scramble. Competition for access to Chinese markets was an important factor in determining the course of Western imperialism throughout much of Asia. The quest for a protected trade route to China, for example, impelled the French to extend their control over neighboring Indochina. By 1893, the Union of French Indochina included the formerly independent states of Laos, Cambodia, Annam, and Tonkin—the latter two better known by their contemporary name of Vietnam.

■ **Map 23.2 Imperialism in Asia, 1914**

The impact of the new imperialism on Asia was not as dramatic as in Africa, but the spread of Western rule is significant nonetheless. This map shows a key development: the entry of non-European powers—Japan and the United States—into the imperialist game. What it does not show is the extent of Western and Japanese influence in China. Profoundly destabilized by foreign intervention, China in 1914 was in the midst of revolution.

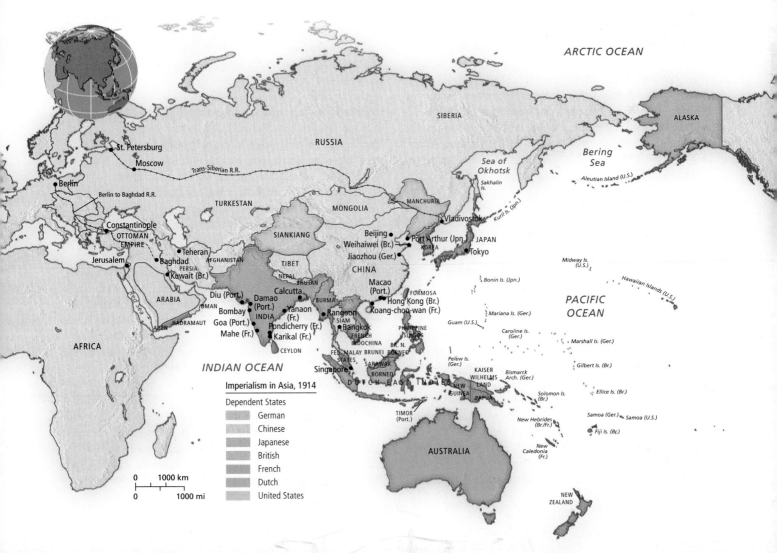

The United States and Empire

The U.S. embrace of empire may seem surprising, given its own history of rebellion from British colonial rule. American imperialism was, in fact, somewhat furtive. American policymakers tended to label their imperial territories "dependencies" rather than colonies, and few politicians in the United States spoke openly about the "American empire." Yet nineteenth-century American history was the story of imperial expansion and consolidation. War with Mexico in 1846 resulted in the acquisition of California (as well as New Mexico and part of Arizona) and so extended the reach of the United States from the Atlantic to the Pacific. The completion of the transcontinental Union Pacific railroad in 1869 both symbolized this coast-to-coast dominion and accelerated the pace of westward settlement. The conquest of the continent, however, depended on the defeat of its indigenous peoples. The decades from 1860 through 1890 were punctuated by a series of Indian Wars throughout the American West. As in Africa, however, even those Indians who acquired repeating rifles, such as Crazy Horse's troops who wiped out General George Armstrong Custer (1839–1876) at Little Big Horn in 1876, could not hold out for long against the industrial might of the United States.

With its borders touching the Pacific Ocean, the United States emerged as an imperialist power in Asia. In 1853, Commodore Matthew Perry used the potent threat of his squadron of four warships to force the opening of Japan to American commerce, and during the 1860s and 1870s the United States participated with the European powers in chipping away at China's national sovereignty to ensure favorable terms of trade there. By the end of the century, the United States had annexed Hawaii and part of Samoa, and as a result of the Spanish-American War had acquired Guam, the Philippines, Cuba, and Puerto Rico.

The Continued Expansion of the Russian Empire

Russia was also a key player in the game of Asian empire during this era. By 1914, the Russian Empire stretched from Warsaw in central Europe to Vladivostok on the Sea of Japan—8,660,000 square miles, or one-seventh of the global land surface. Ethnic Russians comprised only 45 percent of the population of this vast empire.

Beginning in the sixteenth century, Russian peasants had made their way into Siberia, seeking land and freedom from the obligations of serfdom. After the tsarist regime abolished the death penalty in 1744, these peasant colonialists were joined by less willing settlers: Deportation to Siberia became a common punishment for criminals, religious dissenters, and political dissidents. In the nineteenth century, immigration into Siberia accelerated, as peasants fled the debts imposed on them by the emancipation legislation of 1861 (see Chapter 21) and as the construction of the Trans-Siberian railway was completed in the 1890s. Between 1800 and 1914, seven million Russians settled in or were deported to Siberia.

As in the United States, the indigenous population of this land was rapidly displaced. Until 1826 Siberian aborigines were traded as slaves. Two additional factors were even more devastating. First, the immigrants brought with them new epidemic diseases, which decimated the native population. And second, the booming fur trade depleted the animal herds that served as the aborigines' main food source.

During the nineteenth century Russia also expanded its control southward into central Asia, primarily as a preemptive response to the expansion of British power in India. Fearing that the British might push northward, the Russians pushed south. By 1885, the Black Sea region, the Caucasus, and Turkestan had all fallen to Russian imperial control. Over the next three decades the oil fields of the Caucasus would become a crucial part of the Russian industrial economy.

As the tsarist regime expanded its Asian empire, it increasingly encroached upon Chinese territory, a move that contributed to the destabilization of China and to growing hostilities between Russia and Japan. By 1860, Russia had gained from China a sizable chunk of land along the Pacific coast and began pressing into Manchuria. Manchuria, however, was a region also coveted by Japanese imperialists. The growing antagonism between Russia and Japan led to the outbreak of the Russo-Japanese War in 1904 and, as we noted in Chapter 22, to a dramatic Japanese victory. Military defeat by a people regarded as racially inferior shocked Russians and led to demands for radical political change. With Tsar Nicholas II's regime clearly weakened and his troops tied up in Manchuria, this domestic discontent exploded in the Russian Revolution of 1905. The return of his soldiers from the Manchurian front enabled Nicholas to withstand this challenge to his authoritarian rule. His regime, however, was fundamentally weakened: Imperialism could be a risky business.

Japanese Industrial and Imperial Expansion

Japan's victory over Russia in 1905 vividly illustrated its remarkable rise to global power and its emergence as an imperialist player. Until 1853, Japan had remained sealed off from the West, a result of a decision made by the Japanese emperor in the 1630s to close Japanese ports to all foreigners except a small contingent of Dutch and Chinese traders confined to the city of Nagasaki. But by the 1850s, Japan's isolation annoyed both the United States and the European powers with interests in Asia. American whalers, for example, fished off the coast of Japan and desired to use its ports to supply their ships, while American commercial interests in California, aiming to establish a steamer route across the Pacific, also looked longingly at Japanese ports. The Japanese government rebuffed all Western overtures until

1853, when Commodore Perry's warships forced Japan to open two of its ports to American ships. The next fifteen years were tumultuous, as Western powers pushed to expand their economic influence in Japan and as Japanese elites fought over the question of how to respond to the West. Anti-Western terrorism became endemic, civil war broke out, and a political revolution ensued.

In 1868, Japan emerged from this turbulent time with a new government. For more than 200 years effective political control had rested in the hands not of the Japanese emperor, but rather of the "Shogun," the military governor of Japan. When the Shogun adopted pro-Western policies, Japan's warrior nobility tossed him from power and restored the young Emperor Mutsuhito (1867–1912) to effective rule—the Meiji Restoration. Even more dramatically, these anti-Western elites determined that the only way to resist Western domination was by adopting Western industrial and military technologies and techniques. The next four decades witnessed a thoroughgoing revolution from the top as Japan's feudalist political system was dismantled, replaced by a modern centralized state modeled

on France. Young Japanese men traveled to Europe and the United States to be educated in Western ways. Western technologies and techniques helped modernize the Japanese economy.

Modernization was not an end in itself, however. The purpose of opening Japan to the West was to build up its national wealth, and with this wealth, to remake Japan as a global military power. Thus funds poured into building a modern navy, modeled on Britain's, and a powerful conscript-based army, modeled on Germany's. Beginning in the 1890s, Japan used its now formidable military force to push its way into the imperialist game. War with China in 1894 and Russia in 1904 led to the Japanese seizure of Taiwan and Korea, and to expanded Japanese economic influence in Manchuria. One Japanese writer, Tokutomi Soho (1863–1957) proclaimed that Japan's imperial conquests showed that "civilization is not a monopoly of the white man."[13] Certainly imperialist violence was not a white man's monopoly: The Japanese brutally punished Koreans and Taiwanese who dared to protest against their new rulers.

■ Japanese Sailors Waiting for Battle Against Russia, 1904

The Japanese began the war with a surprise attack on Russian ships in Port Arthur. Many in Britain and the United States admired the Japanese for the audacity of their offensive—rather ironically, given the moral outrage that greeted a similar surprise attack carried out by the Japanese against American forces at Pearl Harbor in 1941.

"A DREAM OF THE FUTURE"

In 1878, Tachibana Mitsuomi published his "Dream of the Future" in Hochi Shimbun, *the newspaper that he edited. Tachibana's dream is a nightmare. It reveals the anxiety prevalent in Japan during its time of rapid modernization and increasing contact with Western economies and ideas. In this excerpt, Tachibana projects the consequences of an imaginary decision to lift regulations on the importation of Western capital. In actual fact, no such decision was made. The Japanese government borrowed technology, techniques, and institutions from the West, but restrained the inflow of Western capital, thus retaining control over the Japanese economy.*

Tachibana's story opens with his bewilderment at suddenly finding himself on a busy street in Tokyo in 1967:

The houses in the surrounding streets were splendidly built and some of them three, and others five stories high; flags from every merchant's house were waving in the air; all kinds of precious articles were displayed in the shops and carriages and horses were incessantly passing to and fro. Indeed, a most flourishing trade was actually before my eyes. Greatly puzzled at this, I went into a shop and found that the master of the shop was a White man with blue eyes and red hair, wearing handsome clean clothes and sitting in an easy position by a desk; and that those wearing scanty and torn apparel and in the employment of the master of the house, were none but the yellow-coloured and high-cheek-boned brethren of ours.... I was informed that ... all the large houses in the main streets [were] occupied by the Whites....

". . . I then passed into the [side] streets and on looking at the state of the houses, I saw none but immense numbers of my countrymen flocking together like sheep or pigs, in a few poorly-built houses . . . their scanty dress leaving portions of their body uncovered . . . their wives were weeping from the cold, and the children crying from hunger, the husbands being employed by the Western people, and were earning scarcely sufficient wages to fill the mouths of their families. . . .

"I, seeing this, could hardly keep from weeping and was sorely puzzled why my countrymen should have fallen to such misery . . . I saw a respectable looking gray-haired old man standing on the bridge . . . I approached him and after bowing to him, I asked, 'Is this country Japan? Is this the capital, Tokei [Tokyo]? How is it that the Western people alone are enjoying such great wealth, whilst the Japanese are in such a miserable state? . . .'"

The old man explains to Tochibana that the Japanese "were outdone by the superior strength of capital and intellect" from the West. As a result of lifting regulations on Western investment and ownership within Japan, "those who have control over the wealth of Japan . . . are none but the Western people." Tochibana concludes, "At this, I was very sad and deeply affected, and I was on the point of bursting into tears, when I suddenly awoke and found that it was all a dream."

Source: From Tachibana Mitsuomi, "A Dream of the Future," *Hochi Shimbun,* October 17, 1878. For the full version and a commentary, refer to Ian Inkster, *Japanese Industrialisation: Historical and Cultural Perspectives* (Routledge: London and New York, 2001), pp. 1–6.

Scrambling in China

While Japan used its encounter with the West to modernize and militarize its society, China proved far less successful in withstanding Western encroachment. Throughout the nineteenth century, Chinese national sovereignty slowly eroded, as European powers, soon joined by Russia, the United States, and Japan, jostled for access to China's markets and resources.

For much of the nineteenth century, China's encounter with the West was structured by the treaty port system, a diplomatic and trading arrangement first forced on China by the British after their victory in the Opium War in 1842. The treaty port system granted to foreign representatives the right to live and trade in specific ports (and eventually in railheads within the Chinese interior). The system was inherently unequal. Low customs duties ensured that the profits flowed out from rather than into China. Even more significant, the principle of "extraterritoriality" declared

foreign residents subject only to their own country's laws and so placed Westerners entirely outside the Chinese legal system, while granting Chinese residents in Western countries no such equivalent rights. Thus the provisions of the treaty port system worked to diminish Chinese national sovereignty.

The Western powers realized that the treaty port system was profitable but risky. If the Chinese government was forced to cede too much of its sovereignty to foreign interests, it might cease to control the country—and revolutions are rarely good for business. In 1858, Lord Elgin, who supervised British affairs in China, warned European traders to be careful not to "kill the goose that lays the golden eggs, throw the country into confusion and imperil the most lucrative trade you have in the world."[14] Taking to heart Elgin's warning, Western governments agreed to put the goose on life support—to assist the Chinese government in reforming its financial, administrative, and military systems. By 1890, China appeared to have stabilized as these reforms proceeded apace under the supervision of the Empress Dowager Cixi (Tzu Hsi) (1835–1908).

This stability proved to be short-lived, however. Western actions after 1895 fatally weakened China's central government. The Sino-Japanese War of 1894–1895 revealed China to be far weaker than the Western powers had realized. Over the next five years, these powers scrambled to create spheres of influence throughout China. The European powers and the United States did agree in 1899 to back the American "open door" policy, which opposed the formal partitioning of China (as had just occurred in Africa), but Western economic and political involvement continued to expand.

Chinese opposition to this intensified Western encroachment provoked greater outside interference—and the collapse of the Manchu dynasty that had governed China since the seventeenth century. In 1900, a secret society devoted to purging China of Western influence began attacking foreigners. The Boxer Rebellion (a rough translation of "Harmonious Fists," a name that refers to the society's commitment to the discipline of martial arts) received the covert support of the Chinese government. With more than 200 missionaries and several thousand Chinese Christians killed, and European diplomatic headquarters under attack in Beijing, the West responded in fury. A combined military force, drawing 16,000 soldiers from Russia, Germany, Austria-Hungary, France, Britain, Japan and the United States, crushed the rebellion and sacked Beijing. Required to pay a large indemnity to the West and to grant further trade and territorial concessions to its invaders, the Chinese central government was fatally weakened. In 1911, revolution engulfed China and propelled it into four decades of political and social tumult.

"White Australia"

The story of imperialist conquest in Asia also extends to the island continent of Australia. Discovered and claimed for the British Crown by Captain James Cook in 1770, Australia was used by Britain as a dumping ground for convicts for the next several decades. But with the establishment and expansion of the wool industry in the decades after 1830, the six British colonies established in Australia became a center of British immigration. In 1901, these colonies were joined together in the Commonwealth of Australia, part of the British Empire but a self-governing political entity—and a self-defined "Western" nation, despite its geographical location in the Eastern Hemisphere. Many Australians, including the new nation's first prime minister, Edmund Barton, identified the "West" as "white." Barton, who campaigned on a platform calling for a "White Australia," regarded his country as an outpost of Western civilization.

At the very start of Britain's occupation of Australia in 1787, King George III had forbidden anyone to "wantonly destroy [the Aboriginal peoples] or give them any unnecessary interruption in the exercise of their several occupations."[15] But the landing of whites intent on building cities, planting farms, and fencing in land for pastures clearly interrupted the nomadic way of life for the estimated 500,000 inhabitants of Australia, living in scattered tribal groupings. In 1795, the first major clash between Aborigines and British settlers occurred. Over the next hundred years, these clashes were frequent—and disastrous for the Aboriginal populations.

The British were divided over how to treat the Aborigines. To many British settlers, and as the decades passed, to many in the growing group of Australia-born whites, the Aborigines constituted a clear and violent threat that had to be eradicated. Massacres of Aborigines resulted. Christian and humanitarian groups, as well as the British government in London, opposed this sort of violence and insisted that the Aborigines should be westernized and Christianized. From the 1820s on, mission stations were established for housing and educating Aboriginal children. Forcibly removed from their homes, these children were educated in British ways and then at age 15 placed in employment as apprentices and domestic servants. Despite these missions, few Aborigines assimilated to the Western way of life. Thus the final decades of the nineteenth century saw a shift in official policy from assimilation to "protection." Aborigines and mixed-race individuals were declared legal wards of the state and required to live on reserves. Not until 1967 did Aborigines receive Australian citizenship.

White Australians also perceived Asian immigrants as a threat to their Western identity. By the 1850s, tens of thousands of Chinese had emigrated to Australia. Arriving as indentured servants, they worked under brutal conditions. Many, for example, labored in the gold mines, where they received one-twelfth of the wages paid to a European. As the numbers of Chinese immigrants grew, so, too, did anti-Chinese sentiment. Most British immigrants and white native Australians, often fiercely divided in their vision of what sort of nation Australia should be, agreed that it should be colored white. One newspaper editor noted, "The Chinese question never fails. At every meeting, somebody in the hall has a word to say in regard to it, and visions of millions of the barbarians swooping upon the colony in a solid body rise in the mental horizons of every man present."[16] In 1888, the Australian government turned back ships containing Chinese immigrants; restrictive immigration legislation soon followed.

A GLIMPSE OF THINGS TO COME: THE BOER WAR

Writing at the time of the Opium War (1840–1842), a British journalist in China urged the Chinese to accept what he regarded as the crucial lesson of history: "Ever since the dispersion of man, the richest stream of human

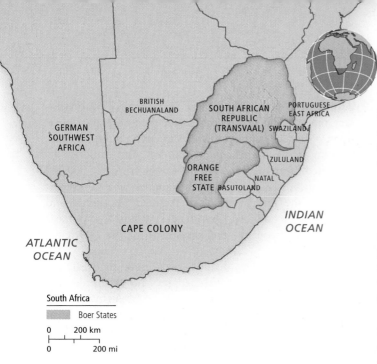

South Africa
▨ Boer States

0   200 km
0   200 mi

■ **Map 23.3 South Africa**
After the defeat of the Boer states—the Transvaal and the Orange Free State—in the Boer War, the Union of South Africa comprised the Cape Colony and the two Boer republics.

blessings has, in the will of Providence, followed a western course." To many Europeans, Australians, and Americans, the rapid expansion of Western imperial control over much of the world after 1870 confirmed this lesson. At the very end of the nineteenth century, however, the British found themselves embroiled in a bloody imperial conflict that challenged this complacent view. The Boer War of 1899–1902 shook British self-confidence and in many ways foreshadowed both the total warfare and the crumbling of empires that would mark the experience of the West in the twentieth century.

The Boer War was the culmination of a century of hostility among British imperialists, Dutch settlers (called Boers, the Dutch word for "farmer"), and indigenous Africans in the southern triangle of Africa. Germany's move into southwest Africa in 1884 worsened this conflict: The British in the Cape Colony feared that the Boers would work with Germany to limit British expansion in the region. But even more important was the discovery in 1886 of diamonds and gold in the Transvaal, an independent Boer republic. British investors in the profitable diamond and gold mines resented Boer taxation and labor policies, and pressed the British government to use military force to place the Boer republics under British rule.

In 1899, these imperialists got the war they had demanded, but it turned out to be rather different from what they expected. Skilled riflemen who were fighting for their very homes, the Boers proved to be fierce enemies who successfully adopted guerilla tactics against their numerically superior foe. By the spring of 1901, the war had reached a stalemate. The British military command in South Africa then decided to smoke out the Boer fighters through a scorched-earth policy: British troops burned more than 30,000 farms to the ground and confined the Boer women

and children, and their black African servants, in poorly provisioned concentration camps. Diseases such as diphtheria and typhus soon took their toll. Almost 20,000 Boer women and children, and at least 14,000 blacks, died in these camps.

The British finally defeated the Boers in April 1902, but this victory was limited. The Boer states were brought under British control but the Boers (or Afrikaners, as they were increasingly called) outnumbered other whites in the newly created Union of South Africa (see Map 23.3). After South Africa received self-government in 1910, the Afrikaners dominated the political system and created a nation founded on segregation and racist oppression. More immediately, Britain emerged from the war with both its military and its humanitarian reputation severely tarnished. The war aroused strong opposition inside Britain and made clear that popular support for imperialism could be rapidly eroded if the costs of imperial conquest proved too high. The conflict between the war's opponents and supporters inside Britain was one that would be repeated within imperialist countries many times over the course of the next several decades as nationalist challenges against imperial rule multiplied and as the imperial idea grew less and less persuasive. More ominously, the sight of noncombatants confined—and dying—in concentration camps would soon become all too familiar. The Boer War thus served as a fitting opening to the twentieth century.

CHRONOLOGY

The Struggle for Control in South Africa

1806	Britain takes control of the Cape Colony from the Dutch
1837	Boers establish independent republics of Transvaal and Orange Free State
1884	German annexation of Southwest Africa
1886	Gold discovered in the Transvaal
1899	Anglo-Boer War begins
1910	Self-government granted to South Africa

CONCLUSION

Reshaping the West: Expansion and Fragmentation

Africans and Asians who saw their political and social structures topple under the imperialist onslaught would probably have agreed with the Austrian poet Hugo von Hoffmansthal (1874–1929) when he wrote in 1905 that "what other generations believed to be firm is in fact sliding." Hoffmansthal, however, was commenting not on Africa or Asia or any other region of imperialist conquest, but rather on the Western cultural and intellectual landscape, which, like colonial political boundaries, underwent enormous and disturbing change in the period between 1870 and the outbreak of World War I in 1914. In this era, matter itself began to slide, as the Newtonian conception of the world gave way to a new, much more unsettling picture of the physical universe. At the same time, changes in medical practice, the revolt against positivism, and the triumph of Darwin's evolutionary theory helped undermine established assumptions and contributed to the sense that the foundations of Western culture were shifting; so, too, did the birth of modernism as well as broader cultural changes such as the move of middle-class women into the public sphere and the redefinition of sexual boundaries.

In the decades after 1870, then, a series of encounters reshaped the West. Its geographic boundaries expanded as non-European regions such as the United States emerged as significant economic and imperial powers. With Australians claiming Western identity, "the West" even spilled over into the Eastern Hemisphere. Yet fragmentation as well as expansion characterized the Western experience after 1870. At the same time that some social thinkers were proclaiming white cultural superiority, European artists such as Gauguin and Picasso were embracing the visual forms of non-European, nonwhite societies in an effort to push open the boundaries of Western culture. While scientific and technological achievements convinced many Europeans and Americans that the West was destined to conquer the globe, others regarded these scientific and technological changes with profound uneasiness.

The next chapter will show that the sense that old certainties were slipping led some Europeans to welcome the outbreak of war in 1914 as a way to restore heroic values and clear purpose to Western society. The trenches of World War I, however, provided little solidity. Many nineteenth-century political, economic, and cultural structures slid into ruin under the impact of total war.

Suggestions for Further Reading

For a comprehensive list of suggested readings, please go to www.ablongman.com/levack/chapter23

Adas, Michael. *Machines as the Measure of Men: Science, Technology, and Ideologies of Western Dominance.* 1989. A superb study of the way in which the ideology of empire was inextricably connected with cultural and intellectual developments within the West.

Betts, Raymond F. *The False Dawn: European Imperialism in the Nineteenth Century.* 1975. A general survey that looks at the ideas that underlay imperialism as well as the events that shaped it.

Bowler, Peter. *Evolution: The History of an Idea.* 1989. Looks at the development of evolutionary theory both before and after Darwin.

Butler, Christopher. *Early Modernism: Literature, Music, and Painting in Europe, 1900–1916.* 1994. Wide-ranging and nicely illustrated.

Dijkstra, Bram. *Idols of Perversity: Fantasies of Feminine Evil in Fin-de-Siècle Culture.* 1986. This richly illustrated work shows how anxiety over the changing role of women permeated artistic production at the end of the nineteenth century.

Dodge, Ernest. *Islands and Empires: The Western Impact on the Pacific and East Asia.* 1976. A useful study of Asian imperialism.

Ellis, John. *The Social History of the Machine Gun.* 1975. Lively, nicely illustrated, and informative.

Gould, Stephen Jay. *The Mismeasure of Man.* 1996. A compelling look at the manipulation of scientific data and statistics to provide "proof" for racist and elitist assumptions.

Headrick, Daniel R. *The Tools of Empire: Technology and European Imperialism in the Nineteenth Century.* 1981. Highlights the important role played by technology in determining both the timing and success of Western imperialism.

Hochschild, Adam. *King Leopold's Ghost.* 1998. Blistering account of Leopold's imperialist rule in the Congo.

Pick, Daniel. *Faces of Degeneration: A European Disorder c. 1848–1918.* 1993. Argues that concern over degeneration formed a central theme in European culture in the second half of the nineteenth century.

Showalter, Elaine. *Sexual Anarchy: Gender and Culture at the Fin de Siècle.* 1990. An illuminating look at the turbulence that characterized gender relations in the fin de siècle.

Sperber, Jonathan. *Popular Catholicism in Nineteenth-Century Germany.* 1984. A look at the religious dimensions of popular culture.

Thornton, A. P. *The Imperial Idea and Its Enemies: A Study in British Power.* 1959; reprinted 1985. An older but still-important look at imperialist ideology and opposition.

Vandervort, Bruce. *Wars of Imperial Conquest in Africa, 1830–1914.* 1998. An up-to-date study by a military historian.

Wesseling, H. L. *Divide and Rule: The Partition of Africa 1880–1914.* 1996. A solid survey of complex developments.

Notes

1. Winston Churchill, *The River War: An Account of the Reconquest of the Sudan* (New York, 1933); quoted in Daniel Headrick, *The Tools of Empire: Technology and European Imperialism in the Nineteenth Century* (1981), 118.
2. Quoted in H. Stuart Hughes, *Consciousness and Society: The Reorientation of European Social Thought 1890–1930* (1958), 332.
3. Quoted in Hughes, 296.
4. Quoted in Anne McClintock, *Imperial Leather: Race, Gender, and Sexuality in the Colonial Contest* (1995), 50.
5. Quoted in Shearer West, *Fin De Siècle,* (1993) 24.
6. Quoted in Christopher Butler, *Early Modernism: Literature, Music, and Painting in Europe, 1900–1916* (1994), 2.
7. Stephen Kern, *The Culture of Time and Space, 1880–1918* (1983), 195.
8. From *Elementary Forms.* Quoted in Hughes, 284–285.
9. Quoted in William Schneider, *An Empire for the Masses: The French Popular Image of Africa, 1870–1900* (1982), 72.
10. *West African Studies* (1901), 329–330.
11. Headrick, 101. Headrick is the historian who identified the crucial role of the steamship, the quinine prophylaxis, and the breech-loading, repeating rifle in the conquest of Africa.
12. Quoted in Thomas Pakenham, *The Scramble for Africa 1876–1912* (1991), 22.
13. Quoted in W. G. Beasley, *Japanese Imperialism, 1894–1945* (1987), 31–33.
14. Quoted in Beasley, 19.
15. Quoted in F. K. Crowley (ed.), *A New History of Australia* (1974), 6.
16. Quoted in Crowley, 207.

The First World War

O N THE MORNING OF JULY 1, 1916, IN THE FIELDS OF NORTHERN FRANCE near the Somme River, tens of thousands of young British soldiers crawled out of ditches and began to walk across a muddy expanse filled with shards of metal and decomposing human bodies. Encumbered with backpacks weighing more than sixty pounds, the men trudged forward. For the past week their heavy artillery had pummeled the Germans who lay on the other side of the mud. Thus they expected little opposition. In less than sixty seconds, expectations and reality horribly diverged. The German troops, who had waited out the bombardment in the safety of "dugouts"—fortified bunkers scooped from the earth beneath the trenches—raced to their gunnery positions and raked the evenly spaced lines of British soldiers with machine-gun fire. The slowly walking men made easy targets. Those who were lucky enough to make it to the enemy lines found their way blocked by barbed-wire fences—still intact, despite the bombardment. Standing in front of the wire, they were quickly mown down. Over 20,000 British soldiers died that day, thousands within the first minutes of the attack. Another 40,000 were wounded. Yet the attack went on. Between July 1 and November 18, 1916, when the Battle of the Somme finally ended, almost 420,000 British soldiers were killed or wounded. Their French allies lost 200,000 men to death or injury. German casualties are estimated at 450,000.

Such carnage became commonplace during the First World War. At the Battle of Verdun, which began before the Somme conflict and continued after, the French and Germans suffered total casualties of at least 750,000, while in the disastrous Gallipoli offensive of 1915, ANZAC (Australia and New Zealand) troops experienced a casualty rate of 65 percent. Between 1914 and 1918, European commanders sent more than eight million men to their deaths in a series of often futile attacks. The total number of casualties—killed, wounded, and missing—reached over 37 million.

Death on the Western Front: This movie still comes from *The Battle of the Somme,* a documentary filmed during the battle and the first "war movie" shown in Britain.

These casualty figures were in part the products of the Industrial Revolution. Between 1914 and 1918 the nations of the West used their factories to churn out ever more efficient tools of killing. The need for machine guns, artillery shells, poison gas canisters, and other implements of modern warfare meant that World War I was the first total war°, a war that demanded that combatant nations mobilize their industrial economies as well as their armies, and thus a war that erased the distinction between civilian and soldier. In total war, victory depended on the woman in the munitions factory as well as the man on the front lines.

The First World War challenged many core assumptions of Western culture and reshaped economic and political structures. By shattering the authoritarian empires of eastern and central Europe and integrating the United States more fully in European affairs, the war ensured that commitment to democratic values became central to one dominant twentieth-century definition of "the West." But the war also strengthened antidemocratic forces: It catapulted into power a communist regime in Russia, intensified eastern Europe's ethnic and nationalist conflicts, and undermined many of the economic structures on which Western stability and prosperity rested. The years after the war, then, would see an acceleration of the fragmentation of Western cultural and social life already underway in the prewar period.

Three questions inform this chapter's examination of the origins and experience of the First World War: (1) What factors led Europe into war in 1914? (2) What were the characteristics of the war experience on both the front lines and on the home front? (3) What were the consequences of this war for the European and the global social, political, and international order?

The Origins of the First World War

O n June 28, 1914, the heir to the throne of Austrian-Hungarian Empire, Archduke Franz Ferdinand (1863–1914), was assassinated by ethnic Serbian terrorists. Austrian officials accused the Serbian government of involvement with the assassination. One month after the archduke's death, Austria declared war on Serbia. One week later, Europe was at war. Germany entered the war on Austria's side. These two Central Powers°, as they were known, squared off against not only small Serbia but also the colossal weight of Russia, France, and Britain, called the Allies°. Soon the Ottoman Empire and Bulgaria joined the Central Powers, with Greece, Romania, Italy, and Portugal jumping in on the Allied side. By the time the war ended in late 1918, the conflict had embraced nations from around the globe.

The origins of the First World War have fascinated historians ever since. Why did the murder of one man on the streets of a Balkan city lead to the deaths of millions in theaters of war ranging from muddy ditches in northern

■ **Arrest of Gavrilo Princip**

Princip was only 18 years old when he assassinated the Archduke Franz Ferdinand and set into motion the sequence of events that led to the First World War. Because of his young age, he did not receive the death penalty but instead was sentenced to twenty years in prison. He did not serve out his term; he died at age 22 of tuberculosis.

France to beaches along the Mediterranean, from the mountains of Italy to the deserts of northern Africa and the depths of the Atlantic? To understand the war's origins, we need to examine four interlocking developments: first, the destabilizing effects of nationalist political movements in eastern Europe; second, the heightened international economic and military competition among the European powers, which resulted in the creation of rival alliance systems; third, the widening gap between the expectations of traditional diplomacy and the requirements of an industrialized military; and finally, a strengthening "will to war," the conviction among both policymakers and ordinary people that war would provide a resolution to social and cultural crisis.

NATIONALISM IN EASTERN EUROPE: AUSTRIA-HUNGARY AND THE PROBLEM OF SERBIA

The roots of the First World War extend deep into the soil of nationalist conflict in eastern Europe. Western European national identities coalesced in accordance with existing political boundaries; in eastern Europe, however, the "nation" was defined by ethnic, religious, or linguistic identities rather than political citizenship. More than 27 million subjects of the Habsburg monarchy, for example, did not identify themselves with the Austrian-Hungarian Empire's dominant German or Magyar (Hungarian) peoples.[1] For the Czechs or Slovenians or Serbs, translating national into political identity—creating a "nation-state"—demanded the breakup of empires and a radical redrawing of political boundaries. Unlike in much of western Europe, then, in the East nationalism served as an explosive rather than a unifying force.

The divisive impact of nationalism explains why officials within the vast Austrian-Hungarian Empire regarded the small state of Serbia as a major threat. As a multiethnic, multilinguistic empire, Austria-Hungary's very survival depended on damping down the fires of nationalism wherever they flamed up. Yet much of Serbian politics centered on fanning the nationalist flame. In 1903, a group of Serbian army officers had shot Serbia's despised king and queen, chopped their bodies into little bits, and threw the pieces out the window. The new king, a member of a rival Serbian royal dynasty, recognized that his position on the throne was precarious, to say the least. To remain in power he catered to the demands of radical nationalists, who sought the unification of all Serbs in eastern Europe into a Greater Serbian state. Given the fact that over seven million Serbs lived not in Serbia but in the confines of Austria-Hungary, it is not surprising that the Austrian monarchy regarded the call for Serbian unification as a direct threat to its existence.

The hostile relations between Serbia and Austria-Hungary led directly to the outbreak of World War I. In 1908 Austria annexed Bosnia, a region with a large Serbian population. The Serbian government responded by encouraging the formation of Bosnian Serb separatist groups. After one such group, the Black Hand, succeeded in assassinating Archduke Franz Ferdinand in the summer of 1914, Austrian officials decided to crush Serbia once and for all. On July 23 a representative of the Empire presented the Serbs with an ultimatum, a set of demands that would have given Austria-Hungary the right to an unprecedented degree of involvement in Serbian internal affairs. Austrian diplomats informed the Serbian government that anything short of unconditional acceptance of the impossible ultimatum within just forty-eight hours would be taken as a declaration of war. Serbian officials agreed to comply with every demand except one. On July 28 Austria-Hungary declared war on Serbia.

INTERNATIONAL COMPETITION AND THE ALLIANCE SYSTEM

But why did war between Austria-Hungary and Serbia mean war across Europe? To understand what transformed this Austro-Serbian conflict into a continental war, we need to look beyond the unsettling impact of nationalism in eastern Europe to the heightened international competition that divided Europe into rival alliance systems. Concerned with protecting and enhancing the economic and military might of their states in an increasingly unsettled international climate, diplomats wove a web of alliances across Europe. As we will see, these alliances helped escalate a regional conflict into a European and then a global war.

One crucial factor in the growing intensity of international competition in the prewar years was Germany's unification as a state in 1871. By creating a military and economic powerhouse in the middle of Europe, the unification of the German states upset the balance of power on the Continent. Until 1890, however, the diplomatic maneuvers of Otto von Bismarck (1815–1898), the chancellor of the new nation, ensured a certain degree of stability. Bismarck recognized that Germany's position in the center of Europe made it vulnerable to encirclement by hostile powers. To avoid such an encirclement, Bismarck patched up relations with Austria in the aftermath of the Austrian-Prussian War, an effort that resulted in the signing of the Dual Alliance between Germany and the Austrian Empire in 1879. In 1882, the Dual Alliance became the Triple Alliance° when Italy joined the two Central Powers in a defensive treaty. At the same time, Bismarck was careful to maintain an alliance with Russia. By the terms of the Reinsurance Treaty of 1887, Russia and Germany agreed to remain neutral if either was attacked. Bismarck thus ensured that if Germany were to go to war against its old enemy, France, it would not face battle on two fronts.

But in 1888, a new emperor, Kaiser William II (r. 1888–1918), succeeded to the German throne. William, an ambitious and impatient young man, dismissed Bismarck in 1890 and launched Germany down a more dangerous path. The new kaiser made a fatal break with Bismarck's policies in two areas. First, William let the Reinsurance Treaty with Russia lapse, thus allowing fiercely anti-German France to form a partnership with Russia, formalized as the Franco-Russian Alliance of 1894. Germany now faced exactly the sort of encirclement by hostile powers, and the resulting threat of a two-front war, that Bismarck had sought to avoid.

Second, William favored a new "world policy" for Germany that pushed Britain toward allying with Russia and France. Whereas Bismarck had insisted that Germany's interests were confined to Europe, William and many prominent Germans wanted to see Germany claim its "place in the sun" as a global imperial and naval power. In 1898 Germany passed a naval law mandating the construction of nineteen battle ships; a second law passed in 1900 doubled the number of ships. At the same time Germany adopted a more aggressive stance in Africa.

Such policies were guaranteed to aggravate and alienate Britain. As an island nation with a vast overseas empire, Britain based its military defense system on its naval supremacy. From the British point of view, a strong German navy was nothing less than a direct challenge to British national security, just as an expanding German empire was bound to come into conflict with British imperial interests.

Hostility toward German ambitions overcame Britain's long tradition of "splendid isolation" from continental entanglements. In the first decade of the twentieth century, a series of military, imperial, and economic arrangements formed ever-tighter links between Britain and both Russia and France. These arrangements cleared the way for the formation of the Triple Entente° among France, Russia, and Britain. An informal association rather than a formal alliance, the Triple Entente did not require Britain to join in a war against Germany. There is no doubt, however, that British officials increasingly viewed Germany as the major threat to British interests.

By the first decade of the twentieth century, then, Europe had split into two opposing camps: the Triple Alliance versus the Triple Entente. To German policymakers, it appeared that Germany stood surrounded by hostile powers. With Italy regarded as unreliable, Germany's alliance with Austria-Hungary took on greater and greater importance. Strengthening this crucial ally became paramount. These considerations guided German policymaking in July 1914. When Austrian officials debated their response to the assassination of Franz Ferdinand, Kaiser William and his chancellor Theobold von Bethmann-Hollweg (1856–1921) urged a quick and decisive blow against Serbia. According to the Austrian ambassador, the kaiser told him "he would

regret if we did not make use of the present moment, which is all in our favour."[2] In what some historians have described as an act akin to issuing a "blank check," the kaiser assured the ambassador that Germany would stand by Austria, even at the risk of a war with Russia.

Both German and Austrian policymakers recognized that an attack on Serbia translated into a threat against Russian interests. Eager to expand Russian influence in the Balkan region, the Russian Empire had for decades positioned itself as the champion of Slavic nationalism in the Balkans and as the protector of small independent Slavic states such as Serbia. Its loss in the Russo-Japanese War of 1905 (discussed in Chapter 23) had exposed Russia's military weaknesses, but by 1914 the tsarist empire was re-arming quickly. German officials gambled that Russia was not yet strong enough to risk war on Serbia's behalf. But what if they were wrong and Russia did mobilize? Then, as Bethmann-Hollweg explained, certainly Germany's chances of winning were "better now than in one or two years' time," when Russia would be a more formidable foe.[3]

The escalation of the Austro-Serbian conflict into a European war is partly explained, then, by the existence of rival alliances. Germany's support for Austria emboldened Austrian policymakers to embark on an aggressive attack on Serbia. The links between Serbia and Russia made it very likely that this attack against Serbia would pull in the Russian Empire, which of course did not stand alone but was allied with France. No open and formal alliance required Britain to join a continental war, but a series of treaties with France and Russia demonstrated that British policymakers viewed Germany as a major threat to their imperial, military, and economic interests.

MOBILIZATION PLANS AND THE INDUSTRIALIZED MILITARY

Alliances alone do not explain the transformation of the Austro-Serbian conflict into a European war, however. Consider the case of Italy. Although a member of the Triple Alliance, Italy did not join Germany and Austria in August 1914. In fact, when Italy did enter the war in 1915, it did so on the opposing side. Even more significantly, no alliance required either Russia or Britain to enter the fray. To understand why these powers entered the war when they did, we need to look not only at the alliance systems but also at a third factor in the origins of World War I—the widening gap between the expectations of traditional diplomacy and the requirements of an increasingly industrialized military. This growing gap ensured that when preparations for war were underway in the summer of 1914, control of the situation slipped out of the hands of the diplomats and their political superiors and into the grasp of the generals. The generals had planned for a European war. Once set in motion, their plans began to dictate events (see Map 24.1).

In the decades before 1914 military planning was dominated by a new reality, the railroad. The criss-crossing of the European continent with train tracks gave military planners a new and incredibly powerful weapon: the ability to move large numbers of men quickly to precise locations. The speed with which nations could now throw armies into battle almost obliterated the distinction between mobilization and actual war. *Mobilization* refers to the transformation of a standing army into a fighting force—calling up reserves, requisitioning supplies, enlisting of volunteers or draftees, moving troops to battle stations. Traditionally, mobilization meant preparation for a possible fight, a process that took months and could be halted if the diplomats succeeded in avoiding war. But the railroads accelerated the mobilization process and thereby changed the very nature of military plans. Aware that the enemy could also mobilize quickly, military planners stressed the importance of preventive attacks, of striking

■ **Map 24.1 Europe, August 1914**

In August 1914 each of the Central Powers faced the challenge of war on two fronts, but the entry of the Ottoman Empire into the war on the side of the Central Powers in November 1914 blocked Allied supply lines to Russia through the Mediterranean.

Europe, August 1914

The "Central Powers"

States formerly associated with the Central Powers, but remaining neutral on the outbreak of war, and later joining the Allies

The "Entente" or "Allies", following the German attack on Belgium and the Austrian attack on Serbia

Neutral, later joining the Central Powers

Neutral, later joining Allies

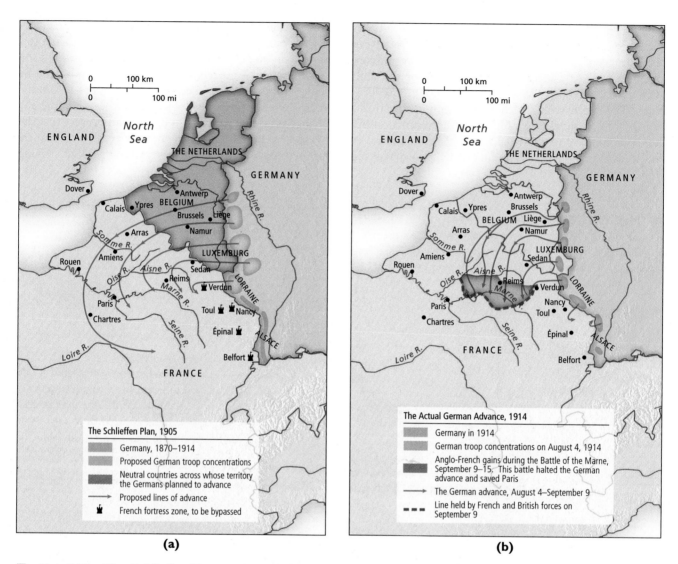

(a)   **(b)**

■ **Map 24.2   The Schlieffen Plan, 1905 (a) and The Actual German Advance, 1914 (b)**

Count Alfred von Schlieffen's original plan of 1905 called for the sleeves of the German soldiers on the right flank to brush the English Channel—in a daring move, the German army would sweep in a huge arching movement west. In the fall of 1914 Helmut von Moltke modified Schlieffen's plan: The crucial right flank was only three times stronger than the left, rather than eight times stronger as Schlieffen stipulated, and Moltke moved his troops north and east of Paris instead of south and west. Military historians today still argue over whether Schlieffen's original plan could have succeeded.

before being struck. Once a nation mobilized, therefore, the momentum toward war became almost irresistible.

These factors help explain the origins and impact of the military blueprint that structured German actions—and Allied reactions—in the summer of 1914. This scheme was the Schlieffen Plan°. The Franco-Russian Alliance meant that beginning in 1894, German military planners had to prepare for the possibility of a two-front war. The Schlieffen Plan was devised for just that eventuality. It aimed for a quick knockout blow against France, which would then allow the German army to concentrate on defeating the much larger force of Russia. The rationale here was that

Russia's mobilization would take time. Its territory was so vast, and its industrial infrastructure so underdeveloped, that Russian troops would not pose an immediate threat to German borders. According to the Schlieffen Plan, the smaller Austrian army would hold off the slowly mobilizing Russians while the German army moved with lightning speed against France (see Map 24.2).

The need for speed dictated the next step in the plan—an attack against France via Belgium. German planners knew that the French expected any German attack to come through Alsace and Lorraine (the provinces taken from France by the victorious Germans after the Franco-

Prussian War in 1870). The Schlieffen Plan called for the bulk of the German army to avoid France's heavily fortified northeastern border and instead swing to the west. Moving rapidly in a wide arc, the German army would flood into France through Belgium, encircle Paris, and scoop up the French forces before their generals knew what had hit them. With France out of the fight, the German troops would then board trains and head back to the Eastern Front to join their Austrian allies in defeating the Russians.

The need for speed—the key factor in the Schlieffen Plan—placed enormous pressure on German politicians to treat a Russian declaration of mobilization as a declaration of war itself. And that is what happened. Only two days elapsed between Russia's order of mobilization and the German declaration of war. As soon as Russia began to mobilize, German military leaders pressured their political counterparts to break off diplomatic negotiations so that the troop-laden trains could set off.

Moreover, the plan for a speedy thrust into France meant that Germany went ahead with its invasion of Belgium—a decision that brought Britain into the war. Belgium was a neutral nation, with its neutrality protected by Britain under a long-standing treaty. German policymakers gambled that Britain would stay out of the conflict, but their gamble failed. Germany's unprovoked and brutal invasion of Belgium provided the British government with the public-pleasing moral justification it needed to enter the war with mass support. Thus, just six weeks after an Austrian archduke died in Sarajevo, British and German soldiers were killing each other in the mud of northern France.

CHRONOLOGY

The Outbreak of the First World War, 1914

June 28	Assassination of Archduke Franz Ferdinand
July 28	Austrian-Hungarian declaration of war against Serbia
July 30	Russian mobilization
July 31	French, Austrian, and German mobilization
August 1	German declaration of war on Russia
August 3	German declaration of war on France
August 4	German invasion of Belgium; British declaration of war against Germany

THE WILL TO WAR

The events that pushed those soldiers into that mud were dictated not by diplomatic maneuvers but by the needs of an industrialized military. Unable to rein in the new forces of industrial warfare, diplomats also faced new pressures from public opinion. This public pressure, or the "will to war," constitutes the fourth factor that helps explain the outbreak of World War I in 1914.

Still drawn largely from the aristocracy, diplomats moved from elaborate hall to exclusive dinner, secure in their belief that with their secret agreements and coded

■ **German Volunteers**

In western Europe, the public welcomed the news that war had begun. The middle-class young men in this photograph are marching up *Unter den Linden*, the main street of Berlin, on their way to volunteer to fight. Enthusiasm for the war was less marked in working-class and peasant communities.

dispatches they could manipulate international affairs. Mired in traditional protocol, they also remained enmeshed in traditional assumptions. Prominent among these assumptions was the notion of balancing power among the principal European states. But they sought to maintain a balance of power in a world increasingly unbalanced by the forces of nationalism, mass politics, and industrial change. To these men, the traditions of secret diplomacy made perfect sense. They believed only a small elite possessed the education, temperament, and background to understand and control international affairs. Increasingly, however, foreign affairs interested and excited the mass public, whose assumptions about the course of international events clashed strongly with those of the career diplomats.

A number of developments accounted for this mass interest in foreign affairs. First, new technologies such as the telegraph, telephone, and camera collapsed distances and made international news much more immediate and accessible. Second, the rise of the popular press—cheap newspapers marketed to a semiliterate public—changed the coverage of foreign affairs. The competition to attract readers increased the pressure on editors and reporters to simplify and color their coverage, to make the often dull, dense, gray complexities of foreign relations into a compelling drama of Good Guys versus Bad Guys. Finally, the emergence of mass nationalism played an important role in shaping public opinion. Well-schooled in national identity, the European masses by 1914 viewed international relations as a vast nationalistic competition. They wanted evidence that "we" were ahead of "them."

Public opinion, therefore, constituted a new ingredient in international affairs in the years before the outbreak of World War I. Public opinion also constituted a real, although impossible-to-measure factor in the war's outbreak. In the last weeks of July, pro-war crowds gathered in large cities. In Berlin, for example, a crowd of 30,000 young men and women paraded through the streets on the evening of July 25, singing patriotic songs and massing around statues of German heroes. Not all Europeans greeted the prospect of war with enthusiasm. Middle-class men and women, particularly students, predominated in the cheering crowds. In the countryside, farmers and villagers were more fearful, while in working-class neighborhoods anti-war demonstrations received solid support in July. The declaration of war, however, silenced these demonstrations. Opposition to the war was very much a minority movement after August 1914, even among working-class socialists. The German Social Democratic Party (SPD), for example, sponsored anti-war parades in July, but when war was declared in August, voted overwhelmingly to approve war appropriations. Socialist parties throughout Europe did likewise; national loyalties proved far stronger than class solidarity. In Britain, a total of 2.5 million men volunteered to fight in the war, with 300,000 enlisting in the first month.

What made the idea of war so appealing to so many men and women in 1914? For some Europeans, war constituted a purging force, a powerful cleanser that would scour the impurities and corruptions from European society. As Chapter 23 explained, the years before 1914 witnessed a widespread cultural crisis in Europe, marked by fears of racial degeneration and gender confusion. War seemed to provide an opportunity for men to reassert their virility and their superiority. It also offered them the chance to be part of something bigger than themselves—to move beyond the boundaries of their often-restricted lives and join in what was presented as a great national crusade. As Carl Zuckmayer, a German playwright and novelist and a volunteer in the conflict, explained later, men like him welcomed the war as bringing

WAR AS A UNIFYING FORCE

Many Europeans welcomed the outbreak of war because it offered a chance to step aside from peacetime quarrels and factions. This excerpt from The Diary of a French Army Chaplain, *first published in 1915, illustrates the way political party competition was forgotten as French society mobilized for war. The author, Felix Klein, contrasts the prewar political infighting of the French legislature with the spirit of unity expressed in the declaration of war on August 4, 1914.*

Where, but a few weeks ago, could be found a more grievous spectacle than the first sittings of the new Chamber? And where, even in turning over the annals of many Parliaments, could be found a more admirable scene than that it offered on the 4th August. . . . And in this hot-bed of dissensions, quarrels, selfish desires, boundless ambitions, what trace remained of groups, of rivalries, of hates? Unanimous the respect with which the Presidential message was received; unanimous the adhesion to the Chief of the Government and his noble declaration: "It is the liberties of Europe that are being attacked of which France and her allies and friends are proud to be the defenders. . . ." And without debate, with no dissentient voice, all the laws of national defense, with the heavy sacrifices they imply, are at once voted. . . .

The fact is that we know ourselves no longer; barriers are falling on every side which, both in public and private life, divided us into hostile clans. . . . The relations between citizens are transformed. In the squares, in the streets, in the trains, outside the stations, on the thresholds of houses, each accosts the other, talks, gives news, exchanges impressions; each feels the same anxiety, the same hopes, the same wish to be useful, the same acceptance of the hardest sacrifices.

Source: From *Diary of a French Army Chaplain* by Felix Klein. London: Melrose, 1915.

"liberation . . . from that which we—consciously or unconsciously—felt as the saturation, the stuffy air, the petrifaction of our world."[4]

For political leaders, war provided the opportunity to mask social conflicts, to displace domestic hostilities onto the battlefield. We saw in Chapter 22 that the decades before 1914 were characterized by the rise of aggressive and often violent trade union movements and the increasing strength of socialist political parties, as well as anarchist-inspired assassinations and ethnic terrorism. To many European elites, their society seemed on the verge of disintegration. But, as the future British prime minister Winston Churchill explained, war united societies with "a higher principle of hatred."

The war for which university students cheered and for which the politicians and generals had planned was not anything like the war that actually happened, however. Most anticipated a short war. Theorists argued that in the new industrial age, the cost of waging war was so high that no nation would be able to sustain a conflict for very long. Everything depended on throwing as many men and as much materiel as possible into the battlefield at the very beginning. The men who marched off in August 1914 expected that they would be home by Christmas. Instead, if they survived, which few of them did, they would spend not only that Christmas, but the next three, in the midst of unspeakable and unprecedented horror.

The Experience of War

Expecting a German attack through Alsace and Lorraine, French military commanders in August 1914 poured their troops into these provinces. Counting on *élan*, the French military spirit, to see them to victory, the French troops swung into battle sporting bright red pants and flashy blue tunics. At their head rode the cream of the French military education system, the graduates of the elite Saint-Cyr military academy, who charged forward wearing their parade dress of white gloves and plumed hats. All that color and dash made easy targets for the German machine guns. As one military historian has written, "Never have machine-gunners had such a heyday. The French stubble-fields became transformed into gay carpets of red and blue."[5] Those "gay carpets," colored with the blood and broken bodies of young French men, signaled that this would be a war that shattered expectations, a war of revolutionary possibilities and devastating slaughter. It was a war fought not only in northern France—what became known as the "Western Front"—and in the Balkans, but throughout eastern Europe, down into Africa, across Asia, and out into the Atlantic Ocean. It eventually drew in the United States, Japan, and many of the countries of Central and South America. As the economic demands of total war escalated, governments assumed unprecedented powers, women stepped into new roles, and social tensions rose. Thus at the same time the war spread beyond European borders, it also transformed relations within Europe.

THE WESTERN FRONT: STALEMATE IN THE TRENCHES

Implementing a modified version of the Schlieffen Plan (see Map 24.2), the German troops swept into Belgium in August 1914. By the first week of September the German troops had swung into France and seemed poised to take Paris. The Germans had overstretched their supply lines, however, and in a remarkable military feat, French and British forces turned back the German offensive at the Marne River. They had saved Paris, but they were unable to push the German army out of France. By the middle of October, the German, British, and French forces were huddling in trenches that eventually extended more than 300 miles from the Belgian coast to the borders of Switzerland. There they stayed for the next four years.

■ French Soldiers

These French soldiers are stationed in a listening post near the front lines. Note the typical trench features: barbed wire at the top, the sandbag walls, the omnipresent and always necessary shovel.

The Troglodyte War

Literary scholar Paul Fussell has used the phrase "the troglodyte war" to sum up what the soldiers experienced on the Western Front.[6] Like prehistoric cavemen, the men on both sides of the conflict found themselves confined to underground dwellings. As British poet and World War I veteran Siegfried Sassoon explained, "when all is said and done, this war was a matter of holes and ditches."

From the strategic point of view, these holes and ditches—the trenches—were defensive fortifications, and the long stalemate on the Western Front shows that they worked well. Despite numerous attempts between the fall of 1914 and the spring of 1918, neither side was able to break through the enemy line. The defensive advantages of the trench system are easy to comprehend. Attacking infantry units faced the dreadful task of walking forward against troops armed with machine guns and sheltered behind wide barbed-wire fences and a thick wall of dirt and sandbags (see Map 24.3).

A discussion of trench strategy, however, conveys nothing of the appalling misery summed up by the term "trench warfare." Imagine standing in a ditch that is about seven or eight feet deep and about three or four feet wide. The walls of the ditches are packed mud, propped up with sandbags. Wooden boards cover the floor, but the mud squelches between them. The top side of the ditch facing the enemy is reinforced with piled sandbags and barbed-wire barricades, thus deepening your sense of being underground. Moreover, the trenches do not run in tidy straight lines. If they did, an enemy machine gunner in the right position would be able to slaughter an entire platoon in a matter of seconds. Instead, the trenches zigzag at sharp angles, restricting the range of fire for enemy snipers but also ensuring that everywhere you look you see a wall of mud. Because you are in northern France, it is probably raining. Thus you are standing not on but *in* mud—if you are lucky. In some parts of the line, soldiers stand in muddy water up to a foot deep. On the other side of your sandbag defenses stretches no-man's-land°, the territory dividing the British and French trench systems from the German. Pocked with deep craters from heavy shelling, often a sea of mud churned up by the artillery, no-man's-land is littered with stinking corpses in various states of decomposition—all that is left of the soldiers who died during previous attacks. Your constant com-

EXPECTATIONS VS. REALITY

···················

Written by two young upper-middle class British writers, the following poems illustrate the shift from the initial enthusiasm for the war to later disillusionment and despair. In the first poem, written just as the war began, Rupert Brooke welcomes the war as an ennobling and purifying force that will bring genuine peace. In contrast, Wilfred Owen's later piece flatly describes a soldier asphyxiated by poison gas. Brooke died of blood-poisoning on his way to Gallipoli in 1915; Owen was killed in battle in 1918, just days before the war ended.

1914. *PEACE* BY RUPERT BROOKE

Now, God be thanked Who has matched us with His hour,
And caught our youth, and wakened us from sleeping,
With hand made sure, clear eye, and sharpened power,
To turn, as swimmers into cleanness leaping,
Glad from a world grown old and cold and weary
Leave the sick hearts that honor could not move,
And half-men, and their dirty songs and dreary,
And all the little emptiness of love.

DULCE ET DECORUM EST BY WILFRED OWEN

Bent double, like old beggars under sacks,
Knock-kneed, coughing like hags,
we cursed through sludge,
Till on the haunting flares we turned our backs
And towards our distant rest began to trudge.
Men marched asleep. Many had lost their boots

But limped on, blood-shod. All went lame; all blind;
Drunk with fatigue; deaf even to the hoots
Of tired, outstripped Five-Nines that dropped behind.
Gas! Gas! Quick, boys!—An ecstasy of fumbling,

Fitting the clumsy helmets just in time;
But someone still was yelling out and stumbling
And flound'ring like a man in fire or lime. . .
Dim, through the misty panes and thick green light,
As under a green sea, I saw him drowning.
In all my dreams, before my helpless sight,
He plunges at me, guttering, choking, drowning.

If in some smothering dreams you too could pace
Behind the wagon that we flung him in,
And watch the white eyes writhing in his face,
His hanging face, like a devil's sick of sin;
If you could hear, at every jolt, the blood
Come gargling from the froth-corrupted lungs,
Obscene as cancer, bitter as the cud
Of vile, incurable sores on innocent tongues,—
My friend, you would not tell with such high zest
To children ardent for some desperate glory,
The old Lie: "Dulce et decorum est
Pro patria mori."*

————
* *"It is good and right to die for one's country."*

Sources: From "Peace" from *"1914" Five Sonnets* by Rupert Brooke. London: Sidgwick & Jackson, 1915; "Dulce et Decorum Est" from *Poems* by Wilfred Owen, with an Introduction by Siegfried Sassoon. London: Chatto and Windus, 1920.

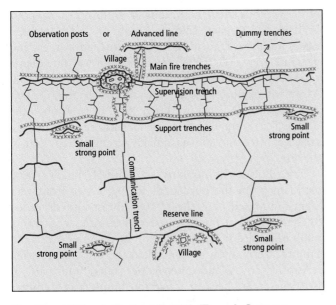

■ Map 24.3 A Typical British Trench System

The trench system consisted of three parallel lines: the front or fire trenches, the support trenches, and the reserve trenches, all connected by intersecting communications trenches. If the enemy succeeded in gaining the front trenches, the defending forces could withdraw to the support or even the reserve trenches, and still hold the line. (Source: From Tony Ashworth, *Trench Warfare, 1914–1918: The Live and Let Live System*, Pan Books, 2000. Copyright © 1980 by Tony Ashworth. Reprinted by permission of Macmillan, London, UK.

panions are lice (the term *lousy* was coined on the Western Front) and rats. For the rats, the war is an endless feast as they grow enormously fat, nibbling their way through the piles of dead.

From 1915 on, the horror of the Western Front escalated with the introduction of a new killing tool—poison gas, first deployed against enemy troops by the Germans in the spring of 1915. The Allies condemned the use of poison gas as inhumane, but within a matter of months the British and French, too, were firing poison gas canisters across the lines. The consequences were appalling: blinded eyes, blistered skin, seared lungs, death by asphyxiation. Gas proved to be an unreliable weapon, however. A sudden wind shift, and artillery units found they had asphyxiated their own troops. By 1916, with the gas mask a standard part of every soldier's uniform, military companies resembled hordes of insects. And, like insects, they were easily squashed. In the summer of 1915 an average of 300 British men became casualties on the Western Front every day, not because they were wounded in an attack but because they were picked off by snipers, felled by an exploding shell, or wasted by disease brought on by living in the mud amidst putrefying corpses.[7]

The Offensives

The offensives, the attacks launched by both sides on the Western Front, sent the numbers of dead and wounded soaring. None of the elderly commanders—the Germans Helmut von Moltke and Erich von Falkenhayn, the French Joseph Joffre and Ferdinand Foch, and the British Douglas Haig and John French—knew what to make of trench warfare. Both Haig and French had been cavalry generals, and expected war to be fought at a gallop. Schooled to believe that war is about attacking, they sought vainly to move this conflict out of the ditches by throwing vast masses of both artillery and men against the enemy lines. But time and time again these mass attacks were foiled by the machine gun. One British captain described the compelling power of this weapon: "To the south of the wood Germans could be seen, silhouetted against the sky-line, moving forward. I fired at them and watched them fall, chuckling with joy at the technical efficiency of the machine."[8]

The Battle of the Somme, described in the opening of this chapter, provides a classic illustration of a failed offensive. The Somme, however, was only one of a number of fruitless attacks launched by both sides on the Western Front. By the end of 1917, the death tolls on the Western Front were astonishing, yet neither side had gained much ground. Soldiers, who enlisted not for a specific term or tour of duty but "for the duration"—until the war ended—became convinced that only the dead escaped from the trenches.

THE WAR IN EASTERN EUROPE

The Western Front was only one in a number of theaters of war. Floundering in the snows of the Italian Alps, the Italian and Austrian armies fought each other along a stationary front for two brutal years after Italy, enticed by the promise of territorial gain, joined the war on the Allies' side. Characterized by futile offensives and essential immobility, the war in Italy mirrored the conflict on the Western Front. In eastern Europe, however, a different plot unfolded. For three years, massive armies surged back and forth, as the plains and mountains of eastern Europe echoed with the tumult of spectacular advances, headlong retreats, and finally political revolution.

The Eastern Front: A War of Movement

Much of the movement in eastern Europe consisted of Russians running—running forward in surprising advances, running back in terrifying retreats. When the war began in August 1914, Russia shocked its enemies by fielding a much stronger army much more quickly than German and Austrian military planners had expected. In a two-pronged onslaught, Russian troops headed against the Germans in East Prussia and against the Austrians in Galicia, the northeastern region of the Austrian empire. Surprised by the speed of the Russian advance, German troops in East Prussia at first fell back, but brilliant maneuvering by the German commanders Paul von Hindenburg (1847–1934) and Erich von Ludendorff (1865–1937) turned the Russian tide at the

Battle of Tannenberg at the end of August. Within two weeks the Germans had shoved the Russian troops back across the border. In the subsequent months, the Germans advanced steadily into Russian imperial territory. At the same time, a combined German and Austrian assault forced the Russian army to retreat from Austrian Galicia—and over 300 miles into its own territory. Russian casualties in the offensive stood at 2.5 million. Over the next two years the pattern of Russian advances and retreats continued. Russian soldiers pushed into Austria-Hungary in June 1916, but could not sustain the attack. The summer of 1917 saw another initially successful Russian advance, but it too soon disintegrated into a retreat (see Map 24.4).

These defeats revealed that Russia's economic and political structures could not withstand the pressures of total war. Russian supply lines were so overextended that the poorly fed and inadequately clothed Russian troops found themselves without ammunition and unable to press ahead. Demoralized by defeat and by the daily grind

of life without adequate rations or uniforms or weapons or barracks, Russian soldiers began to desert in ever-larger numbers. On the home front Russian workers and peasants grew ever more impatient with wartime deprivations and demands. This disaffection led to revolution. As we will explore in detail later in this chapter, the tsar was forced to abdicate in March 1917. In November, the Bolsheviks, a small group of socialist revolutionaries, seized control and moved quickly to pull Russia out of the war.

The Bolshevik military withdrawal finally freed Germany from the burden of waging a two-front war. Signed in March 1918, the Treaty of Brest-Litovsk° ceded to Germany all of Russia's western territories, containing a full one-third of the population of the prewar Russian Empire. Germany now controlled the imperial Russian territories in Poland, the Baltic states, and part of Byelorussia. But because it had to commit large numbers of troops to controlling this new territory, Germany

■ **Map 24.4   The Eastern Front, 1915–1918**
Unlike the Western Front, the Eastern Front was far from stationary. By 1918, the Central Powers occupied Serbia, Romania, and much of European Russia.

reaped less advantage from this victory than might have been expected.

The Forgotten Front: The Balkans

The new Balkan states were no strangers to war by 1914. After shrugging off Ottoman control, Greece, Bulgaria, Romania, and Serbia fought each other in the First and Second Balkan Wars of 1912 and 1913. In southeastern Europe, World War I was thus in many ways the "Third Balkan War," yet another installment in an ongoing competition for territory and power. Bulgaria joined the Central Powers in 1915, hoping to gain back the territory it had lost in the Second Balkan War. To protect its hold on this territory, Romania entered the war on the Allies' side in August 1916 and quickly found itself crushed between invading Bulgarian, German, and Austrian-Hungarian troops.

The Serbian experience was even more bleak. In the first year of the war Austrian and Serbian troops jostled back and forth for control of the country, but in October 1915 Bulgarian, German, and Austrian forces advanced into Serbia from three different directions. By November, the Serbian army had been pushed to the Albanian border. Two hundred thousand Serbian soldiers fled over the snow-swept mountains of Albania to the Adriatic Sea, in a disastrous "Winter March." Serbia was occupied by Austrian troops and placed under military rule, as were the adjoining nations of Albania and Montenegro. Like most military occupations, this one was brutal. By the war's end, approximately 25 percent of Serbian citizens lay dead.

CHRONOLOGY

Major Developments in the First World War, 1914–1916

1914

September	First Battle of the Marne: Anglo-French forces halt German advance on the Western Front
	Battles of Tannenburg and the Masurian Lakes: Germans halt Russian advance on the Eastern Front
October–November	First Battle of Ypres: German offensive, no gains, trenches dug on the Western Front

1915

	Stalemate continues on Western Front
April	Allied landing on Gallipoli: British and ANZAC troops quickly pinned down
May	Russian retreat from Austria
June	First battle between Italy and Austria; stalemate continues for next two years
October–December	German-Bulgarian invasion of Serbia; Serbian "Winter March"

1916

January	Allied withdrawal from Gallipoli
February–December	Battle of Verdun: German offensive, no gains
July–November	Battle of the Somme: British offensive, no gains, stalemate continues on the Western Front

■ **The Winter March**

Of the 200,000 soldiers who attempted the "Winter March" in 1915, at least 40,000 died and another 60,000 were wounded.

THE WORLD AT WAR

The imperialist expansion of the later nineteenth century ensured that as soon as the war began, it jumped outside European borders. The British and French empires supplied the Allies with invaluable military and manpower resources. Australia, New Zealand, Canada, India, South Africa, and Ireland supplied no less than 40 percent of Britain's military manpower during the war. More than 650,000 men from Indochina, Algeria, and French West Africa assisted the French war effort. (One of these men was Ho Chi Minh, who would later lead the Vietnamese struggle against France and then the United States.)

Fighting fronts multiplied around the globe as the major combatants struggled for imperial as well as European supremacy (see Map 24.5). Portugal joined the Allies largely because it hoped to expand its colonial possessions in Africa. Japan, too, entered the war for colonial gain. When the war began in August 1914, Japan seized the opportunity to snatch German colonial possessions in China. In return, Japan contributed to the Allied war effort by using its navy to protect Allied troop and supply ships in both the Pacific and the Mediterranean. By the end of 1914, most of Germany's colonies in the Far East had been occupied by Japanese and ANZAC troops.

The Middle East also became a key theater. When the Ottoman Empire joined the war on the side of Germany and Austria-Hungary in 1914, it posed a serious threat to Britain's economic and military interests in the Mediter-

■ **Map 24.5   The World at War**

Imperialist relationships and global economics ensured that a European conflict became a world war. In Africa both Portuguese and South African troops fought a bush war against German and native soldiers. The entry of the Ottoman Empire on the side of the Central Powers in November 1914 extended the conflict into the Middle East. Japan, the first non-European power to enter the war, occupied German colonial territories in Asia and the Pacific region. When the United States joined the Allies in April 1917, a number of Latin American countries also declared war on Germany.

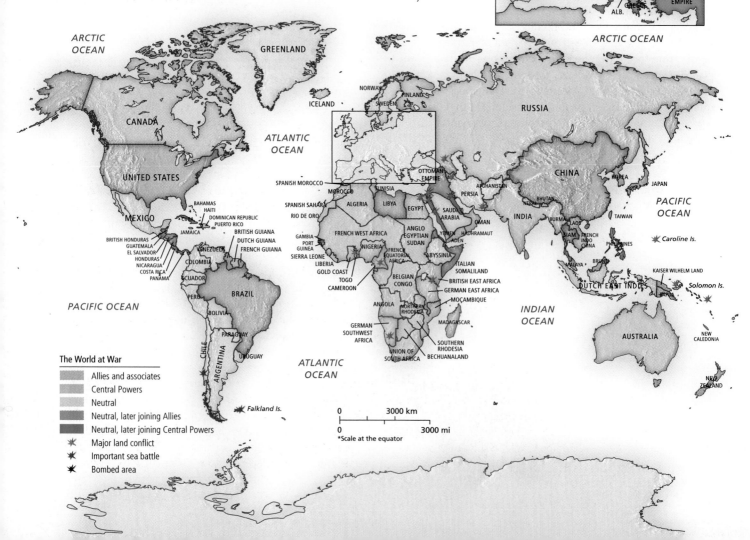

■ Sikh Cavalry Officers

Sikh cavalry officers from India patrol on the Western Front. India provided 1.3 million men to assist the British war effort. Indian troops fought—and more than 49,000 Indian soldiers died—in battles in the Middle East, in East Africa, and on the Western Front.

ranean and Middle East. Britain was desperate to protect Allied access both to the Suez Canal—a vital link to the soldiers and supplies of India, Australia, and New Zealand—and to Persian oil fields, an important source of fuel for the British navy. But by 1915 Ottoman armies had beaten back Allied attempts to advance through Arabia. They also occupied the Sinai peninsula, and threatened Britain's control of Egypt.

Struggling to establish a foothold on the shifting sands of the Middle East, the Allies joined with Arab groups seeking to free themselves from Ottoman rule. Led by a British soldier named T. E. Lawrence (1888–1935)—better known as "Lawrence of Arabia"—and inspired by promises of postwar national independence, Arab nationalists used guerilla warfare to undermine the Ottoman Empire's hold on the Arabian peninsula. This strategy proved successful. By 1917 British troops had pushed Ottoman forces out of Sinai, Arabian nationalists had lifted Ottoman control from almost the entire coastal region of the Arabian peninsula bordering the Red Sea, and Lawrence had captured Jerusalem.

THE END OF THE WAR

Despite the losses of its ally in the Middle East, at the beginning of 1918 Germany looked to be in winning position. Engulfed in revolution, Russia had dropped out of the war and relieved Germany of the burden of fighting on two fronts. With Serbia and Romania both occupied by their forces, the Central Powers could claim to have won the war in eastern Europe. Yet Germany was far weaker

than any map of its eastern conquests in 1917 could indicate. Germany was being strangled from the sea.

The War at Sea and the Entry of the United States

While infantrymen rotted in trenches and froze in mountain passes, the German and British navies fought a critical war at sea. German submarines sought to cut Britain's imperial lifeline and starve out its civilian population by sinking ships before they could reach British ports. Almost 14,000 British sailors and civilians died in these submarine attacks. In turn, British destroyers stretched a blockade across all ocean and sea passageways to Germany and its allies. The Allied blockade proved effective in preventing food and other essential raw materials from reaching Germany, Austria-Hungary and their associates. Food shortages sparked riots in more than thirty German cities in 1916. When the potato crop that year failed and eliminated one of the only sources of nutrition left, children's rations were limited to *one-tenth* of their actual needs.

Desperate to win the war quickly, German policymakers in 1917 took a huge gamble when they decided to up the tempo of their submarine war against Britain. Suspecting that supposedly neutral American passenger ships were delivering essential war materiel to Britain, they ordered their submarines to sink without warning any ship heading for British shores. The Germans were well aware that attacking American ships would very likely pull the United States into the war. In May 1915, a German submarine had torpedoed the British passenger liner *Lusitania* and killed almost 1,200 people, including 128 Americans. The furious response from the United States had forced Germany to restrict its submarine attacks. By 1917, however, Germany stood on the brink of economic collapse, and German policymakers decided they had no choice but to resume unrestricted submarine warfare. They gambled they could defeat Britain in a last-ditch effort before the addition of the United States to the Allies could make much of a difference. Over the next eight months German submarines sank 500 British merchant ships.

The United States declared war on Germany in April 1917. Outrage over American deaths at sea served as the most immediate cause of American entry into the war. Four other factors, however, also played a role. First, Franco-British news stories about German atrocities during the invasion of Belgium had persuaded many Americans that right rested on the Allied side. Second, the Russian Revolution of March 1917 removed an important obstacle to American cooperation with the Allies—the tsarist regime. Americans had balked at the idea of allying with the repressive government of Tsar Nicholas II, but the March Revolution, which overthrew Nicholas, reminded many in the United States of the American Revolution and offered American policymakers a more ideologically acceptable wartime partner. Third, by the time President Woodrow Wilson asked the U.S. Congress for a declaration of war, the American economy was thoroughly intertwined with that of the Allies. Trade between the United States and the Allied nations had grown from $825 million in 1914 to more than

$3 billion in 1916, and American bankers had loaned more than $2 billion to the Allied governments. Finally, the German government committed a serious blunder in the spring of 1917 when it offered to back Mexico in recovering New Mexico, Arizona, and Texas in exchange for Mexican support should war break out between Germany and the United States. American interception of a telegram sent by the German foreign minister Arthur Zimmermann exposed this offer and inflamed anti-German sentiment in the United States. The German resumption of unrestricted submarine warfare, then, simply put flame to kindling that was already in place.

The U.S. declaration of war (followed by those of Brazil, Costa Rica, Cuba, Guatemala, Haiti, Honduras, Nicaragua, and Panama) provided an immediate psychological boost for the Allies, but several months passed before American troops arrived on the battlefield in significant numbers. By July 1918, however, the United States was sending 300,000 fresh soldiers to Europe each month. The Allies now had access to an almost unlimited supply of materiel and men. Eventually nearly two million American soldiers were sent to Europe and almost 49,000 American soldiers died in battle.

Back in Motion: The Western Front in 1918
Faced with the prospect of having to fight fresh American forces, German policymakers decided to gamble one more time. On March 2, 1918—before the bulk of the U.S. army had been deployed—the German army launched a massive

■ **Harlem Hell Fighters**
The American expeditionary forces sent to France contained 200,000 black soldiers. This photograph shows the "Harlem Hellfighters," an all-black, all-volunteer regiment that served in front-line combat longer than any other American unit, saw half its men die, and received more than 170 medals of honor from the French government.

ground assault against British and French lines. The gamble almost succeeded. In just thirty minutes the German troops broke through the British front line; in seven days, German soldiers advanced forty miles; by April the German army stood just fifty miles from Paris.

What explains this sudden shift on the Western Front from a conflict characterized by stalemate and deadlock to a war of rapid and decisive movement? The answer is that after three and a half years of relentless, pointless slaughter, the German High Command in 1918 finally developed strategies that matched offensive techniques with industrialized killing technology. As we have seen, in the first years of the war commanders remained committed to offensive techniques suited to an age of preindustrial warfare—the mass charge, the cavalry attack. What they failed to realize was that industrial technologies such as the machine gun had transformed the power of defensive war. Certainly Western commanders were well-acquainted with the power of the machine gun. In the imperial conflicts discussed in Chapter 23, the machine gun enabled small European forces to mow down enormous indigenous armies. But on the Western Front, both sides possessed the machine gun. In other words, both sides were good on defense but poor on offense.

In 1918, however, the Germans came up with a new offensive strategy. They did not simply throw masses of men against machine guns. Instead of a frontal assault dictated by commanders sitting well behind the lines, Germany's offensive of 1918 consisted of a series of small group attacks aiming to cut behind British and French positions rather than straight on against them. In addition, the Germans in 1918 scrapped the massive preliminary artillery barrage that signaled when and where an attack was about to begin. In place of the barrage they employed sudden gas and artillery bursts throughout the offensive. The rapid German advance in the spring of 1918 showed that technique had caught up with technology.

In July, however, the Allies stopped the German advance; in August they broke through the German lines and began to push the German army backward. Throughout the summer the push continued. By September the Western Front, which had stood so stationary for so long, was being rolled eastward at a rapid clip. The final German gamble failed for three reasons: First, the German advance was so rapid that it overstrained German manpower and supply lines; second, the Allies learned from their enemies and adopted the same new offensive strategies; and third, the Allies figured out how to make effective use of a new offensive technology—the tank. Developed in Britain, the tank obliterated the defensive advantages of machine-gun-fortified trenches. A twentieth-century offense met a twentieth-century defense,

CHRONOLOGY

The End of the War, 1917–1918

1917	Stalemate continues on the Western Front
March	Collapse of the Russian imperial government
April	U.S. declaration of war on Germany
November	Bolshevik Revolution in Russia
December	Bolsheviks sign armistice with Germany; capture of Jerusalem by British troops
1918	
March	Treaty of Brest-Litovsk
March–July	German offensive on Western Front, rapid gains
July–November	Allied counteroffensive begins
September	Bulgaria and Allies sign armistice
November 3	Austria-Hungary sues for peace with Allies
November 9	Kaiser Wilhelm abdicates
November 11	Fighting ends on Western Front at 11:00 A.M.

and the war turned mobile. Reinforced with fresh American troops and the promise of more to come, the Allied forces surged forward against the hungry and demoralized Germans. When the Bulgarian, Ottoman, and Austrian armies collapsed in September and October, Germany stood alone. On November 11, 1918, German leaders signed an armistice and the war ended.

THE HOME FRONT

Four years of warfare had transformed the societies to which the soldiers returned. The term "home front" was coined during these years to highlight the fact that this war was fought not only by soldiers on the front lines, but also by civilians at home. Industrialization had created total war, a war that demanded that the productive capacity of a nation be utilized in the war effort, a war that recast and in some cases revolutionized not only the economic but also the political and social relations of the nations involved.

War in the Factories

World War I was the first industrial war. Everywhere we look on the Western Front we see the products of industrialization. Poison gas, the machine gun, barbed wire, canned foods, mass-produced uniforms and boots, and of course shovels all poured out of Europe's factories and helped shape this distinctive style of warfare. Even more important, industrialization made it possible for governments to deploy the vast masses of men mobilized in this conflict. Consider this comparison: The Battle of Waterloo, which ended the Napoleonic Wars in 1815, involved 170,000 men; the Battle of Sedan, which ended the Franco-Prussian War in 1870, involved 300,000 soldiers. The first Battle of the Marne, however, fought between the Germans and the French in September 1914, involved one million combatants. Only industrialized production could keep these huge armies supplied with weapons, ammunition, and other necessities.

It soon became clear that this war would be won in the factories as much as on the front lines. Those nations that collapsed did so at least in part because they lost the war at home. In Austria-Hungary, factories could not produce enough uniforms to clothe the empire's soldiers. Similarly, Russia's underdeveloped industrial sector and infrastructure meant that its soldiers failed to receive needed supplies. In the end, the Allies (minus Russia) won the war in large part because of their greater economic power. The contrast between the United States, with its vast industrial potential, and Germany, unable to feed its population, was pivotal, but even before U.S. entry, Germany was in trouble. Despite inflicting huge human and economic losses, the German submarine attacks were unable to stop the British empire from supplying Britain's factories with the raw materials they needed to crank out rifles, bullets, poison gas canisters, artillery shells, trucks, ambulances, and all the other makings of modern war.

At first, no government realized the crucial role that industrial labor would play in this war. Both military and political leaders believed that the war would end quickly, and that success depended on throwing as many men as possible into the front lines. In France, even munitions factories were shut down and their workers sent to the front. Governments practiced "business as usual"—letting the free market decide wages, prices, and supply—with disastrous results. Soaring rates of inflation, the rapid expansion of the black market, growing public resentment over war profiteering (the practice of private businessmen making huge profits off the war), and, most crucially, shortages of essential military supplies, including shells, proved that a total war economy needed total regulation.

Beginning in 1915, both the Allied and Central Powers governments gradually assumed the power to requisition supplies, dictate wages, limit profits, and forbid workers to change jobs. In Germany, the increasing regulation of the economy was called "war socialism," a misleading term because it was big business rather than ordinary workers who benefited. In Germany, the army worked in partnership with large industrial firms to ensure the supply of war materiel to the front lines, while the Auxiliary Service Law of 1916 drafted all men age 17 to 60 for war work. Measures such as these greatly expanded the size

and power of the central governments in the combatant states. For example, in 1914 the British office in charge of military purchases employed twenty clerks. By 1918, it had become the Department of Munitions, an enormous bureaucratic empire with 65,000 employees overseeing over three million men and women working in government-owned and -operated munitions plants.

The Individual and the State

One of the most striking aspects of the war experience on the home front was this expansion of governmental power. Even in Britain, bastion of liberalism, the demands of total war seriously restricted individual freedom. Flying in the face of tradition, in 1916 Britain's government imposed the draft—a clear example of the requirements of the state overriding the desires of the individual. By the war's end, governments had moved further, not only dictating all as-

■ **War Propaganda**

"Daddy, What Did You Do in the Great War?" This British poster achieved postwar notoriety for its rather crude attempt to embarrass men into volunteering to fight.

pects of economic life but also controlling many areas of social and intellectual choice. The British government restricted the hours that pubs could be open, as a way of encouraging workers to show up for work sober. It also tampered with time itself, introducing Daylight Saving Time as a means of maximizing war production.

To ensure that their citizens remained committed to the war effort, governments regulated the production and distribution of ideas. First, they eliminated ideas they viewed as dangerous. Pacifists and war objectors faced prison sentences and even execution. The French prime minister Georges Clemenceau (1841–1929) adopted a particularly harsh stance toward all dissenting opinion. Journalists and rival politicians—even the former prime minister—who dared suggest that France negotiate with Germany rather than fight on for total victory were thrown in prison. Second, governments worked to create ideas that would encourage a total war mentality. The First World War demonstrated the importance of propaganda as a political and social tool. Newspapers were carefully censored and photographs doctored to ensure that the public received a positive image of the war. In Britain, the government produced a series of now-legendary posters to shame men into enlisting. In Germany, giant wooden statues of the war hero Hindenburg were paraded around the nation to rally war enthusiasm.

The Politics of Total War

The war's reliance on industrial production greatly empowered industrial producers—the workers. In 1915 both France and Britain abandoned political party competition and formed coalition governments, which included socialist and working-class representatives. At the same time, political leaders welcomed labor unionists as partners in shaping the wartime economy. In return, French and British union leaders agreed to a ban on labor strikes and the "deskilling" of certain jobs—a measure that allowed unskilled laborers, particularly women, to take the place of skilled workers at much lower rates of pay.

Despite these "no strike" agreements, both Britain and France witnessed a sharp rise in the number of labor strikes in 1916 and in 1917. Faced with the potential of disintegration on the home front, political leaders in Britain and France reacted similarly. Both countries witnessed the emergence of war governments committed to total victory. In Britain, David Lloyd George (1863–1945) became prime minister at the end of 1916. A Welsh artisan's son who had fought hard to reach the top of Britain's class-bound, English-dominated political system, Lloyd George was not a man to settle for a compromise peace. One year later, Georges Clemenceau became prime minister of France. Nicknamed the "Tiger," Clemenceau demanded victory. When asked to detail his government's program, he replied simply, "*Je fais la guerre!*" ("I make war!").

Making war, however, was not possible without public support, as officials in both France and Britain realized. They cultivated this support in two ways. First, they sought to depict the war as a struggle between democracy and authoritarianism—a crusade not simply for national power or economic gain but for a better world. Second, they recognized that if civilian morale were to be sustained, the basic needs of ordinary citizens had to be met. Both governments intervened regularly in the economy to ensure that workers received higher wages, better working conditions, and a fair distribution of food stocks.

The situation in Germany differed significantly. The working class in Germany was never as successfully integrated into the political process as it was in Britain and in France. The parliamentary political voice of the working class, the Social Democratic Party (SPD), was not invited to participate in a coalition government. Instead, until the very last weeks of the war German political leadership remained in the hands of the conservative aristocracy. Increasingly, the aristocratic generals Hindenburg and Ludendorff—the heroes of the Battle of Tannenberg—called the political shots. The army and big industrial firms seized control of German economic life. Given the power to set prices and profit margins, industrialists—not surprisingly—made a killing. Their incomes soared, while ordinary workers were ground down by escalating inflation and chronic food shortages. By 1917, industrial unrest had slowed German war production, and civilian discontent had reached dangerous levels. Unlike the British and the French, the German government proved unable to control the unrest. The success of the Allied blockade meant Germans were starving. In contrast, living standards among employed workers in France and in Britain rose during the war.

War Against Civilians

Total war meant that the productive labor of the civilian was just as crucial as the killing work of the soldier. A logical, if horrifying, consequence of this fact was the deliberate targeting of civilian populations by military forces. The First World War eroded the distinction between civilian and combatant; as we will see in Chapter 26, in the Second World War this distinction almost disappeared. During World War I, both the German submarine attacks on passenger ships and the Allied blockade of Germany were aimed at civilians. Warfare on civilians also came from the skies. In the spring of 1915, the Germans began a series of zeppelin or airship raids against British cities. From airship decks, the zeppelin crews dropped bombs and grenades on civilian centers. Two years later, after the Germans shifted from zeppelins to airplanes, the British followed suit with air attacks against German cities. By the war's end, 7,300 British and German civilians had been killed and wounded in air attacks.

■ Turkish Massacre of Armenians
The Turkish massacre of more than one million Armenians illustrates the destructive consequences of combining nationalist hatred with total war. This criminal horror is often seen as foreshadowing the Jewish Holocaust during World War II.

The most horrifying civilian suffering, however, occurred on the Eastern Front, where hundreds of thousands of Serbs, Montenegrins, Romanians, and others died from starvation, disease, and brutal military occupation. The Armenian population living in the Turkish heartland of the Ottoman Empire also experienced intense suffering. Massacres of Armenians had punctuated the two decades before the outbreak of the war. Recognizing that Armenian loyalty to imperial rule was shaky, the Ottomans decided to eliminate the Armenian population

from Turkey and the conquered territories of southern Russia through forced deportation and wholesale slaughter. Over one million Armenian men, women, and children died.

A MODERNIST WAR

On both the home front and the front lines, the war introduced men and women to new realities—often horrifying, sometimes liberating, always unsettling. But for

■ *We Are Making a New World* by Paul Nash (1918)
Nash's wartime paintings turned the landscape genre from an evocation of natural beauty into a cry of pain.

■ **Returning to the Trenches by Christopher Nevinson (1914–1915)**
Nevinson's work demonstrates the close parallels between wartime reality and modernist representation.

some Europeans, the war confirmed rather than revolutionized their perceptions. In disturbing ways, the landscape of the war conformed to the canvases that modernist artists had painted in the decades before 1914. We saw in Chapter 23 that in these earlier decades, modernist styles and idioms were condemned as outrageous, degenerate, and removed from reality. By 1918, however, these forms seemed to offer an accurate, even realistic means of conveying the horror of the war experience. As the British cultural historian Samuel Hynes has argued, "modernism had not changed, but reality had."[9]

During the war many modernist artists abandoned "art for art's sake," the idea that art had no moral purpose or social responsibility, that it conveyed no message. Instead, they used their art to communicate their moral outrage against the war. Paul Nash (1889–1940), a British landscape painter and army volunteer, explained in 1918, "I am no longer an artist, interested and curious, I am a messenger who will bring back word from the men who are fighting to those who want the war to go on forever. . . . may it burn their lousy souls."[10] Before the war, Nash had painted pastoral scenes; his wartime experience, however, pushed him to employ modernist techniques. Nash's *We Are Making a New World* (1918)—a title dripping in irony—is one of the finest paintings produced during the war.

The war itself sometimes seemed like a modernist painting that had escaped its frame. The qualities that characterized a modernist painting—fragmentation, surprising juxtaposition, an emphasis on the isolation and the incommunicability of each individual's perception—also characterized a soldier's experience in the trenches. His vision is fragmented. Confined on all sides by mud walls, he can see only a bit of sky. When sent "over the top," he knows

only his own little part.* He cannot see the battlefield, or comprehend the battle plan, in its entirety. Every day he encounters surprising juxtapositions: a tired soldier resting against the wall of a trench out of which juts the arm of a corpse, for example. And in letters home he finds he simply cannot communicate to his parents or to his lover the reality in which he is living and expects to die.

Like modernist artists, soldiers quickly learned to question accepted truths, to mistrust the past, and to doubt the power of human reason. Recruited with promises of glory, they watched rats eat the bodies of their friends. While the generals clung to their history books, which taught that offensives won wars, soldiers died in great numbers. Not surprisingly, the modernist rejection of history resonated in the trenches. The past seemed to offer little of value in this new kind of war. Similarly, the war revealed the absurdity of the nineteenth-century faith in human reason. As the weeks, months, and years wore on, and the death tolls climbed higher and higher, many soldiers were struck by the senselessness, the sheer irrationality, of the conflict. The war, in fact, seemed to be governed not by rational men but rather by unthinking machines.

The mechanical nature of this war became a dominant theme in soldiers' accounts, just as machines dominated prewar modernist art. In this conflict, soldiers not only used machines, they became machines. Seeking the chance to be heroes, men volunteered to fight, and found themselves reduced to interchangeable parts in a colossal war machine. Like the gears on a machine, army companies moved in

---

* Now either a cliché applied to fund-raising drives or a colloquialism for "outrageous," the phrase over the top originated in World War I to describe the action of climbing out of a trench to mount an attack.

circles: from the firing trenches to the reserve trenches to the support trenches to behind the lines and back to the firing trenches. Thus in works such as *Returning to the Trenches*, British artist Christopher Nevinson (1889–1946) used modernist techniques to represent the reality of mechanized war. In Nevinson's work, the men cease to be individuals. Welded into a single machine, they are propelled into the trenches by a force beyond their control, components of a purely mechanized landscape. French war veteran and writer Georges Duhamel (1884–1966) even likened the front-line ambulances to factory repair shops. The function of the ambulances was to repair the broken-down parts (the soldiers) of the war machine and get them back into production.

War and Revolution

The machinery of total war tore at the social and political fabric of European societies. As seams began to fray and gaping holes appeared, many welcomed what they saw as the opportunity to tear apart the old cloth and create something entirely new. Some of these revolutionaries were Marxists aiming to build a socialist world order. Others were nationalists, determined to assert the rights of their ethnic or linguistic group. But it was not only in politics that total war opened the door to revolutionary change. Even relations between men and women faced a revolutionary challenge. Nor did all revolutionaries belong to underground terrorist groups. One individual who dared to demand a new world order was the president of the United States, Woodrow Wilson. The peace settlement, however, fell far short of creating a new Europe. Many of the conflicts that had caused the war remained unresolved, with disastrous consequences for the next generation.

THE WORLD TURNED UPSIDE DOWN

By the war's end, changes in the relations among classes and between men and women caused many Europeans to feel as if their world had turned upside down. Total war not only expanded the power of the state, it also enhanced the position of the working class. The result was a growing radicalism among European workers, as they realized the possibilities of their own collective power and the potential of the state as an instrument of social change. The fact that by 1917 many of these workers were women also had revolutionary implications. In the work world and in society at large, gender roles, like class relations, underwent a marked shift.

In the trenches and on the battlefields, the war had a leveling effect. For many young middle- and upper-class soldiers, the war provided their first sustained contact with both manual labor and manual laborers. In letters home, they testified to a newfound respect for both, as the horrors of the war experience broke down rigid class barriers.

On the home front, however, social relations grew more rather than less hostile. During the war years, inflation

THE BREAKDOWN OF CLASS BARRIERS

For many young middle- and upper-class officers, their time in the trenches offered their first sustained contact with men of the working class. Marc Bloch, who became one of the best-known historians of medieval Europe, was one of these young officers in the French army. In this excerpt from his war memoirs, Bloch records both his contempt for his commanders and his growing respect for his men.

I was by no means always satisfied with our officers. Often I found them insufficiently concerned with their men's well-being, too ignorant of their physical condition, and too uninterested to find out. The words "Let them cope". . . were still too often on their lips. . . .

When I remember the face of Corporal M., I cannot restrain a smile. He was a miner, stocky and rather heavy-footed, with a square face. . . . Though an indefatigable walker, he was unaccustomed to shoes, so he traveled the roads of Lorraine and Champagne barefoot. He was so careless and so stupid that it now seems to me I did little

during the first six weeks of the campaign but hunt for him from one end of the camp to the other, to transmit orders he never understood. But I should not forget that the last thing I did not succeed in making him understand, on the morning of September 10, was that his place was not at the head of the platoon. When we went into action that day, he fell, whether killed or wounded I do not know. . . .

Of all my comrades who fell in Champagne or the Argonne, there is none I mourned more than F., who was the sergeant of my second half platoon. F.'s line of work was not one usually considered important. He ran a shop for a wine merchant near the Bastille. He had scant education and could barely read. Yet no one has done more to make me understand the beauty of a truly noble and sensitive soul. . . . Unquestionably his main desire and his greatest effort was to ensure that his half platoon should "get along well together." When I lost him, I lost a moral support.

Source: From Marc Bloch, *Memoirs of War, 1914–15*, translated by Carole Fink (Cornell University Press, 1980), 161–166. Reprinted with the permission of Cambridge University Press.

■ Women in the War
Women often served at the front in extremely dangerous conditions. The two women in this photograph set up a dressing station to treat the wounded just five yards behind the trenches.

eroded the savings of the middle class and left bourgeois men and women desperately seeking ways to maintain their social and economic status. In Germany and throughout eastern Europe, drastic food shortages and falling real wages produced a revolutionary situation. By contrast, in both Britain and France, a rising standard of living demonstrated to workers the benefits of an active and interventionist state. After the disastrous "business as usual" approach of the first year of the war, the French and British governments recognized that maintaining civilian morale was crucial if industrial and agricultural production levels were to increase. The results were high wage rates and improved working conditions. In state-owned munitions factories, workers for the first time received benefits such as communal kitchens and day care. Food rationing (although not implemented until quite late in the war) actually improved the diets of many poor families. Yet the result of these new policies was not social peace. Class hostilities rose as workers, having finally tasted the economic pie, fought for a bigger piece, while the middle class fought to defend its shrinking share. Many workers began to demand that the state act on their behalf during peacetime as well.

Many of these workers were women. By 1916, labor shortages in key military industries, combined with the need to free up as many men as possible for fighting, meant that governments on both sides actively recruited women for the paid workforce. Women were suddenly everywhere in very visible roles: as bus drivers, elevator operators, train conductors, and sales clerks. In eastern Europe, the agricultural labor force came to consist almost entirely of women. In western Europe, women joined labor unions in unprece-

dented numbers. They took on extremely dangerous positions in munitions factories; they worked just behind the front lines as ambulance drivers and nurses; in 1917 and 1918, they often led the way in walking off the job to demand better conditions.

The impact of the war on women's roles should not be exaggerated, however. Throughout the war, more women continued to work in domestic service—as cooks, maids, nannies—than in any other sector of the economy. The great majority of those women who did move into skilled industrial employment were not new to the world of paid employment. Before 1914 they had worked in different, lower-paying jobs. And they certainly were not treated as men's equals. In government-run factories in Britain, women were paid as little as 50 percent of men's wages for the same job.

Nevertheless, for many women, the war constituted a profoundly liberating experience. With their husbands away, many wives made decisions on their own for the first time. The average wages of female munitions workers in Britain were three times higher than their prewar earnings. But just as crucially, the war validated women's claims to citizenship. Total war made the female civilian into a combatant. For example, the *Win the War Cookery Book* (1917) urged British housewives to view the preparation of meals in a time of food shortages as part of the war effort: "The British fighting line shifts and extends now *you* are in it. The struggle is not only on land and sea; it is in *your* larder, *your* kitchen and *your* dining room. Every meal you serve is now literally a battle."[11] With "women's work" as central to national survival as

Shell Shock: From Woman's Malady to Soldier's Affliction

Broken in mind as well as body, the casualties of World War I forced medical practitioners to think anew about the connections among emotional anguish, physical disabilities, and gender roles. Doctors discovered to their horror and surprise that in the trenches of total war, men's bodies began to act like women's. Pouring into hospital units came thousands of men with the symptoms of a malady that before the war was considered a woman's disease—hysteria.

The word *hysteria* comes from the Greek word *hystera*, for "womb" or "uterus," and for much of Western history doctors believed that women were doomed to suffer from hysteria because of their physical makeup—because they were afflicted with wombs. Physicians long considered the uterus to be an inherently weak and unstable organ, prone even to detach itself from its proper place and wander about the body causing havoc. By the end of the nineteenth century, however, the diagnosis had changed. Doctors continued to regard hysteria as primarily a woman's disease but they were more inclined to view it as a neurosis, a mental and emotional disorder. The symptoms varied enormously but included bouts of shrieking, emotional problems such as depression or breakdown, and physical ailments without any clear physical cause—ranging from abnormal fatigue or insomnia to the inability to walk.

With war came thousands of soldiers with the symptoms of hysteria—men who could not stop shaking, men with healthy limbs who could not move, men certain that rats were nibbling at their bodies. At first, doctors dismissed such symptoms as signs of cowardice: These were men faking illness to avoid doing their duty. But by 1916, with such men accounting for 40 percent of the casualties in British combat zones alone, doctors realized they were dealing with an epidemic of male hysteria.

The war illustrated that hysteria was linked not to the uterus or the weak female nervous system but rather to an environment of immobility and passivity. Neither the length of time a soldier had served nor the intensity or horror of his combat experience were significant in producing breakdowns. Instead, the most important factor was his level of immobility. Men on the Western Front suddenly found themselves in positions of passivity and confinement. Deprived of the ability to make decisions, to determine their future, to act, many men broke down.

Yet the reincarnation of what had been considered a woman's malady as a soldier's affliction did not lead doctors to reexamine their understanding of the woman's body or the woman's role. Instead, they reconfigured the disease. Hysteria became "shell shock." The treatment differed as well. Convinced that female hysteria was a result of the overstimulation of the nervous system, doctors prescribed total rest cures for their female patients. Women found themselves confined to rooms with bare walls and shuttered windows, forbidden to read or to receive visitors. In contrast, doctors ordered male soldiers with shell shock to engage in intense physical and mental activity. Thus, despite the upheaval in gender roles caused by total war, doctors continued to view women's bodies as inherently passive and men's as naturally active. The findings of medical science remained linked to cultural conventions. ■

■ Shell Shock

French troops under artillery fire during the Battle of Verdun, 1916. Such battles produced psychological as well as physical casualties.

For Discussion

Why does the contrast between the medical treatment of hysteria and that of shell shock indicate that the war had a limited impact on gender roles? What evidence in this chapter points to the opposite conclusion?

men's work, women were regarded as an integral part of the national community.

Middle-class women, especially, testified to the freedom the war brought. Before 1914, the position of middle-class women in Europe had undergone important changes, as Chapter 22 detailed. From 1870 on, the numbers of women in higher education and paid employment expanded, women increasingly served in local government, and a European-wide women's suffrage campaign emerged. Despite the rise of these strong challenges to the ideology of separate spheres, however, the predominant idea remained that women were biologically suited for the private confines of home and family, and men for the public arena of work and politics. Many middle-class girls continued to live lives marked by immobility and passivity—sheltered within the family home, subject to paternal authority, waiting for a marriage proposal. The war, however, threw women into the public space. The middle-class girl who before 1914 was forbidden to travel without a chaperone might be driving an ambulance, splashing through the mud and blood, or washing the bodies of naked working-class soldiers.

At the same time that the war smashed many of the boundaries to which women had been confined, it sharply narrowed the world of the middle-class male soldier. While women were in charge and on the move—driving buses, flying transport planes, ferrying the wounded— men were stuck in the mud, confined to narrow ditches, waiting for orders. Expecting to be heroes, men of action, they found themselves instead living the sort of immobile, passive lives that had characterized the prewar middle-class women's experience. Ironically, then, at the same time the war gave women new power, it introduced many men, particularly middle-class men, to new levels of powerlessness. In total war, even gender roles turned upside down.

Yet when the war ended, some of these radical changes proved to be very temporary indeed. The much-heralded wartime movement of women into skilled factory jobs and public positions such as bus drivers and train conductors was rapidly reversed. For example, by the terms of the British Restoration of Pre-War Practices Act (1919), women who had taken up skilled factory jobs received two weeks' pay and a train ticket home.

Other changes appeared more permanent. In France in 1919, there were ten times as many female law students and three times as many female medical students as there had been in 1914. British women over age 30 received the vote on a limited basis while in the United States, Germany, and most of the new states in eastern Europe, the achievement of female suffrage was more complete. (Women in France, Italy, Switzerland, and Greece remained unenfranchised.) Cultural changes also seemed to signal a gender revolution. Women began to smoke in public; trousers became acceptable female attire;

hemlines rose dramatically; the corset and bustle disappeared for good.

THE RUSSIAN REVOLUTIONS

Tsarist Russia also disappeared. It began the war already sharply divided, its 125 million inhabitants splintered into more than one hundred different national groups—from Inuits in the north to Kazakhs in the southeast to Germans in the west. Ethnic hostilities sapped Russia's defenses from the very start. In Poland, for example, many of the four million Jews under Russian imperial rule welcomed the German army as liberators from tsarist violence and repression. In the regions of Latvia and Lithuania, anti-Russian sentiment flared high, and nationalists saw the war as opening the door to national independence.

The war brought political chaos to Russia. Nicholas II (r. 1894–1917), a man of limited intelligence and a remarkable capacity for self-delusion, insisted on going to the front and commanding his army. He left political affairs in the hands of his wife Alexandra (1872–1918) and her spiritual mentor Grigorii Rasputin (1869–1916). Rasputin is one of the more intriguing characters in twentieth-century history. An illiterate, unwashed faith healer from a peasant background, he possessed a well-documented and still-unexplained ability to stop the bleeding of Alexei, the young hemophiliac heir to the throne. To many high-ranking Russians, however, Rasputin was not a miracle worker but a traitor. Because Rasputin opposed the war against Germany, they perceived him as a voice of treason whispering in the German-born tsarina's ear. In 1916 Russian noblemen murdered Rasputin, in hopes of restoring authority and stability to the tsarist government.

The March Revolution

Rasputin's removal was not enough to stop the forces of revolution stirred up by total war. The political disarray he observed at the highest levels of government dumbfounded the French ambassador, who wrote in January 1917, "I am obliged to report that, at the present moment, the Russian Empire is run by lunatics."[12] The lack of effective political leadership, combined with Russian losses on the battlefield, brought to a boil the simmering disaffection with the tsarist government. Almost two million Russian soldiers had died and many more had been wounded or taken prisoner. Economic and communications networks had broken down, bread prices were rising, and people were hungry. Even members of the tsarist government began to ask not *if* revolution would occur, but *when.*

The answer came on March 8, 1917. A group of women workers in Petrograd staged a demonstration to protest against inadequate food supplies. Over the course of the next few days, similar demonstrations flickered across the city; on March 11, they coalesced into a major revolutionary fire when the troops who were ordered to put down the

REVOLUTION IN THE FRONT LINES

At age 25, Maria Botchkareva, a poor Russian woman who had been forced to work as a prostitute, volunteered for service as a soldier. Women served as nurses, ambulance drivers, and transport plane pilots on both sides of the war, but only in Russia did women serve in combat, and even there the presence of a woman on the front lines was quite exceptional. Botchkareva earned a well-deserved reputation as a fierce fighter, and was honored for her bravery. In 1917, she was serving at the front with her company when she heard startling news from the capital.

The first swallow to warn us of the approaching storm was a soldier from our Company who had returned from a leave of absence at Petrograd: "Oh my! If you but knew, boys, what is going on in the rear! Revolution! Everywhere they talk of overthrowing the Tsar. The capital is aflame with revolution.". . . Finally, the joyous news arrived. The Commander gathered the entire Regiment to read to us the glorious words. . . . The miracle had happened! Tsarism, which enslaved us and thrived on the blood and marrow of the toiler, had fallen. Freedom, Equality and Brotherhood! How sweet were these words to our ears! We were transported. There were tears of joy, embraces, dancing. It all seemed a dream, a wonderful dream. Who ever believed that the hated regime would be destroyed so easily and in our own time?

The Commander read to us the manifesto, which concluded with a fervent appeal to us to hold the line with greater vigilance than ever, now that we were free citizens, to defend our newly won liberty from the attacks of the Kaiser and his slaves. . . . Then came Order No. 1, signed by the Petrograd Soviet of Workmen and Soldiers. Soldiers and officers were now equal, it declared. All the citizens of Free Russia were equal henceforth. . . .

We were dazzled by this shower of brilliant phrases. The men went about as if intoxicated. For four days the festival continued unabated. . . . There were meetings, meetings, and meetings. . . . All duty was abandoned. . . . The front became a veritable insane asylum.

One day, in the first week of the revolution, I ordered a soldier to take up duty at the listening-post. He refused.

Source: From Maria Botchkareva, *Yashka: My Life as Peasant, Officer and Exile* (New York: Frederick A. Stokes Company, 1919), 139–145.

protest joined it instead. Governmental orders lost all authority, and on March 15 Tsar Nicholas was forced to abdicate. The Russian Revolution had begun.

Who now controlled Russia? Two competing centers of power soon emerged: the Provisional Government and the Petrograd Soviet. On March 12, the Duma, or Russian parliament, created a Provisional Government from among its members. Like the Duma, the new Provisional Government was dominated by members of the gentry and middle classes: professionals, businessmen, intellectuals, bureaucrats. These men tended to be liberals who believed that Russia was now moving along the path toward a parliamentary democracy. They quickly enacted important reforms such as universal suffrage, the eight-hour workday, and civic equality for all citizens.

But at the same time that the Provisional Government was struggling to bring order to the chaos of revolutionary Russia, across the empire industrial workers and soldiers formed soviets°, or councils, to articulate their grievances and hopes. As Russian revolutionary socialists in exile across Europe returned to their homeland in the weeks after the March Revolution began, they assumed leading roles in the Petrograd Soviet, which soon became a powerful political rival to the less radical Provisional Government.

The revolution, however, did not originate with nor was it controlled by either the liberals in the Provisional Government or the socialists in the Petrograd Soviet.

Nicholas II was overthrown by a popular revolution, and at the core of this popular revolution stood a simply stated demand: "Peace, Land, Bread." Soldiers—and most Russians—wanted an immediate end to a war that had long ceased to make any sense to them. Peasants, as always, wanted land, their guarantee of survival in a chaotic world. And city dwellers wanted bread—food in sufficient quantities and at affordable prices.

The Provisional Government could not satisfy these demands. It did promise the gradual redistribution of royal and monastic lands, but peasants, inspired by the revolution and unconstrained by the liberal regard for law and the rights of private property, wanted land immediately. More important, by the summer of 1917 no Russian government could have provided bread without providing peace. Russia no longer had the resources both to continue its war effort and to reconstruct its economy. The population of the cities began to dwindle as food disappeared from the shops, factories ceased operation because of shortages of raw materials, and currency had little value. Peace appeared impossible, however. Not only did Russia have commitments to its allies, but German armies stood deep within Russian territory. A separate peace with Germany would mean huge territorial losses. And so the war continued.

But so, too, did the revolution. Peasants effected their own land reform by simply seizing the land they wanted.

■ **Red Square**
Lenin inspires the crowds gathered in Moscow's Red Square on May Day 1918.

Soldiers declared their own peace by deserting in huge numbers. (Of every 1,000-man troop sent to the front, fewer than 250 men actually made it into combat. The rest deserted.) The Provisional Government grew increasingly unpopular. Not even the appointment of the popular socialist and Petrograd Soviet member Alexander Kerensky (1881–1970) as prime minister could stabilize the government's position.

The November Revolution

This tumultuous situation created the opportunity for the Bolsheviks°, one of the socialist factions in the Petrograd Soviet, to emerge as a powerful revolutionary force. In April 1917, the Bolshevik leader, Vladimir Lenin (1870–1924), returned from almost twenty years in exile. While still in his teens, Lenin had committed himself to revolution, after his older brother was executed for trying to assassinate Tsar Alexander III. Iron-willed and ruthlessly pragmatic, Lenin argued that a committed group of professional revolutionaries could force a working-class revolution on Russia immediately.

By the fall of 1917, Bolshevik membership had grown from 10,000 to 250,000, and the party had achieved a majority in the Petrograd Soviet. Lenin now demanded the immediate overthrow of the Provisional Government. "Insurrection is an art," he declared, something to be made, not something that happens spontaneously. By promising "Peace, Land, Bread," Lenin would take control. On November 9, Bolshevik fighters captured the Winter Palace in Petrograd, where the Provisional Government had been sitting.

The *second* Russian Revolution was underway. The Bolsheviks declared a policy of land and peace—land partition with no payment of compensation to estate owners

and an immediate peace with Germany, regardless of the cost. (And as we have seen, the cost was high: According to the terms of the Treaty of Brest-Litovsk, signed with Germany in 1918, Russia lost its western territories.) Not everyone in Russia was won over by promises of peace and land, however. Confronted with a diverse array of opponents, the Bolsheviks turned to the methods of terror. After an assassination attempt against Lenin in August 1918, the Bolshevik secret police received the power to execute without trial. More than 500 individuals were shot in a single day in Petrograd.

During the next two years, the Bolsheviks waged a brutal war against domestic and international opponents of their Communist Revolution. This civil war proved Lenin's

CHRONOLOGY	
Revolution in Russia, 1917–1921	
1917	
March 8	St. Petersburg/Petrograd women's protest; revolution begins
March 12	Establishment of Provisional Government
March 15	Abdication of Tsar Nicholas II
November 9	Bolshevik overthrow of the Provisional Government
1918–1921	Civil war

Revolutionary Justice: The Nontrial of Nicholas and Alexandra

On July 16, 1918, Bolshevik revolutionaries shot and killed Nicholas II, Tsar of Russia; his wife, the Tsarina Alexandra; his heir, 14-year-old Alexei; their four daughters—Olga (age 23), Tatiana (age 21), Maria (age 19), and Anastasia (age 17); their three servants; and their physician. When news of the deaths reached other countries, the killings were condemned as murders. The Bolsheviks, however, termed them executions, acts of revolutionary justice.

When Nicholas II abdicated on March 15, 1917, after twenty-three years on the throne, he expected to embark on a life of exile in Britain. Instead, the Provisional Government placed the tsar and his family under house arrest, and appointed a Commission of Inquiry to investigate the persistent rumors that the tsar's German-born wife had conspired with Germany to destroy Russia. The Commission found no evidence to convict the tsar or his wife of treason, but by the autumn of 1917, its findings were irrelevant. The war with Germany was effectively over, whereas the war against all that the tsar had stood for had just begun.

The civil war that followed the Bolshevik Revolution proved fatal for the royal family. Faced with counter-revolutionary challenges on all sides, the Bolsheviks feared that if Nicholas escaped, he would serve as a symbolic center for these antirevolutionary forces. They decided to move him to a region firmly under Bolshevik control. In April 1918, a special train transported the tsar and his family to Ekaterinburg (about 900 miles east of Moscow), where they were placed in the hands of the Bolshevik-dominated Ural Regional Soviet. Meanwhile, the revolutionary Bolshevik government prepared to try Nicholas publicly for his crimes against the Russian people. The charge was no longer secret contacts with Germany—the Bolsheviks themselves had negotiated with Germany and ended Russia's participation in the war—but rather the tsar's both real and symbolic leadership of a politically repressive regime. Leon Trotsky, the head of the Petrograd Soviet, planned to present the case against Nicholas.

But the case was never made. By July, an anti-Bolshevik army was approaching Ekaterinburg from the east. If these troops freed the imperial family, they would score a crucial victory. Told that Ekaterinburg might fall to the enemy within days, the Ural Soviet decided to execute the tsar and his family immediately, most likely with Lenin's approval.

Pavel Medvedev, one of the tsar's guards, later offered a detailed account of the events of the evening of July 16. His interviewer recorded what Medvedev had told him:

> [He said,] The Tsar, the Tsaritsa [Tsarina], the Tsar's four daughters, the doctor, the cook and the lackey came out of their rooms. The Tsar was carrying the heir [Alexei] in his arms. . . . In my presence there were no tears, no sobs and no questions. . . .

Medvedev then testified that he was ordered out of the room. When he returned a few minutes later:

> . . . he saw all the members of the Tsar's family lying on the floor with numerous wounds to their bodies. The blood was gushing. The heir was still alive—and moaning. [The commander] walked over to him and shot him two or three times at point blank range. The heir fell still.[13]

What Medvedev's understated account did not relate were the more gruesome details of the execution. In an effort to preserve part of the family fortune, the tsar's daughters were wearing corsets into which had been sewn diamonds. When they were shot, the bullets, in the words of one eyewitness, "ricocheted, jumping around the room like hail."[14] Even after several pistols were emptied, one of the girls remained alive. The guards resorted to bayonets.

The killing of not only the tsar but also his wife and children was a startling act, as the Bolsheviks themselves recognized. The Ural Regional Soviet announced the tsar's execution, but said nothing about his family, while the official statement from Moscow reported that "the wife and son of Nicholas Romanov were sent to a safe place."[15]

These omissions and lies reveal the Bolsheviks' own uneasiness with the killings. Why, then, was the entire family shot? The Bolsheviks' determination to win the civil war regardless of the cost provides part of the answer. According to Trotsky, Lenin "believed we shouldn't leave the Whites [the anti-Bolshevik forces] a live banner to rally around."[16] Any of the tsar's children could have served as such a banner. The rapid approach of the White army meant the royal family had to be disposed of quickly. But Trotsky also viewed the killings as an essential and absolute break with the past. In his words, "the execution of the Tsar's family was needed not only to frighten, horrify, and to dishearten the enemy, but also in order to shake up our own ranks, to show them that there was no turning back, that ahead lay either complete victory or complete ruin."[17] For the Bolsheviks, there was no middle ground.

The killing of Tsar Nicholas and his family thus forms part of the pattern of escalating violence that characterized the First World War's revolutionary aftermath. But in the blood of these killings we can also see reflected two ideas that had a powerful impact on postwar political life—first, the subordination of law to the revolutionary State; second, the concept of collective guilt.

The Bolsheviks offered a different idea of justice. As a Bolshevik publication explained in a discussion of the tsar's killing:

> *Many formal aspects of bourgeois justice may have been violated. . . . However, worker-peasant power was manifested in the process, making no exception for the All-Russian murderer, shooting as if he were an ordinary brigand. . . . Nicholas the Bloody is no more.*[18]

In the Bolshevik model, the law was not separate from but rather subordinate to the state. Legal rights and requirements—the "formal aspects of bourgeois justice"—could be suspended in the service of "worker peasant power," as embodied in the revolutionary state.

This concept of the law subordinate to the state helps us understand the tsar's execution without trial; the concept of collective guilt provides a context for the killing of his children. The Bolshevik model of socialism assumed that *class* constituted objective reality. Simply by belonging to a certain social class, an individual could be—and was—designated an enemy of the revolution. The Bolshevik constitution equated citizenship with social class. Workers and peasants received the vote, but seven categories of people, such as those who lived off investment interest, were disenfranchised. For the next two decades, aristocratic and middle-class origins served as an indelible ink, marking a person permanently as an enemy of the revolutionary state—regardless of that person's own actions or inclinations. Thus, from the Bolshevik perspective, the tsar's children bore the taint of their royal origins. When their continuing existence threatened the revolution, they were shot. Over the next four decades, the concept of collective guilt would result in the deaths of millions in the new Soviet Union.

When World War I ended and representatives of the Allied victors met in Paris in 1919 to build the new postwar world, they sought to establish nationalist-based democracies, in which the rule of law would guarantee the rights of individuals. These two interlinked concepts of law and human rights became for many the defining features of "the West," of democracy, and of civilization itself. The Bolsheviks challenged this definition. They offered instead a definition of democracy based on class and an understanding of the law resting on the demands of continuing revolution. ■

Questions of Justice

1. In what ways did the Bolshevik refusal to accept bourgeois principles of justice mean that the newly established Soviet Union placed itself outside the boundaries of the West?

2. Compare and contrast attitudes toward the law and "revolutionary justice" in the "nontrial" of Tsar Nicholas with those revealed in the trials of Charles I in seventeenth-century England and Louis XVI in eighteenth-century France. (See "Justice in History" in Chapters 15 and 19.) What factors explain the differences?

Taking It Further

Kozlov, Vladimir, and Vladimir Khrustalëv. *The Last Diary of Tsaritsa Alexandra.* 1997. Translation of the tsarina's diary from 1918.

Rosenberg, William, ed. *Bolshevik Visions: First Phase of the Cultural Revolution in Soviet Russia.* 1990. The section on "Proletarian Legality" explores the Bolsheviks' effort to develop a legal system that embodied their revolutionary ideals.

Steinberg, Mark, and Vladimir Khrustalëv. *The Fall of the Romanovs.* 1999. Detailed account of the last two years of the tsar and his family, based on recently opened archives.

■ **Tsar Nicholas II and Family**
Tsar Nicholas II, the Tsarina Alexandra, and their family.

■ **Spartacist Revolution**

The effort to establish a soviet government in Berlin took the form of street fighting. This photograph shows one street skirmish that occurred in the city's newspaper district.

promises of "Peace, Land, Bread" to be hollow. Peasant farms were transformed into battlefields as five years of civil war killed off more combatants than had World War I. In the resulting famine, death tolls reached as high as five million. Yet, as the next chapter shows, the Bolsheviks emerged victorious. The Russian Empire was remade as the Soviet Union, a communist state.

THE SPREADING REVOLUTION

The victory of the Bolsheviks in Russia inspired socialists across Europe and around the world. In January 1919, communists in Buenos Aires, Argentina, led by Russian immigrants, controlled the city for three days until they were crushed by the Argentine army. British dockworkers struck in support of the Bolshevik Revolution, and in French cities general strikes caused chaos. In Austria, revolutionaries attempted to take control of government buildings in Vienna but were quickly defeated by the Austrian army. In Hungary, Bela Kun, a journalist who had come to admire the Bolsheviks while a prisoner of war in Russia, established a short-lived soviet regime in the spring of 1919.

Revolution also swept through defeated Germany. Disillusion with the kaiser's regime had set in long before Germany had lost the war. Defeat simply accentuated the desire for radical political change. But the first revolutionary step in Germany was a response not to popular desire but to American demands. In October 1918, Germany's military commanders recommended that the German government enter into peace negotiations. U.S. President Woodrow Wilson, however, saw the war as a democratic crusade and so refused to allow the Allies to negotiate with representatives of the kaiser's authoritarian regime. To placate Wilson, the kaiser was forced to overhaul Germany's political system. For the first time, representatives of left-wing and centrist parties—including the SPD, the largest socialist party in Europe—were invited to join the government.

This "revolution from above" coincided with and was challenged by a "revolution from below." Inspired by the success of the Bolshevik Revolution, many German workers rejected the SPD's vision of socialism as too moderate. The members of the SPD believed in working for gradual social reform through parliamentary action and debate. A much more radical alternative was offered by a breakaway socialist faction called the Spartacists (after Spartacus, the gladiator who led a slave revolt against Rome in the first century B.C.E.). Directed by Karl Liebknecht (1871–1919) and Rosa Luxemburg (1870–1919), the Spartacists wanted Germany to follow Russia down the path to communist revolution. In Berlin, thousands rallied behind Liebknecht and Luxemburg. By November 8, communists had declared the establishment of a Soviet republic in the province of Bavaria; the Red Flag—symbol of communism—was flying over eleven German cities; and revolutionaries had seized control of all the main railroad junctions.

On November 9, the head of the SPD, Friedrich Ebert (1871–1925), became chancellor of Germany and the kaiser abdicated. One of Ebert's colleagues in the SPD triumphantly proclaimed from the window of the Reichstag building in Berlin that Germany was now a parliamentary democracy. Almost at that very moment, Karl Liebknecht stood at another window (in the occupied royal palace) and announced that Germany was now a revolutionary communist state. With two opposing versions of revolution on offer, civil war raged until the spring of 1919, when the SPD defeated the communists for control of the new Germany.

THE NATIONALIST REVOLUTIONS

In both Germany and Russia, the war created the opportunity for *social* revolution. In other areas, both within and outside Europe, the war kindled the fires of *nationalist* revolution. As the war progressed, both sides used nationalism against the enemy. The British, for example, fostered Arab nationalism to undermine Ottoman strength while the

Germans sought to encourage uprisings in both India and Ireland as a way to weaken Britain. For peoples seeking political statehood, the war held great promise.

The Disintegration of Austria-Hungary

Nationalist divisions plagued Austria-Hungary from the very start of the war. On the average, of every 100 soldiers mobilized, twenty-five spoke German, twenty-three Magyar, thirteen Czech, nine Serbo-Croatian, eight Polish, eight Ukrainian, seven Romanian, five Slovak, three Slovene, and one Italian.[19] Such linguistic confusion created overwhelming administrative and logistical difficulties. But much more important, this linguistic diversity symbolized a lack of the fundamental national cohesion needed to unite the empire's peoples behind the war effort. Large sections of the population of the Austrian-Hungarian Empire opposed the war; both Czech and Serb soldiers defected to the Russian side. Throughout the war years, minority groups within the empire faced brutal repression. Over 500 Bosnian Serbs and hundreds of Ukrainians were shot without trial because they sympathized with the enemy.

When the war turned decisively against the Central Powers in 1918, Austria-Hungary broke into pieces. In May, mutinies erupted among Slovenian, Ruthenian, Serbian, and Czech troops. Throughout the summer of 1918, the Allied army advanced up from Greece through the Balkan peninsula, and restored independent status to Serbia, Albania, and Montenegro. Inspired by the resurrection of these nationalist states and sure that Austria-Hungary was defeated, nationalist politicians made their move. By the end of October, they had declared independent governments in Poland, Hungary, Czechoslovakia, and what would become Yugoslavia.

Promises in the Middle East

World War I also resulted in the collapse of the Ottoman Empire. When war broke out in 1914, Ottoman control still stretched far into the Middle East, embracing Palestine and the western coast of the Red Sea. As we have seen, this region became a key battleground, with both oil and the Suez Canal as strong lures for the armies of both sides. Allied victory and the collapse of the Ottoman Empire opened the door to revolutionary change. As in eastern Europe, a new map would have to be drawn and new political structures erected.

The defeat of the Ottoman forces in this region owed an enormous debt to the revolutionary impact of Arab nationalism. By the late nineteenth century, Arab intellectuals had begun to dream of overthrowing Ottoman rule. When war came, Arab nationalists joined with the Allies to defeat the Ottoman forces. The British welcomed Arab support with promises of Arab national independence after the war.

But the British also promised to support a Jewish state in the same region. Eager to win the backing of the American Jewish community for U.S. participation in the war, the British government in 1917 issued the Balfour Declaration°, a pledge of British support for a Jewish national homeland in Palestine. With Jews often the first victims of escalating hatred and ethnic violence, the Zionist argument that Jews needed their own nation-state seemed more and more compelling to many Europeans. To the 700,000 Arabs living in Palestine, however, the Balfour Declaration was a betrayal. Contradictory promises of an independent Palestinian homeland made to both Arabs and Jews set the stage for disaster in future decades.

War and the European Empires

The Middle East was not the only region in which the war heightened nationalist aspirations. In Ireland, revolutionary nationalists saw the war as an opportunity for revolt. Counting on the war to distract the British, they mounted an armed rebellion on Easter Monday in 1916. Quickly and brutally suppressed, the "Easter Rising" was fairly unusual: Few colonial territories saw armed uprisings during the war years. But throughout the regions of European empires, the desire for political independence gained in strength as the war changed economic relationships and strengthened nationalist identities.

The war eroded many of the economic connections between European nations and their empires. Germany's submarine warfare and the Allies' blockade sharply limited both the imports of colonial raw materials and foods into Europe and the exports of European industrial products to the imperial territories. The war thus stimulated the development of more diversified and industrialized—and therefore more independent—economies in regions such as Australia, India, South Africa, and much of South America.

Less directly, but just as important, the war undermined the sense of superiority that had bolstered European imperialism. In the latter decades of the nineteenth century, imperialist ideologues defended empire making as the spread of a superior civilization to primitive regions and peoples. They described inhabitants of Asia, Africa, and South America as barbarians who needed the guidance and discipline of the more advanced European white races. But by 1918, in the wake of the war, at least some Europeans were asking, "Who is the barbarian now?"

In what the British called the "white Dominions"— Australia, New Zealand, Canada, and South Africa—the war accelerated the formation of national as opposed to imperial identities. By 1914, these regions had already received a great deal of autonomy within the structure of the British Empire, with the nonwhite populations firmly subjugated to the white colonial classes. When the British government declared war against Germany, the Dominions found themselves at war as well. Serving as part of the British forces, the Dominion regiments nonetheless remained distinct— Canadians fought alongside Canadians, Australians with Australians. The performance of these Dominion troops during the war became a matter of intense national pride.

For example, in 1915, British political and military leaders devised a plan to win the war by heading up the Gallipoli peninsula to the Ottoman capital of Constantinople. (See Map 24.4). On April 25, British and ANZAC troops moved onto the peninsula. At one of the landing sites, the troops were put ashore on the wrong beach, a narrow stretch of sand butting against tall cliffs on the top of which sat Turkish soldiers armed with machine guns. It was an impossible situation, yet for the next six months they clung there, heroically if futilely, until at last British commanders admitted defeat and evacuated the peninsula. For many Australians, the word *Gallipoli* became synonymous with national suffering and national courage. The heroism of their soldiers (and what they perceived as the stupidity of the British planners) accentuated their sense of themselves as Australian rather than British.

The war proved even more influential—and more destabilizing—in imperial territories without large white populations. Small nationalist movements existed in many of these regions before 1914, but the war strengthened and energized them. In Egypt, British requisitions of food, livestock, and forced labor aroused great resentment and fostered the birth of the Wafd, a nationalist group fighting for Egyptian independence. Throughout the British empire, Muslims faced divided loyalties. If they fought for Britain, they fought against their religious leader, the caliph, sultan of the Ottoman Empire. Discontent spread among non-Muslims as well. In countries such as India, which lost almost 50,000 of its soldiers in the war, more and more people—Hindu and Muslim—began to question the right of a small group of men in a government far, far away to involve their people in a war.

The nationalist cause in India took on added impetus in 1916 when a British-educated lawyer returned from South Africa, where he had spent twenty years fighting to improve the lot of indentured Indian laborers. As the war was drawing to a close, Mohandas Gandhi (1869–1948) introduced India and the world to a new form of revolution. He called on his followers to fight the British not with armed weapons but with moral force—with nonviolent protest and civil disobedience. Unlike many revolutionaries (such as Lenin), Gandhi did not believe that a small elite could or should dictate the course of events. He transformed Indian nationalism from the pastime of Western-educated intellectuals to a mass movement. By the end of the war, he and his followers stood ready to challenge British rule over India.

WILSON'S REVOLUTION

At the beginning of 1919, the representatives of the victorious Allied nations gathered in Paris to draw up the treaties that would wrap up the war. Yet their aims were far higher

■ Wilson and the Peace
Setting sail for the Paris Peace Conference on December 4, 1918, Wilson believed he was also embarking on a journey in which he would lead Europe into political democracy and international peace.

than simply ending the war; they wished to construct a new Europe and to reconfigure the conduct of international affairs. At the center of this high endeavor was the American college-professor-turned-president Woodrow Wilson. Like the Bolsheviks, Wilson offered a vision of a radical new future. He based *his* version of revolutionary change on the ideal of national self-determination—a world in which "every people should be left free to determine its own polity, its own way of development, unhindered, unthreatened, unafraid, the little along with the great and powerful." The map of Europe would be redrawn, the old empires replaced with independent, ethnically homogenous, democratic nation-states (see Map 24.6).

These new nation-states would interact differently from the empires of the past. In what he called his Fourteen Points, Wilson demanded a revolution in international affairs. He argued that "Points" such as freedom of the seas, freedom of trade, and open diplomacy (an end to secret treaties) would break down barriers and guarantee peace and prosperity for all peoples. The cornerstone of this new world order would be an international organization, the League of Nations°, which would oversee the implementation of these new measures and would have the power to resolve disputes between nations. Wilson and other planners of the postwar era envisioned the league as a truly revolutionary organization, one that would guarantee that World War I was "the war to end all wars." To replace the system of secret diplomacy and Great Power alliances that had led to the horrors of total war, the league offered an international forum in which all states, big and small, European and non-European, would have a voice and in which negotiations would be conducted openly and democratically. War would become outmoded.

THE FAILURE OF THE PEACE SETTLEMENT

At the end of the war, then, Europe seemed to stand on the brink of revolutionary change. But as we shall see in Chapter 25, soaring social and political expectations went unrealized, as Europeans sought not to build a new world but to reconstruct the one the war had obliterated. The peace treaties that ended the war played a crucial role in shattering the

■ **Map 24.6 Europe and the Middle East after World War I**
A comparison of this map with Map 24.1 on page 793 illustrates the vital role played by the war in shaping eastern Europe and the Middle East.

dreams of a new Europe and in undermining the international political and economic stability of the postwar era. In Paris in 1919 and 1920, the Allies and their defeated enemies signed a series of treaties named after the French palaces in which they were signed—the Treaty of Versailles, with Germany; the Treaty of St. Germain, with Austria; the Treaty of Neuilly, with Bulgaria; the Treaty of Trianon, with Hungary; and the Treaty of Sèvres, with Turkey. In drawing up the treaties, the Allies' writers sought to create a new international order based on three features: a democratic Germany, national self-determination in eastern Europe, and the League of Nations. They failed in all three areas.

The Treaty of Versailles and German Democracy

At the center of the new Europe envisioned by Woodrow Wilson was to be a new democratic Germany. French leader Georges Clemenceau did not share this vision. He had lived through two German invasions of his homeland and wished to ensure that Germany could never again threaten France. Clemenceau proposed the creation of a Rhineland state out of Germany's industrialized western region, both as a neutral buffer zone between France and Germany and as a way to reduce Germany's economic power. The British leader, David Lloyd George, who had just won an election on the campaign slogan "Hang the Kaiser" and who had promised his people that he would squeeze Germany "until the pips squeak," publicly supported Clemenceau's hardline approach to the peace settlement with Germany. In private, however, he expressed fear that such an approach would backfire by feeding the flames of German resentment and undermining the structures of German democracy.

Lloyd George's fears proved well-grounded. The German people bitterly resented the Versailles Treaty°, which they perceived as unjustly punitive. By the terms of the treaty, Germany lost all of its overseas colonies, 13 percent of its European territory, 10 percent of its population, and its ability to wage war. The German army was limited to a defensive force of 100,000 men and was allowed no aircraft or tanks. Clemenceau failed in his effort to create a separate Rhineland state, but the Rhineland was demilitarized, emptied of German soldiers and fortifications. In addition, the coalfields of the Saar region were ceded to France for fifteen years. Even more significantly, the Versailles Treaty declared that German aggression had caused the war, and therefore that Germany must recompense the Allies for its cost. In 1921, the Allies presented Germany with a bill for reparations° of 132 billion marks ($31.5 billion). As we will see in the next chapter, this reparations clause set up an economic cycle that was to prove devastating for both global prosperity and German democratic politics.

The Failure of National Self-Determination

The map of Europe drawn by the peace treaties appeared to signal the establishment of a new international order.

The old authoritarian empires of eastern and central Europe disappeared, replaced with independent nation-states. In keeping with the principle of national self-determination, Poland once again became an independent nation, with pieces carved out of the German, Austrian, and Russian empires. One entirely new state was formed out of the rubble of the Austrian-Hungarian Empire—Czechoslovakia. Romania, Greece, and Italy all expanded as a result of serving on the winners' side, while Serbia became the heart of the new Yugoslavia. The defeated nations shrunk, some dramatically. Austria, for example, became a mere rump of what had been the mighty Habsburg Empire, while Hungary was reduced to one-third of its prewar size. All that remained of the Ottoman Empire was Turkey.

These changes were heralded as the victory of "national self-determination." But as Woodrow Wilson's own secretary of state, Robert Lansing, complained, "This phrase is simply loaded with dynamite. It will raise hopes which can never be realized." Wilson had called for "every people" to be left free to determine its political destiny—but who constituted "a people"? Did, for example, the Macedonians? Should there be an independent Macedonia? Macedonians said yes, but the Paris peace negotiators answered no. Macedonia was enveloped by Yugoslavia and Greece, and in consequence, throughout the 1920s and 1930s Macedonians waged a terrorist campaign in the Balkans. Wilson's peaceful new world seemed far, far away when in 1923, a Macedonian nationalist group kidnapped the Bulgarian prime minister, chopped off his head, and sliced off his limbs.

The Macedonians were far from the only dissatisfied ethnic group in eastern Europe. Even after the peace settlements redrew the map, no fewer than 30 million eastern Europeans remained members of minority groups. Less than 70 percent of Hungarians, for example, lived in Hungary—more than three million were scattered in other states. Over nine million Germans resided outside the borders of Germany. In the newly created Czechoslovakia, one-third of the population was neither Czech nor Slovak. The new state of Yugoslavia contained an uneasy mixture of several ethnic groups, most resentful of the dominant Serbs. Rather than satisfying nationalist ambitions, then, the peace settlements served to inflame them, thus creating a volatile situation for the post–World War I world.

The Limits of the League

True to Wilson's vision of a new international order, the treaty makers included the Covenant of the League of Nations in each of the treaties. The league, however, never realized Wilson's high hopes of making war obsolete. Three factors help explain the league's failure. First, it did not represent every state. When the league met for the first time in 1920, three significant world powers had no representative present: Germany and the Soviet Union were excluded, and, in a stunning defeat for President

Wilson, the U.S. Senate rejected membership. The failure of these three states to participate in the League at its beginning stripped the organization of much of its potential influence. Second, the League had no military power. Although it could levy economic sanctions against states that flouted its decisions, it could do nothing more. Finally, the will to make the League work was lacking.

With Wilson removed from the picture, European leaders were free to pursue their own rather more traditional visions of what the League should be. French politicians, for example, believed that the League's primary reason for existence was to enforce the provisions of the Versailles Treaty—in other words, to punish Germany rather than to restructure international relations.

CONCLUSION

The War and the West

Sparked by nationalist fervor, international competition, and a widespread will to believe that in war lay the solution to political divisions and cultural fears, World War I quickly slipped out of the control of both the diplomats and the generals. Industrialization changed the face of combat. Total war smashed the boundaries of the battlefield, eroded the distinction between soldier and civilian, and demanded an overhaul of each combatant nation's political, economic, and social structures.

The idea of "the West" also changed as a result of the impact of this war. The entry of American forces in the final year of the war signaled that in the twentieth century, the United States would have to be factored into any definition of "Western culture" or "Western civilization." At the same time, the spread of the war to the Middle East and Africa and the significant role played by soldiers from imperial territories such as Tunisia, India, and Australia demonstrated the global framework that complicated and constrained Western affairs. The war's revolutionary aftermath also had profound consequences for formulations of "Western identity." With the triumph of the Bolshevik Revolution, two versions of modernity now presented themselves—one associated with the United States and capitalism, and the other represented by the new Soviet Union and its communist ideology. Soviet communism's intellectual roots lay in Marxism, a quintessentially Western ideology, one shaped by Western ideals of evolutionary progress and the triumph of human reason. But after the Russian Revolution, communism was increasingly viewed in the West as something foreign, essentially Eastern, the Other against which the West identified itself.

The carnage of World War I also challenged the faith of many Europeans that through industrial development the West was progressing morally as well as materially. In the final decades of the nineteenth century, European and American soldiers had used repeating rifles and machine guns to conquer huge sections of the globe in the name of Western civilization. In 1914, European and American soldiers turned their machine guns on each other. The world the war had created was one of unprecedented destruction. Millions lay dead, with millions more maimed for life. Vast sections of northern France and eastern Europe had been turned into giant cemeteries filled with rotting men and rusting metal. Across central and eastern Europe, starvation continued to claim thousands of victims, while a worldwide influenza epidemic, spread in part by the marching armies, ratcheted up the death tolls even higher. In the new world shaped by relentless conflicts such as the Battle of the Somme, the pessimism and sense of despair that had already invaded much of the arts in the decade before the war became more characteristic of the wider culture. For many Europeans, the optimism and confidence of nineteenth-century liberalism died in the trenches.

Yet, paradoxically, the war also fostered high hopes. Wilson declared that this had been the war to end all wars. The fires of revolution burned high and many in the West believed that on top of the ashes of empire they would now build a better world. The task of reconstruction, however, proved immense; as we shall see in Chapter 25, in many areas, retrenchment replaced revolution. Seeking stability in an increasingly unsettled world, many

Europeans and Americans did their best to return to prewar patterns. The failure of the peace settlement ensured that the "war to end all wars" set the stage for the next, far more destructive total war.

Suggestions for Further Reading

For a comprehensive list of suggested readings, please go to www.ablongman.com/levack/chapter24

Cork, Richard. *A Bitter Truth: Avant-Garde Art and the Great War*. 1994. A beautifully illustrated work that looks at the cultural impact of the war.

Eksteins, Modris. *Rites of Spring: The Great War and the Birth of the Modern Age*. 1989. Explores the links among modernism, the war experience, and modernity.

Ferguson, Niall. *The Pity of War*. 1999. A bold reconsideration of many accepted interpretations of the origins and experience of the war.

Fitzpatrick, Sheila. *The Russian Revolution, 1917–1932*. 1994. As the title indicates, Fitzpatrick sees the revolutions of 1917 as the opening battle in a more than ten-year struggle to shape the new Russia.

Gilbert, Martin. *The First World War: A Complete History*. 1994. A comprehensive account, packed with illuminating detail.

Gilbert, Martin. *The Routledge Atlas of the First World War*. 1994. Much more than a set of maps, Gilbert's atlas provides a very clear and useful survey of both the causes and results of the war.

Higonnet, Margaret. *Lines of Fire: Women's Visions of World War I*. 1998. An important study of women's experiences.

Joll, James. *The Origins of the First World War*. 1984. One of the best and most carefully balanced studies of this complicated question.

Read, Christopher. *From Tsar to Soviets: The Russian People and Their Revolution, 1917–1921*. 1996. An up-to-date study of the popular revolution and its fate.

Winter, J. M. *The Experience of World War I*. 1989. Despite the title, this richly illustrated work not only covers the war itself but also explores the factors that led to its outbreak and outlines its chief consequences.

Winter, J. M., and R. M. Wall, eds. *The Upheaval of War: Family, Work and Welfare in Europe, 1914–1918*. Cambridge, 1988. A series of essays examining the home front experiences.

Notes

1. Figures from Alan Sharp, "The Genie That Would Not Go Back into the Bottle: National Self-Determination and the Legacy of the First World War and the Peace Settlement," in Seamus Dunn and T. G. Fraser, eds., *Europe and Ethnicity*, (1996), p. 10.
2. Quotation from Karl Kautsky et. al. eds., *The Outbreak of the World War: German Documents* (1924), 76.
3. Quoted in Niall Ferguson, *The Pity of War* (1999), 152.
4. Quoted in Eric Leeds, *No Man's Land: Combat and Identity in World War I* (1979), 17.
5. Allister Horne, *The Price of Glory: Verdun, 1916* (1967), 27.
6. Paul Fussell, *The Great War and Modern Memory* (1975).
7. Figure from Tony Ashworth, *Trench Warfare 1914–1918* (1980), 15–16.
8. Quoted in Martin Gilbert, *A History of the Twentieth Century, Vol. 1* (1997), 417.
9. Samuel Hynes, *A War Imagined: The First World War and English Culture* (1991), 195.
10. Quoted in Richard Cork, *A Bitter Truth* (1994), 198.
11. Quoted in Sheila Rowbotham, *A Century of Women* (1997), 72.
12. Quoted in W. Bruce Lincoln, *Red Victory: A History of the Russian Civil War* (1989), 32.
13. Quoted in Edvard Radzinsky, *The Last Tsar*, trans. Marian Schwartz (1993), 336.
14. From the written account of Yakov Yurovsky, quoted in Radzinsky, *The Last Tsar*, 355.
15. Quoted in William Henry Chamberlin, *The Russian Revolution, 1917–1921. Volume 2. From The Civil War to the Consolidation of Power* (1987), 91.
16. Quoted in Lincoln, *Red Victory*, 151.
17. *Ibid.*, Quoted in Lincoln, 155.
18. Quoted in Radzinsky, *The Last Tsar*, 326.
19. Figures from Robert O. Paxton, *Europe in the Twentieth Century*, 3rd ed. (1997), 109.

Reconstruction, Reaction, and Continuing Revolution: The 1920s and 1930s

O N SEPTEMBER 14, 1927, AN OPEN CAR ACCELERATED DOWN A STREET IN Nice in southern France. In its passenger seat sat a woman, who let her long silk shawl whip in the wind. This woman in free-flowing clothing, speeding down the streets in a convertible, provides a fitting image for Western culture in the decade after World War I. Entranced by the automobile, Americans and Europeans embraced its promise of mobility and freedom. They perceived themselves as moving ahead, breaking through traditional barriers and heading off into new directions. Even more fitting was the identity of that female passenger: Isadora Duncan, by 1927 one of the most famous artists in Europe. In the years before World War I, the American-born Duncan had rejected classical ballet as an artificial form that restricted and deformed the female body. She cast aside ballet's confining toe shoes and tutus, and opted for bare feet and simple tunics. For Duncan, dance was not a force imposed on the body from outside; instead, dance flowed from the body itself. In her break with the highly regulated system of classical ballet, her quest for more natural forms, and her desire to liberate women, both physically and artistically, Duncan serves as an apt symbol for modernity. Moreover, as an American, Duncan appeared to personify the new culture that for many Europeans represented the world of the future. Even her clothing—loose tunics, free-flowing scarves, fluid shawls—symbolized a love of freedom and movement.

Yet freedom is sometimes dangerous and movement can be violent. On that autumn day in 1927 Duncan's long scarf became entangled in the wheel of her car and strangled the dancer. Gruesome as it is, the image of Duncan's sudden death serves as an appropriate introduction to the history of the West in the 1920s and 1930s, the turbulent interlude between two tragic world wars. The

Chapter Outline

- Cultural Despair and Desire
- Out of the Trenches: Reconstructing National and Gender Politics in the 1920s
- The Rise of the Radical Right
- The Polarization of Politics in the 1930s
- European Empires in the Interwar Era

"This Hand Guides the Reich: German Youth Follow It in the Ranks of the Hitler Youth": In this German propaganda poster from the 1930s, the Nazi government promises order and strong leadership, and at the same time allies itself with youth and vigor. During the 1930s, governments from across the political spectrum borrowed techniques from mass advertising to spread their ideas and win support.

American president Woodrow Wilson had hailed World War I as the "final war for human liberty." Many Europeans agreed; they thought that the war would propel their society down a new road, yet in much of Europe the drive toward freedom ended quickly. The interwar period saw the strangulation of democracy in eastern and southern Europe and the rise of political and cultural ideologies that viewed human liberty as an illusion and mass murder as a tool of the state.

These developments had profound implications for the idea of the West. In the Wilsonian vision, "the West" stood as a culture that promoted individual freedom through democratic politics and capitalist economics. But the success of antidemocratic and anticapitalist ideologies in capturing the hopes and allegiances of large numbers of Europeans illustrated that Wilson's definition of the West was only one among many, and that the link between "Western" and "democratic" remained fragile.

Understanding the developments that shaped the interwar era demands close consideration of the way Europeans responded to the revolutionary aftermath of World War I. Hopes for radical social and political change often clashed with the desire to restore the prewar order. Five questions will guide our examination of this confusing period: (1) What was the impact of the war on European cultural life? (2) In what ways did reconstruction rather than revolution characterize the postwar period? (3) What circumstances explain the emergence of the Radical Right? (4) What factors led to the polarization of European politics in the 1930s? (5) How did the interaction between Europe and the world outside the West change after the war?

Cultural Despair and Desire

To many Europeans in the 1920s and 1930s, World War I seemed to have torn a huge and irreparable gash in the fabric of culture and society. It appeared as the sudden and horrifying end to an age of science and progress, an era of technological improvement and social optimism. Yet this perception of a radical cultural break masked fundamental continuities. As we observed in Chapter 23, beginning in the 1870s, anxiety intermingled with optimism in European culture, and widespread fear of degeneration and decay marked Western society. Well before World War I, modernist painters, musicians, and poets were pushing beyond the limits of nineteenth-century art and articulating disturbing visions of a world in purposeless flux. The real change in the years after the war was that modernism's fragmented canvases and dissonant choruses no longer seemed alien; they echoed the

sensibilities of societies shattered by total war. But the war had also injected art with an often passionate political intensity. Excitement as well as anxiety thus marked the art and the age. The interwar era was a time of contradictions, one in which many Europeans despaired at the future of their society but many others dreamed of building a new and better world.

THE WASTE LAND

Within just a few years of the war's end, war memorials were erected in cities, towns, and villages throughout France and Britain. Significantly, these memorials rarely celebrated the Allies' victory; instead, they focused on dead soldiers. Slaughter, not success, was the dominant theme. At Verdun, for example, the memorial was an ossuary, a gigantic receptacle for the skulls and bones of 130,000 men. In some ways, European culture after the war took on the form of an ossuary, as intellectuals and artists looked at the death tolls from the war, and concluded that the end product of human reason and scientific endeavor was mass destruction.

In the English-speaking world, the American expatriate poet T. S. Eliot (1888–1965) supplied the most evocative portrait of postwar disillusion. In 1922, Eliot published a lengthy poem called "The Waste Land," which became a metaphor used by many Europeans to express their own sense of the waste wrought by the war. Arising out of Eliot's own personal anguish, "The Waste Land" contains no straightforward narrative. Instead, like a Cubist collage painting, it comprises fragments of conversation, literary allusions, disjointed quotations, mythological references, all clashing and combining in a modernist cry of despair.

The heightened anxiety and loss of certainty that characterized much of Western literature after the war is also clear in the realms of theology and philosophy. In the nineteenth century, theologians emphasized the harmony of religion and science. Their argument that God is present in the world, guiding its rational and progressive evolution, was difficult to sustain in a society that had experienced the absurd slaughter of World War I. In his postwar writings, the Swiss theologian Karl Barth (1886–1968) emphasized human sinfulness and argued that an immense gulf separated humanity from God. Neither scientific analysis nor historical inquiry could bridge the gap. Reaching God demanded a radical leap of faith.

Barth's German colleague Rudolf Bultmann (1884–1976) made the leap of faith even more radical. Bultmann argued that the Jesus Christ depicted in the New Testament—the foundation of Christianity—was largely fictional. In Bultmann's view, the Gospels were something like Eliot's "Waste Land" poem, a collection of fragments originating from myth and folk tale, layered on one another and capable of multiple interpretations. Rational inquiry and scien-

THE WASTE LAND

T. S. Eliot's "The Waste Land" comprises 434 lines; the excerpt given here is thus just one small piece of a much larger and complex poetic work that provides an evocative portrait of a despairing age. One of its central images, drawn from the English legends of King Arthur, is of an impotent and sickly king, reigning over a dried-up land.

April is the cruellest month, breeding
Lilacs out of the dead land, mixing
Memory and desire, stirring
Dull roots with spring rain.
Winter kept us warm, covering
Earth in forgetful snow, feeding
A little life with dried tubers.
. . . .

But at my back in a cold blast I hear
The rattle of the bones, and chuckle spread
   from ear to ear.

A rat crept softly through the vegetation
Dragging its slimy belly on the bank
While I was fishing in the dull canal
On a winter evening round behind the gashouse
Musing upon the king my brother's wreck
And on the king my father's death before him.
White bodies naked on the low damp ground
And bones cast in a little low dry garret,
Rattled by the rat's foot only, year to year.

Source: From "The Waste Land" by T. S. Eliot. First published in 1922. Reprinted by permission of Faber and Faber Ltd.

---

tific methods cannot deliver a certain image of the historical Jesus, who remains essentially unknowable, obscured by the myths built up over centuries. Yet Bultmann, a Lutheran pastor, did not discard his Christian beliefs. Instead, he argued that within and through the Christian mythology rests ultimate spiritual—although not scientific or historical—truth.

Bultmann's form of Christianity is often called Christian existentialism° because Bultmann put a Christian twist on the existentialist philosophy taught by his friend, the philosopher Martin Heidegger (1889–1976). At the core of existentialism was a profound despair. The human condition is one of anxiety and alienation, even *Nausea*, as Heidegger's student Jean-Paul Sartre (1905–1980) entitled one of his most famous works. For Barth and Bultmann, the way out from this anxiety was through submission to God. As an atheist, Heidegger found this route blocked. Instead, he taught that the individual must struggle to rise above mere existence to a consciousness of the genuine and authentic. Sartre's version of existentialism was more pessimistic. At a time when, as we will see, dictatorships were rising across Europe, Sartre insisted that the fundamental fact of human existence is that "man is condemned to be free" in a universe devoid of meaning or reason. Yet Sartre, too, offered a way out from this prison of freedom: Individuals must recognize that they are free to make choices, and then must do so. During World War II, Sartre's own heroic acts in the French Resistance against the Nazis exemplified his insistence on the necessity of making moral choices in an absurd world.

A sense of absurdity and waste dominates much of the visual art of the period. War veteran Otto Dix (1891–1969) filled his canvases with crippled ex-soldiers. The vivid colors and distorted figures of the Expressionist style enabled Dix to articulate his outrage at the world he saw about him. In *Flanders,* painted in 1934, Dix depicted a nightmare of trench soldiers, rotting like blasted trees. Here there is no heroism, only horror (see page 830).

BUILDING SOMETHING BETTER

Stuck in the mud, the soldiers in Dix's *Flanders* provide a haunting image of European culture in the interwar years. A very different image takes shape when we examine the work of Dix's contemporaries in the *Bauhaus.* Established in Berlin in 1919 as a school for architects, craftsmen, and designers, the Bauhaus epitomized not the despair but rather the near-utopianism of much of European culture after the war. Bauhaus sought to eliminate the barriers between "art" (what we put on our walls or see in museums) and "craft" (what we actually use in daily life: furniture, textiles, dishes, and the like), and so to enhance daily living by making it more effective, efficient, and beautiful. Its founder, Walter Gropius (1883–1969), hoped his students would become nothing less than "the architects of a new civilization."[1]

Gropius's belief that the arts could serve a social purpose was commonly shared in the interwar years. As the British poet W. H. Auden (1907–1973) explained, although good poetry is "not concerned with telling people what to do," it should "[lead] us to the point where it is possible for us to make a rational and moral choice."[2] Many artists abandoned the prewar modernist ideal of "art for art's sake," and produced work steeped in political passion and a desire for a better world. The murals of the Mexican artist Diego Rivera (1906–1957) exemplify this postwar turn toward political engagement.

Much of the near-utopianism of European culture focused on the transforming power of technology. The "machine aesthetic" triumphed most completely in the Soviet Union, where the Bolsheviks encouraged artistic experiment and innovation as part of their revolution. The engineer became the image of a communist hero, and industrial motifs permeated Soviet culture in the 1920s. In the revolutionary theater of Vsevelod Meyerhold, mechanical gestures replaced naturalistic expressions and sets consisted of scaffolding. Similarly, a factory whistle opens the chorus of Dmitri Shostakovich's *Second Symphony* (1927), written to praise industrial labor.

Postwar architecture in the West also provides a vivid illustration of this mechanical faith. A house, explained the Swiss architect Le Corbusier (1887–1965), was "a machine for living in." Le Corbusier and his fellow modernist architects stripped their buildings of all ornament and frequently exposed the essential machinery—the supporting beams, the heating ducts, the elevator shafts. Concrete, steel, and glass became the building materials of choice as modernist skyscrapers—glittering rectangles—transformed urban skylines and testified to the triumph of the human-made.

Closely related to the worship of the machine in the interwar period was a celebration of movement and speed.

The automobile evolved from a rich man's toy to a middle-class necessity, made possible by the assembly-line techniques developed in Henry Ford's Detroit factories. The assembly line, which reduced the entire industrial workforce of a factory to a single efficient machine, was imported from the United States into Europe in the later 1920s. The airline industry also took off in this era. In 1919 the first air passenger service between London and Paris began; the next decade saw Europe's major cities linked by air networks. The car and the plane became potent symbols of a new age of possibility and opportunity. In 1927, when the American Charles Lindbergh (1902–1974) became the first person to fly across the Atlantic alone, he was hailed not only as a national but as an international hero, an icon of human resourcefulness and technological mastery.

The idea that Western society was moving rapidly and that anything was possible in a world of change shaped much of the culture of the interwar era. Take the popular dance craze of the 1920s—the Charleston. Arms outstretched and legs firing like pistons, the entire body becomes a fast-moving machine. Another American import, Hollywood's "moving pictures," even more clearly represented and stimulated the ideal of a society in motion. The Italians and the French had dominated the movie industry before 1914, but during the war film production in Europe halted. American filmmakers quickly filled the void. After the war, moviegoing became a truly popular pastime—and most of the movies on the screen were made in America.

■ **Otto Dix, *Flanders* (1934–1935)**

In this painting, the Flanders landscape is literally shaped by the bodies of soldiers. Like these soldiers—and much of postwar European culture—Dix could not escape the war. His paintings reveal a man permanently wounded.

Diego Rivera, *The Distribution of Arms* (1928)
Like many other artists in the 1920s and 1930s, Diego Rivera combined political activism with his artistic pursuits. A member of the Mexican Communist Party, Rivera's pro-Soviet sympathies are evident in this mural depicting a workers' revolution.

Hollywood presented European audiences with an appealing, if unrealistic, picture of the United States as a land of fabulous wealth, technological modernity, and unlimited mobility.

Out of the Trenches: Reconstructing National and Gender Politics in the 1920s

As we saw at the end of Chapter 24, in the years immediately following World War I Europe stood on the brink of revolutionary change. The war toppled empires and redrew the map of eastern and central Europe. Gender roles turned upside down, imperial patterns shattered, and social expectations were raised. The American president Woodrow Wilson promised a radically new world of peace and democracy. In Russia, the Bolshevik Revolution offered an even more radical vision of communist freedom. Despite these expectations and fears, however, retrenchment rather than revolution characterized much of the immediate postwar period. In many areas, World War I was the turning point that failed to turn, as Europeans sought to reconstruct the structures toppled by total war.

THE RECONSTRUCTION OF RUSSIA: FROM TSAR TO COMMISSAR

Even in the newly formed Soviet Union, the nation that epitomized revolution, important aspects of prewar society re-emerged in the postwar period. By 1922 and against all odds, the Bolsheviks had won the civil war and established their authority over most of the regions of the old tsarist empire. The Bolsheviks also re-established many features of the tsarist regime: authoritarian rule built on violent coercion, a highly centralized state, a large bureaucratic elite living in conditions of privilege that cut it off from ordinary people, and a peasant economy.

How do we explain the continuity of authoritarian rule in Russia? The first crucial factor was the impact of civil and international war. Across Russia in 1919 the Bolsheviks faced fierce opposition from rival bands of socialists, middle-class liberals, and aristocratic supporters of the tsar. These opponents of the Bolshevik revolution—called the "Whites" to distinguish them from the "Red" Bolsheviks—were supported by foreign troops. Fearing the spread of communist revolution, fourteen different countries (including the United States, Britain, France, and Japan) sent more than 100,000 soldiers to fight in Russia. In addition to these forces, the new Bolshevik state confronted numerous attempts by non-Russian nationalists to throw off the yoke of Russian rule. This was warfare at its most savage. When Ukrainian peasants resisted Russian

■ "Whites" and "Reds"

These U.S. sailors, on board the cruiser *Des Moines* in 1919, are on their way to fight against the Bolsheviks in Russia. They disembarked at Archangel, a northern Russian port held by the Allied armies. Even with the assistance of American and west European troops, the "Whites" were unable to defeat the Bolsheviks, and the "Reds" won the Russian Civil War.

control, the Bolsheviks resorted to methods of mass reprisal. Entire villages were burned, the men executed, the women and children sent to slower deaths in prison camps. The Bolsheviks did not have a monopoly on murder, however. White forces in the Ukraine massacred over 100,000 Jews.

As the scale of savagery escalated, so too did Russia's economic disintegration. In the cities, residents faced anarchic conditions. Transportation systems shut down, the water supply ceased to run, and furniture became the only source of fuel. When the furniture ran out, entire families froze to death inside apartment blocks. The urban areas emptied as their inhabitants fled to the countryside. By 1921, Moscow had lost half its residents and Petrograd (formerly St. Petersburg) had lost two-thirds. Yet conditions in the countryside were also brutal. To feed the cities, the Bolsheviks adopted the policy of "War Communism": requisitioning (stealing) food and seed stores from the peasants. The peasants resisted, both actively, in violent revolt, and passively, by reducing the amount they planted. Food shortages and other war-related hardships increased the population's vulnerability to epidemic disease. Between 1918 and 1921, the number of deaths from the combined impact of the civil war, starvation, and typhus surpassed the number of those who died in World War I.

The need to impose order on this chaotic situation led the Bolsheviks to adopt increasingly authoritarian measures. Like the Jacobins in 1792 during the French Revolutionary Wars, the Bolsheviks turned to terror to defeat their enemies, both domestic and foreign. In the first six years of Bolshevik rule, the Cheka (Lenin's secret police force) executed at least 200,000 people. In contrast, in the fifty years before the Bolsheviks came to power, 14,000 Russians had died at the hands of the tsarist secret police.

But the antidemocratic nature of the Bolshevik regime was not solely a response to the pressures of war. Ideology is the second crucial factor that helps explain the continuity of authoritarian rule in post-tsarist Russia. Faced with the task of building a communist state in an isolated, economically backward, peasant society, the Bolshevik leader Vladimir Lenin modified Marxist theory. In a peasant society, Lenin argued, the agent of revolutionary change could not be the working class: There simply were not enough industrial workers in Russia. Instead, the Bolshevik or Communist Party, an elite of highly disciplined, politically aware and committed individuals, would be the "vanguard" of revolution. Debate and disagreement could not be permitted—at the Tenth Communist Party Congress in 1921, party leaders agreed to Lenin's proposal to ban all political factions. Because the masses could not be trusted to make their own decisions, government officials, strictly controlled by the party, would make these decisions for them. The number of bureaucrats multiplied, and by 1925, had become a privileged elite, with access to the best jobs, food, clothing, and apartments. The rule of the tsar had been replaced not with democracy but with the rule of the commissar, the Communist Party functionary.

In the economic sphere, as in the political system, important continuities shaped the Russian experience. By 1921 the Bolshevik policy of "War Communism" had produced famine in the countryside and widespread peasant unrest. Material necessity forced Lenin to backpedal from communist ideology and announce a New Economic Policy (NEP)°. Under NEP, peasants were allowed to sell their produce for profit. Although the state continued to control heavy industry, transport, and banking, NEP encouraged the proliferation of small private businesses and farms—just as the tsar's economic policymakers had done before the war.

THE RECONSTRUCTION OF NATIONAL POLITICS IN EASTERN AND CENTRAL EUROPE

U.S. President Woodrow Wilson's vision of a new international order based on democratic politics offered the war-torn states of Europe a sharp alternative to Bolshevik one-party rule. But in the new states of eastern Europe, democracy proved to be fragile, and in most cases short-lived. Much of old Europe survived the war intact.

The Defeat of Democracy in Eastern Europe

After the peace negotiations concluded in 1922, postwar eastern Europe certainly looked markedly different from its prewar counterpart (see Map 25.1). The Russian, Austrian-Hungarian, and Ottoman Empires had all disappeared, replaced by a jigsaw puzzle of small independent nations. But lines on the map did not change key political and economic realities. Three important threads tied these new states to their prewar past: ethnic disputes, economic underdevelopment, and antidemocratic politics.

As we saw at the end of Chapter 24, the Allies paid lip service to the ideal of national self-determination but found it impossible to create ethnically homogenous nation-states in eastern Europe. As a result, nationalist-ethnic divisions continued to haunt postwar political structures. In the new Yugoslavia, for example, ethnic struggles dominated interwar politics. Croats and Slovenes had expected a federalist system that would grant them local autonomy. Instead, they found themselves in a centralized state under Serbian control. As a result, Croat representatives refused even to sit in the new parliament.

Economic difficulties also threatened eastern European stability. In many regions, eastern Europe remained a world

■ Map 25.1   Europe in the 1920s and 1930s

The map shows the consequences of not only World War I but also such successor conflicts as the Irish-English struggles, which resulted in the formation of the Irish Free State; the war between Bolshevick Russia and its enemies, which widened the western frontiers of the Soviet state; and the Turkish uprising, which kept Turkey intact and independent.

of peasants and aristocratic landlords. In Romania, Poland, and Hungary, at least 60 percent of the population worked the land; in Bulgaria and Yugoslavia the figure was 80 percent—versus 20 percent in industrialized Britain. With little industrial growth in these regions and few cities to absorb labor, unemployment rates and land hunger were both high.

Thus ethnic divisions and economic underdevelopment helped destabilize eastern Europe's new democratic political systems. The result was the collapse of democracy across eastern Europe. As the chronology (right) shows, with the exception of Czechoslovakia, every eastern European nation returned to authoritarian politics during the 1920s or early 1930s. In Poland, for example, democracy crumbled in 1926 when the World War I hero Marshal Josef Pilsudski (1867–1935) seized power in a military coup, after parliamentary representatives proved unable to overcome class and ethnic divisions. Pilsudski told the squabbling legislators, "The time has come to treat you like children, because you behave like children."[3] In Yugoslavia, the death of democracy was even more dramatic. Years of escalating ethnic violence peaked in 1928 when a popular Croatian political leader was shot to death on the floor of the legislature. The ensuing ethnic unrest gave King Alexander (a Serb) the excuse he needed to abolish the constitution and replace parliamentary democracy with a royal dictatorship. A brutal repression of Alexander's opponents followed. In Bulgaria, Albania, Hungary, and Romania, too, continuing ethnic conflicts and economic underdevelopment ensured the destruction of democracy.

The Weakness of the Weimar Republic

In Germany, as in the new states of eastern Europe, the appearance of radical change masked crucial continuities between the pre- and postwar eras. The kaiser's empire gave way to the Weimar Republic°, led by a democratically elected parliamentary government. This democratic political structure, however, sat uneasily atop fundamentally antidemocratic social and political foundations.

The survival of authoritarian attitudes and institutions resulted in part from the civil war that raged throughout Germany in the fall of 1918 and the first months of 1919. In this struggle, communists, inspired by the Bolshevik Revolution, fought their one-time colleagues in the more moderate socialist party (the SPD) for control of the new Germany. Anxious to impose order on a potentially anarchic situation, the SPD leaders who now controlled the German government chose not to replace the existing state bureaucracy—the elite corps of aristocratic civil servants that had served the kaiser—but to work with it. To put down the communist threat, they also abandoned their longstanding loathing of the German military and deployed both regular army units and the "Free Corps" (volunteer paramilitary units, often comprising demobilized soldiers addicted to violence). By the spring of 1919, this strange alliance of moderate socialists, traditional aristo-

> ### CHRONOLOGY
>
> ## The Return of Authoritarian Rule to Eastern Europe
>
> | | |
> |---|---|
> | 1923 | Boris III establishes a royalist dictatorship in Bulgaria |
> | 1926 | Marshal Josef Pilsudski establishes a military dictatorship in Poland |
> | 1928 | A new constitution gives King Zog in Albania almost unlimited powers |
> | 1929 | Alexander I establishes a royal dictatorship in Yugoslavia |
> | 1932 | Fascist leader Gyula Gombos appointed prime minister in Hungary |
> | 1938 | King Carol establishes a royal dictatorship in Romania |

crats, and military men had triumphed. In January 1919, Free Corps officers murdered the communist leaders Karl Liebknecht and Rosa Luxemburg in Berlin. Three months later, an equally savage repression crushed the communist soviet in Munich, with the Free Corps killing more than 600 people.

The SPD had won. Yet it lost. By allying with the aristocratic civil service, the army, and the Free Corps, the SPD crushed more than the communist revolution; it also crushed its own chances of achieving significant social change. The officers in the army and the bureaucrats in the civil service were representatives of the old Germany, vehemently opposed to not only communism but also parliamentary democracy. Continuing in positions of authority and influence, they constituted a formidable anti-democratic force at the very heart of the new Germany. The approximately 400,000 men who made up the Free Corps also regarded democratic ideals and the new German republic with contempt—"an attempt of the slime to govern."[4] The attitude of the Free Corps men is summed up in their slogan: "Everything would still have been all right if we had shot more people."[5]

The antidemocratic nature of the Free Corps became clear in 1920, after the Allies imposed restrictions on the size of Germany's military force and most Free Corps units were officially dissolved. Disaffected corpsmen joined the rightwing politician Wolfgang Kapp (1858–1922) and the World War I hero Erich von Ludendorff in an effort to overthrow the Weimar regime. This "Kapp Putsch" quickly fizzled out, defeated by both divisions in the ranks of the rebels and a general strike, but the threat posed by the Free

Corps did not disappear. Disguising themselves as athletic societies, haulage companies, and even circuses, many corps units continued their violent anti-Weimar activities. In 1923, some of these corpsmen tried once again to overthrow the Weimar government by force, with another "putsch," this time originating in a beer hall in Munich and led by a former army corporal named Adolf Hitler. Like the Kapp Putsch, Hitler's "Beer Hall Putsch°" did not succeed. The laughably light sentences imposed on its participants, however, made clear the strength of anti-Republican sentiments not only among disgruntled Free Corps men but also far up the ranks of the Weimar judicial system.

Antidemocratic forces in the Weimar Republic fed on the widespread resentment among Germans aroused by severity of the Versailles Treaty. Many Germans could not separate the birth of the Republic from the national humiliation imposed by Versailles. They blamed the moderate socialist government that signed the treaty for this humiliation. Army officers encouraged the idea that Germany could have kept on fighting had it not been "stabbed in the back" by the socialists. This "stab-in-the-back" legend helped undermine support not only for the SPD's moderate socialism but even for democracy itself.

The Death of Money: The Causes and Consequences of Hyperinflation

The shaky foundations of democracy in Weimar Germany were eroded further by the dramatic events of 1923. In that year, the German mark collapsed completely and paper money ceased to have any value. Germans used wheelbarrows full of cash to purchase a single loaf of bread. In later years, Germans spoke of 1923 as "the time when money died." With the death of money came the collapse of many other assumptions. Inflation not only gutted the currency but it also exposed as hollow many of the conventions and standards by which many Germans had ordered their lives. The result was a long-lasting cultural crisis that paved the way for the collapse of German democracy in the 1930s.

What the Germans experienced in 1923 was a phenomenon economists labeled hyperinflation°, the unintended by-product of the Weimar government's effort to force the Allies to reconsider reparations. In 1922, the Weimar government halted the payment of reparations and demanded a new economic settlement. The French responded by sending troops to occupy the Ruhr Valley, Germany's principal coal-mining and industrial region, and to seize coal as a form of reparations payment. To the surprise and dismay of French politicians, however, German coal miners simply refused to head down into the mines. This policy of passive resistance received the full support of the German government. It vowed to pay the coal miners for not working, and it raised the funds to do so by printing money. By January 1923, the mark, which in 1914 could be traded for the American dollar at a rate of 4:1, had plummeted to an exchange rate of 22,400:1. Within a few weeks, Germans were being paid three times a day, so they could run out and spend their wages before prices rose once again. And prices did keep rising. By October, the exchange rate from mark to dollar was at 440,000,000:1.

Despite—or in some ways because of—the economic disaster of hyperinflation, the Weimar government's strategy worked. The French army pulled out of the Ruhr Valley and in 1924 Allied and German representatives renegotiated reparations. The resulting Dawes Plan stretched the payments over a longer period. But the social costs of this victory were enormous. Middle-class men and women, who had lived frugally and saved carefully all their lives, found their retirement accounts completely wiped out in the course of a single afternoon. Peasant families who had scrimped for years to acquire dowries for their daughters found that they had only enough money to buy half a loaf of bread. The world turned topsy-turvy; old rules no longer applied. Respectable families were forced to send their daughters out as prostitutes to service the American tourists who lived in luxury for just pennies a day. Small businessmen went bankrupt while large industrialists, with their much greater resources, borrowed freely and expanded ruthlessly.

By the end of 1924, the German economy had stabilized; the later 1920s were years of relative prosperity. Yet for many Germans, the Weimar Republic was now indelibly stained by the memory of hyperinflation. For these Germans, democracy meant disorder and degradation. They looked with longing back to the prewar period, an era of supposed social stability and national power.

CHRONOLOGY

The Instability of the Early Weimar Republic

1918	Civil war: moderate socialists fight communists
1919	
January	Free Corps murder Karl Liebknecht and Rosa Luxemburg
March	Communist soviet in Munich crushed
1920	Kapp Putsch
1922	French occupation of the Ruhr
1923	Hyperinflation destroys German economy; Beer Hall Putsch
1924	Dawes Plan

The Trial of Adolf Hitler

On February 24, 1924, Adolf Hitler appeared in court in Munich to confront a charge of high treason following his pathetic attempt three months earlier to overthrow the Weimar government by armed rebellion. The trial marked a crucial point in Hitler's career. It gave him a national platform and, even more important, convinced him of the futility of an armed offensive against the state. From 1925 on, Hitler would work through the parliamentary system in order to destroy it. But the trial of Adolf Hitler is also significant in what it reveals about the power of antidemocratic forces in the new Germany. The trial made clear that many in positions of authority and responsibility in the Weimar Republic shared Hitler's contempt for the democratic state. By treating Hitler not as a traitorous thug but rather as an honorable patriot, his prosecutors helped weaken the already fragile structures of German democracy.

Hitler's attempt to overthrow the Weimar Republic by force occurred at the height of hyperinflation and the ensuing political chaos. By November 8, 1923, when Hitler took up arms, the German mark was worth only one trillionth of its prewar value. As its currency eroded, the Weimar Republic saw its political legitimacy seeping away as well. Separatist movements in several states threatened the sovereignty of the central government in Berlin. Separatist politics attracted the

support of many men from aristocratic backgrounds, members of the traditional conservative elite who viewed Weimar democracy as a foreign and unwelcome import.

Hitler had little interest in the separatist movement, but he believed he could channel its antidemocratic sentiments into a national revolution. He attracted a number of supporters, including one of the most important men in Germany, the World War I hero General Erich von Ludendorff. Seeking to avoid the blame for Germany's defeat in 1918, Ludendorff insisted that his army could have won the war had it not been stabbed in the back by the Social Democratic politicians who now ran the government. Like many German conservatives—and like Hitler—he viewed the Weimar Republic as illegitimate.

On November 8 Hitler made his move. His men surrounded a Munich beer hall where 2,000 supporters of Bavarian separatism had gathered. Hitler declared that both the Bavarian and the national governments had been overthrown and that he was now the head of a new German state, with Ludendorff as his commander-in-chief. Around noon the next day, Hitler, Ludendorff, and several thousand of their followers marched toward the regional government buildings located on one of Munich's main squares. Armed police blocked their passage. In the ensuing firefight, seventeen men were killed. Despite the bullets

whizzing through the air, Ludendorff marched through the police cordon and stood in the square awaiting arrest. Hitler ran away. Police found him two days later, cowering in a supporter's country house about thirty-five miles outside of Munich.

The Beer Hall Putsch had clearly, utterly, completely failed. In jail awaiting trial, Hitler contemplated suicide. Yet later he described his defeat as "perhaps the greatest stroke of luck in my life." The defeat meant a trial; the trial meant a national audience—and an opportunity for Hitler to present his case against the Weimar Republic. He admitted that he had conspired to overthrow the democratically elected Republican government, but he insisted he was not therefore guilty of treason. The real treason had occurred in November 1918, when the Social Democratic government had surrendered to the Allies: "I confess to the deed, but I do not confess to the crime of high treason. There can be no question of treason in an action which aims to undo the betrayal of this country in 1918. . . . I consider myself not a traitor but a German." He argued that he was not aiming for personal power: "In what small terms small minds think! . . . What I had in mind from the very first day was a thousand times more important than becoming a minister. I wanted to become the destroyer of Marxism." Thus Hitler depicted himself as a patriot, a nationalist motivated by love of Germany and hatred

Hitler in Landsberg Prison, 1924
This photo of Hitler during his short imprisonment was made into a postcard, to be purchased by his supporters.

of communists and socialists. "The eternal court of history," according to Hitler, would judge him and his fellow defendants "as Germans who wanted the best for their people and their Fatherland, who were willing to fight and to die."[6]

Despite Hitler's own admission of conspiring against the government, the presiding judge could convince the three lay judges (who took the place of a jury) to render a guilty verdict only by arguing that Hitler would most likely be pardoned soon. The reluctance of the judges to convict Hitler highlights the extraordinary sympathy shown to him and his political ideas throughout the trial and during his imprisonment. The chief prosecutor offered a rather surprising description of an accused traitor: "Hitler is a highly gifted man, who has risen from humble beginnings to achieve a respected position in public life, the result of much hard work and dedication. . . . As a soldier he did his duty to the utmost. He cannot be accused of having used the position he created for himself in any self-serving way." In delivering the verdict, the judge emphasized Hitler's "pure patriotic motives and honorable intentions." Rather than being deported as a foreign national convicted of a serious crime (Hitler was still an Austrian citizen), Hitler was given a slight sentence of five years, which made him eligible for parole in just six months. In prison he was treated like a visiting dignitary—

exempted from work and exercise requirements, provided with prisoners to clean his rooms, even given a special table, decorated with a swastika banner, in the dining hall. When he was released in September, his parole report described him favorably as "a man of order."[7]

Hitler's gentle treatment reveals the precarious state of democratic institutions in Germany after World War I. Many high-ranking Germans in positions of power and influence (such as judges and prosecutors) viewed parliamentary democracy with loathing. The trial also reveals the willingness of conservative aristocrats to ally with Radical Right groups such as the Nazis. Still not very strong, the Nazis in 1923 were easily reined in. A decade later, however, the conservatives who thought they could ride Hitler to power suddenly found that they were no longer in control.

Questions of Justice

1. Imagine you are a German war veteran reading about this case in the newspaper in 1924. Why might you be attracted to the party of Adolf Hitler?
2. Compare Hitler's trial with that of Alfred Dreyfus in France in 1895 (see "Justice in History" in Chapter 22). How did both trials reveal key points of instability within the political systems in which they occurred?

Taking It Further

Gordon, Harold Jr. *Hitler and the Beer Hall Putsch.* 1972. This lengthy study (over 600 pages) provides a detailed account of the putsch and its aftermath.

The Hitler Trial before the People's Court in Munich, trans. H. Francis Freniece, Lucie Karcic, and Philip Fandek (3 vols.). 1976. English translation of the court transcripts.

THE RECONSTRUCTION OF GENDER

Many of the patterns that shaped interwar national politics also characterized the politics of gender in these years. World War I wrought a profound upheaval in gender roles in European society. The demands of total war had meant that women moved into economic areas previously designated as "men only." Middle-class conventions collapsed as women shrugged off both their corsets and their chaperones, and jumped into the drivers' seats of ambulances and buses. The war, therefore, seemed an important turning point in the history of women in the West. But here again the turning point failed to turn. Important changes in women's expectations did occur, but nineteenth-century gender roles were quickly reconstructed after the war.

The New Woman

At first sight, the postwar period seems an era of profound change in the roles of women. In the films, magazines, novels, and popular music of the 1920s, the "New Woman" took center stage. Living, working, and traveling on her own, sexually active, she stepped out of the confines of

■ **The "New Woman"**
Almost every aspect of the "New Woman" captured in this 1928 French photograph caused offense to traditionalists: short skirts and bobbed hair; smoking in public, the association with a car and therefore with mobility and illicit sex—all crossing the border into masculine terrain.

home and family. Women's dress reinforced this idea of a new woman. Whereas nineteenth-century women's clothing had accentuated the womanly body while restricting the woman's movement, the clothing of the 1920s ignored a woman's curves and became much less confining. Complementing this revolution in clothing came a revolution in hairstyle. Women chopped off the long locks regarded for generations as a sign of femaleness and sported fashionable new bobs.

This perception of the New Woman rested on important changes in women's political and economic expectations. By 1920 women in the United States and many European countries had received the right to vote in national elections and to hold national office. In all the industrialized countries, the expansion of both the health care and service sectors meant new jobs for women as nurses, social workers, secretaries, telephone exchange operators, and clerks. Women's higher education opportunities also widened in this period.

The biggest change affecting the lives of ordinary women was the spreading practice of limiting family size. We saw in Chapter 22 that by the 1870s middle-class women in Western nations were practicing forms of birth control. In the 1920s and 1930s, an increasing number of working-class women began to do so as well. In Britain, for example, between 1911 and 1931 the average number of children per family fell from 3.4 to 2.2, with most of this decrease resulting from changes in working-class family size. Fewer pregnancies and fewer mouths to feed meant a significant improvement in women's health and living standards.

The Reconstruction of Traditional Roles

Despite these important changes, however, women's roles actually altered little in the two decades after World War I. These years witnessed a strong reaction against the wartime gender upheaval and a concerted effort to reconstruct nineteenth-century masculine and feminine ideals.

Both the war's lengthy casualty lists and the drop in the average family size provoked widespread fear about declining populations—and thus declining national strength. Governments, religious leaders, and commercial entrepreneurs joined together to convince women that their destiny lay in motherhood. Sale and purchase of birth control devices became illegal during the 1920s in France, Belgium, Italy, and Spain. France outlawed abortions in 1920. In Britain after 1929, a woman who had an abortion could be sentenced to life imprisonment.

To encourage population growth, governments also turned to more positive incentives ranging from the symbolic to the economic. Mother's Day, an American invention, crossed into Europe during the 1920s. In France from 1920 on, women who gave birth to at least five children received a bronze medal; those who bore seven or more children earned the silver; and mothers who produced ten offspring brought home the gold. German women had an easier time: They needed only seven children to get the gold. Of more lasting importance was the expansion of welfare services—family allowances, subsidized or state-provided housing, school lunches, health insurance, prenatal and well-baby clinics—with the express aim of strengthening the family, encouraging women to stay at home, and raising the birth rate. Eugenics played an important role in this legislation. National leaders wanted to increase not only the quantity but the quality of the population. On the positive side, this meant improving the health of babies and mothers. More ominously, much of the rhetoric focused on separating the "fit" from the "unfit," with both class and race among the factors that determined who was "fit" to produce children for the nation.

Despite the calls for women to remain at home, many women had to work in paid employment. In the work world, just as in the family, traditional roles were strengthened after World War I. Most working women returned to jobs in domestic service or to factory positions labeled unskilled and therefore low-paying. Women tended to be barred from management positions, assigned to the most repetitive tasks, and paid by piecework, with the result that the wage gap between male and female laborers remained wide. In both Germany and Britain, unemployment benefits were frequently denied to married women workers, even though they had regularly paid into the insurance system while they were working. The numbers of women employed in the clerical and service sectors did rise in this era, but the movement of women into these positions meant such jobs were reclassified as "women's work," a guarantee of low pay and little power.

Women and the Bolshevik Revolution

In sharp contrast to these efforts to buttress the traditional family structures, in Russia the Bolsheviks promised to revolutionize gender roles. Lenin believed that the family was a middle-class institution doomed to "wither away." In the ideal communist society, marriage would be a mutually beneficial—and in many cases temporary—arrangement between two equally educated and equally waged partners, and both housework and child care would move from the private domestic household into the public sphere of paid employment. To create such a society, the Bolsheviks turned to legislation. One month after seizing power, they legalized divorce and civil marriages. In October 1918, a new family legal code declared women and men equal under the law, made divorce readily available, and abolished the distinction between legitimate and illegitimate children. To free women from housework—described by Lenin as "barbarously unproductive, petty, nervewracking, and stultifying drudgery"[8]—the Bolsheviks established communal child care centers, laundries, and dining rooms. In 1920, just as other nations were outlawing abortion, the practice became legal in Bolshevik Russia.

By 1922, however, the newly created Soviet Union seemed about to self-destruct, and as we have already seen, Lenin retreated from rigorous communist economic ideology to institute the New Economic Policy. NEP also meant significant reversals in the gender revolution. By 1923, the dining halls had been closed and more than half of the day care centers had shut down. The decade of the 1920s was a time of high unemployment for Soviet women. Those who did find jobs received wages that averaged only 65 percent that of men's. An increasing number turned to prostitution. In addition, the traditional patriarchal peasant household—with women in a clearly subordinate role—remained firmly intact. Even in revolutionary Russia, therefore, certain continuities linked the pre- and postwar experience of women.

The Rise of the Radical Right

As the revolution in gender roles was reversed, as Lenin's communist revolution shifted into a lower gear, and as Wilson's democratic revolution ran out of gas, a very different sort of revolution was occurring in Italy, a region long on the periphery of European power. The fascist revolution introduced Europe to a new sort of politics, the politics of the Radical Right. Like conservatism, the new Radical Right ideologies—fascism° and its younger cousin, Nazism—dismissed equality as a socialist myth and emphasized the importance of authority. But neither fascism nor Nazism was conservative. These radical political systems sought to use the new technologies of the mass media to mobilize their societies for a program of violent nationalism.

THE FASCIST ALTERNATIVE

Conceived in the coupling of wartime exhilaration and postwar despair, fascism offered an alternative to the existing political ideologies. Fascism was more than a set of political ideas, however. As presented by its creator, Benito Mussolini (1883–1945), fascism was an ongoing performance, a spectacular sound-and-lights show with a cast of millions.

Mussolini's Rise to Power

Fascism originated in Italy. In 1915 after a fierce internal debate that widened the already huge gaps in Italian society, Italy entered the war on the side of the Allies. Many pro-war Italians believed that parliamentary politics, with its emphasis on compromise, committees, and endless discussion, was sapping the vitality from Italian society. Calling for violent action, they viewed the war as a cleansing force, a powerful disinfectant that would leave Italian society stronger

THE CULT OF THE LEADER

The personality cult characterized not only the Radical Right ideologies of Italian fascism and German Nazism, but also the ideological system that stood at the opposite end of the political spectrum: Stalinist communism. Searching for a way to mobilize the masses without granting to them actual political power, Mussolini, Hitler, and Stalin erected around themselves leadership cults. Their own images came to embody the nation. As the following set of excerpts shows, the cults of Mussolini, Hitler, and Stalin took on religious dimensions, with all three men adored as secular saviors.

I. DESCRIPTION OF MUSSOLINI'S VISIT TO TRIESTE IN 1938

Finally we have seen and heard Him! . . . These first reactions, expressed with indescribable joy, eyes moved to tears and an ineffable, agonizing joy . . . It is not easy to describe the expression on most faces, on those of the little people as on those of the educated, of the mass as a whole. Expressions of wonderful contentment and pride among those who saw Him pass close by—especially among the dockworkers He visited yesterday—and those whose eyes He met, those who caught His eye. "Never such eyes! The way he looks at you is irresistible! He smiled at me . . . I was close, I could almost touch him . . . When I saw him my legs trembled" . . . and a thousand other similar statements show and confirm the enormous fascination exercised by his person.

II. DESCRIPTION OF AN EARLY NAZI RALLY BY LOUISE SOLMITZ, SCHOOLTEACHER

The April sun shone hot like summer and turned everything into a picture of gay expectation. There was immaculate order and discipline . . . the hours passed. . . . Expectations rose. There stood Hitler in a simple black coat and looked over the crowd. Waiting. A forest of swastika pennants swished up, the jubilation of this moment was given vent in a roaring salute. . . . How many look up to him with a touching faith! As their helper, their savior, their deliverer from unbearable distress—to him who rescues the Prussian prince, the scholar, the clergyman, the farmer, the worker, the unemployed, who leads them from the parties back into the nation.

III. SPEECH BY A WOMAN DELEGATE AT A WORKERS' CONFERENCE IN THE SOVIET UNION

Thank you comrade Stalin, our leader, our father, for a happy, merry kolkhoz life!

He, our Stalin, put the steering-wheel of the tractor in our hand. . . . He, the great Stalin, carefully listens to all of us in this meeting, loves us with a great Stalinist love (*tumultuous applause*), day and night thinks of our prosperity, of our culture, of our work . . .

Long live our friend, our teacher, the beloved leader of the world proletariat, comrade Stalin! (*Tumultuous applause, rising to an ovation. Shouts of 'Hurrah!'*)

Sources: "I. Description of Mussolini's Visit to Trieste in 1938," reprinted by permission of the publisher from *The Sacralization of Politics in Fascist Italy* by Emilio Gentile, translated by Keith Botsford, p. 147, Cambridge, Mass.; Harvard University Press. Copyright © 1996 by the President and Fellows of Harvard College. "II. Description of an Early Nazi Rally by Louise Solmitz, Schoolteacher," copyright © 1988 by Claudia Koonz. From *Mothers in the Fatherland: Women, the Family, and Nazi Politics* by Claudia Koonz. Reprinted by permission of St. Martin's Press, LLC. "III. Speech by a Woman Delegate at a Worker's Conference in the Soviet Union," from *Stalin's Peasants: Resistance and Survival in the Russian Village after Collectivization* by Sheila Fitzpatrick. Copyright © 1996 by Oxford University Press, Inc. Published by Oxford University Press, Inc.

and more powerful. Mussolini, a socialist journalist, shared these views. Because the Socialist Party opposed Italy's entry into the war, Mussolini broke with the socialists, joined the army in 1915, and fought courageously until he was wounded in 1917. When the war ended, he sought to create a new form of politics that would translate the military camaraderie and the exhilaration of violent action from the trenches to peacetime society. The result was fascism. Mussolini condemned conservatism, liberalism, and socialism as all outdated. Socialism exalted the working class; liberalism viewed the individual as the core of society; conservatism clung to social hierarchy. Fascism, however, identified the *nation* as the dominant social reality. With a strong leader at the wheel, with violent action as its fuel, the fascist nation would crash through social and economic barriers and transport its people into a new and more powerful age.

In March 1919, Mussolini and a little more than 100 men and some women gathered in Milan and declared themselves the fascist movement. Like Mussolini, many of these "fascists of the first hour" were war veterans; a number had served in the *arditi*, elite commando units that fought behind enemy lines. The arditi uniform, a severe black shirt, became the fascist badge of identity. The arditi slogan, *"me ne frego"* ("I don't give a damn") became the blackshirts' creed, a fitting summary of their willingness to throw aside conventional standards and politics.

Just three and a half years after the first fascist meeting in Milan, Mussolini became prime minister of Italy. His astonishing rise to power occurred against a backdrop of social turmoil. In 1919 and 1920, more than one million workers were on strike, factory occupations became commonplace, and a wave of land seizures spread across the countryside. Increasingly frightened that revolution would engulf Italy just as it had destroyed tsarist Russia, large landowners and industrialists, as well as the professional and commercial middle classes, looked to Mussolini's fascists for help. Fascist squads disrupted Socialist Party meetings, vandalized the offices of socialist newspapers, broke up strikes, beat up trade unionists, and protected aristocratic estates from attack. By 1922, the fascists were a formidable political force and Mussolini was engaged in negotiations aimed at bringing the fascists into a coalition government. Fascist violence proved persuasive. In October 1922, King Victor Emmanuel III (1900–1946) asked Mussolini to become not only a member of the government but its prime minister. Mussolini agreed. In a carefully orchestrated display of muscle, fascists from all over Italy converged in the "March on Rome," a piece of street theater designed to demonstrate Mussolini's mass support, as well as the disciplined might of his followers.

The Fascist Revolution in Italy

Over the next four years Mussolini used both legal and illegal methods, including murder, to eliminate his political rivals and remake Italy as a one-party state. By 1926,

he had succeeded. Party politics, an independent press, and the trade union movement ceased to exist. Victor Emmanuel remained on the throne, the official head of state, but power lay in Mussolini's hands. The restored death penalty and a strong police apparatus stood ready to enforce Mussolini's will.

In a sharp break with previous governments, Mussolini won the support of the Catholic Church. For more than fifty years, successive popes had regarded themselves as prisoners in the Vatican, surrounded by a hostile, secular state. In the mid-1920s, Mussolini, a self-proclaimed atheist, suddenly recognized the Church as a possible ally. After consecrating his marriage in a religious ceremony and arranging the baptism of his children, he ordered crucifixes placed in all schools and courtrooms and increased the amount of state funds flowing into the Church coffers. In the Lateran Pact of 1929, Mussolini declared Catholicism the state religion and guaranteed the Church freedom to control spiritual matters. In exchange, Pope Pius XI (r. 1922–1939) became the first Catholic prelate to recognize the Italian state. The pope declared Mussolini "a man sent by Providence" to defeat socialism, feminism, and other threats to the social order.

As Mussolini's alliance with the Church indicated, Mussolini's supposedly radical revolution reinforced traditional elite interests. Fascist economic theory, such as it

■ **The March on Rome, October 28, 1922**
The fascist march on Rome was a carefully orchestrated show of power, not an armed rebellion. Mussolini had already been offered the premiership of Italy, as is clear from his clothing: He has changed his black shirt for a proper suit.

was, promised to replace capitalist competition and the profit motive with corporatism: committees (or "corporations") made up of representatives of workers, employers, and the state were to direct the economy for the good of the nation. In actuality, workers' rights disappeared from fascist Italy while private property and industrial profits remained untouched. At the same time, landed aristocrats prospered. Early fascist promises of land redistribution were quickly forgotten, and the end of democracy meant that the control of local government rested not with elected officials but rather with Mussolini's appointees—usually drawn from the ranks of the traditional agrarian elite.

Mussolini's revolution, then, was not about leveling society. Mussolini had no intention of giving *actual* political power to ordinary people; he did, however, recognize the importance of giving them the *illusion* of power. Participation was the key. The fascist revolution offered individuals a sense of power by giving them the chance to participate in the life of the nation. A series of "after-work" occupational and recreational groups served as a channel for fascist propaganda and connected ordinary people more closely to the fascist state, while at the same time occupying their leisure hours. By 1939, four million Italians were participating in fascist sporting clubs, holiday camps, and cultural outings.

The "Cult of the Duce" also provided an important means of fostering a sense of participation in the life of the nation. Mussolini insisted, "I am Fascism." Carefully choreographed public appearances gave ordinary Italians the chance to see, hear, and adore their Duce ("Leader"), and through contact with his person, to feel a part of the new Italy. To stimulate public adoration of himself, Mussolini paid careful attention to his public image. He ordered that the press ignore his birthdays and the births of his grandchildren: The Duce could not be seen to age. Instead, in photograph after photograph, Mussolini appeared as a man of action. Depicted in planes, in trains, and in racing cars, he was always on the move, always pressing forward. At the same time, Mussolini combined up-to-date advertising and the latest mass media technologies with age-old rituals inspired largely by the Catholic Church. Huge public rallies set in massive arenas, carefully staged with lighting and music, inspired his followers. A popular fascist slogan summed up the leadership cult: "Believe, Obey, Fight." Italians were not to think or question; they were to *believe*. What were they to believe? Another slogan provides the answer: "Mussolini is always right."

THE GREAT DEPRESSION AND THE SPREAD OF FASCISM AFTER 1929

The simple certainty offered by a slogan such as Mussolini's proved highly appealing throughout much of Europe after 1929. During the 1930s, fascist movements emerged in almost every European state. The key factor in the spread of

CHRONOLOGY

Mussolini's Rise to Power

1915–1917	Serves in the Italian army
1919	Participates in the creation of the fascist movement
1921	Fascist Party wins thirty-five seats in parliament
1922	Becomes prime minister
1925–1926	Abolishes party politics and establishes himself as dictator
1929	Signs Lateran Accords with the Roman Catholic Church

fascism was the Great Depression°. On October 24, 1929, the American stock market collapsed. Over the next two years, the American economic crisis evolved into a global depression. Banks closed, businesses collapsed, and unemployment rates rose to devastating levels. Even by the end of the 1930s, the production rates of many nations remained low. Desperate people looked for desperate answers. Fascism provided some of these.

Why did the Depression spread so quickly and last so long? The explanation lies with the changing role of the United States in Europe. World War I accelerated the shift of the world's economic center away from Europe and toward America. New York's stock market emerged to rival London's, and U.S. businesses increasingly displaced European competitors as the chief suppliers of industrial goods to regions such as Latin America. While European nations sold off their domestic and foreign assets and borrowed heavily to pay for the war, the United States moved from the position of debtor to creditor nation. By the end of 1918 Allied nations owed the United States more than $9 billion—and American officials made it clear that they expected this money to be repaid in full, with interest.

The problem of wartime indebtedness quickly became entangled with the issue of German reparations. Britain, France, and Italy could pay off their debts to the United States only if Germany paid reparations to them. Hyperinflation and the near-collapse of the German economy in 1923 made clear, however, that the reparations schedule established by the Versailles Treaty would have to be revised. In 1924 and again in 1928 American and European financial representatives met to reconfigure (and in 1928 to reduce) the payments. American credit became the fuel that kept the European economy burning. From 1925 on, American investors loaned money to Germany, which used the money to pay reparations to the Allies, which in turn used the money to pay back the United States. The system worked for a short time. Fueled by loans, the German economy kicked into gear. Currencies stabilized, production rose, and American money flowed not only into Germany but into all of Europe. If these loans dried up, however, Europe faced disaster.

In 1929 that disaster struck. With the collapse of the U.S. stock market, savings portfolios lost between 60 and 75 percent of their value almost overnight. Scrambling to scrape up any assets, American creditors liquidated their European investments, and European economies tumbled. Germany, the country whose economy was most directly linked to the United States, saw its industrial output fall by 46 percent, while its number of jobless grew to over six million.

The political and social disarray that accompanied the Great Depression enhanced the appeal of fascist promises of stability, order, and national strength. In the 1930s, fascist movements emerged across Europe. Although few succeeded in seizing the reins of government, the emergence of popular fascist movements placed enormous pressure on existing authoritarian regimes and forced them to adopt many fascist trappings. For example, Romania's King Carol II (r. 1930–1940) faced a strong challenge to his rule from the Iron Guard, the first mass fascist movement in the Balkans. To compete with the Guard, Carol embraced its language of national renewal, as well as typically fascist features such as uniformed paramilitaries, a youth group, and mass rallies. In 1938 he abolished all political parties, placed the judicial system under military control, and declared himself a royal dictator. He then dissolved the Iron Guard and had its leader garroted.

THE NAZI REVOLUTION

In Germany, the Nazi Party offered a different version of Radical Right ideology. Just as the emergence of fascism was inextricably linked to the career of one man, Benito Mussolini, so Nazism° cannot be separated from Adolf Hitler (1889–1945). To understand the Nazi Revolution in Germany, we need first to explore Hitler's rise to power and then to examine the impact of Nazi rule on ordinary people.

Hitler's Rise to Power

Hitler, an ardent German nationalist, was not a citizen of Germany for most of his life. Born in Austria, Hitler came of age in Vienna, where he made a meager living as a painter while absorbing the anti-Semitic German nationalism that permeated the capital city of the Habsburg Empire. When World War I broke out, Hitler grabbed at the chance to fight the war in a German rather than an Austrian uniform. He regarded army life as "the greatest of all experiences." Hitler served as a German soldier for almost the entire length of the war until he was temporarily blinded by poison gas in 1918. After the war he settled in Munich, home to large bands of unemployed war veterans. Munich became a fertile breeding ground of far right-wing political factions that espoused various versions of German nationalism laced with antidemocratic, antisocialist, and often anti-Semitic imagery and ideas.

The Nazi Party began as one of these small fringe groups, with Hitler quickly emerging as its leader. *Nazi* is shorthand for *National Socialist German Workers' Party,* but this title is misleading—the Nazis were *not* a socialist party. Like fascism, Nazism was fiercely opposed to socialism, communism, trade unionism, and any political analysis that emphasized class conflict or workers' rights. Hitler, however, inserted these common fascist ideas into an astonishing apocalyptic story. In the tale told by Hitler, Germany was destined to become a powerful empire controlling central and eastern Europe. This new age would dawn only after a mighty battle between the racially superior Germans and their numerically superior enemy: the forces of "Judeo-Bolshevism." In Hitler's distorted vision, communism and Jewishness were two parts of the same evil whole. He saw the Bolshevik victory in Russia and the call for communist world revolution as part of a much larger struggle for Jewish world domination. Like Mussolini, Hitler exalted the nation, but Hitler's Nazism, much more so than Mussolini's fascism, focused on *race* as the key social reality. To Hitler, all history was the history of racial struggle, and in that racial struggle, the Jews were always the principal enemy. Hitler regarded Jewishness as a biological rather than a religious identity, as a sort of toxic infection that could be passed on to future generations and that posed a threat to the racially pure "Aryans"—white northern Europeans. (*Aryan* is actually a linguistic term referring to the Indo-Aryan or Indo-European language groups. Hitler misapplied the term to racial groups to lend a supposedly scientific authority to his racism.)

In its early days Nazism appealed to men like Hitler, individuals without much power or, apparently, much chance of getting it—demobilized and now unemployed soldiers, small shopkeepers wiped out by postwar inflation, lower middle-class office clerks anxious to preserve their shaky social status, and workers who had lost their jobs. Nazism offered a simple explanation of history, a promise of future glory, and a clear and identifiable scapegoat for both personal and national woes. By the time of the Beer Hall Putsch in November 1923, party membership stood at about 55,000.

As we saw earlier in the discussion of postwar Germany, the Beer Hall Putsch failed in its aim to overthrow the Weimar Republic, but it did bring Hitler before a national audience. Both his speeches during the ensuing trial for treason and *Mein Kampf* (My Struggle), the book he wrote while in prison, publicized his racialized view of German political history. After Hitler emerged from prison, he concentrated on transforming the Nazis into a persuasive political force. To infiltrate German society at all levels, Nazis formed university and professional groups, labor unions, and agrarian organizations, while the Nazi paramilitary organization, the SA (the *Sturmabteilung*), terrorized opponents. The party held meetings and rallies incessantly, not just during election periods, and so ensured that Germany was saturated with its message. Even so, in the elections of 1928, Nazi candidates won only 2.6 percent of the vote.

It was the Great Depression that gave the Nazis their chance at power. After 1929, unemployment rates skyrocketed and the Weimar political system began to collapse. No German political leader was able to put together a viable governing coalition. Parliamentary power dwindled; in all of 1932 the federal parliament was in session for only thirteen days. As the mechanisms of parliamentary democracy faltered, the German chancellor Heinrich Bruning was increasingly forced to rely on a stopgap measure in the German constitution—the presidential emergency decree. The constitution declared that in emergency situations, decrees signed by the German president could become law without parliamentary consent. But this practice meant that power shifted from the parliament to the president, the World War I hero General Paul von Hindenburg. Already in his eighties, Hindenburg was a weak man easily manipulated by a small circle of aristocratic advisors and cronies.

In this unstable political climate, political polarization accelerated. In elections in 1930 both the Communist and Nazi parties attracted an increasing number of votes as Germans looked for extreme solutions to extreme problems. By July 1932, the Nazis had become the largest party in the parliament, winning the support of 37 percent of the German voters. Support for their communist rivals also continued to grow.

Terrified of the threat posed by communism and convinced that Hitler could be easily controlled, a small group of conservative politicians persuaded Hindenburg to offer Hitler the position of chancellor in January 1933. One of the group, Baron Franz von Papen, reassured a friend that Hitler posed "no danger at all. We have hired him for our act. In two months' time we'll have pushed Hitler so far into the corner, he'll be squeaking."[9] But von Papen was wrong.

Within six months Hitler had destroyed what remained of democracy in Germany and established a Nazi dictatorship. Almost as soon as he took office he persuaded Hindenburg to pass an emergency decree mandating the seizure of all Communist Party presses and buildings. Then in February a mentally unstable Dutch transient set fire to the German parliament building. Declaring that the fire was part of a communist plot against the state, Hitler demanded the power to imprison without warrant or trial. Mass arrests of more than 25,000 of his political opponents

CHRONOLOGY

Hitler's Rise to Power

1914–1918	Serves in the German army
1919–1923	Establishes himself as a right-wing activist in Munich
1923	Fails to overthrow the government with the Beer Hall Putsch
1929	Collapse of the U.S. stock market; onset of Great Depression
1930	Nazis win 107 seats in German parliament
1932	Nazis win 230 seats; become largest party in German parliament
1933	
January	Becomes chancellor
February	Uses Reichstag fire as pretext to gain emergency powers
March	Uses the Enabling Act to destroy democracy in Germany

followed—not only communists but also social democrats and anyone who dared oppose him openly. At the end of March, German politicians, cowed by Nazi threats of imprisonment, passed the Enabling Act. This key act gave Hitler the power to suspend the Constitution and pass legislation without a parliamentary majority. By the summer of 1933, parliamentary political life had ceased to exist in Germany.

The Nazi dictatorship was designed to give maximum power to Hitler. Often presented as a model of authoritarian efficiency, it was actually a confusing mass of overlapping bureaucracies, in which ambitious officials competed with each other for power and influence. This planned chaos ensured that none of Hitler's deputies acquired too much authority. It also enhanced the mystery of the state. The individual citizen attempting to make a complaint or resolve a problem would soon feel like he was engaged in a battle with a multilimbed monster.

This multilimbed monster, however, had only one head: Adolf Hitler. The entire system was designed to make clear that there was only one man in charge, one leader—the *Führer*. Like Mussolini, Hitler realized the importance of personalizing his rule. During election campaigns before 1933 and in the early years of power after, Hitler was constantly on the move, using cars and planes to hit city after city, to deliver speech after speech, to touch person after person. In 1932 and 1933, he conducted election campaigns from the sky, often visiting four or five cities in a single night. He always arrived late, so that his plane could fly above the packed stadium, the focus of every upturned face. Leaders of the Hitler Youth were required to take this oath: "Adolf Hitler is Germany and Germany is Adolf Hitler. He who pledges himself to Hitler pledges himself to Germany."[10]

National Recovery

Jews, communists, socialists, and other groups defined as enemies of the state faced the constant threat of persecution and imprisonment under the Nazi regime during the 1930s. But for many Germans not in these groups, life got better. Nazi rule brought economic prosperity, restoration of national pride, and a cultural revolution that linked the power of nostalgia to the dynamism of modernity.

Economic depression gave the Nazis the chance at power; economic prosperity enabled them to hold on to this power. Because Hitler perceived himself as a revolutionary, bound by no existing rules, he was able to adopt the

■ **Hitler Opening the Construction of the German Autobahn, 1933**

Hitler's program of public works was designed both to provide employment and to rebuild Germany as a world power. One of his most cherished projects was the Autobahn, the highway system of modern Germany. The Autobahn was not only of economic importance, in terms of providing an efficient means of moving goods and people across Germany, but also of great symbolic significance: It associated Nazi Germany with mobility and modernity.

aggressive and ultimately successful economic policy suggested by Hjalmar Schacht (1877–1970), his finance minister. The rules of economic orthodoxy dictated that in times of depression, a government should cut spending and maintain a balanced budget. Schacht broke the rules and instead embarked on a program of massive state expenditure. The result was the most impressive economic recovery in Europe. Industrial output rose by almost 30 percent while unemployment dropped from 44 percent in 1932 to 14.1 percent in 1934 to under 1 percent in 1938. In contrast, double-digit unemployment rates persisted in Britain while in France industrial production remained below 1929 levels through the 1930s. Under the Nazis, social welfare programs expanded and the "Strength through Joy" program (directly inspired by Mussolini's "after-work" organizations) provided workers with cheap vacations, theater and concert tickets, and weekend outings. Although real wages fell under Nazi rule and independent trade unions were outlawed, the fact that jobs were now available in abundance made Hitler an economic savior to many Germans.

Many also viewed him as a national savior, a leader who restored Germany's pride and power. Payment of war reparations, demanded by the humiliating Versailles Treaty, halted in 1930 because of the global economic crisis. Hitler never resumed payment. He also ignored the treaty's military restrictions and rebuilt Germany's armed forces. By 1938, parades featuring row after row of smartly uniformed troops, impressive displays of tanks, and flybys of military aircraft all signaled the revitalization of German military might. For many ordinary Germans, traumatized and shamed by the sequence of national disasters—military defeat, loss of territory, hyperinflation, political and fiscal crises, unemployment—the sight of troops goose-stepping under the German flag meant a personal as well as a national renaissance. As one Nazi song proclaimed, "And now the me is part of the great We."[11]

To create the "great We," Hitler utilized modern techniques and technology. In his election campaigns in the early 1930s he demonstrated that, like Mussolini, he understood the power of the new mass media. For just one election, his staff distributed 50,000 records of his speeches. The Nazis published a glossy illustrated magazine, produced their own films, and littered cities with campaign posters. Impressed by Mussolini's use of the radio to popularize fascism, Hitler subsidized the production of radios in Germany so that by the end of the 1930s most Germans had access to a radio—and to Hitler's radio talks. He also recognized the power of the cinema, and hired the brilliant filmmaker Leni Riefenstahl (1902–2003) to film Nazi rallies. These still-astonishing films show an overwhelming mass spectacle, in which an entire nation appears to be marching in step behind Hitler.

But Hitler also recognized the power of nostalgia for many Germans. He used modern techniques and technologies to establish the Nazis as bulwarks of tradition. In speeches, posters, and films, the Nazis painted a picture of a mythic Germany, an idyllic community peopled by sturdy blond peasants, small shopkeepers, and independent craftsmen. The Nazis promised that under their leadership, individual Germans would regain meaning and purpose as part of a single national community. International corporations, large department stores, and supermarket chains were all demonized as elements of a vast Jewish-controlled conspiracy to deprive ordinary people of their livelihoods.

Campaigns of Repression and Terror

Part of the appeal of the "great We" that Hitler was creating relied on the demonization and violent repression of the "not Us," those defined as outside or opposed to the nation. Hitler used the existing German police force as well as his own paramilitary troops—the brownshirted SA and the blackshirted SS (the *Schutzstaffeln*)—to terrorize those he defined as enemies of the nation. The Nazis first targeted political opponents. By 1934 half of the 300,000 German Communist Party members were in prison or dead; most of the rest had fled the country. The Nazis also persecuted specific religious groups on the basis of their actual or presumed opposition to the Nazi state. Roman Catholics were banned from government service and subject to constant harassment, and about half of Germany's 20,000 Jehovah's Witnesses were sent to concentration camps.

The groups that the Nazis deemed biologically inferior suffered most severely. Beginning in 1933, the Nazi regime forced the sterilization of the Roma (Gypsies), the mentally and physically handicapped, and mixed-race children (in most cases, the offspring of German women and black African soldiers serving in the French occupation force in the Rhineland). By 1939, 370,000 men and women had been sterilized.

The Jewish community—less than 1 percent of the German population—bore the brunt of Nazi racial attacks. To Nazi anti-Semites, Hitler's accession to the German chancellorship was like the opening of hunting season. They beat up Jews in the streets, vandalized Jewish shops and homes, threatened German Christians who associated with Jews, and violently enforced boycotts of Jewish businesses. Anti-Jewish legislation piled up in an effort to convince Germans of the separateness, the "non-Germanness," of Jewish cultural and racial identity. In 1933, "non-Aryans" (Jews) were dismissed from the civil service and the legal profession, and the number of Jewish students in high schools and universities was restricted. Every organization in Germany—youth clubs, sports teams, labor unions, charitable societies—was subject to "Nazification," which meant Jewish members had to be dismissed and Nazis appointed to leadership roles. In 1935, the "Nuremberg Laws" labeled as Jewish anyone with three or more Jewish grandparents. Marriage or sexual relations between German Jews and non-Jews now became a serious crime.

WOMEN AND THE RADICAL RIGHT

Much of the appeal of both fascism and Nazism lay in the promise to restore order to societies on the verge of disintegration. Restoration of order meant the return of women to their proper place. According to Nazi propaganda, "the soil provides the food, the woman supplies the population, and the men make the action."[12] Hitler proclaimed, "the Nazi Revolution will be an entirely male event." Mussolini agreed: "Woman must obey. . . . In our State, she must not count."[13]

In Nazi Germany, the restoration of order translated into a series of financial and cultural incentives to encourage women to stay at home and produce babies. Incentives ranged from marriage loans (available only if the wife quit her job) to income tax deductions to the opportunity to participate in housewives' discussion, welfare, and leisure groups. Disincentives were also utilized. One of the first actions of the new Nazi government was to dismiss women from the civil service. Women physicians could work only in their husbands' practices. By 1937, both women physicians and women Ph.D.s had lost the right to be addressed as "Doctor" or "Professor." The Nazis abolished coeducation and replaced female principals with males. Birth control became illegal and penalties for abortion increased while prosecutions doubled.

In Italy, Mussolini's government focused its legislation on both men and women. Unmarried men over age 30 had to pay double income tax (priests were exempt), homosexual relations between men were outlawed, and fatherhood became a prerequisite for men in high-ranking public office. As in the democracies, the fascist government established a wide-ranging social welfare program: Family allowances, maternity leaves, birth and marriage loans, and family health clinics were all established to strengthen the Italian "race." Quotas limited the number of women employed in both the civil service and in private business, while women found themselves excluded entirely from jobs defined as "virile," a varied list that included boat captains, diplomats, high school principals, and history teachers.

The Polarization of Politics in the 1930s

To Europeans and Americans disenchanted with the response of the democracies to the challenge of the Great Depression, fascist Italy and Nazi Germany offered powerful alternatives. The Soviet Union provided yet another option. While the capitalist nations struggled with high unemployment rates and falling industrial output, the

Soviet Union appeared to be performing economic miracles. Politics in the West thus became polarized between communism on the left and fascism and Nazism on the right. In both the United States and Europe, however, politicians and policymakers sought to maintain the middle ground, to retain democratic values in a time of extremist ideologies.

THE SOVIET UNION UNDER STALIN: REVOLUTION RECONSTRUCTED, TERROR EXTENDED

Many Europeans looked with envy at the Soviet Union in the 1930s. Unemployment had disappeared; huge industrial cities transformed the landscape; the development of new industries such as chemicals and automobiles, together with a full-scale exploitation of the Soviet Union's massive natural resources (gold, timber, coal), sent production indices soaring. But this economic transformation rested on dead bodies, millions of dead bodies. During the 1930s, mass murder became an integral part of the Soviet regime under Joseph Stalin (1879–1953).

Stalin's Rise to Power

By 1928, Stalin was the uncontested head of the party. At the time of Lenin's death in 1924, however, few observers would have predicted Stalin's success. A stalwart Bolshevik, he was overshadowed by more charismatic, intellectually able colleagues. How, then, did Stalin seize control of the Communist party and the Soviet state?

One key factor in Stalin's rise to power was the changing nature of the Communist Party. The party that made the revolution in 1917 comprised only 24,000 members. Following a massive recruitment campaign to honor Lenin's memory, party membership in 1929 stood at over one and a half million—and only 8,000 of these had been members in 1917. In other words, the vast majority of communists in 1929 had not fought in the revolution. For them, communism was not a revolutionary ideology challenging the tsarist political order; it was itself the political order. Party membership was not a revolutionary act; it was a guarantee of privileged status and career opportunities. Moreover, unlike the original Bolshevik revolutionaries, most of the new members were not well-educated or well-versed in communist ideology. In fact, 25 percent of the party membership was functionally illiterate.

As party secretary from 1922 on, Stalin had led the recruitment drive that enlisted many of these new party members. Other party leaders dismissed Stalin as the "card-index Bolshevik"—the paper-pusher, the gray guy with the boring job. But Stalin, an astute politician, recognized that

CHRONOLOGY

Stalin's Rise to Power

1917	
March	Popular Russian Revolution
November	Bolshevik Revolution
1918–1921	Russian Civil War
1921	New Economic Policy (NEP) begins
1922	Stalin appointed General Secretary of the Central Committee of the Communist Party
1924	Death of Lenin
1925–1928	Leadership disputes; Stalin emerges as the head of the Communist Party
1929	NEP ended; collectivization begins
1934	The Congress of Victors
1934–1938	The Great Purge

his card index held enormous power. Not only did he determine the fate of party membership applications, he also decided who got promoted to what and where. Thus, throughout the 1920s Stalin slowly built up a broad base of support within the party. Vast numbers of ordinary communists owed their party membership, and in many cases their livelihoods, to Stalin.

While Stalin expanded his support at the grassroots, a fierce ideological struggle at the highest levels of the Communist Party distracted his rivals for the party leadership. By the time of Lenin's death, the New Economic Policy (NEP) had restored economic stability to the Soviet Union. The nation, however, remained far behind its capitalist competitors in both agricultural and industrial productivity. All communists agreed on the need to launch the Soviet economy into industrialization. The problem was, how could this backward nation obtain the capital it needed for industrial development? One faction of the party, led by Leon Trotsky (1879–1940), argued that the answer was to squeeze the necessary capital out of the peasantry through high taxation and even, if necessary, the confiscation of crops. Trotsky wanted to abandon NEP and its encouragement of small private farming initiatives. The opposing faction, led by Nikolai Bukharin (1888–1938), pointed to the lessons taught by western European industrialization. In the West, industrial capital came from agricultural profits. Bukharin insisted on the need for gradualism: Agricultural development must precede industrialization. "Enrich the peasant," Bukharin argued.

Stalin at first backed Bukharin and those who wished to continue on the NEP course, because he perceived that the more immediate threat to his ambitions came from the charismatic Trotsky. Once Trotsky had been expelled from the party, however, Stalin reversed course and turned on Bukharin. Painting this veteran Bolshevik as an antisocialist, Stalin pushed Bukharin to the margins of Soviet politics. In 1928, Stalin emerged as the sole leader of the party and as a fierce advocate of the abandonment of NEP, the total socialization of the Soviet economy, and a fast march forward into full-scale industrialization.

The "Revolution from Above": Collectivization and Industrialization, 1928–1934

As party leader, Stalin placed the Soviet Union firmly back on a revolutionary course, with the aim of catapulting the Soviet Union into the ranks of the industrialized nations. The first step in what was called "the revolution from above" was collectivization°, the replacement of private and village farms with large cooperative agricultural enterprises run by communist managers according to directives received from the central government. Collectivization had both economic and political aims. Regarded as more modern and efficient, collective farms were expected to produce an agricultural surplus and thereby raise the capital needed for industrialization. But in addition, collectivization would realize communist ideals by eradicating the profit motive, abolishing private property, and transforming the peasants into modern state employees.

The peasants resisted this transformation, however. They burned their crops and slaughtered their livestock. Famine followed. The numbers of deaths resulting from collectivization and the famine of 1931–1932 remain the subject of intense controversy; the available quantitative evidence points to death figures between five million and seven million. Ukraine and Kazakhstan were hardest hit. Almost 40 percent of the Kazakh population died from starvation or typhus; the number of dead in Ukraine alone may have reached four million.[14] Perhaps as many as ten million peasants were deported in these years; many of these died either on the way to or in forced labor camps.

While class war raged in the countryside, city dwellers embarked on the second stage of the "revolution from above"—industrialization. In 1931 Stalin articulated the task facing the Soviet Union: "We are fifty or a hundred years behind the advanced countries. We must catch up this distance in ten years. Either we do it or we go under."[15]

■ "Pictures Can't Lie . . ."

Stalin was not Lenin's closest associate, nor did Lenin select him as his successor. To claim and consolidate his position as sole leader of the Communist Party and of the Soviet Union, Stalin had to falsify history and present himself as Lenin's chosen heir. Murder and mass executions could remove competitors from the present, but to erase them from the past, Stalin turned to the airbrush and the scissors rather than the gun. Pictures showing other Bolsheviks standing next to Lenin were cropped, leaving him with Stalin, or if such a pairing could not be achieved, standing alone. This illustration shows the process at work. Compare the photo shown on page 815 of Chapter 24 with the photo on the right. In the first photo, taken just seconds before the one shown here, Lev Kamenev and Leon Trotsky—leading Bolsheviks and rivals with Stalin for the party leadership after Lenin's death—stand on the steps to Lenin's left. But in this picture, Kamenev and Trotsky have been cut out and some steps have been drawn in. Stalin sought to airbrush Trotsky and Kamenev out of Soviet history, just as he eliminated them from Soviet politics. Trotsky was forced into exile in 1929 and murdered in 1940, Kamenev was executed in 1936.

Doing it demanded, first, unprecedented levels of labor output. Despite the massive investment in heavy industry, the Soviet Union throughout the 1930s remained undermechanized. What it lacked in technology, however, it possessed in population. Thus Soviet industry was highly labor-intensive. To ensure that workers produced at the levels needed, the Soviet state under Stalin imposed fierce labor discipline. Only productive workers received ration cards. Internal passports restricted workers' freedom of movement. If fired, a worker was automatically evicted from his or her apartment and deprived of a ration card.

Catching up with the West also demanded reducing already-low levels of personal consumption. Eighty percent of all investment went into heavy industry, while domestic construction and light industry—clothing, for example, or furniture—were ignored. Scarcity became the norm, long lines and constant shortages part of every urban resident's existence. Economists estimate that Soviet citizens endured a 40 percent fall in their already low standard of living between 1929 and 1932.

Yet in the midst of this suffering was great enthusiasm. For young communists in the 1930s, these years of hardship were also years of heroism, an era in which they believed they were building a new society. They volunteered to organize collective farms, to work in conditions of extreme brutality at construction sites, to labor long hours in factories and mines. Babies born in this decade received names like "Little-Five-Years" (for girls) and "Plan" (for boys), reflecting their parents' enthusiasm for the series of Five-Year-Plans issued by the central government as outlines for the new world order. Much of this enthusiasm was stirred up by propaganda campaigns aimed at persuading laborers to work ever harder and sacrifice ever more. Ordinary workers who achieved record-breaking feats of production were featured in newspaper articles and rewarded with medals, special ceremonies, and material gifts. Immense publicity focused on the gargantuan engineering achievements of the era—the cities built atop swampland, the hydroelectric projects with their enormous dams and power plants, the Moscow subway system. Such publicity made party members feel part of a huge and powerful endeavor. A popular song announced, "We were born to make fairy tales come true."[16]

Just as important as the propaganda campaigns was the reality of unprecedented opportunity. The Soviet Union in the 1930s has been called "the quicksand society," one in which traditional structures and relations (and people too) were swallowed up at a breathtaking pace. Yet as these traditional structures disappeared, new ones emerged, bringing tremendous geographic and social mobility to Soviet society. For example, Nikita Khrushchev (1894–1971), who would succeed Stalin as the head of the party and state in the 1950s, was the son of a poor peasant.

No propaganda campaign and no amount of effort from enthusiastic young communists, however, could provide the Soviet Union with the labor it needed to catch up with the West in ten years. Forced labor was crucial. Throughout the 1930s, as many as five million men, women, and children—peasants, political opponents of Stalin, religious dissenters, ethnic minorities—labored in prison camps.[17] By some estimates, forced labor accounted for no less than 25 percent of all construction work in the Soviet Union in the 1930s. Many of the huge engineering triumphs of the decade rested on the backs of prisoners and deportees.

By the end of the 1930s, Stalin's "revolution from above" had achieved its aim. The pouring of resources into heavy industry and the wringing of every ounce of labor out of an exhausted, cold, and hungry populace succeeded in building the foundations of an industrial society. This society would stand the test of total war in the 1940s.

But Stalin's revolution failed to convert Soviet agriculture into a modern, prosperous sector of the economy. Rural regions remained backward. Peasant villages, for example, were not electrified until the later 1950s. Most peasants regarded the collective farm as belonging not to them or to the community but to the state, just another in a long line of harsh landlords. Under Stalin, peasants were second-class citizens, ineligible for internal passports, with little access to the benefits of Soviet industrialization. Like

■ **Forced Labor in the Soviet Union**

Deported peasants and political prisoners construct the Stalin-Belomor canal in northern Russia in 1933. Death rates were high as slave laborers toiled in brutal conditions to achieve Stalin's industrial goals. At least 30,000 prisoners died on this project.

their ancestors under serfdom, peasants at the end of the 1930s found themselves tied to a particular village, saddled with forced labor obligations, and compelled to spend the bulk of their time farming for someone else's profit. Most peasants viewed the state, and Stalin, as the enemy, to be ignored when possible, tricked if necessary, and endured no matter what.

Stalin's Consolidation of Power: The Great Purge and Soviet Society, 1934–1939

By the mid-1930s, the worst seemed to be over. Most villages were collectivized and the mass violence had ended. The 17th Party Congress in 1934 was known as the "Congress of Victors," as the party celebrated its industrial successes and the achievement of collectivization. But for many of the men and women at this Congress the worst was yet to come. Within five years, half of the 2,000 delegates had been arrested; of the 149 elected members of the Congress's Central Committee, 98 were shot dead. These Congress delegates, and hundreds of thousands of other Soviet citizens, were victims of the "Great Purge°." In the purge, Stalin's effort to eliminate any possible rival to his power converged with widespread paranoia and economic crisis to produce a nationwide witch hunt and mass executions.

The beginning of the purge is often dated from December 1, 1934, when Leningrad Communist Party Chief Sergei Kirov was assassinated. Some historians argue that Stalin himself engineered Kirov's assassination because he feared the Leningrad chief's popularity. Stalin's exact role in the assassination remains opaque, but it is clear that once Kirov was dead Stalin used the murder for his own political ends. The hunt for Kirov's killers became the pretext for a purge of the Communist Party. The investigation into the assassination sparked a wave of arrests and executions, first in Leningrad, and soon throughout the entire Soviet Union.

The early victims of the purge tended to be top-ranking Communist Party officials, many of whom had opposed Stalin on various issues during the 1920s. By charging these powerful men with conspiring against the communist state, Stalin reduced the chances that any competitor might oust him. In a series of three spectacular show trials attended by journalists from all over the world, leading Bolsheviks— some of the Soviet Union's most respected men such as Nikolai Bukharin—pleaded guilty to charges of conspiracy and sabotage, and were immediately executed. Numerous smaller trials replicated the process throughout the Soviet Union. Non-Russians suffered heavily. By the end of the 1930s, for example, 260 of the 300 party secretaries in Georgia had been killed. The purge also swept the armed forces. Those executed included three of the five Soviet marshals, thirteen of fifteen army commanders, and fifty-seven of eighty corps commanders.

Two factors spread the purge beyond the top ranks of the party and military. First, the purge coincided with the military resurgence of Germany as well as heightened hostilities between the Soviet Union and Japan. By the later 1930s the Soviet press carried frequent articles about the possibility of a two-front war, and lent credence to popular fears of spies. With the show trials indicating that even the highest-level Bolsheviks were not to be trusted, people began to suspect that traitors lurked within every factory and local party gathering. Second, the purge came at a time of agricultural crisis and the beginnings of an industrial slowdown. In 1936, exceptionally bad weather resulted in a dangerously poor harvest. By 1937, food was once again in short supply. At the same time the shortcomings of an overly centralized and poorly run economy were multiplying. Subject to an endless stream of ever-changing and often irrational program and policy directives, managers falsified key economic statistics, while poorly trained workers misused machines and cut all available corners. People were anxious and hungry, and eager to find someone to blame for breakdowns and failures. The purge made it easy to point the finger, to charge this manager with deliberately failing to order tractors or that engineer with implementing the wrong system of crop rotation to sabotage production.

Thus the Great Purge quickly spun out of control to embrace low-level party members, managers in state agencies, factory directors, and engineers. Family members, neighbors, clients, and friends all became victims. So, too, did the "usual suspects"—anyone with a black mark on his or her record, one-time well-to-do farmers, former priests and nuns, anyone who had opposed the Bolsheviks or Stalin at any time or place. Many were killed without trial, others executed after a legal show. Many of those purged were deported to slave labor camps to be worked to death on Stalin's vast construction projects. Death estimates vary widely; at least 750,000 people died, with the numbers of those arrested, imprisoned, or deported running into the millions.[18]

The Great Purge consolidated Stalin's hold on the Soviet Union. It not only eliminated all potential competitors, it also tied huge numbers of people more tightly to Stalin and his version of revolution. The shocking thing about the Great Purge was its popularity. The purge hit primarily urban managers. For the most part, ordinary workers and peasants were safe from its onslaught. These ordinary citizens, who had been ordered about, reprimanded, fined, insulted, and assaulted by these self-same managers, tended to believe that the purge's victims got what they deserved. Moreover, the purge can also be seen as a huge job creation program. Individuals who moved into the positions left vacant by the purge's victims had an enormous material as well as psychological stake in viewing the purge as an act of justice.

Stalin and the Nation

The popularity of the purge was also closely linked with the emergence of a Stalin-centered personality cult. By the time the purge began, the cult was an omnipresent part of Soviet urban life. Huge posters and statues ensured that Stalin's figure remained constantly in front of Soviet citizens. Every scientific, technological, or economic advance in the Soviet Union was linked to the person and power of Stalin. Textbooks rewrote the history of the Bolshevik Revolution to highlight Stalin's contribution. The scores of letters personally addressed to Stalin that poured into central government offices testify to the success of this cult. To many Soviet citizens, Stalin personified the nation.

Increasingly it was the *nation*—not the worker, not socialism, not the revolution—that was emphasized. Lenin had condemned Russian nationalism as a middle-class ideology to be eradicated along with capitalism. The working class, not the nation, was what mattered. But Stalin reversed this aspect of Lenin's revolution. In the 1930s, "Russia" and "the motherland/fatherland" both reappeared in political discourse. The tsarist past, which Lenin had condemned or ignored, was resurrected to emphasize Russian greatness. The imperial anthem resounded once again, while films and books praised strong Russian leaders such as Peter the Great. While this resurgence of Russian nationalism was popular in Russia itself, it spelled real difficulties for the 50 percent of the Soviet population who lived outside of Russia and who found it necessary to repress their own sense of national identity—or face deportation.

Exalting the motherland went hand in hand with exalting the mother. Just as Stalin resurrected Russian nationalism in the 1930s, so he sought to resurrect the Russian family. He promoted the family as a vital prop of the national order, an institution to be strengthened rather than encouraged to wither away (as Lenin had insisted). In 1936, Stalin's regime outlawed abortion and made divorce more difficult. Like Western leaders, Stalin also sought to increase the national birth rate by granting pregnant women maternity stipends and increasing the number of prenatal health clinics. There was no effort to pull women out of the workforce, however. Of the more than four million new workers entering the labor force between 1932 and 1937, 82 percent were women. The Soviet Union continued to provide women with access to higher education and professional jobs—women worked as doctors, engineers, scientists, and high-ranking public officials. (And women were deported and executed in huge numbers—one could argue that Stalin was an equal-opportunity killer.)

THE SEARCH FOR MIDDLE GROUND

The apparent economic successes of fascism and Nazism on the right, and Stalinism on the left, polarized European politics. For many Europeans in the 1930s, it seemed that the middle ground was collapsing beneath their feet, that democracy had failed and that they had no choice but to scramble to one extreme or the other. Yet in both western Europe and in the United States, important steps were taken to assure that democracy not only survived but that it eventually delivered a decent standard of living to the great mass of ordinary people.

A Third Way?
The Social Democratic Alternative

The effort to meet the challenge of the depression without embracing either the Radical Right or Stalinism accelerated the development of the political model that would dominate western Europe after World War II: social democracy°. In a social democracy, a democratically elected parliamentary government assumes the role of ensuring a decent standard of living for its citizens. To achieve this goal, the government assumes two important functions—first, regulating an economy containing both private enterprise and nationalized or state-controlled corporations; and second, overseeing a welfare state, which guarantees the citizen access to unemployment and sickness benefits, pensions, family allowances, and health services. Although social democracy did not triumph in western Europe until after the massive bloodletting of another total war, the interwar years witnessed important steps toward this third path, an alternative to the extremes of both the Radical Right and Stalinism.

One of the most striking experiments in changing the relationship between democratic governments and the economy occurred in the United States. Franklin Delano Roosevelt (1882–1945) became president in 1932 at the height of the Great Depression, when unemployment stood at 24 percent (15 million workers were without jobs) and Washington, D.C., witnessed federal troops called out to quell rioting among unemployed veterans. Promising a "New Deal" of "Relief, Recovery, Reform," Roosevelt tackled the depression with an activist governmental policy that included agricultural subsidies, public works programs, and the Social Security Act of 1935, which laid the foundations of the U.S. welfare program.

Yet even with this sharp upswing in governmental activity, unemployment remained high—ten million workers were without jobs in 1939—and the gross national product (GNP) did not recover to 1929 levels until 1941. In the view of some economists, Roosevelt failed to solve the problem of unemployment because he remained committed to the ideal of a balanced budget. In contrast, the British economist John Maynard Keynes (1883–1946) insisted that in times of depression, the state should not reduce spending and endeavor to live within its budget, but instead should adopt a program of deficit spending to stimulate economic growth. Only when prosperity returned, Keynes advised, should governments increase taxes and cut expenditures to recover the deficits.

The experience of Sweden appeared to confirm Keynes's theory. The Swedish Social Democratic Party took office in 1932 with the intention of using the powers of central government to revive the depressed economy. The government allowed its budget deficit to climb while it financed a massive public works campaign, as well as an increase in welfare benefits ranging from unemployment insurance to maternity allowances to subsidized housing. By 1937 unemployment was shrinking rapidly as the manufacturing sector boomed.

Throughout most of western Europe, however, governments proved far more reluctant to advocate radically new policies, despite an expansion of the state's role in economic affairs. In Britain, for example, social spending did rise during the interwar decades. Government spending on social benefits—ranging from old-age pensions to health and unemployment insurance to school meals—grew from 4.2 percent of the gross national product in 1910 to 11.3 percent of the GNP by 1938. In addition, a housing program made two million new houses available to families on low incomes. In general, however, the British government remained reluctant to intervene in the economy. Britain's limited economic recovery in the later 1930s was based largely on private initiatives such as an expansion in housing construction and the emergence of new industries aimed at domestic consumption (radios and other small electronics, household goods, automobiles). In the areas hardest hit by depression—the heavy export industries such as coal, shipbuilding, textiles, and steel, located primarily in northern Britain—the lack of government intervention meant continuing high unemployment rates and widespread poverty and deprivation throughout the 1930s.

The Popular Front in France

The limited success of democratic governments in addressing the problems of the Great Depression meant that many experienced the 1930s as a hard, hungry decade when democracy failed to deliver a decent standard of living. The example of France illustrates both the political polarization occurring in Europe in the 1930s and the sharp limits on governments seeking both to maintain democratic politics and to improve the living conditions of their citizens. The Great Depression hit France later than most other European nations, but by 1931 the nation was experiencing a sharp economic downturn. France lacked such basic welfare benefits as old-age pensions and unemployment insurance. As the economy plummeted, therefore, social unrest rose, and so, too, did the appeal of the fascist movement. In 1934, right-wing antigovernment riots left seventeen dead and more than 2,000 injured.

The increasing strength of fascism, combined with the deepening national emergency, led to the formation of the Popular Front, a coalition comprising the centrist Radical Party, the moderate leftist Socialist Party, and the Stalinist Communist Party. In 1936, the Popular Front won the national elections. The Socialist Party leader Leon Blum (1872–1950) took office as prime minister in the midst of a general strike involving two million workers. He settled the

strike to the workers' benefit by granting them a 15 percent pay raise and the right to collective bargaining. Over the next year, Blum nationalized the key war industries and gave workers further pay increases, paid holidays, and a forty-hour work week.

For many French voters, Blum's policies of social reform represented not a new democratic alternative but rather the first step on the road to Stalinism. Thus they cried, "Better Hitler than Blum!"—in other words, better the Radical Right than the Stalinist Left. The response of the global business community was a massive pullout of capital from France, resulting in a major financial crisis and the devaluation of the French franc. Dependent on foreign loans, Blum's government faced sharp pressure to pull back from its program of social and economic reforms. When it tried to do so, its working-class constituency rose in revolt. In May 1937 the suppression of a left-wing demonstration left seven dead and 200 injured. Blum resigned the next month. The Popular Front in France quickly disintegrated.

THE SPANISH CIVIL WAR

Spain became the arena in which the struggle of Europe's polarized political forces turned into outright war. In 1931, a democratically elected republican government replaced the Spanish monarchy and in 1936, a Popular Front government, comprising both socialists and communists, took office. In July, army officers led a right-wing rebellion against this government.

The struggle between the left-wing Republican government and the right-wing rebels quickly became an international issue. Both fascist Italy and Nazi Germany supported the rebellion, enabling General Francisco Franco (1892–1975) and his crack Moroccan troops to cross into Spain from their station in North Africa and launch an all-out offensive against the Republic. The Republican government appealed to the democracies for aid, but the only government that came to its assistance was that of the Soviet Union. Soviet tanks and aircraft enabled the besieged city of Madrid to hold out against Franco's forces but at the same time the Soviet intervention split the Republican movement, with anarchists and socialists resisting Stalinist control. Unnerved by the Soviet involvement, the governments of France, Britain, and the United States remained neutral. Appalled by this official inaction, many citizens of these countries served in the International Brigade, which fought for the cause of democracy in Spain.

The Spanish Civil War raged until March 1939, when the last remnants of the Republican forces finally surrendered to Franco. Four hundred thousand men and women died in the war; in the following four years, another 200,000 were executed. The war resulted in the death of democracy in Spain and the establishment of an authoritarian government led by Franco. Even more crucially, Spain became a

■ The Spanish Civil War

The Spanish Civil War mobilized women as well as men. These soldiers, fighting in the uniform of the anarchist militia, are defending the barricades of Barcelona against rebel attack.

potent symbol for all of Europe. To both fascists and their democratic opponents, Franco's victory served as one more step in the forward march of the Radical Right.

European Empires in the Interwar Era

The polarization of European politics was one important consequence of the First World War. The war also had significant—but contradictory—consequences for the structures of European empires. On the one hand, the war seemed to strengthen European imperialism: Both France and Britain emerged from the war with their empires expanded and their commitment to imperialism intact. On the other hand, the economic, social, and political changes wrought by the war accelerated the formation of mass nationalist movements that challenged imperial control.

THE EXPANSION OF EMPIRE

During the final years of World War I, the Allies claimed to be fighting for national self-determination, but they had no intention of allowing the nations under their imperial rule to determine themselves. Belgium and Portugal retained their African colonies, and Britain and France divided up Germany's African possessions between themselves. In Asia, some of the spoils went to Japan, Australia, and New Zealand (see Map 25.2).

Similarly, in the Middle East the victorious Allies carved up the Ottoman Empire but replaced it with French and British control. Arab leaders had fought for the Allies against their Ottoman rulers with the expectation that when the war ended they would govern independent Arab kingdoms. These expectations seemed on the brink of fulfillment in October 1918, when the Arab leader Husein's son Faisal entered Damascus at the head of an Arab nationalist army. But less than two years later, in what the Arabs called *am an-nakba*—"the year of catastrophe"—Faisal was deposed by the French. The League of Nations devised a new system of "Mandates," by which territories that the league recognized as states but deemed "not yet able to stand by themselves under the strenuous conditions of the modern world" were placed under Western supervision. France took over Syria and Lebanon; Britain established control of Iraq, Palestine, and Transjordan. The British also retained a dominant influence in both Egypt and the new state of Saudi Arabia.

The British thus emerged from the war with a firmer hold on the Middle East. At the same time, the war altered the imperial structures within Britain's so-called white settlement colonies. As Chapter 24 explained, Canada, Australia, New Zealand, and South Africa emerged from the war with a strong sense of their own unique national identities. In 1931 the Statute of Westminster confirmed this sense by placing the parliaments of these states on an equal footing with the British Parliament—no longer would London reign supreme within what was increasingly called the British Commonwealth°. Because both the British and their former colonial subjects viewed the Commonwealth states as *extensions of* the West, this loosening of imperial control was hailed as a triumph of Western culture and civilization rather than as a challenge to ideas of Western superiority and to the structures of Western empire.

During the interwar period, European imperial nations placed new emphasis on the necessity and desirability of their imperial connections. The Belgian government promoted the Congo as a "model colony," while Portugal embarked on an intensive economic development campaign in its imperial territories. Throughout the 1920s and 1930s, the French government promoted colonial investments so that by 1940, over 45 percent of French overseas investment went to its empire. In Britain, a series of colonial

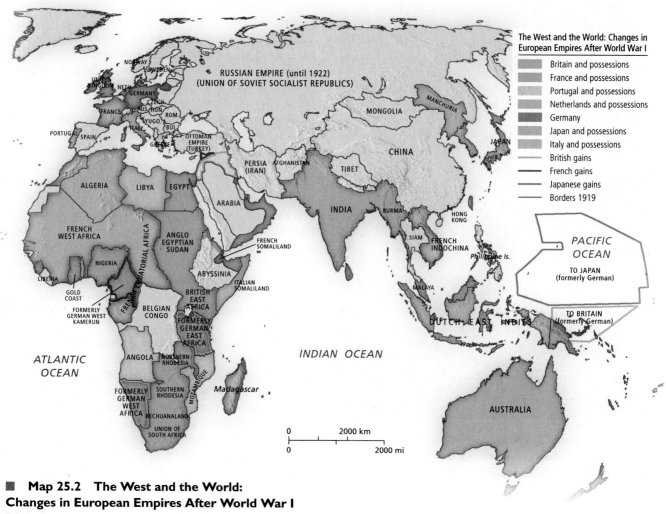

■ **Map 25.2   The West and the World:**
Changes in European Empires After World War I
Britain, France, and Japan were the principal beneficiaries of Germany's loss
of empire after World War I.

exhibitions impressed on the British public the importance of the empire to Britain's economic prosperity, while popular British filmmakers and novelists found that imperial settings formed the perfect backdrop for tales of heroic Englishmen triumphing against all odds. In both Britain and France, imperial history became a required part of school curricula, thus indoctrinating the post–World War I generations in the values of empire.

THE EROSION OF EMPIRE

This period also witnessed the emergence of important challenges to the imperial idea. For Britain, one of the most dramatic of these challenges occurred in its oldest and closest imperial territory. In 1921, ground down by over two years of guerilla warfare waged with consummate skill by the Irish Republican Army (IRA), the British government offered independence to most of Ireland. (Ireland's six

northern counties, dominated by Protestants who opposed Irish independence, remained part of Britain.) The Irish victory was unique; throughout the regions of empire, however, shifting global economic relationships and communist ideology accelerated the spread of mass nationalist movements and so worked to erode imperial control.

Economics and Mass Nationalism

The economic demands of total war had forced Europe's imperial powers to utilize fully their colonial resources, a strategy that brought with it unintended but far-reaching social changes, including the increasing migration of workers, the expansion of cities, and the enveloping of once isolated villages in the global economic web. These unsettling changes provoked resistance, often in the form of anti-Western agitation, because colonial subjects equated Western social, political, and cultural styles with imperialist oppression. In Africa, anti-Western religious movements increased in number and popularity in this era. Conversions to Islam multiplied. In the growing cities, immigrants who were cut off from their village and its religious practices found that Islam provided an alternative cultural identity to that on offer from their European rulers.

The Great Depression further accelerated the spread of mass nationalism throughout Asia and Africa. Because of the Depression, the prices of primary products fell sharply. The result was disastrous for the undeveloped regions of the world that relied on income from the sales of agricultural products and raw materials. At the same time, the benefits of imperial governance diminished. Looking for ways to reduce expenditures, European governments cut funds to colonial schools, public services, and health care. Direct taxation rates rose while unemployment rates soared. In response, nationalist movements exploded. For example, challenges to French imperialist rule escalated during the 1930s in Tunisia, Algeria, Indochina, and Trinidad.

The Impact of Communism: The Case of China

Economics accounted for only part of the spread of nationalism in imperial territories in the interwar era. Communist ideology also played a role. Lenin had argued that imperialism was the logical outcome of capitalism and its quest for markets, and thus that anticapitalism and anti-imperialism went hand in hand. Under Lenin, the Soviet Union declared itself the defender of oppressed nationalities everywhere, and provided assistance to nationalist independence movements in Indonesia, Indochina, Burma, and most significantly, China.

Soviet advisors helped form the Chinese communist Party in 1921. The communists quickly formed an alliance with the Guomindang, a Western-oriented reform movement seeking to bring order to revolution-torn China through industrial and political modernization. By 1925, when Chiang Kai-Shek (1887–1975) became the Guomindang leader, Soviet political and military advisors had helped reorganize the Guomindang, reform its army, and solidify its power base. Chiang was able to establish Guomindang rule over most of China. Despite Chiang's Soviet links, Americans and Europeans with economic interests in the region welcomed China's stabilization under the Guomindang. Emboldened by Western support, Chiang broke with the communists in 1927. Communism, however, remained a potent force in China even after this break. Led by Mao Zedong (1893–1976), China's communists would revolutionize Chinese society after World War II and offer a potent challenge to Western models of modernity.

THE QUESTION OF WESTERNIZATION: THE CASES OF TURKEY AND INDIA

The question of the relationship between modernity and the West was a crucial one for nationalists in non-Western regions. These nationalists sought not only political independence but also economic modernization. They wanted to establish prosperous nations on a level equal with Europe and the United States. But could modernization be achieved without Westernization? Developments in Turkey and India offer two different answers to this question.

To Mustafa Kemal Pasha (1881–1938), the leader of Turkey, "modernity" and "the West" seemed inseparable. A war hero, Kemal led a postwar nationalist revolt that defeated the Anglo-French plan to partition the Ottoman Empire's Turkish heartland among themselves. Kemal forced a new peace settlement in which Turkey remained intact and independent. Kemal had no intentions of letting Western powers govern in Turkey, but he was not anti-Western. He viewed the West as modern, and he intended to modernize Turkey. As a state-led industrialization program began to transform the economy, Kemal declared Turkey a secular republic and abolished both the sultanate and the Islamic caliphate. He also attempted to westernize Turkish culture. He outlawed polygamy, granted women civil and legal rights, and required all Turks to take surnames—he became known as Kemal "Ataturk" ("the Turk"). The Latin alphabet replaced Arabic script and a mass literacy program was established. Schoolmasters who dared use Arabic lettering were arrested. Ataturk even insisted that citizens of the new state change their clothes. Western suits replaced Eastern robes, and the bowler hat replaced the fez, which Ataturk claimed was "an emblem of ignorance, negligence, fanaticism, hatred of progress and civilization."[19]

Westernization and modernization, however, did not mean democratization. Despite setting up a parliament elected by universal suffrage, Ataturk made full use of emergency executive powers to govern with an iron grip over a one-party state. He also continued the Ottoman policies of repression toward Turkey's Armenian minority.

In India, the nationalism of Mohandas Gandhi (1869–1948) offered a striking contrast to Ataturk's pro-Western approach. Gandhi transformed the Indian National Congress into a mass nationalist movement by appealing to Indian customs and religious identity. He was not opposed to modernization, but he argued that modernization did not necessarily mean Westernization, that India could follow its own path. Thus Gandhi (a lawyer educated in England) rejected Western dress and presented himself in the role of the religious ascetic, a familiar and deeply honored figure in Indian culture. In his insistence that the nationalist struggle be one of "moral force" rather than a physical fight, Gandhi drew on the Hindu tradition of nonviolence. He was careful, however, not to equate "Indian" with "Hindu." He worked hard to incorporate the minority Muslim community into the nationalist movement, and he broke with the traditional Hindu caste system by campaigning for the rights of those deemed "untouchable." Ordinary Indians surged into the movement,

GANDHI ON TRIAL

When World War I ended, Mohandas Gandhi transformed the Indian National Congress into a mass movement. He and his supporters embarked on a campaign of noncooperation with British rule. The campaign was designed to undermine British political and economic structures in India, while at the same time building the nationalist cause on the moral foundations of nonviolence. In 1922, however, a number of violent episodes occurred, including the murder and subsequent burning of twenty-one Indian policemen by nationalists in the town of Chauri-Chaura. Gandhi declared that he would fast until the violence stopped. Following further mass civil disobedience (and more violence in Bombay and Madras), Gandhi was arrested. The following excerpt is from Gandhi's confession at his trial, and shows clearly why Gandhi won the admiration of so many in the Western world.

I wish to endorse all the blame that the Advocate General has thrown on my shoulders in connection with the Bombay occurrences, the Madras occurrences, and the Chauri-Chaura occurrences . . . He is quite right when he says that as a man of responsibility, a man having received a fair share of education, having had a fair share of experience in this world, I should know the consequences of every one of my acts. I knew them. I knew that I was playing with fire. I ran the risk, and if I were set free I would still do the same. I would be failing in my duty if I did not do so . . . I wanted to avoid violence; I want to avoid violence. Non-violence is the first article of my faith. It is the last article of my faith. But I had to make my choice; I had either to submit to a system which I consider has done irreparable harm to my country, or to incur the risk of the mad fury of my people bursting forth when they understood the truth from my lips. I know that my people have sometimes gone mad; I am deeply sorry for it; and I am therefore here to submit, not to a light penalty but to the highest penalty. I do not ask for mercy.

Source: From a speech by Mohandas K. Ghandi at his defense trial, March 18, 1922.

---

calling Gandhi "Mahatma," or "great-souled," a term of great respect.

Unable to decide whether to arrest Gandhi as a dangerous revolutionary or to negotiate with him as a representative of the Indian people, the British did both. In 1931, Gandhi and the viceroy of India (literally the "vice-king," the highest British official in India) met on equal terms for a series of eight meetings. A few months later Gandhi was in prison, along with 66,000 of his nationalist colleagues. Successive British governments did pass a series of measures granting Indians increasing degrees of self-government, but Gandhi and the Indian National Congress demanded full and immediate national independence. The resulting impasse led to escalating unrest and terrorist activity, despite Gandhi's personal commitment to nonviolence. India remained the jewel in Britain's imperial crown, but the glue holding it in place was deteriorating rapidly by the end of the 1930s.

THE POWER OF THE PRIMITIVE

Gandhi's rejection of any notion of Western superiority was not unique. Just as nationalists outside of the West began to challenge the idea of Western supremacy in this era, so too did Westerners themselves. For nineteenth-century European culture, "civilization" was what gave the West the right to rule the rest of the world. But after Verdun and the Somme, many Europeans found it hard to believe in the superiority of Western civilization. One of the bestsellers in Europe during the 1920s was Oswald Spengler's *The Decline of the West* (1919), in which Spengler argued that western European civilization was marching along a path of inevitable decline. The poet Ezra Pound was more succinct; he described European civilization as "an old bitch, gone in the teeth."

Developments in psychology further undermined the idea of Western superiority by eroding the boundaries between so-called primitive and modern cultures. In his postwar writings, Sigmund Freud (1856–1939) emphasized that human nature was fundamentally aggressive, even bestial. Freud's three-part theory of personality, developed in the 1920s, argued that within each individual the *id*, the unconscious force of primitive instinct, battles against the controls of the *ego*, or conscious rationality, and the *superego*, the moral values imposed by society. Although Freud taught that the continuity of civilization depended on the repression of the id, many Freudian popularizers insisted that the individual should allow his or her primitive self to run free. The work of Freud's one-time disciple Carl Jung (1875–1961) also stressed the links between the primitive and the modern. Jung contended that careful study of an individual's dreams will show that they share common images and forms—"archetypes"—with ancient mythologies and world religions. These archetypes point to the existence of the "collective unconscious," shared by all human beings, regardless of when or where they lived. Thus, in Jung's analysis the boundary between "civilized" and "primitive," "West" and "not West," disappeared.

■ The Power of the Primitive

When the American dancer Josephine Baker first hit the stage in Paris in 1925, her audience embraced her as the image of African savagery, even though Baker was a city kid from Philadelphia. A Parisian sensation from the moment she arrived, Baker's frenetic and passionate style of dancing, as well as her willingness to appear on stage wearing nothing but a belt of bananas, seemed to epitomize for many Europeans the essential freedom they believed their urbanized culture had lost, and that both the United States and Africa retained. As Baker's belt of bananas, designed by her white French employer, makes clear, much of this idealization of the primitive was deeply embedded in racist stereotypes. But it is also clear that both Baker's blackness and her Americanness represented a positive image of liberation to many Parisians.

In the work of other thinkers and artists, that boundary remained intact, but Western notions of cultural superiority were turned upside down. The belief that white Western culture was anemic, washed out, and washed up led to a new openness to alternative intellectual and artistic traditions. This era saw a lasting transformation of popular music as the energetic rhythms of African-American jazz worked their way into white musical traditions. Many writers argued that the West needed to look to outside its borders for vibrancy and vitality. The German novelist Herman Hesse (1877–1962) condemned modern industrial society as spiritually barren and celebrated Eastern mysticism as a source of power and wisdom. Similarly, the *Négritude* movement stressed the history and intrinsic value of black African culture. Founded in Paris in 1935 by French colonial students from Africa and the West Indies, Négritude condemned European culture as weak and corrupted, and called for blacks to recreate a separate cultural and political identity. The movement's leading figures, such as Leopold Senghor (1906–2001), who later became the first president of independent Senegal, vehemently opposed the continuation of European empires and demanded African self-rule. Drawing together Africans, Afro-Caribbeans, and black Americans, Négritude assumed the existence of a common black culture that transcended national and colonial boundaries. The movement stole the white racists' stereotype of the "happy dancing savage" and refigured it as positive: Black culture fostered the emotion, creativity, and human connections that white Western industrial society destroyed.

CONCLUSION

The Kingdom of Corpses

In 1921, the Goncourt Prize, the most prestigious award in French literature, was awarded not to a native French writer but to a colonial: René Maran, born in the French colony of Martinique. Even more striking than Maran's receiving the prize was the content of the novel for which he was honored. In *Batouala*, Maran mounted a fierce onslaught against Western culture: "Civilization, civilization, pride of the Europeans and charnel house of innocents . . . You build your kingdom on corpses."[20]

For many in the West, Maran's description of Europe as a kingdom of corpses seemed apt in the aftermath of total war. The 1920s and 1930s witnessed a dramatic re-evaluation of Western cultural and political assumptions. Both Soviet communism on the left and Nazism and fascism on the right rejected such key Western ideals as individual rights and the rule of law. Such extremist ideologies seemed persuasive in the climate of despair produced not only by the war, but by the postwar failure of democracy in eastern Europe and the collapse of the global economy after 1929. As a result, the kingdom of corpses grew: in Nazi Germany, in Spain, and most dramatically in the Soviet Union. The kingdom of corpses was, however, a particularly expansionist domain. As the 1930s ended, the West and the world stood on the brink of another total war, one in which the numbers of dead would spiral to nearly incomprehensible levels.

Suggestions for Further Reading

For a comprehensive list of suggested readings, please go to www.ablongman.com/levack/chapter25

Bookbinder, Paul. *Weimar Germany: The Republic of the Reasonable.* 1996. An innovative interpretation.

Brendon, Piers. *The Dark Valley: A Panorama of the 1930s.* 2000. Fast-paced but carefully researched and comprehensive overview of the histories of the United States, Germany, Italy, France, Britain, Japan, Russia, and Spain.

Carrère D'Encausse, Hélène. *Stalin: Order through Terror.* Vol. 2, *A History of the Soviet Union, 1917–1953.* 1981. A brief but convincing account of the way Stalin seized and held power in the Soviet Union.

Fischer, Conan. *The Rise of the Nazis.* 1995. Summarizes recent research and includes a section of primary documents.

Fitzpatrick, Sheila. *Everyday Stalinism. Ordinary Life in Extraordinary Times: Soviet Russia in the 1930s.* 1999. Explores the daily life of the ordinary urban worker in Stalinist Russia.

Fitzpatrick, Sheila. *Stalin's Peasants: Resistance and Survival in the Russian Village after Collectivization.* 1995. Superb history from the bottom up.

Getty, J. Arch, and Oleg V. Naumov. *The Road to Terror: Stalin and the Self-Destruction of the Bolsheviks, 1932–1939.* 1999. Interweaves recently discovered documents with an up-to-date interpretation of the Great Purge.

Gilbert, Bentley Brinkerhoff. *Britain 1914–1945: The Aftermath of Power.* 1996. Short, readable overview, designed for beginning students.

Jackson, Julian. *The Popular Front in France: Defending Democracy, 1934–1938.* 1988. A political and cultural history.

Kershaw, Ian. *Hitler.* 1991. A highly acclaimed recent biography.

Mack Smith, Denis. *Mussolini: A Biography.* 1983. An engaging read.

Pedersen, Susan. *Family, Dependence, and the Origins of the Welfare State: Britain and France, 1914–1945.* 1993. Shows how welfare policy was inextricably linked to demographic and eugenic concerns.

Rothschild, Joseph. *East Central Europe between the Wars.* 1974. An older source, but still one of the best accounts of this tumultuous region in this tumultuous time.

Thomas, Hugh. *The Spanish Civil War.* 1977. An authoritative account.

Whittam, John. *Fascist Italy.* 1995. A short synthesis of recent research. Includes a section of primary documents and an excellent bibliographic essay.

Notes

1. Quoted in Peter Gay, *Weimar Culture* (1970), 99.
2. Quoted in T. W. Heyck, *The Peoples of the British Isles from 1870 to the Present* (1992), 200.
3. Quoted in Martin Gilbert, *A History of the Twentieth Century, Vol. I* (1997), 700.
4. Quoted in Michael Burleigh, *The Third Reich: A New History* (2000), 36.
5. Quoted in Burleigh, 52.
6. Quoted in Joachim Fest, *Hitler* (1973), 190–193.
7. Quoted in Fest, 192, 218.
8. Quoted in Wendy Goldman, *Women, the State, and Revolution: Soviet Family Policy and Social Life, 1917–1936* (1993), 5.
9. Quoted in Claudia Koonz, *Mothers in the Fatherland* (1987), 130.
10. Quoted in Fest, 445.
11. Quoted in Koonz, 194.

12. Quoted in Koonz, 178.

13. Quoted in Koonz, 56; Victoria DeGrazia, *How Fascism Ruled Women: Italy, 1922–1945* (1992), 234.

14. See J. Arch Getty and Roberta Manning, *Stalinist Terror: New Perspectives* (1993), 11, 265, 268, 280, 290.

15. Quoted in Mark Mazower, *Dark Continent: Europe's Twentieth Century* (1998), 123.

16. Quoted in Sheila Fitzpatrick, *Everyday Stalinism*, 68.

17. See Stephen G. Wheatcroft, "More Light on the Scale of Repression and Excess Mortality in the Soviet Union in the 1930s," in Getty and Manning, *Stalinist Terror*, 275–290.

18. "Appendix 1: Numbers of Victims of the Terror," in J. Arch Getty and Oleg V. Naumov, *The Road to Terror: Stalin and the Self-Destruction of the Bolsheviks, 1932–1939* (1999), 587–594.

19. Quoted in Felix Gilbert, *The End of the European Era* (1991), 162.

20. Quoted in Tyler Stovall, *Paris Noir: African Americans in the City of Light* (1996), 32.

World War II and Its Aftermath, 1931–1949

O N JUNE 22, 1940, FRENCH DELEGATES SIGNED AN ARMISTICE ACKNOWL-edging their army's defeat by the forces of Nazi Germany. After sweeping through Norway, Denmark, the Netherlands, and Belgium in a startling spring offensive, the German army had conquered France in just six weeks. Nazi Germany now dominated the European continent. To mark this achievement, Chancellor Adolf Hitler announced plans for the rebuilding of the German Empire. These plans included the physical transformation of Berlin and forty other cities. The past would be wiped out, replaced by the new Nazi order. Hitler's urban redesigns called for the construction of triumphal arches and monumental public buildings to proclaim to the world the power of the German state, and for broad, straight streets to serve as visual reminders of Nazi values—discipline over freedom, regimentation over spontaneity, uniformity over individualism.

Five years later, Berlin and much of Germany had been leveled—not by Nazi urban planners, however, but by Soviet artillery and by British and American bombs. The rebuilding of German cities after World War II took place in a context far removed from Hitler's grandiose and gruesome visions of race-based imperial rule. On top of the rubble of the past, a new European order emerged. This new order was based not on a German continental empire, as Hitler had hoped, but rather on German partition and the division of Europe into two opposing camps—western Europe allied with the United States, eastern Europe dominated by the Soviet Union.

This chapter examines the way that World War II transformed European society, politics, and culture. The war was not confined to Europe, however. In Hitler's quest to conquer the European continent, he joined hands with an un-likely ally: Japan. Japan's desire for a Pacific empire clashed with American and

Chapter Outline

- The Coming of War
- Europe at War, 1939–1941
- The World at War, 1941–1945
- The Home Fronts
- A Dubious Peace, 1945–1949

Wilhelm Becker, *Bombing Raid in Berlin* (1943): The intentional and intensive bombing of civilian centers was one of the defining characteristics of the Second World War.

British interests in the region and transformed World War II into a global conflict. Japanese imperial ambitions arose from the efforts of governing elites to insulate their nation's economic and political structures from Western influence. The Pacific war constituted the most brutal in a long series of violent clashes resulting from the encounter between the West and the world. Understanding World War II, then, demands that we look not only at Germany and the results of the twisted perversions of Nazi ideology but also at global power relations, patterns of economic dependency, and the changing relationship between the West and the rest of the world.

To examine this second round of total war, this chapter focuses on five questions: (1) What were the expectations concerning war in the 1920s and 1930s, and how did these hopes and fears lead to armed conflict in both Europe and Asia? (2) How did Nazi Germany conquer the continent of Europe by 1941? (3) Why did the Allies win in 1945? (4) What did total war mean on the home fronts? (5) How and why did Europe step directly from World War II into the Cold War?

The Coming of War

The 1914–1918 war had been proclaimed the "war to end all wars." Instead, a little more than twenty years later, total war once again engulfed Europe and then the world. Adolf Hitler's ambitions for a German Empire in eastern Europe account for the immediate outbreak of war in September 1939. But other, longer-term factors also contributed, and help explain the origins of World War II. During the 1930s, the uneasy peace was broken by a series of military conflicts. These confrontations underlined the fragility of the post–World War I international settlement and foreshadowed the horrors to come in World War II.

AN UNEASY PEACE

The origins of the Second World War are closely tied to the settlement of the First. Rather than ending war for all time, the treaties negotiated after 1918 created an uneasy peace, one that could not be sustained. As we have already seen, much of Hitler's appeal to his German followers lay in his openly displayed contempt for the economic and military terms of the Versailles Treaty. But the peace settlement of World War I led to World War II in other, less direct ways as well. First, the redrawing of the map of eastern and central Europe fostered political instability in these regions. The mapmakers failed to fulfill the nationalist ambitions of many groups—the Macedonians, the Croats, the Ukrainians, and a host of others—and created as many territorial resentments as they resolved. For ex-

ample, Germans could not forget that parts of Silesia now belonged to Poland, and Hungarians mourned the loss of traditionally Hungarian lands to Czechoslovakia, Romania, and Yugoslavia. Demands for boundary revisions, as well as ethnic hostilities and economic weaknesses, debilitated the new central and eastern European states carved out of the prewar Austrian-Hungarian, Russian, and German Empires.

Second, the League of Nations, created to replace the competitive alliance systems that many blamed for starting World War I, could not realize the high hopes of its planners. Poorly organized, lacking military power, boycotted by the United States and at various times excluding the key nations of Germany and the Soviet Union, the league proved too weak to serve as the basis of a new international order. Instead, alliances, such as that between the French and Polish governments or the "Little Entente" of Czechoslovakia, Yugoslavia, and Romania, formed the framework of a more traditional and very precarious international system.

Finally, the peace settlements created resentments among the war's winners as well as its losers. Italian nationalists argued that their nation's contribution to the Allies' victory should have been more fully compensated, and looked longingly at territories granted to Yugoslavia, Austria, and Albania. Japanese nationalists, too, felt betrayed by the peace. Japan had cooperated fully with Britain and the United States during the First World War, and expected this cooperation to be rewarded in the postwar era. Instead, many Japanese contended that the peace settlement disregarded Japan's economic needs and international ambitions. The results of the postwar Washington Conference, for example, enraged Japanese nationalists. The conference, convened in Washington, D.C., in 1921, assembled representatives of the war's nine victorious powers—Britain, France, Italy, the United States, Belgium, the Netherlands, Portugal, China, and Japan—who pledged themselves to uphold China's territorial integrity and political independence. European and especially American capital poured into China during the 1920s while Western advisers assisted in the reform of the Chinese tax and currency systems. Japanese nationalists viewed a united, Western-oriented China not as a guarantor of regional stability but rather as a threat to Japanese political power and economic development.

THE 1930s: PRELUDE TO WORLD WAR II

The onset of the Great Depression in 1929 heightened international instability. Throughout Europe economic nationalism intensified as nations responded to economic collapse by throwing up tariff walls in an effort to protect their own industries. In addition, leaders sought escape from economic difficulties through territorial expansion. In Japan, for example, the collapse of export markets for

Japanese raw silk and cotton cloth made it difficult for the Japanese to pay for their vital imports of oil and other industrial resources. Anti-Western Japanese nationalists contended that Western capitalism was terminally ill and that the time had come for Japan to embark on a course of aggressive imperialist expansion to ensure its access to vital resources. In 1931, Japanese forces seized Manchuria.

Similarly, Mussolini proclaimed empire as the answer to Italy's economic woes, as well as a way to recreate the glories of ancient Rome. Seeking to expand Italy's North African empire and to avenge Italy's humiliating defeat at the Battle of Adowa in 1896, when Ethiopian troops had beaten back an Italian invasion, Mussolini ordered his army into Ethiopia in 1935. The Italian forces inflicted on the Ethiopian people many of the horrors soon to come to the European continent, including the saturation bombing of civilians, the use of poison gas, and the establishment of concentration camps. At the end of June 1936, Ethiopia's now-exiled Emperor Haile Selassie (1892–1975) addressed the Assembly of the League of Nations and warned, "It is us today. It will be you tomorrow."[1]

One year after Italian troops invaded Ethiopia, civil war broke out in Spain. As Chapter 25 explained, the war between the elected republican government and General Franco's rebels quickly became an international conflict. Hitler and Mussolini sent troops and equipment to assist Franco, and Stalin responded by sending aid to communists fighting on the republican side. Reluctant to ally with Stalin, the governments of France, Britain, and the United States remained neutral, and seemed, therefore, to signal that aggressors could act with impunity.

While the Spanish Civil War raged, the Japanese resumed their advance in China. The Japanese conquest was brutal. In what became known as the Rape of Nanking (Nanjing), soldiers used babies for bayonet practice, gang-raped as many as 20,000 young girls and women, and left the bodies of the dead to rot in the street. The League of Nations had condemned Japan's seizure of Manchuria in 1931 but could do little else.

Against this backdrop of military aggression and the democracies' inaction, Hitler made his first moves to establish a German Empire in Europe (see Map 26.1). In 1933, he withdrew Germany from the League of Nations and two years later announced the creation of a German air force and the return of mass conscription—in deliberate violation of the terms of the Versailles Treaty. In 1936, Hitler al-

CHRONOLOGY

On the Road to World War II

1919	Versailles Treaty
1921–1922	Washington Conference
1929	Onset of the Great Depression
1931	Japan invades Manchuria
1933	Hitler becomes chancellor of Germany
1935	Hitler announces a German air force and military conscription; Italy invades Ethiopia
1936	German troops occupy the Rhineland; civil war breaks out in Spain; Hitler and Mussolini form the Rome-Berlin Axis
1937	Japan advances against China; Rape of Nanking
1938	
March	Germany annexes Austria (the *Anschluss*)
September	Munich Conference: Germany occupies the Sudetenland
1939	
March 15	Germany invades Czechoslovakia
August 23	German-Soviet Non-Aggression Pact
September 1	Germany invades Poland
September 3	Great Britain and France declare war on Germany

lied with Mussolini in the Rome-Berlin Axis° and again violated his treaty obligations when he sent German troops into the Rhineland, the industrially rich region on Germany's western border. Yet France and Britain did not respond. Two years later, in March 1938, Germany broke the Versailles Treaty once more by annexing Austria after an intense Austrian Nazi propaganda campaign punctuated by violence.

After the successful *Anschluss* ("joining") of Germany and Austria, Hitler demanded that the Sudetenland, the western portion of Czechoslovakia inhabited by a German-speaking majority, be joined to Germany as well. He seemed finally to have gone too far. France and the Soviet Union had pledged to protect the territorial integrity of Czechoslovakia. In September 1938, Europe stood on the brink of war. The urgency of the situation impelled Britain's prime minister Neville Chamberlain (1869–1940) to board an airplane for the first time in his life and fly to Munich to negotiate with Hitler. After intense negotiations that excluded the Czech government, Chamberlain and French prime minister Edouard Daladier agreed to grant Hitler the right to occupy the Sudetenland immediately. Assured by Hitler that this "Munich Agreement" satisfied all his territorial demands, Chamberlain flew home to a rapturous welcome. Crowds cheered and church bells rang when he claimed to have achieved "peace in our time."

"Peace in our time" lasted for six months. In March 1939, German troops occupied the rest of Czechoslovakia and Hitler's promises proved to be worthless. On August 23, Hitler took out an insurance policy against fighting a two-front war by persuading Stalin to sign the German-Soviet Non-Aggression Pact°. The pact publicly pledged the two powers not to attack each other; it also secretly divided Poland between them and promised Stalin substantial territorial gains—much of eastern Poland and the Baltic regions of Latvia, Estonia, and parts of Lithuania. On September 1, 1939, German troops invaded Poland. The British and French declared war against Germany on September 3. Two weeks after German troops crossed

Poland's borders in the west, the Soviets pushed in from the east and imposed a regime of murderous brutality. The Second World War had begun.

EVALUATING APPEASEMENT

Could Hitler have been stopped before he catapulted Europe into World War II? The debate over this question has centered on British policy during the 1930s. France advocated an aggressive policy toward Germany in the 1920s, even to the point of sending troops into the Rhineland in 1923 to seize reparations. But during the 1930s, debilitating economic and political crises left France too weak to respond strongly to Hitler. With the United States remaining aloof from European affairs and the now-communist Soviet Union regarded as a pariah state, Britain assumed the initiative in responding to Hitler's rise to power and his increasingly aggressive actions.

■ **Map 26.1   The Expansion of Germany in the 1930s**
Beginning with the remilitarization of the Rhineland in 1936, Hitler embarked on a program of German territorial expansion. This map also indicates the expansion of the Soviet Union into Poland as a result of the secret terms of the German-Soviet Non-Aggression Pact.

■ **Pablo Picasso's *Guernica* (1937)**
The bombing of the undefended city of Guernica during the Spanish Civil War has come to symbolize the horror of modern aerial warfare, and Picasso's depiction of this horrific event has become one
of the most well-known works of the twentieth century.

After World War II broke out, one term came to be equated with passivity and cowardice in the face of aggression. That term was appeasement°—the policy of conciliation and negotiation that British policymakers, particularly Neville Chamberlain, pursued in their dealings with Hitler in the 1930s. Chamberlain, however, was not a coward and was far from passive. Convinced he had a mission to save Europe from war, he actively sought to accommodate Hitler. Chamberlain thought like the businessmen who voted for him. He believed that through negotiation a suitable agreement—the "best price"—can always be found. His fundamental failure was not passivity or cowardice but rather his insistence that Hitler was a man like himself. Chamberlain could not believe that Hitler would find a war worth the price Germany would need to pay.

For Chamberlain, and many other Europeans, the alternative to appeasement was a total war that would surely destroy Western civilization. They remembered the last war with horror, and agreed that the next war would be even worse, for it would be an air war. The years after 1918 saw the aviation industry come into its own in Europe and the United States, and both military experts and ordinary people recognized the disastrous potential of airborne bombs. Stanley Baldwin (1867–1947), Chamberlain's predecessor as prime minister, told the British public that there was no defense against a bomber force: "The bomber will always get through." The horrendous civilian casualties inflicted by the Italian air force in Ethiopia and by the bombing of Spanish cities in the Spanish Civil War convinced many

Europeans that Baldwin was right, and that war was completely unacceptable. Just two years after the British Peace Pledge Union was founded in 1934, it had 100,000 supporters pledged not to fight in a war.

Motivated by the desire to avoid another horrible war, appeasement also rested on two additional pillars—first, the assumption that many of Germany's grievances were legitimate; second, the belief that only a strong Germany could neutralize the threat posed by Soviet communism. During the 1920s, many historians, political scientists, and policymakers studied the diplomatic records concerning the outbreak of World War I and concluded that the treaty makers at Versailles were wrong in blaming Germany for starting the war. During the 1920s, then, British leaders sought to renegotiate reparations, to press the French into softening their anti-German policies, and to draw Germany back into the network of international diplomatic relations. Hitler's rise to power gave added impetus to a policy already in place. British leaders argued that they could rob Hitler of much of his appeal by rectifying legitimate German grievances.

British policymakers' fear of communism reinforced their desire to stabilize Germany. Many politicians applauded Hitler's moves against German communists and welcomed the military resurgence of Germany as a strong bulwark against the threat posed by Soviet Russia. The startling announcement of the German-Soviet Non-Aggression Pact in the summer of 1939 revealed the hollowness of this bulwark, just as the German invasion of

Czechoslovakia in March had exposed Hitler's promises of peace as worthless.

Europe at War, 1939–1941

German soldiers crossed the Polish border on September 1, 1939; just two years later, Hitler appeared to have achieved his goal of establishing a Nazi Empire in Europe. By the autumn of 1941, almost all of continental Europe was either allied to or occupied by Nazi Germany.

A NEW KIND OF WARFARE

During these two years, the German army moved from triumph to triumph as a result of its mastery of the new technology of offensive warfare. Executing a strategy of attack that fully utilized the products of modern industry, the German military demonstrated the power of a mobile, mechanized offensive force. Germany's only defeat during these years came in the Battle of Britain, when Germany confronted a mobile, mechanized defense. Like Germany's victories, this defeat highlighted the central role of industrial production in modern warfare.

The Conquest of Poland

In its attack on Poland, the German army made use of a new kind of warfare. As Chapter 24 explained, in World War I a full frontal infantry assault proved no match for a deeply entrenched defensive force armed with machine guns. In the 1920s and 1930s, military strategists theorized that the way to avoid the stalemate of trench warfare was to use both the airplane and the tank to construct an "armored fist" strong and swift enough to break through even the most well-fortified enemy defenses. The bomber plane provided a mobile bombardment, one that shattered enemy defenses, broke vital communication links, and clogged key transport routes. Simultaneously, motorized infantry and tank formations punched through enemy lines.

Germany's swift conquest of Poland provided the world with a stunning demonstration of this new offensive strategy. Most of the German army, like all of the Polish, moved on foot or by horseback, as soldiers had done for centuries.

IN THE TANKS

If World War I was the war of the trenches, then World War II was the war of the tanks. In the Battle of Kursk on the eastern front, for example, the Russians and Germans sent a thousand tanks into combat on a single day (July 12, 1943). In the first two years of the war, just the sight of these armored monsters crashing through barriers could demoralize an entire infantry regiment. By 1942, however, both sides had developed effective antitank defensive systems. For the men in the tanks, the experience of combat was harrowing.

ALAN GILMOUR, 48TH ROYAL TANK REGIMENT (BRITAIN), TUNISIA, 1943

In the low padded compartment . . . we crouch, the two of us shapeless figures engulfed in a miasma of smoke and dust through which the facia lights barely penetrate. Behind us in the turret the crew are choking with the fumes of cordite which the fans are powerless to dissipate. Cut off from visible contact with the outside world, the wireless operator, wedged in his seat, cannot possibly know in which direction the vehicle is moving. To all five of us, the intercom, our lifeline, relays a bedlam of orders, distortions, and cries from another world.

NAT FRANKEL, AMERICAN PRIVATE, FRANCE, 1944

It takes twenty minutes for a medium tank to incinerate; and the flames burn slowly, so figure it takes ten minutes for a hearty man within to perish. You wouldn't even be able to struggle for chances are both exits would be sheeted with flame and smoke. You would sit, read *Good Housekeeping*, and die like a dog. Steel coffins indeed!

ANONYMOUS BRITISH TANK COMPANY COMMANDER, ITALIAN FRONT, 1944

We were ordered to make the attack in the face of an anti-tank screen firing down the line of advance. We knew that we should not get far. . . . armour-piercing shot seemed to come from all directions. . . . the tanks were knocked out one by one. Most of them burst into flames immediately. A few were disabled, the turrets jammed or the tank made immobile. As the survivors jumped out, some of them made a dash across the open. . . . but they were almost all mown down by German machine gun fire.

Sources: From Bryan Perrett, *Through Mud and Blood: Infantry*. Published by Robert Hale, 1975. Reprinted by permission of Watson, Little, Ltd., licensing agents.; from Nat Frankel and Larry Smith, *Patton's Best: An Informal History of the 4th Armored Division*. Hawthorne Books, New York, 1978.; and from Douglas Orgill, *The Gothic Line*, Heinemann, 1967. Reprinted by permission of John Johnson Limited.

Fast-moving motorized divisions, however, bludgeoned through the Polish defenses, penetrated deep into enemy territory, and secured key positions. While these units wreaked havoc on the ground, the Luftwaffe—the German air force—rained ruin from the air. Thirteen hundred planes shrieked across the Polish skies and in just one day destroyed the far smaller, less modern Polish air force, most of whose planes never left the ground. Warsaw surrendered after just ten days.

Blitzkrieg in Western Europe

Western newspaper reporters christened this new style of warfare blitzkrieg°—lightning war. Western Europeans experienced blitzkrieg firsthand in the spring of 1940. The German army invaded Denmark and Norway in early April, routed the French and British troops sent to aid the Norwegians, and moved into western Europe in May. The Netherlands fell in just four days; Belgium, supported by French and British units as in World War I, held out for two weeks.

On May 27, 1940, the British army and several divisions of the French force found themselves trapped in a small pocket on the northern French coast called Dunkirk. Their destruction seemed certain. But over the next week, the only Allied success in the campaign unfolded. The British Royal Air Force (RAF) succeeded in holding off the Luftwaffe and enabling the British navy and a flotilla of fishing and recreational boats manned by British civilians to evacuate these troops. By June 4, 110,000 French and almost 240,000 British soldiers had been brought safely back to Britain. But, as the newly appointed British prime minister Winston Churchill (1874–1965) reminded his cheering people, "wars are not won by evacuation."

Over the next two weeks the Germans steadily advanced through northern France, and on June 14, German soldiers marched into Paris. The French Assembly voted to disband and to hand over power to the World War I war hero Marshal Philippe Pétain (1856–1951), who established an authoritarian government. On June 22 this new Vichy regime° (named after the city Pétain chose for his capital) signed an armistice with Germany that pledged French collaboration with the Nazi regime. Theoretically, Pétain's authority extended over all of France, but in actuality the Vichy regime was confined to the south, with Germany occupying France's western and northern regions, including Paris, as well as the Atlantic seaboard. One million French soldiers became prisoners of war. Germany, with its allies and satellites, held most of the continent.

The Battle of Britain

After the fall of France, Hitler hoped that Britain would accept Germany's domination of the continent and agree to a negotiated peace. But his hopes went unrealized. Military disaster in Norway had thoroughly discredited Prime Minister Chamberlain and his halfhearted approach to war making. A member of Chamberlain's own party, Leo Amery, spoke for the nation when he shouted at Chamberlain, "In the name of God, go!" Chamberlain went. Party politics were suspended for the duration of the war, and the British government passed to an all-party coalition headed by Winston Churchill, a vocal critic of Britain's appeasement policy since 1933. Never a humble man, Churchill wrote that when he accepted the position of prime minister, "I felt as if I were walking with Destiny, and that all my past life had been but a preparation for this hour and this trial . . . I was sure I should not fail." In his first speech as prime minister, Churchill promised, "Victory—victory at all costs."

Faced with the British refusal to negotiate, Hitler ordered his General Staff to prepare for a land invasion of Britain. But placing German troops in the English Channel while Britain's Royal Air Force (RAF) still flew the skies would be a certain military disaster. Thus, a precondition of invasion was the destruction of the RAF. On July 10, German bomber raids on English southern coastal cities opened the Battle of Britain, a battle waged in the air—and in the factories. Fortunately for Britain, from 1935 on the government's defense policy had accorded priority to the RAF. In the summer of 1940, British factories each month produced twice the number of fighter aircraft coming out of German plants in the same period. Preparing for air attack, the British had constructed a shield comprising fighter

■ **Victory Celebration, July 1940**
Young German girls in Berlin prepare a carpet of flowers for Hitler.

planes, anti-aircraft gun installations, and a chain of radar stations. These preparations, its higher production rates of aircraft, and the fact that RAF pilots were fighting in the skies above their homes gave the British the advantage. On September 17, 1940, Hitler announced that the invasion of Britain was postponed indefinitely.

THE INVASION OF THE SOVIET UNION

War against Britain had never been one of Hitler's central goals, however. His dreams of the "Third Reich," a renewed Germanic European empire that was to last a thousand years, centered on conquest of the Soviet Union. Hitler believed that the rich agricultural and industrial resources of the vast Russian empire rightly belonged to the superior German race. He also believed that Soviet communism was an evil force and a potential threat to German stability and prosperity. Moreover, as the next chapter will show, one of Hitler's aims in invading the Soviet Union was to realize his dream of a new racial order in Europe. This dream demanded a war against the Jews, the majority of whom lived in Poland and the Soviet Union.

A Crucial Postponement

In July 1940, at the very start of the Battle of Britain, Hitler ordered his military advisers to begin planning a Soviet invasion. By December the plan was set: German troops were to invade the Soviet Union in April 1941. But they did not. Hitler postponed the invasion for two crucial months because the ambitions of an incompetent ally—Mussolini—threatened to undermine the economic base of the Nazi war machine.

Italy was ill-equipped to fight a broad-based war. Its military budget was only one-tenth the size of Germany's, its tanks and aircraft were outdated, it had no aircraft carriers or anti-aircraft defenses, and most crucially, it lacked an adequate industrial base. Yet in 1940 Mussolini's hopes of rebuilding the Roman Empire drove him to launch just such a war. In July 1940, Italian troops invaded British imperial territories in North Africa, and in October Mussolini's soldiers marched into Greece. But by the spring of 1941, the Italian advance was in trouble. The British army in North Africa pushed the Italians back into Libya while the Greeks mounted a fierce resistance against the invaders.

Hitler feared the consolidation of British power in Africa and was even more terrified that Mussolini's adventurism would pull the British into eastern Europe. If Britain were able to build air bases in Greece, the Balkans would lie open to British bombing runs. The British could then cripple the German war effort. Germany received 50 percent of its cereal and livestock from the Balkan region, 45 percent of its aluminum ore from Greece, and 90 percent of its tin from Yugoslavia. Most crucially, the oil fields of Romania

CHRONOLOGY

Europe at War

1939	
September	German-Soviet conquest of Poland
1940	
April 9	German blitzkrieg against Denmark and Norway begins
May 10	Germans attack western Europe
June 22	Fall of France
July 10	Battle of Britain begins
September 7	London Blitz begins
September 17	Hitler cancels plans for invasion of Britain
1941	
March	U.S. Congress passes Lend-Lease Act
April	German invasion of the Soviet Union postponed; German offensives in Yugoslavia, Greece, and North Africa
June 22	German invasion of the Soviet Union begins
September	German siege of Leningrad begins
December	German advance halted outside Moscow

constituted Germany's chief source of this vital war-making resource. Without oil, there would be no blitz in blitzkrieg.

These economic considerations led Hitler to delay the invasion of the Soviet Union while the German army mopped up Mussolini's mess in the Balkans and North Africa. In April 1941, German armored units punched through Yugoslavian defenses and encircled the hapless Yugoslav army. Greece came next. The British sent troops, as well as state-of-the-art tanks and airplanes to aid the Greeks, but by the end of April Greece was in German hands. Meanwhile, in North Africa German field marshal Erwin Rommel's (1891–1944) Afrika Korps recaptured all the territory taken by the British the previous year.

In the summer of 1941, then, Germany stood triumphant, with dramatic victories in North Africa and the Balkans (see Map 26.2). But these victories came at a high price. They had postponed the German invasion of the Soviet Union. By the winter of 1941, the delay in beginning the Soviet invasion would imperil the German army.

Early Success

On June 22, 1941, the largest invading force the world had yet seen began to cross the Soviet borders. Three million German soldiers, equipped with 2,770 modern aircraft and

3,350 tanks, went into battle. In a matter of days, most of the Soviet air force was destroyed. By October 1941, only four months after the invasion began, German tanks were within eighty miles of Moscow, Kiev had fallen, and Leningrad was besieged. An astonishing 45 percent of the Soviet population was under German occupation, and the Germans controlled access to much of the Soviet Union's natural and industrial resources, including over 45 percent of its grain and 65 percent of its coal, iron and steel.

The early German victories in the Soviet campaign illustrated the power of blitzkrieg. Although the bulk of the German army traveled on foot or horseback (the Germans went into the Soviet Union with 700,000 horses), its spear-head force consisted of tank and motorized infantry divisions. This force shattered the Soviet defensive line and then moved quickly to seize key targets. Two additional factors contributed to the initial German success. First, Stalin's stubborn refusal to believe that Hitler would violate the Non-Aggression Pact and attack the Soviet Union weakened Russian resistance. Soviet intelligence sources sent in more than eighty warnings of an imminent German attack; all, however, were classified as "doubtful" and a number of the messengers were punished, some even executed. Even as German troops poured over the border and German bombs fell on Soviet cities, Stalin distrusted the news of a German invasion and ignored his generals' pleas for a counterassault.

■ **Map 26.2 The Nazi Empire in 1942**

By 1942, Nazi Germany occupied or was allied to not only most European countries but also much of North Africa and the Middle East. Spain, Portugal, Ireland, Iceland, Sweden, and Switzerland remained neutral. Great Britain and the Soviet Union east of Moscow remained unconquered.

■ **Stuck in the Mud**

Climate and geography proved unbeatable foes for the German Army in the Soviet Union. The thaw following an October snowfall turned the roads to mud, and greatly slowed the German advance. The onset of real winter the following month brought far worse conditions.

A second factor that contributed to the early German victories was the popularity of the invasion among many of the peoples being invaded. The initial German advance occurred in territories where Stalin's rule had brought enormous suffering. In areas that had come under Soviet rule in the previous two years—eastern Poland and the Baltic states—anti-Soviet sentiment was especially high. Ceded to the Soviets by the German-Soviet Non-Aggression Pact, these regions were still bleeding from the imposition of Stalinist terror after 1939. Over two million ethnic Poles had been thrown into cattle cars and sent to Siberian labor camps. Thousands had been shot, including 10,000 Polish army officers who were marched to the Katyn forest and gunned down in front of mass graves. To many in these regions, then, the Germans at first seemed like liberators.

The Fatal Winter

On October 10, Hitler's spokesman announced to the foreign press corps that the destruction of the Soviet Union was assured. German newspapers proclaimed, "CAMPAIGN IN THE EAST DECIDED!"[2] But within just a few months, the German advance had stalled. Leningrad resisted its besiegers and Moscow remained beyond the Germans' reach.

Three obstacles halted the German invasion: stiffening Soviet resistance, the difficulty of supplying the Germans' overstretched lines, and the Russian weather. German troops rapidly squandered the huge reserves of anti-Stalinist sentiment in occupied Soviet territory by treating the local populations with fierce cruelty. Both SS and German army units moved through Soviet territories like a plague of locusts, stripping the regions of livestock, grain, and fuel. The Nazi governor of Ukraine insisted, "I will pump every last thing out of this country."[3] By 1941, both Ukraine and Galicia were devastated by human-made famine. German atrocities in the occupied territories

strengthened the will to resist among the Soviets still in the Germans' path. Anti-German partisan units worked behind the German lines, sabotaging their transportation routes, hijacking their supplies, and murdering their patrols. They found the Germans especially vulnerable to this sort of attack because of their overstretched supply lines. Ironically, the Germans had succeeded too well: Since June they had advanced so far so fast that they overstrained their supply and communication lines.

The weather worsened these logistical problems. An early October snowfall, which then melted, turned Russia's dirt roads to impassable mud. By the time the ground froze several weeks later, the German forces, like Napoleon's army 130 years earlier, found themselves fighting the Russian winter. Subzero temperatures wreaked havoc with transportation lines. Horses froze to death, and machinery refused to start. Men fared just as badly. Dressed in lightweight spring uniforms and forced to camp out in the cold, German soldiers fell victim to frostbite. By the end of the winter, the casualty list numbered more than 30 percent of the German East Army.

At the close of the winter of 1941–1942, the German army still occupied huge sections of the Soviet Union and controlled the vast majority of its agricultural and industrial resources. Over three million Soviet soldiers had been killed and another three million captured. But the failure to deal the Soviets a quick death blow in 1941 gave Stalin and his military high command a crucial advantage—*time*. In the zones soon to be occupied by the German army, Soviet laborers dismantled entire factories and shipped them eastward to areas out of German bombing range. Between August and October 1941, 80 percent of the Soviet war industry was in pieces, scattered among railway cars, heading to safety in Siberia. With time, these factories could be rebuilt and the colossal productive power of the Soviet Union geared for the war effort. And that is what happened.

By 1943, Russia was outproducing Germany: 24,000 tanks versus 17,000; 130,000 artillery pieces versus 27,000; 35,000 combat aircraft versus 25,000. In a total war, in which victory occurs on the assembly line as well as on the front line, these were ominous statistics for Hitler and his dreams of a German Empire.

The World at War, 1941–1945

In December 1941, as the German advance slowed in the Soviet Union, Japanese expansionism in the Pacific fused with the war in Europe and drew the United States into the conflict. Neither Japan nor Germany could compete with the United States on the factory floor. Over the next four years, as millions of soldiers, sailors, and civilians lost their lives in a gargantuan and complicated conflict, industrial production continued to supply a crucial advantage to the Allies.

THE GLOBALIZATION OF THE WAR

Even before 1941, Europe's imperialist legacy ensured that World War II was not confined to Europe. As we have seen, Mussolini's desire to expand his North African empire pushed the fighting almost immediately outside European borders. In addition, Britain would never have been able to stand alone against the German-occupied continent without access to the manpower and materials of its colonies and Commonwealth. German efforts to block British access to these resources spread the war into the Atlantic, where British merchant marines battled desperately against German submarines to keep open the sea lanes into Britain.

Britain also drew heavily on the resources of the United States. Throughout 1941 the United States maintained a precarious balance between neutrality and support for the British war effort, as American naval escorts accompanied supply ships loaded with goods for Britain across the Atlantic. In March, the U.S. Congress passed the Lend-Lease Act°, which guaranteed to supply Britain all needed military supplies, with payment postponed until after the war ended. The passage of Lend-Lease was one of the most important decisions in all of World War II. It gave first Britain and then the Soviets access to the incredible might of American industry.

At the same time that the United States was drawing closer to Britain, its relations with Japan were growing increasingly hostile. In 1941 the Japanese occupied Indochina, and the United States responded by placing an embargo on trade in oil with Japan. Threatened with the loss of a key resource, Japanese policymakers viewed this boycott as tantamount to an act of war. Japan's imperial ambitions demanded that it move decisively before its oil ran out. The South Pacific, a treasure house of mineral and other resources, beckoned.

Between December 7 and 10, 1941, Japanese forces attacked American, British, and Dutch territories in the Pacific—Hong Kong, Wake and Guam islands, the Philippines, Malaya, Molucca in the Dutch East Indies, and most dramatically, the U.S. Pacific fleet base at Pearl

■ **The Surrender of Singapore**

In one of the most humiliating moments in British military history, General Arthur Percival surrenders the Union Jack, and Singapore, to the Japanese in February 1942. Over 130,000 troops were taken prisoner by a Japanese force containing half that number. The Japanese had captured the island's water reservoirs and so had placed Percival in a helpless situation.

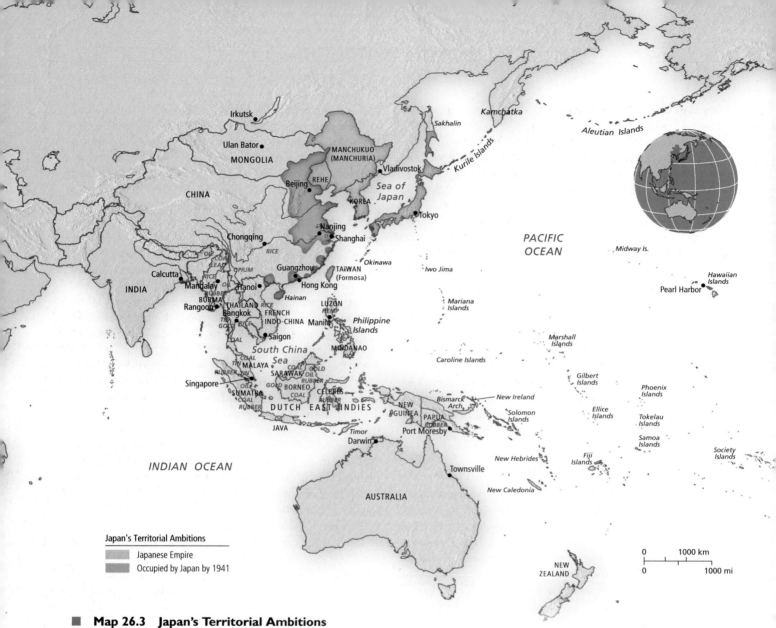

■ Map 26.3 Japan's Territorial Ambitions

Lacking its own supply of natural resources, Japan embarked on imperial conquest.

Harbor. After an attack that lasted only a few hours, the American Pacific fleet in Hawaii lay gutted. Guam fell immediately; Wake held out until December 23; Hong Kong surrendered on Christmas Day; by February, Malaya had been defeated. On February 15, 1942, the garrison of 130,000 British, Indian, Australian, and local troops surrendered Singapore to a Japanese force less than half its size. By May, this astounding success had been cemented with the conquest of Indonesia, Burma, and the Philippines. In just a few months, the Japanese had established themselves as imperial overlords of the South Pacific, with its wealth of raw materials (see Map 26.3).

The audacity of the Japanese attack impressed Hitler. Although he had long feared American industrial power, he declared war on the United States on December 11, 1941. In Europe Germany now faced the alliance of Britain, the Soviet Union, and the United States. Even against such an alliance, Germany appeared to occupy a

strong position. By January a spectacular offensive in North Africa had brought Rommel's forces within two hundred miles of the strategically vital Suez Canal. And in June the German army resumed its advance in the Soviet Union. Within a few months German troops stood at the borders of Russia's oil fields in the southern Caucasus. With Germany on the offensive in the east and Japan controlling the Pacific, the Allies looked poised to lose the war.

FROM ALLIED DEFEAT TO ALLIED VICTORY

Twelve months later the situation had changed, and the Allies were on the road to eventual victory. This road, however, proved long and arduous. The period from 1943 through 1945 was marked by horrendous human suffering, unprecedented attacks on civilians, and cataclysmic military battles. Yet in the end American and Soviet industrial supremacy, allied with a superior military strategy, pushed the balance in the Allies' favor.

The Turning Point: Midway and Stalingrad

The second half of 1942 proved the turning point as two very different battles helped transform the course of the war. In the Pacific, victory at the Battle of Midway gave the U.S. forces a decisive advantage. In Europe, the Battle of Stalingrad dealt Germany a blow from which it never recovered.

The Battle of Midway was the result of the Japanese effort to ensure its air supremacy by drawing the U.S. Pacific fleet's aircraft carriers into battle. To do so, the Japanese attacked Midway Island, a U.S. outpost in the Pacific, on June 4, 1942. By midmorning the Japanese had shot down two-thirds of the American planes. But then an American dive-bomber group, which earlier in the morning had overflown its target and gotten lost, suddenly found itself above the main Japanese carriers. Caught in the act of refueling and rearming the strike force, their decks cluttered with gas lines and bombs, the carriers made remarkably combustible targets. In five minutes, three of Japan's four carriers were destroyed; the fourth was sunk later in the day. Japan's First Air Fleet was decimated. The destruction of the Japanese fleet dealt Japan a blow from which it could not recover. The United States possessed the industrial resources to rebuild its lost ships and airplanes. Japan did not. In five explosive minutes the course of the Pacific war changed.

The Battle of Stalingrad could not have been more different from the Battle of Midway. Extending over months, it tested human endurance to its very limits. In July 1942 the German army was sweeping southward toward the oil-rich Caucasus. Hitler ordered the southern offensive split into two, with one arm reaching up to conquer Stalingrad on the Volga River. The conquest of Stalingrad would give the Germans control over the main waterway for the transport of oil and food from the Caucasus to the rest of the Soviet Union. These resources were vital to the Soviet war effort now that Ukraine was held by Germany. But by dividing his offensive, Hitler widened his front from 500 to 2,500 miles. By the time the German Sixth Army reached Stalingrad on August 23, German resources were fatally overstretched.

Recognizing Germany's vulnerability, Stalin's generals assured him they could attack the exposed German lines and then encircle the German Sixth Army—but only if Stalingrad's defenders could hold on for almost two months while they assembled the necessary men and machinery. An epic urban battle ensued, with the Russian and German soldiers fighting street by street, house by house, room by room. By November, the Russians had surrounded the Germans. When the German commander, General Friedrich von Paulus (d. 1953), requested permission to surrender, Hitler replied, "The army will hold its position to the last soldier and the last cartridge."[4] Paulus finally

CHRONOLOGY

1942: The Turning Point

1941

December 7	Japan bombs Pearl Harbor
December 11	Germany declares war on United States

1942

January 21	Rommel's Second Offensive begins in North Africa
February 15	Surrender of British forces to Japan at Singapore
April 22	British retreat from Burma
May 6	Japan completes conquest of the Philippines
June 4	Battle of Midway
August 7	First U.S. Marine landing on Guadalcanal
August 23	German Sixth Army reaches Stalingrad
October 23	Battle of El Alamein begins
November 8	Anglo-American landing in North Africa begins
November 23	German Sixth Army cut off at Stalingrad

disobeyed orders and surrendered on January 30, 1943, but by then his army had almost ceased to exist. The Germans were never able to make up the losses in manpower, material, or morale they suffered at Stalingrad. The colossal struggle turned the course of the European war, as the Battle of Midway turned the course of the Pacific war.

The Allies on the Offensive

The Allies were now on the offensive. In 1942 British bomber command ordered the intensive bombing of German civilian centers. Soon joined by the American air force, the RAF bombers brought the war home to the German people. In October 1942 Rommel's North Afrika Korps suffered a decisive defeat to the British at the Battle of El Alamein. In November, a joint landing of British and American troops in French North Africa forced the Germans to send reinforcements to Rommel. After fierce fighting, the Anglo-American forces finally claimed victory in North Africa in the spring of 1943.

The Allies followed their victory in North Africa with an invasion of Italy. This campaign was a response, first, to Stalin's pleas that his Allies open a "Second Front" in Europe and so relieve the pressure on Russian troops and, second, to Churchill's desire to protect British economic and imperial interests in the Mediterranean. The Italian offensive began on July 10, 1943, when Anglo-American forces landed in Sicily, prepared to push up into what Churchill called the "soft underbelly" of German-controlled Europe. Within just fifteen days, Mussolini had been overthrown in a high-level coup and his successor opened peace negotiations with the Allies. But then German muscle hardened the "soft underbelly": The German army occupied Italy. British and American soldiers faced a long, brutal, slow-moving push up the peninsula. Ridged with mountains and laced with rivers, Italy formed a natural defensive fortress. In an eight-month period, the Allied forces advanced only seventy miles.

The European war was decided, then, not in the mountains of Italy but on the eastern front. Beginning in the summer of 1943, the Russians steadily pushed back the Germans. By the spring of 1944 the Red Army had reached the borders of Poland. In August Soviet troops turned south into Romania and Hungary. By February 1945 they were within 100 miles of Berlin (see Map 26.4).

Two interconnected factors proved vital in the Soviet victory over the Germans in the east. The first was the evolution of Soviet military strategy. By 1943, the Red Army had learned important lessons from being on the receiving end of blitzkrieg. It had not only increased its tank units, but it had concentrated these into armies in which motorized infantry regiments accompanied massive numbers of tanks, antitank battalions, and mobile antiaircraft artillery. In addition, a vast expansion in the number of radios and field telephones overcame the organizational chaos that had greeted the German invasion in 1941.

These changes in technique and technology were closely connected to achievements in industrial production, the

■ **Map 26.4   Allied Victory in Europe, 1942–1945**
Beginning in late 1942, Allied forces moved onto the offensive.

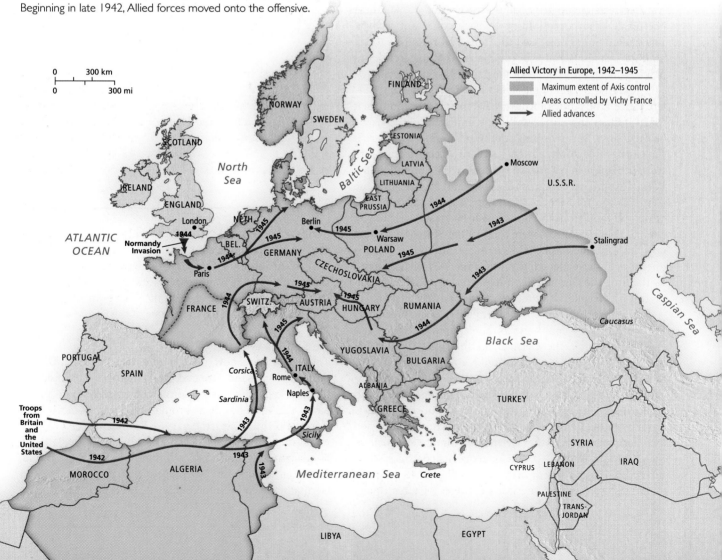

second key factor in the Soviet victory. Mobile armored forces depended on factories churning out steel, rubber, oil, and all the various machine parts needed by a modern army. Access to the industrial wealth of the United States provided the Soviet Union with assistance in this task. By 1943, Lend-Lease deliveries of aircraft and tanks were pouring into Soviet ports. Lend-Lease supplied the Soviet Union with the basics needed to keep its army moving: rails and locomotives, jeeps, trucks and gasoline, plus 15 million pairs of boots. Yet the Soviets did not rely only on imports. The Soviet industrial effort was enormous. In 1943, Russia manufactured four times as many tanks as it imported, and Soviet production of tanks and antitank guns was double that of Germany.

The Fall of Germany

As the Red Army closed in on Germany from the east, the British and Americans pushed in from the west. On June 6, 1944, the Allies carried out the largest amphibious operation the world had ever seen. Five seaborne divisions (two American, two British, and one Canadian) and three airborne divisions (two American and one British) crossed the English Channel and landed on a sixty-mile stretch of coastline in northern France. The "D-Day" landings illustrated the Allied advantage in manpower and material. Against the Allies' eight divisions, the Germans had four; against the Allies' 5,000 fighter planes, the Germans could send up 169.

CHRONOLOGY	
The Long March Toward Allied Victory	
1943	
February	German surrender at Stalingrad; Red Army goes on the offensive; Allied round-the-clock bombing of Germany begins; Japanese surrender at Guadalcanal
May	German surrender in North Africa
July 10	Allied invasion of Italy begins
1944	
January	Lifting of the siege of Leningrad
June 4	Allies liberate Rome
June 6	D-Day landings; Allied offensive in France begins
August 24–26	Allied liberation of Paris
September	Allies liberate the Netherlands, Belgium, Luxembourg
October	U.S. invasion of Philippines

Yet the strength of the German resistance—particularly on Omaha Beach, where the U.S. landing encountered more than 4,000 casualties—signaled that the road to Berlin would not be easy. The Allies faced the formidable task of uprooting the Germans from territory where they had planted themselves five years earlier. For ten long months, the British, American, Canadian, and imperial

■ **The Battle for Berlin**
On April 20, 1945, Hitler celebrated his fifty-sixth birthday, and made a rare visit out of his Berlin bunker to visit with the troops defending his city. As this photograph shows, these "soldiers" were just children. Ten days later, Hitler committed suicide.

The GI

On January 26, 1942, the first soldiers from the United States arrived in Britain to prepare for the invasion of Nazi-controlled Europe. By the spring of 1944, Britain was host to a million and a half American soldiers, sailors, and airmen, awaiting the opening of the Second Front in Europe. The coming of the "Yanks" to war-weary, bomb-blasted Britain was an event of more than military significance. For the majority of individuals on both sides, it was their first prolonged encounter with another culture, another way of life. Cultural clashes were commonplace. Forgetting that most essential items were strictly rationed, the GIs (slang that comes from the military label "government issue") at times infuriated their hosts with insensitive complaints about cold rooms, inadequate food, and the shabby style of British dress. The British found the Americans naive, supremely self-confident, alarmingly friendly, and most of all, BIG.

The *bigness* of the GI is a constant theme in British descriptions and recollections. One British man, urging greater toleration for the GIs, explained to his countrymen, "An American is like a large dog trying to be friendly with everyone in the room, whilst wrecking everything with its tail wagging." A Lancashire nurse recalled her first sight of GIs: "They all seemed to be handsome six-footers with friendly grins and toothpaste advert teeth." But we know that not every GI stationed in Britain was tall and husky; the average height of American servicemen in this era was 5' 10". How do we explain this focus on the bigness of the GI body?

A number of factors helped shape British perceptions. First, the bigness of America in general was a constant obsession of both the GIs and their British hosts. *Meet the U.S. Army,* a publication distributed in British schools, told the children, "In the USA, you can get in a car—a high-powered car at that—and drive for a week or more in a comparatively straight line without running into the sea." Second, the Americans *looked better.* The GI's uniform was of a higher-quality fabric and a closer fit than that of the average British soldier's: American privates often found that their flashy uniforms led not only British civilians but even British soldiers to mistake them for officers. Third, compared to the British, the Americans were big eaters and big spenders. An American private earned five times as much as his British counterpart—and spent it with abandon. British pubgoers were sometimes dismayed to find that American soldiers had already consumed the pub's entire stock of beer. Undisciplined by rationing, American appetites seemed huge to the British. One soldier enjoyed his dinner in a British home: "Only afterwards did I discover that I had eaten the family's special rations for a *month.*" GIs also had access to items such as chocolate and canned fruit that had long been unobtainable in Britain. And finally, different cultural norms magnified the impact of the GI's presence. Americans spoke more loudly. They used exaggerated expressions that struck the more understated British as boastful. They tended to lounge, to slouch, to lean against walls, to throw their bodies around in ways that startled many British, schooled in more restrained patterns of public behavior. All of these factors combined to ensure that the GI made an indelible impression on British culture.

Embraced with enthusiasm by many British citizens (particularly women), derided by others (particularly men) as "overfed, overpaid, oversexed, and over here," the GI's body became a symbol, a shorthand reference to American power, influence, and plenty. As World War II ended and the Cold War began, and as the United States took on a new role as the undisputed leader of the "West," the American soldier became a familiar figure throughout western Europe, the visible reminder of the reconfiguration of military and economic dominance.[5] ∎

For Discussion

What other bodies became symbols or shorthand references during World War II? What did these bodies symbolize?

■ **Wartime Encounters**
British women entertain GIs heading for the front line in France.

troops fought a series of hard-won battles. By March 1945, as the Russian army approached Berlin from the east, the British and American armies reached Germany's Rhine border and by mid-April stood within fifty miles of Berlin.

The Allies agreed, however, to leave the conquest of Berlin to the Soviet Army. In this climactic battle of the European war, 320,000 Germans, many of them young boys, fought three million Soviet troops. Even so, it took eleven days before the city's commander surrendered on May 2. Two days earlier, Hitler had taken a cyanide capsule and then shot himself with his service pistol. On May 7, 1945, General Alfred Jodl (1890–1946) signed the unconditional surrender of German forces.

The Fall of Japan

When Germany surrendered, the war in the Pacific was still raging. After the Midway battle of 1942, the United States steadily, but slowly, agonizingly, pushed the Japanese back island by island. Japanese industry could not make up for the weapons and ammunition expended in these brutal battles. In contrast, American factories were just gearing up. Whereas in 1940 American assembly lines produced only a little more than 2,000 aircraft, by 1944 they had manufactured over 96,000 bombers and fighters. American productivity per worker hour was five times that of Japan.

While U.S. troops moved, island by island, closer to the Japanese mainland, British and Indian troops rebuffed a Japanese attempt to invade India and pushed the Japanese out of Burma. Australian forces, with American assistance, held the line at New Guinea and forestalled a Japanese invasion of Australia. By February 1945, when U.S. Marines landed on the small island of Iwo Jima, just 380 miles from Japan's home islands, the Japanese war effort was in tatters and an Allied victory was ensured.

Obtaining this victory was not easy. In the month of fighting for Iwo Jima, one-third of the American landing force was killed or wounded. The April conquest of Okinawa was even more hard-won. Outnumbered two to one, the Japanese endured a week-long preliminary bombardment designed to pulverize their defenses and suffered unbelievable casualties—110,000 of the 120,000 soldiers on the island died. They were still able to inflict serious losses on the attacking force: 50,000 Americans were killed or wounded. (Nobody bothered to count how many Okinawans died in a battle they had done nothing to provoke: Estimates range as high as 160,000.)

The conquest of Iwo Jima and Okinawa gave the United States the bases it needed to launch a relentless bombardment of Japanese cities. By July 1945, much of Japan lay in waste. At the same time, a U.S. naval blockade cut Japan off from its supply lines. Already in its death throes, the Japanese war effort was abruptly terminated in August

CHRONOLOGY

The End of World War II

1945

March 16	American victory on Iwo Jima
April	Berlin encircled by Red Army
April 11	American troops reach Elbe River in Germany
April 30	Hitler commits suicide
May 7	Official German surrender
June 22	American victory at Okinawa
August 6	U.S. drops atomic bomb on Hiroshima
August 8	Soviet Union enters war against Japan
August 9	United States drops atomic bomb on Nagasaki
September 2	Official Japanese surrender

when the United States dropped atomic bombs on the cities of Hiroshima and Nagasaki (see Chapter 27), and the Soviet army finally entered the Pacific war with an attack on Japanese forces in China. On August 15, the Japanese emperor Hirohito (1901–1989) announced his country's surrender.

The Home Fronts

While soldiers fought and died in numerous theaters of war, European civilian life was transformed to meet the demands of total war. As governments mobilized their economies for the war effort, gender roles shifted and the demand for radical social change grew. Far more than in World War I, the distinction between the home front and the front lines collapsed, with bombing raids and enemy occupation bringing war onto the civilian's doorstep.

THE OTHER WARS

During World War II in Europe the home front was not a place of safety or normalcy but a place where other wars were fought. Civilians joined the Resistance against Nazi occupation; rival political and ethnic groups engaged in savage struggles for dominance; and both Allied and Axis bombers targeted noncombatants. At the same time, Europeans living in the areas occupied by the Germans endured an increasingly repressive regime.

The Limits of Resistance

Throughout the war individuals and groups in occupied Europe performed heroically, hiding Jews and others on the run, sabotaging equipment, disrupting transportation systems, and relaying secret information to the Allies. In the Soviet Union and in mountainous regions of Yugoslavia, Italy, and southern France, where the terrain offered shelter for guerillas, anti-Nazi fighters formed partisan groups that attacked German army units.

Both men and women participated in the Resistance, the struggle against Nazi rule. In Yugoslavia, 100,000 women fought as soldiers in the partisan ranks: 25,000 were killed and 40,000 injured. Most women in the Resistance were not in combat units. Instead, they played gender stereotypes to great advantage: They hid bombs in baby carriages, tucked vital messages under their shopping, disarmed Germans with feminine charm. One Italian partisan used to catch rides on German trucks to deliver her illegal communications: "What was there to fear? You only had to give them a few smiles."[6] With men at risk of being rounded up for forced labor in Germany, women often shouldered the burden of distributing clandestine publications, delivering supplies and arms, and finding safe houses.

But only a minority of Europeans, men or women, fought in the Resistance. As the Dutch historian Louis de Jong has noted of European actions and attitudes under Nazi occupation, "Unwilling adjustment was the rule, intentional resistance the exception."[7] Why did so few Europeans join the Resistance? Important factors include the Germans' military might, their success at infiltrating Resistance organizations, and their willingness to use brutal force to crush any threat. The German network of concentration camps throughout occupied Europe possessed enormous deterrent value. Concerned for their own and their families' safety, most Europeans hoped simply to keep their heads down and survive the war.

The German practice of exacting collective retribution for Resistance actions particularly undercut mass support for anti-German efforts. In 1942, for example, British intelligence forces parachuted Czech agents into German-held Czechoslovakia. The agents assassinated the chief SS official in the region, Reinhard Heydrich (1904–1942), but they were immediately betrayed by one of their own. In retaliation, the Germans massacred the entire population of the village of Lidice. Similarly, an assassination attempt against Hitler in 1944 led to mass arrests and the executions of an estimated 5,000 Germans.

In Germany itself and in countries allied to rather than conquered by the Germans, potential resisters had to convince themselves that patriotism demanded working against their own government. In France until 1943, resistance meant opposing the lawfully instituted but collaborationist Vichy government of Marshal Pétain. As a World War I hero, Pétain had an almost godlike reputation in France and was popular even with those who did not share his au-

thoritarian conservatism. As a result, in the early years of the war many French men and women viewed the members of the Resistance as traitors against France, rather than as heroes fighting against the Nazis. By 1943, however, an alternative focus of national loyalty had emerged: the Free French headed by General Charles De Gaulle (1890–1970), a career military man who had gone into exile rather than accept the armistice with Nazi Germany. After the Anglo-American landing in North Africa in November 1942, De Gaulle claimed Algeria as a power base and declared himself the head of a Free French provisional government. French patriots could declare themselves loyal to this alternative government, and fight in the Resistance against both Nazi rule and Vichy collaboration.

In many areas—for example, much of Italy after the German army occupied the country in 1943—a genuine spirit of unity characterized the Resistance struggle, with socialists, communists, and Catholics working together not only to defeat the Nazis but also to create the foundations of a better society. In other areas, divisions within the Resistance limited its impact. Conservative army officers fighting to preserve the prewar status quo clashed with

■ The Resistance
A Yugoslav partisan signals his defiance before he is hanged by his German captors.

LIVING UNDER THE BOMBS

·················

During the 1930s, European statesmen and politicians condemned the aerial bombing of civilian populations as an act of barbarity and criminality. Once World War II began, the targeting of civilians in order to break home front morale and impede industrial production became commonplace. Analysts disagree about the military effectiveness of urban bombing, but no one can dispute the human horror.

In this first excerpt, an elderly air warden from Hull, one of Britain's northern port cities, is speaking. One night, when he returned from his post, he found that his street:

Was as flat as this 'ere wharfside—there was just my 'ouse like—well, part of my 'ouse. My missus were just making me a cup of tea for when I come 'ome. She were in the passage between the kitchen and the wash'ouse, where it blowed 'er. She were burnt right up to 'er waist. 'Er legs were just two cinders. And 'er face—The only thing I could recognize 'er by was one of 'er boots—I'd 'ave lost fifteen 'omes if I could 'ave kept my missus. We used to read together. I can't read mesen [myself]. She used to read to me like. We'd 'ave our armchairs on either side o' the fire, and she read me bits out o' the paper. We 'ad a paper every evening. Every evening.

In the following excerpt, a German woman, 19 years old on July 28, 1943, recalls the bombing of Hamburg and the firestorm it induced:

We came to a door which was burning just like a ring in a circus through which a lion has to jump. . . . I struggled to run against the wind in the middle of the street but could only reach a house on the corner. . . . We got to the Loschplatz [park] all right but I couldn't go across the Eiffestrasse [street] because the asphalt had melted. There were people on the roadway, some already dead, some still lying alive but stuck in the asphalt. They must have rushed on to the roadway without thinking. Their feet had got stuck and then they put out their hands to try to get out again. They were on their hands and knees screaming.

Sources: Excerpt from a Mass-Observation typescript report, filed at Mass-Observations offices, no. 844, August 23, 1941. Copyright © by the Trustees of the Mass-Observation Archive. Reprinted by permission.; and from Martin Middlebrook, *The Battle of Hamburg*, Allen Lane, 1980. Reprinted by permission of the author.

---

guerilla groups that espoused radical political goals. Fighting among Resistance factions shaded into civil war. In Ukraine, nationalists fought against communist partisans as well as the Germans. In Greece, the communist-dominated National Liberation Front battled not only the Nazis but also a rival Resistance group, the royalist National Greek Democratic Union.

Civil War in Yugoslavia

The fiercest struggle occurred in Yugoslavia, where political and ethnic divisions split both the country and the Resistance. Wartime Yugoslavia experienced a bloodletting unmatched anywhere in Europe except in the German-occupied regions of Poland and the Soviet Union. Parts of the country such as Slovenia and Macedonia were occupied by German or German-allied armies and endured brutal repression. The scale of violence peaked in the fascist state of Croatia, created after the German invasion of 1941. This Nazi-sponsored regime immediately embarked on a savage program of ethnic homogenization, with a ferocious campaign of terror against Jews, Bosnian Muslims, and Serbs.

In Yugoslavia, therefore, the Resistance was not simply or even primarily aimed at the Germans. Guerilla bands of Serbian soldiers called *Chetniks* supported the now-exiled Yugoslav monarchy and regarded the Croatian regime as their main enemy, although, like the Croatian fascists, the Chetniks also slaughtered both Muslims and Jews. In the midst of this bloody free-for-all, a second Resistance group emerged, one based not on ethnicity but on political ideology. Led by communist Josip Broz (1892–1980), alias "Tito," these partisans saw the war as a chance for social revolution and promised equality for all in a reunited Yugoslavia. Tito's partisans focused on fighting Germans (diverting ten German divisions from the eastern front), but they also fought their fellow Yugoslavs, with the royalist Chetniks fiercely opposing Tito's aim of a communist state.

Tito's partisans won the civil war. In 1944 they fought alongside the Soviet army and liberated Yugoslavia from German control. With 90 percent of the vote in the first postwar election, Tito assumed control of the new communist state of Yugoslavia, a position he held for the next thirty-five years. Beneath the uniform surface created by communist ideology, however, the jagged edges of ethnic division remained sharp.

The Bombing War

For many Europeans, World War II was the war of the bomber. The new technologies and techniques of military aviation ensured that the men, women, and children living in areas targeted by enemy bombers suffered severely. In Britain, until late 1941, civilian deaths outnumbered military, and most of these deaths came from bombing raids. During the autumn of 1940, Londoners endured the "Blitz"—seventy-six consecutive nights of mass bombing.

By May 1941, almost every main industrial city in Britain had been bombed, and 43,000 noncombatants lay dead.

While German bombers were killing British civilians, British bombers, joined in 1943 by the American air force, retaliated in kind, and as the war wore on, developed new techniques of airborne destruction. In May 1942, British planes destroyed Cologne with the world's first 1,000-bomber raid. At the end of July 1943, the British introduced the world to the horror of the firestorm with the bombing of Hamburg. In this human-made catastrophe, fires caused by incendiary bombs combine with winds to suck the oxygen out of the air and raise temperatures to combustible levels. As one survivor recalled, "The smallest children lay like fried eels on the pavement."[8] In a single night, 45,000 of Hamburg's residents were killed. In total, over 500,000 German civilians died in bombing attacks. Twenty percent of the dead were children.

Under Occupation

In occupied Europe, Nazi racial ideology shaped the experience of both soldiers and civilians. The Nazis drew a sharp line between the peoples of western Europe—the Dutch, Norwegian, Danes, and Flemish, all considered of racially superior "Germanic stock"—and the Slavs of eastern Europe. The ferocity of Nazi brutality increased exponentially in the eastern occupied regions. The Nazis drew the sharpest line of all at the Jews, and as Chapter 27 details, sought to murder every Jew in Europe.

The German treatment of prisoners of war (POWs) illustrates the contrast between the western and eastern European experience during World War II. By the end of 1941, 2.5 million Soviet soldiers had been captured. By February 1942, two million of these had died, both from starvation and from epidemic diseases nurtured by the poor conditions in the camps. In contrast, of the over one million French soldiers captured by the Germans in 1940, nineteen out of twenty returned home at the end of the war. When dealing with western European POWs, the Germans abided by international rules; in eastern Europe, World War II was a game without rules and without limits.

In the "General Government" (the portion of Poland not directly annexed to Germany but rather treated as an enemy state under occupation), civilians struggled to survive in barbaric conditions. Political, economic, and intellectual elites faced imprisonment or execution; ordinary Poles endured extreme hunger, hard labor, constant shortages, and the omnipresent threat of death. By the time the war ended in 1945, more than 20 percent of Poland's population had died. Poland's substantial Jewish population endured a hell beyond imagining.

In the occupied regions of the Soviet Union, conditions also reached barbaric levels. Almost 63,000 Soviet civilians were killed in the first five weeks after the German invasion. In planning for the invasion, German policymakers assumed that after a quick and easy victory, the industrial and

particularly the agricultural resources of the Soviet Union would be theirs for the taking. They intended to strip the conquered nation of its food, with no provision made for feeding the defeated Soviets. According to Alfred Rosenberg (1893–1946), the Nazi minister of the eastern occupied territories, the deaths of "many tens of millions" from starvation was to be regarded as "a stern necessity, beyond the realm of all sentiment."[9] Although German plans for a quick conquest in the Soviet Union were soon shattered, German willingness to regard the Soviet population as expendable remained unchanged.

The German occupation of western Europe was less heavy-handed, particularly during the first half of the war. The Nazis believed that "Germanic" peoples such as the Dutch could be taught to become good Nazis and therefore spared them the extreme violence and mindless brutality that characterized the German occupation in the east. Moreover, in western Europe the Germans sought to work with rather than to annihilate political and economic elites. For example, in both Belgium and the Netherlands civil servants continued to do their prewar jobs. Nonetheless, the German occupation in the west, even in the first two years of the war, was far from lenient. The Nazis forced occupied countries to pay exorbitant sums to cover the costs of their own occupation. In addition, they were required to sell both manufactured products and raw materials to Germany at artificially low prices. Anyone who spoke out against the Nazis faced imprisonment or death. The occupation grew even more harsh after 1943 as German military losses piled up, stocks of food and essential supplies dwindled, and German demands for civilian labor increased.

Foreign Laborers in Germany

For millions of European men and women, the war meant forced labor in Germany. With the need to free up German men for the front lines, the Nazis faced crucial labor shortages in almost every sector of the economy. Placing the economy on an all-out war footing would have meant imposing unpopular measures such as the conscription of women for industrial labor, lengthening working hours, and prohibiting holidays. The Nazis chose instead to recruit labor from conquered territories. Within days of the invasion of Poland, Polish POWs were working in German fields. By August 1944, German farmers and factory owners employed over 5.7 million foreign civilian laborers (one-third of whom were women) and almost two million POWs. These foreign workers accounted for more than half the labor in German agriculture and in German munitions plants, and one-third of the labor force in key war industries such as mining, chemicals, and metals.

Hostile, hungry, often untrained for the jobs in which they were placed, foreign workers proved to be less productive than German laborers. Nevertheless, foreign labor played a crucial role in wartime Germany, not only in fueling the German war machine, but also in maintaining

German civilian morale. Foreign labor cushioned German civilians from the impact of total war and reassured them that they belonged to a superior race. Many German factory owners were relieved to find they now had a labor force with few political rights. The director of one aircraft manufacturing firm explained, "The great advantage of employing foreigners . . . is that we only have to give orders. There is no refusal, no need to negotiate."[10] The labor of foreigners also benefited the German working class. Nazi regulations stipulated that German workers were to regard themselves as the masters of the foreign laborers working alongside them. Thus ordinary Germans held positions of privilege and power. Some families even found themselves able to afford new luxuries. Beginning in 1942, the Nazi regime brought Russian women into Germany to serve as maids in German households. As a result, according to a report in January 1943, "even those households with many children, whose financial situation previously did not permit them to hire domestic help, can now afford to maintain a worker."[11]

WOMEN'S WORK

The obliteration of the distinction between soldier and civilian, between the home front and the front lines, meant that this was a women's war. As we have seen, women joined the ranks of the Resistance (and in the Soviet Union, the regular army as well). Women also tended to bear the brunt of home front deprivation, as they were the ones who had to get a meal on the table and clothe their children in the face of severe rationing. Basic household goods such as frying pans, toothbrushes, bicycle tires, baby bottles, and batteries almost disappeared; food was in short supply; clothing had to be recycled. It was Europe's women who became experts at "make do and mend," as British government pamphlets advised.

British women were fully mobilized. They did not serve in combat, but they were drafted for service in civilian defense, war-related industry, or the armed forces. Women accounted for 25 percent of the civilians who worked in Britain's Air Raid Protection services as wardens, rescuers, and telephone operators. All citizens—male or female—working less than 55 hours per week had to perform compulsory fire-watching duties from 1941 on. The numbers of women employed in male-dominated industries such as metals and chemicals rose dramatically.

Only the Soviet Union mobilized women more fully than Britain. Soviet women constituted 80 percent of the agricultural and 50 percent of the industrial labor force. All Soviet adult men and women under age 45 who were not engaged in essential war work were required to work eleven hours a day constructing defenses. Unlike in Britain, Russian women also served in combat. By 1944, 246,000 women were in front-line units. For all Soviet citizens, male and female, life on the home front meant endless labor, inadequate food supplies, and constant surveillance under martial law. Stalin demanded an all-out war against not only the German invaders but also anyone at home who undermined the war effort in any way. The Soviet government established a compulsory sixty-hour workweek and issued ration cards only to those who worked.

Until 1943, the German home front contrasted sharply with that of Britain and the Soviet Union. The Nazi policy toward female employment rested on Hitler's conviction that Germany had lost World War I in part because of the collapse of morale on the home front. As a result, Hitler placed a high priority on maintaining civilian morale. Generous allowances for soldiers meant that their wives,

■ **The Women's War**
Russian women dig trench defenses at the outskirts of Moscow in 1941. No other state mobilized its women as fully as did the Soviet Union.

unlike in Britain, did not have to work to feed their families. In the first years of the war, the Nazi government rationed clothing and food supplies but did not dramatically cut consumption levels. Most significantly, Hitler hesitated to conscript middle-class German women for industrial labor. For Hitler, ideology came before economics. He believed that the future of the "German race" depended on middle-class women being protected from the strains of paid labor so that they could bear healthy Aryan babies.

In Germany the use of foreign labor took the place of the full-scale mobilization of women. Top-ranking Nazis explicitly linked the use of foreign workers to gender considerations. At the end of 1941, for example, Hermann Göring (1893–1946) announced that Soviet workers would be brought into Germany to guarantee "that in future, the German women should not be so much in evidence in the work process."[12] The number of women in the German workforce actually fell by 500,000 between 1939 and 1941. German women who did work were prohibited from working long hours or at night, and from performing heavy physical labor. Instead, eastern European workers (many of them women) were given the tough jobs and the poor hours. At the Krupp metalworks factory, for example, German women worked for six hours at light jobs during the day; Russian women did the heavy labor during the twelve-hour night shift.

Military necessity eventually undercut Nazi gender ideology. The fall of Stalingrad marked a turning point in Nazi policy toward German women at work. With losses on the Eastern front averaging 150,000 men per month, the German army desperately needed more men. At the same time, the German war economy demanded more workers. In response, Hitler's deputy Joseph Goebbels (1897–1945) declared that Germany must fight a total war, which meant total mobilization of the home front. The final, desperate year of the war saw a concentrated use of female labor in Nazi Germany.

Of all the combatant states, the United States stands out as unique with regard to the home front. The United States never fully mobilized its economy, and over 70 percent of its adult women remained outside the paid workforce. Rationing was comparatively minimal and consumption levels in the United States high. In fact, for many families, the war years brought prosperity after years of economic depression. But most important, American cities were never bombed, and thus the United States was able to maintain a clear distinction between soldier and civilian, man and woman—a distinction that was blurred in other combatant nations.

WHAT ARE WE FIGHTING FOR?

To mobilize their populations for total war, governments had to convince their citizens of the importance of the war effort. Maintaining morale and motivating both civilians and soldiers to endure deprivation and danger demanded that leaders supply a persuasive answer to the question: What are we fighting for?

Myth Making and Morale Building

All nations—democratic or authoritarian—rely on myths, on stories of national origins and identity, to unify disparate individuals, classes, and groups. In times of total war, such myths become crucial. During World War II, the process of myth making was institutionalized by government agencies responsible for propaganda. In Britain, the newly formed Ministry of Information (democracies tend to shy away from using the word *propaganda*) took on the task of propping up civilian morale. Staffed by upper-class men, the MOI's efforts often betrayed its class composition: Many of its posters and leaflets adopted a hectoring tone, subjecting ordinary citizens to a barrage of do's and don'ts. Far more effective were the speeches of Prime Minister Winston Churchill, whose romantic vision of Britain as a still-great power destined to triumph was exactly the myth that the beleaguered British needed. In Germany, strict censorship had already subordinated the arts and entertainment industries to the demands of the state. The war heightened this control as censorship tightened even further, paper shortages limited the production of books and periodicals, and the threat of being drafted for the eastern front kept artists in line.

In all the combatant nations, governments enlisted artists, entertainers, and the technologies of the mass media for myth making and morale building. The British artist Henry Moore's (1898–1986) drawings of ordinary people in air raid shelters (completed under an official commission) evoke the survival of civilized values in the midst of unspeakable degradation. Perhaps the most famous musical work from the war is Dmitri Shostakovich's (1906–1975) *Seventh Symphony*—now universally known as the *Leningrad Symphony* and a symbol of human resilience. Shostakovich composed the early drafts of this work in Leningrad while German shells were falling, and it was actually performed in Leningrad in August 1942, while the city was still under siege.

During the war, film came into its own as an artistic form capable of creating important myths of national unity. Laurence Olivier's version of Shakespeare's *Henry V* (1944) comforted British moviegoers with its classic story of a stirring English military victory against huge odds. In Italy, a group of filmmakers known as the Neo-Realists created a set of films that dramatized the Resistance spirit of national unity. Shot on location, with amateur actors and realistic sets, films such as Roberto Rossellini's *Open City* (1945) depicted lower-class life with honesty and respect, and called for the creation of a better society from the rubble of the old.

■ **Henry Moore, *Tube Shelter Perspective* (1941)**
Inadequate public provision of air raid shelters forced working-class Londoners to take matters into their own hands. They began to use London subway stations for shelter during nighttime bombing raids. Impressed by the resilience and good humor of these ordinary people, Moore paid homage to their courage in a series of striking drawings.

Planning for Reconstruction

Rossellini's call for the creation of a new society was echoed throughout Europe during the war. Across Europe a consensus emerged on the need for social democracy, a society in which the state intervenes in economic life to ensure both public welfare and social justice. As early as December 1942, a government committee set out a radical plan for a new Britain. In rather unusual language for an official document, the committee's report identified "five giants on the road to reconstruction": Want, Disease, Ignorance, Squalor, and Idleness. To slay these giants, the committee recommended that the state assume responsibility for ensuring full employment and a minimum standard of living for all through the provision of family allowances, social welfare programs, and a national health service. The Beveridge Report (named after the committee's chairman) became a bestseller in Britain and the basis for a number of postwar European social welfare plans. Churchill, however, reacted lukewarmly to its proposals—a major reason for his defeat

in the election of June 1945. The Labour Party, which enthusiastically endorsed the Beveridge Report and campaigned with slogans such as "Fair Shares for All," won by a landslide. Similarly, Charles De Gaulle, a political conservative, found that in order for his Free French Committee to be recognized as the provisional government of France, he had to display a commitment to democracy and radical social reform. Thus he espoused women's suffrage, and his government promised not only free medical services and expanded family allowances, but also the nationalization of key industries and economic planning.

Four factors explain this radical reorientation of European politics. First, and most important, as the war dragged on and the death tolls mounted, European men and women demanded that their suffering be worthwhile. They wanted to know that they were fighting not to rebuild the depressed and divided societies of the 1930s, but to construct a new Europe. Second, the war (and the ongoing revelations of Nazi atrocities) completely discredited the politics of the far right. This sort of politics, whether fascist, Nazi, or conservative-authoritarian, disappeared from legitimate political discussion. But in Europe (although not in the United States) the liberal ideal of the free and self-interested individual competing in an unregulated economy also lay in ruins, the victim of the prewar Great Depression. The new Europe, then, had to be built along different lines. The third factor that explains the radical reorientation of European politics was the combatant nations' success in mobilizing their economies for total war. If governments could regulate economies to fight wars, why could they not regulate economies for peacetime prosperity? Finally, the important role of socialists and communists in the Resistance enhanced the respectability of radical political ideas. Out of the Resistance came a determination to break the mold of prewar politics and create a new Europe. In France, for example, the Resistance Charter of 1944 demanded the construction of a "more just social order" through the nationalization of key industries, the establishment of a comprehensive social security system, and the recognition of the rights of workers to participate in management.

More generally, the Resistance raised key questions about the role of the individual in modern society. In the 1930s, many Europeans had been persuaded by Hitler, Mussolini, and other far-right theorists that the individual was not important, that only the state mattered. But what the Resistance revealed is the power of human choice and the need for individual action in a world run amuck. Despite—even because of—the horrors of the war, Europeans such as the French writer Albert Camus (1913–1960) emerged convinced of the power of human action: "A pessimist with respect to the human condition, I am an optimist with respect to man." Thus democracy reclaimed the activist state from fascism and Nazism on the one hand, and Stalinism on the other. Europeans saw that the power of the state could be used to improve the well-being of its citizens without at the same time trampling on the rights of the individual.

A Dubious Peace, 1945–1949

Reconstruction seemed far off in 1945, however. World War II ended, but the killing did not. In 1947, Winston Churchill asked, "What is Europe now?" and he answered in the bleakest terms: "A rubble-heap, a charnel house, a breeding ground of pestilence and hate."[13] Postwar purges and deportations ensured that the death totals continued to mount after 1945, and in many regions, particularly in eastern Europe and Southeast Asia, World War II gave way to civil and imperial wars. Most significantly, as the "hot" war waned, the Cold War between the Soviet Union and the United States began.

DEVASTATION, DEATH, AND CONTINUING WAR

If there was peace in Europe and Asia in 1945, it was the "peace of a graveyard," with an estimated 55 million people dead. These deaths were not distributed equally among combatant nations. The greatest losses occurred in the regions Hitler marked as the ground for his new racial empire. Estimates for Soviet deaths—both civilian and military—run up to 25 million.

In the immediate postwar period, the death statistics continued to rise as the victors turned with vengeful fury against the vanquished. In Czechoslovakia, purges killed 30,000 collaborators between 1945 and 1948. In Yugoslavia, Tito ordered the massacre of anticommunists. No one knows how many died: Some estimates range as high as 60,000.

For those left alive, the task of rebuilding was overwhelming. In the Soviet Union, 70 percent of the factories and 60 percent of the transportation facilities had been destroyed. In some German cities, almost every house was uninhabitable. Throughout Europe and Japan, the bombers had rendered most highways, rail tracks, and waterways unusable. With laborers, seed, fertilizer, and basic farming equipment all in short supply, agricultural production in 1945 stood below 50 percent of prewar levels. Less visible, but just as devastating, was the destruction of the financial system. Britain had become the world's largest debtor

nation. Few European currencies were worth much. In occupied Germany, cigarettes replaced marks as the unit of exchange.

One of the most serious problems facing Europe was that of the refugees or displaced persons (DPs). The war, and Hitler's attempt at racial reordering, had uprooted millions from their homes. The DP problem grew even larger as a result of the peace settlement. The Soviet Union kept the Polish territories it had claimed in 1939 and in recompense, Poland received a large chunk of what had been prewar Germany. The new Polish government then expelled the German inhabitants from this region. In Czechoslovakia, Romania, Yugoslavia, and Hungary, too, ethnic Germans were forced out of their homes and onto the road toward Germany. Over 11 million Germans suffered from this forced deportation. As many as two million, suffering from inadequate food, clothing, and shelter, died en route to Germany.

■ **Victors' Vengeance**
The bodies of Mussolini and his mistress hang in the Piazza Loreto in Milan. One year earlier, this piazza was the site of the shooting of Italian hostages by the German military.

Ethnic Germans were not the only ones to endure forced deportation as part of the postwar settlement. Between 1945 and 1948, seven million refugees from other ethnic groups were forcibly transferred, as eastern European governments found a brutal solution to the ethnic divisions that had destabilized prewar political structures. The deportations, together with the Nazis' slaughter of the Jewish population in these regions (see Chapter 27), transformed the ethnic map of Europe. Thus, Poland, whose prewar ethnic minorities composed 32 percent of its population, emerged with a postwar minority population of 3 percent.

Mass deportations also occurred in the Soviet Union. As the Red Army slowly pushed the Germans out of Soviet territory, many of the inhabitants of these regions found that liberation from German occupation did not mean freedom. Following the "liberation" of the Caucasus in the fall of 1943 and the spring of 1944, Stalin accused hundreds of thousands of men, women, and children of collaborating with the Germans. The accused were loaded onto freezing freight cars without adequate supplies of food, water, or warm clothing, and shipped eastward. Entire ethnic groups, such as the Chechens, were accused of collaboration and deported. An estimated 25 percent of these people died on the journey or in the first few years of barren existence in their new homes. Deportations continued after 1945. In the late 1940s and early 1950s, tens of thousands were shipped out of Ukraine, Byelorussia, Moldavia, Latvia, Lithuania, and Estonia.

These deportations can be understood as a continuation of war—a war carried out by governments against groups marked as dangerous because of their ethnic makeup. Other forms of war also continued after 1945. In the Baltic states, the "Forest Brothers" opposed the reimposition of Soviet rule over their homelands by waging guerilla warfare against the government. In Lithuania, partisan fighters posed such a military threat that more than 70,000 Soviet troops were deployed against them in 1948. Similarly, Ukrainian nationalists kept up a guerrilla war against the Soviets until the early 1950s. In many regions, World War II led directly to civil war as compatriots with clashing visions of the postwar future battled each other. In Greece civil war between communist and anticommunist forces raged until 1949, while in Trieste (along the Italian-Yugoslav border) civil war continued until 1954. In Poland, sporadic fighting between the new communist regime and anticommunist guerrilla units based in the marshes and forests continued until 1956.

IMPERIAL ENCOUNTERS

World War II also sparked a series of bloody colonial encounters. In the Pacific region, many colonial nationalists had sided with the Japanese against the British, Dutch, and French, whom they regarded not as defenders of democracy but as imperial overlords. The Japanese internment of the Dutch population in Indonesia in 1942 allowed nationalists to assume positions in the country's government. In Burma, the student-based nationalist movement, led by Aung San (1915–1947), supported the Japanese invasion. Similarly, the Indian nationalist Subhas Chandra Bose (1897–1945) formed a National Army that fought alongside the Japanese and against the British. Of the 45,000 Indian troops captured by the Japanese in the conquests of Malaya and Singapore, 40,000 chose to join Bose's army.

When World War II ended, nationalist elites in colonial regions resisted Western efforts to reimpose imperial rule. They pointed to the inherent contradiction between the Allies' claim to be fighting for democracy and the fact that many Allied nations were imperialist states that denied democratic rule to the colonial regions they controlled. The result was a series of bloody colonial conflicts. In Indonesia, war raged from 1945 to 1949, when the Dutch finally abandoned their attempt to regain control of the region. In Indochina, the nationalist leader Ho Chi Minh (1890–1969) adopted the U.S. Declaration of Independence for his model when he proclaimed Indochinese independence from French colonial rule in September, 1945. A thirty-year war in Vietnam followed, first against the French and then against the Americans.

This era also witnessed a dramatic contraction of the British Empire. Throughout the war Churchill had placed a high priority on preserving the British Empire intact, but World War II had significantly weakened the British state, with its forces stretched to the breaking point. Clement Attlee (1883–1967), who succeeded Churchill as prime minister in July 1945, sought to retain Britain's hold on its essential imperial interests by jettisoning those that Britain no longer needed—or could no longer afford. In just two years—1947 and 1948—Britain relinquished control of India, Burma, and Palestine.

As in much of eastern and central Europe, ethnic and religious hatred devastated these regions in the late 1940s. The proclamation of the new state of Israel in 1948 coincided with the first in a series of Arab-Israeli wars, which left in its wake 500,000 Arab refugees. In India, the Muslim nationalists led by Muhammad Ali Jinnah (1876–1948) refused to accept citizenship in an independent state dominated by Hindus, and won from the British the creation of a separate Muslim state—Pakistan. The partition of the subcontinent led to mass slaughter. Sikhs, frustrated in their desires for an independent Sikh state, saw their Punjabi homeland divided between the two new nations and responded with violence, while Hindus and Muslims also clashed fiercely. More than ten million people fled their homes and became refugees—Muslims fearing Hindu rule, Hindus fearing Muslim rule, Sikhs fearing both. Mahatma Gandhi traveled from village to village in some of the most devastated areas and begged for an end to the killing, but the death tolls reached 250,000—and included Gandhi himself, who was shot by an assassin just six months after Indian independence was proclaimed.

FROM HOT TO COLD WAR

The conflict that aroused the most alarm and posed the greatest threat to the dubious peace after 1945 was the Cold War°, the struggle for global supremacy between the United States and the Soviet Union. Within just a few years of the defeat of Germany and Japan, the allies became enemies, and what Winston Churchill called an "Iron Curtain" dropped between eastern and western Europe. The divisions of the Cold War were rooted in World War II, nurtured by the fears and hopes it aroused.

Interests, Aims, and Armies

Stalin's principal concern in planning for the postwar period was to secure the Soviet Union's western border, to construct for his nation a cushion or buffer zone that could absorb the impact of any future invasion from the west, such as had occurred twice in Stalin's lifetime. The buffer zone Stalin demanded comprised the states of eastern Europe.

Stalin's demand that eastern Europe be regarded as a Soviet sphere of influence conflicted with his allies' public commitment to establish representative democratic political structures throughout Europe. Like Woodrow Wilson in World War I, U.S. president Franklin D. Roosevelt believed that the establishment of European democracies, committed to the liberal economic principles and practices, was crucial for American international security and economic prosperity. British prime minister Winston Churchill's major concerns were the postwar balance of power in Europe and the maintenance of the British Empire. He recognized that once Germany was defeated, a power vacuum would exist in central and eastern Europe and he feared that the Soviets might prove too eager to fill that vacuum. The possibility of Soviet expansion in the Balkans alarmed Churchill, who viewed a Soviet presence in the region as a threat to British military and economic interests in Greece and throughout the Mediterranean.

Fraying Seams, 1943–1945

The "Big Three°," then, came to the negotiating table with clashing interests and aims; even before the war ended, the fabric of the alliance was under strain. In face-to-face meetings—at Tehran in November 1943 and at Yalta in February 1945—disagreements on key questions were already fraying the seams of the alliance. These questions included German reparations and the political and territorial shape of postwar Poland.

Reluctant to place too much pressure on these fraying seams, Roosevelt opted for postponing the hard decisions.

He was not seeking simply to sidestep controversy. Rather, he hoped that the controversial questions would be settled after the war by a new international body, the United Nations (UN). In Roosevelt's vision, such a body could succeed where the now-discredited League of Nations had failed: It could guarantee that conciliation and negotiation would replace armed conflict in settling disputes between countries. Roosevelt recognized that if the Soviet Union refused to participate in the United Nations, the UN, like the league, would be a failure. Therefore he sought to avoid confrontations that might give Stalin a reason to block Soviet membership in the UN.

Roosevelt also hoped that new international economic structures would provide a framework for settling the disputes that divided the Allies. In 1944 leading American and European economists gathered in New Hampshire to construct a system for postwar economic revival. Well aware of the economic chaos that had followed World War I, and desperate to avoid a repeat of the Great Depression of the 1930s, they drew up the Bretton Woods Agreement°, which became the basic framework for the Western postwar economic order. To keep the global economy running smoothly, Bretton Woods established the American dollar as the world's reserve currency and fixed the currency exchange rates of its forty-four participating nations. It also established two new international economic institutions—the International Monetary Fund (IMF), to maintain the stability of member currencies, and the World Bank, to encourage global economic development.

Through the establishment of such international organizations as the IMF and the UN, Roosevelt sought "the end of the system of unilateral action, the exclusive alliances, the spheres of influence, the balances of power, and all the expedients that have been tried for centuries and have always failed." Yet neither Stalin nor Churchill shared Roosevelt's vision. Standing on opposite ends of the political spectrum, the Russian communist and the English aristocrat both continued to believe in precisely those "spheres of influence, the balances of power" that Roosevelt proclaimed outmoded. In the worldview of both Stalin and Churchill, armed force, not a new international organization, would determine the shape of the postwar world. As Stalin pointed out to Tito, the Yugoslav communist leader, "Everyone imposes his own system as far as his armies can reach. It cannot be otherwise."

By 1945, Stalin's army had a long reach. To prevent Soviet domination of eastern Europe, Churchill had earlier in the war pressed for an Anglo-American invasion of the Balkans. When the Big Three met in Tehran in 1943, however, they agreed that the Anglo-American invasion would be a single, concentrated attack across the English Channel into France (the D-Day invasion of June 1944). Although the decision led to a successful offensive and the defeat of Germany, it left the Balkans open to the Red Army. By the time the Big Three met in Yalta in the spring of 1945, the communist partisans under Tito controlled Yugoslavia, and the Soviet Army had occupied Romania, Bulgaria, Hungary, and much of Czechoslovakia. A conquering army possesses strongly persuasive powers. The Red Army's presence in eastern Europe ensured that American and British objections to Soviet actions remained confined to words only. No American or British policy-maker—political or military—was prepared to advocate an armed confrontation with the Soviet Union in 1945.

At Yalta, then, the presence of the Red Army in eastern Europe weakened the negotiating positions of Churchill and Roosevelt. Roosevelt's desire to obtain Stalin's commitment to enter the war against Japan also reduced his bargaining power. The result was a series of problematic compromises. Stalin signed a declaration promising free elections in eastern Europe; at the same time, Roosevelt and Churchill agreed that such freely elected governments should be pro-Soviet.

The Yalta agreements also left undecided the future of Germany. With his country devastated by the ruinous German invasion and occupation, Stalin insisted that Germany be forced to pay reparations to the Soviet Union. Both Roosevelt and Churchill feared that a weak or partitioned German state would invite Soviet expansion into central Europe. The Big Three left open the question of German reparations but stipulated the division of Germany, and the symbolically and strategically vital city of Berlin, into occupation zones controlled by the United States, the Soviet Union, France, and Britain.

CHRONOLOGY

The Outbreak of the Cold War

1943		
	November	Tehran Conference
1944		
	August	Soviet Army advances into Balkans
	October	Soviets link up with Tito's partisans in Yugoslavia
1945		
	January	Soviet Army advances into Poland
	February	Yalta Conference
	July	Potsdam Conference
	August	United States drops atomic bombs on Hiroshima and Nagasaki
1946		
	March	Churchill gives his "Iron Curtain" speech in Missouri
1947		
	February	Truman Doctrine announced
	June	Marshall Plan announced
1948		Stalinist terror in eastern Europe underway
1949		
	April	Formation of North Atlantic Treaty Organization (NATO)
	May	Official formation of West Germany (Federal Republic of Germany)
	August	Soviet atomic bomb test

Ripping Apart, 1945–1946

In July 1945, when the Allied leaders met again in the German city of Potsdam, Stalin faced two unfamiliar negotiating partners. The new U.S. president Harry Truman (1884–1972) replaced Roosevelt, who had died in April, and midway through the summit, the new prime minister, Labour Party leader Clement Attlee, arrived to take Churchill's place. These leadership changes complicated the Big Three negotiations. Attlee lacked Churchill's prestige, and Stalin had far less rapport with Truman than he had enjoyed with Roosevelt. More important, during the conference Truman received a telegram informing him of the world's first successful atomic bomb test, a development

that reduced Western incentives for placating Stalin. (See Chapter 27.)

But in July 1945 Cold War divisions were not yet solid. Throughout the rest of 1945 and 1946 Truman continued to hope to resolve the differences dividing the one-time allies and resisted the idea of a permanent American military presence in Europe. Stalin, too, was unwilling to push too far. He feared American military might, he hoped to retain access to western economic assistance and expertise, and he wanted to scale back military expenditures. Thus he proceeded with rapid demilitarization: Soviet army strength went from 12 million men in 1945 to 3 million by 1948. At the same time, Stalin adopted a policy of passivity for communist parties operating in regions that he viewed as part of the Western sphere of influence. He refused to assist

■ **The Big Three I (Yalta, February 1945)**
From 1941 until April 1945, the Big Three meant Stalin, Roosevelt, and Churchill. At the very end of
the war, however, the composition of the Big Three suddenly changed, as Harry Truman replaced
Roosevelt and Clement Attlee replaced Churchill.

Greek communists seeking to overthrow the British-backed monarchical regime, and he ordered communist parties in western Europe to participate with noncommunists in coalition governments.

During this period, however, the British pushed Truman to adopt a hard line toward Stalin and his demands. British foreign policy was in the hands of the foreign secretary, Ernest Bevin (1881–1951). A labor leader with a history of fighting against communist efforts to control British unions, Bevin was a fierce anti-Stalinist. He was also an ardent British nationalist who regarded the maintenance of the British Empire, particularly in the Mediterranean and the Middle East, as crucial to preserving Britain's Great Power status in the postwar world. Bevin thus urged the United States to stand tough when the Soviets demanded a stake in what had been Italy's North African empire and he urged a strong response when Stalin delayed pulling Russian troops out of Iran. (Soviet and British troops had occupied Iran during the war to keep its oil supplies out of German hands.)

The alliance finally fell apart not over the Mediterranean or the Middle East but over Germany. At Potsdam, Truman and Attlee had agreed to Stalin's demand for German reparations. By 1946, however, British and American authorities became convinced that Germany faced mass starvation. To feed the Germans in the British zone, Attlee's government had to impose bread rationing on the British public—a drastic step never taken during the war itself. The British and Americans decided that the immediate priority must be German economic recovery. They combined their zones into a single economic unit and stopped reparations deliveries to the Soviets. All pretense of a united Allied policy in Germany was dropped, making almost inevitable the eventual division of Germany into two hostile states. The French soon merged their occupation zone with that of the British and Americans, and in 1949 this territory became the Federal Republic of Germany (West Germany), while the Soviet-occupied zone became the German Democratic Republic (East Germany).

Torn in Two, 1947–1949

Within just a few years of the war's end, therefore, clashing aims and interests had shredded the wartime alliance. Because the Cold War was not a shooting war, it is difficult to pinpoint its precise start, but two key developments of 1947—the Truman Doctrine°—and the Marshall Plan°—played crucial roles in transforming allies into enemies.

Like the division of Germany, the Truman Doctrine was linked to Britain's postwar economic crisis. In February 1947 Attlee's government informed Truman's administration that it could not afford to continue its fight against communist rebels in Greece. The United States immediately assumed Britain's role in the Mediterranean. Truman used this development to issue the Truman Doctrine, a broad policy statement committing the American government "to support free people who are resisting attempted subjugation by armed minorities or by outside pressures."[14] The Truman Doctrine inaugurated the policy of containment°—resisting communist expansion wherever in the world it occurred. After the declaration of the Truman Doctrine, the ideological division of Europe proceeded swiftly. Under strong pressure from American political and financial interests, the French and Italian governing coalitions expelled their communist members in May 1947.

The Marshall Plan furthered the division of Europe into two hostile camps. In June 1947, U.S. secretary of state General George Marshall (1880–1959) proposed that the United States underwrite Europe's economic recovery. Initially, Marshall's proposal received little attention in the United States, but in Britain, Foreign Secretary Ernest Bevin heard a report of it on the radio. Believing that British interests demanded a firm American commitment to Europe, Bevin perceived the Marshall Plan as the first step toward establishing this ongoing U.S. presence. He called the plan "a lifeline to sinking men." Bevin's French counterpart, Foreign Minister Georges Bidault (1899–1983), shared his enthusiasm, and together they helped make the Marshall Plan a reality. With representatives from twelve other European states, Bevin and Bidault drew up a list of European resources and requirements, and devised a four-year plan for European economic reconstruction. In 1948, the first food shipments from the United States reached European ports. Eventually $17 billion in aid poured into Europe. A new international body, the Organization for European Economic Cooperation (OEEC), worked to coordinate aid, eliminate trade barriers, and stabilize currencies. The formation of the OEEC was the first step in integrating western European economies, a process that eventually led to the establishment of the European Union (EU), as we will see in Chapters 28 and 29.

The Marshall Plan helped unify western Europe, but at the same time it accelerated the division of East and West. Stalin saw the Marshall Plan as an effort to undercut Soviet influence in Europe, and he was right. Marshall's intentions were explicitly anticommunist. A tour of Europe's still-devastated regions in the spring of 1947 had convinced Marshall that if the United States did not jump-start Europe's economies, its peoples would turn readily to communism. Marshall Plan aid was available to any country that chose to accept it, including the Soviet Union and the nations of eastern Europe. Participating states, however, were required to join in the OEEC—a requirement the Soviets would not accept. Stalin had already refused to participate in the Bretton Woods system, which he saw as an instrument of American economic domination.

In April 1949 nine western European nations[18] joined together with the United States and Canada in the North Atlantic Treaty Organization (NATO)°, a military alliance specifically aimed at repelling a Soviet invasion of western Europe. Months later, on August 29, 1949, the Soviet Union conducted a successful test explosion of an atomic bomb. Over the next few years, Stalin forced his eastern European satellites into an anti-Western military alliance, finalized as the Warsaw Pact° in 1955. Europe was divided into hostile military blocs, each possessing an atomic arsenal.

Terror in Eastern Europe

The onset of the Cold War accelerated a Stalinist campaign of terror already underway in eastern Europe. Stalin launched the terror in the Soviet satellite states in direct response to developments in Yugoslavia. Led by Tito, Yugoslav communists resisted Stalin's efforts to dictate their foreign and domestic policies. This quarrel became a permanent break in 1948, when Stalin lost all control over Yugoslavia. Alarmed, Stalin sought to eliminate any potential Tito imitators from the rest of eastern Europe. The Cold War provided Stalin with additional weaponry in this battle against any possible threat to his personal power. Stalin insisted that a Western conspiracy to divide and conquer the Soviet bloc could be defeated only by a thoroughgoing purge of the communist ranks.

Over the next five years, Stalin prodded eastern European governments to institute a campaign of terror in their countries. Arrested, charged with sabotage and espionage for the West, and savagely tortured, prominent communists were convicted in public show trials at which they recited the confessions that had been prepared for them. The terror quickly spread beyond the ranks of prominent communists. Factory supervisors were assigned quotas; they knew if they did not come up with a required number of names of "criminals," they would be imprisoned. In Budapest, frightened citizens watched the police vans that slid through the street every Monday, Wednesday, and Friday night at 2 A.M., picking up the next allotment of victims. The security forces targeted anyone remotely connected to "the West," including veterans of the Spanish Civil War and members of international organizations such as the Boy Scouts. Jews, considered "cosmopolitan" and therefore potentially pro-Western, were particularly suspect. For eastern Europeans, World War II had ended, but the peace never really began.

Show Time: The Trial of Rudolf Slánský

On the night of July 31, 1951, Rudolf Slánský–general secretary of the Communist Party of Czechoslovakia (CPC) and the second most powerful man in Prague—left his 50th birthday party, and headed home, a frightened man. Outwardly, nothing was wrong. The CPC had celebrated the day in style. The communist president, Klement Gottwald, presented to Slánský the medal of the Order of Socialism, the highest honor awarded in Czechoslovakia. Telegrams of congratulations poured in from all over the country. But the huge stack of congratulatory telegrams contained no greeting from Stalin. Slánský knew he was in trouble.

At another place and in another time, Slánský's fear could be dismissed as mere paranoia. But in the upper ranks of the Communist Party in Czechoslovakia in 1951, signs of Stalin's approval or disapproval were literally a matter of life or death. The Stalinist purge of eastern Europe was well underway, with thousands arrested, tortured, imprisoned, or killed.

Slánský knew he was vulnerable on three counts. First, he held a rank high enough to ensure a spectacular show trial. As the Soviet Great Purge of the 1930s had demonstrated, trials and executions of leading communists worked both to terrorize Stalin's potential rivals and, by rousing ordinary citizens to perpetual vigilance, to cement mass loyalty to the regime. But for a trial to be a genuine show, the defendant had to be worth showing.

Slánský, as the CPC general secretary, was the perfect defendant.

Slánský was a target for Stalin's purge, second, because he was a Czech, and Stalin viewed his Czech colleagues with particular suspicion. Czechoslovakia was the only state in eastern Europe with a history of successful democracy and without Soviet troops in occupation after 1945. Moreover, the CPC had participated with noncommunists in a coalition government longer than any other eastern European communist party.

Such differences linked the CPC to the ideology of "national communism," which taught that the Soviet path to communism was not the only one, that each nation must find its own route. "National communism" became a heresy in Stalin's eyes after his break with the Yugoslav communist leader Tito in 1948. Tito had dared to lead Yugoslavia down a different path, and had dared to defy Stalin's leadership. Determined to prevent any additional defections from his eastern European empire, Stalin embarked on a quest for real or potential "titoists". To save his own skin, CPC leader Klement Gottwald needed to demonstrate his willingness to uproot titoism from his party and his government. Slánský became that demonstration.

Finally, Slánský was vulnerable because he was a Jew. When the purges in eastern Europe began in 1948, anti-Semitism played no prominent role, but by 1950 the intersection of Middle Eastern power plays, Cold War hostilities, Stalin's paranoia, and the still-powerful tradition of Jew-hating in eastern European culture made Jewish communists particularly suspect. Aiming to establish a Soviet presence in the Middle East after the war, Stalin had tried to persuade the new state of Israel to align with the Soviet Union by offering the new Israeli government diplomatic recognition and arms deals. But Stalin's efforts failed. By 1950, Israel had become an ally of the United States. Stalin responded with fury. All Jews came under suspicion of "Zionist" (that is, pro-Israel and therefore pro-Western) tendencies.

Stalin's failure to send Slánský a birthday telegram signaled that Slánský was now on the list of suspects. Over the following months Soviet advisors and homegrown Czech torturers pressured prisoners already caught in the net of the purge to confess that they were part of a Slánský-led conspiracy to overthrow the communist government and to turn Czechoslovakia against the Soviet Union. These torture-induced confessions were then used to prepare a flimsy case against Slánský and thirteen other men (eleven of them Jews).

Shortly before midnight on November 24, 1951, security agents arrested Slánský at his home. A lifelong atheist, Slánský could say nothing except "Jesus Maria." He knew what was coming. Instrumental in initiating the Stalinist purge in Czechoslovakia, Slánský had approved the arrests and torture of many of his colleagues. Ironically, he had drafted the telegram asking Stalin to send Soviet advisors to

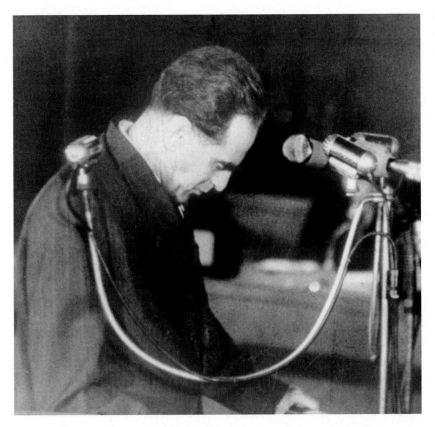

assist in the Czech purge—the very same advisors who decided to target Slánský.

For the next year, Slánský endured mental and physical torture, directed by these advisors. Common torture tactics included beatings and kickings; prolonged periods without sleep, food or water; all-night interrogation sessions; and being forced to stand in one place or march in circles for days on end. One interrogator recalled, "Instead of getting evidence, we were told that they were villains and that we had to break them."[15] Breaking Slánský took six months; the remaining months were spent defining and refining the details of his imaginary crimes against the communist regime, and rehearsing for the all-important show trial.

Slánský's trial, which began on November 20, 1952, was in every sense a show. Before the trial began, party officials had already determined the verdict and the sentences. Prosecutors, defense attorneys, judges, and the accused spoke the lines of a script written by security agents. Thus, one year after his arrest, Slánský stood up in court and pled guilty to the crimes of high treason, espionage, and sabotage. A founding member of the CPC, he said he had conspired to overthrow the communist government. A resistance fighter during World War II, he confessed to working with the Nazis against the communists. A zealous Stalinist, he announced that he was a titoist-Zionist, who had plotted to hand Czechoslovakia to the Americans.

Why did Slánský make such a ludicrous confession? Fear of further torture is clearly one motive, but other factors also came into play. Communists such as Slánský believed that the interests of the party always came first, ahead of individual rights, ahead of abstractions such as "truth." Slánský may have believed that his confession, false though it was, served the party. As one experienced interrogator noted about a different defendant, "He'll confess; he's got a good attitude toward the party."[16] In addition, Slánský may have been promised, as were other show trial defendants, that his life would be spared and his family protected if he confessed.

In his closing statement, Slánský said, "I deserve no other end to my criminal life than that proposed by the state prosecutor."[17] The prosecutor demanded the death penalty. Slánský was executed on December 3, 1952. Ten of his co-accused also hanged. Their families were stripped of their party memberships and privileges, deported with only the barest essentials to designated districts, and assigned to manual labor. ■

Questions of Justice

What sort of justice was served in the trial of Rudolf Slánský?

Taking It Further

Lukes, Igor. "The Rudolf Slánský Affair: New Evidence." *Slavic Review* 58, 1 (Spring 1999): 160–187. Illuminating study of the role of Cold War intrigue in determining Slánský's fate.

Kaplan, Karel. *Report on the Murder of the General Secretary.* 1990. Kaplan emigrated from Czechoslovakia to West Germany in the late 1970s, with a stack of hidden documents, and wrote this report.

CURTAINS AND CAMPS

The Cold War gave rise to a new set of metaphors, as politicians, diplomats, and journalists struggled to find ways to explain the new world order. Two of the most compelling metaphors arose very early: the "Iron Curtain," coined by Winston Churchill in 1946, and "the two camps," used in a speech by Stalin's spokesman Andrei Zhdanov in 1947.

In 1946, Churchill was still the leader of Britain's Conservative Party, but was no longer prime minister. On a visit to the United States, he gave a pivotal speech that warned of a divided Europe.

From Stettin in the Baltic to Trieste in the Adriatic, an iron curtain has descended across the Continent. Behind that line lie all the capitals of the ancient states of Central and Eastern Europe. Warsaw, Berlin, Prague, Vienna, Budapest, Belgrade, Bucharest and Sofia, all these famous cities and the populations around them lie in what I must call the Soviet sphere, and all are subject in one form or another, not only to Soviet influence but to a very high and, in many cases, increasing measure of control from Moscow. . . .

At the founding meeting of the Cominform in September 1947, Zhdanov delivered a speech that clearly articulated the postwar division of the world into two hostile blocs.

In the post-war period sharp changes have taken place in the international situation . . . Two opposite political lines took shape: at one pole, the policy of the USSR and the democratic countries, aimed at undermining imperialism and strengthening democracy; at the other pole the policy of the USA and Britain, aimed at strengthening imperialism and strangling democracy. . . .

Thus two camps have come into being . . .

The Truman-Marshall Plan is only one component part . . . of a general plan of worldwide expansionist policy that is being carried out by the USA in all parts of the world . . . Yesterday's aggressors, the capitalist magnates of Germany and Japan, are being groomed by America for a new role, that of serving as an instrument of the USA's imperialist policy in Europe and Asia. . . . Under these conditions it is essential for the anti-imperialist and democratic camp to close ranks, work out a common programme of actions and develop its own tactics against the main forces of the imperialist camp. . . .

Sources: From a speech by Winston Churchill, delivered to Westminster College, Fulton, Missouri, March 5, 1946.; and from G. Procacci (ed.), *The Cominform: Minutes of the Three Conferences 1947, 1948, 1949*, Milan, 1994.

CONCLUSION

The New Europe, The New West

Adolf Hitler had promised his allies and his enemies that he would create a new Europe. And so he did. As Europeans emerged from their bomb shelters, returned home from their army units, or searched desperately for family members among the DP camps, they faced an uncertain future in a radically changed world. World War II and the Cold War that succeeded it created a new European—and a new global—order, but one dramatically different from that envisioned by Hitler.

World War II also reshaped the dominant idea of the "West." Hitler offered a set of ideas that promised a dramatic reconfiguration of Western values along racist, authoritarian lines. In the Nazi vision, the West comprised white, northern Europeans, marching in step to the dictates of the antidemocratic state. The wartime encounter with this vision was crucial; from it emerged a sharpened commitment within the West to the processes and values of democracy.

But to present the Second World War as a conflict between democracy and Nazism is to oversimplify. To defeat Nazi Germany, the democracies of Britain and the United States allied with Stalin's Soviet Union, a dictatorial regime that matched Hitler's Germany in its contempt for democratic values and human rights and surpassed it in state-sanctioned mass murder. The Soviet Union emerged from the war as the dominant power in eastern Europe; the presence of the Red Army obliterated any chance to establish democratic governments in this region.

The tensions inherent in the Anglo-American alliance with the Soviets led directly to the Cold War, the ideological and political conflict that dominated the post–World War II world and that once again forced a redefinition of the West. From 1949 until 1989, it was easy to draw the West on any map: One simply shaded in the United States and those countries allied to it. But at the same time a new division emerged. World War II marked the beginning of the end of European imperial control over the non-European world. As a result, the postwar era would see growing tensions between "North" and "South"—between the industrially developed nations and the underdeveloped regions seeking to shrug off their colonial past.

Much of the impetus for imperial control over non-European regions came from the conviction of European supremacy. During the war, however, Japanese victories had exposed the illusion of European military invincibility. And after the war, the gradual realization of the full horror of what became known as the Holocaust—Hitler's war against the Jews—demolished any lingering claim to European cultural superiority. Few could doubt the technological preeminence of the nation that emerged as "Leader of the Western World" (the United States), but in the aftermath of the atomic bombings of Japanese cities, disturbing questions surfaced about the implications and consequences of such technologies in a democratic society. These two key developments of the war, the Holocaust and Hiroshima, are the subject of the next chapter.

Suggestions for Further Reading

···················· ▬ ····················

For a comprehensive list of suggested readings, please go to www.ablongman.com/levack/chapter26

Calder, Angus. *The People's War: Britain, 1939–1945.* 1969. Lengthy but worth the effort for students wishing to explore the war's impact on British society. (Those who want a shorter account can turn to Robert Mackay, *The Test of War: Inside Britain 1939–45* [1999].)

Gross, Jan T., ed. *The Politics of Retribution in Europe: World War II and Its Aftermath.* 2000. This series of essays makes clear that war did not end in Europe in May 1945.

Iriye, Akira. *The Origins of the Second World War in Asia and the Pacific.* 1987. Part of Longman's Origins of Modern Wars series aimed at university students, this short and readable study highlights the major issues and events.

Keegan, John. *The Second World War.* 1989. Provides clear explanations of military technologies and techniques; packed with useful maps and vivid illustrations.

Kitchen, Martin. *Nazi Germany at War.* 1995. A short and nicely organized survey of the German home front.

Milward, A. S. *War, Economy, and Society, 1939–1945.* 1977. A solid survey by a leading economic historian.

Moore, Bob, ed. *Resistance in Western Europe.* 2000. A collection of essays that explores recent research on this controversial topic.

Overy, Richard. *Russia's War: A History of the Soviet War Effort, 1941–1945.* 1997. A compelling account, written to accompany the television documentary *Russia's War.*

Paxton, Robert. *Vichy France: Old Guard and New Order, 1940–1944.* 1972. A now-classic study of the aims and evolution of France's collaborationist government.

Rock, William R. *British Appeasement in the 1930s.* 1977. A balanced and concise appraisal.

de Senarclens, P. *From Yalta to the Iron Curtain: The Great Powers and the Origins of the Cold War.* 1995. A look at the diplomatic, political and military concerns that created the Cold War.

Weinberg, Gerhard. *A World at Arms: A Global History of World War II.* 1994. Places the war within a global rather than simply a European context.

Wyman, Mark. *DPs: Europe's Displaced Persons, 1945–1951.* 1989. An important study of an often-neglected topic.

Notes

1. Quoted in Piers Brendon, *The Dark Valley: A Panorama of the 1930s* (2000), p. 282.
2. Quoted in Richard Overy, *Russia's War* (1998), p. 95.
3. Quoted in Mark Mazower, *Dark Continent: Europe's Twentieth Century* (1999), p. 157.
4. Quoted in Joachim Fest, *Hitler* (1973), p. 665.
5. Quotations from Juliet Gardiner, *"Over Here"—The GIs in Wartime Britain* (1992), p. 62, 53, 132.
6. Quoted in Jane Slaughter, *Women in the Italian Resistance 1943–1945* (1997), p. 63.
7. Quoted in Bob Moore, ed., *Resistance in Western Europe* (2000), p. 210.
8. Quoted in Richard Rhodes, *The Making of the Atomic Bomb* (1988), p. 474.
9. Quoted in Ulrich Herbert, *Hitler's Foreign Workers* (1997), p. 139.
10. Quoted in Herbert, p. 306.
11. Quotations from Herbert, pp. 149, 189.
12. Quoted in Herbert, p. 149.
13. Quoted in Derek Urwin, *A Political History of Western Europe Since 1945* (1997), p. 320.
14. Quoted in Robert Paxton, *Europe in the Twentieth Century* (1997), p. 512.
15. Quoted in Karel Kaplan, *Report on the Murder of the General Secretary* (1990), p. 159.
16. Quoted in Kaplan, p. 242.
17. Quoted in Kaplan, p. 231.
18. The original signatories of the NATO treaty were Iceland, Norway, Great Britain, Belgium, the Netherlands, Luxembourg, France, Italy, and Portugal. Greece and Turkey joined the alliance in 1951, West Germany in 1954, Spain in 1982. Sweden, Finland, Switzerland, Austria, Yugoslavia, and Albania remained nonaligned with either the United States or the Soviet Union.

The Holocaust, the Bomb, and the Legacy of Mass Killing

I N THE WEEKS IMMEDIATELY PRECEDING AND FOLLOWING THE END OF THE SECOND World War in Europe, many Allied soldiers faced their most difficult assignment yet. Hardened combat veterans, accustomed to scenes of slaughter and destruction, broke down and wept as they encountered a landscape of horror beyond their wildest nightmares: the world of the Nazi concentration and death camps. As one American war correspondent put it, "we had penetrated at last to the center of the black heart, to the very crawling inside of the vicious heart."[1] The American soldiers who opened the gates of the camp in Mauthausen, Austria, never forgot their first sight of the prisoners there: "By the thousands they came streaming . . . Hollow, pallid ghosts from graves and tombs, terrifying, rot-colored figures of misery marked by disease, deeply ingrained filth, inner decay. . . . squat skeletons in rags and crazy grins."[2]

Similarly, the British troops who liberated Bergen-Belsen in Germany were marked indelibly by what they encountered within the camp's walls. By the end of 1944, Bergen-Belsen had become the dumping ground for tens of thousands of prisoners evacuated from camps in eastern Europe, as the Nazi SS desperately retreated in front of the advancing Soviet army. Already sick and starving, these prisoners were jammed, 1,200 at a time, into barracks built to accommodate a few hundred. By March 1945, both drinking water and food had disappeared, human excrement dripped from bunk beds until it coated the floors of the barracks, and dead bodies piled up everywhere. In these conditions, the only living beings to flourish were the microorganisms that cause typhus. When the British entered Bergen-Belsen, they found 60,000 emaciated and diseased prisoners, half of them Jews. Floundering in this sea of human want, British soldiers, doctors, and nurses did what they could; even so, 28,000 of Bergen-Belsen's inmates died in the weeks following liberation. The photographs of the mass graves taken by the Allies when they opened the camps produced an enduring image of mass

Chapter Outline

- Toward the Final Solution: From Emigration to Extermination

- Responding to the Holocaust

- The Race for the Atom Bomb

- The Dawn of the Nuclear Age

The Crematoria at Buchenwald: The Nazis used industrial technologies, such as industrial-scale bake ovens, to commit mass murder. At Buchenwald, one of the many camps within the Nazi system of concentration and death camps, victims' bodies were cremated..

■ **Mass Grave at Bergen-Belsen**

This concentration camp was liberated by British soldiers on April 15, 1945.

killing, one that has become emblematic of what is now called the Holocaust°, the murder of approximately six million European Jews, and three to five million other victims, including Polish and Russian Christians, Jehovah's Witnesses, Roma (Gypsies), homosexuals, and political opponents of the Nazi regime.

A few months later, another compelling photographic image stunned the world: the mushroom cloud. In August 1945, U.S. planes dropped two atomic bombs on the Japanese cities of Hiroshima and Nagasaki. Tens of thousands died within seconds, and the mushroom cloud immediately became seared on Western consciousness. Yet the image of the billowing cloud, monstrous and beautiful, focused not on mass death but rather on the power and mystery of the new atomic age. Soon, however, other images entered Western consciousness: staggering figures, barely recognizable as human, with their melted eyeballs dripping from their sockets and their flesh peeling off in sheets, the stumbling and blinded survivors of the atomic bombs. As Europeans and Americans encountered the awesome destructive power of first-rate physics allied to military might, they were forced to confront the possibility of mass killing on an unprecedented, even incomprehensible, scale. With the development of the hydrogen bomb in the early 1950s, governments possessed the ability to destroy not just single cities, but entire civilizations and perhaps the world itself.

How can we understand the events that led to both the Holocaust and Hiroshima? Hitler's war against the Jews and the atomic bombings in Japan were not equivalent acts.

Both, however, ensured the centrality of *mass killing* in any discussion of the experience or meaning of the twentieth century. The assembly-line techniques of mass murder developed by the Nazis and, in very different ways, the sheer efficiency of the atom bomb in obliterating urban populations forced both individuals and their political leaders to confront the destructive potential of modern technologies and techniques. Both also challenged key assumptions about the identity of the "West" and so demanded the creation of new frameworks—cultural, political, and international—in the postwar world. In their use of Western science and technology to achieve fundamentally irrational and evil ends, the Nazi death camps upset settled assumptions about both the benevolent role of science in society and the supposed moral superiority of Western civilization. In very different ways, the Bomb, too, caused widespread questioning about basic Western ideals and values. Originating in the desire to save the West from Nazi domination, its use against Japan continues to provoke heated controversy about Western motivations and to raise important questions about the implications of advanced technology for democratic decision making.

To explain how these two events helped shape Western identity and consciousness since World War II, this chapter will address four questions: (1) How and why did the Nazis devise a plan aimed at killing every Jew in Europe? (2) How did Europeans and Americans respond to the Nazi effort to annihilate the Jews—both at the time, and in the decades since the death camps were revealed to the world? (3) What were the factors that led to the Allies' decision to drop atomic bombs on Japanese cities? (4) What were the consequences of this decision?

Toward the Final Solution: From Emigration to Extermination

························ ▬ ························

Central to an examination of the Holocaust is the question of *origins:* When and why was the plan for the annihilation of Europe's Jewish population first conceived? The question is not as simple as it may first appear. Anti-Semitism was a central component of both Adolf Hitler's worldview and Nazi ideology, yet anti-Semitism alone cannot explain the Holocaust, nor was the Holocaust the product of a detailed plan carefully plotted out by Hitler long before he came to power. The decision to murder the Jews evolved over time. More specifically, the Holocaust originated as a response to, and by-product of, total war.

ANTI-SEMITISM: THE NECESSARY PRECONDITION

Anti-Semitism alone cannot explain the Holocaust, but it was its necessary precondition. As Chapter 22 explained, modern anti-Semitism emerged in the nineteenth century. The lifting of discriminatory laws in this period benefited Jews, many of whom moved into the mainstream of European economic, political, and intellectual life, particularly in areas such as Austria and Germany. At the same time, however, the spread of industrialization created an unstable economic and social climate. Those people who viewed themselves as victims in the new modern world—the small shopkeeper put out of business by the large department store, the skilled artisan replaced by new technology, the farmer who watched agricultural prices plummet in the new global marketplace—looked for someone to blame for their woes.

They did not have far to look. European Christians had long blamed Jews for evils of all kinds. Christian doctrine identified the Jews as responsible for the crucifixion of Jesus, while during the Middle Ages Jews were widely believed to have caused the bubonic plague. In the less industrialized regions of Europe, such as outlying portions of the Russian and Austrian-Hungarian Empires, religious anti-Semitism remained powerful until well into the twentieth century. In the more urban and industrial regions, however, this traditional, religion-based hatred of Jews loosened its grip on European culture. Instead, the rise of quasi-scientific theories of racial difference ensured that in a more secular society, Jews were regarded with suspicion not only because of their religion but more so because of their race, a supposed biological fact that could not be altered or escaped.

The rise of racist pseudoscience interacted with the spread of both socialist and mass nationalistic politics to produce a virulently anti-Semitic atmosphere throughout much of Europe by the beginning of the twentieth century. The fact that many Jewish intellectuals had embraced Karl Marx's critique of capitalist society and that a number of leading socialist politicians were Jewish led some desperate Europeans to lump together Jewishness and socialism as partners in a plot to destroy European stability. At the same time, nationalism became a potent force in European politics. Increasingly, ethnic and national identity were seen as inseparable: Germans should have a Germany, Serbs a Serbia, Bulgarians a Bulgaria, and so on. But in this world of competing ethnic nationalisms, where did Jews belong? If national identity depended on ethnicity, then, ominously, the answer was: Not here.

Already firmly established by 1914, modern anti-Semitism flourished in the chaos of post–World War I Europe. The Bolshevik victory in the newly established Soviet Union sparked widespread fear that socialist or communist revolutions would spread across Europe. To desperate, hate-filled men like Adolf Hitler, "the Jew" and "the communist" were indistinguishable. More generally, the existence of large ethnic minorities in the new nation-states established after the war ensured that ethnic tensions continued to rage in central and eastern Europe, with Jews frequently spotlighted as outsiders and potential threats. In addition, the onset of worldwide economic depression in 1929 intensified the quest for scapegoats. Jews, who played a prominent role in European banking industries, were easy targets.

Modern or racial anti-Semitism had thus infected much of European society in the years before Hitler took power in Germany. It was particularly virulent in central and eastern Europe, where traditional peasant societies continued to exist and where ethnic nationalism proved especially potent. Once the Holocaust was underway, Hitler would find ready allies for his war against the Jews among these populations. But the existence of anti-Semitism does not explain the origins or the course of the Holocaust. In order to understand what actually happened, we need to place the Holocaust within the context of both Hitler's racial state and World War II.

INTENSIFIED PERSECUTION OF THE JEWS IN GERMANY, 1938–1939

Hitler talked of exterminating European Jews in his writings and speeches, but he had no specific plan for killing all European Jews when he came to power in 1933. He did clearly identify Jews as a threat to German revival, and he instituted practices designed to drive Jews out of Germany. We saw in Chapter 25 that as soon as the Nazis assumed power, they began to implement a series of laws and policies aimed at constructing what they viewed as a "racially pure" German state. Not only Jews but also the Roma (Gypsies) and the handicapped were singled out for persecution on the grounds that they posed a threat to the health of the supposed German race. By 1938, these policies had driven about 25 percent of Germany's Jews elsewhere; more than 350,000 Jewish German citizens, however, remained.

That year marked an intensification of Nazi persecution of German Jews. With the economic recovery of Germany well underway, the Nazis were less dependent on foreign trade and less vulnerable to the threat of foreign sanctions. And, as we saw in Chapter 26, Nazi Germany achieved two remarkable foreign policy victories in 1938—the Anschluss with Austria in March and the seizure of the Sudetenland from Czechoslovakia in September. The willingness of Western nations to yield on these issues helped persuade Hitler that he could pursue his anti-Semitic programs more aggressively. In 1938 Jews were excluded from all commercial activity and forced to register all property holdings. Jewish firms either were forced to shut down or were taken over by the state or by "Aryan"-owned firms.

On the night of November 9, 1938, anti-Jewish violence in Germany reached new heights. The assassination of a German official in the Paris embassy by a 17-year-old Jewish student provided the pretext for Nazi-encouraged anti-Jewish rioting across Germany. Over 300 synagogues were burned. Although Jews were the victims of the rioting, looting, and vandalism, over 35,000 Jews were sent to concentration camps, and the Nazi government levied a fine of one billion marks against the Jewish community. Because so many windows and store fronts were destroyed in the frenzy of violence—the value of broken glass alone was put at 24 million marks—the episode became known as Kristallnacht°: the Night of the Broken Glass. But more than glass shattered that night. One hundred German Jews were murdered. In the subsequent weeks, one thousand of the Jews sent to the prison camps died.

Faced with the increasing tempo of Nazi persecution, another 150,000 German Jews fled the Reich after Kristallnacht. Yet by September 1939, not only had emigration failed to remove all Jews from Germany, but the numbers of Jews under German control had actually risen. The unification of Germany and Austria in 1938, followed by the seizure first of the Sudetenland and then all Czechoslovakia, meant 300,000 more Jews in the expanded Germany.

These numbers skyrocketed with the outbreak of war. The invasion of Poland brought almost two million more Jews under German control. Pushing Jews to emigrate no longer seemed a workable solution to what the Nazis defined as the "Jewish Problem." As a result, a new sense of urgency characterized the Nazis' effort to find a way to clear Jews out of German-occupied territories. But even more

CHRONOLOGY

The Holocaust

1939

| September | World War II begins; racial reordering of Poland underway |

1941

June 22	German invasion of Soviet Union; Einsatzgruppen actions underway
October	Himmler orders halt to all Jewish emigration
December	Chelmno death camp begins operation

1942

| January 20 | Wannsee Conference |

1943

| February | German surrender at Stalingrad; Soviet army on the offensive |
| April | Warsaw Ghetto uprising |

1944

| June 6 | D-Day; British, French, and American armies on the offensive |
| November | Forced marches from death camps to Germany underway |

1945

| January | Auschwitz liberated by Soviet army |
| April | Hitler's suicide; Soviet army enters Berlin; British army liberates Bergen-Belsen |

important, the fact of war itself made a radicalization of policy and a turn toward murderous violence much more acceptable.

THE GERMAN DRIVE EASTWARD AND THE RADICALIZATION OF THE "FINAL SOLUTION"

The rapid German conquest of Poland in September 1939 not only initiated World War II, as Chapter 26 detailed, but also inaugurated the Nazis' war against the Jews. The German occupation of Poland marked the first step toward the Nazi construction of a new racial order in Europe. In the Nazi vision, Germany was destined to expand its holdings eastward—space for the superior race. The Slavic populations of eastern Europe, defined in Hitler's racist hierarchy as biologically inferior, were to serve as a vast labor pool. Jews were to be "eliminated" from the region. At this point, however, "elimination" did not yet mean total extermination but instead referred to vaguely articulated plans for mass deportations.

As a first step to begin building this new racial world order, the Nazi government divided defeated Poland in two. Germany directly annexed the northern and western regions of Poland and moved in German settlers to join ethnic Germans already living in these areas, displacing huge numbers of Poles from their homes and lands. The rest of German-occupied Poland formed the "General Government," a region envisaged as a huge work camp, home to an army of Polish slave labor that would help create the economic foundations of a vast German empire.

In the General Government, the Nazis embarked on a wholesale destruction of Polish society and culture. Universities and high schools were closed; businesses, farms, and bank accounts were seized; Polish place names were replaced with German. SS squads toured the countryside, searching for so-called "Aryan"-looking babies and children. Tens of thousands of blonde, blue-eyed Polish youngsters were kidnapped and sent to Germany, where they underwent a series of pseudoscientific tests to judge their "racial type." If they passed, they were given German names, forced to speak German, and given for adoption to SS-approved German couples. Mass murder accompanied mass kidnapping. To reduce the Polish people to slaves, the Nazis murdered Polish intellectuals and professionals, whose very existence contradicted Hitler's insistence that Poles were biologically suited only for manual labor.

Within the context of this larger plan of racial reordering, Nazi policy toward the Jews initially focused on "ghettoization." Polish Jews were forcibly expelled from their homes and confined in ghettos that were sealed off from the non-Jewish population. They were soon joined by Jews deported from Germany and Austria. Packed into overcrowded apartments, with inadequate food rations and appalling sanitary conditions, Jews lived in a nightmare of disease, starvation, and death. In Warsaw, for example, the Jewish ghetto comprised only 100 square blocks surrounded by a nine-foot wall. In this small area were crammed 400,000 people, living in rooms that contained on average six to nine individuals. The daily ration was 336 calories—far below starvation levels.

In the period between the invasion of Poland on September 1, 1939, and the invasion of the Soviet Union on June 22, 1941, an estimated 30,000 Jews were either directly murdered or died of starvation and disease as a result of Nazi policies. Yet the suffering had only begun.

■ The New Racial Order

A Nazi soldier assesses the racial characteristics of two young Polish children; their proud mother seems unaware that if her children are judged "Aryan" enough, they will be taken from her and given to a German family.

Some time in the spring or summer of 1941, the Nazis' definition of what they termed the Final Solution° to the "Jewish problem" shifted from emigration and expulsion to extermination. Historians disagree on the exact timing, but it is clear that the Nazi invasion of the Soviet Union provided the catalyst for the shift. Hitler may have already decided on genocide in the months of planning leading up to the June invasion. Alternatively, the decision to murder all the Jews in Europe may not have been taken until after the invasion was underway. It is clear that by the summer of 1941 SS squads were shooting thousands of Jews at a time. In October SS leader Heinrich Himmler (1900–1945) ordered that no Jew be allowed to emigrate from German-controlled territory. The doors of German-occupied Europe slammed shut; genocide was now the official German policy.

In planning for war with the Soviets, Hitler had determined that this would be no conventional military conflict between nation-states. Instead, it would be a battle of races and ideologies. From the early 1920s, Hitler had insisted that two key obstacles blocked the road to a revived German empire—communism and the Jewish people. Hence, war against the Soviet Union, the world's first communist state and home to millions of Jews, was no ordinary war. In Hitler's feverish and hate-filled imagination, Jews were the chief "carriers" of the communist or Bolshevik "virus." He thus perceived the war against the Soviet Union as a struggle to the death against "Judeo-Bolshevism," a powerful enemy that threatened to undermine not only Germany's military and economic strength but even its cultural identity. In such a war, the only rule would be that of absolute destruction. Only the most ferocious would survive.

THE WAR AGAINST THE JEWS

On June 22, 1941, the Nazi army invaded the Soviet Union. Marching with the forces of the regular army were special mobile units of the SS called Einsatzgruppen° ("strike forces"). With the army providing logistical support, these small motorized units (about 3,000 men in all) took on the task of liquidating the enemies of the Nazi Reich—which meant killing not only communist leaders and activists but also, and especially, Jews. Such a task was immense: Over five million Jews lived in the Soviet Union in 1941, and about four million of these lived in the territories invaded by the Germans.

In their war against the Jews, the Einsatzgruppen found ready allies among large sectors of the occupied population. The earliest stages of the German invasion of the Soviet Union took place in the territories that had been seized by the Soviets in 1939 as a result of the German-Soviet Non-Aggression Pact. The local populations often welcomed the German troops as liberators, and aided the SS in hunting down and killing Jews. In Lvov in eastern Galicia, for example, anti-Soviet Ukrainian fighters turned on the large Jewish community and in two days of violence killed at least 7,000 Jews—*before* the Einsatzgruppen had even arrived.

The ferocity of the war against the Jews intensified in the fall and early winter of 1941–1942. Two interconnected factors help explain this intensification. First, as Chapter 26 detailed, in these months the German military offensive ground to a halt. Second, the brutality with which the German occupiers treated the defeated populations in the occupied territories stirred up armed resistance in the form of guerrilla warfare. Seeking a scapegoat for their military losses, Germans blamed the Jews (many of whom did join guerilla combat units).

The horror of what has come to be known as Babi Yar helps illustrate the way in which German military frustration interacted with the slaughter of Jews. In the fall of 1941, German troops surrounded the city of Kiev. Despite sure defeat, Soviet forces held out for almost a month and then planted delayed-action bombs in the city, so that when the German troops entered on September 24, hundreds of Germans died in explosions and the resulting fires. Furious, the German officials blamed the Jews for the explosions. They rounded up all the Jews they could find—mostly old men, women, and young children—and drove them to Babi Yar, a ravine outside the city. The unarmed Jews were stripped, brutally beaten, and herded in small groups down a path into the ravine. Once at the bottom, they were shoved onto the ground and shot, one by one. Their bodies stacked up in layers. The corpses eventually numbered nearly 34,000.

Babi Yar was not unique. In Riga, Latvia, for example, 20,000 Jews perished in two separate actions in November and December 1941. In Lithuania, 10,000 Jews died in massacres in Kovno and 25,000 in Vilna. Estimates of the final death count of the Einsatzgruppen actions range from 1.5 to 2 million. Most of these murders followed the same general pattern: Jews were forcibly rounded up and marched in batches to a field or woods. The first batch was ordered to dig a large ditch. They were then stripped of their clothing, lined up on the edge of the ditch, and shot. Subsequent batches were lined up and shot as well, so that by the end of a day's worth of killing, the ditch would be filled with dead and dying bodies. It was then covered with a thin layer of soil, transformed from a ditch into a mass grave.

■ *Einsatzgruppen* **Action**
A soldier shoots the last remaining Jew in a Ukrainian village.

THE "JAGER REPORT"

Karl Jager was a German businessman who joined the SS in 1932. In 1941 he was appointed commander of Einsatzkommando 3 of Einsatzgruppe A, the unit ordered to rid Lithuania of Jews. The following is an excerpt from his nine-page report on his squad's activities in the summer and fall of 1941. The first six pages contain a day-by-day tally of the number of "executions" (murders) carried out. The final total: 137,346 Jews killed. Jager became a farm laborer after the war, but in 1959 he was arrested; he hanged himself before he could be tried for war crimes.

KAUEN [KAUNAS], 1 DECEMBER 1941.
SECRET REICH BUSINESS!

. . . . Today I can confirm that our objective, to solve the Jewish problem for Lithuania, has been achieved by EK 3. In Lithuania there are no more Jews . . . It was only possible to achieve our objective . . . by forming a raiding squad consisting of specially selected men led by SS-Obersturmführer Hamann, who grasped my aims completely and understood the importance of ensuring cooperation with the Lithuanian partisans and the relevant civilian authorities.

The execution of such actions is first and foremost a matter of organization. The decision to clear each district of Jews systematically required a thorough preparation of each individual action and a reconnaissance of the prevailing conditions in the district concerned. The Jews had to be assembled at one or several places. Depending on the number of Jews a place for the graves had to be found and then the graves dug. . . .

In Rokiskis 3,208 people had to be transported 4½ km before they could be liquidated. In order to get this work done within 24 hours, over sixty of the eighty available Lithuanian partisans had to be detailed for cordon duty. The rest, who had to be relieved constantly, carried out the work together with my men . . . It was only through the efficient use of time that it was possible to carry out up to five actions of week, while still coping with any work that arose in Kauen, so that no backlog was allowed to build up.

The actions in Kauen itself, where there was an adequate number of reasonably well-trained partisans available, were like parade-ground shootings in comparison with the often enormous difficulties which had to be faced elsewhere.

All the officers and men in my Kommando took an active part in the major actions in Kauen . . . I consider the Jewish action more or less terminated as far as Einsatzkommando 3 is concerned.

Source: Reprinted with the permission of The Free Press, a Division of Simon & Schuster Adult Publishing Group, from *"The Good Old Days": The Holocaust as Seen by Its Perpetrators and Bystanders* by Ernst Klee, Willi Dressen, and Volker Reiss, translated by Deborah Burnstone. Copyright © 1988 by S. Fischer Verlag, GmbH. Translation, copyright © 1991 by Deborah Burnstone.

THE EVOLUTION OF THE DEATH CAMPS

On January 20, 1942, senior German officials met in a villa in Wannsee, outside Berlin, to devise a plan for destroying European Jewry. SS Lieutenant Colonel Adolf Eichmann (1906–1962) listed the number of Jews in every country; even the Jewish populations in neutral countries such as Sweden and Ireland were added to the target list. The Wannsee Conference marked the beginning of a more systematic approach to killing European Jews, one that built on the experience gained by the Einsatzgruppen in the Soviet war.

To accomplish their task of mass murder, the Einsatzgruppen had become killing machines. By trial and error, they discovered the most efficient ways of identifying and rounding up Jews, shooting them quickly, and burying the bodies. But the Einsatzgruppen actions also revealed the limits of conventional methods of killing. Shooting unarmed civilians, particularly women and children, proved to be emotionally wearing on even the best-trained and carefully indoctrinated men. Most of the Einsatzgruppen killings occurred at very close range; the shooters were often covered with blood and pieces of flesh by the day's end. A systematic approach needed to be wedded to more advanced technology that would comfortably distance the killers from those they killed. This perceived need resulted in a key Nazi innovation, the death camp. The death camps emerged from the synthesis of three already existing realities in German-governed Europe—the "euthanasia" program, forced emigration and population resettlement, and the concentration camp system.[3]

"Life Unworthy of Life": The "Euthanasia" Program

The technologies and techniques of mass murder used in the Polish death camps were first developed in the so-called "euthanasia" campaign within Germany. (*Euthanasia* means mercy killing; no element of mercy motivated the Nazis.) This campaign grew out of the Nazi perception of biology as destiny. To shape the new Germany, the Nazis sought not only to eliminate the "racially impure"—the Jews—from German society but also to weed out non-Jewish Germans who were deemed unfit to be members of including the use of both gas for asphyxiating their victims and crematoria for disposing of the bodies.

Moving People into Place

In addition to these technologies, the functioning of the death camps depended on a workable policy of forced emigration and population resettlement. Once the decision was made to exterminate all the Jews in Europe, the Nazis made use of the policies of deportation and ghettoization that they had developed in Poland over the previous two-and-a-half years. From 1939 on, the Nazis forcibly resettled Poles to make room for Germans and experimented with confining Jews in ghettos. Beginning in 1942, these policies of deportation and ghettoization were extended across Europe to catch the continent's Jewish peoples in an ever-widening net. Faced with moving much larger populations across a much broader area, the Nazis made systematic use of the European railroad system to transport their victims efficiently.

In early 1942 the trains conveying Jewish victims to the death camps began to rumble across Europe. The Polish ghettos were systematically emptied as their inhabitants were sent in batches to their deaths. Individuals selected for extermination were ordered to gather at the railway station for deportation to "work camps" further east. They were then crammed onto cattle cars, more than 100 people per car, all standing up for the entire journey. Deprived of food and water, with hardly any air, and no sanitary facilities, often for several days, many Jews died en route. Those who survived emerged into the nightmare world of the death camps (see Map 27.1).

The Camps

The death camps grew most directly out of the already existing system of concentration camps, the third element needed to implement the "Final Solution." Beginning in 1933, the Nazi government set up concentration camps, in which the inmates were often forced to endure brutal manual labor. Communists, Jehovah's Witnesses, the Roma, and anyone else defined as an enemy of the regime soon filled their barracks. By the end of 1938 the concentration camp system held about 30,000 prisoners. After the war began in 1939, the concentration camps expanded dramatically in both size and number, and increasingly served as vital reserves of forced labor for German industry. Scattered throughout Nazi-controlled Europe, concentration camps became an essential part of the Nazi war economy. Firms that used camp labor included well-known businesses such as Bayer, Krupp, BMW, and Volkswagen. Some firms, such as the huge chemical conglomerate I. G. Farben, established factories inside or right next to camps.

Concentration camp inmates died in huge numbers from the brutal physical labor, torture, and diseases brought on by malnutrition and inadequate housing and sanitary fa-

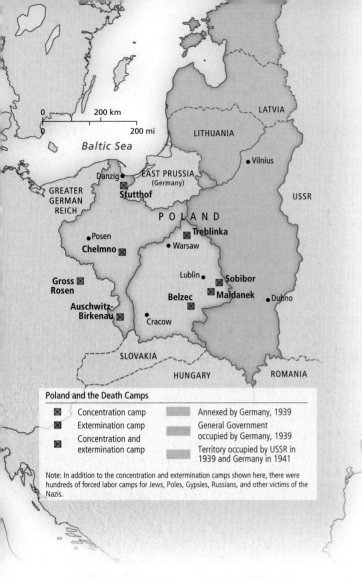

■ Map 27.1 Poland and the Death Camps

The Nazis set up a vast network of concentration and labor camps across Europe, but built death camps only in Poland.

the "Master Race." Beginning in the winter of 1939, government officials and medical personnel began the secret and systematic killing of the mentally and physically impaired, many of them young children. All across Germany doctors were required to identify the handicapped in their care. Individuals judged unfit to be Germans—what the Nazis labeled "life unworthy of life"—were sent to killing centers within Germany, where they were gassed and their bodies burned in crematoria. At least 80,000 Germans were killed.

After two years of secret mass murder, Hitler ordered the killing centers shut down because an increasing number of German citizens grew suspicious and began to protest against the program. (Throughout the war, however, Nazi officials continued to encourage German doctors to withhold medical care and food from patients they judged "unworthy of life.") In 1941, the killing centers' personnel were transferred to Poland to assist in setting up and running the death camps there. They took with them the technologies and techniques of mass murder that they had developed, cilities. At some camps, the SS guards indulged regularly in mass murder. The notorious Mauthausen camp in Austria centered on a stone quarry. Prisoners worked eleven hours a day, carrying—often at a run—impossibly heavy loads of rock up a steep staircase of 186 steps. When bored, the guards played a game they called "parachutes": They pushed the prisoners off the quarry edge to be smashed on the rocks below. At Mauthausen prisoners were also regularly shot en masse, drowned in groups of thirty in the shower rooms, and gassed. Gassings took place first in specially equipped vans and, from August 1941 on, in a gas chamber.

Mauthausen illustrated the way in which a labor camp also became a camp for mass killing. But it was in Poland, in a short period between late 1941 and early 1942, that the Germans developed the death camp, a specialized concentration camp with only one purpose—murder, primarily the murder of Jews.

Auschwitz and the Death Camp System

In the Polish camps of Chelmno, Treblinka, Belzec, and Sobibor, the only living inhabitants, besides the SS staff and their Ukrainian POW assistants, were small groups of slave laborers employed in sorting through the victims' belongings and disposing of the bodies. Jews went straight from the transport trains into a reception room, where they were told to undress, and then herded into a "shower room"—actually a gas chamber. Carbon monoxide gas, piped in from gas or diesel engines running outside the chamber, killed the victims. After the gas had done its work, the bodies were either buried or burned. Shut down in late 1943,

these camps, together with that of a fifth camp, Maidanek, killed more than two million Jews.

Maidanek combined a prison and labor camp with a death camp. So, too, did Auschwitz°, which stood at the center of the death camp system. The history of Auschwitz helps explain the way a concentration camp evolved into a death camp, with the use of the technologies of mass murder developed in the "euthanasia" program within Germany and the techniques of mass concentration and deportation perfected in the occupation of Poland. Auschwitz originated in 1940 as a concentration camp for Polish, then Soviet, prisoners of war. It became a huge industrial complex involving both state-owned and private industry and covering several square miles, with barracks for 70,000 prisoners who slaved in its coal mines, synthetic rubber and oil factories, and several smaller military industries. Its inmate population soon comprised not only Poles and Russians but also a cross-section of peoples from across Europe. A special section of the camp was reserved for the Roma after December 1942, when Himmler ordered all European Gypsies to be deported to Auschwitz. Given hardly enough food for survival (the official diet permitted a prisoner to remain alive for an average of three months), Auschwitz's inmates endured daily hard labor in the mines and factories and the constant, indiscriminate brutality of their captors.

In the middle of 1942, Auschwitz's cruel empire expanded to encompass a death camp as well. The previous fall, Nazi experiments had shown how effective the pesticide Zyklon-B was in killing Soviet prisoners of war.

■ **Walking to the Gas Chambers at Auschwitz**
For most Jews, their first glimpse of Auschwitz was their last. Only a small percentage survived the initial selection process.

Jewish Victims of the Nazis

Region	Jews in 1939	Jews murdered
Poland	3.35 million	3 million
Soviet Union	2.2 million	1.3 million*
Romania	750,000	350,000
Germany	500,000	200,000
Hungary	450,000†	300,000
France	350,000	75,000
Czechoslovakia	255,000	185–190,000
Austria	185,000	65,000
Netherlands	140,000‡	105,000
Belgium	90,000	40,000
Greece	77,000	60,000
Yugoslavia	75,000	60,000
Italy	57,000	7,500
Bulgaria	50,000§	—
Denmark	8,000	
Luxembourg	3,000	800
Finland	2,000	—
Norway	1,800	760

*Figure includes 200,000 Baltic Jews.

†In 1938.

‡Figure includes 30,000 German and Austrian refugees.

§In prewar borders.

Beginning in the summer of 1942, trainloads of Jews arrived in Birkenau, the death camp built within the Auschwitz complex. Those deemed strong enough (never more than 20 percent of a typical transport) were selected for hard labor in the main camp; the rest perished in Birkenau's gas chambers, poisoned with Zyklon-B. The writer Elie Wiesel, deported to Birkenau-Auschwitz with his family when he was fifteen, recalled the selection process:

> "Men to the left! Women to the right!" Eight words spoken quietly, indifferently, without emotion. Eight short, simple words. Yet that was the moment when I parted from my mother.[4]

Wiesel's mother and younger sister, and hundreds of thousands of others, went immediately to the gas chamber. Their bodies were burned in one of Auschwitz's five crematoria. At least one million people were gassed at Auschwitz, most of them Jews.

The gas chambers stopped operating at Auschwitz in November 1944. Faced with imminent defeat in the war, the Nazis scrambled to cover up the evidence of their crimes. Himmler ordered Auschwitz destroyed. The SS sent the remaining prisoners from Auschwitz and other camps on brutal forced marches westward. Exact figures are impossible to calculate, but it is estimated that of the more than

700,000 inmates in the Nazi camp system in January 1945, at least one-third died in the following few months, either on the march or in the overcrowded disease-ridden German camps in which they were crammed. Half of these dead were Jews.

These final victims joined the millions who starved or died of disease in the ghettoes, suffocated in the cattle cars, or were shot in mass graves, worked to death in the labor camps, or asphyxiated in the gas chambers. Children were especially vulnerable. Of the Jewish children living in 1939 in the regions already or soon to be under German control, only 11 percent survived. In total, the Holocaust claimed the lives of approximately six million Jews. The numbers of Roma victims remains unclear. Somewhere between 200,000 and 600,000 died in what the Roma call the *Porajmos*—the Devouring. Jews and Gypsies were the only groups singled out for total extermination based on their supposed biological identity. But Hitler's drive to create his new Germany claimed three to five million other victims as well. Five to fifteen thousand homosexuals perished. So, too, did as many as three million Polish Christians.

Responding to the Holocaust

In their effort to destroy European Jewry, the Nazis were not completely unaided or completely unhindered. Victims, bystanders, accomplices, and perpetrators all faced crucial choices when confronted with the Holocaust.

JEWISH RESISTANCE

One of the most frequently asked questions about the Holocaust is, why did the Jews not respond more aggressively to the Nazi threat? Jewish leaders, in particular the members of the Jewish Councils (groups of Jewish leaders appointed by the Nazis to implement their directives in the ghettos), have been harshly condemned for cooperating with the Nazis. Their options were few, however. Resistance almost always meant certain death. Instead, they followed orders, hoping that by doing so they would save not only themselves and their families, but also their communities. In most cases, they were hoping to buy time, to ensure the survival of at least part of European Jewry. As we saw in Chapter 26, few Europeans—Jew or non-Jew—violently resisted the Nazis; armed rebellion against Nazi oppression was the choice of only a small minority in all subjugated countries.

Some Jews did opt for violent resistance. Thousands of Jews fought in the underground resistance throughout Europe; in a number of ghettos violent uprisings marked the Jewish response to deportations; in occupied Poland, Jews formed more than thirty guerilla groups; rebellions

■ The Resistance

Increasingly aware that the Nazi fiction of "resettlement" was in fact a death sentence, Jews such as these refugees from the Vilna ghetto fled to the forests. Formed into partisan units, they waged guerilla warfare against the German army.

even occurred in the death camps of Treblinka, Sobibor, and Auschwitz. In the best-known case of violent resistance, the Jews in the Warsaw ghetto rose up in the spring of 1943 after a series of deportations that decimated the ghetto's population. Armed with only one or two submachine guns and a scattering of pistols, rifles, hand grenades, and gasoline bombs, Jewish fighters held off the far superior German military force for over a month. In the end, however, the ghetto was leveled, and all its survivors deported to the death camps.

The majority of Jews relied on other means of resisting the Nazis. Because the Nazis viewed Jews as sub-humans that had to be exterminated, any action that affirmed their human identity was, for Europe's Jews, a form of resistance. When Jews in the Polish ghettos formed schools, lending libraries, drama companies, and chamber music groups, they proclaimed their own humanity and so directly confronted Nazi lies. Every bar mitzvah (the Jewish coming-of-age ceremony), every poetry reading, every song, every dance, every family meal, every birth celebration and funeral service conducted by Jews in this time of horror marked an act of profound and fundamental resistance to Nazi degradation.

THE WIDENING CIRCLE OF RESPONSIBILITY

Who participated in the effort to exterminate the Jews? It is clear that the most direct responsibility for the Holocaust lies with Hitler, high-ranking Nazi officials, the Einsatzgruppen, and the Death's Head SS, which ran the death camps. But the circle of responsibility extended far beyond the ranks of these elites.

The complicity of ordinary Germans in the Holocaust has been a subject of great controversy. Many people simply tried not to watch while the horror unfolded. The villagers living around the Mauthausen camp, for example, saw the shuffling columns of starving and beaten prisoners regularly walking the almost three miles from the train station to the camp. Those living near the camp heard the screams, woke to find ashes coating their farms, gagged at the stench of burning human bodies—and learned not to look. One farmer nearby did write a letter of complaint, noting that prisoners were often shot and left to die in the ditch bordering her farm: "I request that it be arranged that such inhuman deeds be discontinued, or else be done where one does not see it."[5]

Many other Germans were more directly involved. Recent research has established that members not only of the SS but also of regular German army units and even reserve police battalions regularly rounded up and murdered Jews. Moreover, German civilians (many, if not most, of whom were *not* members of the Nazi Party) participated in the vast administrative machine needed to perpetrate the Holocaust. The deportations, for example, constituted a colossal operation involving local civil servants; bank, post office, and insurance clerks; and countless others. Consider, for example, the participation of the officials, engineers, and travel agents of the German rail network in the transportation of Jews to the death camps. These ordinary Germans handled preparations for mass deportations as a business arrangement. With money confiscated from Jews, the SS paid four pennies per kilometer for each Jewish "passenger," with children under age 10 traveling at half-fare, and children under age 4 for free. The SS purchased only

A GHETTO DIARY

·················

Zelig Kalmanovich (1881–1943), a Jewish scholar, recorded his observations, his deepening sense of Jewish identity, and his abiding faith in God in a diary that he kept while living in the Vilna ghetto. His diary bears witness to the horrendous choices that confronted Jews during the Holocaust. As the following excerpt records, Jews found themselves carrying out the selection of Nazi victims. It also makes clear that men like Kalmanovich were under no illusions about the destiny of those Jews selected for "transport": He knew that selection meant death.

SUNDAY, OCTOBER 11 [1942]

[The eve of Simhat or Simchath Torah, a Jewish holiday] . . . There was singing and dancing . . . I said a few words: "Our song and dance are a form of worship. Our rejoicing is due to Him who decrees life and death. Here in the midst of this small congregation, in the poor and ruined synagogue, we are united with the whole house of Israel . . ."

[SUNDAY], OCTOBER 25 [1942]

. . . All our Jewish brethren in the Vilna district were gathered into one ghetto . . . Our policemen were sent with passes to be distributed among the . . . workers, and to turn over the rest of the people, "the superfluous," [those without work permits] to the hands of the authorities to do with them what is customary these days. The young men took upon themselves this difficult task. They donned their official caps, with the "Star of David" upon them, went there and did what they were supposed to do. The result was that more than 400 people perished: the aged, the infirm, the sick, and retarded children. Thus 1,500 women and children were saved. Had outsiders, God forbid, carried out this action, 2,000 people would have perished.

The [Jewish] commandant said: "To be sure, our hands are stained with the blood of our brethren, but we had to take upon ourselves this dreadful task. We are clean before the bar of history. We shall watch over the remaining. Who knows if any more victims will be demanded from us here, as they were demanded there. We shall give them only the old and the sick. Children we will not give them. They are our hope."

Source: From the Diary of Zelig Kalmanovich, YIVO Archives, New York, Sutzkever-Kaczerginski Collection. Reprinted by permission of the YIVO Institute for Jewish Research.

---

one-way tickets; Jewish "travelers" did not make return journeys from the gas chambers.

By mechanizing and dividing up the labor of killing, the Nazis made it easier for any single individual involved to escape a sense of personal responsibility or criminal culpability. Few Germans were able to see the entire process at work; few wanted to know. Each could claim, "I was only doing my job."

The circle of responsibility embraces more than Germany. As described earlier, the Einsatzgruppen relied on local people for assistance in slaughtering the Jews in the Russian, Ukrainian, and Baltic regions. In western Europe, a different situation prevailed. The occupied west contained a network of concentration and labor camps that by the spring of 1945 housed a starving and disease-ridden inmate population. But those territories had no death camps nor were Jews shot en masse there. Nevertheless, the Nazis relied heavily on local populations to implement the process that delivered western Jews to the death camps. In countries such as France, the Netherlands, and Belgium, local bureaucrats and police officers took charge of registering, rounding up, and finally deporting Jews.

Some governments in both western and eastern Europe *did*, however, endeavor to slow or sidetrack the German war against the Jews. In the most dramatic case of resistance, the Danes rallied as a people to sneak most of the 8,000 Jews in Denmark across the narrow sea to safety in neutral Sweden. Fascist Italy, too, proved a haven for many Jews. Anti-Semitism was not part of the fascist platform in Italy until 1938, and even then it remained essentially foreign and secondary. Despite the alliance with Germany, Italians undercut anti-Jewish measures by noncompliance, obstruction, and evasion.

Even in nations with anti-Semitic governments at the helm, the "Final Solution" ran into obstacles. In Vichy France, as in German satellite countries in eastern Europe such as Romania, Hungary, and Bulgaria, officials who had proved willing to pass anti-Jewish legislation, and even to turn over Jews of other nationalities to the Germans, hesitated to comply with orders for mass roundups and deportations of their own Jewish citizens. Nationalism apparently outweighed racism in these instances. In Bulgaria, efforts to delay the deportations proved successful: Most Bulgarian Jews survived. In Hungary, the Jewish community remained intact throughout most of the war, only to be targeted for extermination at Auschwitz in the spring and summer of 1944. Of Hungary's 750,000 Jews, at least 300,000 died. The rest survived only because the Russian invasion forced the Germans to abandon Auschwitz.

Just as most of the nations of Europe bear some measure of responsibility for the Holocaust, so too does the Christian Church, both Protestant and Catholic. Certainly individual Christians displayed great heroism in resisting the Nazis. For example, the German Lutheran theologian Dietrich Bonhoeffer (1906–1945) assumed a leading role in resisting the Nazi co-option of the Lutheran church. He directed an underground seminary that worked to train pastors independently of Nazi control, and in 1945, he participated in a failed plot to assassinate Hitler. Bonhoeffer was executed by the Nazis shortly before the end of World War II.

Yet the courage and conviction displayed by Bonhoeffer was unusual. Other German Protestant leaders did little to stop the Nazi effort to murder European Jewry. From 1933 on, the established church of Germany, the Lutheran Church (to which 60 percent of the population belonged), was led by a Hitler appointee, Ludwig Muller, a former army chaplain and an ardent Nazi. No Protestant bishop found the courage to take a public stand against Hitler's anti-Jewish policies. Protestant military chaplains did protest the army's involvement in killing Jews, but they did so on behalf of the *soldiers,* who found the task of murder an emotional strain. Moreover, both Protestant and Roman Catholic clergymen assisted the Nazi regime in identifying German Jews by providing the baptismal and marriage records used to prove "Aryan" status.

The record of the Roman Catholic Church is ambiguous. On the one hand, in localities such as Slovakia and Croatia, Catholic churchmen participated enthusiastically in explicitly anti-Semitic fascist governments. On the other hand, as we noted in Chapter 25, German Catholics faced persecution under the Nazi regime. The Catholic Center Party was outlawed and the Civil Service Law of 1933 purged from government posts not only Jews but also Catholic Center Party activists. Throughout the 1930s, Catholic schools faced a constant onslaught from enthusiastic local Nazi officials who sought to replace religious education with Nazi propaganda. Church doctrine also placed Roman Catholics in direct opposition to Nazi eugenics programs, particularly the forcible sterilization of the handicapped and of mixed-race children. Yet, while many Roman Catholic clergy and laypeople took courageous stands in defense of their religious beliefs, few acted on behalf of the Jews. The largely Catholic outcry against the regime's "euthanasia" policies forced the Nazis to halt the program; no such outcry emerged in response to the deportation of German Jews.

Many Catholics looked to the pope for guidance through the darkness of the war years. The question of the papacy's passivity in the face of the Holocaust is highly controversial. From 1933 on, the Catholic leadership had struggled with the question of how to respond to the Nazi regime's anti-Semitic policies. In 1937, the aging Pope Pius XI (r. 1922–1939) issued the encyclical *Mit brennender Sorge* ("With Deep Anxiety"), a clear condemnation of Hitler's government. Significantly, however, the encyclical focused on the Nazis' mistreatment of Catholics, not Jews.

Pius XI died in February 1939. His successor, Pius XII (r. 1939–1958), was an austere, authoritarian figure who knew Germany well. He had served there as *papal nuncio* (the Vatican's diplomatic representative) from 1917 to 1929, and in 1933 he had negotiated the Vatican's *concordat* or treaty with Hitler's regime. In exchange for Hitler's promise (soon broken) to allow Catholics religious freedom and his guarantee to safeguard Catholic schools, the Vatican agreed to follow a policy of noninterference in the Nazi regime's political and social policies. As a result, the Catholic Center Party, an important anti-Nazi voice in German politics, was silenced.

Once the war began, Pius XII adopted a policy of careful neutrality, one that prohibited him from clearly condemning the Nazi murder of Jews, even though the Vatican's sophisticated diplomatic and intelligence network ensured that it was well-informed of the mass killings from very early on. In his Christmas Eve radio address of 1942, Pius XII came close to condemning Nazi Germany when he called on all peoples to vow to serve God, a vow owed, he insisted, "to those hundreds of thousands who, without any fault of their own, sometimes only by reason of their nationality or race, are marked down for death or gradual extinction." The pope did not, however, explicitly name Hitler, or Nazi Germany, or the Jews.

THE ALLIES' RESPONSE

How did the Allied governments respond to the Nazis' war against the Jews? To answer this question, we must ask when and what the Allies learned about the Holocaust. A crime of such unprecedented proportions could not and did not take place in total secrecy. In fact, British code breakers translated German military radio transmissions throughout the summer of 1941. As the German army—and the Einsatzgruppen—moved into the Soviet Union, British officials confronted intercepted messages such as this one from August 27: "Regiment South shot 914 Jews; the special action staff with police battalion 320 shot 4,200 Jews."

From nearly the beginning of the Nazi effort to exterminate European Jewry, then, Allied leaders had access to surprisingly accurate and horrific information about the Holocaust. By June 1942, this information included details about the death camps. That month, Polish authorities in exile in London released a report, based on information smuggled out by the Polish underground, describing the Nazis' effort to exterminate Polish Jews. This report not only discussed large-scale gassings but also emphasized that such gassings were part of a coordinated plan. The report erred, however, in estimating that 700,000 Jews had been murdered. By June 1942, the Nazi regime was responsible for the deaths of at least two million Jews.

Such information quickly became accessible to ordinary people. From 1941 on, British and American newspaper readers and radio listeners received numerous reports about Jewish massacres and, after 1942, they heard or read about the existence of the death camps. For example, the Babi Yar massacre was reported in the Western press two months after it occurred. These reports had to compete with other war news, however. In addition, many of these articles were written in a skeptical tone, as both reporters and editors had a difficult time believing that such atrocities could be taking place. Newspaper readers, faced with horror on a scale they simply could not conceive, retreated to comfortable positions. They assured themselves that the reports must be exaggerated, that atrocities always take place during wars, that things simply could not be so bad. Many recalled that during World War I, atrocity stories had circulated that later were revealed to be simply propaganda. But even when they believed what they were reading, people often could not grasp its full meaning. As theologian and Dutch Protestant leader W. A. Visser't Hooft explained, "people could find no place in their consciousness for such an unimaginable horror . . . It is possible to live in a twilight between knowing and not knowing."[6]

But not everyone remained in the twilight. British and American Jewish groups mobilized to force the Allied governments to do something to help European Jews before it was too late. Pressure from Jewish and non-Jewish public-interest groups did succeed in pushing the British and American governments to issue an inter-Allied declaration in December 1942 that in no uncertain terms announced and condemned Hitler's effort to exterminate European Jewry. This declaration was broadcast all over the world.

Yet despite official and public acknowledgment of the mass murder of Jews, the Allies did not act directly to stop the killings. Should the Allies be considered bystanders in the crime of the Holocaust? As we saw in Chapter 26, the Soviets put an enormous amount of effort into evacuating factories from their western territories to safety in the east—but Stalin's government made no effort to evacuate Jews. Even more controversial is the failure of the United States and Britain to act more decisively on behalf of Europe's Jews. Some scholars, for example, have highlighted the role of anti-immigration sentiment in limiting the western Allies' response. Scarred by the experience of the Great Depression, both Americans and British often proved reluctant to welcome refugees. If Jewish refugees were rescued, where would they go? Who would pay for their maintenance? Who would find them jobs? By the fall of 1941, however, such questions meant little: Himmler's order that no Jew leave German-occupied territory alive halted Jewish immigration.

The key question is: How did the western Allies respond to the Holocaust from 1942 on? Many historians have contended that anti-Semitism in both British and American society structured the Allies' strategic priorities and prevented political leaders from exploring alternative strategies, such as sending in commando units, bombing the rail lines into the death camps, or even bombing the camps themselves.

Other historians argue these alternatives were not militarily feasible, and that the Allies did the only thing they could do on the Jews' behalf—win the war as quickly as possible.

AFTER AUSCHWITZ: REMEMBERING THE HOLOCAUST

In the months after the war ended, Allied leaders struggled to bring Nazi leaders to trial to account for their crimes. What one participant called "the greatest trial in history" opened on November 14, 1945. For eleven months, a tribunal of four judges and four alternates—American, British, French, and Soviet—sat in a courtroom in the German city of Nuremberg to judge nineteen prominent German military, political, and industrial leaders. In 403 open sessions they heard 94 witnesses and pored over the written testimonies of 143 more. (The published proceedings of the trial take up forty-two volumes.) The cascade of information, broadcast by the crowds of journalists packed into the courtroom, offered the world its first encounter with the Holocaust. The Nuremberg trials° of 1945–1946 highlighted the Nazi onslaught against European Jewry as one of the most horrendous of the Nazis' many "crimes against humanity," a category first introduced into international law by the Nuremberg tribunal. The Nuremberg indictment noted that "Jews were systematically persecuted since 1933" and that "Since 1 September 1939 . . . millions of Jews from Germany and from the occupied Western Countries were sent to the Eastern Countries for extermination." The main charge against the defendants, however, was not attempted genocide but rather conspiring to destroy the peace of Europe via an aggressive war that carried the murder of millions in its wake. The centrality of Hitler's anti-Semitism to both his worldview and his war-making did not become clear in the trials.

In the moral and physical exhaustion that followed the end of World War II, as in the Nuremberg trials, the Holocaust tended to recede from view. Nevertheless, reaction to the Holocaust did play a central role in one of the most dramatic consequences of the war—the establishment of the state of Israel. Many Holocaust survivors embraced Zionism, the ideology of Jewish nationalism (see Chapter 22). From 1945 on, European Jewish refugees poured into British-controlled Palestine. Many soon found themselves waging guerilla warfare against the British, who sought to limit Jewish immigration in order to pacify the local Muslim and Christian populations and to maintain political stability in the region. Faced with mounting violence as well as growing international pressure to grant Jewish demands for statehood, the British turned the problem over to the United Nations in spring of 1947. At the end of that year, the UN adopted a plan calling for the partition of Palestine into Jewish and Arab sectors forming a Jewish and Arab state. Faced with opposition to the plan from the surrounding Arab nations, the British pulled out their troops in May 1948 without transferring authority to either Jews or Arabs. Jewish leaders immediately proclaimed the new state of Israel and the region erupted into an all-out war between Israel and the surrounding Arab nations. After nine months of fighting, an uneasy peace descended, based on a partition of Palestine among Israel, Jordan (which held the region around Jerusalem known as the West Bank), and Egypt (which occupied the Gaza Strip). Approximately 750,000 Palestinian Arabs became stateless refugees, an embittered population confined to camps in Syria, Lebanon, and Jordan, as well as the West Bank and Gaza (see Map 27.2). Not all Holocaust survivors emigrated to Israel, but most of the tens of thousands who turned instead to the United States supported Israel with financial contributions and emotional commitment.

Just as the fact and memory of the Holocaust helped shape the new nation of Israel, so too did it influence the new West Germany. In communist-controlled East Germany, state censorship of political and historical studies guaranteed that the Holocaust was shunted aside as a fascist crime that had little to do with the new communist nation. In contrast, the government of West Germany in 1952 acknowledged German responsibility for the Holocaust when it agreed to pay reparations to individual Jews, to the state of Israel, and to Jewish communities throughout the world.

Despite these developments, the Western world did not begin to grapple with the meaning and memory of the Holocaust until the early 1960s. The reception of *The Diary of Anne Frank*, a simple day-by-day account written by a young Dutch Jewish girl during World War II, illustrates the way in which the central facts of the Holocaust were easily evaded. Published in 1947 and translated into over fifty languages, the book became an international bestseller as well as the basis of a much-acclaimed stage play and movie in the late 1950s. Hiding with her family in a secret annex located behind her father's factory in Amsterdam, Anne used her diary to try to find order and meaning in a world gone mad. The diary abruptly ends on August 1, 1944; three days later Anne and her family were arrested. Anne Frank died of typhus in Bergen-Belsen, shortly before British troops liberated the camp. By telling the story of a horrifying tragedy through the eyes of one ordinary yet extraordinarily appealing young girl, the book forced its readers to confront evil—but not, in fact, to confront the Holocaust. Both the play and film version depicted Anne as a universal symbol of innocence destroyed by the evil of war, not as a Jewish girl killed because she was Jewish.

But in 1960, the world was forced to confront the Holocaust in a very dramatic way. That year the prime minister of Israel captured the world's attention by announcing that the Israeli secret service had found and kidnapped Adolf Eichmann, a leading Nazi administra-

tor charged with overseeing "Jewish Affairs" during World War II. Worldwide coverage of Eichmann's subsequent trial presented for the first time to a large audience the basic narrative of the Holocaust. In the years that followed, the Holocaust became the subject of numerous historical, literary, and artistic works.

For writers and artists in West Germany, the Holocaust became closely connected to questions of collective guilt and national identity. What did it mean to be German in the post-Holocaust world? Nobel Prize–winning novelists Heinrich Böll (1917–1985) and Günter Grass (b. 1927) struggled to find answers. Called "the conscience of a nation," Böll conveyed the dehumanization wrought by the war in a series of carefully crafted novels. Grass's work has been more varied, ranging from sculpture to plays to novels and short stories. From his first and most well-known novel, *The Tin Drum* (1959), in which a small boy caught in

■ Map 27.2   Israel and Its Neighbors, 1949

The map inset outlines the United Nations' plan to partition Palestine into Jewish and Arab sectors, with Jerusalem as an international zone. This plan was not implemented.

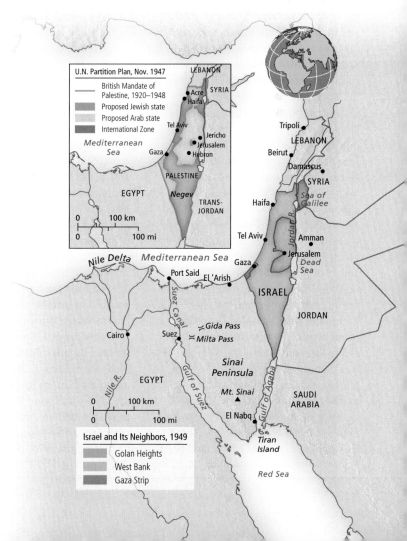

The Trial of Adolf Eichmann

On May 23, 1960, David Ben-Gurion (1886–1973), the prime minister of Israel, made a spectacular announcement: Israeli secret service agents had kidnapped Adolf Eichmann, a wanted Nazi war criminal, and smuggled him into Israel to await trial. Eichmann, the head of the Gestapo's Jewish Affairs unit, had implemented Nazi policies on Jewish emigration and deportation. His office sorted through the complicated bureaucratic procedures to ensure that the trains laden with Jews kept to their schedules and delivered their human cargo to the gas chambers on time. It was to Eichmann that Jewish leaders came to plead for emigration visas and for work permits. It was with Eichmann that Jewish leaders negotiated about the timing, size, and composition of deportations. For many Jews, then, Eichmann represented German power and came to personify Nazi evil. He had disappeared in the chaotic final days of World War II and eventually made his way to Argentina, where, as "Ricardo Klement," he lived a quiet, respectable life with his wife and children—until 1960.

From the moment of Ben Gurion's sensational announcement, the Eichmann case occupied the attention of the world. Six hundred foreign correspondents attended the trial, which was one of the first to be filmed by television cameras. Over 1,500 documents were submitted and 120 witnesses testified in the 114 sessions held between April 11 and August 14, 1961. Three judges, each of whom had been

born in Germany and had emigrated to Palestine in 1933, heard the evidence. On December 15, they sentenced Eichmann to death. He died by hanging on May 31, 1962, the first execution in Israel, which had abolished capital punishment for all crimes except genocide.

The Eichmann trial told the story of Jewish suffering during World War II to the widest possible audience. Both Ben-Gurion and the chief prosecutor Gideon Hausner stated publicly that the trial aimed to construct "a living record of a gigantic human and national disaster," and so educate both young Israelis and the entire world in the causes and consequences of the Holocaust.[7] As Hausner explained in his emotional opening statement, he saw himself as the spokesman for "six million accusers . . . [whose] ashes were piled up in the hills of Auschwitz and in the fields of Treblinka, or washed away by the rivers of Poland."[8] Hausner (who, like many Israelis, had lost most of his relatives in the Nazi death camps) called more than 100 witnesses, many of them death camp survivors. Their testimony, published or broadcast throughout the world, painted an unforgettable and detailed picture of the horror of genocide.

By the time the prosecution rested its case, no one could doubt that Eichmann was a guilty man, one who had played an essential role in the murder of millions. Yet the Eichmann trial attracted an enormous amount of criticism, and continues to arouse great controversy. Critics charged that

to achieve moral justice for Holocaust victims and survivors, the Israeli court committed a legal injustice against Eichmann. The trial was not only made possible by a violation of international law (Eichmann's kidnapping), it also was filled with irregularities, including the introduction of testimony that did not pertain to the specific crimes charged. Critics also disputed Israel's legal right to try Eichmann: The crimes had not occurred in Israeli territory, nor were Eichmann's victims Israeli citizens. (Israel did not exist until 1948.)

In reply to these critics, Hausner and other supporters of the prosecution insisted that justice demanded that Eichmann be brought to trial, and that the Israeli government had pursued the only course of action open to it. In the Eichmann trial, then, we confront a case in which what was legal on the one hand and what was just on the other appeared very much at odds. There is no doubt that Eichmann was guilty of horrendous crimes; there is also no doubt that the Israeli government stepped beyond the boundaries of international law in kidnapping Eichmann.

The Eichmann trial also raised important questions about the nature of the Holocaust. Was it a crime perpetrated by a few very evil men, or did the evil penetrate deep into German, and European, society? The prosecution's case sought to depict Eichmann as a monster, a brilliant and demonic mastermind responsible for the deaths of millions of Jews. As Hausner con-

■ **Eichmann on Trial**

Eichmann sits on the left in a cage of bulletproof glass.

tended, "it was [Eichmann's] word that put gas chambers into action; he lifted the telephone, and railway trains left for the extermination centers; his signature it was that sealed the doom of tens of thousands."[9] Such a depiction provided a comforting explanation for the Holocaust—it was perpetrated not by ordinary human beings but by monstrous devils.

Yet many trial observers and subsequent historians argued that such a depiction was simply wrong. This argument appeared in forceful terms in the most well-known critique of the prosecution—Hannah Arendt's *Eichmann in Jerusalem: A Report on the Banality of Evil*, published in 1963. Arendt (1906–1975), a Jewish philosopher who had fled Nazi Europe in 1941, argued that the evidence provided in the trial showed Eichmann to be a fairly commonplace man, motivated by ambition as much as by ideology, a rather plodding bureaucrat obsessed with trivial details—in other words, an ordinary man, capable of extraordinary evil.

Must ordinary men be held responsible for following evil orders? This is the final question raised by the Eichmann trial. Defense attorney Robert Servatius insisted that the Holocaust was an "act of state," a crime carried out by a political regime, for which no civil servant could bear the blame. Eichmann only followed orders. Servatius concluded his arguments by asking Eichmann how he viewed "this question of guilt." Eichmann replied,

> Where there is no responsibility, there can be no guilt. . . . The questions of responsibility and conscience are for the leadership of the state. . . . I condemn and regret the act of extermination of the Jews which the leadership of the German state ordered. But I myself could not jump over my own shadow. I was a tool in the hands of superior powers and authorities.[10]

Eichmann's judges disagreed. In declaring Eichmann guilty of genocide, they argued,

> We reject absolutely the accused's version that he was nothing more than a 'small cog' in the extermination machine. . . . He was not a puppet in the hands of others. His place was among those who pulled the strings.[11] ■

Questions of Justice

1. Even if Eichmann's assertion that he was simply "a tool in the hands of superior powers and authorities" could be proven correct, to what degree was he culpable for his actions?

2. In the Eichmann case, the letter of the law and justice appeared to be at odds. In what situations—if any—must the law be broken to ensure that justice prevails?

Taking It Further

Laqueur, Walter. "Hannah Arendt in Jerusalem: The Controversy Revisited," in Lyman H. Legters, ed., *Western Society After the Holocaust.* 1983. Examines the impact of Arendt's critique of the trial.

The Trial of Adolf Eichmann: Record of Proceedings in the District Court of Jerusalem. Vols. 1–9, 1993–1995. The basic primary source.

■ **Anselm Kiefer, *Germany's Spiritual Heroes* (1973)**
In much of his work, Kiefer struggled with the legacy of German history.

the trauma of the Nazi era refuses to grow up, to *My Century* (1999), one hundred short tales that convey his personal history of Germany in the twentieth century, Grass explored the moral issues posed by Germany's past.

In contrast to Böll and Grass (both of whom were POWs), the artist Anselm Kiefer, born in 1945, had no direct experience of World War II. Yet, as Kiefer's works show, Germans born after the war continued to grapple with its legacy for personal and national identity. Adding straw, sand, shells, and clay to large canvases or woodcuts, Kiefer built up multitextured works that commented both ironically and allusively on the troubled German past. Painted on six strips of burlap sewn together, *Germany's Spiritual Heroes* (1973) evokes both a crematorium and a memorial hall, and so challenges the viewer to question the national myths that made Germany vulnerable to Nazi ideology. A decade after he painted this work, Kiefer completed a set of paintings that offered haunting images of the death camps.

By the 1980s, many West Germans argued that the Holocaust had come to assume far too large a place in German cultural identity. In journal and newspaper articles, historians fought a well-publicized battle (the *Historikerstreit*) over the proper place of the Holocaust in history. Conservative historians argued that the Holocaust, while an act of enormous criminality, was far from unique; other countries had experienced other outbreaks of mass slaughter. They insisted that Germany, like other nations, needed a usable past rather than "a negative myth of absolute evil."[12]

The Historikerstreit revealed that historians disagree about the meaning of the Holocaust. Was it a unique incident in Western civilization, or was it one more episode in the lengthy history of mass slaughter? Perhaps the best answer is: It was both. The Holocaust does not stand alone as an example of the way in which ideology can fuel mass murder. Chapter 25 showed how Joseph Stalin's political ideas and personal paranoia led to mass death in the Soviet Union. At least two million people died "unnatural deaths" in the Soviet Union during the 1930s, with 750,000 of these executed in the Great Purge alone. An additional four to five million people starved in the famine of 1932, the direct consequence of Stalin's collectivization drive. In the decades after the Holocaust, the world encountered other tragic examples of ideological frenzy resulting in mass death. In the late 1950s, an estimated 30 million Chinese died as a result of the Chinese Communist leader Mao Zedong's (1893–1976) decision to catapult his nation into industrialization through what he called the "Great Leap Forward." Twenty years later in Cambodia, the Khmer Rouge, a communist group inspired by Mao, declared that all city dwellers were enemies of the communist peasant utopia they sought to establish. In less than four years, 1.7 million people—20 percent of the Cambodian population—died as a result of this idea.

The Holocaust occurred at the intersection of modern nationalism and modern war, as did many other episodes of twentieth-century mass murder. During the First World War, the Armenian minority population in Turkey was accused of collaborating with the invading Russian enemy. Six hundred thousand Armenian men, women, and children were massacred, and another 400,000 died in the course of forced deportations. In World War II, 487,000 Serbs in the Nazi-allied state of Croatia fell victim to state-sanctioned ethnic slaughter. Viewed in this context, Hitler's effort to destroy the Jews of Europe was a particularly horrendous act in an ongoing tragedy.

Yet the Turks did not aim to kill every Armenian in Europe, nor did the Croatian fascists hope to eradicate Serbians from the continent. Hitler wanted to kill every Jewish man, woman, and child in Europe. Moreover, the Holocaust was not just a product of ideological or nationalist passion; it was also the result of careful calculation. In the death camps we encounter some of the most highly developed products of human reason used for evil and irrational ends. The gas chamber, for example, is a triumph of industrial *technology*—a sophisticated construction designed to deliver complex chemical products efficiently. But far more important is the centrality of industrial *techniques* to the Holocaust—the adaptation of the assembly line to facilitate mass murder. The Nazis approached the slaughter of a people as an engineering problem, one to be solved with the rational application of both machinery and method. They constructed a vast machine of death, with slave laborers as the key components, each with identification numbers tattooed onto their forearms, a type of human "bar coding." Like manufacturers everywhere, the Nazis sought to eliminate bottlenecks in the "production" process: Mass graves had to be dug when the crematoria could not keep up with the output from the gas chambers. And, like businessmen, the Nazis strove to make profitable use of every aspect of their raw material. The victims' hair, gold tooth fillings, and clothes were all recycled into the Nazi economy. Within these death factories constructed according to the highest standards of efficiency, the human raw material moved along a murderous assembly line—from arrival through selection to the undressing rooms to the gas chamber to the crematoria.

The Nazi death machine thus uniquely challenged, and continues to challenge, the widely held belief that rationality and progress are automatically linked, and that the dominant position of rationality in Western culture assures the West's claim to the label "civilized." For who would agree that the Nazis were civilized? By using the tools of civilization for barbaric ends, the Nazis called into question the very meaning of Western civilization. As one historian has argued, "the realisation that some men will construct a factory in which to kill other men raises the gravest questions about man himself. We have entered an age which we cannot avoid labeling 'After Auschwitz.'"[13]

The Race for the Atom Bomb

Western civilization has also entered an era that we cannot avoid labeling "After the Atom Bomb." During the summer of 1945, Western civilization came face-to-face with the destructive potential of scientific rationality not only in the remains of the Nazi death camps but also in the radioactive rubble of two Japanese cities, Hiroshima and Nagasaki. After the atom bomb the world would never be the same. Scientific theory and military technology had together produced weapons of awesome destructive capability that created an entirely new global balance of power—and the horror of mass death. But before we examine both the immediate and long-term consequences of the atomic bombings, we need to explore two central questions: What factors led scientists to pressure the Allied governments into creating weapons of such destructive power? Once these bombs had been made, why were they dropped on Japanese cities?

SPLITTING THE ATOM

The atom bomb resulted from the profound intellectual revolution occurring in science in the first decades of the twentieth century. At its most basic level, this revolution overthrew the mechanistic explanation of the universe that had held sway since the first scientific revolution in the seventeenth century (see Chapter 16). The triumph of the theories of Isaac Newton had ensured that for 200 years, educated Westerners regarded the natural world as a precise and predictable machine. But Newton's theories could not account for new realities such as X rays, radioactivity, and the discovery that atoms were not solid but actually made up of mobile electrons, nuclei, and empty space. In the first half of the twentieth century, scientists began to replace Newton's now-discredited universe with a new, more complicated model based on Albert Einstein's theory of relativity. As Chapter 23 explained, Einstein's model replaced Newton's static universe with a world in which space, time, matter, and energy are all interchangeable.

The effort to construct an entirely new understanding of the cosmos electrified the discipline of physics and attracted some of the most brilliant young thinkers of the twentieth century. Students traveled across Europe and the United States in pursuit of the best teachers and in hopes of joining research teams in both university and state-funded laboratories.

Much of the funding for all of this scientific activity came from governments. World War I, with its poison gas and bomber planes, had shown that in the new technological age, military victory depended as much on science as it did on soldiers. As one observer said in 1919, "The decisive assaults upon mankind now proceed from the drawing boards and the laboratory." Realizing the practical potential of scientific research, governments began to pour funds into university science departments and to establish research laboratories.

In the 1920s few of these political leaders realized that Einstein's concept of matter as "frozen energy" had profound implications for military technology. But in theory, if the energy could be "thawed out," then this energy could be released—a process that would produce a terrific explosion.

■ **Hiroshima After the Atom Bomb**
The buildings left standing had been reinforced against earthquakes.

But could this theory become reality? In 1936, the distinguished British scientist Ernest Rutherford (1871–1937) answered that question with a resounding "no" when he dismissed as "moonshine" the idea of unlocking the atom to release energy. Yet, just four years earlier, a scientist working in Rutherford's own laboratory had in fact found the key to unlocking the atom's energy. In 1932, James Chadwick (1891–1974) discovered that atoms contain not only positively charged protons and negatively charged electrons, but also neutrons. Because neutrons possess no electrical charge, they are not repelled by either an atom's protons or its electrons. Bombarded with heavy neutrons, an atom's nucleus could, in theory, be split open—a process called nuclear fission. Moreover, the split nucleus would itself emit neutrons, which would then burst open other atoms, which in turn would emit further neutrons . . . and on and on in a nuclear chain reaction. The result: a colossal burst of energy, an explosion, an atom bomb.

The atom bomb, however, remained purely theoretical—or pure "moonshine," in Rutherford's words—until 1938, when two scientists working in Berlin proved Rutherford wrong. Otto Hahn (1879–1968) and Fritz Strassmann (1902–1980) bombarded uranium with a stream of neutrons, and broke open the uranium atom. Matter had been

unlocked. As one historian has noted, "Physicists viewed the discovery of nuclear fission like the finding of a lost treasure map."[14] Within a year, over 100 articles on the implications of this discovery were published in scientific journals around the world.

One of the many scientists who recognized the path-breaking nature of the Hahn-Strassmann experiment was the brilliant Hungarian physicist Leo Szilard (1898–1964). Szilard had emigrated to Germany to take advantage of the first-rate scientific opportunities available in interwar Berlin. In 1933, however, Szilard, who was Jewish, recognized that he had no place in the new Nazi Reich. Like many German and eastern European Jewish scientists (including Albert Einstein and Sigmund Freud), Szilard fled to the West. He emigrated first to England, and then, in 1937, to the United States.

An avid reader of British science fiction writer H. G. Wells, Szilard had always been intrigued by the atomic bombs that Wells imagined in his stories. Once Hahn and Strassman published the results of their experiment with nuclear fission, Szilard recognized that the atom bomb had moved from the world of fiction into the realm of actual possibility. The discovery of nuclear fission in Germany occurred within just three weeks of the events of Kristallnacht, the night on which Nazis murdered more than 100 Jews, terrorized countless others, and burned Jewish businesses, homes, and synagogues. Appalled by the thought of Nazi Germany gaining access to the atomic bomb, Szilard began a vigorous campaign for a Western nuclear weapons program.

THE THREAT OF THE GERMAN BOMB

Szilard was just one of a large number of central and eastern European scientists who emigrated to Britain or the United States during the 1930s. Ironically, during the 1920s, many eastern European Jewish scientists had made their way to Germany, because it was perceived as far more enlightened and far less anti-Semitic than countries such as Poland and Hungary. But this situation changed abruptly in 1933. One of the Nazis' first measures on taking power was to limit the number of Jews employed in universities and the civil service. The University of Göttingen dismissed its top seven scientists, all of them Jewish. At the same time, Jewish scientists found themselves subject to professional persecution and verbal abuse. The Nazis derided Einstein's work, for example, as "Jewish world-bluff."

Acutely aware of the threat that Nazism posed to civilization, many of these émigré scientists were convinced after 1938 that Germany, with its stellar tradition of scientific research and magnificent laboratories, possessed the potential for developing an atom bomb. They and other scientists in the West began to pressure the British and American governments to devote the necessary resources to an atomic weapons program. In 1939, Leo Szilard met with Einstein (who by then was living in the United States) and asked him to use his considerable prestige to influence President Roosevelt. Einstein agreed, and six weeks after the start of the war in Europe, Roosevelt received a letter, signed by Einstein but actually written by Szilard, that warned both of the possibility of "extremely powerful bombs of a new type," and of rumors that Germany was building up its uranium supplies.

Roosevelt declared that "this requires action," but the United States was not yet at war in 1939 and little was done to respond to Szilard and Einstein's warnings. It was left to Britain to take the initial lead in the quest for the atom bomb. There, two refugee scientists, Otto Frisch (1904–1979) and Rudolph Peierls (1907–1995), had been barred (because of their German citizenship) from participating in the top-secret development of radar. They turned instead to exploring the means of developing and detonating an atom bomb. By April 1940, their work had impressed the British government enough to spark the creation of a committee to oversee atomic energy research.

American officials in the spring of 1941 dismissed the British atomic research project as "a wild goose chase." But by the summer of that year, the British had convinced the Americans that an atom bomb could be constructed. In October, Roosevelt suggested to British prime minister Winston Churchill that Britain and the United States pool their efforts and create an atomic partnership. The result was the Manhattan Project°.

THE BEST AND THE BRIGHTEST: THE MANHATTAN PROJECT

The Manhattan Project, the code name for the joint British-American effort to construct an atom bomb, was an extraordinary endeavor, the biggest and most expensive weapons

■ **Albert Einstein and Leo Szilard**
In 1946, Einstein and Szilard reenacted the signing of their letter to Roosevelt for the cameras.

research and development project up to that point in history. Comprising thirty-seven installations in nineteen American states and in Canada, it employed 120,000 individuals. Yet this colossal effort was top-secret. Until U.S. president Harry Truman announced the drop of an atom bomb on Hiroshima in August 1945, few American, British, or Canadian citizens had any inkling that nuclear weapons had jumped from the pages of science fiction and into the world of brutal fact.

The Manhattan Project recruited the best and the brightest, the very top scientists in their fields. In 1943, twenty of the thirty-three nuclear physicists regarded as "leaders in the field" worked on the Manhattan Project. Many of these scientists were astonishingly young; the average age of the scientists working at the core of the project in Los Alamos, New Mexico, was 25.

The Manhattan Project was run by the American military, although its scientific research was directed by the brilliant Berkeley professor of physics, Robert Oppenheimer (1904–1967). In late 1942, Brigadier General Leslie Groves (1896–1970), an engineer who had overseen construction of the Pentagon building in Washington, D.C., became the project's officer-in-charge. The scientists successfully resisted Groves's efforts to place them in military uniform and assign them military rank, but they quickly discovered that they were now servants of the state. Oppenheimer himself found that his telephone conversations were bugged, his movements monitored, his mail screened. His wife's Communist Party membership, and his own left-wing political leanings, made him the subject of intense military scrutiny.

For most of the project scientists, the discomforts of life in Los Alamos (and in other installations in Oak Ridge, Tennessee, and Hanford, Washington) and the unfamiliar military regulations were small prices to pay to participate in what they perceived as the race against Nazi Germany. Throughout 1942, Oppenheimer, Szilard, and other scientists worried that Allied progress was too slow, and that Germany might construct an atom bomb first.

Then, on December 2, 1942, the Italian physicist Enrico Fermi (1901–1954) and other scientists working at the University of Chicago produced a nuclear chain reaction. Once this breakthrough occurred, progress on the atom bomb moved ahead quickly. At 5:29 A.M., on July 16, 1945, the world's first atomic explosion was detonated over the desert of New Mexico. Oppenheimer gave this test explosion its code name—Trinity. American scientist Isidor Rabi (1898–1988) described the sight:

CHRONOLOGY

The Road to the Atom Bomb

1932	Discovery of the neutron
1933	Hitler appointed chancellor of Germany; emigration of many leading eastern European and German scientists to Britain and the United States
1938	First successful splitting of the atom
1939	Szilard and Einstein's letter to President Roosevelt
1940	Creation of British atomic bomb project
1941	Establishment of joint Anglo-American atomic bomb project
1942	Manhattan Project underway; first nuclear chain reaction
1945	
February	Bombing of Dresden
March	Bombing of Tokyo
May	German surrender; end of war in Europe
July	Potsdam Conference; Trinity test explosion
August 6	Atom bomb dropped on Hiroshima
August 8	Soviet declaration of war on Japan
August 9	Atom bomb dropped on Nagasaki
August 15	Japanese surrender

Suddenly, there was an enormous flash of light, the brightest light I have ever seen or that I think anyone has ever seen. It blasted; it pounced; it bored its way right through you . . . Finally, it was over, diminishing, and we looked toward the place where the bomb had been; there was an enormous ball of fire which grew and grew and it rolled as it grew . . . It looked menacing. It seemed to come toward one. A new thing had just been born.

Robert Oppenheimer recalled a line from the Hindu scripture, the *Bhagavad Gita:* "Now I am become Death, the destroyer of worlds." Kenneth Bainbridge (1904–1996), an experimental physicist from Harvard and director of the test, put it more simply: "Now we are all sons-of-bitches," he told Oppenheimer.[15]

THE DECISION TO DROP THE BOMB

By the time of the Trinity test, Nazi Germany had fallen to the Allies. Months before V-E Day (Victory-in-Europe Day—May 8, 1945), Allied military leaders had realized that the Allies would defeat Germany without an atom bomb. In the spring of 1945, as the Allied armies pushed across

■ **The Mushroom Cloud**
The detonation of the atomic bomb over Hiroshima on August 6, 1945, produced what would become one of the most familiar images of the post–World War II age.

Europe, a special intelligence unit discovered that the Germans had never come close to developing atomic weapons. Hence, the original aim of the Manhattan Project, to beat the Germans to a superweapon, was no longer valid by 1945. But almost a year earlier, American military planners had already shifted the atomic target to Japan (see Map 27.3).

By August 1945, Japan was staggering under the combined effects of an American naval blockade and nightly bombing raids. In addition, the Soviet Union stood poised to enter the Pacific War on the Allies' side. Japan had clearly lost the war, and important members of the Japanese cabinet began to press for peace, although Japan's military leaders were determined to fight on to the bitter end. The end, however, was clear. The question was not if but when Japan would surrender.

Given this situation, the decision to use atom bombs against Japan generated controversy from the very start. In the weeks before Hiroshima, scientists at the University of Chicago section of the project (including Leo Szilard) protested against plans to drop the bomb on Japan without warning. Important American military officials such as General Dwight Eisenhower (1890–1969), supreme commander of the Allied forces in Europe, and General Douglas MacArthur (1880–1964), supreme commander of the Allied forces in the Pacific, opposed the use of the atom bombs as (in MacArthur's words) "completely unnecessary."[16]

The decision to drop the bombs involved several considerations. Historians have highlighted four factors that influenced the decision: the desire to save American lives, domestic pressure for Japan's unconditional surrender, international political concerns, and the widespread use of mass air bombing in both Europe and the Pacific during the war.

First, both Truman and his advisers aimed to end the war quickly and thereby save the lives of American servicemen. By the summer of 1945 U.S. forces had reversed Japan's expansion into the Pacific, destroyed most of Japan's navy, and blockaded Japan itself. But these victories exacted a high price. In the spring campaigns on the islands of Iwo Jima and Okinawa, almost 20,000 Americans and 90,000 Japanese lost their lives.

The fierce Japanese resistance encountered at Iwo Jima and Okinawa convinced military planners, ordinary servicemen, and the American public that an invasion of Japan's home islands would result in horrifying casualties. In mid-June 1945, the Joint War Plans Committee estimated that a November invasion of Japan's southern island of Kyushu, followed by a March invasion of the main island of Honshu, would result in 40,000 Americans killed, 150,000 wounded, and 3,500 missing. Admiral William Leahy (1875–1959) noted to President Truman that if casualty rates at Kyushu were as high as those on Okinawa, then the numbers of Americans killed in the first phase of the invasion could reach as high as 50,000.

The desire to end the war quickly and so avoid the deaths of American servicemen thus played an important role in the decision to drop the atom bomb. An invasion of the Japanese home islands was, however, not a foregone conclusion in the spring and summer of 1945. Admiral Leahy, who opposed using the Bomb, argued that the blockade of Japan would end the war *without* an invasion. In 1946, the U.S. Strategic Bombing Survey concluded that Leahy was correct: "Certainly prior to 31 December 1945, and in all probability prior to 1 November 1945 [the scheduled date of the Kyushu invasion], Japan would have surrendered . . . even if no invasion had been planned or contemplated."

Of course, the Strategic Bombing Survey officials had the benefit of hindsight, an advantage denied to Truman and his advisers. But it is clear that there were alternatives to

Map 27.3 Japan in 1945

By the summer of 1945, American bombing raids had decimated many Japanese cities, including Tokyo. Hiroshima escaped unscathed until August 6, 1945. Nagasaki received the second atom bomb on August 9 only because clouds obscured the primary target of Kokura.

both an invasion and the atom bomb. Continuing the blockade and conventional bombing of Japan constituted one such alternative; another was exploring diplomatic avenues for ending the war. American and British policymakers knew that in April, members of the Japanese government had approached the Soviet Union with tentative offers of a Japanese surrender, on the condition that the Japanese emperor be allowed to remain on his throne.

Why were these peace initiatives not pursued? Domestic politics proved to be a crucial constraining factor. The demand for Japan's "unconditional surrender" was extremely popular with both the British and American publics, and most historians agree that Truman—in office only a few months and with far less prestige than Roosevelt—would have found it politically impossible to abandon such a popular policy. The memory of Japan's surprise attack on the American air force base in Pearl Harbor, Hawaii, in 1941, combined with the savagery with which the Pacific war had been waged, ensured that Americans wanted nothing less than Japan's unconditional surrender. Moreover, by the spring of 1945, the Manhattan Project had cost almost two billion dollars. To have spent such a sum of money, and then not to use the resulting weapon while American lives were being lost every day in a dreadful conflict, was, finally, unacceptable.

International politics also played a role in the dropping of the Bomb—specifically, the desire to impress the Soviet Union with American power. By 1945, as Chapter 26 detailed, the fundamental conflicts that divided the Allies could no longer be papered over. It is significant that although Britain and the United States cooperated in the Manhattan Project, they excluded the other principal member of the alliance, the Soviet Union. Concerns over Soviet expansion into both eastern Europe and Asia dominated the thoughts of Truman and his advisers in the final year of the war. American and British officials hoped that the use of the atom bomb, by ending the war quickly, would not only save Allied lives but also stall the Soviet advance in the Pacific. (The Soviets declared war on Japan on August 8, 1945.) Both American and British leaders gambled that a dramatic demonstration of the awesome destructive power of the atom bomb would force the Soviets to recognize that the United States held the winning card and that they must therefore play the postwar game according to American rules.

Finally, the decision to drop the atom bombs must be seen within the context of total war, and, in particular, the strategic mass bombing of civilian centers. In 1939, both Roosevelt and British prime minister Neville Chamberlain publicly condemned aerial bombing of noncombatants as an unacceptable atrocity. But after the German Luftwaffe began bombarding British cities in the fall of 1940, the British Royal Air Force retaliated with air attacks on German civilian centers. Flying in massive formations, bomber planes dropped incendiary bombs and set Germany ablaze. Tens of thousands of noncombatants died in these attacks. The most notorious occurred in 1945, when the Allies destroyed Dresden. A German city with great historical but no military or industrial value, Dresden housed thousands of refugees and over 26,000 American POWs. The bombing, together with the subsequent firestorm, resulted in 130,000 casualties.

In the first years of the war, American military officials had hesitated to follow the British lead in targeting civilian centers. But by 1945 the U.S. air command had adopted massive bombing raids as a key strategy in the war against Japan. In a single March evening, American planes bombed residential areas in Tokyo. Eighty-five thousand Japanese civilians died in the firestorm that night. In the next five months, American bombers hit sixty-six Japanese cities, burned 180 square miles, and killed approximately 330,000 Japanese.

By 1945, then, killing huge numbers of noncombatants had become commonplace. Years of immersion in the savage barbarity of World War II made the use of atom bombs acceptable. The atom bomb's appeal was not in its potential to kill tens of thousands in a single night; conventional bombs were already doing that, and doing it rather effectively. But the idea of massive casualties, caused by a single bomb, dropped by a single plane, promised to have an enormous psychological impact on the Japanese, and so to end the war more quickly.

The Dawn of the Nuclear Age

At 8:15 A.M. on August 6, 1945, a light "brighter than a thousand suns" flashed above the city of Hiroshima. For the first time ever, an atom bomb had been dropped on human beings. Ten days later, Japan surrendered to the Allies, and World War II ended. But the detonation of the atom bomb signaled more than the end of the war; it was a flashpoint of both a new political phase—the emerging Cold War—and a new cultural era. What, then, were the results, both immediate and long-term, of the atomic bombings of Hiroshima and Nagasaki? How did the cultural and political landscape shift after the atom bomb?

"THE GREATEST THING IN HISTORY"

On the day the first bomb was dropped, Truman received a telegram announcing the atomic bombing of Hiroshima: "Results clear-cut successful in all respects." Truman exulted, "This is the greatest thing in history."[17] The atom bomb dropped on Hiroshima caused greater damage than its creators had predicted. Temperatures at the site of the atomic explosion reached 5,400 degrees Fahrenheit. All those exposed within two miles of the center suffered primary thermal burns—their blood literally boiled and their skin peeled off in strips. The combined impact of the blast wave and the thermal flash started fires, which quickly coalesced into a firestorm. Of the 76,000 buildings in Hiroshima, 70,000 were damaged or destroyed. Human losses matched the material damage. Of a wartime population of 400,000, 140,000 died by the end of 1945, with another 60,000 dying in the next five years, primarily due to radiation poisoning. Scientists calculated that the atom bomb produced casualties 6,500 times more efficiently than an ordinary bomb.

Selected in May for atomic bombing, Hiroshima had been deliberately preserved from aerial attack to heighten the Bomb's psychological impact as well as to ensure that the atom bomb's force could be reliably measured. Government press releases about the bombing inaccurately described the city as "an important Japanese army base." Hiroshima did house 43,000 soldiers (a little over 3,000 of whom were killed by the atom bomb), but it was in fact an industrial city, populated by ordinary civilians.

The Japanese reacted to the Hiroshima bombing with incomprehension and confusion. They literally did not know what had hit them. One Japanese woman recalled, "I just could not understand why our surroundings had changed so greatly in one instant . . . I thought it might have been something which had nothing to do with the war, the collapse of the earth which it was said would take place at the end of the world."[18] Within the high levels of the Japanese government, gradual realization of the atomic bomb's power, coupled with U.S. threats of sending a "rain of ruin" on Japan if it did not surrender, strengthened the position of those officials who recognized that Japan must now give up. A hardline faction of the military, however, wished to fight on.

On August 8, the Soviet Union declared war on Japan. The next day, a second atom bomb fell on Japan. Not even named on the original target list, Nagasaki received the second atom bomb by chance. Because the original objective, Kokura, was shielded by heavy cloud cover, the pilot turned toward his secondary target. The atom bomb in Nagasaki killed 70,000 outright, with another 70,000 dying over the next five years. On August 10, Emperor Hirohito met with his military leaders. Viewed in the West as an implacable war lord, Hirohito was actually a man with fairly limited political power who had been pressing for peace since June. Now he insisted the time had come to surrender.

Negotiations between the Allies and the Japanese cabinet over the position of the emperor in a postwar Japan continued until August 15, when peace was announced. In Hiroshima and Nagasaki, however, another battle was raging, this time against an unseen and at first unrecognized enemy—radiation. On September 5, 1945, a journalist for the London *Daily Express* reported,

> In Hiroshima . . . people are still dying, mysteriously and horribly—people who were uninjured in the cataclysm from an unknown something which I can only describe as the atomic plague.[19]

The lingering horror of radiation sickness, accounts of which were at first dismissed by many Americans as Japanese propaganda, signaled that the atom bomb was not just a bigger weapon, not simply more bang for the buck. A revolutionary new force, it introduced the world to new horrors and new possibilities.

COLD WAR CONCERNS AND THE NUCLEAR ARMS RACE

The scientists who created the atom bomb recognized that it had the potential to revolutionize international power relations. The eminent Danish scientist Niels Bohr (1886–1962) urged both Roosevelt and Churchill in 1944 to inform Stalin of the Manhattan Project and prepare a postwar plan for international control of atomic weapons. Bohr feared that failure to include the Soviets in the development

"A GOOD DOSE OF PROPAGANDA"

The following is an excerpt from a declassified transcript (originally marked "Top Secret") of a telephone conversation between General Leslie Groves, the head of the Manhattan Project, and Lt. Col. Rea, a military physician at Oak Ridge Hospital. Groves, concerned about media reports of radiation sickness among Hiroshima survivors, called on Rea for reassurance and advice. The excerpt begins with Groves quoting from a disturbing report.

Groves: Then it goes on: "Radioactivity caused by the fission of the uranium used in atomic bombs is taking a toll of mounting deaths and causing reconstruction workers in Hiroshima to suffer various sicknesses and ill health."

Rea: I would say this: You yourself, as far as radioactivity is concerned, it isn't anything immediate, it's a prolonged thing. I think what these people have, they just got a good thermal burn, that's what it is. . . .

Groves: Now then, he says—this is the thing I wanted to ask you about particularly—"an examination of soldiers working on reconstruction projects one week after the bombing showed that their white corpuscles had diminished by half and a severe deficiency of red corpuscles."

Rea: I read that, too—I think there's something hookum about that.

Groves: Would they both go down?

Rea: They may, yes, they may, but that's awfully quick, pretty terrifically quick. Of course it depends—but I wonder if you aren't getting a good dose of propaganda . . . Of course those Jap scientists over there aren't so dumb either and they are making a play on this, too. They evidently know what the possibility is. Personally, I discounted a lot of it, as it's too early, and in the second place, I think that a lot of these deaths they are getting are just delayed thermal burns.

. . .

Groves: This is the kind of thing that hurts us—"The Japanese, who were reported today by Tokyo radio, to have died mysteriously a few days after the atomic bomb blast, probably were the victims of a phenomenon which is well known in the great radiation laboratories of America." That, of course, is what does us the damage.

Rea: I would say this: You will have to get some big-wig to put a counter-statement in the paper.

Source: Excerpts from Groves, 201 File. Manhattan Engineer District Records. National Archives.

---

of the atomic bomb would fuel Soviet suspicion of the West and result in a frightening race to amass nuclear arms.

After the Japanese bombings, many Manhattan Project scientists and other leading intellectuals—including Albert Einstein and Leo Szilard—joined with Bohr in demanding that a radical new world order be created. The resulting "scientists' movement" attempted to use the great prestige of nuclear scientists after Hiroshima to influence the reconstruction of postwar political structures. The movement called for the development of transnational institutions that would not only control the world's supply of nuclear weapons but also work to redistribute the world's wealth more rationally and reduce nationalistic competition. The alternative, scientists warned, was World War III—a nuclear conflict that could destroy civilization.

The efforts of the scientists to head off a nuclear arms race proved futile. To political leaders in the United States and Britain, demands that the U.S. government turn over its nuclear weapons technology to an international body seemed misguided, at best. The Manhattan Project, although rooted in fear of a German atom bomb, was also shaped by American and British convictions that the Soviet Union would be the West's principal postwar adversary. General Groves, the military head of the Manhattan Project, recalled that "there was never . . . any illusion on

my part but that Russia was our enemy, and the Project was conducted on that basis."[20] Churchill, Roosevelt, and Truman all viewed the atom bomb not only as a war-winning weapon, but also as a postwar diplomatic tool, a device to control the Soviets once peace was declared.

Possession of the atomic "secret" thus shaped Anglo-American attitudes and actions toward the Soviet Union in the final months of the war. Truman scheduled the Potsdam Conference, the "Big Three" summit called to negotiate postwar power relations, to coincide with the Trinity test explosion. He knew that if the test was successful, he would have a weighty bargaining chip in his negotiations with Stalin. The Trinity test report transformed Truman's very demeanor at Potsdam. According to Churchill, Truman "was a changed man. He told the Russians just where they got on and off, and generally bossed the whole meeting." As Truman's adviser James Byrnes (1882–1972) explained, Truman gambled that the Bomb would "put us in a position to dictate our own terms at the end of the war."[21]

The gamble did not pay off. The Soviets responded not by acquiescing to Anglo-American demands but by accelerating their own nuclear weapons research. American policymakers wagered that the Soviets would be unable to develop atomic weapons for at least ten years. They did not realize, however, how advanced the Soviet atomic project already was. Soviet scientists were some of the best in the world and Stalin authorized the spending of huge sums of money on the project. In addition, Soviet spies on the Manhattan Project had passed crucial scientific information on to Russian scientists who, like their Western counterparts, were motivated by a mixture of patriotism and scientific curiosity to press forward rapidly toward an atomic weapon. Fear also played a role: Soviet atomic scientists knew that if they failed, their lives were forfeit. When Stalin's deputy Beria warned against giving scientists too much freedom, Stalin replied, "Leave them in peace. We can always shoot them later."[22]

In August, 1949, the Soviets detonated "Joe I," the first Soviet atom bomb. The nuclear arms race° was on. Within three years the atom bomb was outmoded. The United States won the race for the hydrogen bomb, a weapon more than one thousand times more destructive than the atomic bombs used against Japan. The United States detonated the world's first hydrogen bomb in November 1952, but the Soviets followed in August 1953 with a technologically more sophisticated device. In the second half of the 1950s the nuclear arms race veered onto a new track, with the focus less on the bombs themselves than on their delivery systems. In August 1957, the Soviets tested the world's first intercontinental ballistic missile (ICBM); the U.S. version followed one year later. By the mid-1960s, both the United States and the Soviet Union had replaced the manned bomber plane with nuclear submarines and missiles.

The nuclear arms race had important consequences for the postwar world. In international relations, the nuclear arms race raised the stakes of the Cold War conflict, as both superpowers sought to ensure that their nuclear arsenal equaled or surpassed that of their rival. It also enhanced the position of the superpowers vis-à-vis other allied and rival powers. Other nations did acquire access to nuclear weapons, but none could afford the vast nuclear stockpiles built up by the Soviet Union and the United States. The nations belonging to the two rival Cold War alliances, NATO and the Warsaw Pact, relied on the superpowers for their nuclear defense. Curiously, however, possession of nuclear weapons also limited Soviet and American power. The nuclear threat proved to be a restraining force; behind every potential military action rested the question, "Is this worth the risk of a nuclear war?"

Another consequence of the nuclear arms race was a far-reaching militarization of ordinary life. In a nuclear conflict, to be attacked is to be destroyed; hence, the only possibility of victory rests in launching a surprise attack, in hitting the enemy before it has a chance to hit you. In the 1950s, then, citizens on both sides of the Cold War divide learned that destruction might rain from the skies at any moment. In the United States, the Soviet Union, and Britain, civil-defense campaigns sought to buttress civilian morale by preparing them for nuclear war. American

CHRONOLOGY

The Nuclear Arms Race

1942	Manhattan Project underway; Soviet spies keep Stalin informed
1945	Hiroshima and Nagasaki bombings; acceleration of Soviet atomic bomb project
1949	First test of Soviet atomic bomb
1952	First test of British atomic bomb
	First test of American hydrogen bomb
1953	First test of Soviet hydrogen bomb
1957	First test of British hydrogen bomb
	First test of Soviet ICBM
1958	Formation of Campaign for Nuclear Disarmament (CND) in Britain; first test of American ICBM
1960	First test of French atomic bomb
1964	First test of Chinese atomic bomb

schoolchildren practiced diving under their desks and covering their heads with their hands—"duck-and-cover drills"—to ready them for nuclear attack. Soviet citizens were taught how to dig shelters in which to shield themselves from post-attack radiation.

The superpowers clearly dominated the nuclear race, yet other nations also sought to enter the contest. For many nations, the possession of nuclear weapons technology seemed an important guarantor of national prestige and power. By the end of the twentieth century, the nuclear club included as its members not only the Soviet Union and the United States but also Britain, France, China, Israel, India, Pakistan, and, it is believed, South Africa and Brazil.

LEARNING TO LIVE WITH THE BOMB

Nuclear weapons presented a cultural as well as political and military challenge. While the science behind the bomb eluded the grasp of all but those with advanced scientific educations, the implications of this new weapon were much more readily accessible. From the moment that the Hiroshima bombing was announced, people recognized that the world stood on the brink of an unknown era. Amidst the rejoicing and relief over the war's ending arose fear and apprehension about the dawn of the atomic age. As the

American magazine *Time* noted in its end-of-the-year issue, "What the world would best remember of 1945 was the deadly mushroom clouds over Hiroshima and Nagasaki . . . In their giant shadows . . . all men were pygmies."

With astonishing swiftness, speculations emerged about new and bigger bombs, and the annihilation of entire civilizations. In 1945 Manhattan Project scientists had only begun to explore the possibility of a hydrogen bomb; yet popular culture immediately grasped that Hiroshima was only the beginning. Within just a few months after the atomic bombings, for example, American newspapers featured stories predicting atomic wars that would devastate not just single cities but the entire Earth, leaving behind "a barren waste, in which the survivors of the race will hide in caves or live among ruins."[23]

Threads of sparkling hope interwove with these somber expressions of fear. The fact of the atom bomb made the realization of other seemingly farfetched dreams seem possible. Abundant energy "too cheap to meter," a cure for cancer and inherited diseases, plentiful harvests and giant fruits, deserts turned to lush tropical paradises—all were promised in the immediate aftermath of the destruction of Hiroshima and Nagasaki.

By the 1960s, World War III had not devastated civilization, nor had the world been transformed into paradise, yet Europeans and Americans found themselves struggling to come to terms with the new nuclear age. A growing understanding of radiation and its dangers introduced new fears into ordinary life. The Australian Nevil Shute's (1899–1960) *On the Beach,* published first as a novel in 1959 and then produced as a film in 1962, articulated the widespread cultural anxiety. In Shute's unrealistic but unforgettable fiction, the inhabitants of a southern Australian community await inevitable death from invisible clouds of radiation already responsible for obliterating human life on the rest of the planet.

Scientists scoffed at Shute's fictional radiation clouds, but his novel seemed convincing to many readers who had learned during the previous decade that poisonous clouds were far more than fantasy in the nuclear age. Aboveground nuclear testing in the American West, various South Pacific island clusters, and the Soviet Union had introduced a new word into the world's vocabulary: *fallout.* Scientists had assumed that the radioactive effects of a nuclear explosion would be confined to the blast area, but they were wrong. These explosions ejected into the air radioactive particles, which formed pinkish clouds that drifted across the skies and later settled to the ground in the form of fallout, often appearing as a light dust or ash—or, to children, a sort of snow in which they delighted to play. In 1954, fallout rained down on four Japanese fishermen caught unaware near a U.S. hydrogen bomb test. The resulting death of one of the fishermen became a worldwide scandal that sparked awareness of and protests against nuclear testing.

■ **Nuclear Protest**

CND supporters gather in Trafalgar Square, London, for the annual Easter march to the British nuclear weapons research establishment at Aldermaston. The circular CND symbol quickly transcended the movement itself and became a global peace symbol.

The most significant of these protests emerged in Britain at the start of 1958 when a group of middle-class men and women formed the Campaign for Nuclear Disarmament (CND). Its founders—journalists and intellectuals with a long history of participation in respectable protest and humanitarian campaigns—envisioned CND as an elite pressure group that would lobby Parliament to abandon Britain's separate nuclear weapons program. Much to their surprise and discomfort, CND mushroomed into the first significant postwar mass movement, drawing up to 100,000 supporters onto its annual Easter march and expressing an unfocused but deeply felt sense of uneasiness with the nuclear age. It quickly sparked the formation of similar campaigns in western Europe and the United States, while its symbol, a circle containing a broken cross (actually a combination of the semaphore signals for

N [nuclear] and D [disarmament]), became an instantly recognizable global icon of postwar protest. In many ways, CND foreshadowed the larger and more well-known protests of the 1960s (see Chapter 28). Its young, blue-jeans-clad marchers, stepping to the beat of jazz bands, voiced their anger at having been sidelined while the superpowers played a dangerous nuclear game.

In this period, the Bomb also permeated American and European cultural consciousness. Because figurative painting seemed utterly incapable of capturing the power and terror of the atomic age, the bomb reinforced the hold of abstract art over the avant-garde. But abstract art itself changed. Rejecting the very formal, carefully composed, geometric abstractions that had characterized much of modernist art in the period before the war, Abstract Expressionists sought to develop more spontaneous, emotional styles. Jackson Pollack (1912–1956), for example, invented an entirely new way of painting. Placing the canvas on the ground, he moved around and in it, dripping or pouring paint. Such a technique rested on intuition rather than intellect, and demanded that the artist almost throw himself into the painting itself. As Pollack explained, "New needs need new techniques . . . The modern painter cannot express his age, the airplane, the atom bomb . . . in the old forms."[24] In Pollack's works, the canvas has no clear center, no focal point. Instead, it disintegrates, like matter itself.

Musicians, too, responded to the challenge of the nuclear age. For Polish composer Krzysztof Penderecki (b. 1933), the revolution in warfare wrought at Hiroshima demanded radical changes in musical composition. He created new notational devices and constructed a work for no fewer than fifty-two stringed instruments. Penderecki's *Threnody* [a song of lamentation] *for the Victims of Hiroshima* was praised as one of the best musical works of the year when it was performed in Warsaw in 1961. Probably the best-known musical response to Hiroshima, Penderecki's piece, with its polytonal dissonances, absorbs its listener into a world of pain and anger.

Most people confronted their nuclear fears not in concert halls or art galleries, but rather in movie theaters. Here various nuclear-spawned terrors, including giant spiders, ants, and turtles, wreaked weekly havoc on the Western world. Fittingly enough, many of these films were produced in Japan.

Throughout the 1950s, nuclear war and the postnuclear struggle for survival also filled the pages of popular fiction.

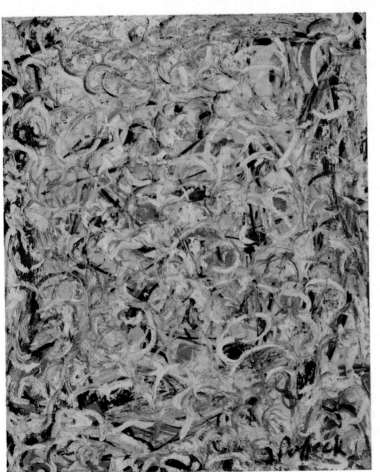

■ **Jackson Pollack, *Shimmering Substance* (1946)**

Many of Pollack's postwar works—huge paintings that pulse with power—show an obsession with heat and light, surely no coincidence in the dawn of the nuclear age.

■ **Peter Sellers as Dr. Strangelove**
This blackly comic character's strange love for the technologies of mass destruction linked together Nazism and the nuclear age.

Probably the most important "nuclear" novel, however, confined mention of atomic bombs to a single sentence. In *The Lord of the Flies* (1954), British author William Golding (1911–1993) told the simple and brutal story of the conflict between savagery and civilization. Fleeing an England under atomic attack, a group of upper-class boarding-school boys are stranded on an island. Their moral deterioration poses basic questions about the meaning of civilization, a question brought to the forefront of Western culture by the use of advanced science to obliterate civilian populations.

The Lord of the Flies showed how quickly the veneer of civilization disintegrates in a world without advanced technology; other cultural productions of the postwar period spotlight technology itself as a threat to civilization. The fear of technology out of control served as the dramatic impulse behind two notable films released in 1964. The first, *Fail-Safe,* used a compelling but conventional narrative to dramatize the failure of supposedly "fail-safe" weapons-control devices and the resulting nuclear devastation of Moscow and New York. But it took filmmaker Stanley Kubrick's (1928–1999) masterpiece, *Dr. Strangelove; or, How I Learned to Stop Worrying and Love the Bomb* (1964), to capture the widespread fear of a nuclear war sparked by accident, by a combination of human error and technological determinism. Unlike *Fail-Safe* (and most films about nuclear war), *Dr. Strangelove* was a comedy; it subverted conventional Cold War orthodoxies by daring to laugh at nuclear war. In its pervasive sense of uneasiness with the power delivered by science into human hands, we can discern the cultural fallout of the nuclear age.

CONCLUSION
The West, Progress, and Power

The title character of Kubrick's film, Dr. Strangelove, is a German scientist who cannot resist thrusting his arm forward in a Nazi salute and yelling, "Heil Hitler!" at inappropriate moments. In these scenes of black comedy, Kubrick linked the Nazi obsession with power to the postwar quest for nuclear dominance. It is a linkage that resonates in Western culture after Auschwitz and the atom bomb. As one scholar has argued, two images "have haunted mankind since the Second World War—the barbed wire and emaciated figures of Hitler's death camps, and the blinding white flash over the city of Hiroshima."[25]

Just as the Holocaust raised crucial questions about the meaning of Western civilization, so too did the bombings of Hiroshima and Nagasaki and their nuclear aftermath. With the best of intentions, some of the greatest minds in the Western world had produced weapons designed to kill and maim tens of thousands of civilians. For centuries, the use of the methods of scientific inquiry to uncover truth and achieve both material and moral progress had supported Westerners' self-identification and their sense of cultural superiority. The carnage of

World War I had eroded these assumptions; World War II and particularly the Holocaust and the atom bomb threatened to level them entirely. The war years demonstrated that the best of science could produce the worst of weapons, that technology and technique could combine in factories designed for mass murder. The task of accepting this knowledge, and facing up to its implications, helped shape Western culture after 1945.

Suggestions for Further Reading

For a comprehensive list of suggested readings, please go to www.ablongman.com/levack/chapter27

Alperovitz, Gar. *Atomic Diplomacy: Hiroshima and Potsdam. The Use of the Atomic Bomb and the American Confrontation with Soviet Power.* 1994. The first edition of this book, published in 1965, sparked an ongoing scholarly debate about the role of Cold War concerns in shaping U.S. decision making at the end of World War II.

Arad, Yitzhak, ed. *The Pictorial History of the Holocaust.* 1990. An excellent introduction.

Browning, Christopher. *Ordinary Men: Reserve Police Battalion 101 and the Final Solution in Poland.* 1992. A powerful account of the participation of a group of "ordinary men" in mass murder.

Frayn, Michael. *Copenhagen.* 1998. A remarkable play in which Frayn dramatizes a meeting (which actually did occur) between the German atomic physicist Werner Hiesenberg and his Danish anti-Nazi colleague Niels Bohr. Contains both extremely clear explanations of the workings of atomic physics and a provocative exploration of the moral issues involved in the making of the atom bomb.

Friedlander, Saul. *Nazi Germany and the Jews, 1933–1939.* 1998. An important study of the evolution of Nazi anti-Semitic policy before the war.

Hersey, John. *Hiroshima.* 1985. This edition of Hersey's classic account (first published in 1946) contains an added chapter that tells the stories of the survivors forty years after the bombing.

Hilberg, Raul. *Perpetrators, Victims, Bystanders: The Jewish Catastrophe, 1933–1945.* 1992. As his title indicates, Hilberg looks at the three principal sets of participants in the Holocaust.

Marrus, Michael R. *The Holocaust in History.* 1987. A clearly written, concise account of historians' efforts to understand the Holocaust. Highly recommended.

Niewyk, Donald L., ed. *The Holocaust: Problems and Perspectives of Interpretation.* 1992. Looks at areas of dispute such as the origins of the Holocaust, the extent of Jewish resistance, and the possibilities of rescue.

Nobile, Philip, ed. *Judgment at the Smithsonian: The Bombing of Hiroshima and Nagasaki.* 1995. Includes an extremely sensible essay by historian Barton Bernstein on both the historiography and popular mythology of the bombings.

Rhodes, Richard. *Masters of Death: The SS-Einsatzgruppen and the Invention of the Holocaust.* 2002. Compelling account of the Einsatzgruppen actions during the German invasion of the Soviet Union.

Rhodes, Richard. *The Making of the Atomic Bomb.* 1986. A lengthy but very readable account; very good at explaining the complicated science involved.

Sherwin, Martin J. *A World Destroyed: Hiroshima and the Origins of the Arms Race.* 1987. Focuses on the diplomatic and political context.

Notes

1. Quoted in Robert H. Abzug, *Inside the Vicious Heart: Americans and the Liberation of Nazi Concentration Camps* (1985), p. 19.
2. Quoted in Gordon Horwitz, *In the Shadow of Death, Living Outside the Gates of Mauthausen* (1991), p. 167.
3. This argument is made by Christopher Browning in *The Path to Genocide: Essays on the Launching of the Final Solution* (1992).
4. Elie Wiesel, *Night,* (1958), p. 39.
5. Quoted in Horwitz, p. 35.
6. Quoted in Walter Laqueur, *The Terrible Secret: An Investigation into the Suppression of Information about Hitler's "Final Solution"* (1982), p. 100.
7. Gideon Hausner, *Justice in Jerusalem* (1966), p. 291.
8. Hausner, pp. 323–324.
9. From Hausner's opening statement; quoted in Moshe Pearlman, *The Capture and Trial of Adolf Eichmann* (1963), p. 149.
10. Quoted in Pearlman, pp. 463–465.
11. Quoted in Pearlman, p. 603; Hausner, p. 422.
12. The quotation is from Ernst Nolte, translated and quoted by Charles Maier, in *The Unmasterable Past: History, Holocaust, and German National Identity* (1997), p. 32.
13. Karl A. Schleunes, *The Twisted Road to Auschwitz: Nazi Policy Toward German Jews, 1933–39* (1970), p. 1.
14. Martin J. Sherwin, *A World Destroyed: Hiroshima and the Origins of the Arms Race* (1987), p. 17.
15. Quoted in Richard Rhodes, *The Making of the Atomic Bomb* (1986), pp. 672, 675, 676.

16. Quoted in Ronald Takaki, *Hiroshima: Why America Dropped the Bomb* (1995), p. 3.
17. Quoted in Takaki, p. 46.
18. Quoted in Robert Jay Lifton, *Death in Life: The Survivors of Hiroshima* (1967), pp. 22-23.
19. Quoted in Paul Boyer, *By the Bomb's Early Light: American Thought and Culture at the Dawn of the Atomic Age* (1985), p. 187.
20. Quoted in Sherwin, p. 62.
21. Churchill to Henry L. Stimson, Stimson Diary; quoted in Sherwin, p. 199.
22. Quoted in John Lewis Gaddis, *We Now Know: Rethinking Cold War History* (1997), p. 96.
23. Quotation from the *Chicago Tribune;* quoted in Boyer, p. 15.
24. Quoted in Jonathan Fineberg, *Art Since 1940: Strategies of Being* (1995), p. 89.
25. Michael Bess, *Realism, Utopia, and the Mushroom Cloud* (1993), p. xv.

INFORMATION LIBRE

Redefining the West After World War II

O N ONE APPARENTLY ORDINARY DAY IN AUGUST 1961, WESTERN EUROPEAN television viewers witnessed an extraordinary sight. While the news cameras rolled, policemen from East Berlin played tug-of-war with firemen from West Berlin. Between them was not a length of rope, but rather a middle-aged German woman. This horrifying contest had been set in motion by the construction of the Berlin Wall. Appalled by the growing numbers of East German citizens who were fleeing communist rule through the gateway of West Berlin, the East German and Soviet authorities decided to shut the gate. In the early morning hours of August 13, East German workers erected a barbed-wire fence along Berlin's east-west dividing line. In some cases, this line ran right through apartment buildings. For the next few weeks, these apartments provided literal "windows to the west." West Berlin firemen waited with blankets ready to catch anyone willing to jump out of a window—and out of communist eastern Europe. These windows closed quickly. The communist authorities bricked them up; later they leveled entire apartment buildings to create a moat in front of what was now the armed fortress of East Berlin. The barbed-wire fence became a concrete wall buttressed by gun towers, lit by searchlights and patrolled by armed guards with "shoot to kill" orders.

The unidentified woman in this scene, literally caught between West and East, serves as an appropriate symbol for Europe during the 1950s and 1960s. In these decades, the Cold War between the United States and the Soviet Union influenced European politics, culture, and society. European governments and their populations found their freedom of maneuver checked by Cold War constraints. The woman's desperation to reach the West reminds us that American influence in western Europe should not be equated with Soviet control of eastern Europe: Cultural and economic dominance are not the same as political tyranny.

Chapter Outline

- The Cold War, the West, and the World

- Imperial Encounters: Decolonization in a Cold War Context

- After Stalin: The Soviet Union and Eastern Europe in the 1950s and 1960s

- The West: Integration and Affluence

- Culture and Society in the Age of Consumption

Protest Poster, Paris 1968: Many of the protest movements of the 1960s questioned the democratic nature of Western governments. Protesters in Paris in 1968 used posters such as this one to articulate their sense that, despite constitutional guarantees and universal suffrage, Western political systems actually suppressed free speech.

■ **Tug-of-War at the Berlin Wall**
Caught by the television cameras, this woman sought to escape through her window into West Berlin. She succeeded.

Nevertheless, many Europeans in the West as well as the East felt that they no longer controlled their own societies.

The Cold War was an encounter of two clashing ideologies, as much a battle of ideas and values as weapons and warriors. Both sides laid claim to universal cultures—to have achieved a way of life that would benefit *all* human societies. This ideological encounter forced a redefinition of "the West." Previous chapters have described the way in which this cultural construct shifted over time. By the late nineteenth century, Christianity, although still important, played a less central role in defining "the West" than did a mix of other factors, including the possession of industrial technology, the illusion of white superiority based on pseudoscientific racist theorizing, and faith in both capitalist economics and liberal political values. The Cold War added an anti-Soviet stance and a fear of communist ideology to the mix. These additions at times eroded the Western commitment to democracy, particularly within the developing world.

Significantly, the Cold War turned "hot" not in Europe but in places such as Korea, Cuba, and Vietnam. The developing world served as the site of crucial Cold War conflicts

in this era. The postwar years witnessed the widening of the economic gap between "North" and "South"—between the industrialized nations, largely located in the Northern Hemisphere, and the economically underdeveloped regions (many but certainly not all of which were situated south of the equator), now shrugging off colonial rule and seeking both political independence and economic prosperity. Thus, as Europeans encountered each other across the Cold War divide, they also encountered non-Europeans across a huge economic gulf. Two very different contests—North versus South and West versus East—quickly became entangled with each other as the Cold War moved beyond Europe's borders to the developing regions.

These encounters created postwar Western culture. To understand their impact, this chapter addresses five questions: (1) What shape did the global Cold War assume after 1949? (2) What was the impact of decolonization on both the former imperial powers in western Europe and on the global balance of power? (3) What patterns characterized the history of the Soviet Union and eastern Europe after the death of Stalin? (4) What developments produced the unprecedented political stability and economic prosperity in western Europe in this era? (5) How do we explain social and cultural trends in this time of fast-paced change?

The Cold War, the West, and the World

The specter of a Third World War loomed over Europe in the 1950s. An American anthropologist living in a small French village, for example, found his neighbors reluctant to make any long-range plans. As one farmer explained, "Plant an apricot orchard so the Russians and Americans can use it as a battlefield? Thanks, [I'm] not so dumb."[1] The postwar era saw the leaders of the superpowers struggling with the new horrible possibilities created by nuclear weapons. At the same time, anticolonial nationalist movements and Cold War rivalries flowed together in an unstable and at times combustible mixture.

THE COLD WAR GOES GLOBAL: THE CHINESE REVOLUTION AND THE KOREAN WAR, 1949–1953

China provided the first example of this inflammable mixture. In 1949, the Communists under Mao Zedong won their decades-long battle to assume control of China. Mao followed in Stalin's footsteps, establishing a one-party state and identifying entire social classes as "enemies of the people." To many Western observers, particularly in the United States, Mao's victory heralded a disturbing expansion of communist power. As Mao triumphantly proclaimed, "The East is Red!" The United States refused to recognize China's communist government as legitimate, and international tensions deepened.

In 1950, this vision of a Red East turned the Cold War hot in Korea. A part of the Japanese empire since 1910, Korea regained political independence after Japan's defeat in 1945, but was immediately divided. A Soviet-allied communist regime took over North Korea, and an anti-communist state propped up by the United States was established in the south. In 1950, Stalin gave in to pressure from North Korea's leader, Kim Il-Sung (1912–1994), and agreed to supply arms for an invasion of South Korea. This civil war was quickly swallowed up by the Cold War. A UN-sponsored, largely American army fought alongside South Korean troops, while soldiers from Communist China supported North Korea.

The Korean War accelerated the globalization of the Cold War. U.S. policymakers became convinced that communism was on the march throughout Asia and had to be stopped. As a result of the Korean conflict, the French government was able to persuade Truman's administration to support its struggle against communist nationalists in Indochina, thus drawing the United States into supporting a colonial regime and onto the path that would lead to its war in Vietnam. The conflict in Korea also welded Japan firmly into the Western alliance. As the U.S. army turned to the Japanese for vital military supplies, over $3.5 billion poured into and rejuvenated the Japanese economy. (American military orders for trucks guaranteed the success of a struggling new Japanese firm called Toyota.) Transformed from an occupied enemy to a staunch ally and an economic powerhouse, Japan became the dam holding back "the red tide that threatens to engulf the world."[2] Thus, in a curious way, Japan—geographically as far "East" as one can get—became a part of the "West."

The Korean War demonstrated not only the globalization of the Cold War but also its limits. After three years of fighting and more than three million deaths, Korea remained divided. Stalin refused to send the Red Army into the conflict, and Truman resisted pressure to invade Communist China. This restraint was imposed, at least in part, by new military realities. By 1950, both sides possessed the atomic bomb. Both realized that expanding the war would almost guarantee the use of nuclear weapons. The question, "Is this worth a nuclear war?" proved inescapable.

Often seen as an American affair, the Korean War did involve small numbers of European troops. Far more important, it fostered intense political controversy within western Europe and raised important questions about the role of the United States in European affairs. Fearing that the war's outbreak signaled a more aggressive Soviet policy in Europe as well as Asia, western European leaders pushed for the transformation of NATO from a loose defensive alliance to a coordinated and formidable fighting

CHRONOLOGY

The Cold War, 1950–1962

1950	Outbreak of the Korean War
1953	First American and Soviet hydrogen bomb tests; death of Joseph Stalin; end of the Korean War
1955	First Geneva summit
1956	Hungarian uprising and its repression by Soviet troops
1957	Launch of *Sputnik*
1959	Khrushchev's visit to the United States
1961	Berlin Wall built
1962	Cuban Missile Crisis

force. This transformation, however, came at a price. As the U.S. military budget exploded from $13.5 billion to $50 billion per year, Truman's administration demanded that its European allies strengthen their own military forces and permit the rearmament of West Germany. Konrad Adenauer (1876–1967), West Germany's first chancellor, argued that only a rearmed West Germany could prevent the forcible reunification of Germany on Soviet terms, but with the trauma of German conquest and occupation so recently behind them, many Europeans were horrified by German rearmament. Britain's prime minister Clement Attlee warned, "The policy of using Satan to defeat Sin is very dangerous." Even within West Germany the proposal aroused strong opposition. After four years of controversy and a failed effort to create a western European army (the European Defense Community, or EDC), West Germany rearmed, as the United States had initially demanded, under the NATO umbrella.

BRIDGES AND BRINKMANSHIP: THE COLD WAR, 1953–1963

In 1953, both sides in the Cold War changed leaders. Stalin died in March 1953, just a few months after a new Republican administration headed by President Dwight Eisenhower (1890–1969) took office in the United States. This change of leadership heralded a new phase in the Cold War in which both sides sought to build bridges—to improve communications, find common ground, and thereby ease tensions. But at the same time, both players utilized the contradictory strategy of brinkmanship°, which relied on the threat of nuclear war. Eisenhower's Secretary of State John Foster Dulles (1888–1959) articulated the classic brinkmanship argument: "If you try to run away from [nuclear war], if you are scared to go to the brink, you are lost."[3] With the Cold War veering sharply back and forth between bridge building and brinkmanship, the period from 1953 until 1963 was characterized by heightened hopes and deepening fears, by thawing superpower relations followed by the icy blasts of renewed hostilities.

Summit Talks and Spy Planes

Eisenhower was elected in 1952 with a promise of an aggressive new approach to foreign affairs. He and Dulles rejected Truman's policy of *containing* communism as defeatist, a "negative, futile and immoral policy . . . which abandons countless human beings to a despotism and Godless terrorism."[4] Instead, they committed the United States to *roll back* communism and insisted that communist aggression would be met with massive nuclear retaliation.

The new American brinkmanship was matched on the other side of the Cold War divide. After a period of uncertain leadership following Stalin's death in 1953, Nikita Khrushchev (1955–1964) emerged in 1955 as the new Soviet leader. Loud and boisterous, given to off-the-cuff remarks and spontaneous displays of emotion, Khrushchev contrasted sharply with the disciplined, reserved Stalin. (It is hard to imagine Stalin taking off his shoe and beating it on a table, as Khrushchev did in front of the television cameras at an assembly of the United Nations.) Khrushchev played a dangerous game of nuclear bluff, in which he persistently and often quite successfully convinced allies and foes alike that the Soviet Union possessed a far stronger nuclear force than it actually did.

Both Khrushchev and Eisenhower, however, recognized that the hydrogen bomb made total war unwinnable and both sought ways to break out of the positions into which they were frozen by Cold War hostilities. In July 1955, representatives of Britain, France, the United States, and the Soviet Union met in Geneva for the first summit of the Cold War. Although this summit produced no substantial policies, it marked a crucial psychological step, a bridge across the Cold War divide. In April 1956, Khrushchev traveled on a state visit to Britain—the first Cold War visit of a Soviet leader to a Western nation.

The Cold War froze once again in October 1956, when Khrushchev sent tanks into Hungary to crush a nationalist rebellion there. Less than one year later, the Soviets launched into space the first human-made satellite, *Sputnik*. The crushing of the Hungarian Revolution showed that the Soviets would permit no challenge to their authority in eastern Europe, while the success of *Sputnik* seemed to shift the military balance of power. Khrushchev claimed—falsely—that the Soviets possessed an advanced intercontinental ballistic missile (ICBM) force and that Soviet factories were producing rockets "like sausages from a machine."[5] Many in the West feared that the Soviets were winning the Cold War. To western

Europeans, *Sputnik* had ominous implications. The development of ICBMs meant that American cities were vulnerable to a Soviet nuclear strike. Europeans began to ask themselves whether the United States would actually risk Chicago to save Paris: If the Soviets invaded western Europe with conventional forces, would the Americans respond with nuclear weapons and so open their own cities to nuclear retaliation?

Yet in the late 1950s, the Cold War ice seemed to be breaking once again. In 1958 the Soviet Union announced a voluntary suspension on nuclear testing. The United States and Britain followed suit and nuclear test ban talks opened in Geneva. The next year Khrushchev spent twelve days touring the United States—much to his regret, security concerns kept him from visiting Disneyland. The communist leader impressed Americans as a down-to-earth, ordinary sort of guy, a man rather than a monster. Khrushchev

■ **"We Will Bury You!"**

In sharp contrast to the reserved, taciturn Stalin, Khrushchev often exploded in anger. This *Time* magazine cover from September 1961 shows Khrushchev in a familiar bombastic pose, as the Soviet Union announced that it was resuming above-ground testing of its hydrogen bombs. One of Khrushchev's most memorable lines was his warning to the West about the coming economic supremacy of the Soviet system: "We will bury you!"

ended his U.S. visit with the promise of another four-power summit in 1960.

The summit never happened. A few weeks before the summit was to convene in France, the Soviet Union announced it had shot down an American spy plane and captured its pilot. The summit was aborted, and Cold War relations froze solid once again.

On the Brink: The Berlin Wall and the Cuban Missile Crisis

These incidents initiated one of the most dangerous periods in the Cold War. Soviet defense spending rose by one-third from 1959 to 1963. In the United States, Herman Kahn's *On Thermonuclear War* became a bestseller. Kahn argued that although thermonuclear war would mean the deaths of millions, it remained a winnable scenario. General Tommy Powers, the commander of the U.S. Strategic Air Command (the nuclear strike force), insisted, "At the end of the war, if there are two Americans and one Russian, we win." Europeans found this idea less than reassuring.

Many Europeans and Americans expected nuclear war to begin in the divided city of Berlin. Khrushchev once noted, "Berlin is the testicles of the West . . . Every time I want to make the West scream, I squeeze on Berlin."[6] Yet throughout the 1950s, it was the East, not the West, that found Berlin a rather tender spot on the collective communist body politic. Germans from the East regularly crossed into West Berlin to work, shop—and disappear. All totaled, 2.8 million East Germans (one-sixth of the population) fled west through Berlin between 1949 and 1961. This torrent of emigration seriously weakened the East German economy by siphoning off its most productive citizens. Almost 75 percent of those who emigrated were below age 45, and most were skilled workers or professionals. The continuing destabilization of East Germany and pressure from the East German communist leader Walter Ulbricht (1893–1973) pushed Khrushchev to adopt a dramatic solution in 1961— the construction of the Berlin Wall°, literally a concrete symbol of the Cold War divide.

The new American president, John F. Kennedy (1917–1963), asserted that "a wall is a hell of a lot better than a war,"[7] but relations between the superpowers remained very tense. Kennedy had campaigned for the presidency in 1960 on a strong anticommunist platform, warning Americans (incorrectly) of the Soviet Union's nuclear superiority: "We will mold our strength and become first again. Not first if. Not first but. Not first when. But first period."[8] Two weeks after the Wall went up, the Soviet Union ended a three-year moratorium on nuclear testing. Kennedy increased military spending and called for an expanded civil defense program to prepare the American public for nuclear war. In Britain, the Conservative government stepped up its own civil defense program, while across Europe men and women feared that if nuclear war occurred, their countries would become a wasteland.

Such a war was narrowly avoided in the fall of 1962. This time the battleground was not Berlin but Cuba, as once again the Cold War intersected with a nationalist struggle. In 1959, a nationalist revolutionary movement led by Fidel Castro (b. 1926) succeeded in toppling Fulgencio Batista y Zaldivar (1901–1973), Cuba's corrupt but pro-U.S. dictator. At the time of the revolution, Castro was not a communist. Faced with American hostility to his plans for radical land reform, however, Castro drew closer to the Soviet Union, which offered both economic and military assistance—and revolutionary enthusiasm. The Communist deputy premier Anastas Mikoyan (1895–1978) explained to an American official, "You Americans must realize what Cuba means to us old Bolsheviks. . . . it makes us feel like boys again!"[9] By 1962, Castro and Cuba were firmly within the Soviet communist camp.

Against such a background, the Cuban Missile Crisis unfolded. Aware of American efforts to assassinate Castro and emotionally committed to preserving the Cuban Revolution, Khrushchev decided "to throw a hedgehog at Uncle Sam's pants."[10] NATO nuclear missiles, stationed in Turkey, were aimed at Soviet cities; Khrushchev chose to retaliate in kind. In October 1962, Kennedy received photos, taken by a spy plane, of nuclear missile bases under construction in Cuba. When operational, the missiles would be able to reach every major mainland American city except Seattle. What the photographs did not show, and what Kennedy did not know, was that the Soviet forces in Cuba were armed with nuclear weapons—and with the discretionary power to use these weapons if U.S. forces attacked. Some of Kennedy's advisers urged just such an attack, but instead the president used secret diplomatic channels to lead Khrushchev to a compromise. Khrushchev removed the missiles and in exchange, Kennedy guaranteed that the United States would not invade Cuba and agreed to withdraw the NATO missiles from Turkey (while claiming that the removal of the Turkish missiles was unrelated to events in Cuba).

The Cuban Missile Crisis marked a watershed in the history of the Cold War. In the aftermath of the crisis, both the United States and the Soviet Union backed off from brinkmanship. In 1963, the superpowers agreed to stop aboveground nuclear testing with the Nuclear Test Ban Treaty, and set up between them the "hotline," a direct communications link (at first not a telephone but a system of telegraph lines and teleprinters) to encourage immediate personal consultation in the event of a future crisis.

BREAKING THE BLOCS: THE COLD WAR AFTER THE CRISIS

In the decade after the Cuban Missile Crisis, a series of diplomatic shifts reconfigured global alignments. The rigid bipolarization characteristic of the Cold War during the

1950s broke down; by the early 1970s, multiple poles of power had emerged.

Ostpolitik: Stabilizing Central Europe

The first of these diplomatic shifts occurred in central Europe. During the Cuban Missile Crisis, European political leaders on both sides of the Iron Curtain found themselves powerless, faced with what the British historian Arnold Toynbee described as "annihilation without representation." As a result, the crisis accelerated European efforts to forge paths less controlled by Cold War concerns. It was no coincidence that just one year later, in 1963, West Germany's Social Democratic Party (SPD) demanded a new Ostpolitik or "Eastern policy"—the opening of diplomatic and economic relations between West Germany and the Soviet Union and its satellite states.

In 1969, the West Berlin mayor and SPD leader Willy Brandt (1913–1992) became the chancellor of the West German government and proceeded to make Ostpolitik a reality. In treaties with both Poland and the Soviet Union, Brandt's government accepted Germany's wartime territorial losses and opened up economic links. In 1972 East and West Germany recognized the legitimacy of each other's existence and finally resolved the long-standing Berlin crisis: Brandt's government accepted that East Berlin was part of East Germany, while the Soviet Union guaranteed West German civilians access to West Berlin. In 1973, both Germanies entered the United Nations, a triumphant climax to Ostpolitik.

Detente: Controlling the Arms Race

With Ostpolitik, nations such as West Germany, Poland, and East Germany took the initiative in bridging the Cold War divide. But during this era, the leaders of the superpowers also acted to break down the bipolarities of the Cold War. By the end of the 1960s, both the Soviet Union and the United States faced stagnating economies, and both were spending $50 million per day on nuclear weapons. These economic pressures led Soviet and American leaders to embrace detente°, the effort to stabilize superpower relations through negotiations and arms control. In November 1969 Soviet and American negotiators began the Strategic Arms Limitation Talks (SALT). Signed in 1972, the agreement froze the existing weapons balance. With both superpowers possessing sufficient nuclear weaponry to destroy the globe several times over, SALT may seem to have been inconsequential, but it helped arrest the armaments spiral and, more important, revealed a shift in Cold War power relations.

The Sino-Soviet Split and Ping-Pong Diplomacy

This same era witnessed important changes in relations within the communist world. Throughout the 1930s and 1940s, the Chinese Communist leader Mao Zedong was an obedient disciple of Stalin, whom he regarded as an authoritative "elder brother" in the family of communism. But

---

CHRONOLOGY

The Cold War, 1963–1973

1963	Nuclear Test Ban treaty signed; contacts between China and Soviet Union suspended; West German SPD demands a new Ostpolitik
1964	Khrushchev ousted; beginning of the Brezhnev era; first successful Chinese atomic bomb test
1966	SPD joins West German coalition government
1969	Willy Brandt elected chancellor of West Germany; Ostpolitik accelerated; SALT negotiations begin
1970	West Germany signs treaties with Poland and the Soviet Union
1972	West Germany signs treaty with East Germany; SALT I signed; Nixon visits China
1973	West Germany and East Germany join United Nations

---

from the mid-1950s on, the communist family grew more and more dysfunctional, as Mao opposed Khrushchev's efforts to reform the Soviet system (discussed shortly) and rejected Khruschev's aim of "peaceful co-existence" with the West. Khrushchev, in turn, opposed Mao's "Great Leap Forward," an effort to accomplish in a single year what had taken the Soviet Union twenty years to achieve—the transformation of a peasant agricultural society into an industrial powerhouse. An estimated 30 million Chinese starved to death as a result of Mao's fantasies. Mao took these deaths in stride but his Soviet partners were horrified and in 1960, Khrushchev suspended economic aid to China. In 1963 China refused to sign the Nuclear Test Ban Treaty, and all contacts between the two states were broken. By the time the first Chinese atomic bomb exploded in 1964, the split between China and the Soviet Union was open and irrevocable. The Sino-Soviet border became a militarized zone, the site of frequent clashes as a million Soviet and a million Chinese soldiers stood head to head. In 1969 the Soviets deployed nuclear missiles on the border, and Mao ordered underground nuclear shelters built in every Chinese city. The East was still Red, but red came in two clashing shades.

President Richard Nixon (1913–1994) and his national security adviser Henry Kissinger (b. 1923) decided to take advantage of the growing hostilities between China and the Soviets, and act according to the ancient proverb, "The enemy of my enemy is my friend." In the spring of 1971, Nixon announced the lifting of travel and trade restrictions with China. Mao responded to the American initiative by inviting the U.S. Ping-Pong team to make a highly publicized visit to Beijing. In July 1971, Nixon—a politician who had built his career on fervent anticommunism—sent shock waves through the world by announcing that he would visit China. In the 1950s, "East versus West" had formed a basic building block of international relations. With part of the East now reconciled to the West, the shape of international politics looked much less clear.

Imperial Encounters: Decolonization in a Cold War Context

The Chinese Communist victory in 1949, the outbreak of the Korean War in 1950, and the Cuban Missile Crisis of 1962 all illustrated that the Cold War was not confined to European borders. Across Africa and Asia in the 1950s and 1960s the Soviet Union and the United States used economic and military aid, as well as covert action, to cajole and coerce newly independent nations into choosing sides in the global Cold War conflict. The superpowers served as magnetic poles, drawing toward themselves competing nationalist forces and so entangling Cold War concerns with nationalist independence struggles throughout the world (see Map 28.1).

THE END TO EMPIRE

These struggles grew fierce during the postwar era. As Chapter 26 explained, World War II had strengthened colonial nationalist movements, while at the same time eroding the economic and military resources needed by European governments to hang on to their imperial possessions. The immediate postwar era witnessed the birth of several new nations—India and Pakistan in 1947, Israel in 1948, and Indonesia in 1949. But it is a mistake to think that European governments emerged from the Second World War committed to decolonization. Imperial ties seemed more crucial than ever in the economic hard times following the war. Moreover, faced with the reality of superpower domination in Europe, nations such as Britain and France looked to their imperial possessions to give them international power and prestige. As the British foreign minister Ernest Bevin explained, empire provided the means "to develop our own power and influence to equal that of the U.S. of A. and the U.S.S.R."[11]

During the 1950s, then, the British adopted a "yes, but later" approach to African independence. They sought to diminish the force of colonial nationalism by diverting it down channels of constitutional reform and complicated systems of power sharing—and then fiercely and futilely stomping down on nationalists who broke out of these channels. Many African leaders, such as Kwame Nkrumah (1957–1966) in Ghana and Jomo Kenyatta (1963–1978) in Kenya, moved from British prison cells to prime ministerial or presidential offices.

France also resisted decolonization. In 1954, the French army suffered a decisive defeat at Dien Bien Phu in North Vietnam. Dien Bien Phu marked the end of France's eight-year war against the communist nationalist forces of Ho Chi Minh and the end of France's empire in Indochina. Humiliated by this defeat, French army officers responded ferociously to the outbreak of a nationalist revolt in Algeria that same year. Many prominent politicians and ordinary men and women shared the army's view that France had

■ **Imperial Retreat**
On May 7, 1954, French forces surrendered to Vietnamese rebels at Dien Bien Phu. The battle quickly became a symbol of the retreat of Europe from its imperialist strongholds.

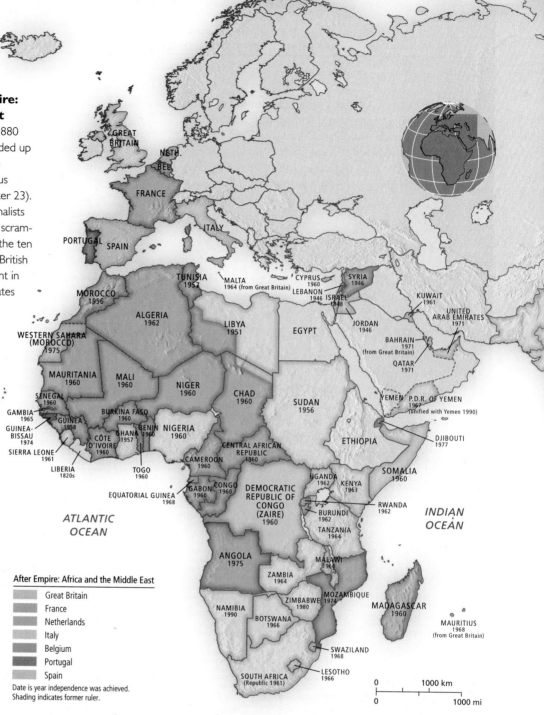

■ Map 28.1 After Empire: Africa and the Middle East

In just three decades, between 1880 and 1919, European nations divided up between them almost the entire African continent in the notorious "scramble for Africa" (see Chapter 23). In just one decade African nationalists effected an even more dramatic scramble *out* of sub-Saharan Africa. In the ten years after Ghana (formerly the British Gold Coast) became independent in 1957, thirty-two independent states were formed.

After Empire: Africa and the Middle East

- Great Britain
- France
- Netherlands
- Italy
- Belgium
- Portugal
- Spain

Date is year independence was achieved.
Shading indicates former ruler.

been pushed too far, and must now stand fast. The result was the Franco-Algerian War, a brutal fight that raged until the early 1960s. Like the Dreyfus Affair of the 1890s (see Chapter 22), the Algerian conflict divided friendships and families. Supporters of the French army in Algeria saw it as a force fighting on behalf of Western civilization against barbarism (both Arab and communist). Critics, pointing to the evidence that the French army used torture against its enemies, argued that the war threatened to corrupt French society.

By the time Algeria claimed independence in 1962, approximately 200,000 Algerian nationalist fighters had been killed or imprisoned, 15,000 French soldiers and auxiliary forces were dead, and almost 23,000 civilians in both France and Algeria had fallen victim to terrorist attack. Another casualty of this conflict was the Fourth Republic, the political structure erected in France after World War II. With France on the brink of civil war in 1958—French army officers were preparing an assault on Paris—Charles De Gaulle forced through a new constitution, which sharply tilted the balance of power in French domestic politics toward the president (conveniently De Gaulle himself).

As the Algerian crisis showed, decolonization was not something that just happened "out there" in the world beyond western Europe; rather it had an often profound impact on European political life. The loss of empire also led to a series of cultural encounters within European societies. Decolonization resulted in an upsurge in immigration. White settlers retreated back to their country of origin, and colonial "losers"—indigenous groups that had allied with the now-defeated colonial powers—fled because they feared discrimination, retribution, or perhaps simply a loss of status. In France, for example, Algerian independence led to the influx not only of Algeria's white French population but also of 80,000 Algerian Harkis whose loyalty to the colonial administration jeopardized their place in the new Algeria. The white settler groups often brought with them hardened racist attitudes, while the presence of nonwhite minority groups, clustered in certain cities, sparked resentment in societies unused to cultural diversity. Thus racism became more overt in European political and social life.

In the United States, too, decolonization had a significant cultural impact. The burgeoning African-American civil rights movement compared the systemic racism of American society to the repression endured by colonial populations. Organizations such as the National Association for the Advancement of Colored People (NAACP), founded in 1910, had long fought against racial discrimination in the United States, but in the 1950s the civil-rights struggle became a mass movement with an innovative program of "freedom rides," lunch counter sit-ins, boycotts, and voter registration campaigns. Martin Luther King Jr. (1929–1968) and other civil-rights leaders directly linked the civil-rights struggle to the colonial independence movements happening at the same time. In King's words, "the determination of Negro Americans to win freedom from all forms of oppression springs from the same deep longing that motivates oppressed peoples all over the world."[12]

THE IMPERIALIST LEGACY

The legacy of imperialist rule lingered long, particularly in areas with large white European settlement such as Rhodesia and South Africa. Despite UN sanctions and a violent black nationalist movement, white settlers in Rhodesia (present-day Zimbabwe) retained a lock on political and economic power until 1980. In South Africa, the white supremacist Afrikaner Nationalist Party assumed control in 1948 and implemented the policies of apartheid°, the rigid segregation of communities based on race. To break down any chance of resistance, the apartheid regime deliberately accentuated tribal divisions among black South Africans and denied them basic human rights. The "No Trial Act" of 1963, for example, gave the government the right to detain anyone, without charge or trial, for as long as it chose.

Imperialism also left a long-lasting economic legacy. European states lost their monopoly on the raw materials and markets of their one-time colonies, yet in the postcolo-

CHRONOLOGY

The End to European Empire

1946	French colonial war in Indochina begins
1947	India, Pakistan, and Burma achieve independence from British rule
1948	State of Israel established; apartheid regime in South Africa comes into power
1949	Indonesia achieves independence from Dutch rule
1954	Defeat of French forces in Indochina; partition of North and South Vietnam; beginning of Franco-Algerian War
1955	Bandung Conference: the "Third World" is born
1956	Suez Crisis
1957	Kwame Nkrumah becomes first prime minister of independent Ghana
1960	Congo achieves independence from Belgian rule; Nigeria achieves independence from British rule; most French colonies in tropical Africa become independent
1962	Algeria achieves independence from French rule
1963	Jomo Kenyatta becomes first prime minister of independent Kenya
1965	U.S. bombing of North Vietnam begins
1967	Suharto ousts Sukarno as leader of Indonesia

nial era, African states grew more economically dependent than ever on the West, a development that anti-Western African nationalists labeled "neo-colonialism." Desperate for cash, newly independent African governments increased production of cash crops for export—cotton, coffee, nuts, sugar—and also expanded their mining industries, producing uranium, lithium, copper, tin, gold, diamonds, and zinc for Western markets. Such exports were extremely vulnerable to fluctuations in demand and prices. At the same time, African nations became ever more dependent on importing manufactured goods from the industrialized West, with aid from Western nations often contingent on trading deals requiring such imports.

For many of the newly independent nations of Africa and Asia, political stability proved as elusive as economic prosperity. To be solid, democratic political structures must rest on a foundation of popular participation, yet almost a century of imperialist rule made such participation very problematic. For example, when the Congo became independent in 1960, it possessed only sixteen university graduates out of a population of 13 million—the result of the Belgian policy of restricting Congolese children to a basic education. In Africa as a whole, 80 percent of the African people could not read or write. Not surprisingly, then, by 1966 military regimes had replaced elected governments in the former colonial territories of Nigeria, Congo Brazzaville, Burkina Faso, Algeria, the Benin Republic, and the Central African Republic. In many newly independent states, competition between rival groups for power led to civil war. Nigeria, which gained independence from Britain in 1960, was overcome by political corruption and regional secession. In its civil war, which began in 1966, at least one million people died, either in battle or from starvation. The Congo stepped directly from Belgian rule in 1960 into a protracted civil war.

COLD WAR EMPIRES

Both superpowers played a role in the Congolese civil war, a good example of the way decolonization became entangled with Cold War rivalries. While Stalin had directed Soviet aid to regimes sharing borders with the Soviet Union (such as North Korea), Khrushchev opted for a far more aggressive approach, using military and economic aid to foster communist movements in Asia, Africa, and South America. Seeking to limit communist expansion, as well as to ensure access to crucial energy and mineral resources, the United States responded by using its economic and military power to cultivate pro-Western (but not always democratic) regimes.

In many regions, superpower influence replaced imperial control. The abrupt withdrawal of Belgium from the Congo in 1960, for example, catapulted that nation into a cauldron of political upheaval and diplomatic maneuvering. Both overt and covert superpower involvement brought the situation to a boil. U.S. intervention included an aborted CIA plot to assassinate the Congo's first elected leader, Patrice Lumumba. (Lumumba was murdered in 1961, but by political rivals rather than American intelligence operatives).

Increasingly in the Middle East, the United States replaced Britain and France as the regional powerbroker. This important reworking of the global power equation became dramatically evident in 1956, when the British and French governments attempted a military invasion of Egypt in an effort to return the Suez Canal to European control. The resulting "Suez Crisis" proved a disaster for France and Britain, when the United States used its economic clout to push Britain to the brink of financial collapse and so force British troops to withdraw.

REJECTING THE WEST

·················

Born in Martinique, Frantz Fanon became a champion of Algerian independence. He died of leukemia in 1961, shortly before an independent Algeria came into being. His writings, published posthumously, articulated clearly the discontent of the colonized. Riveting dissections of the relations of power in Western capitalism, they also helped inspire the protests of 1968.

"The last shall be first and the first last."* Decolonization is the putting into practice of this sentence.... The naked truth of decolonization evokes for us the searing bullets and bloodstained knives which emanate from it. For if the last shall be first, this will only come to pass after a murderous and decisive struggle between the two protagonists.

. . . . As soon as the native begins to pull on his moorings, and to cause anxiety to the settler, he is handed over to well-meaning souls who in cultural congresses point out to him the specificity and wealth of Western values. But . . . it so happens that when the native hears a speech about Western culture he pulls out his knife—or at least he makes sure it is within reach. The violence with which the supremacy of white values is affirmed and the aggressiveness which has permeated the victory of these values over the ways of life and thought of the native mean that, in revenge, the native laughs in mockery when Western values are mentioned in front of him.

. . . . For centuries the capitalists have behaved in the under-developed world like nothing more than war criminals. Deportations, massacres, forced labour and slavery have been the main methods used by capitalism to increase its wealth, its gold or diamond reserves, and to establish its power. . . . So when we hear the head of a European state declare with his hand on his heart that he must come to the help of the poor under-developed peoples, we do not tremble with gratitude. Quite the contrary; we say to ourselves: "It's a just reparation which will be paid to us."

───────

* Fanon is quoting Jesus' words in Matthew 19:30. But as the rest of the excerpt makes clear, Fanon's interpretation of this verse contrasts with the usual Christian emphasis on submission.

Source: From Frantz Fanon, *The Wretched of the Earth*, translated by Constance Farrington. Copyright © 1963 by Présence Africaine. Used by permission.

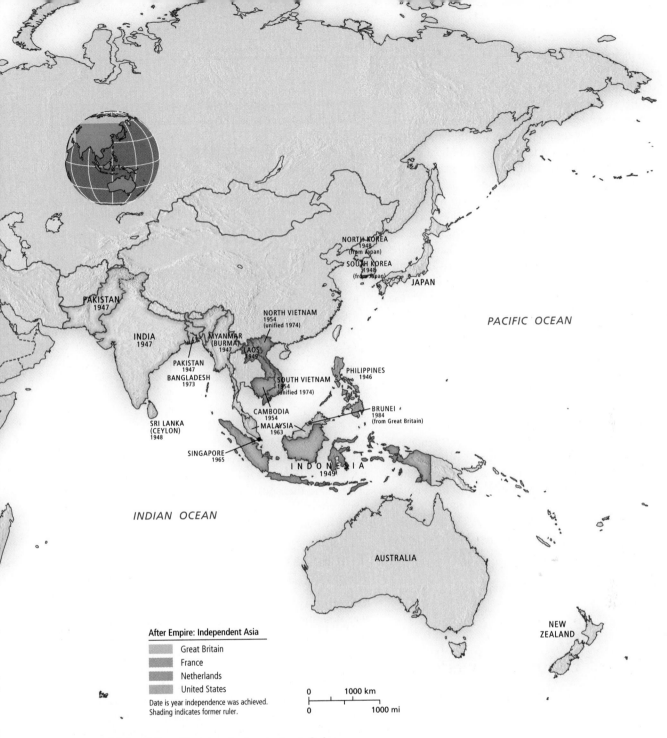

■ Map 28.2   After Empire: Independent Asia

Dates of national formation often give no indication of the continuing political upheaval and violence that afflicted the countries of Asia in the postwar period. The formation of the nations of Vietnam, Laos, and Cambodia in 1953–1954, for example, did not mean an end to warfare in Indochina.

But it was in Vietnam where superpower rivalries were most dramatically superimposed onto a colonial conflict. The withdrawal of French imperial forces from Indochina in 1954 after the French army's humiliating defeat at Dien Bien Phu opened the door to superpower intervention in the region. The Indochinese peninsula was divided, with communist North Vietnam propped up by the Soviet Union, and anticommunist South Vietnam buttressed by American economic and military aid (see Map 28.2). Under the Kennedy presidency (1961–1963), the number of military advisors in Vietnam expanded rapidly, as did American involvement in South Vietnamese politics. When Kennedy's successor, Lyndon Johnson (1908–1973), took office, he issued a clear order, "Win the war!" In 1964, the American Congress granted Johnson the authority to take "all necessary measures" to do so. By 1966, 429,000 American soldiers were fighting in Vietnam. From the U.S. perspective, the Vietnam War was an episode in the Cold War, an effort to block the expansion of communism in Southeast Asia. But to the North Vietnamese leader Ho Chi Minh, the fight against American troops was another chapter in a decades-long struggle against Western colonial rule.

Many newly independent nations sought to resist being pulled into the orbit of either superpower. In 1955, Ahmed Sukarno (1949–1966), the nationalist leader who had led Indonesia out from under Dutch rule six years before, hosted the Bandung Conference of "nonaligned" nations. Bandung signaled the desire of many national leaders to find a place for their nations between or apart from the United States or the Soviet Union. French journalists at the conference gave these nations a collective label—neither the first (Western, capitalist) nor the second (Eastern, communist) but rather the Third World°. Few of these nonaligned nations had much power on their own, but the General Assembly of the United Nations provided them with an important forum for making their voice heard. As the pace of decolonization accelerated, the number of independent nations voting in the UN grew. But genuine independence proved difficult to retain, as the example of Indonesia demonstrates. Despite Sukarno's call for nonalignment, the need for material and military assistance pushed him to lead Indonesia into the Soviet sphere of influence. Then, in 1967, General Mohamed Suharto (b. 1921) succeeded Sukarno after a bloody coup. With his country's rivers clogged with the headless corpses of 100,000 victims, Suharto aligned Indonesia with the West.

After Stalin:
The Soviet Union and Eastern Europe in the 1950s and 1960s

·· ■ ··

Divided by the Cold War, eastern and western Europe followed separate paths in the postwar era (see Map 28.3). Yet despite the ideological divide, certain commonalities linked both sides. Eastern and western Europeans alike lived under the threat of nuclear war, even as both sets of peoples benefited from the Cold War's deflection of military conflict away from the European continent to other parts of the globe. Intra-European rivalries decreased. Populations on both sides of the divide also experienced greater prosperity and a rise in living standards. Thus, in contrast to the sharp bends and turns of international affairs in this era, European domestic politics achieved remarkable stability.

In the East, however, this stability was imposed by force and transposed into stagnation. After a time of tumult

---

CHRONOLOGY

The Soviet Bloc in the Postwar Era

1953	Death of Stalin; relaxation of terror in eastern Europe and Soviet Union; "New Course" in Hungary underway under Nagy
1955	Khrushchev emerges as new Soviet leader
1956	Khrushchev's "Secret Speech," de-Stalinization accelerates; unrest in Poland results in new regime under Gomulka; Hungarian Revolution crushed by Soviet forces
1964	Khrushchev ousted; Brezhnev era begins
1968	Prague Spring crushed

---

associated with de-Stalinization°, or Khrushchev's efforts to reform the communist system, maintaining the status quo became the *raison d'être* of its ruling elites. To sustain the system and their positions in it, they sought to improve the living conditions of their populations without surrendering effective political and economic control.

THE SOVIET UNION: FROM DE-STALINIZATION TO STAGNATION

Emerging as the new Soviet leader in 1955, Khrushchev was determined to prove the superiority of communism over capitalism—to his own people and to the world. A true communist success story, Khrushchev was born to illiterate peasants, began work as a coal miner at age 14, and rose to the top of the Soviet system. Recognized as a man with talent by the Communist Party, he was trained as an engineer and helped build the Moscow subway system. Khrushchev owed everything to the Communist Party, and he never forgot it. Confident in the moral and material superiority of communism, Khrushchev believed that the Soviet Union would win the Cold War on the economic battlefield. But this ultimate victory would take place only if Soviet living standards substantially improved, and only if the Stalinist systems of terror and rigid centralized control were dismantled.

Khrushchev's determination to set communism on a new course became clear in February 1956 when, in a lengthy speech before the Twentieth Congress of the Communist Party, he shocked his listeners by detailing and condemning Stalin's crimes. Although delivered to a closed session, the speech soon appeared in the Western press and gained worldwide attention. This "Secret Speech" marked the beginning of de-Stalinization, a time of greater openness in the Communist bloc as governments dismantled many of the controls on speech and publication, and for the first time in years dissent and debate reappeared in public life.

The most dramatic sign of de-Stalinization was the release of at least four and a half million prisoners from slave labor camps. As one Soviet citizen recalled, their return was disturbing: "in railway trains and stations, there appeared survivors of the camps, with leaden grey hair, sunken eyes, and a faded look; they choked and dragged their feet like old men."[13] These survivors often returned to find their spouses remarried, their children embarrassed by their presence, their world destroyed. Some, such as Alexander Solzhenitsyn, wrote horrifying accounts of their experiences. Solzhenitsyn's books narrated the daily degradation of prison life and provided a detailed map of the network of slave labor camps that he christened "The Gulag Archipelago."

De-Stalinization did not mean an end to all political and cultural repression in the Soviet Union. In 1959 the Gulag still held at least a million prisoners. Religious believers found that conditions worsened under Khrushchev. As part

■ **Map 28.3   Europe in the Cold War**

As this map shows, during the Cold War the "West" was defined culturally and politically, rather than in geographic terms. Greece and Turkey stand far to the east in Europe, yet their membership in NATO placed both within the "West."

of his effort to revitalize communist culture, Khrushchev embarked on a massive offensive against religious practice, which included the razing of churches, the arrest of clergy, the closure of seminaries and monasteries, and even in some cases the forcible removal of children from Christian homes. The number of both Orthodox and Protestant churches dropped by 50 percent. At the same time, anti-Semitism continued to mark communist policy and practice, with Soviet Jews targeted for harassment and repression.

De-Stalinization also failed to remedy the long-term economic weaknesses of the Soviet Union. In 1962, per capita consumption of consumer goods stood at only 40 to 60 percent that of France, West Germany, and Britain. In agriculture, the economic sector where the Soviet Union lagged the furthest behind the West, Khrushchev embarked on an ambitious reform program, which included rapid mechanization, a massive chemical fertilizer program, and the plowing of virgin lands. He refused to retreat from collectivization, however. As a result, the fundamental productivity problem remained unsolved—and in fact worsened in the long term as immense ecological damage was inflicted on the Soviet countryside. Soil erosion increased exponentially, nitrogen runoff from fertilized fields contaminated water supplies, and overirrigation led to salinization and a decline in soil fertility. The full force of these problems would not be felt until the 1980s, but as early as 1963 the Soviet Union had to import Western grain, a humiliating admission of failure for Khrushchev's regime.

Khrushchev's reforms unsettled many high-ranking communists; as a result, he was forced out of office in 1964. After a short period of collective leadership, Leonid Brezhnev (1906–1982) emerged as the new Soviet leader, a position he held until his death in 1982. A polite man with no interest in literature, art, or original ideas, Brezhnev was far more reassuring to Soviet bureaucrats than the flamboyant Khrushchev, whose boisterous embrace of new ideas and ambitious schemes had proven so destabilizing. Fifty-eight years old and already physically ailing when he assumed the party leadership, the increasingly decrepit Brezhnev matched his era.

Under Brezhnev the Soviet economy stagnated. Growth rates in both industrial production and labor productivity slowed during the second half of the 1960s. In the 1970s, growth virtually ceased. This economic stagnation was, however, masked by improving living standards. Brezhnev continued policies implemented by his predecessor such as free higher education and rising wages, while accelerating the expansion of consumer goods. In addition, state subsidies ensured that the cost of utilities, public transport, and rents remained far lower than in the West (although apartments were in short supply), and an extensive welfare system eased pressures on ordinary people.

By the middle of the 1960s, the Soviet Union appeared to have achieved a sort of stability. It was, however, a stability built on repression as well as stagnation. Judging de-Stalinization to be a risky business, Brezhnev and his colleagues embarked on a rehabilitation of Stalin's reputation. As statues of the dictator began to reappear, the limited cultural and intellectual freedoms introduced under Khrushchev vanished. Rigid censorship and repression once again characterized Soviet society. Those who expressed dissident views soon found themselves denied employment and educational opportunities, imprisoned, sent to the Gulag, or confined indefinitely in a psychiatric ward.

Yet dissent did not disappear. Soviet society may have resembled a stagnant pond by the 1970s, but beneath the surface churned dangerous currents that, in the late 1980s, would engulf the entire communist system. Reviving a practice employed by reformers under the tsarist regime, dissidents evaded the censors by *samizdat* or "self-publishing." Novels, plays, poetry, political treatises, and historical studies were circulated privately, copied by hand or duplicated on treasured (and often confiscated) typewriters and photocopiers and distributed more widely.

Nationalism among the non-Russian populations served as the source of much discontent within the Soviet Union during this era. As the Soviet economy grew, Russian managers and technicians were sent to places such as oil-rich Kazakhstan. Russian immigration to the Baltic states was particularly dramatic: In 1970, native Latvians made up only 59 percent of the Latvian population. Resentment of these Russian immigrants, perceived as the privileged representatives of a colonialist power, escalated. Non-Russians increasingly equated centralized economic and political control with Russian dominance rather than with communist ideology. By the mid-1960s, clandestine nationalist political organizations had emerged in almost every non-Russian republic of the Soviet Union.

DIVERSITY AND DISSENT IN EASTERN EUROPE

Despite the uniformity imposed by Soviet-style communist systems during these decades, the nations of eastern Europe developed in different ways. De-Stalinization contributed to this diversification. In his "Secret Speech" of 1955, Khrushchev declared, "it is ridiculous to think that revolutions are made to order"[14] and so signaled that communist nations could follow paths diverging from the road traveled by the Soviet Union.

But just how far from the Soviet road could those paths go? The contrasting fates of Poland and Hungary in 1956 provide the answer. In Poland, popular protests against rigid Stalinist controls proved strong enough in 1956 to bring back into power Władysław Gomułka (1905–1982), an influential Polish communist who had been purged in the Stalinist terror of 1951. Under Gomułka, Poland abandoned the economically disastrous policy of collectivization. Gomułka made clear, however, that Poland could not leave the Warsaw Pact.

Events took a different course in Hungary. Between 1953 and 1956, Hungary pursued a de-Stalinizing "New Course" under the leadership of the reformist communist Imre Nagy (1896–1958). Like Gomułka, Nagy broke with Stalinist economics, permitting a slower pace of industrialization, the production of more consumer goods, and the relaxation of agricultural collectivization. But unlike Gomułka, Nagy proved unable to resist demands for a break with the Soviet Union. By October 1956, hundreds of thousands of Hungarians were on the streets of Budapest, chanting, "We will never again be slaves." On October 31, Hungary withdrew from the Warsaw Pact—or tried to. Four days later, Khrushchev sent in the tanks. As many as 20,000 Hungarians may have died in early November as the Red Army crushed all resistance.[15] Nagy was executed in 1958.

The repression of the Hungarian revolt defined the limits of de-Stalinization in eastern Europe: The Soviet Union's satellite states could not follow paths that led out of the Warsaw Pact. Within the confines of this structure and of the one-party state, however, the governments of eastern Europe continued to pursue different courses. East Germany, for example, became the most industrially advanced and urbanized country in eastern Europe, while Poland's countryside was dotted with family farms. In Hungary, Nagy was succeeded not by a hardline Stalinist but by János Kádár (1912–1989), a reformist communist who had survived torture and imprisonment during the Stalinist purge of the early 1950s. Kádár's Hungary became the most liberal country in the Eastern bloc, with debate encouraged within the Communist Party, censorship loosened on film studios and publishers, and private business ventures encouraged. In sharp contrast, Romanians endured the reign of the "mini-Stalins." Gheorghe Gheorghiu-Dej (1901–1965) and Nicolae Ceaușescu (1918–1989) imposed not only one-party but one-man control over the country through Stalinist methods of terror. Their monomaniacal construction schemes, which dwarfed even Stalin's efforts, destroyed the Romanian economy. Yet at the same time, they pursued a remarkably independent foreign policy that included negotiating economic aid from the United States and France.

Within the diverse experiences of eastern Europeans, certain commonalities characterized the history of this era. Except in Romania and even more oppressive Albania, living standards improved. Educational opportunities expanded, the supply of consumer goods increased, and political repression became less overt. Even so, overcentralization, bureaucratic mismanagement, and political corruption ensured that living standards remained below those of the West. Moreover, the very consumer goods that

■ **De-Stalinization**

On October 31, 1956, Hungarian demonstrators pulled down a huge statue of Joseph Stalin and then dragged it two miles through the city center. Stalin's head still sits at an intersection in Budapest.

were supposed to persuade Soviet and eastern European citizens of the superiority of the communist system instead demonstrated its deficiencies. With a radio, a Hungarian teenager could tune into Radio Free Europe, and through its rock-and-roll programs, hear of a livelier, more abundant society in the West. In East Germany, television watchers could view West German networks and catch a glimpse of Western prosperity.

PRAGUE 1968: THE DESTRUCTION OF SOCIALISM WITH A HUMAN FACE

Discontent and dissent simmered throughout the eastern bloc during the 1960s. Samizdat publishing, so important a feature of the dissident movement in the Soviet Union, also tied together reform movements throughout eastern Europe. In 1968, however, these reform efforts received a fatal blow. When eastern bloc armies crushed a multifaceted popular protest in Czechoslovakia, they also crushed all hopes that the communist system could be reformed.

During the 1960s, a reform movement emerged in the ranks of the Czechoslovakian Communist Party. It included both Slovaks, who believed that the regime's highly centralized policies favored Czechs, and the new elite of highly educated technocrats who resented the power of poorly educated party superiors. At the beginning of 1968, this resentment fueled an intraparty revolution. Longtime communist leader Antonín Novotný (1952–1968) was removed

■ Crushing the Prague Spring, 1968
Confronted with the overwhelming might of the Warsaw Pact armies, many Czechs tried to reason with the invading soldiers, who could do little but shrug and say they were only obeying orders.

from office and replaced by the reformist Communist (and Slovak) Alexander Dubček (1921–1992). Dubček embarked on a program of radical reform, aimed at achieving "socialism with a human face." This more humane socialism included freedom of speech, press, assembly, and travel; the removal of Communist Party controls from social and cultural life; and decentralization of the economy. Dubček's effort to reform the system from the top quickly merged with a wider popular protest movement that had arisen among intellectuals, artists, students, and workers. The result was the "Prague Spring"°—the blossoming of political and social freedoms throughout Czechoslovakia, but especially in the capital city of Prague.

Well aware of the fate of Hungary in 1956, Dubček reassured Brezhnev and the other Soviet leaders that these reforms would not lead Czechoslovakia out of the Warsaw Pact. But by the summer of 1968, many of the ideas of the Prague activists were filtering through to other eastern European countries and to the Soviet Union itself. In Ukraine, nationalist protesters looked to Prague for inspiration, while in Poland, student riots, which broke out in all the major cities, featured placards reading "Poland is awaiting its own Dubček." Frightened communist leaders throughout the eastern bloc demanded that Brezhnev act to stifle the Prague Spring.

On the night of August 20–21, 80,000 troops—drawn not only from the Soviet Union but also Poland, Hungary, and East Germany—crossed the Czech border. They were immediately confused: Czechs had removed road signs and painted over street numbers in order to confound the invaders. Thirty Czechs died on the first day of the invasion,

and hundreds more were injured. The resistance spread. Workers went on strike, 20,000 Czechs marched in Prague to protest the invasion, and children ran in front of the tanks, shaking their fists. But over the next several weeks, the Prague Spring was crushed. The scientists, artists, and intellectuals who had supported the movement found themselves either in prison or unemployed. As one Communist Party journal explained, the new regime "will not permit all flowers to blossom. We will cultivate, water, and protect only one flower, the red rose of Marxism."

But that rose needed an army to hold it up. In the fall of 1968, Brezhnev acknowledged that Soviet domination in eastern Europe rested on force alone when he articulated what came to be known as the "Brezhnev Doctrine." Formally a commitment to support global socialism, the Brezhnev Doctrine was essentially a promise to use the Red Army to stomp on any eastern European effort to achieve fundamental change.

Even more important, after 1968 eastern Europeans recognized the futility of attempting to reform a system that had now been revealed as beyond reform. Many, perhaps most, eastern Europeans retreated to private worlds of friendship and family life (or to the easy escape provided by alcohol). Others, however, refused to give up or to give in to a system they now viewed as utterly corrupt. They sought, in the words of the Czech playwright and dissident Václav Havel (b. 1936), to "live in truth" in the midst of a society based on lies. As the Polish author Konstanty Gebert explained, living in truth raised "a small, portable barricade between me and silence, submission, humiliation, shame. Impregnable for tanks, uncircumventable. As long as I man it, there is, around me, a small area of freedom."

The West: Integration and Affluence

As in eastern Europe, Cold War concerns helped shape postwar societies in western Europe. Fear of communism furthered the integration of Europe's economies and helped define the political centrism characteristic of western Europe in the 1950s and 1960s. The dominant fact of the postwar years was, however, material prosperity as western European economies embarked on two decades of dramatic economic growth and consumer spending.

THE TRIUMPH OF POLITICAL CONSENSUS

In both the United States and Europe during this era, the Cold War constricted the parameters of political debate. Joseph McCarthy (1908–1957), a senator from Wisconsin, catapulted himself to international prominence by charging that communists occupied key positions in the U.S. State Department, the Hollywood establishment, and American universities. Writers, actors, film producers, social activists, scientists, and intellectuals found themselves on trial, stigmatized, unemployable. In western Europe, anticommunism never dominated political culture to this extent; it did, however, accelerate a broad retreat from the radicalism of the immediate postwar years. With the exception of the Scandinavian countries, conservative parties held power throughout western Europe during the 1950s. In West Germany, the Communist Party was banned in 1956. In France and Italy, communist parties remained popular, drawing 20 to 30 percent of the vote, but their exclusion from office after 1947–1948 effectively marginalized them.

With the communists outlawed or isolated, and with the ideologies of the extremist Right such as fascism and Nazism thoroughly discredited by the horrors of the war, western European politics took on a new and marked stability during the 1950s and early 1960s. Even France, severely divided by colonial crises and subject to nineteen different governments between 1948 and 1958, witnessed the emergence of a basic consensus on the outlines and aims of domestic political life. The Cold War placed strong pressure on Social Democratic parties to moderate or even abandon their Marxist ideology, in order to carve out a place for themselves in the anticommunist political culture. In sharp contrast to the interwar years, the parties in power in western Europe in the 1950s and 1960s, and the voters who put them there, agreed on the viability and virtues of parliamentary democracy. The new constitutions of France, West Germany, and Italy guaranteed the protection of individual rights, and French and Italian women achieved suffrage. The democratic ideal of the universal franchise had finally been realized in most of western Europe.

After 1945, citizenship took on a wider meaning in the West. It embraced not only the right to vote but also the right to a decent standard of living. Through the nationalization of key industries, the establishment of public agencies to oversee and encourage investment and trade, and the manipulation of interest rates and currency supplies, governments assumed the task of ensuring full employment and industrial prosperity for their citizens. A slogan of the German Social Democratic Party—"as much competition as possible, as much planning as necessary"—sums up an approach common to much of western Europe at this time. This commitment, however, embraced a variety of national styles. The British stressed the nationalization of heavy industry, while the French emphasized the role of centralized planning. Led by the pragmatic visionary Jean Monnet (1888–1979), France's postwar Planning Commission set economic targets and directed investment. In contrast, in West Germany, where centralized direction of the economy was linked to Nazism, politicians chose a more free-market path to industrial success.

Yet even in West Germany, citizens had access to an extensive welfare system. With the construction of comprehensive welfare states, postwar governments undertook to guarantee their citizens adequate incomes and medical care. By the end of the 1950s, the average western European working class family received 63 percent of its income from wages. The substantial remaining income came from welfare benefits such as family allowances, national health services, sickness and disability insurance, and old-age pensions. In addition, state-run vaccination and inoculation programs, stricter sanitation regulation, and the development of policies to control communicable diseases all meant an improvement in the health of Europe's populations.

The postwar political consensus was reflected in the triumph of centrist politics. Christian Democratic° parties—which have no American or British counterpart—flourished on the Continent during the postwar era. Drawing on a Roman Catholic base for their support and espousing a largely conservative social ideology combined with a progressive commitment to the welfare state, Christian Democratic parties dominated much of European politics in the 1950s and 1960s. Christian Democratic parties played significant roles in the political life of France and Belgium, governed West Germany between 1949 and 1969, and provided every prime minister except two in Italy between 1945 and 1993.

Three factors account for Christian Democracy's success. First, as anticommunists and advocates of the free market, Christian Democrats benefited from Cold War anxieties and more directly from American aid and support. Second, because they were based on religion (Roman Catholicism) rather than class, Christian Democratic parties were able to appeal to both middle-class and working-class voters, and particularly to women, who tended to vote more conservatively than men. But finally and most important, the triumph of Christian Democracy rested on its dramatic transformation from a right-wing to a centrist

---

CHRONOLOGY

Conservatives in Power in Western Europe

1945	Christian Democrat De Gaspari becomes prime minister of Italy
1949	Christian Democrat Adenauer becomes first chancellor of West Germany
1951	Conservatives replace Labour in power in Britain
1958	French Fourth Republic replaced by more authoritarian regime of De Gaulle

political movement. In the interwar period, Christian Democracy, rooted in a religious and political tradition based on hierarchy and authoritarianism, had veered close to fascism. But during World War II, many Catholics served in the resistance movement, where they absorbed progressive political ideas. This war-inspired desire to use the power of the state to improve the lives of ordinary people blended with more traditional Catholic paternalism. After the war the Christian Democrats not only jettisoned their authoritarianism and embraced democracy, they also supported the construction of comprehensive welfare states.

ECONOMIC INTEGRATION: THE COMMON MARKET

Just as western European societies became more politically integrated within their borders, so they became more economically integrated across their borders. The formation of the European Economic Community° (EEC) or Common Market° in 1957 marks a significant moment in not only the economic history of western Europe but also in its wider political and social development. As we will see in Chapter 29, from the 1980s on the states within this economic union moved steadily toward greater political integration as well.

The idea of European union took shape during World War II as Europeans, fighting in conditions of unprecedented horror, looked for ways to guarantee a lasting peace. In 1943, Jean Monnet, who would oversee French economic planning in the postwar era, declared, "there will be no peace in Europe, if the states are reconstituted on the basis of national sovereignty." Resistance fighters, already drawn to radical ideas, embraced Monnet's vision of a Europe no longer divided by national boundaries. In July 1944, resistance leaders from France, Italy, the Netherlands, and a number of other countries met in Geneva and declared their support for a federal, democratic Europe.

No such radical restructuring of Europe occurred, but the push toward greater European union moved forward in the years after the war. Cold War concerns played a significant role. Opposition to Stalin helped western Europeans see themselves as part of a single region with common interests. At the same time, American postwar planners—anxious to restore economic prosperity to Europe in order to lessen the appeal of communism—urged their European colleagues to dismantle trade barriers and coordinate national economic plans. As Chapter 26 explained, recipients of Marshall Plan aid were required to develop transnational institutions to oversee the distribution and use of American funds. Looking back on this early stage of European integration, the Belgian prime minister (and ardent proponent of European union) Paul-Henri Spaak (1899–1972) wrote in the later 1960s, "Europeans, let us be modest. It is the fear

of Stalin and the daring views of Marshall which led us into the right path."[16]

Spaak was a socialist, but many Christian Democrats also promoted European economic union, including Konrad Adenauer, the first chancellor of West Germany; Alcide de Gaspari, the postwar prime minister of Italy; and the French foreign minister Robert Schuman (1886–1963). Schuman's upbringing opened him to an internationalist perspective: Reared in Alsace under both German and French rule, Schuman had served as a German army officer before he entered French politics.

Desperate to break down the nationalist and economic rivalries that had led to World War II, Schuman in 1950 proposed the merger of the German and French coal and steel industries. The resulting European Coal and Steel Community (ECSC), established in 1952, comprised not only Germany and France, but also Italy and the Benelux countries (Belgium, the Netherlands, and Luxembourg). It proved to be an economic success, promoting the efficient exploitation of western European steel and coal resources and stimulating economic growth throughout the member economies. But advocates of European union, such as Schuman and Jean Monnet, saw the ECSC as far more than an economic arrangement. In Monnet's words, the ECSC was "the first expression of the Europe that is being born."[17]

Heartened by the success of the ECSC, the six member nations in 1957 formed the European Economic Community. The EEC sought to establish not only an enormous free trade zone across member boundaries, but also to coordinate policies on wages, prices, immigration, and social security. It worked. Between 1958 and 1970, trade among its six member states rose five times. The rapid movement of goods, services, and even workers ensured that the economies of member states flourished. In contrast, Britain, which had chosen to remain outside the EEC in order to preserve its preferential trading relationships with its former and current colonies, struggled to compete, with growth rates below those of its continental competitors.

THE AGE OF AFFLUENCE

If a European living in 1930 had been transported by a time machine to the Europe of 1965, he or she would probably have been most astonished not by political consensus or European economic unity but by the cornucopia of consumer goods spilling over the lives of ordinary Europeans. On the average, western European economies were growing by 4 percent a year during the 1950s, with some states growing even faster. Growth in Italian industrial production averaged over 8 percent per year, as firms such as Vespa and Olivetti cornered the international market with their motor scooters and typewriters.

It is not surprising that after years of wartime rationing, Europeans went on a spending spree. What is surprising is

THE AGE OF AFFLUENCE

....

Full employment and rising real wages meant that the European working class joined the mass consumer society in the postwar era. In Alan Sillitoe's novel Saturday Night and Sunday Morning, *20-year-old Arthur Seaton seethes with unarticulated anger over continuing class divisions and his own powerlessness; yet, he is well aware of the stark material contrast between the 1930s and the 1950s. Seaton credits the war, not the welfare state, with the material improvements he observes around him. He confronts his father on Monday morning before heading to work:*

"Y ou'll go blind one day, dad," he said, for nothing, taking the words out of the air for sport, ready to play with the consequences of whatever he might cause.

Seaton turned to him uncomprehendingly, his older head still fuddled. It took ten cups of tea and as many Woodbines [cigarettes] to set his temper right after the weekend. "What do you mean?" he demanded, intractable at any time before ten in the morning.

"Sittin' in front of the TV. You stick to it like glue from six to eleven every night. It can't be good for yer. You'll go blind one day. You're bound to. I read it in the *Post* last week that a lad from the Medders went blind . . ."

"Ye're barmy," Seaton said. "Go an tell yer stories somewhere else . . ."

The subject was dropped. His father cut several slices of bread and made sandwiches with cold meat left from Sunday dinner. Arthur teased him a lot, but in a way he was glad to see the TV standing in a corner of the living-room, a glossy panelled box looking, he thought, like something plundered from a spaceship. The old man was happy at last, anyway, and he deserved to be happy, after all the years before the war on the dole [on unemployment benefit], five kids and the miserying that went with no money and no way of getting any. And now he had a sit-down job at the factory, all the Woodbines he could smoke, money for a pint [of beer] if he wanted one, though he didn't as a rule drink, a holiday somewhere, a jaunt on the firm's trip to Blackpool [a seaside resort], and a television-set to look into at home. The difference between before the war and after the war didn't bear thinking about. War was a marvellous thing in many ways, when you thought about how happy it had made so many people in England.

. . . . Once out of doors they were aware of the factory rumbling a hundred yards away . . . The thousands that worked there took home good wages . . . With the wages you got you could save up for a motor-bike or even an old car, or you could go on a ten-day binge and get rid of all you'd saved. Because it was no use saving your money year after year. A mug's game, since the value of it got less and less and in any case you never knew when the Yanks were going to do something daft like dropping the H-bomb on Moscow.

Source: From *Saturday Night and Sunday Morning* by Alan Sillitoe, copyright © 1958 by Alan Sillitoe. Used by permission of Alfred A. Knopf, a division of Random House, Inc.

that this spree simply did not stop. A swift and unprecedented climb in real wages—by 80 percent in England, for example, between 1950 and 1970—helps explain why. So too does the construction of the welfare state. With full employment and comprehensive welfare services offering unprecedented financial security, Europeans shrugged off habits of thrift.

The postwar period witnessed a boom in housing construction. The annual volume of construction rose by 80 percent between 1950 and 1957. With new houses came new household goods. Items such as refrigerators and washing machines, once unaffordable luxuries, now became increasingly common in ordinary homes. In France, for example, the stock of home appliances rose by 400 percent between 1949 and 1957. By the 1970s, half of British families owned their own homes, two-thirds possessed washing machines, three-quarters owned refrigerators, and a whopping 90 percent had television sets.

While such purchases transformed the interiors of European homes and apartments, outside the automobile revolutionized much of both the rural and urban landscape. Highways, few and far between in 1950, cut across the countryside, and parking meters, unknown in Europe before 1959, dotted city streets. In 1964, the archbishop of Florence presided over a thanksgiving service in a gas station to celebrate the completion of a highway linking Milan and Naples. Out-of-town shopping centers, geared to the convenience of car owners, proliferated; city centers decayed.

Spending begot more spending. Credit buying (what the British called "buying on the never-never") became commonplace and made possible even more consumption. Television commercials (first seen in the mid-1950s), the Yellow Pages (first distributed in Europe in the early 1960s), and color advertising supplements in the Sunday newspapers (an innovation, again, of the early 1960s) all encouraged a culture of consumption.

Culture and Society in the Age of Consumption

The new affluence brought with it a sense of new possibilities, together with a fear that the abundance of material goods could actually work to restrict rather than open up opportunities. A variety of cultural and social developments and responses shaped, and were shaped by, western Europeans' efforts to make sense of the new material world.

CULTURAL ENCOUNTERS: AMERICANIZATION AND IMMIGRATION

Affluence meant greater economic interchange, which in turn meant increased interactions across diverse cultures. During the postwar era, two sets of cultural encounters particularly shaped European societies. First, Europeans found themselves inundated with American products, people, and ideas. Second, rising numbers of immigrants from non-Western societies brought to Europe greater cultural diversity.

The American Challenge

In western Europe in the 1950s and 1960s, consumption often meant the consumption of American goods. U.S.-based corporations scattered branch offices throughout western Europe, and U.S.-produced goods filled the shelves of European shops. In France, the best-selling book of the 1960s was entitled *The American Challenge,* and argued that Europe was fast becoming nothing more than a subcontractor for American business.

Western Europeans also struggled with American domination in science and technology. The United States invested more in scientific research and development, produced more graduates in the sciences and engineering than all other Western countries combined, and came out on top in terms of numbers of papers published and patents registered. Between 1945 and 1967, fifty-four scientists from the United States (fourteen foreign-born) won the Nobel Prize; the rest of the world produced sixty-eight scientific winners. Europeans spoke with alarm about the "brain drain" as scientists and academics headed across the Atlantic to the richer universities of the United States.

The United States particularly dominated the realm of popular culture. Immediately after World War II, the U.S. government forced European states to dismantle quotas on American film imports by threatening to withhold much-needed loans. By 1951, American productions accounted for 61 percent of film showings in western Europe. American television, too, quickly established a central position in European mass culture. In the mid-1950s, few

European households had a television, while the average American family was watching more than five hours of programming every day. In the second half of the decade, then, as the number of television owners in Europe began to expand rapidly (more than doubling between 1955 and 1956), American television networks were well-situated to take advantage of this new market. By 1960, CBS, ABC, and NBC were selling their programs to the world. The popular *Lone Ranger* series appeared in twenty-four countries. Language itself seemed subject to American takeover. More than 80 percent of the songs played on Austrian radio in the early 1960s were written by Americans and sung in English. Words such as *babysitter* and *comics* entered directly into German, while French children coveted *les jeans* and *le chewing-gum.*

While the pursuit of profit provided the primary motivating force for the export of these cultural goods, the Cold War also played a role. Seeking to fortify western Europe against communist ideas as well as communist armies, the United States embarked on a full-scale cultural assault during the 1950s. The U.S. Central Intelligence Agency (CIA) covertly funded not only western European anticommunist political parties but also cultural and scientific organizations and publications that it believed would promote values and ideas antithetical to Marxist ideology. Films, art exhibits, books and magazines, radio shows, and scholarly exchange programs all became weapons in the cultural Cold War. Ironically, the effort to fight communism with American culture went hand in hand with censorship, with the works of left-wing authors and composers banned from American-funded libraries and public information centers throughout western Europe. More positively, exhibitions of American modernist paintings were sent on tour to persuade western Europeans that capitalism nurtured artistic innovation. Even rock music was enlisted in the Cold War. In 1958, a writer in a NATO journal argued, "Whenever a rock and roll or calypso tune imbeds itself in a communist mind, it tends to erode other things." By the early 1960s, Radio Free Europe regularly included Western rock music in its programming.

Many Europeans enthusiastically embraced American culture but some Europeans argued that even as Europe was losing its colonial possessions, it was itself undergoing colonization, or at least "coca-colonization," as Coca-Cola and other American products seemed poised to conquer European markets and transform European tastes.[18] Opponents to "coca-colonization" came from both the right and the left of the political spectrum, with conservative nationalists joining pro-Soviet communists in denouncing American influence over European culture.

One of the most powerful voices protesting American hegemony was France's conservative leader Charles De Gaulle. De Gaulle sought to reduce American influence in Europe by pursuing independent foreign and military policies. He extended diplomatic recognition to China in

■ **McDonald's on the Champs-Elysées in Paris**

In the postwar era, the United States functioned as a symbol of modernity. The McDonald's hamburger franchise represented the United States to many Europeans because it typified modernity's standardization and mass consumerism. Assembly-line production lowered costs and made the standardized experience of eating fast food affordable to the masses.

1964 and two years later made a state visit to Moscow. In 1960 France exploded its own atomic bomb and in 1966 French forces withdrew from NATO command, although France remained formally part of the Atlantic alliance. De Gaulle was deeply anticommunist and fiercely opposed to the Soviet Union, but he believed that the more immediate threat to the French way of life came from American culture. Taken in 1960 to view a new highway in California, De Gaulle gazed somberly at the sight of cars weaving in and out on a traffic cloverleaf and commented, "I have the impression that all this will end very badly."[19] De Gaulle's anti-Americanism was largely rooted in his pro-Frenchness: He wanted to reduce American influence in Europe in order to restore France to a position of grandeur and glory. In De Gaulle's imagination, France was "like the princess in the fairy stories or the Madonna in the frescoes, as dedicated to an exalted and exceptional destiny . . . France cannot be France without greatness."[20]

American cultural and economic influence in postwar Europe was very real, yet the fear of Europe becoming a secondhand version of the United States was misplaced. Throughout this era, Europeans consumed American products with great gusto, but in the process they adapted these products to suit their own needs. In the late 1950s, for example, four young working-class men from the northern British seaport of Liverpool latched on to the new American rock and roll, mixed in their own regional musical styles, and transformed popular music not only in Europe but also in the United States. The impact of the Beatles testified to the power of European culture to remake American cultural products. Even McDonald's, when

it arrived in European cities in the 1960s, made subtle changes to the composition of its fast food to appeal to the differing tastes of the new markets. Thus the cultural history of this era is one of reciprocal encounters rather than one-way Americanization.

Immigration and the Challenge of Diversity
At the same time, the immigration of new communities into western European countries brought new and in many cases non-Western cultural traditions into contact with those of the host nation. Immigration was the result of economic prosperity. As their economic growth rates soared in the 1950s, northern and western European nations were experiencing a slowing rate of population increase. Scrambling for workers to fill their fields and factories, staff their new hospitals, and build their new houses and transportation systems, governments undertook to recruit foreign labor. Beginning in 1955, the West German government negotiated a series of immigration contracts with Italy, Greece, Turkey, Yugoslavia, and the North African states. In Britain, both public and private agencies turned for workers to the West Indies, India, and Pakistan. France recruited workers from Spain and Italy, as well as its colonial territories such as Algeria, Morocco, Tunisia, Senegal, Mali, and Guadeloupe. By the beginning of the 1970s, the nations of northern and western Europe were home to approximately nine million immigrants, half of these from the less prosperous Mediterranean states of Portugal, Spain, Italy, and Greece. The other half came from Turkey, Yugoslavia, and countries in Asia, Africa, and the Caribbean.

■ **Immigrants Arriving in Britain, 1956**
Many immigrants from regions within the British Empire had been taught that Britain was the "mother country" or "home." They were shocked to discover that once in Britain, they were regarded as foreign and as inferior.

These workers did the dirtiest, most dangerous, least desirable jobs. They worked the night shifts, emptied the bedpans, dug the ditches, and cleaned the toilets. They lived in substandard housing, often confined to isolated dormitories or inner-city slums, and accepted low, often illegally low, pay rates. The reason they did so is starkly presented in the table below: Despite racial discrimination and economic exploitation, western Europe offered greater economic opportunities than were available in the immigrants' homelands.

Until the 1970s, the majority of these immigrants were single men, who saw themselves, and were seen by their

host countries, as "guestworkers," temporary laborers who would earn money and then return home to their native lands. By the mid-1960s, however, families were beginning to join these men, and a second generation of "immigrants" was being born, a generation who did not know their supposedly "native" land. This generation changed the face of Europe. Chapter 29 will show that by the 1980s European societies had become multiethnic. The emergence of urban subcultures immeasurably enlivened European cultures and economies (and diets); it also complicated domestic politics and raised challenging questions about the relationship between national and ethnic identity. In the 1950s and 1960s, however, few Europeans could yet discern the multicolored patterns that were emerging.

The Appeal of Immigration—Annual Per Capita Gross National Product in the Mid-1960s

Pakistan	$125
Turkey	$353
Jamaica	$520
Spain	$822
Italy	$1,272
Britain	$1,977
France	$2,324

Source: Leslie Page Moch, *Moving Europeans: Migration in Western Europe Since 1650* (1992), p. 177.

THE SECOND SEX?

In 1949, the French writer Simone de Beauvoir (1908–1986) published *The Second Sex*. In this enormously influential critique of gender divisions in Western industrial society, de Beauvoir argued that women remained the "second sex." Despite changes in their political and legal status, women were still defined by their relationship to men rather than by their own actions or achievements. Over the next two decades, the new prosperity pushed women into higher education and the labor force and so, in the long run, worked to undermine the traditional gender roles that de Beauvoir described; in the short run, however, affluence accentuated women's domestic identity.

A number of changes both reflected and reinforced postwar domesticity. The most important were demographic. Marriage rates rose and the marriage age dropped in the postwar years. In the United States, between 1940 and 1957, the fertility rate rose by 50 percent. Europe experienced a baby "boomlet" rather than a baby boom. European birth rates rose in the late 1940s but dropped again in the 1950s (whereas U.S. fertility rates remained high into the 1960s). Nevertheless, although family sizes were small, a higher percentage of western European women than ever before had children.

By exalting women's maternal identity, both religion and popular culture provided a potent ideology for these demographic changes. The Roman Catholic Church of the 1950s placed renewed emphasis on Mary, the paragon of motherhood. Pope Pius XII (r. 1939–1958) particularly encouraged the growth of devotion to Mary during the last years of his papacy. The pope, who believed he had experienced his own personal Marian visitation, proclaimed in 1950 that Mary had ascended bodily into heaven (the Doctrine of the Assumption) and designated 1954 as the Year of Mary. This Marian devotion encouraged women to regard motherhood as a holy calling, and as the very core of female identity.

Popular culture reinforced this religious message. Programming aimed at families dominated the new television schedules and established new images of what families should look like and how they should interact. So, too, did the articles and advertisements of women's magazines. In both, the woman stayed at home, presiding over an expanding array of household machines that, in theory, reduced her housework burden and so freed her to focus on the satisfactions of motherhood.

At the same time, a number of cultural, economic, and technological changes transformed the Western home into a much more private place. Because of the boom in house building, by the mid-1950s couples forced by wartime deprivation to live with their parents could now move into their own apartment or house. Accelerated suburbanization, made possible by the expansion of private car ownership and the spread of highway networks, meant that relatives now lived farther apart. "Family" increasingly meant the nuclear family. Prosperity accentuated the family's isolation. Economic growth translated into a rapid drop in the number of domestic servants as workers turned to better-paying jobs and household appliances took their place. Because the new houses and apartment buildings possessed modern conveniences such as indoor plumbing, communal baths, toilets, and washhouses gradually disappeared. Television moved the social center away from cinemas, cafés, and pubs to the family living room.

Cold War concerns also accentuated the Western woman's domestic role in two very different ways. First, anticommunist propaganda hailed domesticity as a sign of Western superiority, by contrasting the favorable lot of Western women to their Soviet counterparts, who led lives of almost endless labor. The vast majority of Soviet women combined their domestic duties with full-time outside employment, often in jobs involving heavy manual labor, and they spent a substantial portion of each day lining up to purchase scarce goods. Second, the nuclear age made the nuclear family seem all the more important. Feeling increasingly helpless in a superpower-dominated world on

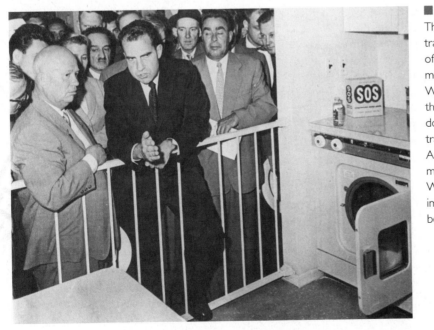

■ **The Kitchen Debate**

The kitchen—stocked with an abundance of attractively packaged foods and a glittering array of time-saving appliances—symbolized not only material plenty but also moral stability. In the Western domestic ideal, the kitchen represented the center of family life, and the woman's proper domain. When Vice President Richard Nixon traveled to Moscow in 1959 to open an American exhibition, he pointed to the display model of a suburban kitchen as evidence of Western superiority. Khrushchev refused to be impressed. Nixon and Khrushchev's argument became known as the "Kitchen Debate."

the brink of nuclear annihilation, Europeans tended to withdraw for shelter to family life.

For some women, this shelter was more like a prison. In *The Captive Wife*, published in 1966, the British sociologist Hannah Gavron (b. 1944) asked, "Have all the great changes in the position of women in the last one hundred and fifty years come to nothing?" In *The Feminine Mystique* (1963), the American journalist Betty Friedan (b. 1921) identified what she called "the problem that had no name," a crisis of identity and purpose among middle-class, educated women confined in the role of housewife and mother.

Whether a nightmare or a dream, the domestic ideal remained removed from the reality of many women's lives in the postwar era. In the poorer social classes, women by necessity continued to work outside the home, as they always had. At the same time, the new culture of consumption demanded that many women, clinging precariously to the middle rungs of the social ladder, take on paid employment to pay for the ever-expanding list of household necessities. In many countries, such as Britain, the number of female workers, including married women with children, rose. In 1951, 21 percent of British married women were in the paid workforce; by 1971 the figure was 47 percent.

In general, a new pattern of employment emerged that reconciled the new domesticity with the needs of expanding economies. It was increasingly expected that single women, including those in the middle class, would work until they married. Many continued to do so until the first child arrived, and resumed paid employment after the last child had left home or at least started school. This work was regarded, however, as secondary to their main job—the making of a home and the rearing of children. Part-time employment, with lower wages and few or no benefits, expanded accordingly. Everywhere pay rates remained unequal. In Britain in 1950, single women earned about half of what their male colleagues were paid; in France two decades later, married women workers earned one-third less than married men. Inequalities in legal status continued as well. Until 1964 and the passage of the Matrimonial Act, a married French woman could not open her own bank account, run a shop, or apply for a passport without her husband's permission. Traditional gender roles remained firmly intact, despite the material and political changes of the postwar era.

HIGH CULTURE IN THE AGE OF CONSUMPTION

Continuity also marked the high culture of the 1950s. Neorealism, which had first appeared in Italian cinema during World War II (see Chapter 26), continued to exert a powerful influence not only in the European film world but also in British and French fiction. For example, the novels of the British "Angry Young Men" of the 1950s, like

Italian movies of the 1940s, presented realistic depictions of working-class lives and concerns. At the same time, both existentialism and modernism retained their dominant position in high culture in the decade after World War II. By the beginning of the 1960s, however, existentialist concerns and modernist assumptions were losing their hold. In very general terms, artists retreated from engagement with the horrors of World War II and the overwhelming challenges of the Cold War. Instead, they produced works that reflected, commented on, and reveled in the cascade of consumer abundance that was transforming western European and American social life.

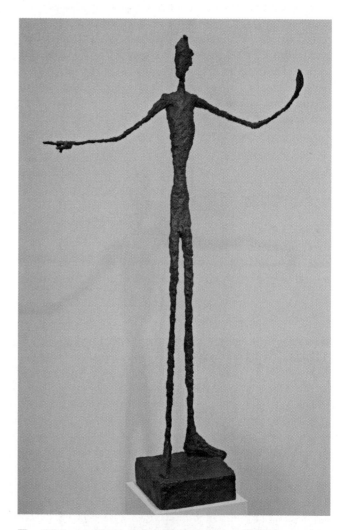

■ **Alberto Giacometti,** *Man Pointing* **(1947)**
Giacometti's sculptures embodied existentialist anguish. His account of this piece's creation seems to be lifted from a Samuel Beckett play or one of Jean-Paul Sartre's novels: "Wanting to create from memory [the figures] I had seen, to my terror the sculptures became smaller and smaller, they had a likeness only when they were small, yet their dimensions revolted me, and tirelessly I began again, only to end several months later at the same point."

Meaning and Absurdity

Forged in the despair of the 1930s and hammered into shape by the horrors of the Second World War, existentialism remained a powerful cultural force in the early post-war era. Jean-Paul Sartre's conviction that existence has no intrinsic meaning, and yet that the individual retains the freedom to act and therefore make meaning, resounded loudly in a world that had experienced both the Holocaust and the Resistance. The existentialist emphasis on individual action as the source of meaning could lead to a life of political activism—Sartre, for example, worked with the French Resistance and became a prominent participant in left-wing political causes in the 1950s and 1960s. On the other hand, existentialism also justified political disengagement. In the Irish-French playwright Samuel Beckett's (1906–1989) existentialist masterpiece *Waiting for Godot* (1952), two tramps sit in an empty universe, waiting for someone who never comes. In this absurd void, politics has no relevance or resonance.

Existentialist themes echo throughout the visual arts in the 1950s. The sculptures of the Swiss artist Alberto Giacometti (1901–1966) are the embodiments of existentialist anguish—fragile, insubstantial, they appear ready to crack under the strain of being. While Giacometti's sculptures embody existentialist terror, the works of the preeminent British painter of the 1950s, Francis Bacon (1909–1992), evoke outright nausea. Bacon's disturbing canvases are case studies in the power of the subconscious. He painted the people he saw around him, but his perceptions were of a society disfigured by slaughter. Slabs of meat, dripping in blood, figure prominently. Bacon explained, "When you go into a butcher's shop . . . you can think of the whole horror of life, of one thing living off another."[21] By the end of the decade, solitary figures, secluded in claustrophobic settings and embodying Sartre's description of human existence as essentially isolated, recurred frequently in Bacon's work.

Moving into Post-Modernism

The works of Bacon and Giacometti remained well under the umbrella of modernism (see Chapter 23). As the consumer revolution poured through Western culture, however, it forced a dramatic transformation in the content and purpose of the visual arts. Fascinated by the plethora of material objects pouring off assembly lines and onto department store shelves, artists began to turn away from ex-

■ **Richard Hamilton, "Just What Is It That Makes Today's Homes So Different, So Appealing?" (1956)**
British artist Richard Hamilton was one of the leading figures in the Pop Art of the 1950s.

istentialist concerns and to focus on the material stuff of everyday existence. Technology, too became a source of artistic inspiration. Works such as "Just What Is It That Makes Today's Homes So Different, So Appealing?" (1956), by British artist Richard Hamilton (b. 1922) signaled this artistic shift. This playful collage satirizes and yet celebrates the postwar emphasis on material consumption and on private family life. Hamilton was a leading force in the Independent Group, a loose association of British artists, designers, and architects that sought in their work to embody the "aesthetics of plenty"—the idea that consumer affluence had smashed the barriers between fine art and popular culture. The Independent Group, along with other movements such as "New Realism" in France and "Capitalist Realism" in West Germany, helped shape what became known as pop art°. Pop artists dismissed the anguish of Bacon and Giacometti as the concerns of an older generation still mired in World War II. Pop art looked outward rather than inward, and focused on the material rather than the spiritual. Pop artists spoke in the vocabulary of mass material culture, and even relied on mass production and mass marketing.

The result was a revolution in Western art. These young artists broke with modernism, and catapulted the art world into what would become postmodernism (as we shall see in Chapter 29). Pop artists challenged accepted ideas about the role of both art and the artist in Western society. Works such as *Flag* (1954–1955) by the American Jasper Johns (b. 1930) raised fundamental questions about the difference between a thing and the artist's interpretation of that thing. *Flag* consists of small pieces of newspapers dipped into wax and then sealed onto fabric in the pattern of the American flag—in other words, the work is not just an image of a flag; it *is* a flag. Where, then, is the line between reality and representation? And if that line disappears, where does the artist stand? When the American pop artist Andy Warhol (1930–1987) called his studio "The Factory" and employed assistants to mass-produce his works, he overturned the modernist idea of the artist as a uniquely inspired individual. His German counterpart Gerhard Richter (b. 1932) went even further when he placed himself in the furniture display of a West German department store and called the resulting "piece" *Living with Pop* (1963). Richter turned the artist, as well as art, into a commodity, something to be bought and sold just like anything else. In the age of consumption, the individual artist's intentions and attitudes became unimportant, and concepts such as artistic genius or lasting meaning became irrelevant.

The demotion of the individual and the abandonment of meaning characteristic of pop art also characterized developments in social thought. Existentialism had elevated the individual as the only source of meaning in an absurd universe. In the late 1950s, however, a new social theory—structuralism°—emerged to challenge existentialism's hold on Western intellectual formations. Rooted in linguistics and anthropology, structuralism transformed a number of academic disciplines, including literary criticism, political theory, sociology, and even history. Structuralism was first introduced to a wide audience by the French anthropologist Claude Levi-Strauss (b. 1908). Levi-Strauss argued that the myths told in all cultures, whether that of Brazilian Indian tribes still using stone-age tools or medieval French peasants or contemporary Londoners, shared certain "deep structures," repeated patterns such as pairings and oppositions that help give order to the cultural world. The actual stories are unimportant. To use a newspaper metaphor offered by the intellectual historian Roland Stromberg, the structuralist is interested not in the content of the articles but in the layout of the page—the arrangement of articles, the juxtaposition of images, the shape of headlines. By analyzing the "layout" of cultures, the structuralist can uncover the basic structures of human thought. In structuralism, then, as in pop art, the individual matters little. Human beings exist within a ready-built structure that shapes and dictates the way they perceive the world.

SCIENCE AND RELIGION IN AN AGE OF MASS CONSUMPTION

At the same time that structuralists depicted the individual as stuck within a cultural and linguistic web, his or her choices firmly constrained by the sticky fibers of that web, radical breakthroughs in the biological sciences posited that perhaps the web lay inside the individual, its fibers comprising chemicals and chromosomes that set sharp limits on individual capabilities. While Levi-Strauss sought to decipher human culture, biologists embarked on the task of decoding humanity's genetic structure. In 1962, the British biologist Francis Crick (b. 1916) and his American colleague James Watson (b. 1928) received the Nobel Prize in Medicine and Physiology for mapping the structure of DNA, the basic building block of genetic material, which they had discovered in 1953. Crick and Watson's model of the "double helix," the intertwined spirals of chemical units that, in a sense, issue the instructions for an individual's development, caught the attention of the world. As biologists and geneticists furthered their investigations into human genetic inheritance, they raised exciting yet potentially disturbing possibilities, such as the cloning of living organisms and genetic manipulation, and added a new dimension to the perennial debate about individual freedom.

Other scientific developments assured human beings more freedom from their physical environment than ever before. Motivated by the Cold War, the space race launched humanity beyond the confines of Earth, culminating in 1969 with the American astronaut Neil Armstrong's moon walk. Medical breakthroughs in this era seemed to promise that infectious diseases could be eradicated. Large-scale production of penicillin transformed ordinary medical care, as did rapid development of vaccines against many childhood killers such as measles. In 1953, the American Jonas Salk announced the first successful clinical trial of a polio vaccine. In this era, blood transfusions become more commonplace, along with the development of organ transplants, following the first successful kidney transplant in Chicago in 1950. Like washing machines and television sets, a long and healthy life suddenly appeared accessible to most people.

While scientists were claiming more control of the physical environment than ever before, the organized churches continued to offer spiritual authority and sustenance. Church attendance, which had declined in most Western countries in the interwar period, rose during the 1950s. In the United States between 1942 and 1960, church membership per capita grew faster than at any time since the 1890s. No European nation shared this dramatic religious upsurge; nevertheless, except in Scandinavia, western Europe experienced what we can call a gentle religious revival. In Britain during the 1950s, church membership, Sunday school enrollment, and the numbers of baptisms and religious marriages all increased. In West Germany, the rate of churchgoing rose among Protestants from 1952 until 1967. Throughout Catholic Europe, the vibrancy of Christian Democratic politics reflected the vital position of the Catholic Church in society.

In the 1960s, however, the situation changed dramatically. Europeans (followed a generation later by their American counterparts) abandoned the churches in favor of the shops, sports fields, and television sets. Declining rates of church attendance, a growing number of civil rather than religious marriage ceremonies, and an increased reluctance to obey Church teaching on issues such as premarital sexual relations all pointed to the secularization of European society. As we will see in Chapter 29, by the 1970s, churchgoing rates in both Protestant and Catholic countries were in freefall. In what had once been called "Christendom," the fastest-growing religious community was Islam.

The churches did not remain stagnant during this time of change. A number of Protestant theologians argued that Christianity could maintain its relevance in this more secular society only by adapting the biblical message to a modern context. The British theologian (and Anglican bishop) John Robinson achieved great notoriety in 1963 when he proclaimed, "God is dead." Most of those who jeered at or cheered for Robinson's statement missed his point: The language in which Christians articulate their faith must be updated to make sense in the modern world.

The biggest change occurred in Roman Catholicism. In 1963 the Second Vatican Council—widely known as Vatican II°—convened in Rome, the first catholic council to meet since 1870. In calling the council, Pope John XXIII (r. 1958–1963) sought to modernize and rejuvenate the Church, a process that, he recognized, would demand "a change in mentalities, ways of thinking and prejudices, all of which have a long history."[22] John did not live to see this change in mentalities take place, but his successor Paul VI (r. 1963–1978) presided over a quiet revolution.

The Church that emerged from Vatican II was a great deal less hierarchical and a great deal more open than its pre–Vatican II predecessor. The council embraced ecumenism, the effort to overcome the divisions between the separate Christian branches. For the first time, Roman Catholics were allowed to receive communion in non-Roman churches (under certain conditions). Reversing Pius XII's emphasis on the absolute power of the papacy, Vatican II granted more authority to local and regional councils. For ordinary Catholics, the most striking changes occurred in the worship service. To make the service more accessible to the laity, Latin was scrapped in favor of the vernacular (in France, services were in French; in Britain, in English; and so on). A number of reforms narrowed the gap between priest and people. During the mass, for example, the priest stood behind the altar, facing the congrega-

tion, rather than in front, with his back to the people, and all worshipers, not only the priest, received the wine at communion.

Vatican II was less revolutionary in its approach to sexual issues and gender roles. The council said nothing about homosexuality (still a largely taboo subject throughout the Western world), reaffirmed the traditional doctrine of clerical celibacy, and insisted that only men could be ordained as priests. It did, however, abandon over one thousand years of Church teaching when it insisted that the purpose of marriage was not simply to produce children but also to establish "an intimate partnership of life and love" between a man and a woman.[23] Following up on this crucial break, the council declared that parents had the right and responsibility to determine how many children they should have and when they should have them—but, in obedience to Paul VI's order that contraception was not a subject suitable for conciliar debate, it left open the question of birth control. Three years later, the pope closed the question. In the papal document *Humanae Vitae* he declared contraceptive use to be contrary to Church teaching.

The issues of clerical celibacy, women's ordination, and contraceptive use would bedevil the Church for the rest of the century. Nevertheless, Vatican II did reinvigorate global Catholicism. It also made clear that, as one popular contemporary folk song put it, "the times they are a'changin.'" A quiet and cautious administrator, Paul seemed an unlikely revolutionary, yet he became the first pope to travel outside Italy since 1809 and the first to fly on an airplane. If the pope could fly, who knew what else might happen?

1968 AND THE END OF THE POSTWAR ERA

Events in 1968 seemed to indicate that the answer might be: Just about anything. As we have already seen, that year eastern Europe witnessed the most serious challenge to Soviet hegemony in eastern Europe since 1956. In the West, too,

"The Whole State Will Be on Trial": The Aldo Moro Kidnapping

On March 16, 1978, while on his way to pray before going to Parliament, the former prime minister of Italy and leader of the Christian Democratic Party, Aldo Moro, was kidnapped in broad daylight in a Roman suburb. In a carefully planned and brilliantly executed operation, a woman driving a white car backed in front of Moro's official dark blue Fiat and caused an accident. She and her male companion sprang from their car and blasted automatic weapons into the front seat of the Fiat, killing Moro's chauffeur and bodyguard. Moro, who had been quietly reading the morning paper when the attack began, was pulled unhurt from the backseat and hurried away in an escape vehicle. Thus began Aldo Moro's horrible ordeal, and one of the most daring instances of organized terrorist violence in the postwar era.

Moro was kidnapped by the Red Brigade, a terrorist group that emerged out of the student protest movement. During the 1960s, many young Italians became convinced that Italy needed fundamental change. These students believed that Italy's traditional left-wing political parties (the Socialists and the Communists) could never transform Italy's political or social structures in any meaningful way. The Communists were sunk in inertia; the Socialists had shown themselves to be just another group of politicians interested in personal power when they joined the Christian Democrats in a governing coalition in 1962. The stu-

dents turned instead to the street protest of the "New Left." In 1967, students occupied the University of Trento. Over the next several months, student protest spread throughout the country.

The New Left ideology of the student movement was broadly Marxist, but opposed to Soviet-style communism. Spontaneity, a mistrust of authority in any form, a rejection of political doctrine (in some cases, a rejection of any books at all), and an insistence on direct democracy all characterized the movement in its first days. By 1970, however, the movement had altered. Heartened by the spread of the most serious labor unrest in Italian industry since World War II, students shifted their focus from the universities to the factories. As students joined striking workers spontaneity disappeared; doctrine and discipline returned with a vengeance. The movement adopted Soviet-style authoritarianism and factionalized into small revolutionary groups, each of which demanded conformity to its brand of ideological purity.

One of these factions was the Red Brigades, led by former student activist Renato Curcio. The Red Brigades declared an "attack on the heart of the state." By targeting politicians, judges, journalists, and professors, the Brigades hoped to terrorize the ruling elite, destabilize the Italian state, and push Italian society into revolution. In 1976 and 1977, fifteen people died and over fifty were wounded in Brigade attacks.

Then, in the spring of 1978, the Red Brigades kidnapped Aldo Moro.

Just a few weeks before, the Italian state had brought to trial fifteen captured Red Brigadiers, including Curcio. Kept in a cage in the courtroom in Turin, the defendants screamed insults and made obscene gestures at the judges and jury. It was from this cage that Curcio shouted to the world, "Moro is in our hands!" Curcio then explained, "The real trial is taking place elsewhere . . . Moro is in the hands of the proletariat, and the whole state will be on trial."

To the Red Brigadiers, Moro represented the kind of compromise-based politics that prevented any fundamental transformation of Italian society. Moro had spent much of his political career working to ensure that Italy's traditional left-wing parties posed no radical threat. During the 1960s, under Moro's leadership, the Christian Democrats had formed coalition governments with the Italian Socialists. Moro believed that by including the Socialists in government, he could tame them—and he was right. Once in office, the Socialists abandoned much of their radical rhetoric and most of their radical goals. In the 1970s, Moro sought to cooperate with the Communists, in hopes of domesticating them just as he had tamed the Socialists a decade earlier. To the Brigades, then, Aldo Moro was "the most authoritative leader, the undisputed theorist and strategist of the

Christian Democratic regime, which for thirty years has oppressed the Italian people."

The so-called trial conducted by the Red Brigades had nothing to do with proving a case against Moro but consisted of repeatedly badgering him with allegations. The goal was to keep Moro in complete terror and to break down his will. After a month the Red Brigades announced the completion of the Aldo Moro trial. The verdict: "ALDO MORO IS GUILTY AND IS THEREFORE CONDEMNED TO DEATH."

On May 9 the Red Brigades brought the affair to a dramatic finale. They telephoned Moro's assistant and told him where to find his boss. The former prime minister's bullet-riddled body

lay in the back of a red Renault station wagon across the street from the American Cultural Center, which stood almost exactly halfway between the headquarters of the Christian Democratic and Italian Communist parties. By leaving Moro's body in this spot, the Brigades expressed their contempt for the entire Italian political establishment. Moreover, by managing to park a car containing Moro's bloody body in plain view in a city swarming with policemen, the Brigadiers taunted the government with their apparent invincibility. From his cage in the Turin courtroom, Renato Curcio declared, "This is only the beginning. You have not understood what will happen in Italy during the coming days and months."

But Curcio was wrong. Moro's death utterly failed to ignite the revolution. Appalled by Moro's murder, Italians from across the political spectrum supported a new antiterrorist offensive mounted by the government. By 1982 many of the Brigadiers had been arrested. Much to the surprise of many Italians, Italian society emerged from its bloody encounter with "revolutionary justice" not only intact, but even, it can be argued, more united than before—exactly the opposite of what the Brigades had intended. ■

Questions of Justice

1. How does the killing of Aldo Moro compare to an earlier episode of "proletarian justice"—the "Nontrial of Nicholas and Alexandra"? (See "Justice in History" in Chapter 24, p. 816.)

2. How might the Aldo Moro affair be considered an episode in the history of the Cold War?

Taking It Further

Drake, Richard. *The Aldo Moro Murder Case.* 1995. Based on the extensive records of two parliamentary inquiries and four sets of criminal trials, this book is the most thorough examination of all the available evidence about the Moro murder.

Wagner-Pacifici, Robin Erica. *The Moro Morality Play: Terrorism as Social Drama.* 1986. This book is less concerned with the evidence of who did what than how the Moro kidnapping constituted one of the most striking social dramas of the twentieth century.

■ **The Death of Aldo Moro**
By killing Moro, the Red Brigades hoped to spark a revolution. Instead, they horrified their potential supporters.

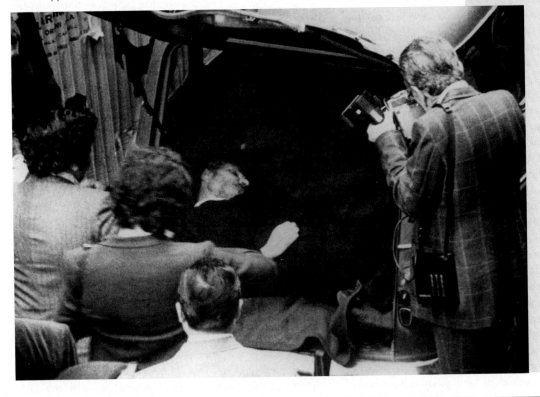

■ **The Protests of 1968**
French student demonstrators and
their supporters gather at the Place
Denfert-Rochereau, Paris.

the end of the 1960s saw the rise of widespread protests against the postwar order. In 1968, demonstrations disrupted university campuses in almost every Western country and in the East and the Third World as well. Students from Addis Ababa to Warsaw, from Berkeley to Berlin, rose up in protest. In Italy half a million students were on strike. In Mexico City, a series of confrontations between students and police resulted in a police massacre that killed 300 students. In France, a student demonstration blossomed into a full-scale social revolt, which for a time looked set to topple De Gaulle's government. The events in Paris began in May, when police used brutal methods to clear a Parisian courtyard occupied by protesting students. The unwarranted violence of the police action, broadcast throughout France in newspaper photographs and television news reports, aroused support for the students from the wider population. Within a few days, eight million French men and women were on strike.

The common theme among these protests was the demand for a voice, for the right of ordinary people to participate in the processes and structures that determined their lives. More specifically, protesters drew on the ideas of the New Left° to articulate a profound uneasiness with the power of the state in the West. Before World War II, activists and thinkers on the left of the political spectrum had sought to expand the power of the state to counterbalance the inegalitarian consequences of capitalism and so make

possible genuine democracy. But by the late 1950s and early 1960s, New Left thinkers, appalled by the excesses of Stalinism and concerned about the growth of state power in the West, warned that the expansive state, with its staff of experts, threatened the individuality and independence of the ordinary citizen. The German philosopher Herbert Marcuse (1898–1979) condemned the "repressive tolerance" of Western democracies. According to Marcuse, debate seemed open, but the range of actual political choices was limited. Throughout the West, the concept of "citizenship" was being degraded, defined by voting alone rather than by active participation in decision making. Building on this idea, the student movement called for "participatory democracy," the revitalization of active citizenship.

Armed with these New Left ideas, student protesters quickly moved beyond the university context to mount a broadly based challenge to the Cold War status quo. In their view, the superpower conflict threatened the world with nuclear annihilation at the same time that it restricted domestic political freedoms and denied individuals an effective political voice. Rejecting both Soviet-style communism and free-market capitalism, they turned for inspiration to the newly emerging nations of the Third World. Idealizing such Third World revolutionaries as Ernesto Che Guevara, one of the leaders of the Cuban revolution, and the Algerian nationalist leader Frantz Fanon, the students identified their struggle for a more open politics with the colo-

ROCK AND REVOLUTION

....

In 1967, the Beatles, already global superstars, released Sgt. Pepper's Lonely Hearts Club Band. *Called the "most influential rock album ever produced,"* Sgt. Pepper's *revolutionized rock music. The complexity of its compositions impressed serious music critics, who for the first time acknowledged that rock music was worth listening to. The album's lyrics, too, received unprecedented praise, with one reviewer comparing the last song on the album ("A Day in the Life") to T. S. Eliot's modernist masterpiece, "The Waste Land" (see Chapter 24). Although not overtly political,* Sgt. Pepper's *illustrates many of the themes of the protests that marked the era in which it was produced. Infused with a sense of playfulness and celebration, the album called its listeners to burst out of the confines of order, authority, and rationality, and embrace instead the values of human community and emotional liberation.*

SHE'S LEAVING HOME

Wednesday morning at five o'clock as the day begins
Silently closing her bedroom door
Leaving the note that she hoped would say more
She goes downstairs to the kitchen clutching her
    handkerchief
Quietly turning the backdoor key
Stepping outside she is free.
She (We gave her most of our lives)
is leaving (Sacrificed most of our lives)
home (We gave her everything money could buy)

She's leaving home after living alone
For so many years. Bye, bye
Father snores as his wife gets into her dressing gown
Picks up the letter that's lying there
Standing alone at the top of the stairs
She breaks down and cries to her husband
Daddy our baby's gone.
Why would she treat us so thoughtlessly
How could she do this to me.
She (We never thought of ourselves)
is leaving (Never a thought for ourselves)
home (We struggled hard all our lives to get by)
She's leaving home after living alone
For so many years. Bye, bye
Friday morning at nine o'clock she is far away
Waiting to keep the appointment she made
Meeting a man from the motor trade.
She (What did we do that was wrong)
is having (We didn't know it was wrong) fun
Fun is the one thing that money can't buy
Something inside that was always denied
For so many years. Bye, bye
She's leaving home bye bye

nial independence movements (see Rejecting the West, on p. 940). Vietnam served as a central issue, with the protesters regarding the U.S. not as "the leader of the free world" but rather as an imperialist oppressor.

Discarding orthodox political solutions went hand in hand with overturning traditional social rules. In their demand for "liberation," the students focused as much on cultural as on economic and political issues. Commentators began to talk about a sexual revolution as practices became commonplace that in the 1950s were labeled immoral or bohemian—couples living together before marriage or individuals engaging in sexual relationships with a variety of partners.

The global protest subsided in the early 1970s, but the movement had a significant impact. As we shall see in the next chapter, two of its offshoots, environmentalism and feminism, mounted a radical challenge to political relations and economic practices throughout the West from the 1970s onward and helped define the contemporary era. The protest movement also survived in the distorted form of terrorism. Frustrated with their failure to effect real change through protest and persuasion, a small minority of student activists turned to organized violence. The Weathermen in the United States, the Red Brigades in Italy, and Baader-Meinhof and the Red Army Faction in West Germany all dived underground and resorted to bombings, assassinations, abductions, and hijackings in an effort to weaken the structures of Western capitalism. In Italy a terrorist culture emerged, with approximately 2,000 acts of terrorism committed each year during the 1970s, including a yearly average of 40 murders and 300 *reported* kidnappings. With its dramatic rejection of the processes of democratic decision making, terrorism challenged some of the most basic assumptions of the postwar order in the West.

CONCLUSION

New Definitions, New Divisions

The Cold War was an ideological encounter, with both sides laying claim to the title "democratic." When Soviet tanks rolled through the streets of Budapest in 1956, they flattened not only the Hungarian Revolution but also any illusions about the democratic nature of Soviet-style communism. Yet the hope that the communist system could be reformed, that Marx's original concern for social justice and political equality could be reclaimed, remained—until twelve years later when the tanks rolled again in an eastern European city. The crushing of the Prague Spring destroyed any hope of a democratic eastern Europe within the confines of the Cold War.

In contrast, democracy took firm root in western Europe during the postwar era, even in nations with antidemocratic cultural traditions such as West Germany and Italy. Yet in 1968, protesters in Paris and in cities throughout the world challenged the easy linkage of "the West" with democracy. They pointed out that the increasing scale and complexity of industrial society deprived ordinary people of opportunities for genuine participation in political decision making. And they pointed to the way that Cold War divisions superseded democratic commitments. Despite its abandonment of democratic practices to reinforce racial apartheid, for example, South Africa considered itself, and was considered by other powers, as part of "the West." Within the Cold War context, "the West" sometimes seemed to mean simply "anti-Soviet."

By the early 1970s, the sharp bipolarities of West versus East had begun to break down. Over the next three decades, economic crisis, combined with revolutionary changes in eastern European and Soviet affairs, would reshape the contemporary world. By the early 1990s, the Cold War was over and nationalist conflicts, often fueled by vicious ethnic and religious hatreds, once again played front and center, after twenty years of being upstaged by superpower hostilities.

Suggestions for Further Reading

For a comprehensive list of suggested readings, please go to www.ablongman.com/levack/chapter28

Ansprenger, Franz. *The Dissolution of Colonial Empires.* 1989. A clear and comprehensive account (that unfortunately includes no maps).

Castles, Stephen, et al. *Here for Good: Western Europe's New Ethnic Minorities.* 1984. A useful exploration of the impact of postwar immigration, despite the rather rigid Marxist analysis.

Crampton, R. J. *Eastern Europe in the Twentieth Century—And After.* 1997. Detailed chapters on the 1950s and 1960s, including a substantial discussion of the Prague Spring.

Cronin, James. *The World the Cold War Made: Order, Chaos, and the Return of History.* 1996. An intelligent and thought-provoking overview of the impact of the Cold War.

Fineberg, Jonathan. *Art Since 1940: Strategies of Being.* 1995. A big, bold, lavishly illustrated volume that makes the unfashionable argument that individuals matter.

Fink, Carole, et al. *1968: The World Transformed.* 1998. A collection of essays that explores both the international and the domestic political context for the turmoil of 1968.

Isaacs, Jeremy, and Taylor Downing. *Cold War: An Illustrated History.* 1998. The companion book to the CNN television series. Filled with memorable photographs.

Judge, Edward, and John Langdon. *A Hard and Bitter Peace: A Global History of the Cold War.* 1999. An extremely useful survey for students. Excellent maps.

Keep, John. *Last of the Empires: A History of the Soviet Union, 1945–1991.* 1995. Looks beyond the Kremlin to explore social, cultural, and economic developments.

Mazrui, Ali, and Michael Tidy. *Nationalism and New States in Africa.* 1984. Offers a thematic rather than chronological account of African state-building.

Poiger, Uta. *Jazz, Rock, and Rebels: Cold War Politics and American Culture in a Divided Germany.* 2000. Explores the interplay among youth culture, Americanization, and political protest.

Stromberg, Roland. *After Everything: Western Intellectual History Since 1945.* 1975. A swiftly moving tour through the major intellectual developments.

Urwin, Derek. *A Political History of Western Europe Since 1945.* 1997. Readable, reasonably up-to-date, and comprehensive.

Zubok, Vladislav, and Constantine Pleshakov. *Inside the Kremlin's Cold War: From Stalin to Khrushchev.* 1996. A close examination of the Cold War on the Soviet side.

Notes

1. Lawrence Wylie, *Village in the Vaucluse* (1964), p. 33.
2. Quotation from *Time* magazine, 1950; quoted in Martin Walker, *The Cold War and the Making of the Modern World* (1993), pp. 66–67.
3. Quoted in Stephen Ambrose, *Rise to Globalism* (1971), p. 225.
4. Quoted in Walker, p. 83.
5. Quoted in Donald W. White, *The American Century* (1996), p. 286.
6. Quoted in Jeremy Isaacs and Taylor Downing, *Cold War: An Illustrated History* (1998), p. 170.
7. Quoted in Isaacs and Downing, p. 182.
8. Quoted in Walker, p. 132.
9. Quoted in John Lewis Gaddis, *We Now Know: Rethinking Cold War Evidence* (1997), p. 181.
10. Quotation from Isaacs and Downing, p. 190.
11. Quoted in John D. Hargreaves, *Decolonization in Africa* (1996), p. 113.
12. Quoted in White, *The American Century* (1996), p. 328.
13. Quoted in John L. H. Keep, *Last of the Empires: A History of the Soviet Union, 1945–1991* (1995), p. 79.
14. Quoted in Walker, p. 105.
15. Official Hungarian statistics reported 3,000 dead. John Lewis Gaddis places the number at 20,000 in *We Now Know: Rethinking Cold War Evidence* (1997).
16. Quoted in Robert Paxton, *Europe in the Twentieth Century* (1997), p. 578.
17. Quoted in Derek Urwin, *A Political History of Western Europe Since 1945* (1997), p. 84.
18. Reinhold Wagnleitner, *Coca-Colonization and the Cold War: The Cultural Mission of the United States in Austria After the Second World War* (1994).
19. Quoted in Richard Kuisel, *Seducing the French: The Dilemma of Americanization* (1993), p. 147.
20. Quoted in Felix Gilbert, *The End of the European Era, 1890 to the Present* (1991), p. 429.
21. Quoted in Jonathan Fineberg, *Art Since 1940: Strategies of Being* (1995), p. 144.
22. Quoted in Adrian Hastings, *Modern Catholicism: Vatican II and After* (1991), p. 29.
23. Quoted in Hastings, p. 267.

The Contemporary Era, 1973 to the Present

O N THE EVENING OF NOVEMBER 9, 1989, EAST GERMAN BORDER GUARDS stationed at the wall that divided East and West Berlin gazed out nervously at an unprecedented sight. Thousands of their fellow citizens had gathered in front of the gates, and were demanding to be let through into the western half of the city. This demand was extraordinary; in the twenty-eight years that the Berlin Wall had stood, over 200 people had been shot trying to cross it. But the autumn of 1989 was no ordinary time. A radically reformist regime had emerged in the Soviet Union and publicly proclaimed that its eastern European allies could no longer rely on the Soviet army to assist them in putting down domestic dissent. Poland and Hungary were in the process of replacing communist governments with pluralist parliamentary systems. And in East Germany, 200,000 disaffected citizens had taken advantage of relaxed border controls in Hungary and Czechoslovakia to flee to the West in just a few weeks, while over one million had joined illegal protest demonstrations.

On November 9, in response to overwhelming public pressure, the East German government announced that it would drastically relax the requirements for obtaining an exit visa to visit or emigrate to the West. In a press conference to announce the upcoming changes, the East Berlin Communist Party boss Gunter Schabowski gave a carelessly worded reply to a reporter's question about the new travel policy—and sparked a revolution. Schabowski indicated, wrongly, that as of the next morning, anyone who wanted to head to the West could obtain an automatic exit visa at the border. The news spread quickly, and huge crowds gathered at the checkpoints that dotted the Berlin Wall. The nervous border guards had no idea what to do. Neither did their superiors, who refused to issue the guards any clear instructions. As the crowds pressed forward, the guards gave in and opened the gates. While television cameras broadcast the scene to an astonished world, tens of thousands of East Germans walked, ran, and danced

And the Wall Came Tumbling Down: Berliners celebrate the fall of the Berlin Wall in November 1989.

across the border that had for so long literally and symbolically divided West from East. Elated with their new freedom and energized with a sense of power and possibility, they then turned on the wall itself. Jumping on top of it, they transformed it from an instrument of coercion and division into a platform for partying. Caught, the East German government saw no way to close the gates. Within a few days, and again without any official approval, ordinary Germans, equipped with hammers and chisels, began to dismantle the wall that the politicians had erected almost three decades earlier.

As extraordinary as the fall of the wall was, the events that followed over the next two years proved even more dramatic—the collapse of communist regimes throughout eastern Europe, the end of the Cold War, the disintegration of the Soviet Union, and the onset of civil war in Yugoslavia and in many formerly Soviet regions. Over the next decade, both governments and ordinary people—not only throughout Europe but across the globe—struggled to build new structures to suit the vastly changed geopolitical landscape. With the collapse of communism and the sundering of the Iron Curtain that had once divided Europe, the meaning of "the West" itself changed, as new enemies emerged to take the place of the Soviet Union. Clearly, then, the dramatic developments of 1989–1991 deserve close study, but they must be set within a context of causes and consequences. To explain that context, this chapter will address three questions: (1) How did economic and political developments in the 1970s and 1980s interact to bring about an end to the international structures of the postwar era and to create a volatile situation within the Soviet bloc? (2) What factors explain not only the outbreak but also the success of the revolutions of 1989–1991, and what were the consequences of these revolutions for the societies of eastern Europe? (3) What were the implications of these developments for the meaning of "the West" itself?

A New and Uncertain Era: The 1970s and 1980s

In the early 1970s, the United States and Europe—both East and West—entered a new era, one defined by economic crisis, widening social divisions, heightened political polarization, and a renewed Cold War.

ECONOMIC CRISIS AND ITS CONSEQUENCES IN THE WEST

Economic crisis was the defining fact of the history of the West after 1973. Before the 1970s, inflation and unemployment seemed to be mutually exclusive—robust economies

featured little or no unemployment but tended toward inflation; slower-moving economies were devoid of inflation, but suffered from high unemployment rates. The 1970s, however, brought an unprecedented combination of high inflation rates (in the double digits in many countries by the end of the 1970s) and high unemployment rates (also reaching the double digits in a number of regions). Commentators labeled this new reality stagflation°—the escalating prices of a boom economy combined with the joblessness of an economy going bust. Between 1974 and 1976 the average annual growth rate within western European nations dropped to zero, a sharp contrast to the 1960s' average of 4.8 percent. The prosperous postwar era appeared to be over. By 1984, one-quarter of western European workers under age 25 were unemployed.

Causes of the Economic Crisis

What caused this economic crisis? There is no easy answer, but clearly war and oil played important roles. In October 1973, Egyptian and Syrian armies attacked Israel. When Soviet forces began airlifting supplies to the invading troops, Israel appealed to the U.S. for military aid. In retaliation for American assistance to Israel, the oil-producing states, or OPEC (Organization of Petroleum Exporting Countries), imposed an embargo on American sales, cut back production, and drove up prices from $3 to $16 per barrel of oil. In 1979 political revolution in Iran sparked an even more dramatic price rise—up to $35 per barrel by 1981. These price increases vastly accelerated the inflationary spiral and dealt the death blow to the easy affluence of the postwar era.

Yet rising oil prices were not the sole cause of the economic crisis of the 1970s and 1980s. Two other factors also contributed. First, in 1973 U.S. President Richard Nixon decided to let the dollar "float," to let market forces rather than fixed currency exchange rates determine the dollar's value against other currencies. This decision gutted the Bretton Woods agreements, which had governed international economic affairs since World War II (see Chapter 26), and introduced a more volatile economic era. Whereas the Bretton Woods system had worked to direct the flow of capital to countries in need of investment, the new unregulated system allowed capital to surge into markets where investors could reap immediate gains. National economies lay vulnerable to speculative attacks. No fewer than sixty-nine countries experienced serious banking crises, and the annual economic growth rates of the developed nations fell by one-third in the decades that followed the collapse of Bretton Woods.

A second factor in the economic crisis of the 1970s was international competition. Both the western European and American economies struggled to compete with the emerging Asian and South and Latin American economies. Western societies possessed aging industries and a politicized workforce that demanded relatively high wages and

Inflation and Economic Performance in the West

	France	Great Britain	Italy	United States	West Germany
Inflation over Previous Year (percent)					
1970	5.2%	6.4%	5.0%	5.9%	3.4%
1975	11.8	24.2	17.0	9.1	6.0
1979	9.1	13.4	14.8	11.3	4.1
Gross Domestic Product (Percentage Growth/Decline over Previous Year)					
1970	+5.7%	+2.3%	+5.3%	–0.3%	+5.1%
1975	+0.2	–0.6	–3.6	–0.1	–1.6
1979	+3.3	+2.4	+2.7	+2.4	+4.2

Source: Martin Walker, *Cold War: A History*, 1993, p. 234.

extensive social services. Increasingly, manufacturing concerns moved south and east, to take advantage of the lack of labor regulation and protection in the developing world.

Heightened Social Tensions

The economic crisis had stark social consequences. As the economic pie grew smaller, competition for slices grew more fierce. The 1970s saw a resurgence of industrial unrest in western Europe. In Britain, conflict with the unions brought down three successive governments in a decade. In both Italy and West Germany, workers became increasingly militant and succeeded in winning large wage increases. These industrial settlements only worsened the problem of inflation. Workers demanded large pay increases to meet the rising cost of living, but employers, faced with having to pay higher wages, raised the prices of their goods and services. And so the cost of living continued to climb.

The new economic climate of austerity also led to heightened racial conflict throughout much of western Europe. As we saw in Chapter 28, postwar governments struggling to cope with labor shortages had encouraged immigration, both from the poorer countries of southern and eastern Europe and from colonial or former colonial regions such as Algeria, India, and Jamaica. By 1971, nine million immigrants were living in northern and western Europe.

With the onset of economic crisis, these immigrant communities soon found themselves under attack. European governments reacted to rising unemployment rates by halting labor immigration. By 1975 West Germany, France, the Netherlands, Britain, Belgium, Sweden, and Switzerland had all banned further immigration. Because it explicitly (although incorrectly) linked the presence of immigrants to unemployment, anti-immigration legislation helped solidify racist attitudes among many sectors of the European population. Violence against immigrants began to escalate. In 1973, thirty-two Algerians were murdered in France. White working-class youths in London indulged in what they termed "paki-bashing": beating up individuals of Southeast Asian descent.

Ironically, anti-immigration legislation actually increased the size of immigrant communities. West Germany saw its number of foreign residents rise by 13 percent between 1974 and 1982; in the same period, France witnessed a 33 percent increase. Foreign workers scrambled to get into western Europe before the doors shut, and once they were in, were reluctant to leave because of the well-grounded fear that they would not be able to return. Family members came too—only Switzerland banned the entry of dependents.

In the 1980s, then, what sociologists call "migration streams" were solidifying into ethnic minority communities—not "guestworkers," but rather a permanent part of western European societies. By 1991, 25 percent of the inhabitants of France were either immigrants or the children or grandchildren of immigrants. For both economic and social reasons, minority groups clustered in certain areas in certain cities. In West Germany in the early 1980s, ethnic minorities constituted 6 percent of the population as a whole, but 24 percent of the population of Frankfurt—and in the city's central district, 80 percent.

The resulting encounters among peoples of different religious and ethnic traditions reshaped European culture. In Britain, for example, Afro-Caribbean styles of dress and music had a profound influence on white working-class youth culture. These encounters also posed a potent challenge to ideas of national identity. By the 1980s, British journalists were writing about "third-generation immigrants," as if someone born in Britain to British citizenship was somehow less British than other British citizens. Such terminology indicated a deep reluctance to classify individuals with brown or black skin as British, an inability to conceive of national identity as anything but white. In France, the highly centralized education system became the site of hostile encounters, as Islamic parents fought for the rights of their daughters to attend school in traditional Muslim headdress, a practice resisted by some French authorities

"YOUNG, BRITISH, AND WHITE"

During the 1980s, racist violence increased in Britain, as throughout much of Europe. Overtly racist political parties, such as the National Front, capitalized on anti-immigrant sentiment to recruit new members for their movements. In this document, the American journalist Bill Buford describes a birthday party held in a pub for one young member of the National Front. The excerpt begins with a dangerous moment: football (soccer) rivalries are threatening to divide the partygoers.

On the far side, some of the new members had started in on their football chants, just as Neil had feared. These appeared to be West Ham supporters. They were then answered, from the other side of the room, by Chelsea supporters.* A contrapuntal chorus of West Ham and Chelsea songs followed, one that sent Neil scurrying through his record collection. It was time to change the music . . . It was time to play the White Power music.

None of the songs was played on any of the established radio stations or sold in any of the conventional shops. It was a mail-order or cash-in-hand music trade, and from the titles you could see why: "Young, British, and White"; "England Belongs to Me"; "Shove the Dove"; "England" and "British Justice." These were the lyrics of "The Voice of Britain":

> Our old people cannot walk the streets alone.
> They fought for this nation and this is what they get back.

They risked their lives for Britain, and now Britain belongs to aliens.
It's about time Britain went and took it back.

This is the voice of Britain.
You'd better believe it.
This is the voice of Britain
C'mon and fly the flag now.

. . .

The music was delivered with the same numbing, crushing percussion that had characterized everything else that had been played that evening . . . There was one refrain I could follow, and that was because it was played repeatedly, and because, each time, everyone joined in. It seemed to be the theme song.

> Two pints of lager† and a packet of crisps.‡
> Wogs§ out! White power!
> Wogs out! White power!
> Wogs out! White power!

It was interesting to contemplate that the high-point of the evening was organized around this simple declaration of needs: a lad needed his lager; a lad needed his packet of crisps; a lad needed his wog.

* West Ham and Chelsea = rival English soccer teams.
† "Lager" = beer.
‡ "Packet of crisps" = bag of potato chips.
§ "Wog" = racially derogatory term for Southeast Asians.

Source: From *Among the Thugs: The Experience, and the Seduction, of Crowd Violence* by Bill Buford. Copyright © 1991, 1990 by William Buford. Used by permission of W. W. Norton & Company, Inc. and The Random House Group Limited.

---

who feared that "Frenchness" would be diluted if immigrants failed to accept the traditions of the host society.

In both France and Britain, immigrants could become or already were legal citizens. In West Germany, Switzerland, and the Scandinavian countries, however, foreign workers remained foreign, with no chance of obtaining citizenship. Thus by the 1980s, a dangerous situation had emerged in these countries, with the children of foreign workers growing up in a society in which they had no political rights. These "foreigners" experienced widespread discrimination in education, housing, and employment. In West Germany in the late 1970s, over 40 percent of foreign workers lived in housing without a bath or shower. (Only 6 percent of German citizens did so.) Forced to live in such substandard accommodation by poverty, immigrants were often then stereotyped as dirty and uncivilized.

Explicitly racist political parties capitalized on the new anti-immigration sentiment. In France, for example, Jean-Marie Le Pen (b. 1928), a veteran of the Algerian war,

created the *Front National* in 1974 as an anti-immigration party. In Le Pen's view, "Everything comes from immigration. Everything goes back to immigration." Unemployment, rising crime rates, an increase in illegitimate births, crowded schools, AIDS—Le Pen blamed it all on non-white immigrants. Appealing particularly to young, male working-class voters, Le Pen's party attracted between 9 and 11 percent of the votes in elections in the mid-1980s, and remained a threatening political presence for the next two decades. In the presidential race of 2002, Le Pen beat out sixteen competitors and came in second only to the incumbent, the Gaullist Party leader Jacques Chirac.

A Changing Political Culture

The economic crisis called into question the main assumptions that had governed political life since World War II. Western Europeans had emerged from the horror of total war in 1945 determined to build better societies. Rejecting the extremes of communism on the left and fascism on the right, they took the centrist social democratic path. Two features characterized social democracies—first, mixed economies that combined nationalization of key industries with private enterprise, and second, an interventionist state that took responsibility for maintaining full employment and providing extensive welfare services. The stagflation of the 1970s, however, seemed to indicate that these social democratic solutions no longer worked.

Alternative answers appeared, clustered under the label of New Conservatism°, epitomized by the Republican Ronald Reagan in the United States (1911–), the Christian Democrat Helmut Kohl in West Germany (1930–), and the Conservative Margaret Thatcher in Britain (1925–). On the most fundamental level, the New Conservatives rejected the postwar emphasis on social improvement in favor of policies intended to create more opportunities for individual achievement. Thatcher even insisted, "There is no such thing as society." In the New Conservative worldview, there was instead the individual, freely competing in a world governed by market forces rather than governmental regulations or state planning. As Kohl demanded during his

■ The New Conservatism

Britain's first female prime minister, Margaret Thatcher, called herself a "conviction" rather than a "consensus" politician. She held office from 1979 to 1990—the longest term of any British prime minister in the twentieth century.

Spending on Social Services as a Percentage of the Gross Domestic Product

	France	West Germany	Sweden	United Kingdom
1960	13.2	15.5	11.0	10.8
1965	15.6	16.5	13.8	11.8
1970	15.1	17.1	18.6	13.1
1975	23.9	23.7	25.0	17.1
1980	26.3	24.0	31.9	18.1
1985	28.7	23.8	30.7	20.3

Source: Susan Pedersen, *Family, Dependence, and the Origins of the Welfare State: Britain and France, 1914–1945*, 1993, p. 416. Reprinted with the permission of Cambridge University Press.

1983 campaign, "Less state, more market; fewer collective burdens, more personal performance; fewer encrusted structures, more mobility, self-initiative, and competition." Privatization of nationalized or state-owned industries constituted a key part of the New Conservative agenda—removing the state from the economy and allowing private enterprises to compete. In Britain under Thatcher, the coal industry, transport, and utilities were all shifted to private ownership.

New Conservatives also mounted an attack on the welfare state, insisting that rising social expenditures, funded by rising taxes, lay at the heart of the economic crisis that had afflicted the West since the early 1970s. They pointed to the fact that the years between 1960 and 1981 had seen a dramatic rise in social spending (for programs such as health, disability, and unemployment insurance; pensions; and family allowances). Minimizing the successes of these social programs in reducing poverty, New Conservatives instead linked rising social expenditures to surging inflation and declining economic growth rates.

New Conservative fiscal policies did not actually break sharply from their social democratic predecessors. Reagan, for example, used deficit spending to finance skyrocketing military budgets (up by 40 percent during his administration). The real break lay in the New Conservatives' willingness to tolerate high unemployment rates in order to lower inflation. By imposing high interest rates on their economies, Thatcher and Reagan engineered a recession in the early 1980s that brought inflation under control. Inflation rates in Britain fell from 18 percent in 1980 to 4.5 percent in 1983. High interest rates, however, overvalued the British pound and the American dollar. As a result, manufacturers found it hard to sell their products abroad and many went under. In Britain, 13 percent of the workforce was unemployed by 1984. In West Germany, too, Kohl's policies of holding down taxes and government expenditures were accompanied by unemployment rates of over 9 percent in the mid-1980s. Inflation-busting came at a high social cost, as riots erupted in English cities in 1981 and beggars reappeared on British streets.

By the end of the 1980s, as a result of falling global oil prices and the Reagan military spending spree that primed the pump of the global economy, Western economies returned to growth (and by 1990, inflation rates had begun to rise again). But the average late-1980s growth rates of 2 to 3 percent per year were lower than those of 5 to 6 percent that had characterized Western economies in the 1950s and 1960s. At the same time, unemployment rates tended to hover between 5 and 7 percent—levels that would have been regarded as unacceptably high in the earlier period. A new political culture, based on lowered expectations, had come into being.

Even Europe's social democratic parties had to adapt to this new political culture. In Sweden, the Social Democrats returned to office in 1982 after eight years out of power, but under the leadership of Olaf Palme (1926–1986), the chastened party followed a centrist path, marked by moderate wage agreements and reductions in tax rates. Socialist governments in Italy, Greece, and Spain during the 1980s also followed the path of reduced health and social security expenditures, rising utility and public transport fees, and wage cuts.

The most dramatic example of social democratic adaptation occurred in France. In 1981, French voters elected Socialist Party leader François Mitterrand (1916–1996) to the presidency. In his first year in office, Mitterrand implemented a series of radical social democratic measures, including a rise in the minimum wage, a reduction in the workweek and an increase in holiday time, and expanded social welfare. He nationalized the country's banking system and imposed higher taxes on the wealthier sections of society. But in 1982, Mitterrand was forced by a series of economic catastrophes—falling exports, rising trade and budget deficits, and soaring inflation rates—to cut social spending, to reverse his nationalization program, and to implement "austerity" measures, which led to higher unemployment rates.

FROM DETENTE TO RENEWED COLD WAR, 1975–1985

At the same time that economic crisis undermined political consensus, rising superpower tensions put an end to the era of detente—and caused greater rifts within western European societies. In the early 1970s, detente had appeared to be flourishing, with the United States and the Soviet Union signing the first major arms control agreement in 1971. The culmination of detente came in 1975 at the Helsinki Conference in Finland. Thirty-two European states, Canada, the United States, and the Soviet Union declared their acceptance of all existing European borders, agreed to a policy of joint notification of all major military exercises (thus reducing the chances of accidental nuclear war), and promised to safeguard the human rights of their citizens.

Ironically, the Helsinki Accords marked the beginning of the end of the detente era. Using the Helsinki human rights clauses to demand political reform, eastern European and Soviet dissidents such as the Soviet scientist and Nobel Peace Prize–winner Andrei Sakharov (1921–1989) began to publicize the human rights abuses committed by their governments. The human rights issue weakened U.S.-Soviet relations, particularly after the election of Jimmy Carter (1976–1980) to the U.S. presidency. Carter insisted on placing human rights at the center of his foreign policy. Soviet leaders reacted in fury to what they perceived as Carter's meddling in their internal affairs—and heightened their persecution of dissidents. Sakharov, for example, was imprisoned in 1979.

As detente crumbled, the arms race accelerated. Alarmed by the Soviet deployment of a new intermediate-range nuclear missile in 1977, western European leaders pressured Carter to approve the development of NATO's own intermediate-range weapon, the cruise missile. In 1979, the governments of West Germany, Britain, Italy, Belgium, and the Netherlands agreed to the deployment of the cruise missiles on their soil. Carter pledged a 5 percent increase in the U.S. defense budget, with even more dramatic increases promised for years to come.

The final blow to detente came in 1979 with the Soviet invasion of Afghanistan. In 1978 Afghan communists had seized control of their government and soon found themselves under attack from Islamic rebels. The prospect of a fundamentalist Islamic regime in Afghanistan alarmed the Soviet government, which feared the spread of Islamic nationalism into its own Central Asian republics. In December 1979, on the same day that NATO announced the deployment of its cruise missiles, the Politburo voted to send troops into Afghanistan (at a meeting in which Soviet leader Leonid Brezhnev was so drunk he could not participate). Calling the invasion "the most serious threat to peace since the Second World War," Carter cut economic and cultural links with the Soviet Union, approved CIA aid for anti-Soviet Islamic guerrilla groups, and warned that if the Soviets moved toward the Middle East, he would not hesitate to use nuclear weapons. The era of detente was over.

With the election of New Conservatives such as Reagan and Thatcher, the renewal of the Cold War took on a greater intensity. Both Reagan and Thatcher viewed detente as a policy of weakness. Pointing to the triumph of communist regimes in Ethiopia, Vietnam, Mozambique, and Angola, they argued that the Soviet Union had gained the advantage over the West in the struggle for global supremacy. Reagan labeled the Soviet Union the "Evil Empire"—a reference to the popular *Star Wars* film series that was first released in the 1970s—and revived the anticommunist attitudes and

The Greenham Common Protests

In the spring of 1983, protesters formed a fourteen-mile-human chain across Greenham Common in England to protest against NATO's deployment of cruise missiles. The protest was part of a much wider movement in western Europe and the United States, which articulated widespread public discontent with the renewal of the Cold War. It also played a pivotal role in British feminism, as female activists established a women-only camp at the Greenham Common military base.

rhetoric of the 1950s. Thatcher strongly supported Reagan's decision to accelerate the arms buildup begun by Carter. Her hard-line anticommunism won her the nickname the "Iron Lady" from Soviet policymakers.

The renewal of the Cold War, like the end of economic prosperity, opened up large rifts within European societies. The NATO decision to deploy cruise missiles proved enormously unpopular with many ordinary Europeans. Hundreds of thousands of protesters turned out in the streets of London, Bonn, Amsterdam, and other cities. Many of these protesters demanded not only the cancellation of the cruise missiles but also a withdrawal from NATO's nuclear umbrella and a reorientation of European political life and international affairs away from nuclear weapons—and away from the United States.

New Challenges and New Identities in the West

In the wake of economic crisis and the renewed Cold War, new cultural and political forces emerged in western Europe and the United States. In the 1970s and 1980s, feminism and radical environmentalism demanded a shift in the political status quo.

Changing Women's Roles

New feminism° emerged directly out of the student protest movement of the 1960s. Female activists grew frustrated at being denied a voice in the movement—"we cook while the men talk of revolution."[1] At the same time, they were increasingly eager to connect analyses of political subordination to experiences of sexual repression. Their efforts to liberate women from political and cultural limits and expectations gave birth to what was, by the 1980s, an international feminist movement.

Economic changes buttressed the new feminism. The numbers of women working outside the home rose in these decades—up by 50 percent in Italy between 1970 and 1985, for example. By the late 1970s, women in France accounted for over 34 percent of the labor force; in Britain, 31 percent; in West Germany, 37 percent. As unemployment took a particularly high toll on male, unionized, full-time, skilled manual laborers, many homes saw the wife emerge as the chief breadwinner.

Demographic changes also supported the new feminism. In 1970, the age at which men and women first married began to climb (reversing the trend of two decades), and birth rates continued to fall. Women were also far more likely to have children outside marriage—25 percent of all

The Pill: Controlling the Female Body

In the postwar period, all sorts of pills appeared on the shelves of American and European pharmacies. Offered in a myriad of colors and sizes, they promised all sorts of remedies for all sorts of ailments. But only one earned the designation "*the* Pill"—the oral contraceptive, first marketed in the United States in 1960. In 1993, the *Economist* (a respected British weekly news magazine) listed the Pill as one of the seven wonders of the modern world. A revolutionary contraceptive, the Pill helped alter the place of the female body in Western culture.

The Pill's entry into the mass market coincided with two other developments. First, sexual practices and attitudes changed significantly among some sectors of the population—particularly middle-class men and women with university educations. Second, the birth rate slowed throughout the United States and western Europe. Thus it is often assumed that the Pill caused both a sexual and demographic revolution.

This assumption is incorrect. Although by 1965 the Pill was the most popular form of birth control in the United States (used by 80 percent of white, non-Catholic, college graduates between ages 20 and 24), in Europe it became a part of women's lives much more slowly. Introduced to Britain in 1961, the Pill was not mass-marketed there until the late 1960s. In France and Czechoslovakia, withdrawal remained the most popular form of birth control until well into the 1970s, when the Pill began to be distributed widely. In Italy, contraceptives of all types, including the Pill, were illegal until 1971. In Ireland, they remain illegal for unmarried men and women. In the Soviet Union, the Pill was never widely accessible. Most Soviet women relied on withdrawal, rhythm, and abortion—on the average, four to six abortions during the childbearing years. Moreover, throughout Europe and the United States, the Pill always remained more popular with the wealthier sectors of society. Because women who wanted to use it were required to visit their doctor every six months, many poor women viewed the Pill as prohibitively expensive (and many single women simply could not obtain a prescription).

The Pill, then, did not cause the sexual revolution. It did, however, have a radical impact. The Pill offered a new, yet ambivalent way of viewing the female body. Other methods of birth control dealt with the consequences of sexual intercourse (the barrier methods, withdrawal, and abortion) or sought to limit its practice (rhythm). The Pill, however, was not an external object to be inserted or applied or fitted. By manipulating the female reproductive cycle, it actually altered the body itself, permitting women to experience what had been defined as an exclusively male prerogative—the detachment of sexual intercourse from pregnancy. At the same time, the Pill allowed women to distance themselves from their bodies. One of the problems with other forms of female contraceptives was that they required women to touch their genitals, a requirement that many European and American women found distasteful.

The Pill also raised important questions about controlling the female body. During the course of the twentieth century, childbirth had altered radically in the Western world. No longer occurring at home and presided over by women, childbirth now occurred in the hospital, where doctors—usually male—were in charge. It had become "medicalized": The birthing woman had become a patient, a medical problem, in need of drugs and other scientific devices. The Pill fit with this process. Although many women hailed it as a liberator that allowed them to control their own bodies, the Pill was initially marketed to doctors very differently. In its advertising, the Searle pharmaceutical company assured doctors that the Pill would allow them to supervise and regulate their patients' birth control practices. The Pill, then, offered the promise of controlling the female body: The question was, who was in charge? ∎

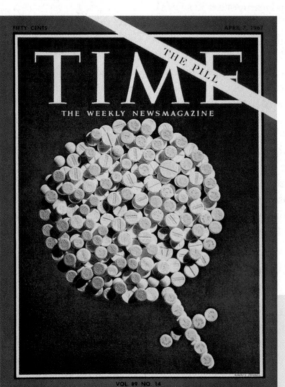

■ **One Little Pill**

In 1967, *Time* magazine's cover story on the Pill was entitled "Freedom from Fear."

For Discussion

Why has the Pill become a powerful symbol of changes in women's roles in the contemporary era?

births in Britain in 1988; in Sweden and Denmark, almost 50 percent. Marriage itself became optional. By the late 1970s, almost half of the couples who married were already cohabiting.

Institutional politics responded slowly to the changes in women's roles. In many countries, women had lost ground since World War II. Whereas thirty women had sat in France's National Assembly in 1945, in 1973 only nine remained. Slowly, these numbers climbed back up. In the British general elections of 1992, twice as many women stood as parliamentary candidates compared to 1979. The most dramatic changes occurred in Scandinavia. By the mid-1980s, women averaged about one-third of the members of parliament in Sweden, and women members accounted for approximately half of Norway's cabinets.

The new feminist movement refused to confine its focus to the world of party politics, recognizing instead that "the personal is political." Much of the new feminist critique focused on the female body—its image, its oppression, its control. Feminists challenged feminine stereotypes through attacks on beauty pageants and critiques of the fashion industry, and sought the reform of legal codes to outlaw spousal rape and to legalize abortion. Legalization of abortion occurred first in northern Europe: in Britain in 1967, in Denmark in 1970. Catholic Europe followed: In Italy abortions became legally available in 1978, in France in 1979.

In the economic and educational spheres, feminists demanded equal pay for equal work and greater access to educational and professional opportunities. They pressed for more generous parental leave policies, family allowances, and child care provisions. In addition, with women accounting for approximately half of the university students in many Western countries, feminists began to alter the content of the curriculum. Challenging the male biases that had regarded women's contributions as irrelevant and women's lives as insignificant, for example, feminist historians brought to light the "hidden history" of women.

Environmental Awareness and Activism

Environmentalists added their voice to the political cacophony of the 1970s and 1980s. Conservationist groups seeking to protect this species or preserve that plant had long existed in the industrial world, but the radical environmentalism that emerged in the later 1960s was something new. Radical environmentalists saw problems such as species elimination or pollution as part of a larger ecological breakdown. They challenged the fundamental structures of industrial economies (whether capitalist or communist), particularly their inherent emphasis on "more, bigger, faster, now." The movement embraced the ideas of unorthodox economists such as Britain's E. F. Schumacher (1911–1977), who insisted that quantitative measures of economic growth (such as the GNP) failed to factor in environmental destruction and social dislocation, and that in many con-

■ **Spaceship Earth**
The photographs of the globe taken by the Apollo space teams in the 1960s provided humanity with a powerful new visual image, one that proved influential in shaping radical environmentalism. Suspended in space, the Earth seemed suddenly vulnerable, its limits very clear, a single spaceship hurtling through a vast infinity.

texts, "small is beautiful." At the heart of radical environmentalism was the concept of natural limits, of "Spaceship Earth"—the vision of the planet as a "single spaceship, without unlimited reservoirs of anything."[2]

New media-savvy organizations like Greenpeace publicized the environmentalist cause with colorful protests, such as sailing in small rubber dinghies to challenge whaling fleets. The most popular of radical environmentalist targets was nuclear power. From the mid-1970s on, protests against the construction of nuclear power plants in western Europe drew tens of thousands of supporters. The movement's slogan, "Nuclear Power? No Thanks," was translated into more than forty languages.

Environmental concern helped create a new sort of political party. By the late 1980s Green Parties had sprouted in fifteen western European countries. The Greens were the most successful in West Germany, where they sat in the legislature from 1983 and formed an important voting bloc. In the late 1990s, the members of the German Green Party joined the government.

Green politics° drew its ideas not only from environmentalism but also from both feminism and the mass protests against NATO's cruise missile deployment in the early 1980s. Strongly opposed to NATO and its reliance on nuclear weapons, the Greens appropriated the antinuclear movement's effort to break away from Cold War categories. To do so, they turned to feminist theory, contending that both the continuing Cold War and the degradation of the natural environment stemmed from the same root as discrimination against women—an obsession with physical power, a glorification of violence, and an unwillingness to tear down hierarchical structures. The Greens articulated a basic challenge to the political status quo: "We are neither left nor right; we are in front."

THE CRISIS OF LEGITIMACY IN THE EAST

Like the West, eastern Europe was rocked by the transformation in the global economy after 1973, but the impact was delayed, its consequences not fully felt until the 1980s. Even during the apparent prosperity of the 1970s, however, both structural economic weaknesses and spreading political disillusion undermined the stability of the Soviet bloc.

The Illusion of Prosperity

While Western countries in the 1970s struggled with stagflation and disappearing economic growth rates, the Soviet Union posted record-breaking production figures. By 1984, for example, the Soviet Union was producing 80 percent more steel and six times more iron ore than the United States. But Soviet prosperity was an illusion. Published growth and productivity statistics had little to do with actual economic performance. The Soviet economy continued to be hampered by overcentralization. The state planning commission, GOSPLAN, had the impossible task of coordinating the production of over four million different products in at least 50,000 factories. "Success" in Soviet industry continued to mean fulfilling arbitrary quotas, regardless of the quality of goods produced, the actual demand for the product, or the cost of producing it. The Soviet command economy also proved far too rigid to keep pace with global economic change. While triumphantly proclaiming its fulfillment of the heavy industrial expansion planned by Khrushchev in the early 1960s, Soviet leaders in the 1970s failed to recognize that increasingly, microchips counted for far more than iron ore—that fiber optics, not steel, would buttress the new modernity. When the first Soviet home computer reached the market in the 1980s, it cost ten times the comparable Western model. The few consumers who could afford the machine soon found that no floppy disks were available to run it.

By the 1980s, the only growth sectors in the Soviet economy were oil and vodka—and then the bottom dropped out of the oil market. After peaking at $35 per barrel in 1981, oil prices began a steady decade-long fall. In 1985, a barrel of oil averaged at $26; a year later, prices had dropped to between $12 and $20 per barrel. For the Soviet economy, the results were catastrophic.

The Soviet leadership was incapable of responding to the economic crisis. Throughout the 1970s, the General Secretary of the Communist Party (and thus the de facto ruler of the Soviet Union) was Leonid Brezhnev, whose increasing physical frailty mirrored that of the country at large. Like many of his colleagues, Brezhnev had been a child at the time of the Russian Revolution; he knew only Soviet rule and had risen into major office very young because of the employment opportunities created by Stalin's Great Purge. In 1982, the average age of members of the Politburo was 68. These men had a vested interest in maintaining the status quo, not in carrying out fundamental reform.

The Soviet Union's satellite states in eastern Europe also lurched from apparent prosperity into economic crisis during this period. During the 1970s, the Soviets provided oil to their eastern European satellites at prices far below the market value and so shielded these economies from some of the tensions afflicting their western European rivals. At the same time, eastern European governments borrowed heavily from Western banks. They used the loans to increase the flow of consumer goods to their populations (and thus to quell dissent) and also to import the latest industrial technologies, in hopes that modernization would invigorate their stagnant economies.

These hopes went unrealized. Western loans did not solve fundamental problems such as overcentralization and the divorce of prices from production costs. Despite an increased standard of living, eastern European consumption levels remained well behind those in the West. And unlike Soviet citizens, eastern Europeans were acutely aware of this fact. Travel restrictions were less severe than in the Soviet Union, and many eastern Europeans had access to Western television and radio stations. In East Germany, the prosperity of West Germany just across the border was a particular source of discontent. While West Germans drove some of the best-made cars in the world, East Germans endured long waiting periods before purchasing the Trabant, a plastic car with a two-cylinder, two-stroke motor that pumped out clouds of polluting exhaust.

In the 1980s, the debt-laden economic structures of eastern Europe began to collapse. Two factors were crucial. First, governments found they had to borrow simply to service their existing debt. Second, as oil prices fell, the Soviet Union responded by charging market value for their oil sales to their satellites, thus depriving these economies of a crucial support. Ordinary people soon felt the impact of this economic crisis, as governments restricted the flow of consumer goods and imposed higher prices.

The Moment of Solidarity, the Moment of Punk

Events in Poland at the end of the decade illustrated how economic discontent and political dissent could create a revolutionary situation. Faced with negative economic growth rates, the Polish government announced price increases for meat and other essentials in July 1980. Poles hit

■ **The Moment of Solidarity**
Lech Wałęsa addresses workers in the Gdansk shipyard in 1980. Note the pictures of the pope and the Virgin Mary—Roman Catholicism served as a vital source of national unity and identity, one opposed to communism.

the streets in angry protest. Workers at the Lenin Shipyard in Gdansk went on strike, a legal impossibility in a communist state. Led by a charismatic and politically savvy electrician named Lech Wałęsa (b. 1943), the striking shipyard workers demanded the right to form a trade union independent of communist control. One month later, they did so—and Solidarity° was born. Solidarity was far more than a trade union, however. When Wałęsa and his co-workers announced their demands, they not only included the right to unionize and strike, but also called for the liberation of political prisoners and an end to censorship. They demanded a rollback of the state's power and sharp restrictions on its repressive apparatus. Within just a few months, ten million Poles had joined the ranks of Solidarity.

Fearing Soviet military intervention, the Polish communist government cracked down. In December 1981 Prime Minister Wojciech Jaruzelski declared martial law, arrested more than 10,000 Solidarity members (including Wałęsa), banned all independent trade unions, and imposed price increases of 75 percent. For the next eighteen months, Poles lived in fear; they could not leave their home city without police permission and phone lines were openly wiretapped.

Like the Hungarian revolution in 1956 and the Prague Spring of 1968, Solidarity seemed to be one more futile and defeated protest in eastern Europe. But two factors made the Solidarity story end very differently. First, Poland's economic crisis continued to deepen. Its debt to the West climbed inexorably upward, food shortages became endemic, unemployment rates rose, and real wages fell. The average Polish worker's monthly wage was half the

cost of living, and the waiting time for an apartment was fifteen years. Second, Solidarity simply refused to be defeated. Both in prison and out, its members resolved to act as if they were free. They met in small groups, published six illegal newspapers and ran a radio station, and organized election boycotts. To a far greater degree than many observers in the West realized at the time, Solidarity remained a political presence and a moral force in Polish society throughout the 1980s, and in 1989 it emerged to lead Poland into democracy.

Before 1989 no other eastern European country experienced a protest movement as dramatic as Solidarity, yet throughout the region economic hardship fed widespread political alienation and a deepening longing for radical change. One sign of the widening gap between the communist authorities and the people they governed was the emergence of punk music as a cultural force among eastern European youth. Punk had first appeared in Britain in the mid-1970s, the product of economic decline and social division. Dressed in clothes that deliberately mocked the consumerism and respectability of mainstream middle-class society—ripped trousers held together with safety pins, dog collars, spiked and outrageously colored hair—punks promoted a do-it-yourself style of rock music that also spat on middle-class standards. Punk rockers rarely had any musical training or expertise; even talent was not actually necessary. All that was needed was rage, which was readily available.

The nihilistic message of bands such as Britain's Sex Pistols—"no future for you, no future for me"—resonated in eastern Europe. With names like Doom, Crisis, Shortage, Paralysis, Sewage, and Dead Organism, Eastern punk bands, like their Western models, often expressed utter despair: "No goal, no future, no hope, no joy!" But this nihilism butted against explicit political protest. At punk concerts in Poland, bands and their audiences stood in silent homage to Solidarity. In Hungary, the members of one punk group received prison sentences for a performance in which they mocked their government as a "rotten, stinking communist gang" while tearing up a live chicken.[3]

Nature and the Nation

The dissatisfaction expressed by punk bands permeated eastern European society, and increasingly took political form. Just as the emergence of radical environmentalism demonstrated a strong current of dissatisfaction with the political order in the West, so similar movements in the East pushed for radical change.

For decades, the conquest of nature had been a key part of Soviet ideology: "We cannot wait for favors from nature; our task is to take from her."[4] Beginning in the 1930s, Soviet engineers sought to fill what they regarded as nature's "empty spaces" with exotic plant and animal life, thus wreaking havoc with the ecological balance of much of the Soviet environment. In the early 1960s, Khrushchev's "Virgin Lands" scheme introduced intensive chemical fertilization and irrigation across huge swathes of Soviet territory, resulting in the fall of lake water levels, the destruction of wetlands, and the salinization of extensive stretches of land. The situation worsened in the 1970s. The rapid expansion of heavy industry focused on churning out products, not on human safety or environmental sustainability. The most basic environmental precautions were ignored within Soviet and eastern European cities; untreated sewage was often dumped directly into lakes and rivers. By 1977, Soviet scientists concluded that Lake Baikal—the most voluminous and deepest freshwater lake in the world, home to more than 800 plant and 1,500 animal species—had experienced irreversible environmental degradation.

As a result of this environmental destruction, environmentalist protest groups emerged in the Soviet Union and throughout eastern Europe. Because Soviet officials regarded the environment as insignificant, they tended to view environmentalist protest as unimportant, as a "safe" outlet for popular frustration. Thus environmentalism became one of the few areas in Soviet society that permitted ordinary people free expression and in which public opinion was allowed a voice. Environmental activism worked like a termite infestation, nibbling away from within at the structures of Soviet communism.

Environmentalism also proved crucial in underlining nationalist identity and fueling nationalist protest. The various national and ethnic groups within the vast Soviet empire watched their forests disappear, their lakes dry up, and their ancient cities bulldozed, as a result of decisions made in faraway Moscow by men they regarded as foreigners—as *Russians* rather than *comrades*. By the 1980s, schools in Latvia issued gas masks as a routine safety precaution because of the dangers of chemical spills. Many Latvians concluded that they would be better off independent of Soviet control.

Revolution in the East

Between 1989 and 1991, revolution engulfed eastern Europe and the Soviet Union. The appointment of Mikhail Gorbachev (1985–1991) as Soviet Communist Party Secretary in 1985 proved pivotal. Gorbachev's efforts to reform the Soviet system led to a series of breathtaking changes: Soviet control over eastern Europe ended, the Cold War came to an abrupt halt, the Soviet Union itself ceased to exist. Ironically, Gorbachev set in motion the first two of these developments precisely to avoid the third. But Gorbachev did not control the story. Ordinary people developed their own plot lines. What Czech dissident Václav Havel called "the power of the powerless" proved to be powerful indeed. In the decade following the revolutions, however, a sense of powerlessness returned to eastern Europe, as economic and social crisis followed in the wake of communism's fall.

GORBACHEV AND RADICAL REFORM

In 1982, the decrepit Leonid Brezhnev died—and so, in rapid succession, did his two successors, Yuri Andropov (1982–1984) and Konstantin Chernenko (1984–1985). The time had come for a generational change. When Mikhail Gorbachev succeeded Chernenko, he was 54 years old. Compared to his elderly colleagues on the Politburo, he looked like a teenager.

Gorbachev's biography encompassed the drama of Soviet history. He was born, in 1931, into the turmoil of collectivization. One-third of the inhabitants of his native village in Stavropol were executed or imprisoned or died from famine or disease in the upheavals of the early 1930s. Both of his grandfathers were arrested on trumped-up charges. Yet Gorbachev's family continued to believe in the Communist dream. During World War II his father served in the Red Army (and was twice wounded), and in 1948 Gorbachev and his father together won the Order of Red Banner of Labor for harvesting almost six times the average crop. Because of this award and his academic abilities, Gorbachev won entry to Moscow University. After earning degrees in economics and law, he rose through the ranks of the provincial Communist Party. In 1978, at age

■ Glasnost

Mikhail Gorbachev meets with workers in Moscow in 1985.

47, he became the youngest member of the Communist Party Central Committee, the key leadership body in the Soviet Union.

Gorbachev came to power in 1985, convinced that the Soviet system was ailing, and that the only way to restore it to health was through radical surgery. What he did not anticipate was that such surgery would in fact kill the patient. His surgical tools were glasnost and perestroika, two Russian terms without direct English equivalents.

Glasnost°, sometimes translated as "openness," "publicity," or "transparency," meant abandoning the deception and censorship that had always characterized the Soviet system, for a policy based on open admission of failures and problems. To Gorbachev, "Broad, timely, and frank information is testimony of faith in people . . . and for their capacity to work things out themselves."[5]

Not surprisingly, Soviet citizens remained wary of Gorbachev's talk of glasnost—until April 1986 and the Chernobyl nuclear power plant disaster. Operator error at the Ukrainian power plant led to the most serious nuclear accident in history. In the days following the accident, thirty-five plant workers died; over the next five years the clean-up effort would claim at least 7,000 lives. The accident placed more than four million inhabitants of Ukraine and Belarus at risk from excess radiation, and spread a radioactive cloud that extended all the way to Scotland. When news of the accident first reached Moscow, party officials acted as they had always done: They denied anything had happened. But monitors in Western countries quickly picked up on the excess radiation spewing into the atmosphere. Gorbachev initiated an about-face and insisted that the accurate information about the disaster be released to the public. Chernobyl became the first Soviet media event. In 1986, 93 percent of the Soviet population had access to a television set and what they saw on their screens convinced them that glasnost was real. A powerful change had occurred in Soviet political culture.

Through glasnost Gorbachev aimed to overcome the alienation and apathy that he perceived as endemic in Soviet culture, to convince citizens of the importance of participating in the structures of political and economic life. At the same time, he sought to change those structures through perestroika°, often translated as "restructuring" or "reconstruction." Gorbachev believed he could reverse his nation's economic decline only through a series of reforms focusing on modernization, decentralization, and the introduction of a limited market.

Gorbachev knew, however, that even limited reforms threatened the vested interests of communist bureaucrats. Thus the success of economic perestroika depended on political perestroika. The culmination of political restructuring came in May 1989, when Soviet voters entered the voting booths to elect the Congress of People's Deputies, and for the first time in Soviet history they had a choice of candidates. All of these candidates were members of the Communist Party, but in 1990, the Communist Party monopoly was ended, and the Soviet Union entered the brave new world of multiparty politics.

A NEW INTERNATIONAL ORDER

Restructuring Soviet economics and politics led almost inevitably to restructuring international relations. By the 1980s, at least 18 percent of the Soviet GNP was absorbed by the arms race; Gorbachev concluded that the Soviet Union simply could not afford the Cold War. In just a five-year period, between 1987 and 1991, the international order was transformed. The Cold War ended, the Soviet Union released its hold on eastern Europe, and the communist regimes put in place in the late 1940s collapsed.

These dramatic changes began with Gorbachev's efforts to reduce Soviet military spending. As soon as Gorbachev took office, he signaled to the West his desire to resume arms control negotiations. In December 1987, Gorbachev and U.S. president Ronald Reagan signed the INF (Intermediate Nuclear Forces) Treaty, agreeing to the total elimination of land-based intermediate-range nuclear missiles. In 1990, the Soviet Union, the United States, and twenty-two European countries agreed to cut conventional forces. A year later, the Soviets and Americans signed the Strategic Arms Reduction Treaty (START I), pledging themselves to a mutual reduction of intercontinental ballistic missiles (ICBMs). At the same time, Gorbachev moved to reduce Soviet military commitments abroad. In 1989, he ended the Soviet war in Afghanistan, pulled the Red Army from Mongolia, and removed Soviet-sponsored Cuban forces from Angola.

Even more remarkable changes occurred within Europe. By the end of 1990, the Red Army had withdrawn from every nation in eastern Europe except East Germany and Poland (and would soon clear out of these countries as well). In 1991, the Warsaw Pact was dissolved.

The Soviet retreat from eastern Europe was linked to Gorbachev's aim of economic perestroika. The Soviet Union could not afford its empire. In his first informal meetings with eastern European leaders in 1985, Gorbachev told them they should no longer expect Soviet tanks to enforce their will on rebellious populations. By the time Gorbachev addressed the UN General Assembly at the end of 1988 and declared that the nations of eastern Europe were free to choose their own paths, dramatic changes were already underway.

Hungary and Poland were the first to jettison communist rule. Even before Gorbachev took power, economic crisis had driven both of these states to embrace fundamental reforms. In the early 1980s Hungary moved toward a Western-oriented, market-driven economy by joining the World Bank and the International Monetary Fund (IMF) and establishing a stock market. Political reforms accompanied these economic changes. In 1983, Hungarian voters for the first time had a choice of candidates (all still Communist Party members); eighteen months later, independent candidates were allowed to run—and many were elected. In Poland, Jaruzelski's government also began experimenting with restoring some measures of a market economy and with political liberalization. Once martial law ended in 1983, censorship loosened considerably.

CHRONOLOGY

Revolution in Eastern Europe

1989

January	Noncommunist parties and unions legalized in Hungary
February	Roundtable talks between Polish government and Solidarity
June	Free elections in Poland
September	Solidarity forms government in Poland; Hungary opens its borders to the West; thousands of East Germans emigrate
November	Fall of Berlin Wall; reformist communists overthrow Zhivkov in Bulgaria
December	Collapse of communist government in Czechoslovakia and East Germany; execution of Ceauşescu in Romania

1990

March	Free elections in East Germany and Hungary
October	Reunification of Germany
December	Wałęsa elected president of Poland

Newspapers published criticisms of governmental policy that would never have been permitted before 1980.

With Gorbachev in power, the pace of reform in both Poland and Hungary accelerated rapidly. In January 1989, Hungary took the leap into political pluralism by legalizing noncommunist political parties and trade unions. In February, Solidarity and Polish communist officials began "round table talks" aimed at restructuring Poland's political system. In June, Poland held the first free elections in the Soviet bloc. Solidarity swept the contest and formed the first noncommunist government in eastern Europe since 1948.

A bewildered world waited to see if Gorbachev would send in the tanks. Only one day before the Polish elections, the Chinese communist government, oblivious to the television cameras that broadcast the horrible scenes around the globe, had used brutal force to crush a student pro-democracy uprising centered in Beijing's Tiananmen Square. Hundreds died. Horrified by the carnage, Gorbachev insisted that "the very possibility of the use or threat of force [in Poland] . . . is totally unacceptable."[6]

With the prop of the Red Army removed, the communist states of eastern Europe were easily toppled. In November 1989, the Berlin Wall fell. The collapse of the wall echoed to the sound of communist governments crashing throughout eastern Europe. In December, after a year of ever-widening protest demonstrations, the communist government in Czechoslovakia resigned. Alexander Dubcek, the hero of the Prague Spring of 1968, returned in triumph to assume the leadership of parliament, and the playwright and leading dissident Václav Havel (1936–) became the Czech president. In March 1990, the Christian Democrats took over the government from the communists in East Germany; seven months later the states of East and West Germany ceased to exist, and a single Germany was reborn. At the end of the year, reform-minded Communist Party members in Bulgaria overthrew the government of Todor Zhivkov, who had been in power for thirty-five years.

All of these revolutions occurred with very little bloodshed. The pace of change in Czechoslovakia was so smooth, in fact, that the events earned the nickname "the Velvet Revolution." But in Romania, the revolutionary cloth came soaked in blood. In December 1989, Romania's dictator Nicolae Ceauşescu ordered the army to fire on a peaceful protest; hundreds died. In a matter of days, however, the soldiers turned against Ceauşescu. Fighting spread across the nation as the dictator's security forces battled with both the demonstrators and the army. Ceauşescu and his wife

■ **Revolution in Eastern Europe**
Students in Prague give the V for Victory signal in November 1989.

went into hiding, but on Christmas Day they were caught and executed by a firing squad. The televised pictures of their dead bodies were broadcast around the world. A new government was formed under Ion Iliescu (b. 1930), a reformist communist who had attended Moscow University with Gorbachev.

FROM SUCCESS TO FAILURE: THE DISINTEGRATION OF THE SOVIET UNION

By 1990, Gorbachev was one of the best-known leaders in the Western world. His leadership was seen as pivotal in accomplishing radical change in eastern Europe with a minimum of bloodshed and in ending the Cold War. But for Gorbachev, these changes in the international structure were means to an end—freeing the Soviet economy for prosperity and thereby saving the communist system. But prosperity eluded his grasp, and the system he sought to save disintegrated. Between 1985 and 1991, Gorbachev's administration started and stopped twelve different national economic plans, in ever-more-desperate attempts to prop up the Soviet economy. Yet these reforms seemed only to worsen the economic crisis. By 1990, food and other essential goods were scarce, prices had risen by 20 percent since the year before, and productivity was falling. In 1991, the average net income in Russia fell by 17 percent. Dramatic increases in the number of prostitutes (accompanied by a tripling of the rate of venereal disease in Moscow), abandoned babies, and the homeless population all signaled a society in the midst of economic breakdown.

By the early 1990s Gorbachev faced fierce opposition not only from hard-line communists who opposed his reforms, but also from more liberal reformers who viewed the communist system as utterly broken, and who wanted to accelerate the shift to a capitalist economy. These reformers found a spokesman in Boris Yeltsin (1931–), a charismatic, hard-drinking, boisterous politician who became the president of Russia (as distinct from the Soviet Union) in 1991. As Gorbachev increasingly began to tack toward the right, Yeltsin emerged as the leader who would keep the revolution on course. When communist hard-liners attempted to overthrow Gorbachev in August of 1991, it was Yeltsin who led the popular resistance movement that defeated the coup attempt.

Gorbachev was finally defeated not by a political coup but by the power of nationalism. Glasnost had allowed separatist nationalist movements within the Soviet Union to surface from the underground, but Gorbachev, despite his commitment to freedom of choice for eastern Europe, firmly opposed the breakup of the Soviet Union. In 1990, he deployed troops to quell nationalist rioting in both Azerbaijan and Georgia, and to counter independence movements in the Baltic states of Latvia, Estonia, and Lithuania. Short of an all-out civil war, however, there was little Gorbachev could do to hold the union together. By

December 1991, the Soviet Union had broken apart (see Map 29.1). On December 25, Gorbachev resigned his office as president of a state that no longer existed.

THE RETURN OF HISTORY: RUSSIA AND EASTERN EUROPE AT THE END OF THE TWENTIETH CENTURY

With the Cold War over and the long struggle between communism and capitalism clearly won by the latter, one best-selling author talked of the "end of history," by which he meant the end of the ideological struggles that had so defined the last two centuries of historical development.[7] But such talk was premature. "History" returned with a vengeance in the 1990s. As nationalism replaced the capitalist-communist struggle, many of the divisive issues that had led to world war in 1914 and 1939 moved back on the center stage. Patterns of prewar politics reasserted themselves.

The Former Soviet Union in Crisis

For many ordinary Russians, the ending of the Soviet regime meant freedom of the worst kind—freedom to be hungry, freedom to be homeless, freedom to be afraid. In January 1992, Yeltsin applied "shock therapy" to the ailing Russian economy. He lifted price controls, abolished subsidies, and privatized state industries. By mid-1994, the state sector of the Russian economy had shrunk to under 40 percent. But the economy did not prosper. Prices climbed dramatically, and the closure of unproductive businesses sent unemployment rates upward, while at the same time cuts in government spending severed welfare lifelines. By 1995, 80 percent of Russians were no longer earning a living wage. Food consumption fell to the same level as the early 1950s, with meat almost disappearing from the diets of many.

The economic situation worsened in 1998, when Russia effectively went bankrupt. The value of the ruble collapsed

■ **Map 29.1   The Former Soviet Union**

In December 1991, the Soviet empire disintegrated. In its place stood fifteen independent and very diverse republics, ranging from tiny and impoverished Moldova to relatively affluent and Europeanized Latvia to Russia itself, still the dominant power in the region, but economically stagnant.

and the state defaulted on its loans. Even Russians with jobs found it difficult to make ends meet. Workers at the Moscow McDonald's, for example, had regarded themselves as privileged: They were paid regularly and well. But overnight in 1998, the value of their paycheck dropped by 70 percent. Workers in state jobs simply weren't paid at all.

For many Russians, capitalism meant lawlessness. Managers of state industries were often able to manipulate privatization for their own private enrichment, so they grew fabulously wealthy, while ordinary employees experienced sharp pay cuts or the loss of their jobs. The prime minister Viktor Chernomyrdin (1938–), for example, moved from his position as the head of the state natural gas monopoly to become the largest shareholder of the privatized natural gas company. By the mid-1990s, a new force had appeared in Russian life—the "Russian Mafia," crime syndicates with international links that used extortion and intimidation to seize control of large sectors of the economy.

In the non-Russian republics, often the situation was even worse. The end of the Soviet Union meant the end of Soviet subsidies for these impoverished regions. Tajikistan, for example, depended on Soviet financial aid to prop up the extensive irrigation system that allowed its farmers to grow cotton for export. The collapse of the Soviet Union meant the collapse of the Tajikistan economy. By the end of the 1990s, almost half of Tajikistan's 6.2 million inhabitants were struggling to survive in the face of severe food shortages. In Moldova, the economy shrank by 60 percent between 1991 and 2001, while life expectancy rates fell by five years. One Moldovan elementary school principal admitted she was "hungry for Soviet days," which she recalled as a time when salaries were steady and health care universally available.[8] In the post-Soviet era, Moldovans resorted to marketing their body organs to Western entrepreneurs for $3,000 each.

The economic and social collapse that followed the end of the Soviet Union fostered a climate of desperation in which extremist nationalism flourished. Independence did not mean stability in the republics of Georgia, Armenia, and Azerbaijan, all of which experienced civil war in the 1990s. In Russia itself, Yeltsin faced strong opposition from nationalist groups who viewed the breakup of the Soviet Union as a humiliation for Mother Russia. In elections at the end of 1993, the party of ultranationalist Vladimir Zhirinovsky (b. 1946) won 23 percent of the vote, more than any other single party.

The sharpest nationalist challenge to Yeltsin came from Chechnya, one of twenty-one autonomous republics within the larger Russian Federation. When the Soviet Union broke up, Chechnya became part of independent Russia. But the Chechens demanded their own state, and in 1991 declared Chechnya independent. The Chechen-Russian dispute simmered until 1994 when Yeltsin committed 30,000 troops to forcing Chechnya back within Russia's embrace.

In the ensuing twenty-month conflict, 80,000 died and 240,000 were wounded—80 percent of these Chechen civilians. Yeltsin negotiated a truce in the summer of 1996, but four years later his successor, Vladimir Putin (1952–), renewed the war against Chechnya.

Eastern Europe After Communism

Like the former Soviet Union, the countries of eastern Europe found the path from communist rule to democracy far from easy. All the states of eastern Europe experienced high inflation rates, high unemployment, and economic instability in the wake of the revolution. The dissolution of the Soviet bloc meant that economic networks established over the last four decades suddenly disintegrated. In addition, Western advisors and the IMF, which controlled access to much-needed loans, insisted that the new governments follow programs of "austerity" aimed at cutting government spending and curbing inflation. The result was economic hardship far beyond what any Western electorate would have endured. In Poland, for example, the new Solidarity-led government instituted the "Big Bang" on New Year's Day, 1990. Controls disappeared and overnight prices jumped between 30 and 600 percent. The inflation rate for 1990 in Poland was a remarkable 550 percent. Even in 1995, when the economy had stabilized, inflation remained at 20 percent, while joblessness stood at 15 percent. In 1996 the Gdansk shipyard, where Solidarity had been born in 1980, closed and half its workers lost their jobs.

But by the second half of the 1990s, it was clear that despite these costs, Poland was succeeding in moving from communism to capitalism. With some measures of market reform already in place before 1988, both Poland and Hungary were the best prepared for the transition from a command to a capitalist economy. The Czech Republic and the Baltic nations also moved fairly rapidly through the most difficult stages of this transition. In countries such as Romania, Bulgaria, Albania, and of course Russia itself, severe economic instability continued, with the majority of their populations experiencing hardship.

Political stability was also hard-won during this decade. The revolutionary coalitions that had led the charge against communist rule in 1989–1990 quickly fragmented as their members moved from the heady idealism of challenging authoritarianism to the nitty-gritty of parliamentary politics. Political parties proliferated: forty-five in Hungary in 1990, sixty-seven in Poland in 1991, seventy-four in Romania in 1992. One unexpected result of the end of the communist monopoly on power was a worsened political position for women. Under communism, a quota system had ensured that women occupied 30 percent of the parliamentary seats in eastern European governments. In the postcommunist era of the mid-1990s, the percentages were far lower, ranging from 7 percent in Romania to 13 percent in Bulgaria and Poland.

Yet signs of emerging political stability were evident in the 1990s. Former communists entered the political mainstream. Given the seriousness of the economic crisis in eastern Europe in the 1990s, it is not surprising that ex-communists soon were back in power as disenchanted voters turned to the people who represented a more stable past. Between 1993 and 1995, the "Velvet Restoration" occurred, as ex-communists returned to power in Lithuania, Hungary, Bulgaria, and Poland. In Romania, they had never left. Yet Western fears that the revolutions of 1989 would be reversed proved groundless. Ex-communists continued with the economic liberalization programs of their opponents, although in many cases opting for a more gradual and thus, they hoped, less socially divisive transition. No former communist regime returned to authoritarian rule or a centralized state-run economy.

A far greater threat to eastern European democracy was posed by the revival not of communism but of pre–World War II political ideas and styles. For example, the claim of Josef Antall, Hungary's prime minister in the early 1990s, to be the leader of "all Hungarians" (two million of whom lived in Romania and another 600,000 in Slovakia) recalled the vehement Hungarian nationalism of the 1920s and 1930s. In Romania escalating discrimination against the Hungarian and Roma minority populations stirred up memories of interwar racist violence. Throughout eastern Europe, anti-Semitic rhetoric returned to political discourse. In 1990, Lech Wałęsa's election campaign was tainted by anti-Jewish references; graffiti appeared on the walls of Warsaw buildings: "Jews to the ovens."

The resurgence of pre–World War II ethnic identities did not always mean violence, however. In Czechoslovakia, Václav Havel's Civic Forum could not bridge the regional-ethnic divide that opened up between the Czech half of the country and Slovakia. In 1993, Czechoslovakia ceased to exist, replaced by the separate nations of the Czech Republic and Slovakia. Significantly, the breakup of Czechoslovakia was accomplished without violence, negotiated in conference rooms rather than fought out in the streets.

The German Problem

The problems that engulfed Germany after its eastern and western halves reunited in October 1990 illustrated the difficulties faced by eastern Europeans as they struggled to adjust to a post–Cold War, post-Soviet world. Almost half the population of East Germany crossed the border into West Germany in the first week after the fall of the Berlin Wall. They returned home dazzled by the consumer delights they saw in store windows and eager for a chance to grab a piece of the capitalist pie. West German chancellor Helmut Kohl recognized the power of these desires, and skillfully forced the pace of reunification. When the two Germanies united at the end of 1990, Kohl became the first chancellor of the new German state.

Kohl trusted that West Germany's economy was strong enough to pull its bankrupt new partner into prosperity, but he proved overly optimistic. The residents of the former East Germany soon found their factories closing and their livelihoods gone. These economic troubles quickly leached over into the western regions of Germany. By 1997, unemployment in Germany stood at 12.8 percent—the highest since World War II. In the eastern regions, over 20 percent of the population was out of work.

For the women of the former East Germany, life in the new Germany meant an intense culture clash. The concept of the male breadwinner/head of household was enshrined in the West German legal code until the end of the 1970s and prominent in West German culture for a long time after. This concept was alien to many East German women. In East Germany, all women were expected to be in full-time employment, the state provided day care and school holiday care, abortion was readily available, and contraceptives were free. In the new united Germany, which adhered to West German legal and cultural traditions, more conventional gender roles and conceptions of sexual morality dominated. For at least some East German women, then, the end of communist rule was not unambiguously liberating.

Economic despair throughout much of the former East Germany resulted in racial violence. Looking for scapegoats, eastern German youths targeted the foreign workers in their cities. Violent attacks against Turkish workers escalated in the 1990s, as did support for neo-Nazi organizations. In 1998, these economic and social problems led German voters to reject Kohl and the Christian Democrats. The Social Democrats, out of office since 1982, took charge under the leadership of Gerhard Schroeder (b. 1944). Schroeder, however, was unable to reverse the economic slide. By 2001, the German economy was standing still, with a GDP growth rate of little over zero.

THE BREAKUP OF YUGOSLAVIA

In Yugoslavia the "return of history" proved most marked and, given the nature of that history, most horrific. When the communist guerilla leader Tito seized control of the Yugoslav state after World War II, he sought to free Yugoslavia from the divisive and bloody battles of its recent past. But in the 1980s and 1990s, the revival of nationalist hostilities within Yugoslavia led to civil war and state-sanctioned mass murder, to scenes of carnage and to mass atrocities not seen in Europe since the 1940s.

Although Yugoslavia had appeared on European maps since the end of World War I, one could argue it did not really exist until after World War II. During the 1920s and 1930s, the subjects of the Serbian monarchy did not regard themselves as "Yugoslavs"; they were Serbs or Croats,

■ **Map 29.2 The Former Yugoslavia**

The breakup of Yugoslavia began in June 1991, with the Slovenian and Croatian declarations of independence. Bosnia and Macedonia soon followed.

Muslims or Montenegrins, Albanians or Slovenians. And during World War II, as we saw in Chapter 26, Serbs and Croats fought each other with a savage intensity–a bitter reminder of the lack of a single national Yugoslav identity.

To construct a united nation out of Yugoslavia's diverse and often hostile cultures, Tito utilized two tools—federalism and communism. A federal political structure consisting of six equal republics prevented Serbia, or any other of the republics, from dominating Yugoslavia. Communism served as a unifying ideology, a cluster of ideas that transcended the divisions of race, religion, and language. Recognizing the divisive and bloody potential of ethnic nationalism, Tito refused to allow it to break through the surface of Yugoslav political life. Aspiring politicians knew that an appeal to ethnic hatred would bar them from career advancement in the communist hierarchy. Ethnic identities and rivalries were declared unacceptable, part of the bourgeois past that had supposedly been left behind.

Yugoslavs often said, however, that their nation consisted of "six nationalities, five languages, four religions, . . . and one Tito." According to this folk wisdom, Tito—not communism, not federalism—was the glue that held together this diverse state. In 1980, Tito died. Ominously, the year after his death saw the outbreak of riots between ethnic Albanians and Serbs in the province of Kosovo. Even more ominously, Tito's death coincided with the onset of serious economic crisis. The drastic rise in oil prices in 1979 undercut the Yugoslav economy, as did its rising debt load. Between 1979 and 1985 real wages fell in Yugoslavia by almost 25 percent. By 1987, inflation was raging at 200 percent per year and two years later it had burst through into hyperinflation—200 percent *per month*.

Under pressure from this economic crisis, the federal structure built by Tito began to collapse, as the wealthier Yugoslav republics such as Croatia sought to loosen the ties that bound them to the poorer republics such as Serbia. Then, in 1989, the revolutions that swept through the Soviet satellite states shattered the hold of communism on Yugoslavia as well. Ethnic nationalism, long simmering under the surface of Yugoslavian political life, poured into the resulting ideological void. New leaders emerged with new agendas. In Serbia, the former communist functionary Slobodan Milosevic (b. 1941) transformed himself into a popular spokesman for aggressive Serbian nationalism. Milosevic used rallies and the mass media, which he controlled, to convince Serbs that their culture was under attack and to paint himself as the defender of that culture. To enhance Serbia's power—and his own—Milosevic fiercely opposed any talk of destroying the Yugoslav federation. Moreover, Milosevic possessed a powerful weapon to enforce his will. The Yugoslav army, the fourth largest fighting force in Europe, was dominated by Serbs.

Thus, when Croatia declared independence in June 1991, the result was civil war (see Map 29.2). Milosevic

A GLOBAL YOUTH CULTURE?

The following excerpt, from an interview with rock singer and Serbian nationalist Sonja Karadzic, first appeared in a Serbian magazine in September 1992, at the height of the war in Bosnia. Daughter of Radovan Karadzic, the political leader of the Bosnian Serbs, Sonja Karadzic condemned her fellow Serbs who had fled the war in Bosnia for the safety of Serbia. She also offered a disturbing definition of "Western civilization": one characterized not by democratic freedom and the protection of human rights, but rather by a culture of violence fostered by American television and films.

If the Americans come to Bosnia, they'll see that our soldiers look at the world like theirs do. We aren't Vietnamese or Iraqis, we are fighters who think in terms of the same images and music as their soldiers do. The Serbian chetnik fighters have grown up with a Coke in their hand and watching the same TV spots as someone their own age in Alabama, and we're into the latest styles just the way guys or girls from Florida are. Together we got our battle ethics from the movies about Mad Max and Terminator, Rambo and Young Guns. And what happened when the war began—we started identifying with the media images and heroes. Our fighters got into battle dress, short Rambo boots and modern weapons of destruction. They call themselves chetniks—but Mad Max Chetniks, Serbian Terminators. And most important, it doesn't matter what sex you are. Nobody is dirty or sloppy or smelly or unshaven—we're still into good cigarettes and Coca-Cola, nice perfume and makeup, and we're up on the latest movies and music. And we still like a good laugh—not the Moslem nonsense down in town. We're building a new lifestyle in a new country.

Fortunately for us only the best fighters, the real ones have stayed. The others have helped us perform a natural selection by running away from the homeland they weren't prepared to defend and build up . . .

For us the Serbian chetniks . . . will always be our heroes, our Serbian Terminators. With fighters like them we are already the victors in this war and leaders in the creation of a new civilization.

Source: From an interview with Sonja Karadzic, by Nenad Stefanovic, *Duga* (Belgrade), September 12–26, 1992. Excerpted and translated by Ann Clymer Bigelow. Reprinted by permission.

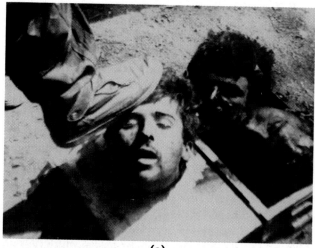

(a)

(b)

■ **Bosnian War Atrocities**

(a) Serbian heads, found after Serb fighters raided a Muslim base in northern Bosnia in 1993. (b) The mass grave of Muslim civilians, Pilica, northwest of Srebrenica, in the spring of 1996. Twelve thousand of the men and boys of Srebrenica tried to flee to safety—about half made it; many of those that didn't were forced by Serb fighters to dig their own graves and then shot in front of them. The citizens of Srebenica who did not flee were told by Bosnian Serbian General Ratko Mladic, "No one will harm you." Mladic then ordered his soldiers to shoot all Muslim men between ages 17 and 60. Reviewing the evidence against Mladic, the UN tribunal noted, "These are truly scenes from hell, written on the darkest pages of human history."

mobilized the Yugoslav army against the Croatian separatists. In 1992 the war spread to Bosnia-Herzegovina after its government, too, declared independence. The war quickly degenerated into an ethnic bloodbath, with memories of World War II shaping the conflict. Serbs viewed Croats as the direct heirs of the murderous Nazi-backed Croatian Ustace regime, responsible for the mass slaughter of Serbs in World War II. In turn, Croats called all Serbs "Chetniks," linking them to the anti-Croat Serbian guerrilla bands of the war years. The presence of paramilitary forces also heightened the brutality of the war. With no military discipline and often possessing criminal records, the volunteers in these units plunged into a fury of plunder, murder, and rape.

This war introduced the world to the horrors of ethnic cleansing° and rape camps. By 1994, all sides within the Bosnian war were practicing ethnic cleansing, although it is clear that Serbs initiated the practice and used it most extensively. To create all-Serb zones within Croatia and Bosnia, Serb paramilitary units embarked on a campaign of terror designed to force Muslims and Croats to abandon their homes and villages. They burned mosques, closed schools, and vandalized houses. Most villagers fled; the paramilitaries tortured and often killed those who stayed. Women were sometimes rounded up and placed in special camps where they were subjected to regular, systematic rape. An estimated 20,000 women, most of them Muslim, endured this peculiarly vicious effort to subjugate and humiliate a people.

Outrage against these atrocities forced Western governments to intervene. In 1994, NATO planes began bombing Serb positions, the first time in its history that NATO had gone into combat. The Dayton Accords, signed in Dayton, Ohio, in December 1995, brought an uneasy peace to Bosnia. The accords declared Bosnia to be one state with two parts—the Muslim-Croat Federation (consisting of 51 percent of Bosnian territory) and the Serbian Republic (holding the remaining 49 percent), each with its own military, taxation, and judicial powers. Keeping the peace in this strange creation was the job of 60,000 UN soldiers.

Peace eluded Serbia during this period, however. The sort of vicious nationalism embodied by Milosevic demanded a constant supply of enemies and a continuous cycle of violence. In 1998, large-scale fighting between Serbs and Albanians erupted in the province of Kosovo. Ethnic cleansing, mass rape, and a huge exodus of refugees began

CHRONOLOGY

The Shattering of Yugoslavia

1989	Slobodan Milosevic becomes president of Yugoslavian Republic of Serbia
1991	
July	Civil war in Croatia begins
1992	
April	Civil war in Bosnia begins
1994	
April	NATO air strikes against Bosnian Serb positions begin
1995	
December	Dayton Accords
1998	Large-scale fighting in Kosovo between Albanians and Serbs
1999	
March	NATO air strikes against Serbia
June	Ceasefire in Kosovo
2000	
October	Milosevic defeated in Serbian elections
2001	
June	Milosevic extradited to the Hague to be tried for genocide

once again. After a NATO bombing campaign in Serbia, NATO and Russian troops moved into Kosovo, and in 2001, a police helicopter transported Milosevic to the Netherlands to be tried for genocide before the International War Crimes Tribunal.

Rethinking the West

At the start of the 1990s, a sense of triumphalism characterized much of Western culture—at its simplest, expressed as "we won the Cold War." But who was "we"? For forty years, the Cold War had provided a clear enemy and thus a clear identity: The West was anticommunist, anti-Soviet, anti–Warsaw Pact. Communism's loss of credibility, the disintegration of the Soviet Union, and the dismantling of the Warsaw Pact all demanded that the West revise itself. New enemies moved into prominent positions, the relationship between the United States and Europe had to be renegotiated, and even the definition of

"Europe" became problematic. At the same time, a series of intellectual and cultural forces challenged many facets of Western identity, while Western nations, like those in the rest of the world, found their scope of autonomous action increasingly limited as they were caught up in the web of global economic, technological, and environmental change.

OLD AND NEW ENEMIES

This textbook has traced the way in which "the West" changed meaning, largely in response to places and peoples defined as "not West." With the ending of the Cold War, the West lost its main enemy—but replacements stood readily at hand. In 1996, the American president Bill Clinton (1946–) identified terrorism as "the enemy of our generation." Terrorism in many ways replaced communism as the new foe against which the West defined itself. Because terrorists seek to achieve political ends through the means of violence and intimidation, terrorism short-circuits the democratic process: Decision-making power shifts from the ballot box to the bomb. Thus terrorism directly opposed what many regarded as the bedrock of Western culture—a commitment to democracy and the rule of the law.

Yet the equation of the West with law and democracy conveniently ignored other, less palatable, products of Western political culture such as fascism, Nazism, and terrorism itself. Terrorism grew out of late nineteenth-century anarchism, which advocated violence as a means of political change (see Chapter 22). Like the Russian populists who assassinated Tsar Alexander II or the Serbian nationalists who shot the Archduke Franz Ferdinand and sparked World War I, contemporary terrorists belonged to groups lacking access to political power. Unable to achieve their goals through political persuasion (lobbying, campaigning, winning votes), they endeavored to destabilize the societies they opposed through acts of terror. Thus small groups of western European and American student activists, disillusioned by the failures of 1968, went underground in the 1970s, embarking on bombing and assassination campaigns. Thwarted nationalism provided even more fertile soil for the growth of terrorism. In Spain, the Basque separatist group Eta engaged in a three-decades-long campaign of terror to achieve its aim of an independent Basque state. In Northern Ireland, assassinations, bombings, and knee-cappings became commonplace after the Irish Republican Army (IRA) turned to terror to pressure the British government to relinquish its control over the province.

Terrorism is thus one of the negative aspects of "Western civilization." Yet, by the 1980s, terrorism was often perceived as the antithesis of the West, as an outside threat, usually bearing an Arabic face. Popular perceptions often linked "terrorism" and "Islam," with Islam defined as emphatically "not West"—fanatical, violent, antidemocratic.

What factors forged this perceived link between Islam and terrorism? One of the most important was the continuing Israeli-Palestinian crisis. Frustrated by the failure of the United Nations to implement its 1947 resolution promising a Palestinian state, Palestinian nationalists in 1964 formed the Palestine Liberation Organization (PLO). Like the IRA or Eta, the PLO saw violence as its only means to its nationalist ends. The PLO's commitment to terrorism deepened after the Arab-Israeli War of 1967, which led to Israel occupying East Jerusalem, all land west of the Jordan River (the West Bank), and the Golan Heights. In response, the PLO took its campaign of terror around the world, bombing airports, targeting tourists, and persuading many in the West that "Arab," "Muslim," and "terrorist" were interchangeable terms.

At the same time, U.S. support for Israel convinced many Muslims that "the West" (often equated simply with the United States) was an enemy. Between 1949 and 1998, Israel received more American aid than any other country. As relations between Palestinians and Israelis deteriorated in the late 1980s and 1990s, Palestinians and their supporters argued that the United States was bankrolling a repressive regime and that Israel was a Western colonialist outpost (see Map 29.3).

The conflict in Israel served as a backdrop to the emergence of a militant, anti-Western form of Islam, fueled by fear of Western culture as well as the West's willingness, during the Cold War, to prop up unpopular and corrupt governments. Events in Iran illustrate this process. In 1979, a popular revolution overthrew the autocratic, U.S.-backed Shah of Iran, and vaulted into power the Ayatollah Khomeini (1901–1989). Khomeini rapidly reversed the westernizing and modernizing policies of the Shah. The Sharia (the religious law of Islam) became the law of the state, and strict Islamic codes of behavior were required for all Iranians. Women, for example, could not appear in public without being veiled. Then in November 1979, Iranian students, obeying instructions from religious leaders, took over the U.S. Embassy in Tehran and captured sixty-six Americans, the bulk of whom spent over a year in captivity—an episode of state-sanctioned terrorism that constituted an appalling tragedy for the hostages, and an international humiliation for the United States. Khomeini decried the United States as the "Great Satan," while the excesses of his regime strengthened the popular perception in the West that Islam fundamentally opposed Western values.

Two additional factors raised anti-Muslim sentiments throughout much of the Western world—oil and immigration. In 1979, OPEC responded to Khomeini's revolution in Iran by raising the base price of petroleum by almost 25 percent, thus (as we have seen earlier) catapulting the West into economic crisis. Although OPEC included non-Arab nations such as Venezuela, for most in the West it was seen as an "Arab cartel," and linked to an image of a resurgent

Islam. Even more important was the emergence in western Europe of permanent minority communities, many of them Muslim. As the minarets of mosques began to poke through the skylines of European cities, some non-Muslim Europeans argued that their own cultures were under threat. The decision of the Ayatollah Khomeini to issue a death sentence against the Anglo-Indian writer Salman Rushdie in 1989 forced many of these tensions and hostilities into the open but provided no easy answers.

During the 1990s, these hostilities grew more fierce as a result of the First Gulf War. In 1991 American and British forces led a twenty-eight country coalition in a military intervention to drive invading Iraqi forces out of tiny but oil-rich Kuwait. The war itself could not be construed as "the West versus Islam" or "the West versus the East": One Arab and Islamic country had invaded another. But in the aftermath of the war, U.S. forces remained in American-controlled bases in Saudi Arabia, home of some of the most holy sites in Islam. For Muslim radicals, the presence of the United States in this region was both an offense against Islam and an insult to Arabian political independence. Anti-Western Islamic movements grew stronger in many

■ **Map 29.3   The Middle East in the Contemporary Era**

Although placed under Palestinian self-rule in 1994, the West Bank and Gaza Strip remain contested areas, sites of frequent confrontations between Palestinians and Israelis.

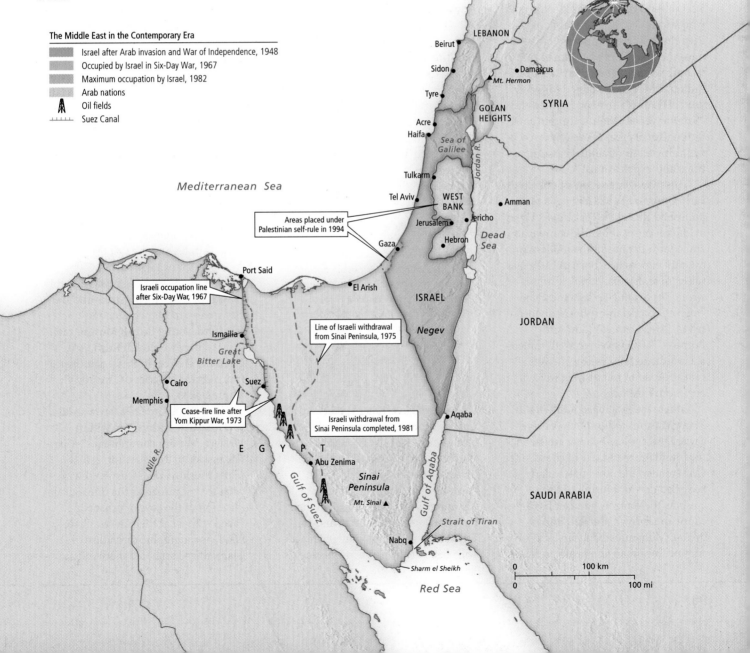

The Sentencing of Salman Rushdie

In February 1989, the Ayatollah Khomeini, political leader of Iran and spiritual head of the Shi'a Muslim community, issued a death sentence against the novelist Salman Rushdie and offered an award of $2.5 million to any faithful Muslim who succeeded in killing him. Rushdie, a British citizen who had never been tried in any Iranian or Islamic court, immediately went into hiding, where he remained for several years. His death sentence ignited the "Satanic Verses Affair," a tumultuous international crisis caused by a resounding clash of cultural assumptions and expectations.

The crisis centered on a book. In the early autumn of 1988 Viking Penguin published Rushdie's *The Satanic Verses,* a difficult novel about the complexities and contradictions of the modern immigrant experience. Born in India and raised in an Islamic home, Rushdie wrote *The Satanic Verses* to describe "migration, metamorphosis, divided selves, love, death, London, and Bombay."[9] The novel received immediate critical acclaim, with reviewers praising it as an astonishing work of postmodernist fiction.

Other readers judged it differently. Many Muslims around the world regarded the book as a direct attack on the foundations of their religious faith. One scene in the novel particularly horrified devout Muslims. In this episode, the central character has a psychotic breakdown and falls into a dream: Muhammad appears as a corrupt businessman and prostitutes in a brothel take on the names of the Prophet's wives.

The novel aroused intense controversy from the moment of its publication. The government of India banned it almost immediately; within a matter of weeks, several other states followed suit. Anti-Rushdie demonstrations in both India and Pakistan turned violent, resulting in fifteen deaths. Bookstores selling the novel received bombing and death threats. In western Europe, hostilities between Muslims and non-Muslims intensified. Then, on February 14, 1989, an announcer on Radio Tehran read aloud the text of a *fatwa,* or decree, issued by the Ayatollah Khomeini:

> I would like to inform all the intrepid Muslims of the world that the author of the book entitled The Satanic Verses, *which has been compiled, printed and published in opposition to Islam, the Prophet and the Koran, as well as those publishers who were aware of its contents, have been sentenced to death. I call on all zealous Muslims to execute them quickly, wherever they find them . . . Whoever is killed on this path will be regarded as a martyr, God willing.*

Western governments reacted quickly against Khomeini's call for Rushdie's death. The twelve nations of the European Community, the United States, Sweden, Norway, Canada, Australia, and Brazil all condemned Khomeini's judgment, recalled their ambassadors from Tehran, and cancelled high-level diplomatic contacts with Iran. British Prime Minister Margaret Thatcher provided police protection for Rushdie and dismissed British Muslim demands to ban the book: "It is an essential part of our democratic system that people who act within the law should be able to express their opinions freely."[10]

Large numbers of Muslims, including many who spoke out against Rushdie's book, also condemned Khomeini's fatwa. Some Muslim scholars contended that the Ayatollah's fatwa was a scholarly opinion, not a legally binding judgment; others argued that Rushdie could not be condemned without a trial, or that because Rushdie lived in a society without an Islamic government, he was not bound by Islamic law.

But many ordinary Muslims ignored these high-level theological and legal disputes and greeted the Ayatollah's fatwa with delight. The news of the Ayatollah's fatwa brought crowds of cheering Muslims into the city streets. In Manchester and Bradford, young British Muslim men insisted they would kill Rushdie if given the chance. In Paris, demonstrators marched to cries of "we are all Khomeinists!"

Why did Khomeini's fatwa arouse such popular enthusiasm within Western Muslim communities? A partial answer to this question is that many Muslims were frustrated with what they regarded as the unequal application of the laws of censorship. Faced with what they saw as a hate-filled, pornographic caricature of Islam, they demanded that Western

■ A Clash of Cultures?

In London, a policeman chases a demonstrator during a protest against the publication of *The Satanic Verses*.

governments use the laws censoring pornography and banning hate crimes to block the publication of Rushdie's book. In Britain, Muslims were particularly outraged that the existing law against blasphemy protected only Christianity, the official state religion.

But the controversy was not simply a dispute about censorship. For some Muslims, Rushdie's *Satanic Verses* epitomized Western secular society, with its scant regard for tradition or religious values. As Dr. Kalim Siddiqui of the pro-Iranian Muslim Institute in Britain proclaimed, "western civilization is fundamentally an immoral civilization. Its 'values' are free of moral constraints."[11] From this perspective, Khomeini's fatwa condemned not just one book or one author, but an entire culture that seemed inherently opposed to Islam. Khomeini had already proven himself a forceful leader in the Iranian hostage crisis of 1979–1980, when he successfully thumbed his nose at American power. Now once again he seemed willing to take on the West to defend Islam.

The anti-Western stance of some radical Muslims was mirrored by the anti-Islam position soon occupied by some Rushdie supporters. In one of the most ironic twists in the entire Satanic Verses Affair, Rushdie's books, which condemned the endemic racism in British society and exposed the falsehood of Western claims to cultural superiority, were championed by individuals who articulated precisely the sort of Western cultural chauvinism against which Rushdie had written so

passionately. For example, Robert Maxwell, a multimillionaire communications tycoon, offered $10 million to any individual "who will, not kill, but civilise the barbarian Ayatollah" by forcing him to recite publicly the Ten Commandments.[12] Many western Europeans agreed with the conclusion drawn in this letter to a British daily newspaper: "The lesson of the Rushdie affair is that it was unwise to let Muslim communities establish themselves in our midst."[13] The lines were drawn, with Islam standing for irrationalism, barbarity, intolerance, and ignorance, while the "West" was linked to democracy, reason, freedom, and civilization. At precisely the moment when the crumbling of communism and the ending of the Cold War deprived the West of one of its defining attributes, the Satanic Verses Affair offered up a new Other against which the West could define itself. ■

Questions of Justice

1. On what grounds are publications censored in secular, Western societies? Given the existence of this censorship, should Rushdie's book have been banned?

2. In what ways does the Satanic Verses Affair illuminate the tensions within many European societies from the 1970s on, as communities struggled to adapt to the challenges of ethnic and religious diversity?

Taking It Further

Bowen, David G., ed. *The Satanic Verses: Bradford Responds*. 1996. This collection of essays and documents helps explains why many British Muslims viewed the British government's failure to censor Rushdie's book as an act of injustice.

regions of the world, including not only the Middle East but also the Philippines, Algeria, Bosnia, and Afghanistan.

The dangerous perception of some sort of fundamental opposition between "Islam" and "the West" led, on September 11, 2001, to one of the most dramatic episodes of terrorism ever. At 8:46 A.M., a jumbo jet hijacked by Muslim Arab terrorists smashed into one of the towers of the World Trade Center in New York City. Twenty minutes later, another hijacked plane hit the second tower. A third plane dove into the Pentagon, the U.S. military headquarters in Washington, D.C., and a fourth crashed in Pennsylvania. Almost 3,000 people died.

In the wake of the horrifying attack, U.S. president George W. Bush (1946–) declared a "war on terrorism." U.S. and European intelligence officers quickly linked the suicide pilots to a terrorist organization run by Osama bin Laden, a wealthy Saudi exile who espoused a fiercely anti-Western form of Islam. Bin Laden was backed by the

■ The Terrorist Age

A fireball erupts from one of the World Trade Center towers as it is struck by the second of two airplanes in New York on September 11, 2001. The terrorist attacks demonstrated the power of global communications in the contemporary world. By the time the first tower collapsed, just a little more than an hour after the first plane crash, television stations around the world were broadcasting live images of the scene. Thus viewers witnessed on their television screens the Hollywood-like scene of the towers' collapse.

Taliban, a revolutionary Muslim group that had won control of Afghanistan in the early 1990s after the Soviet army withdrew from the region. The United States began air attacks against Afghanistan in October 2001. The Taliban regime fell within weeks, but the war against terrorism continued.

In March 2003, this widely ranging war took a new turn when U.S. and British forces, attacked Iraq in the Second Gulf War. No direct connection linked Osama bin Laden to Iraq's government, which was firmly controlled by Saddam Hussein, a secular dictator with a long history of torturing and killing radical Muslims who threatened his personal power. But in the world after "9/11", Saddam Hussein's refusal to allow United Nations' inspections of his weapons factories convinced both the American and British governments that Iraq possessed the ability to launch a terrorist strike, in the form of biological or chemical weapons, against Western targets. The result was the first preemptive war ever waged by U.S. forces and, after a three-week conflict involving both air strikes and land battles, the toppling of Saddam Hussein's dictatorial regime. Many Iraqis cheered the dictator's overthrow, but many Arabs in the surrounding nations condemned the Anglo-American intervention as yet another episode in a long history of Western imperial intrusions on Arab territory.

9/11 thus had important consequences for the West and the world. It not only resulted in military engagements in both Afghanistan and Iraq, but also accelerated the development of the United States as a military colossus. Even before the Second Gulf War, the U.S. defense budget outweighed that of the next nine largest defense budgets of other countries combined. In addition, 9/11 made it clear that terrorism had replaced communism as the West's new enemy, the "Them" against which the "Us" took shape. A series of mysterious anthrax outbreaks in the weeks following the September 2001 attacks provided an alarming demonstration of the risks terrorism posed in urban industrial society. Defense budgets could skyrocket, but there seemed little safety in a world in which every passenger plane could become a weapon of mass murder, and every envelope could contain deadly spores. Finally, in the aftermath of the attacks the question of Western identity was more troublesome than ever. European and American Muslims found their loyalties questioned, their religious beliefs regarded as grounds for suspicion. The long, complex history of Islam in the West was often ignored, replaced by a simplistic "Them" versus "Us" mentality.

THE EUROPEAN UNION

In the wake of 9/11, the status of the United States as the world's only superpower seemed dramatically confirmed; developments in Europe in this era, however, limited American hegemony. With the ending of the Cold War, the nations of western Europe, united under the umbrella of the European Union° (EU), moved to take on a much more important role in global affairs. We saw in Chapter 28 that the EU began in the 1950s as the Common Market or EEC (European Economic Community), an economic free-trade organization of six western European nations. By the end of the millennium, this organization had become a powerful entity possessing not only economic but also political clout, a potential counterweight to the United States.

From the EEC to the EU

During the 1970s and 1980s, the EEC widened both its membership and its areas of cooperation, and thus helped move the nations of western Europe toward greater economic and political unity. Britain, Denmark, and Ireland joined the European Community in 1973, Greece in 1981, Spain and Portugal in 1986. (Austria, Finland, and Sweden joined in the 1990s.) In 1979, a European parliament chosen directly by European voters met for the first time. Throughout these decades, the European Court of Justice gradually began to assert the primacy of the European Community over national law, thus breaching the walls of national sovereignty and pushing western Europe down the road toward political integration. A name change signaled this broadening of aims. The EEC—the European Economic Community—became the EC—the European Community, a political and cultural as well as economic organization.

The development of the EC made it clear that the "West" was no longer American-made. Even before expanding in the 1980s, the EC constituted the largest trading unit and consumer market in the world. By 1980, the U.S. share of global economic output had fallen from 38 percent in 1970 to 25 percent, while the EC saw its share rise in these same years from 26 to 30 percent. The "Western" economy gradually grew less American, and more and more European. The emergence of Europe as the strongest economic competitor to the United States broke the symbolic link between "America" and "modernity." One French businessman noted in 1983, "I remember when I first went to America thirty years ago. Everything looked bigger, newer, faster. Now, everything looks shabbier and older than here."[14]

The pace of change accelerated in the 1980s and 1990s as the Single European Act of 1985 and the Maastricht Agreements of 1991 replaced the European *Community* (EC) with the European *Union* (EU), defined by France's President Mitterrand as "one currency, one culture, one social area, one environment." The establishment of the EU meant visible changes for ordinary Europeans. They saw their national passports replaced by a common EU document, and border controls eliminated. The creation of a single EU currency—the euro, which replaced national currencies in 2002—tore down one of the most significant economic barriers between European countries. In what was labeled the largest peacetime logistical operation in European history, 6 billion notes and 37.5 billion coins re-

placed national currency in twelve EU states. At the same time, the powers of the European Parliament expanded. Member states moved toward establishing common social policies (such as labor rights) and a common defense system, with an EU rapid reaction force of 60,000 men created in 2003.

Old and New Obstacles

At the launch of the euro, the president of the European Central Bank announced that the single currency would "forever banish the horrors of past conflicts," thus underscoring the internationalist idealism that has driven forward European unification since the 1940s.[15] This process of European unification was controversial, however. French voters ratified the Maastricht treaty with a "yes" vote of only 51 percent, while Britain, Denmark, and Sweden refused to join the conversion to the euro, fearing a loss of national sovereignty and economic independence. "Euro-skeptics" questioned the economic value of unification. They pointed out that throughout the 1990s, the U.S. economy continued to outperform that of the EU, and European unemployment rates were often high. France's, for example, hovered between 10 and 12 percent in the mid-1990s. Small traders and independent producers opposed the seemingly endless stream of orders and regulations issued by EU bureaucrats and the way in which economic integration privileged large, international firms over small, local shops. In addition, the process of unification meant the loss of many of the symbols that people treasured as links to their national traditions. In Britain in 2001, a shopkeeper who refused to abandon traditional English ounces and pounds for the metric system (required by EU regulations) became a folk hero, seen by many as an English patriot who refused to give in to faraway faceless bureaucrats in Brussels.

The end of the Cold War posed an even sharper challenge to the EU. Should the European Union (often called simply "Europe") include East as well as West? Attracted by the undoubted prosperity of the EU, the nations of the former Soviet bloc answered that question with a resounding "yes." The leaders of western Europe, however, looked with trepidation at the prospect of joining their countries to eastern Europe's shattered economies and divided societies, and drew up a set of rigorous qualifications for applicant nations. To be recognized as belonging to "Europe," nations applying for EU membership had to meet a set of complex financial requirements that demonstrated both the essential stability of their economies and their commitment to market capitalism. Thus "Europe" was defined, first of all, as capitalist. But a set of political requirements made clear that "Europe" also meant a commitment to democratic politics. Applicants' voting processes, treatment of minority groups, policing methods, and judicial systems were all scrutinized, as the EU used its considerable economic clout to nurture fledgling democratic structures in eastern Europe. In 2003, the EU parliament voted overwhelmingly in favor of expanding the Union to include Estonia, Latvia,

Lithuania, Poland, the Czech Republic, Slovakia, Slovenia, and Hungary, as well as Cyprus and Malta (see Map 29.4).

That same year, however, the Second Gulf War opened a serious fissure in the European Union. While governments in eastern Europe supported the Anglo-American attack on Iraq, those of France, Germany, and Russia strongly opposed military intervention and stymied attempts to gain United Nations approval of military action. The split within Europe over the war revealed that the development of a common European foreign and defense policy would be difficult indeed.

CULTURE AND SOCIETY IN THE POSTMODERN ERA

While the formation of the EU, the end of the Cold War, and the revolutions of 1989 helped redefine the balance of power within the West, intellectual and artistic develop-

ments labeled as "postmodern" challenged the dominance of Western values, styles, and assumptions in global culture. At the same time, technological and economic developments worked in contradictory ways, producing a global culture that was at once more uniform than ever before and yet more fragmented, a collection of distinct subcultures.

The Making of the Postmodern

A grab-bag term covering a huge array of styles and stances, postmodernism° at its core constitutes the rejection of Western cultural supremacy. A diverse group of writers, thinkers, and artists began to challenge the idea that Western science and rationality had constructed a single, universally applicable form of "modernity." Postmodernism in this general sense resulted from the joining of three specific intellectual and cultural streams: postmodernist architecture, postmodernist art, and the literary theories of poststructuralism.

■ **Map 29.4 Contemporary Europe**
The revolutions of 1989 and their aftermath mark a clear turning point in European history, as a comparison of this map and that of "Europe in the Cold War" (p. 943) will show. Significant changes include the breakup of the Soviet Union and Yugoslavia, the replacement of Czechoslovakia by the Czech Republic and Slovakia, and the unification of Germany.

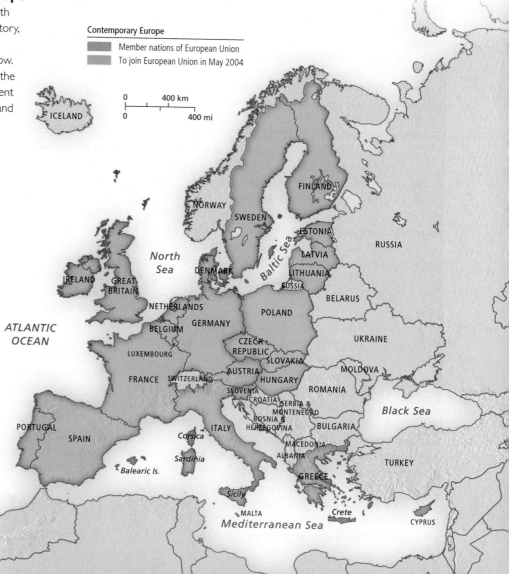

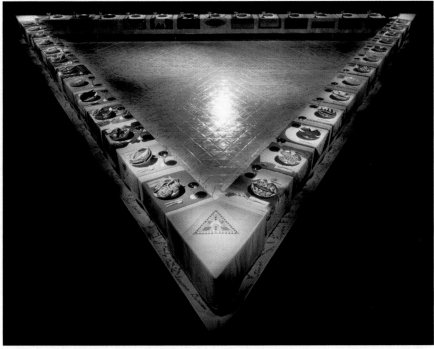

■ **Judy Chicago, *The Dinner Party*, (1973–1979)**

This installation sits on 2,300 white porcelain tiles, across which run the names of 999 women from Western history. Each of the thirty-nine place settings includes a ceramic or painted china plate and a needlework runner that use symbols to portray historical or mythological female figures. Like Chicago's work, much of the feminist art of the 1970s focused on celebrating femaleness, the ways in which women's bodies and experiences set them apart from men. Later in the era, many younger feminists criticized this work for reducing women to some sort of mythic female essence, and instead focused their art on exposing the dynamics of power and oppression in modern societies.

As Chapter 28 explained, with the pop art of the 1960s visual artists moved away from many of the central assumptions of modernism. It was in architecture, however, that postmodernism first clearly took form, perhaps because the failures of modernist architecture were so obvious by the early 1970s. Motivated by an intense faith in both human rationality and modern technology, modernist architects had sought to build new forms of housing that, they believed, would enable people to live better, more beautiful lives. But the concrete high-rises they constructed failed to connect with the needs and emotions of their inhabitants, and many became derelict, crime-ridden, graffiti-scarred tenements.

Faced with this sense of failure, a new generation—the postmodernists—insisted that architects needed to start communicating with ordinary people. The American architect Charles Jencks (b. 1939) argued that because people tend to rely on the familiar to make sense of their world, modernism was wrong to reject traditional forms. For example, most Europeans and Americans connect domestic housing with gabled roofs (ask a child to draw a picture of a house and see if he or she draws a flat roof). Was it surprising, Jencks asked, that the concrete rectangles used by modernists for housing proved profoundly alienating to many people? Postmodernist *anti-elitism* thus led to *eclecticism,* to re-creating and combining forms and styles from past eras (such as gabled roofs), and to efforts to revive local and regional styles. Why should the streets of Tokyo look like the center of London or downtown Chicago? Instead, postmodernists embraced an architecture rooted in the specifics of time and place. In addition to being anti-elitist and eclectic, then, postmodernist architecture was also *anti-universalist:* It condemned modernism for its assumption that the same modern (and Western) ideals and forms fit all individuals and all societies.

The same sorts of criticism of modernism surfaced in the art world, as the wider political context of the late 1960s and early 1970s transformed the visual arts in three ways. First, in the wake of the protests of 1968, artists—many coming out of left-wing activist environments—rejected ideologies based on hierarchy and authority. This rejection led to an attack on the modernist idea of the "avant-garde," a small elite of artistic geniuses fighting to advance the frontiers of aesthetic excellence. Even more than their modernist predecessors, postmodernist artists celebrated the possibilities of the mass media and condemned distinctions between "high" and popular culture. Second, the experience of political protest led many artists to reject the modernist ideal of "art for art's sake," insisting instead that art had to say something to the world around it. To communicate with a wider public, they plundered both the past and popular culture for familiar forms and material. As the art critic Edit DeAk explained, postmodernist art relied on "the shock of recognition instead of the shock of the new."[16] Finally, feminism proved crucial in shaping the new art. Women began to challenge the dominance of men in the art world not only by highlighting the systematic exclusion of women from gallery and museum exhibitions, but also by questioning the aesthetic hierarchy that relegated to the lower status of "craft" traditionally female art forms such as weaving.

By the end of the 1970s, postmodernist practices in art and architecture were both reinforced by and in turn served to strengthen a growing body of literary and cultural theory often called *poststructuralism*. The theory of poststructural-ism was associated with the work of an assorted group of French thinkers, whose ideas were taken up in American universities and then filtered back into European intellectual circles. These thinkers included Jacques Derrida (b. 1930) and Roland Barthes (1915–1980) in literary studies, Michel Foucault (1926–1984) in history, and Jacques Lacan (1901–1981) in psychoanalytic theory.

Like postmodernist theories in architecture and art, poststructuralism began as an exploration into the problems of communication. Jacques Derrida argued that the world we see and experience is a world structured by language—we cannot even understand or express our very selves apart from language. But because there is no inherent match between a word (what Derrida called a "signi-fier") and the thing or idea to which that word refers (the "signified"), communication is never straightforward. An endless variety of meanings and interpretations results, and thus, Derrida argued, we must abandon the idea of a fixed or single truth, of ultimate or universal meaning. In a related argument, Roland Barthes declared the "Death of the Author," by which he meant that the purpose of literary study is not to ask "What does the author mean?" but instead to explore the way in which the reader creates his or her own meanings.

This effort to challenge any center of authority (sometimes called "decentering") linked the poststructuralist concern with communication to its analysis of power. In their work, Michel Foucault and Jacques Lacan looked at hierarchies of authority (not only in the political sphere but also in academic disciplines, for example, or in the medical world), and the way these authorities created and manipulated seemingly objective bodies of knowledge to retain their hold on power.

Postmodernism in its most general form emerged by the later 1980s out of the blending of these poststructuralist theories of communication and power with the critique of modernism already flourishing in architecture and the arts. Thinkers, writers, and artists argued that Western elites had shaped global culture and had ignored or distorted the cultures of non-Western and minority groups. This view of culture as bound up in a global contest for power disturbed many more traditional thinkers (with "modernist" now increasingly perceived as traditional) who continued to insist that criteria of aesthetic excellence ("Beauty") and objective standards of knowledge ("Truth") did exist. These critics warned that cultural "decentering" would destroy the social cohesion and political stability of the West.

Postmodern Cultures and Postindustrial Technologies

In many ways popular culture confirmed postmodern theories. In Britain, for example, the "Big Beat" songs that dominated the club scene in the late 1990s were produced not by vocalists or instrumentalists but by disc jockeys who lifted snatches from old records, played them at different speeds, and combined them with contrasting styles. Like postmodernist paintings, Big Beat contained chunks of the past, recycled in startling new ways. More generally, a series of technological developments meant that popular culture was clearly "decentered," that at the very least a multitude of popular cultures coexisted and that the individual consumer of culture, like Barthes's reader, was free to make meaning as he or she chose. The video cassette recorder (VCR), first marketed in 1975, not only transported film viewing from the public to the private sphere, it also provided the film viewer with the possibility to tailor the film to his or her own preferences—to adjust the volume or choose another soundtrack entirely, to omit or fast-forward through certain scenes, to replay others endlessly. Similarly, the proliferation of cable and satellite television stations during the 1980s and 1990s fragmented the viewing audience and made it impossible to speak of popular culture in the singular.

Postmodernist concerns with communication and codes, with the way in which interpretations can be endlessly modified, and with the abolition of a single center of authority, certainly seemed appropriate for an era that many called "the Information Age" and others called the postindustrial society°. The industrial phase of economic development was characterized by an emphasis on production. But in the postindustrial phase, the *making* of things becomes less important than the *marketing* of them. A postindustrial society, in fact, is characterized less by *things* in general than by *images, ideas, and information*. If the factory symbolized industrial society, then the epitome of the postindustrial era is the home computer, with its capacity to disperse information, market products, and endlessly duplicate yet constantly alter visual and verbal images. By the end of the 1990s, relatively inexpensively priced home computers gave their users access to libraries, art galleries, and retail outlets from across the world, and provided, for entrepreneurs, the opportunity to make (and lose) enormous fortunes by exploiting this new image-oriented means of marketing products and information—all without any central regulating authority. Governments scrambled desperately to impose control on the proliferating technologies of the postindustrial age, but in true postmodern fashion the centers of authority broke down. Existing laws that regulated pornography, for example, proved difficult to apply to the Internet, the vast global communications web.

Similarly, developments in medical technologies raised important questions about authority and ownership. In 1978, Louise Brown was born in Britain, the world's first "test-tube baby." Over the next twenty years, assisted fertility treatment resulted in the births of more than a million babies. As the technology grew more sophisticated, so too did the ethical and political questions. Societies struggled to determine the legality of practices such as commercial surrogate motherhood, in which a woman rents her womb to a couple, and postmenopausal motherhood, in which a woman past childbearing age is implanted with a fertilized egg. Genetic research provoked even more debate about which authorities or what principles should guide scientific research. In 1996, British scientists introduced the world to Dolly the sheep, the first mammal cloned from an adult. Many scientists declared that the cloning of human beings, long part of science fiction and horror stories, was inevitable, even if declared immoral by religious leaders and illegal by political authorities. The announcement in February 2001 that the human genome had been decoded—that scientists had mapped the sequencing of the human genome, or set of instructions in every cell in the human body—immediately raised such questions as: Who owns this information? Who has the authority to decide how it is to be used?

Postmodern Patterns in Religious Life

Postmodern patterns—the fragmentation of cultures, the collapse of centers of authority, the supremacy of image—also characterized Western religious faith and practice after the 1970s. Christianity no longer served as a common cultural bond. In a time of increasing immigration and cultural diversity, Islam was the fastest-growing religious community in western Europe. In Britain, Muslims outnumbered Methodists by two to one. By the end of the twentieth century, established Protestant churches in western Europe faced a serious crisis, with regular churchgoers now a small minority of the population—less than 5 percent, in most countries. The decline of the mainline churches in the United States was also dramatic, although a greater percentage of Americans—25 to 30 percent—attended church regularly. Religious faith became a private matter, the mark of subcultures (often defined by an "Us versus Them" mentality), rather than a bond tying together individuals and groups into a cohesive national culture.

At the same time, however, the long-reigning Pope John Paul II (b. 1920, r. 1978–) experienced unprecedented popularity. The most well-traveled and populist-oriented of twentieth-century popes, John Paul II became a media star, met with the same sort of cheering crowds and T-shirt vendors that accompanied famous rock bands. Much of his popularity rested on his intimate connection with Poland's Solidarity, and therefore with an image of liberation. Born Karol Wojtyła, John Paul was the first non-Italian pope since 1523 and the first-ever Polish pope. Twelve million people—one-third of the Polish population—greeted the pope in Warsaw in 1979 when he made the first visit by any pope to a communist country. Many Solidarity members testified to the importance of this visit in empowering them to challenge the political order fourteen months later. But

CHRONOLOGY

Medical Challenges

1977	First diagnosed case of AIDS
1978	First test-tube baby
1980	Worldwide eradication of smallpox
1982	First use of genetic engineering (insulin manufactured from bacteria)
1983	First artificially created chromosome
1984	HIV identified
1985	First use of laser surgery to clear blocked arteries
1997	Successful cloning of sheep
2001	Human genome decoded

the pope's support for Solidarity did not mean he supported other forms of rebellion against authority. Opposing the promise of continuing change inherent in Vatican II (see Chapter 28), John Paul II adopted a thoroughly authoritarian approach to church government and took an uncompromising stand against birth control, married clergy, and the ordination of women. Confronted with the postmodernist message that authority had fragmented and that no universal truth existed, many Christians found the pope's uncompromising stand a source of great comfort.

Yet, the papacy of John Paul II confirmed as well as contradicted postmodernist ideas; much of the pope's popularity was based on image rather than authority. Despite censoring liberal Catholic theologians, the pope was unable to bring into line an increasingly rebellious flock throughout Europe and the United States. In the United States, millions turned out to cheer the pope waving from an open car (the "popemobile"), yet the percentage of American Catholics using birth control—in direct violation of papal teachings—mirrored that of the population at large. By the 1980s, Catholic Italy boasted the second-lowest birth rate in the world (after China), with the one-child family becoming the norm. It was hard to avoid the conclusion that in much of Western Roman Catholicism, as in much of postmodern society, image ruled while authority dissipated.

THE GLOBAL CHALLENGE

At the same time that postmodern artists and theorists were questioning the validity of Western cultural forms, economic and environmental developments called into doubt other key assumptions of Western societies. Both the globalization of market capitalism and a worldwide environmental crisis crashed down national borders, limited the scope of action open to individual governments, and raised significant questions about the ecological sustainability of Western habits of consumption.

The Global Economy

In the 1990s, a number of technological and economic developments helped make national borders even more permeable and accelerated the globalization of economic production. Personal computers, fax machines, and wireless telephones all ensured that "the office" could be anywhere. Fiber optic cables that transmitted signals 4,000 times faster than their copper predecessors made instant communication across national boundaries a reality.

Technological innovations demanded organizational change. In the postindustrial economy, firms had to be more flexible, able to respond immediately to rapidly changing markets and technologies. They did not want too much capital investment in one way of doing things, in one kind of machinery, in one labor force, in one stock of supplies. Rather than economies of scale, they looked for other economies, such as subcontracting, outsourcing, and downsizing. The worker became more vulnerable. Concepts such as "a job for life" or "loyalty to the firm" had little relevance as companies merged and fragmented, shedding large number of workers in the endless pursuit of efficiency and the competitive edge. In this global economy, multinational corporations, with quick access to cheap Third World labor and raw materials, possessed significant economic power. In 2000, corporations such as

THE WEST AND THE REST

·················

In 1998, economic historian David Landes published The Wealth and Poverty of Nations: Why Some Are So Rich and Some So Poor. *Landes, a professor at Harvard University, had been writing on the history of industrial and technological change since the 1950s. Now he turned his attention to the present, and endeavored to answer one of the most pressing problems of the contemporary era. His introduction laid out the key issues.*

The old division of the world into two power blocs, East and West, has subsided. Now the big challenge and threat is the gap in wealth and health that separates the rich and poor. These are often styled North and South, because the division is geographic; but a more accurate signifier would be the West and the Rest, because the division is also historic. Here is the greatest single problem and danger facing the world of the Third Millennium. The only other worry that comes close is environmental deterioration, and the two are intimately connected, indeed are one. They are one because wealth entails not only consumption but also waste, not only production but also destruction. It is this waste and destruction, which has increased enormously with output and income, that threatens the space we live and move in.

How big is the gap between rich and poor and what is happening to it? Very roughly and briefly: the difference in income per head between the richest industrial nation, say Switzerland, and the poorest nonindustrial country, Mozambique, is about 400 to 1. Two hundred and fifty years ago, this gap between richest and poorest was perhaps 5 to 1, and the difference between Europe and, say, East or South Asia (China or India) was around 1.5 or 2 to 1.

. . . . Our task (the rich countries), in our own interest as well as theirs, is to help the poor become healthier and wealthier. If we do not, they will seek to take what they cannot make; and if they cannot earn by exporting commodities, they will export people. In short, wealth is an irresistible magnet; and poverty is a potentially raging contaminant: it cannot be segregated, and our peace and prosperity depend in the long run on the well-being of others.

. . . the best way to understand a problem is to ask: How and why did we get where we are? How did the rich countries get so rich? Why are the poor countries so poor? Why did Europe ("the West") take the lead in changing the world?

A historical approach does not ensure an answer. Others have thought about these matters and come up with diverse explanations. Most of these fall into two schools. Some see Western wealth and dominion as the triumph of good over bad. The Europeans, they say, were smarter, better organized, harder working; the others were ignorant, arrogant, lazy, backward, superstitious. Others invert the categories. The Europeans, they say, were aggressive, ruthless, greedy, unscrupulous, hypocritical; their victims were happy, innocent, weak—waiting victims and hence thoroughly victimized. We shall see that both of these manichean visions have elements of truth, as well as of ideological fantasy. Things are always more complicated than we would have them.

Source: From *The Wealth and Poverty of Nations: Why Some Are So Rich and Some So Poor* by David S. Landes. Copyright © 1998 by David S. Landes. Used by permission of W. W. Norton & Company, Inc.

North versus South

An Ethiopian farmer wages a losing war against drought and famine.

ExxonMobil and DaimlerChrysler had annual revenues that exceeded the GDP of Norway or Singapore.

Increasingly, however, it was the far more nebulous "markets" that dictated the course of economic and political affairs across the world. In the 1990s, the volatility that had characterized the global economy since the collapse of the Bretton Woods agreements in 1973 became even more intense as currency speculators moved their money in and out of currency markets with astonishing rapidity, and with often devastating consequences for the countries involved. In 1997, for example, Thailand was forced to devalue its currency, and the economic catastrophe of collapsing currencies and stock markets quickly spread to Indonesia, Malaysia, the Philippines, and South Korea. By 1998, the Japanese economy had slid into serious recession.

As the Asian economic crisis revealed, "the markets," rather than elected leaders, played an increasingly important role in determining a country's path. So, too, did the dictates of the World Bank and the IMF, the institutions that directed the flow of aid and loans throughout much of the world. The IMF, for example, insisted that governments receiving loans follow the orthodoxy of "austerity"—cutting government spending on social and welfare programs and restricting the flow of money supply to reduce inflation. Thus economists in offices far away, not elected leaders, called the shots. Moreover, both the World Bank and the IMF embodied the characteristic Western confidence of the postwar era. Local traditions and leaders were ignored, replaced instead by outside economists and agronomists who believed that an infusion of Western economic and technological expertise would set the rest of the world on the path to economic growth.

By the 1990s, the widening gap between "North" and "South," the rich and poor nations of the world, called into question these easy assumptions. Meetings of the World Bank, the IMF, and the "G8" (Japan, the United States, Britain, Canada, France, Germany, Italy, and Russia) were disrupted by "antiglobalization" campaigners who sought to call attention to the social costs of global capitalism, particularly the devastation wrought by what was called the "debt crisis." Over fifty of the world's poorest countries (thirty-six in Africa) were paying off their debts to Western banks and governments by withdrawing money from sanitation, health, and education programs. Relief organiza-tions estimated that as many as seven million children died each year during the 1990s because of the debt crisis.

The Environmental Crisis

The urgency of the environmental crisis also revealed the limitations of Western expertise. By 1985, 257 multilateral treaties mandated some form of environmental protection—restrictions on trade in endangered species, wetlands preservation, forest conservation, regulation of industrial emissions. Almost half of these had been signed since 1970. Yet the degradation of the planet proceeded apace. At the end of the millennium, half of the world's rivers were polluted or running dry, and the number of people displaced by water crises stood at 25 million (versus 21 million war-related refugees). In the 1980s, almost half of the world's tropical forests were cleared, posing a serious threat to the planet's biodiversity.

The destruction of the rain forests contributed to what is perhaps the largest threat facing not only Western but global civilization at the beginning of the third millennium—global warming. Global warming is linked to industrial development. The burning of fossil fuels such as oil and coal (which releases carbon dioxide into the atmosphere) and deforestation (which reduces the "natural sinks" that absorb the gas) together produce the "greenhouse effect"—the trapping of solar radiation in the Earth's atmosphere, with rising temperatures as a result. Faced with predictions of widespread climate change (and resulting economic devastation on a colossal scale), representatives from 160 countries met in Kyoto in 1997 and agreed to cut "greenhouse gas emissions" by 10 percent. In 2001, however, U.S. President George W. Bush rejected the Kyoto Agreements. Without the cooperation of the world's largest producer of greenhouse gases, the Kyoto Agreements' impact would be minimal.

Europeans, both political leaders and ordinary citizens, reacted with fury to Bush's withdrawal from the Kyoto Agreements. They condemned the unilateral American action as that of a superpower out of control, no longer constrained by the Cold War to march in step with its allies.

This perception of the United States as a bullying "hyperpower" was strengthened in 2003 by the Second Gulf War. Across Europe, anti-war rallies drew huge crowds as Europeans protested against what they perceived to be an unwarranted use of American military force. As new divisions and alliances emerged both within and outside of Europe, the meaning of "the West" remained the subject of intense debate.

CONCLUSION
Where Is the West Now?

In England, the most popular fast food is not fish and chips, long the quintessential English national supper, nor is it the Big Mac, as opponents of economic globalization might predict. Instead it is curry, the gift of the minority South Asian immigrant community. In the new millennium, "the West" may no longer serve as an important conceptual border marker. By many of the criteria explored in this textbook—economic, technological, political, and cultural—Tokyo would be defined as a Western city. So, too, would Melbourne—or Budapest or Warsaw. Nevertheless, the economic and social trauma that afflicted Russia and the poorer nations of the former Soviet bloc such as Romania and Bulgaria in the 1990s and after demonstrates that the "West" retains its distinct identity, for clearly the gap between it and the "East" remains wide. The admittedly hesitant, still incomplete spread of the Western ideal of democracy has thrown a fragile bridge across that gap. But perhaps the real divide for the twenty-first century stretches between "North" and "South"—the huge and growing difference between the global Haves and the Have-Nots. Whether any bridge can stretch across that span remains to be seen.

Suggestions for Further Reading

For a comprehensive list of suggested readings, please go to www.ablongman.com/levack/chapter29

Ardagh, John. *Germany and the Germans: The United Germany in the Mid-1990s.* 1996. A snapshot of a society in the midst of social and economic change.

Hughes, H. Stuart. *Sophisticated Rebels. The Political Culture of European Dissent 1968–1987.* 1988. A perceptive and imaginative exploration of "dissenters," ranging from Solidarity and Soviet dissidents to German Greens, Welsh nationalists, and an assortment of novelists and philosophers.

Kavanagh, Dennis. *Thatcherism and British Politics: The End of Consensus?* 1987. Kavanagh answers the question posed in his title with a convincing "yes."

Lewis, Jane, ed. *Women and Social Policies in Europe: Work, Family and the State.* 1993. A series of essays exploring the position of women in western Europe. Packed with statistics and useful tables.

McNeill, John. *Something New Under the Sun: An Environmental History of the Twentieth Century.* 2000. Argues that twentieth-century human economic activity has transformed the ecology of the globe—an ongoing experiment with a potentially devastating outcome.

Ost, David. *Solidarity and the Politics of Anti-Politics: Opposition and Reform in Poland Since 1968.* 1990. Although the bulk of this account was written before the Revolution of 1989, it provides a compelling study of Solidarity's emergence, impact, and ideology.

Rogel, Carole. *The Breakup of Yugoslavia and the War in Bosnia.* 1998. Designed for undergraduates, this work includes a short but detailed historical narrative, biographies of the main personalities, and a set of primary documents.

Rosenberg, Tina. *The Haunted Land: Facing Europe's Ghosts After Communism.* 1995. Winner of the Pulitzer Prize, this disturbing account focuses on the fundamental moral issues facing postcommunist political cultures.

Sandler, Irving. *Art of the Postmodern Era: From the Late 1960s to the Early 1980s,* 1996. Much more broad-ranging than the title suggests, this well-written, blessedly jargon-free work sets both contemporary art and the theories of the postmodern within the wider historical context.

Stokes, Gale. *The Walls Came Tumbling Down: The Collapse of Communism in Eastern Europe.* 1993. A superb account, firmly embedded in history.

Young, John W. *Cold War Europe 1945–1991: A Political History.* 1996. A solid survey.

See also the works by Crampton, Cronin, Isaacs and Downing, Judge and Langdon, Keep, and Urwin listed at the end of Chapter 28.

Notes

1. Quoted in Robert Paxton, *Europe in the Twentieth Century* (1997), p. 613.
2. Kenneth Boulding, "The Economics of the Coming Spaceship Earth," first published in 1966, reprinted in *Toward a Steady-State Economy,* ed. Herman Daly (1973).
3. Quotations from Timothy W. Ryback, *Rock Around the Bloc: A History of Rock Music in Eastern Europe and the Soviet Union* (1990); pp. 184–185, 176.
4. Quoted in D. J. Peterson, *Troubled Lands: The Legacy of Soviet Environmental Destruction* (1993), p. 12.
5. Quoted in Archie Brown, *The Gorbachev Factor* (1996), p. 125.
6. Quoted in R. J. Crampton, *Eastern Europe in the Twentieth Century—And After* (1997), p. 408.
7. Francis Fukuyama, *The End of History and the Last Man* (1992).
8. Quoted in *The Observer* (London), April 8, 2001, p. 20.
9. Salman Rushdie, "Please, Read *Satanic Verses* Before Condemning It," *Illustrated Weekly of India,* October 1988, reprinted in M. M. Ahsan and A. R. Kidwai. *Sacrilege versus Civility: Muslim Perspectives on The Satanic Verses Affair* (1991), p. 63.
10. Quoted in Malise Ruthven, *A Satanic Affair: Salman Rushdie and the Wrath of Islam* (1991). p. 562.
11. Quoted in Ruthven, p. 100.
12. *Bookseller,* London, February 24, 1989; quoted in Lisa Appignanesi and Sara Maitland, *The Rushdie File* (1990), pp. 103–104.
13. *The Sunday Telegraph,* June 24, 1990; quoted in Ahsan and Kidwai, p. 80.
14. Quoted in J. Robert Wegs and Robert Landrech, *Europe Since 1945* (1996) p. 354.
15. Wim Duisenberg, quoted in *The Independent* (London), August 31, 2001, p. 1.
16. Quoted in Irving Sandler, *Art of the Postmodern Era* (1996), p. 4.

Glossary

Allies (p. 790) During World War I, the states allied against the Central Powers of Germany and Austria-Hungary. During World War II, the states allied against the regimes of Nazi Germany, fascist Italy and imperial Japan.

anarchism (p. 740) Ideology that views the state as unnecessary and repressive, and rejects participation in parliamentary politics in favor of direct, usually violent, action.

anticlericalism (p. 771) Opposition to the political influence of the Roman Catholic Church.

apartheid (p. 939) System of racial segregation and discrimination put into place in South Africa in 1948.

appeasement (p. 865) British diplomatic and financial efforts to stabilize Germany in the 1920s and 1930s and so avoid a second world war.

Auschwitz (p. 905) Technically Auschwitz-Birkenau; death camp in Poland that has become the symbol of the Holocaust.

Balfour Declaration (p. 819) Declaration of 1917 that affirmed British support of a Jewish state in Palestine.

Beer Hall Putsch (pp. 835–836) Failed Nazi effort to overthrow the German government by force in 1923.

Berlin Wall (p. 935) Constructed by the East German government, the wall physically cut the city of Berlin in two and prevented East German citizens from access to West Germany; stood from 1961 to 1989.

Big Three (p. 886) Term applied to the British, Soviet, and U.S. leaders during World War II: until 1945, Churchill, Stalin, and Roosevelt; by the summer of 1945, Attlee, Stalin, and Truman.

blitzkrieg (p. 867) "Lightning war;" offensive military tactic making use of airplanes, tanks, and motorized infantry to punch through enemy defenses and secure key territory. First demonstrated by the German army in World War II.

boers (p. 628) Dutch farmers in the colony established by the Dutch Republic in South Africa.

Bolsheviks (p. 815) Minority group of Russian socialists, headed by Lenin, who espoused an immediate transition to a socialist state. It became the Communist Party in the Soviet Union.

Bretton Woods Agreement (p. 886) Agreement signed in 1944 that established the post-World War II economic framework in which the U.S. dollar served as the world's reserve currency.

brinkmanship (p. 933) Style of Cold War confrontation in which each superpower endeavored to convince the other that it was willing to wage nuclear war.

British Commonwealth (p. 853) Loose organization of former British colonies and imperial territories.

capital (p. 664) All the physical assets used in production, including fixed capital, such as machinery, and circulating capital, such as raw materials; more generally the cost of these physical assets.

Central Powers (p. 790) Germany and Austria-Hungary in World War I.

chinoiserie (p. 643) A French word for an eighteenth-century decorative art that combined Chinese and European motifs.

Christian Democracy, Christian Democratic parties (pp. 947–948) Conservative and confessionally based (Roman Catholic) political parties that dominated much of western European politics after World War II.

Cold War (p. 886) Struggle for global supremacy between the United States and the Soviet Union, waged from the end of World War II until 1990.

collectivization (p. 848) The replacement of private and village farms with large cooperative agricultural enterprises run by state-employed managers.

colons (p. 647) White planters in the French Caribbean colony of Saint Domingue (Haiti).

Common Market (p. 948) Originally comprising West Germany, France, Italy, Belgium, Luxembourg, and the Netherlands, the Common Market was formed in 1957 to integrate its members' economic structures and so foster both economic prosperity and international peace. Also called the European Economic Community (EEC).

communism (p. 689) The revolutionary form of socialism developed by Karl Marx and Friedrich Engels that promoted the overthrow of bourgeois or capitalist institutions and the establishment of a dictatorship of the proletariat.

Concert of Europe (p. 688) The joint efforts made by Austria, Prussia, Russia, Britain, and France during the years following the Congress of Vienna to suppress liberal and nationalist movements throughout Europe.

Congress of Vienna (p. 616) A conference of the major powers of Europe in 1814–1815 to establish a new balance of power at the end of the Napoleonic Wars.

conservatism (pp. 687–688) A nineteenth-century ideology intended to prevent a recurrence of the revolutionary changes of the 1790s and the implementation of liberal policies.

containment (p. 889) Cold War policy of blocking communist expansion; inaugurated by the Truman Doctrine in 1947.

creoles (p. 628) People of Spanish descent who had been born in Spanish America.

Cubism (p. 768) Modernist artistic movement of the early twentieth century that emphasized the fragmentation of human perception through visual experiments with geometric forms.

Darwinian theory of evolution (p. 757) Scientific theory associated with nineteenth-century scientist Charles Darwin that highlights the role of variation and natural selection in the evolution of species.

Decembrists (p. 697) Russian liberals who staged a revolt against Tsar Nicholas I on the first day of his reign in December 1825.

de-Christianization (pp. 602–603) A program inaugurated in France in 1793 by the radical Jacobin and former priest Joseph Fouché that closed churches, eliminated religious symbols, and attempted to establish a purely civic religion.

demand (p. 665) The desire of consumers to acquire goods and the need of producers to acquire raw materials and machinery.

de-Stalinization (p. 942) Khrushchev's effort to decentralize political and economic control in the Soviet Union after 1956.

detente (p. 936) During the 1970s, a period of lessened Cold War hostilities and greater reliance on negotiation and compromise.

dialectic (p. 688) The theory that history advanced in stages as the result of the conflict between different ideas or social groups.

dialectical materialism (p. 688) The socialist philosophy of Karl Marx according to which history advanced as the result of material or economic forces and would lead to the creation of a classless society.

division of labor (p. 660) The assignment of one stage of production to a single worker or group of workers to increase efficiency and productive output.

Dreyfus Affair (pp. 733–735) The trials of Captain Alfred Dreyfus on treason charges dominated French political life in the decade after 1894 and revealed fundamental divisions in French society.

Einsatzgruppen (p. 902) Loosely translated as strike force or task force; SS units given the task of murdering Jews and Communist Party members in the areas of the Soviet Union occupied by Germany during World War II.

empires (p. 622) Large political formations consisting of different kingdoms or territories outside the boundaries of the states that control them.

enclosure (p. 663) The consolidation of scattered agricultural holdings into large, compact fields which were then closed off by hedges, bushes, or walls, giving farmers complete control over the uses of their land.

ethnic cleansing (p. 985) A term introduced during the wars in Yugoslavia in the 1990s; the systematic use of murder, rape, and violence by one ethnic group against members of other ethnic groups in order to establish control over a territory.

European Economic Community (EEC) (p. 948) Originally comprising West Germany, France, Italy, Belgium, Luxembourg, and the Netherlands, the EEC was formed in 1957 to integrate its members' economic structures and so foster both economic prosperity and international peace. Also called the Common Market.

European Union (EU) (p. 991) A successor organization to the EEC; the effort to integrate European political, economic, cultural, and military structures and policies.

existentialism (pp. 829, 955) Twentieth-century philosophy that emerged in the interwar era and influenced many thinkers and artists after World War II. Existentialism emphasizes individual freedom in a world devoid of meaning or coherence.

Expressionism (p. 769) Modernist artistic movement of the early twentieth century that used bold colors and experimental forms to express emotional realities.

factories (p. 624) Trading posts established by European powers in foreign lands.

fascism (p. 839) Twentieth-century political ideology that rejected the existing alternatives of conservatism, communism, socialism, and liberalism. Fascists stressed the authoritarian power of the state, the efficacy of violent action, the need to build a national community, and the use of new technologies of influence and control.

federalists (p. 594) The name assigned by radical Jacobins to provincial rebels who opposed the centralization of the state during the French Revolution.

feminism, feminist movement (p. 744) International movement that emerged in the second half of the nineteenth century and demanded broader political, legal, and economic rights for women.

Final Solution (p. 901) Nazi term for the effort to murder every Jew in Europe during World War II.

fin-de-siecle (p. 760) French term for the "turn of the century"; used to refer to the cultural crisis of the late nineteenth century.

German-Soviet Non-Aggression Pact (p. 864) Signed by Stalin and Hitler in 1939, the agreement publicly pledged Germany and the Soviet Union not to attack each other, and secretly divided up Poland and the Baltic states between the two powers.

Girondins (pp. 593–594) The more conservative members of the Jacobin party who favored greater economic freedom and opposed further centralization of state power during the French Revolution.

glasnost (p. 977) Loosely translated as openness or honesty; Gorbachev's effort after 1985 to break with the secrecy that had characterized Soviet political life.

Great Depression in Trade and Agriculture (p. 722) Downturn in prices and profits, particularly in the agricultural sector, in Europe from 1873 through the 1880s.

Great Depression (p. 842) Calamitous drop in prices, reduction in trade, and rise in unemployment that devastated the global economy in 1929.

Great Purge (p. 850) Period of mass arrests and executions particularly aimed at Communist Party members. Lasting from 1934 to 1939, the Great Purge enabled Stalin to consolidate his one-man rule over the Soviet Union.

Green movement, Green politics (p. 973) A new style of politics and set of political ideas resulting from the confluence of environmentalism, feminism, and anti-nuclear protests of the 1970s.

Holocaust (p. 898) Adolf Hitler's effort to murder all the Jews in Europe during World War II.

hyperinflation (p. 835) Catastrophic price increases and currency devaluation, such as that which occurred in Germany in 1923.

ideologies (p. 686) Theories of society and government that form the basis of political programs.

Ideologues (p. 608) A group of liberal writers and philosophers in France who objected to Napoleon's religious policy on the grounds that it would inaugurate a return of religious superstition.

industrial capitalism (p. 672) A form of capitalism characterized by the ownership of factories by private individuals and the employment of wage labor.

Jacobins (p. 590) A French political party supporting a democratic republic that found support in political clubs throughout the country and dominated the National Convention from 1792 until 1794.

Jim Crow (p. 743) Series of laws mandating racial segregation throughout the American South.

Kristallnacht (p. 900) The "Night of the Broken Glass"—on November 9, 1938, Nazi-directed mobs burned the synagogues and vandalized the homes and businesses of the German Jewish community.

laissez-faire (p. 686) The principle that governments should not regulate or otherwise intervene in the economy unless it is necessary to protect property rights and public order.

League of Nations (p. 821) Association of states set up after World War I to resolve international conflicts through open and peaceful negotiation.

Lend-Lease Act (p. 871) Passed in March 1941, the act gave Britain access to American industrial products during World War II, with payment postponed for the duration of the war.

liberalism (pp. 686–687) An ideology based on the conviction that individual freedom is of supreme importance and the main responsibility of government is to protect that freedom.

Mafia (p. 710) Organizations of armed men who took control of local politics and the economy in late nineteenth-century Sicily.

Manhattan Project (p. 917) Code name given to the secret Anglo-American project that resulted in the construction of the atom bomb during World War II.

Marshall Plan (p. 889) The use of U.S. economic aid to restore stability to Europe after World War II and so undercut the appeal of communist ideology.

metropolis (p. 622) The parent country of a colony or imperial possession.

modernism (p. 765) Term applied to artistic and literary movements from the late nineteenth century through the 1950s. Modernists sought to create new aesthetic forms and values.

Montagnards (pp. 593–594) Members of the radical faction within the Jacobin party who advocated the centralization of state power during the French Revolution and instituted the Reign of Terror.

nabobs (p. 643) Members of the British East India Company who made fortunes in India and returned to Britain, flaunting their wealth.

Napoleonic Code (p. 608) The name given to the Civil Code of 1804, promulgated by Napoleon, which gave France a uniform and authoritative code of law.

nation (p. 689) A large community of people who possess a sense of unity based on a belief that they have a common homeland and share a similar culture.

nationalism (p. 689) The belief that the people who form a nation should have their own political institutions and that the interests of the nation should be defended and promoted at all costs.

national self-determination (p. 689) The doctrine advanced by nationalists that any group that considers itself a nation has the right to be ruled only by the members of their own nation and to have all members of the nation included in that state.

nation-state (p. 689) A political structure sought by nationalists in which the boundaries of the state and the nation are identical, so that all the members of a nation are governed by the same political authorities.

NATO (North Atlantic Treaty Organization) (p. 889) Defensive anti-Soviet alliance of the United States, Canada, and the nations of western Europe established in 1949.

nawabs (p. 640) Native provincial governors in eighteenth-century India.

Nazism (p. 843) Twentieth-century political ideology associated with Adolf Hitler that adopted many fascist ideas but with a central focus on racism and particularly anti-Semitism.

NEP (New Economic Plan) (p. 832) Lenin's economic turnaround in 1921 that allowed and even encouraged small private businesses and farms in the Soviet Union.

New Conservatism (p. 969) Political ideology that emerged at the end of the 1970s combining the free market approach of nineteenth-century liberalism with social conservatism.

new feminism (p. 971) Re-emergence of the feminist movement in the 1970s.

new imperialism (p. 771) The third phase of modern European imperialism, that occurred in the late nineteenth and early twentieth centuries and extended Western control over almost all of Africa and much of Asia.

New Left (p. 960) Leftwing political and cultural movement that emerged in the late 1950s and early 1960s; sought to develop a form of socialism that rejected the over-centralization, authoritarianism, and inhumanity of Stalinism.

no-man's-land (p. 798) The area between the combatants' trenches on the Western Front during World War I.

nuclear arms race (p. 923) Product of the Cold War between the United States and the Soviet Union; each superpower endeavored to achieve military superiority through the acquisition of ever-more sophisticated nuclear bombs and nuclear weapons delivery systems.

Nuremberg trials (p. 910) Post-World War II trials of members of the Nazi Party and German military; conducted by an international tribunal.

perestroika (p. 977) Loosely translated as "restructuring;" Gorbachev's effort to decentralize, reform, and thereby strengthen Soviet economic and political structures.

pop art (p. 955) Effort by artists in the 1950s and 1960s both to utilize and to critique the material plenty of post-World War II popular culture.

popular sovereignty (p. 602) The claim that political power came from the people and that the people constituted the highest political power in the state.

positivism (pp. 691–692) The philosophy developed by August Comte in the nineteenth century according to which human society passed through a series of stages, leading to the final positive stage in which the accumulation of scientific data would enable thinkers to discover the laws of human behavior and bring about the improvement of society.

postindustrialism, postindustrial society (p. 994) A service-rather than manufacturing-based economy characterized by an emphasis on marketing and information and by a proliferation of communications technologies.

postmodernism (pp. 992, 995) Umbrella term covering a variety of artistic styles and intellectual theories and practices; in general, a rejection of a single, universal, Western style of modernity.

Prague Spring (p. 946) Short-lived popular effort in 1968 to reform Czechoslovakia's political structures; associated with the phrase "socialism with a human face."

proletariat (p. 689) The word used by Karl Marx and Friedrich Engels to identify the class of workers who received their income from wages.

protectionism (p. 631) The policy of shielding domestic industries from foreign competition through a policy of levying tariffs on imported goods.

Reign of Terror (p. 595) A purging of alleged enemies of the French state between 1793 and 1794, superintended by the Committee of Public Safety, that resulted in the execution of 17,000 people.

reparations (p. 822) Payments imposed upon Germany after World War I by the Versailles Treaty to cover the costs of the war.

revisionism, socialist revisionism (p. 739) The belief that an equal society can be built through participation in parliamentary politics rather than through violent revolution.

romanticism (pp. 692–695) An artistic and literary movement of the late eighteenth and nineteenth centuries that involved a protest against classicism, appealed to the passions rather than the intellect, and emphasized the beauty and power of nature.

Rome-Berlin Axis (p. 863) Alliance between Mussolini's Italy and Hitler's Germany formed in 1936.

Schlieffen Plan (p. 794) German military plan devised in 1905 that called for a sweeping attack on France through Belgium and the Netherlands.

Scramble for Africa (p. 774) The frenzied imposition of European control over most of Africa that occurred between 1870 and 1914.

Second Industrial Revolution (p. 723) A new phase in the industrialization of the processes of production and consumption, underway in Europe in the 1870s.

sepoys (p. 642) Indian troops serving in the armed forces of the British East India Company.

Social Darwinism (p. 759) The later-nineteenth-century application of the theory of evolution to entire human societies.

social democracy (pp. 851, 883, 969) Political system in which a democratically elected parliamentary government endeavors to ensure a decent standard of living for its citizens through both economic regulation and the maintenance of a welfare state.

Solidarity (p. 975) Trade union and political party in Poland that led an unsuccessful effort to reform the Polish communist state in 1981; survived to lead Poland's first non-communist government since World War II in 1989.

soviets (p. 814) Workers' and soldiers' councils formed in Russia during the Revolution of 1917.

stagflation (p. 966) Term coined in the 1970s to describe an economy troubled by both high inflation and high unemployment rates.

states (p. 622) Consolidated territorial areas that have their own political institutions and recognize no higher political authority.

structuralism (p. 956) Influential post-World War II social theory that explored the common structures of language and thought.

suffragettes (p. 749) Feminist movement that emerged in Britain in the early twentieth century. Unlike the suffragists, who sought to achieve the vote for women through rational persuasion, the suffragettes adopted the tactics of violent protest.

supply (p. 665) The amounts of capital, labor, and food that are needed to produce goods for the market as well as the quantities of those goods themselves.

syndicalism (p. 740) Ideology of the late nineteenth and early twentieth century that sought to achieve a working-class revolution through economic action, particularly through mass labor strikes.

Third World (p. 942) Term coined in 1955 to describe nations that did not align with either the Soviet Union or the United States; commonly used to describe the industrially underdeveloped nations.

total war (pp. 790, 805) A war that demands extensive state regulation of economic production, distribution, and consumption.

Treaty of Brest-Litovsk (p. 800) Treaty between Germany and Bolshevik-controlled Russia, signed in March, 1918, that ceded to Germany all of Russia's western territories.

Triple Alliance (p. 791) Defensive alliance of Germany, Austria-Hungary, and Italy, signed in 1882.

Triple Entente (p. 792) Informal defensive agreement linking France, Great Britain, and Russia before World War I.

Truman Doctrine (p. 889) Named after U.S. president Harry Truman, the doctrine that in 1947 inaugurated the Cold War policy of resisting the expansion of communist control.

universal male suffrage (p. 592) The granting of the right to vote to all adult males.

Utilitarians (p. 687) Nineteenth-century British liberals who promoted social and economic policies that in their view would provide the greatest good for the greatest number of people.

Vatican II (p. 957) Popular term for the Second Vatican Council that convened in 1963 and introduced a series of changes within the Roman Catholic Church.

Versailles Treaty (p. 822) Treaty between Germany and the victorious Allies after World War I.

Vichy, Vichy regime, Vichy government (p. 867) Authoritarian state established in France after defeat by the German army in 1940.

Warsaw Pact (p. 889) Military alliance of the Soviet Union and its eastern European satellite states in the Cold War era.

Weimar Republic (p. 834) The democratic German state constructed after defeat in World War I and destroyed by the Nazis in 1933.

Zionism (p. 743) Nationalist movement that emerged in the late nineteenth century and sought to establish a Jewish political state in Palestine (the Biblical Zion).

Credits

Unless otherwise acknowledged, all photographs are the property of Pearson Education, Inc. Page abbreviations are as follows: (T) Top, (B) Bottom, (L) Left, (R) Right, (C) Center.

The Human Body in History title panel image: Cameraphoto/ Art Resource, NY
Justice in History title panel image: Don Mason/Corbis

What Is the West?
2 Canali Photobank; 4 European Space Agency/Photo Researchers, Inc.; 6 Courtesy of Adler Planetarium & Astronomy Museum, Chicago, Illinois (W-264); 7 American Museum of Natural History Library (AMNH#314372)

Chapter 18
584 Erich Lessing/Art Resource, NY; 591 AKG London; 592 (B) Bibliothèque Nationale de France, Paris (80C 103369); 593 Bibliothèque Nationale de France, Paris (45B M89); 597 Giraudon/Art Resource, NY; 599 Réunion des Musées Nationaux/Art Resource, NY; 601 Annenberg Rare Book & Manuscript Library, University of Pennsylvania (Révolutions de Paris No. 161: Aug 4–11, 1792); 603 Photothèque des Musées de las Ville de Paris/Cliché: Andreani; 604 Giraudon/Art Resource, NY; 605 Réunion des Musées Nationaux/Art Resource, NY; 610 Réunion des Musées Nationaux/Art Resource, NY; 613 Erich Lessing/Art Resource, NY

Chapter 19
620 Victoria & Albert Museum, London/Art Resource, NY; 626 Private Collection Pairs/Dagli Orti/The Art Archive; 627 British Museum/Art Resource, NY; 629 Benson Latin American Collection, University of Texas-Austin; 637 Benson Latin American Collection, University of Texas-Austin; 640 Bridgeman Art Library; 643 Bridgeman Art Library; 644 Erich Lessing/Art Resource, NY; 646 The Library of Congress; 648 Art Resource, NY; 650 Museo Bolivar Caracas/Dagli Orti/The Art Archive

Chapter 20
654 Guildhall Library, Corporation of London/Bridgeman Art Library; 656 From *The White Slaves of England,* 1853; 659 Science Museum, London/Science and Society Picture Library; 660 From *History of the Cotton Manufacture in Great Britain,* 1836; 662 *Lewis Carroll's Album.* The Gernsheim Collection, Harry Ransom Research Center, University of Texas-Austin; 668 Deutsche Bahn Museum, Nurnberg; 670 AKG London; 674 Rickett Collection of Slides/The Slide Center; 677 *Punch,* 1847; 678 Sheffield Archives and Local Studies Library; 679 Rickitt Collection of Slides/The Slide Center; 680 © National Gallery, London

Chapter 21
684 Gemälde von Anton von Werner, 1995. Friedrichsruh, Bismarck-Museum, Bildarchiv Preussischer Kulturbesitz, Berlin; 689 The Granger Collection, New York; 693 Southampton Art Gallery/Bridgeman Art Library; 694 Bridgeman Art Library; 696 Réunion des Musées Nationaux/Art Resource, NY; 698 Giraudon/Art Resource, NY; 701 The Royal Archives © 2003 Her Majesty Queen Elizabeth II; 705 AKG London; 710 Hulton Archive/Getty Images; 711 AKG London; 717 AKG London

Chapter 22
720 The Library of Congress (811714 262-7307); 723 Roger-Viollet/Getty Images; 724 Hulton Archive/Getty Images; 725 The Mansell Collection/Time Life Pictures/Getty Images; 729 Courtesy Special Auction Services, England; 730 Eastphoto/ Sovfoto; 731 Hulton Archive/Getty Images; 735 Hulton Archive/Getty Images; 738 Hulton Archive/Getty Images; 740 By permission of the People's History Museum; 745 Bridgeman Art Library; 746 By permission of the People's History Museum

Chapter 23
752 Erich Lessing/Art Resource, NY; 755 Erich Lessing/Art Resource, NY; 757 Cambridge University Library, Darwin Archive; 760 New York Public Library, Astor, Lenox and Tilden Foundations; 763 The Granger Collection, New York; 765 Schloss Immendorf, Austria/Bridgeman Art Library; 766 (L) Mary Evans Picture Library; (B) Corey Suppes/Ballparks.com; 767 (TR) AKG London; (BR) Science Museum, London/Science & Society Picture Library; 768 (L) Victoria & Albert Museum/Art Resource, NY; (R) Graphische Sammlung Albertina, Vienna, Austria/Bridgeman Art Library; 769 Eastphoto/ Sovfoto; 770 Manchester City Art Galleries, UK/Bridgeman Art Library; 772 Wisconsin Historical Society (WHi-3104); 773 Hulton Archive/Getty Images; 774 © The Museum of Modern Art, New York/Art Resource, NY/© Estate of Pablo Picasso/ Artists Rights Society (ARS), New York; 777 Anti-Slavery International; 781 Robert Hunt Picture Library

Chapter 24
788 Imperial War Museum, London; 790 Hulton Archive/Getty Images; 795 Ullstein Bilderdienst; 797 Imperial War Museum, London; 801 Robert Hunt Picture Library; 803 Imperial War Museum, London; 804 Hulton Archive/Getty Images; 806 Imperial War Museum, London; 808 (T) Hulton Archive/Getty Images; (B) Imperial War Museum, London; 809 National Gallery of Canada, Ottawa (No. 4800); 811 Imperial War Museum, London; 812 Hulton-Deutsch Collection/Corbis; 815 Hulton Archive/Getty Images; 817 Corbis; 818 AKG London; 820 AP/Wide World Photos

Chapter 25
826 Institute of Contemporary History and Wiener Library; 830 Bildarchiv Preussischer Kulturbesitz; 831 Schalwijk/Art Resource, NY/Reproduction authorized by Nacional Bellas Artes y Literatura/ © 2003 Banco de México, Diego Rivera & Frida Kahlo Museums Trust. Av. Cinco de Mayo No. 2, Col. Centro, Del. Cuauhtémoc 06059, México, D.F.; 832 Hulton Archive/Getty Images; 837 AKG London; 838 Photographie J. H. Lartigue/© Ministère de la Culture-France/A.A.J.H.L.; 841 AKG London; 845 AKG London; 848 David King/Sovfoto; 849 TASS/Sovfoto; 853 Robert Capa/Magnum Photos, Inc.; 857 AKG London

Chapter 26
860 Courtesy of the National Museum of the U.S. Army; 865 Art Resource, NY/© 2003 The Estate of Pablo Picasso/Artists Rights Society (ARS) New York; 867 Suddeutscher Verlag Bildarchiv; 870 AKG London; 871 TRH Pictures; 875 Popperfoto; 876 Hulton Archive/Getty Images; 878 Foto-Tanjug; 881 Sovfoto;

C-1

883 © Henry Moore Foundation. © Tate Gallery, London/Art Resource, NY; **884** AKG London; **888** Courtesy Franklin D. Roosevelt Library; **891** CTK Photo

Chapter 27
896 United States Holocaust Memorial Museum, Washington, D.C.; **898** Hulton Archive/Getty Images; **901** Bundesarchiv Bild (101I/12/11/19); **902** AKG London; **905** AKG London; **907** United States Holocaust Memorial Museum, Washington, D.C. Courtesy of Moshe Kaganovich; **913** Bettmann/Corbis; **914** Anselm Kiefer, *Deutscheslands Geisteshelden*, 1973, oil, paint, and charcoal on burlap. 121 × 268 ½ in. The Broad Art Foundation/The Gagosian Gallery, New York; **916** Hulton Archive/Getty Images; **917** Time Life Films, Inc./Time Life Pictures/Getty Images; **919** Hulton Archive/Getty Images; **924** Philip Jones Griffiths/Magnum Photos, Inc.; **925** © 2003 Museum of Modern Art, New York/Art Resource, NY/© 2003 The Pollock-Krasner Foundation/Artists Rights Society (ARS), New York; **926** Photofest

Chapter 28
930 Photos12; **932** Camera Press, London/Retna, Ltd.; **934** Time Life Pictures/Getty Images; **937** Camera Press, London/

Retna, Ltd.; **945** Hulton Archive/Getty Images; **946** CTK Photo; **951** Todd A. Gipstein/Corbis; **952** Hulton Archive/Getty Images; **953** William Safire/Bettmann/Corbis; **954** © 2003 Museum of Modern Art, New York/Art Resource, NY/© 2003 Artists Rights Society (ARS), New York/ADAGP, Paris; **955** Kunsthalle, Tubingen/Bridgeman Art Library/© 2003 Artists Rights Society (ARS), New York/DACS, London; **959** Hulton Archive/Getty Images; **960** Hulton Archive/Getty Images

Chapter 29
964 Lionel Cironneau/AP/Wide World Photos; **969** Reuters/Corbis; **971** AP/Wide World Photos; **972** Time Life Pictures/Getty Images; **973** Courtesy NASA; **975** Jean Gaumy/Magnum Photo, Inc.; **977** Tass/Sovfoto; **979** AP/Wide World Photos; **984** **(L)** Gyori Antoine/Corbis Sygma; **(R)** Scott Peterson/Getty Images; **989** Hulton Archive/Getty Images; **990** Todd Hollis/AP/Wide World Photos; **993** Through the Flower/© 2003 Judy Chicago/Artists Rights Society (ARS), New York; **997** Neil Cooper/Panos Pictures

Index

Art(s): Asian influences on, 643; romanticism in, 679, 692–695; modernism in, 752 (illus.), 765–769; primitive, 774, 774 (illus.); between world wars, 828–831; politics in, 829–830; works on Holocaust, 911–914; Abstract Expressionist, 925; after Second World War, 954–956; meaning and absurdity in, 955; Pop Art and, 955–956, 955 (illus.); postmodern, 955–956, 992–994; feminist, 993, 993 (illus.); poststructuralism in, 994

Artillery. See Weapons

"Aryans": Nazis and, 843, 846, 901, 901 (illus.)

Asia: trade routes in, 623; British colonies in, 624; French in, 625; Dutch in, 628; Spanish in, 628; Portugal and, 629; Europeans and, 630, 640–645; Seven Years' War and, 632; art influences from, 643–644; bathing in, 644; Opium War in, 681; imperialism by, 771; new imperialism and, 778–783, 779 (map); United States and, 780; immigrants to Australia from, 783; First World War and, 802; colonies in, 853; mass nationalism in, 855; Second World War in, 861–862; after Second World War, 885–886; independence in, 940 (map); recession in, 997. See also Middle East

Assassinations: anarchism and, 740

Assemblies: French Estates General as, 587; in Russia, 730. See also specific legislative bodies

Assembly line, 669

Assembly of Notables (France), 587

Assignats (French paper money), 598

Aswan, 599 (illus.)

Ataturk, Kemal. See Kemal Pasha, Mustafa ("Ataturk")

Athletics. See Sports

Atlantic region: economy of, 634–639; slave trade in, 636–639; cultural encounters in, 639

Atom(s), 916–917

Atomic bomb, 898, 915–921; at Hiroshima, 877, 896 (illus.), 898, 919 (illus.); at Nagasaki, 877, 898; splitting atom and, 915–916; threat of German, 917; Manhattan Project and, 917–918; decision to use, 918–921; Soviets and, 922–923. See also Hydrogen bomb; Nuclear power

Atomic theory, 755–756

Atomic weight, 756

Attlee, Clement, 885, 887, 933

Auclert, Hubertine, 748

Auden, W. H., 829

Auerstedt, battle at, 611

Aung San (Burma), 885

Auschwitz: Nazi death camp at, 905–906; Jewish resistance at, 907

Ausgleich (Settlement, 1867): in Austria-Hungary, 715

Austerlitz, Battle of, 611

Australia: Britain and, 624; immigration to, 726; whites in, 783; First World War and, 802, 819; colonies of, 853; in Second World War, 877

Austria: war with France, 592; Napoleon and, 609; after Congress of Vienna, 615 (map), 616; War of the Austrian Succession and, 632; industrialization in, 666, 668; in Holy Alliance, 688; revolutions of 1848 in, 703–704, 705; Italian unification and, 709; German unification and, 711; anti-Semitism in, 742; women's suffrage in, 748; First World War and, 790, 800; German alliance

with, 791, 792; revolutionary efforts in, 818; after First World War, 822; treaty after First World War, 822; Anschluss with Germany and, 863, 900

Austria-Hungary, 714–715; free education in, 727; mass politics in, 741; First World War and, 791, 822; nationalism in, 791; disintegration of, 819

Austrian Habsburg Monarchy: empire of, 622. See also Habsburg Empire; Habsburg Monarchy

Austrian Netherlands: revolts in, 599; Napoleon and, 609, 615; Dutch Republic and, 698. See also Dutch Republic (United Provinces of the Netherlands); Netherlands

Austro-Hungarian Empire. See Austria-Hungary

Austro-Prussian War, 711

Austro-Serbian conflict. See First World War

Authoritarianism: of Napoleon, 607; in eastern Europe, 834; in Germany, 834–835; in Spain, 852–853

Authority: vs. image, 995. See also Government(s); Politics; Power (political)

Autobahn (Germany), 845 (illus.)

Automobile, 772, 827; between world wars, 830; in Japan, 933; after Second World War, 949

Auxiliary Service Law (Germany, 1916), 806

Avant-garde, 925, 993

Axis powers, 863

Azerbaijan, republic of, 981

Baader-Meinhof (West Germany), 961

Babeuf, François-Noël, 689

Babi Yar: slaughter of Jews at, 902; West informed about, 910

Baby "boomlet": in Europe, 953

Bacon, Francis (painter), 955

Bacteria: Pasteur and, 754

Bainbridge, Kenneth, 918

Baker, Josephine, 857 (illus.)

Bakunin, Mikhail, 740

Balance of payments: in Britain, 681

Balance of power: Russia, Ottoman Empire, Crimean War, and, 715–716; in Western Hemisphere, 715–717; German Empire, Paris Commune, and, 716–717; in Africa, 776; German unification and, 791; in postwar Europe, 886; superpowers in, 940

Baldwin, Stanley, 865

Balfour Declaration, 819

Balkan region: Russian imperialism in, 715–716; First World War and, 790, 801; wars in, 822; fascism in, 843; Second World War and, 868; Soviet Union and, 886; Red Army and, 886–887. See also Eastern Europe

Balkan Wars (1912 and 1913), 801

Baltic region: in First World War, 800; "Forest Brothers" in, 885; Russian immigration to, 944; independence movements in, 979–980; capitalism in, 981; EU and, 991–992

Bandits: in Italy, 710

Bandung Conference, 942

Bankruptcy: of former soviet Union, 980–981

Banks and banking: industrialization and, 664, 668; crises in 1970s, 966

Barras, Paul, 595

Barres, Maurice, 735

Barth, Karl, 828

Barthes, Roland, 994

Barton, Edmund, 783

Basque separatists, 986

Bastille: storming of, 584 (illus.), 585–586, 588; anniversary of fall, 602, 603 (illus.)

Bathing: in Eastern and Western cultures, 644

Batista y Zaldivar, Fulgencio, 935

Batouala (Maran), 857

Battle of Britain, 867–868

"Battle of the Somme, The," 788 (illus.)

Battles. See specific battles and wars

Bauhaus (art school), 829

Beagle (ship), 757

Beale, Dorothea, 747

Beatles, 951, 961

Beauvoir, Simone de, 952–953

Bebel, August, 738

Beckett, Samuel, 955

Beer Hall Putsch (Germany), 835, 836–837, 843

Beethoven, Ludwig van, 606, 692

Behavior: "normal," 764; U.S. vs. British, 876

Beijing: Western sack of, 783

Belarus: Chernobyl disaster and, 977. See also Byelorussia

Belgium, 609; railroads in, 662; industrialization in, 666, 668; constitutional monarchy in, 687; nationalist revolution in, 698; revolt against Dutch and, 698; revolution of 1830 in, 698; Congo and, 777, 853, 940; First World War and, 794–795; colonies of, 853; Second World War and, 861, 867; Holocaust and, 908; in Benelux countries, 948

Belzec: as Nazi death camp, 905

Benelux countries: ECSC and, 948

Bengal, 632, 681

Ben-Gurion, David: on Eichmann, 812

Benin Republic, 940

Bentham, Jeremy, 687

Bergen-Belsen, 897; mass graves at, 897–898, 898 (illus.)

Berlin: Napoleon in, 611; growth of, 725; Soviets and, 874, 877; battle for, 875 (illus.), 877; postwar division of, 887. See also East Berlin; West Berlin

Berlin Conference (1871), 777

Berlin Wall, 931, 935; escape from, 931, 932 (illus.); fall of, 964 (illus.), 965–966

Bernstein, Eduard, 739

Bethmann-Hollweg, Theobold von, 792

Beveridge Report (Britain), 883

Bevin, Ernest, 888, 889, 937

Bicycles, 725 (illus.)

Bidault, Georges, 889

"Big Beat" songs, 994

Big Three: meetings by, 886, 888 (illus.); atomic bomb and, 922

Bill of Rights (England), 589

Bill of Rights (U.S.), 713

Billroth, Theodor, 755 (illus.)

Bin Laden, Osama, 990

Biological sciences: breakthroughs and, 956

Biological weapons: in Iraq, 990

Birkenau: as death camp, 906

Birth control, 744, 838; illegality after First World War, 838; in Nazi Germany, 846; Roman Catholic Church on, 957; methods of, 972; Pill as, 972

Birth rate: of slaves, 638; increase in, 663; decline in, 744; after Second World War, 953

Birth rates, 971

Bismarck, Otto von, 684 (illus.), 711, 711 (illus.), 716, 731, 791; dismissal of, 792

Common Market and, 948; affluence in, 948–949; American postwar influence in, 950–951; crisis in 1970s and 1980s, 966–970; New Conservatism and, 969–970; environmentalism and, 973; women in, 973; in Poland, 975; of reunified Germany, 982; of Yugoslavia, 983; in postindustrial age, 994; global, 996–997; currency devaluations and, 997. See also Agriculture; Food; Great Depression (1870s); Great Depression (1930s); Industrial Revolution; Poverty; Production; Wealth

ECSC. See European Coal and Steel Community (ECSC)

EDC. See European Defense Community (EDC)

Edison, Thomas, 723–724

Education: French Revolution (1789) and, 600; nation-building and, 727; for women, 747, 838, 846, 973; in Africa, 940; in eastern Europe, 945. See also Universities and colleges

EEC. See European Economic Community (EEC)

Ego: Freud on, 856

Egypt: France and, 611, 624; First World War and, 803; independence and, 820; England and, 853; Israel and, 911, 966; Suez Crisis and, 940

Eichmann, Adolf, 903, 911, 912–913, 913 (illus.)

Eichmann in Jerusalem: A Report on the Banality of Evil (Arendt), 913

Eiffel, Gustave, 723

Eiffel Tower, 723, 724 (illus.)

Eighteenth Amendment (U.S.), 748

Einsatzgruppen (SS units): Jews killed by, 902, 902 (illus.), 903, 907, 908

Einstein, Albert, 756, 916, 917, 917 (illus.); theory of relativity, 915; on nuclear weapons controls, 922

Eisenhower, Dwight, 933–934; atomic bomb and, 919

El Alamein, Battle of, 873

Elba: exile of Napoleon to, 614

Elections: in France, 598. See also Voting rights

Electricity, 723–724; in Soviet Union, 849

Elgin, Lord, 782

Eliot, T. S., 961; "The Waste Land," 828, 829

Elisabeth (Austria-Hungary): assassination of, 740

Elites: in Soviet Union, 832; in Germany, 834; in fascist Italy, 841–842; colonial, 885. See also Classes

Ellis, Havelock, 764

Emancipation: of slaves, 638–639; of African Americans, 743–744

Emigration: forced, of Africans, 621; of German Jews, 900. See also Immigrants and immigration

Emissions regulation, 997

Empires: Napoleonic, 609–613, 612 (map); European colonial, 621–630, 625 (map); wars over, 630–634; in Asia, 640–645; industry, trade, and, 680–682; nation-states in, 691; Austria-Hungary as, 714–715, 727, 741; ideology, balance of power, and, 715–717; economics and, 772; critics of, 774; after First World War, 819–820, 822, 833 (map), 854 (map); between world wars, 853–857; challenges to, 854–855; German, 863–864; Nazi, 863–864, 869 (map); after Second World War, 885–886; decolonization and, 937–942;

Africa after European, 938 (map); Asia after European, 938 (map); in Cold War, 940–942. See also Imperialism; Kings and kingdoms; New imperialism; specific empires

Employment: in railroads, 662; in Germany, 845; inflation and, 967. See also Children; Labor; Women

Enabling Act (Germany), 844

Enclosure, 663

Encounters (cultural): in Atlantic region, 639. See also Culture(s)

Endangered species, 997

Energy. See Power (energy)

Engels, Friedrich, 672, 676, 688, 690

Engineering: in Soviet Union, 849. See also Technology

Engines: steam, 658

England (Britain): French Revolution (1789) and, 590; Napoleon and, 609; Battle of Trafalgar and, 611; Great Britain and, 622; trading posts (factories) in India, 624; mutiny on Bounty and, 626–627, 627 (illus.); slave trade and, 629, 638; navy of, 630; Dutch wars with, 631; mercantile wars of, 631; Spanish wars with, 631; France and, 631–634; Canadian control by, 632–633; Seven Years' War and, 632–633; Caribbean region and, 633 (map); North America and, 633 (map); common law ideals in, 639; India and, 640–642, 641 (map), 779; Black Hole of Calcutta and, 641; nabobs and, 642; American Revolution and, 645–646; Hispaniola and, 647; Ireland and, 648–649, 854; in United Kingdom, 649; Industrial Revolution in, 657–666; coal in, 658; transportation in, 661; railroads in, 662; population growth in, 662–663; banking in, 664; capital in, 664; Scientific Revolution in, 664; exports from, 665; industry and, 666 (map); aristocracy in, 667; raw materials in, 667; trade within, 667; regional industrialization in, 669; economic growth in, 672; living standards in, 672; child labor in, 673–676; women in, 673–676, 747, 748, 749, 954; Luddites in, 677; Peterloo Massacre in, 678; class consciousness in, 678–679; industry in, 680; Opium War and, 681; nation-state in, 690; liberal reform in, 699–702; Monroe Doctrine and, 715; Russian imperialism and, 716; nationalism in, 736–737; society in, 736–737; labor unions in, 739–740, 740 (illus.); Darwinian theory and, 758–759; Vorticist painters in, 765, 768 (illus.); soccer in, 766–767, 766 (illus.), 767 (illus.); Boer War and, 784; First World War and, 790, 796, 822; Germany and, 792, 863, 887, 888; Mediterranean and Middle East interests of, 802–803; submarine warfare against, 803–804; home front in First World War and, 806–807; Arab nationalism and, 818; Balfour Declaration and, 819; in 1930s, 852; African colonies of, 853; in Middle East, 853; Second World War and, 864, 868, 882, 884; appeasement and, 864–865; RAF of, 867; Battle of Britain and, 867–868; U.S. assistance in Second World War, 871; U.S. soldiers in, 876, 876 (illus.); bombings by, 880; plans for post-Second World War period, 883; postwar policies and, 888; Holocaust and, 909–910; Palestine and, 910; atomic research

in, 917; Campaign for Nuclear Disarmament (CND) in, 924; African independence and, 937; Suez Crisis and, 940; nationalization of industry in, 947; immigrant labor in, 951, 952 (illus.); "Angry Young Men" in, 954; church attendance in, 956–957; Afro-Caribbeans in, 967; National Front in, 968; unemployment in, 969; punk in, 975–976; Muslims in, 995. See also British Empire

English Bill of Rights, 589

English language, 950

Enlightenment: French Revolution (1789) and, 595; Asian political systems and, 645; liberal ideas and, 686–687; scientific rationalism and, 691

Entrepreneurs: rural "domestic system" and, 659; industrialization and, 664–665; continental Europe and, 667; in United States, 669

Environment and environmentalism: industrial, 673, 679–680; Soviet Union and, 944, 961, 976; student protests and, 961; activism for, 973–974; multilateral treaties protecting, 997; crisis in, 997–998

Epidemics: disease control and, 754. See also Disease

Episcopalian Church. See Church of England

Equality: in France, 588–590; ideals of, 639; socialism and, 688–689

Equiano, Olaudah, 621

Essay on the Principle of Population (Malthus), 670, 671

Estates (France), 587–588

Estates General (France): French Revolution (1789) and, 587–588

Estonia: Second World War and, 864; independence of, 979

Eta (Basque separatists), 986

Ethiopia: Italian invasion of, 732, 863; defeat of Italy by, 777

Ethnic cleansing, 985

Ethnic Germans, 822; as DPs, 884

Ethnic groups: in Atlantic world, 639; in Habsburg Empire, 714; tensions over, 727; in Russia, 813; after First World War, 822; in eastern Europe, 834, 982; in postwar Europe, 884–885; Jews and, 899; in European countries, 952; in western Europe, 967; in Yugoslavia, 983. See also Multinational empires

EU. See European Union (EU)

Eugenics programs: in Nazi Germany, 909

Euro, 991

European Coal and Steel Community (ECSC), 948

European Community (EC), 991

European Court of Justice, 991

European Defense Community (EDC), 933

Europe and Europeans: after Congress of Vienna, 615 (map); empires in, 621–622, 625 (map); Atlantic economy and, 635 (map); Asia and, 640–645; attitudes toward Asia, 642–646; bathing and, 644; continental industrialization and, 666–670; revolutions in (1815–1871), 686; ideological revolts and, 694–699; revolts and rebellions in (1815–1848), 695–699, 699 (map); in late 19th century, 728 (map); religion and, 769–771; culture vs. indigenous cultures, 773; in August, 1914, 793 (map); superior feelings of, 819; after First World War, 821 (map);

939–940. *See also* Colonies and colonization; Decolonization; Empires

Imports: tariffs on, 631

Income: consumer demand and, 665–666; industrialization and, 672; in West, 947

Indentured servants: in American colonies, 623; French, 624

Independence: of American colonies, 645–646; South American movements and, 649–650, 681; Greek, 696–697; Belgian, 698; in Austria-Hungary, 819; of Turkey, 855; for India, 856; in British Empire, 885; of Algeria, 938; in Africa, 938 (map); in Middle East, 938 (map); in Asia, 940 (map); in Third World nations, 942; movements in former Soviet Union, 979–980. *See also* Revolts and rebellions

Independent Group: in arts, 955

India: Britain and, 624, 640, 641–642, 641 (map), 680–681, 771, 779; French factories in, 624; Dutch factories in, 628; Portugal and, 629; French-British conflicts in, 634; Europeans and, 640–642, 643; Sepoy Mutiny in, 641–642; prejudice against nabobs and, 642; bathing and, 644; First World War and, 802, 803 (illus.); Gandhi and, 820; westernization in, 855; in Second World War, 877, 885; independence of, 885, 937; Pakistan and, 885

Indian National Congress, 856

Indian Ocean region: British superiority in, 633, 633 (map)

Indians. *See* American Indians

Indian Wars: in United States, 780

Indigenous peoples: in Portuguese Empire, 630; "Scramble for Africa" and, 775 (map); in Siberia, 780; in United States, 780; in Australia, 783

Individual: liberalism and, 691; in First World War, 806–807; in modern society, 883; rights of, in West, 947

Indochina: France and, 779, 855; First World War and, 802; independence and, 855, 937; after Second World War, 885; U.S. involvement in, 933; division of, 941. *See also* Vietnam

Indonesia: Dutch in, 628, 628 (illus.); nationalist independence movement in, 855; Japan and, 872; colonial conflict in, 885; in Second World War, 885; independence and, 937, 942

Industrial capitalism, 672–673; socialists and, 688

Industrialization: social unrest and, 727; in Russia, 729; First World War and, 806; in Soviet Union, 848–850. *See also* Industrial Revolution

Industrial Revolution, 654 (illus.), 655–656; nature of, 656–662; in Britain, 657–666, 666 (map); factories and, 659–661; transportation and, 661–662; causes of, 662–666; population increase and, 663; in continental Europe, 666–670; in United States, 668–669; regionalism and, 669–670; effects of, 670–680; classes and, 676–679; socialism and, 688; Second, 723–725, 771–772. *See also* Industrialization

Industrial technology, 656, 657–658

Industry: in rural areas, 659; handicraft workshop and, 660; capital in, 664; trade, empire, and, 680–682; in Latin America, 682; expansion of, 722–723; organizational forms in, 724; protection of, 724; in cities, 737; in Nazi

Germany, 845; Soviet, 849, 974; in western Europe, 852; Japanese, 877; in China, 936; British nationalization of, 947; environmentalism and, 973; in postindustrial age, 994; emissions regulations and, 997. *See also* Industrial Revolution

Inflation: in First World War, 806; in Germany, 835; labor issues and, 967; and Western economies, 967 (illus.); unemployment and, 969; in 1970s, 970; in Poland, 981; in Yugoslavia, 983

Information: on Holocaust, 909–910

Information Age, 994

INF Treaty. *See* Intermediate Nuclear Force (INF) Treaty

Inheritance: in France, 589, 590; evolution and, 758–759; of acquired traits, 759, 760

Inquiry into the Nature and Causes of the Wealth of Nations, An (Smith). *See* Wealth of Nations, The (Smith)

Inquisition. *See* Spanish Inquisition

Institute of Egypt, 611

Intellectual thought: in Atlantic world, 639; social thought and, 756–757; structuralism in, 956; postmodern, 992–994. *See also* Art(s); Culture(s); Ideologies; Science; Scientific Revolution

Interchangeable parts, 669

Intercontinental ballistic missiles (ICBMs), 923, 934, 978

Interest rates: in 1980s, 969

Intermarriage: between whites and indigenous peoples, 630; in Latin America, 639. *See also* Marriage

Intermediate Nuclear Force (INF) Treaty, 978

Intermediate-range nuclear missiles, 970, 978

International affairs. *See* Diplomacy

International Brigade: in Spanish Civil War, 852

International economic competition, 966–967

International Monetary Fund (IMF), 886, 997

International organizations: League of Nations as, 821, 822–823; after Second World War, 886, 889; Marshall Plan and, 948. *See also* United Nations (UN); specific organizations

International War Crimes Tribunal: Milosevic and, 985

Internet, 994

Interpretation of Dreams, The (Freud), 756

Intolerable Acts (1774), 646

Inventors and inventions: textile machinery and, 657; steam engine and, 658; industrialization and, 665; in United States, 669; in Second Industrial Revolution, 723–724

Investment: for industrialization, 664; in Russia, 723; by West, 772; in Soviet industry, 849; in China, 862

IRA. *See* Irish Republican Army (IRA)

Iran: after Second World War, 888; revolution in, 986

Iraq: England and, 853; Second Gulf War and, 990. *See also* First Gulf War

Ireland: rebellion in, 648–649; in United Kingdom, 649; industrialization in, 669; Catholic voting rights and, 700; potato famine in, 700; nationalism in, 736; First World War and, 802; revolt in, 819; independence of, 854

Irish Free State, 833 (map)

Irish Republican Army (IRA), 854, 986

Irish Republican Brotherhood, 736

Iron Curtain, 886, 892

Iron Guard (Romania), 843

Iron industry, 658, 659 (illus.); railroads and, 662; continental industrialization and, 668; in France, 669; in Germany, 669

"Iron Lady": Thatcher as, 971

"Iron law of wages," 687

Irrational thought, 756–757

Isabella II (Spain), 695

Islam: slavery in, 636; European attitudes toward, 642; African conversions to, 855; growth of, 957; militant, 986; terrorism and, 986. *See also* Muslims

Israel: Arab-Israeli wars and, 885, 966, 986; Soviet Union and, 890; creation of, 910–911, 937; Holocaust survivors in, 911; and neighbors, 911 (map). *See also* Jews and Judaism

Italy: France and, 599; Napoleon and, 609, 611; nationalism in, 612–613, 732–733; after Congress of Vienna, 615 (map); industrialization in, 666; revolutions of 1848 in, 705–708; unification of, 708–710, 709 (map); education in, 727; socialism in, 732, 733; Libya annexed by, 733; women in, 748, 846; Futurist painters in, 765; empire of, 772; First World War and, 790, 792, 822, 862; Mussolini in, 839–842; fascist revolution in, 841–842; Second World War and, 863, 868; Nazi occupation of, 878; Resistance in, 878; Holocaust and, 908; constitution of, 947; in ECSC, 948; neorealist films in, 954; kidnapping of Aldo Moro in, 958–959; student protests in, 960; terrorism in, 961; Catholic image vs. authority in, 995

Ivory, 772

Iwo Jima: in Second World War, 877, 919

"J'accuse!" (Zola), 734

Jacobins (France), 590–591, 598; French Revolution (1789) and, 593–595; Napoleon and, 605

Jager, Karl: "Jager Report" of, 903

Jakarta, 628, 628 (illus.), 640

Jamaica, 631

James I (England), 649

James II (England), 686

Jamestown, 623

Japan: Dutch factories in, 628; Europeans and, 640; Russo-Japanese War and, 730, 781 (illus.); Manchuria and, 780; U.S. and, 780, 871; expansion by, 780–781; Sino-Japanese War and, 783; First World War and, 802, 862; colonies of, 853, 885; Second World War and, 861–862, 862–863, 933; Rape of Nanking (Nanjing) and, 863; territorial ambitions of, 871–872, 872 (map); conquest of Singapore by, 871 (illus.); Battle of Midway and, 873; atomic bombings of, 877, 919–921, 919 (illus.), 920 (illus.); fall of, 877; Soviet declaration of war against, 920; surrender of, 920, 921; in 1945, 920 (map)

Japanese empire: after First World War, 854 (map)

Jaruzelski, Wojciech, 975

Java: in mercantilist empire, 778

Jazz, 857

Jefferson, Thomas, 713; Declaration of Independence and, 646

Jehovah's Witnesses: Nazi Germany and, 846, 898, 904

Contemporary Political Map of the World

160°W 140°W 120°W 100°W 80°W 60°W 40°W 20°W

80°N
60°N
40°N
Tropic of Cancer
20°N
0° Equator
20°S
Tropic of Capricorn
40°S
60°S
Antarctic Circle
80°S

GREENLAND
(KALAALLIT NUNAAT)
(Den.)

Arctic

ICELAND

IRELA

ALASKA
(U.S.)

CANADA

UNITED STATES

ATLANTIC
OCEAN

AZORES (Port.)

PORTU

MO

CANARY IS. (Sp.)

WESTERN SAHARA
(Mor.)

HAWAII (U.S.)

MEXICO

BAHAMAS
DOMINICAN
REPUBLIC
HAITI
CUBA
PUERTO RICO (U.S.)
JAMAICA
ST. KITTS AND NEVIS
BELIZE
ANTIGUA AND BARBUDA
GUADELOUPE (Fr.)
DOMINICA
GUATEMALA
HONDURAS
MARTINIQUE (Fr.)
ST. VINCENT AND THE GRENADINES
EL SALVADOR
NICARAGUA
ST. LUCIA
BARBADOS
GRENADA
TRINIDAD AND TOBAGO
COSTA RICA
GUYANA
PANAMA
SURINAME
VENEZUELA
FRENCH GUIANA (Fr.)
COLOMBIA

CAPE
VERDE

MAURITA

SENEGAL
THE GAMBIA
GUINEA-BISSAU
GUINEA
SIERRA LEONE
LIBERIA
CÔTE D'IV
BURKINA

PACIFIC OCEAN

GALÁPAGOS IS.
(Ec.)

ECUADOR

PERU

BRAZIL

WESTERN
SAMOA
AMERICAN
SAMOA (U.S.)
TONGA

FRENCH
POLYNESIA (Fr.)

BOLIVIA

PARAGUAY

CHILE

URUGUAY

ARGENTINA

ATLANT
OCEA

0   1,500   3,000 Miles
0   1,500   3,000 Kilometers

FALKLAND IS. (U.K.)

**Contemporary
Political Map
of the World**